Nutrition Counseling Skills

Assessment, Treatment, and Evaluation

Second Edition

Linda G. Snetselaar, PhD, RD, LD
Department of Preventive Medicine
and Internal Medicine
University of Iowa
Iowa City, Iowa

AN ASPEN PUBLICATION®
Aspen Publishers, Inc.   1989

Rockville, Maryland
Royal Tunbridge Wells

Library of Congress Cataloging-in-Publication Data

Snetselaar, Linda G.
Nutrition counseling skills.

"An Aspen publication."
Includes bibliographies and index.
1. Obesity—Psychological aspects. 2. Health
counseling. I. Title. [DNLM: 1. Counseling. 2. Food
Habits. 3. Nutrition. QU 145 S67in]
RC628.S646   1989   616.3 '98 '0019   88-24060
ISBN: 0-8342-0009-0

The authors have made every effort to ensure the accuracy of the information herein.
However, appropriate information sources should be consulted, especially for new or unfamiliar procedures. It is the responsibility of every practitioner to evaluate the appropriateness of a particular opinion in the context of actual clinical situations and with due
considerations to new developments. Authors, editors, and the publisher cannot be held
responsible for any typographical or other errors found in this book.

Editorial Services: Ruth Bloom

Library of Congress Catalog Card Number: 88-24060
ISBN: 0-8342-0009-0

Printed in the United States of America

1   2   3   4   5

*To
my husband
Gary
and my friends
and colleagues
Dru and Lisa*

Contributors

Johanna T. Dwyer, DSc, RD
Professor of Medicine at Tufts University Medical School
Director, Frances Stern Nutrition Center
New England Medical Center Hospital
Jamaica Plain, Massachusetts

Marilyn E. Farrand, MS, RD
Public Health Nutrition Consultant for
    Cardiovascular Disease Programs
McLean, Virginia

John R. Kramer, PhD
Assistant Research Scientist
Department of Psychiatry
University of Iowa
Iowa City, Iowa

Sandra N. Powers, RD
Assistant in Medicine
Department of Medicine
Vanderbilt University Medical Center North
Nashville, Tennessee

Phyllis J. Stumbo, RD, PhD, LD
Research Dietitian
Clinical Research Center
University of Iowa
Iowa City, Iowa

Table of Contents

Foreword ix

Preface x

Acknowledgments xi

PART I: THE BASICS OF INTERVIEWING AND COUNSELING
         SKILLS FOR NUTRITION COUNSELING 1

Chapter 1— Overview of Nutrition Counseling.. 3

        Definition of Nutrition Counseling 3
        History of Nutrition Counseling... 3
        Importance of Nutrition Counseling.. 9
        Counseling Skills 12
        Counseling Spectrum 15

Chapter 2— Interviewing Skills 18

        Effective Counselor-Client Relationships 18
        Nonverbal Communication 21
        Verbal Communication... 34
        Listening Responses 36
        Action Responses 38
        Teaching Responses 46
        Choosing the Appropriate Response.. 49

Chapter 3— Counseling Skills 55

        Initial Information 55
        Assessment 56
        Treatment Planning.. 58
        Strategy Implementation.. 68
        Evaluation 81

PART II: TOOLS FOR NUTRITION COUNSELING **89**

Chapter   4— Assessing and Monitoring Dietary Behaviors............................   **91**
Johanna T. Dwyer

    Assessment   91
    Monitoring   103
    Enhancing Adherence   114

Chapter   5— Computer Assisted Nutrition Counseling.....................................   **123**
Sandra N. Powers and Phyllis J. Stumbo

    Choosing Appropriate Software for Nutrition Counseling   124
    Data Base Considerations for Nutrition Counseling   131
    Spreadsheet Applications for Nutrition Counseling   134
    Using the Computer To Facilitate Dietary Compliance   143

Chapter   6— Designing Instructional Plans **151**

    Objectives   151
    Teaching Steps   153
    Materials and Activities   157
    Conclusion   157

Chapter   7— Stress: An Overview **167**
John R. Kramer

    The Conceptualization and Measurement of Stress   167
    Stress and Illness: General Considerations   177
    Stress and Illness: The Example of Diabetes   178
    Stress Management   182
    Conclusion   190

PART III: APPLICATION OF INTERVIEWING AND COUNSELING
           SKILLS **201**

Chapter   8— Nutrition Counseling in Treatment of Obesity **205**

    Theories and Facts about Nutrition and Obesity   205
    Adherence with Weight Loss Programs   206
    Inappropriate Eating Behaviors   208
    Assessment of Eating Behaviors   209
    Treatment Strategies   212
    Client Eating Questionnaire for Low-Calorie Eating Patterns
       in Treating Obesity   217

Chapter 9— **Nutrition Counseling in Prevention and Treatment of Coronary Heart Disease**... **231**

Theories and Facts about Nutrition and Coronary Heart Disease.. 235
Research on Compliance with Eating Patterns Low in Fat and Cholesterol.. 239
Inappropriate Eating Behaviors 240

Chapter 10— **Nutrition Counseling in Treatment of Diabetes** **286**

Theories and Facts about Nutrition and Non-Insulin-Dependent Diabetes 287
Theories and Facts about Nutrition and Insulin-Dependent Diabetes.. 287
Research on Adherence with Eating Patterns Controlled for Carbohydrate, Protein, and Fat.. 315
Inappropriate Eating Behaviors 317
Assessment of Eating Behaviors.. 318
Treatment Strategies 319

Chapter 11— **Nutrition Counseling in Treatment of Renal Diseases**................ **348**

Theories and Facts about Nutrition and Chronic Renal Failure.. 349
Research on Adherence with Eating Patterns in Treatment of Renal Disease 353
Inappropriate Eating Behaviors 353
Assessment of Eating Behaviors.. 354
Treatment Strategies 356

Chapter 12— **Nutrition Counseling in Treatment of Hypertension**................... **382**

Theories and Facts about Nutrition and Hypertension 383
Research on Adherence to Eating Patterns in Treatment of Hypertension 388
Inappropriate Eating Behaviors 389
Assessment of Eating Behaviors.. 390
Treatment Strategies 392

Chapter 13— **Nutrition Counseling for Cancer Risk Prevention**....................... **406**

Theories and Facts about Nutrition and Cancer........................ 406
Research on Adherence to Eating Patterns in Cancer Risk Prevention 406
Inappropriate Eating Behaviors 408
Assessment of Eating Behaviors.. 408
Treatment Strategies 408

**Chapter 14— Nutrition Counseling in Treatment of Anorexia Nervosa and
Bulimia** **422**

Theories and Facts about Anorexia Nervosa 423
Theories and Facts about Bulimia 424
Adherence to Treatment Programs for Anorexia and Bulimia .. 425
Inappropriate Eating Behaviors 426
Assessment of Eating Behaviors... 427
Treatment Strategies 428

Chapter 15— Nutrition Counseling in Management of Pregnancy.................... **437**

Theories and Facts about Diet in Pregnancy 437
Research on Adherence to Appropriate Eating Patterns in
Pregnancy 438
Assessment of Eating Behaviors... 442
Treatment Strategies 445

PART IV: ENDING COUNSELING SESSIONS **467**

Chapter 16— Evaluation and Follow-Up.. **469**

Evaluation of Counselor Progress.. 469
Evaluation of Client Progress... 470
Strategies To Maintain Dietary Adherence................................ 470
Reinstitution of Intervention or Treatment 471
The Termination Process 472

Appendix A — Checklist of Counselor Self-Image **475**

Appendix B — Checklist of Nutrition Counselor's Nonverbal Behavior **477**

Appendix C — Measures of Nutritional Status... **479**

Appendix D — Behavioral Chart **486**

Appendix E — Behavioral Log.. **487**

Appendix F — Logs of Thoughts Related to Food **488**

Appendix G — Daily Record of Cognitive Restructuring **491**

**Appendix H — Food Composition Table (Fat and Cholesterol Content of
Certain Foods)**.. **492**

Appendix I — Answers to Chapter Reviews.. **502**

Index **508**

About the Author

Foreword

Nutrition counselors play a leading role in interpreting the results of nutrition research and subsequent diet recommendations for other health professionals, patients, and the general public. Current interest in food and in food habits is high, and changes in the American diet are being advocated. Nutrition is at the forefront of efforts to prevent and treat the major chronic diseases in the United States—obesity, elevated blood lipids, elevated blood pressure, and diabetes—as well as other less prevalent disorders. The potential role of nutrition for the prevention of some types of cancer is being assessed. To use this information most effectively, nutrition counselors need to have both knowledge of food and nutrition, and the skills to help people to change their eating habits. By integrating knowledge and skills, nutrition counselors can promote optimal nutrition and influence the overall health of our nation.

Marilyn E. Farrand, RD
Public Health Nutritionist

Preface

This text focuses on increasing the effectiveness of nutrition counselors as facilitators of behavioral change. The term "nutrition counselor" describes all health professionals involved in counseling clients or patients to provide dietary information or facilitate dietary adherence. Nutrition counselors may be registered dietitians or other health professionals—medical doctors, nurses, psychologists, or behavior therapists—who interact with registered dietitians.

Readers of this text will acquire or enhance the following abilities:

1. demonstrate effective use of tools for nutrition counseling and interviewing skills
2. select and apply appropriate strategies when presented with nutrition problems
3. evaluate progress, achievements, and failures in both clients and themselves
4. adapt counseling strategies based on self-evaluations and client evaluations.

Nutrition Counseling Skills was written to supplement a major course in nutrition principles. It does not replace discussions on basic nutrition, and the information in the text will be most useful to readers with a thorough understanding of the subject as taught in a college curriculum. The intent of the text is to (1) apply interviewing and counseling skills and strategies to the discipline of nutrition and (2) provide for their practice in situations that require specific dietary modifications. Ideally, a course in counseling psychology will expand the knowledge and skills presented in this text.

Each chapter begins with objectives; the notes at the end of each chapter serve as a list of reference materials for further study. Part I covers basic theories on interviewing and counseling skills. Part II reviews nutrition assessment techniques, the use of the computer to counsel effectively, the organization of counseling sessions through lesson planning and a discussion on stress management. Part III demonstrates how to use counseling skills and nutrition tools in specific nutrition situations in which eating behaviors may pose problems. Part IV provides suggestions for evaluating and terminating counseling sessions.

The text frequently uses the term "eating pattern" in place of "diet." The rationale for this change in terminology is that "diet" tends to denote the following of an eating regimen for a short time with degression to old habits as an eventual outcome. In treating or preventing chronic disease, changes in eating behaviors are long term, and the nutrition counselor's goal is to assist the client or patient in maintaining change over time.

Linda G. Snetselaar
October 1988

Acknowledgments

The author acknowledges the expertise of the following, without whose help this book would not have been possible:

Barry Bratton, PhD
Lisa Brooks, RD, MA, LD
Jacqueline Dunbar, PhD
Harold Engen, EdD
Barry Ginsberg, MD, PhD
Dru Kurtzman, RD, MS, LD
Kathryn Mahoney, PhD
Sandra Powers, RD, MS
Helmut Schrott, MD
Karen Smith, RD, MS
Phyllis Stumbo, RD, PhD, LD
Rhonda Dale Terry, PhD
Laura Vailas, RD, MS

Appendix H, the result of the Lipid Research Clinic Food Substitution Guide project at the University of Iowa in 1984, was funded in part by the Lipid Research Clinic, Coronary Primary Prevention Trial, and the National Heart, Lung, and Blood Institute, to which the author expresses deep appreciation.

Finally, this book would not have been possible without the interest and enthusiasm of Marilyn Farrand. Her innovative approaches to dietetic practices have supported the idea of applying counseling skills to the dissemination of nutrition information.

The Basics of Interviewing and Counseling Skills for Nutrition Counseling

Part I covers basic ideas on the theoretical aspects of interviewing and counseling skills in relation to nutrition and eating behaviors. Terms used in the field are discussed.

Chapter 1

Overview of Nutrition Counseling

Objectives for Chapter 1

1. Discuss the influence of counseling theory on the client.
2. Describe three theories that influence the nutrition counselor.
3. Discuss two ways in which counseling is important to the work of the nutrition counselor.
4. Identify the components of counseling skills.
5. Diagram the counseling spectrum.

DEFINITION OF NUTRITION COUNSELING

Nutrition has been described as both a science and an art. The nutrition counselor's goals are to convert theory into practice and science into art. This ability requires a great deal of knowledge and skill.[1]

Nutrition is a profession requiring knowledge of diverse subjects, and counselors in the field must be well versed in many areas, including biochemistry, physiology, botany, and agriculture as well as nutrition. To use this knowledge to change food behaviors, they also must have an understanding of the art of helping others, the art of counseling.

What is nutrition counseling? Mason et al. define it as "helping people with present or potential nutrition problems, whether they exist because of lack of knowledge, or motivation, or both."[2]

HISTORY OF NUTRITION COUNSELING

Over the years nutrition advice has been a part of nearly every culture. Early Greek physicians recognized the role of food in the treatment of disease.[3] In America in the early 1800s Thomas Jefferson described his eating habits in a letter to his doctor in what may be one of the first diet records[4] (Exhibit 1-1). After World War II, advances in chemical knowledge allowed nutrition researchers to define metabolic requirements.[5] This marked the beginning of looking at patterns of nutrients needed by all persons in relation to their age, sex, and activity. These patterns are vital to the assessment phase of counseling.

Exhibit 1-1 A Colonial Era Diet Report

> " ... *I have lived temperately, eating little animal food, & that... as a condiment for the vegetables, which constitute my principal diet. I double however the doctor's glass and a half of wine."*
>
> *From Thomas Jefferson to his Doctor*
>
> *Source:* Courtesy of the Thomas Jefferson Memorial Foundation, Monticello, Charlottesville, Virginia.

Selling and Ferraro, in discussing the psychology of diet and nutrition in 1945, recommended what at that time must have been a rather unconventional view:

1. knowing the client's personality
2. knowing the client's psychological surroundings
3. eliminating emotional tension
4. assisting the client in knowing his own limitations
5. arranging the diet so that it has the effect of encouraging the client
6. allowing for occasional cheating [on the diet].[6]

In 1945 this advice was obscured by the flood of scientific knowledge relating nutrition to disease. Only minor efforts were expended to put these critical ideas into practice.

Nutrition advice has changed over the years in terms of the counselors' roles during a session. In the past, the role fell more on the authoritarian side of a continuum; today a counselor must be able to function in all roles at appropriate times (Figure 1-1). Ivey et al. describe the role of counseling as knowing which strategy to use for which individual given specific conditions.[7]

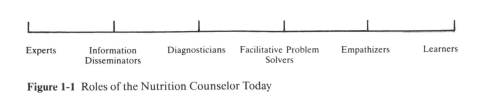

Figure 1-1 Roles of the Nutrition Counselor Today

Pioneers in the Field

In the early 1900s Frances Stearn started a food clinic at the New England Medical Center. Her work continues today with dietitians who work to emphasize the counseling aspects of nutrition.

In 1973 Margaret Ohlson stressed the importance of creating an interviewing atmosphere in which the client can respond freely. This can occur only when the counselor's listening skills are attuned to hearing what the client is saying. Ohlson warns against a common problem in dietetic counseling sessions: speaking at the expense of missing important factors during the interview.[8]

Selling and Ferraro say there no longer is any justification for prescribing a diet without also recognizing the psychological factors in a case. They recommend a diagnostic study to determine the right psychodietetic approach.[9] Indeed, the thrust in counseling today is matching the treatment to each individual case.[10]

Theories Influence Clients

As in every discipline, theories form the basis for developing the counseling skills of nutrition practitioners and other health professionals responsible for client education and have led them to view counseling as a means of changing eating habits. Both clients and counselors use theories and beliefs in determining what will take place during an interview.

Clients approach nutrition counseling sessions with mind-sets about themselves and the world around them. They present "a history of being healed or hurt by others, of being accepted or rejected, of dominating others or treating them as equals, of seeing people as ends or means."[11] They also come with a positive or negative self-image and a record of success or failure in diet modification. From this stem their personal theories of what counseling is and should be.

Most practitioners have faced a client who slouches down in the chair, slams a diet instruction sheet on the desk, and demands: "Well, what are you going to do to get me to follow this diet?" This client sees the counselor as an expert, the person with all of the answers—and an adversary. A second client may walk into the office, sit down, and speak only when spoken to. Still a third client arrives commenting, "Well, how can we work out this problem I've been having with my diet?"

All three clients see the world through different eyes. The first does not want any responsibility, the second may be afraid of authority figures, and the last sees the counselor as an advocate, as someone who can help increase self-directed solutions to problems with diet. Lorr lists five descriptors of client perception of counselors: (1) accepting, (2) understanding, (3) independence-encouraging, (4) authoritarian, and (5) critical-hostile.[12]

Clients may be programmed before the interview to see the nutrition counselor as rejecting, dominating, and hostile. Consequently, they resort to behavior they have used in the past in dealing with an unapproachable person. Other clients, on the basis of past experience, see counselors as friendly, supportive, respectful, and positive. Both of these situations can create self-fulfilling prophecies. Counselors can become trapped into behaving in accordance with the clients' theory of the world. Thus, it is important to be open with a client and to discuss interpersonal factors that may affect both client and counselor. Gerber recommends discussing frankly and openly any interpersonal factors that may negatively affect counseling for dietary change.[13]

Clients also come to a nutrition counseling session with feelings about themselves. They want to succeed in changing yet seek to sabotage any efforts toward change so their routines will stay the same.[14] Clients may say, "New eating habits may be healthy, but what changes will they make in my family life?" A familiar image of themselves as overweight can give obese persons a sense of identity and security that they can lose when the pounds come off: "Why should I change my feeling of security to a feeling of having to shape up to what people want me to be?" Clients may come to counselors feeling confused, disturbed, and self-defeated by new knowledge that their health is threatened.[15]

In summary, clients come to counseling with:

1. attitudes and beliefs about people
2. ideas and feelings about counselors and counseling
3. self-images
4. basic incongruities in desired outcomes:
   - wanting to continue along a familiar course
   - wanting to make changes to improve health and well-being.[16]

Counseling is a skill that can correct or validate clients' preconceived beliefs. It enables counselors to behave as decent, empathic persons in spite of the "provocation to be less or the seduction to be more than they are."[17]

Theories Influence Counselors

The many different theories that can influence the way a nutrition counselor conducts a session can be categorized in many different ways. Briefly, five of the theories are (1) person-centered therapy, (2) rational emotive therapy (RET), (3) behavioral therapy, (4) Gestalt therapy, and (5) family therapy.

An analysis of their characteristics as they apply to the nutrition counseling session follows. Note that the ideas in many of these theories overlap.

Person-Centered Therapy

Carl Rogers is the founder of person-centered therapy, originally client-centered therapy.[18] It is based on three major concepts:

1. All individuals are a composite of their physical being, their thoughts, and their behaviors.
2. Individuals function as an organized system, so alterations in one part may produce changes in another part.
3. Individuals react to everything they perceive; this is their reality.

When counselors try to change dietary behaviors, they also must be concerned with clients' thoughts, as behavioral alterations may produce changes in the clients' physical being as well as the cognitive (thoughtful) being. Counselors must also assess client perceptions thoroughly because what clients perceive as reality influences their ability to follow an eating pattern. The skill of listening is very important to this therapy.

The goals of client-centered therapy include:

- promoting a more confident and self-directed person
- promoting a more realistic self-perception
- promoting a positive attitude about self.[19]

Modern Rogerian, person-centered therapy focuses on each person's worth and dignity. The emphasis is on the ability to direct one's own life and move toward self-actualization, growth, and health.[20]

Nutrition counselors should provide the tools to help clients solve their own problems by assessing their current dietary behavior and establishing realistic goals for change. Practitioners also can assess clients' thoughts about their body image and food behaviors. Changing thoughts from negative to positive is a first step toward the client's mastery of positive self-reinforcement skills.

Rational Emotive Therapy

Rational emotive therapy was developed by Albert Ellis, who determined that irrationality was the most frequent source of individual's problems and that self-talk (the monologues individuals have with themselves) was the major cause of emotion-related difficulties.[21] The major purposes of RET are to demonstrate to clients that self-talk, the source of their problems, should be reevaluated and eliminated along with illogical ideas.[22] Clients' major goal in RET is to look to themselves for positive reinforcement for behaviors.

For example, in dietary counseling a hyperlipidemic client says:

"I knew I shouldn't eat that piece of cream pie, but I did. After eating it, I decided, well, what's the use, you've been such a bad person for eating it. You're just making yourself fat and ugly. It's no use. So I ate the entire pie."

The RET counselor in this case can help change self-talk to more positive thoughts: "I ate one piece. Even if it was high in fat, I don't need to feel guilty. I won't eat another piece and that's great. I'm really doing well. I feel better about myself."

Behavioral Therapy

Behavioral counseling, which can be traced back to Pavlov, Skinner, Wolpe, Krumboltz, and Thoreson, states that people are born in a neutral state. Environment, consisting of significant others and experience, shapes their behavior.

Three modes of learning are basic to behavioral counseling:[23]

1. *Operant conditioning* holds that if spontaneous behavior satisfies a need, it will occur with greater frequency. For example, a person who switches to a high-fiber diet and finds that constipation problems are reduced will probably increase fiber in all meals.
2. *Imitation* does not involve teaching a new behavior; instead, the emphasis is on mimicking. For example, a hyperlipidemic client selects a low-cholesterol, low-fat snack after a spouse or friend has just ordered one in a restaurant.
3. *Modeling* extends the concept of imitation, which tends to be haphazard, by providing a planned demonstration. Modeling implies direct teaching of a certain behavior.[24] For example, an overweight client watches a videotape of someone who has lost a large amount of weight. The model's description or demonstration of successful weight loss behaviors helps the client begin a weight-loss program.

Behavioral counseling obviously varies from client to client, as each individual is responsible for shaping the environment to accommodate changes in behavior. Problem behaviors result from faulty learning, and the goal is to eliminate faulty learning and behavior and substitute more adaptive patterns of behavior.[25]

Gestalt Therapy

Gestalt counseling emphasizes confronting problems. Steps toward solving them involve experiencing them in the present rather than the past or the future.

The major goal in Gestalt therapy is to make clients aware of all the experience they have disowned and recognize that individuals are self-regulating. Being aware of the hidden factors related to a problem is the key to finding an eventual solution.[26]

Using Gestalt therapy to help clients with dietary change involves asking them to recognize how many "disowned" factors can contribute to their dietary problems. Showing clients how to be responsible for regulating their behavior is a practical application of the Gestalt approach to counseling. The goal is for clients to take responsibility for making dietary changes.[27] For example, the client who continuously blames poor glucose control on either parents who don't help him or her control foods or teachers who cause him or her to be under stress is disowning behaviors that he or she could control. Helping the client set reasonable behavioral goals can aid in solving the problem of "disowning."

Family Therapy

Family therapy is a new, not yet fully articulated theory. In it, behavior is examined as a system, and the family is considered a system of relationships that influence a client's behavior. The individual client is always seen in the context of relationships, with emphasis on understanding the total system in which the inappropriate behavior exists. The goal is to help both individuals and families to change themselves and the systems within which they live.[28]

One of the major techniques used in family therapy is to involve the client's entire family in solving problems through open and closed questioning. Role playing may be used to illustrate both the negative aspects of "blaming" and the positive aspects, in which "blame" is considered out of bounds.

The theories described above are only 5 of over 200 orientations to helping clients change their behavior. The interviewing and counseling skills presented in the next two chapters provide a format through which counselors can consider and use ideas based on the five theories above. All theories are concerned with change, the generation of novel ways of thinking, being, deciding, and behaving. Once a client who is trying to change a dietary behavior does so in a small way, the nutrition counselor has a beginning foundation with which to support further change. Integrating tenets of many theories into the treatment of a client's dietary problems is the goal. One theory may work best in promoting change at one stage in a client's treatment; another may work well at a different point.

IMPORTANCE OF NUTRITION COUNSELING

Why is counseling important? Nutrition counseling provides a logical structure via strategies based on a variety of counseling theories for all dietary interviews. It sets the stage for optimum dietary adherence.

Dietary adherence, or how well clients follow practitioners' recommendations, should be the ultimate goal of all nutrition counseling sessions. Research has shown that there are many deterrents to dietary adherence:

1. the restrictiveness of the dietary pattern
2. the required changes in life style and behavior
3. the fact that symptom relief may not be noticeable or may be temporary
4. the interference of diet with family or personal habits
5. other barriers:
   - cost
   - access to proper foods
   - effort necessary for food preparation.[29]

Glanz shows that two positive counseling techniques appear to increase dietary adherence: (1) employing more strategies that influence client behavior and (2) involving clients more during the session.[30] She further specifies several strategies for maintaining dietary changes: (1) tailoring the dietary regimen and information about the regimen; (2) using social support inside and outside the health care setting; (3) providing skills and training in addition to information, such as assertiveness training skills and weighing and measuring skills; (4) ensuring effective client-provider communication; and (5) paying attention to follow-up, monitoring, and reinforcement.[31]

Hosking lists conditions that increase dietary adherence in hypertensive clients on salt-restricted eating patterns:

1. diet programs that are individualized, fully explained, and adapted to the client's preferences and life style
2. regular revisits to the same nutrition counselor
3. involvement of the family
4. reinforcement of the eating pattern from every member of the treatment team.[32]

Several research studies have shown that adherence is better when the counselor is warm and empathetic and shows interest ("Call me if there is a problem") and demonstrates genuine concern ("I will call in a week").[33]

Counseling skills help eliminate the hit-or-miss philosophy that allows little assurance for success. This philosophy also tends to be inefficient because the nutrition counselor must backtrack when strategies fail. To provide structure and organization many counseling models resemble the one described below.[34]

Systems Approach to Nutrition Counseling

Models provide a sequenced path for counselors to follow and list essential components in each step of the process. Figure 1-2 shows one model by which nutrition counselors can avoid missing a vital part of the process.

In this model the counselor wears many hats. The first is that of a diagnostician preparing for the interview by reviewing all available data in the medical record, diet records, diet recalls, diet histories, interviews with family members, and other sources.

The session begins with an explanation of the counseling relationship with enough detail that the client knows precisely what will take place. In this stage the practitioner is a teacher informing the client of what the relationship is.

During the assessment phase, once again in the role of diagnostician, the counselor evaluates the client's nutrition status and relates food intake data to behavioral indicators. The practitioner also must establish a safe, trusting, and caring environment, acting as empathizer. Mason specifies the categories of information necessary for assessment of clients' nutritional status:

1. agricultural data
2. socioeconomic data
3. food consumption patterns
4. dietary surveys
5. special studies on foods
6. vital and health statistics
7. anthropometric studies
8. clinical nutrition survey
9. biochemical studies
10. additional medical information.[35]

As for the information necessary to assess behavior, Mason designates several categories to analyze in determining baseline behaviors:

1. general health practices
2. health, attitudes, beliefs, and information
3. physical activities
4. educational achievements and language skills
5. economic considerations
6. environmental considerations
7. social considerations.[36]

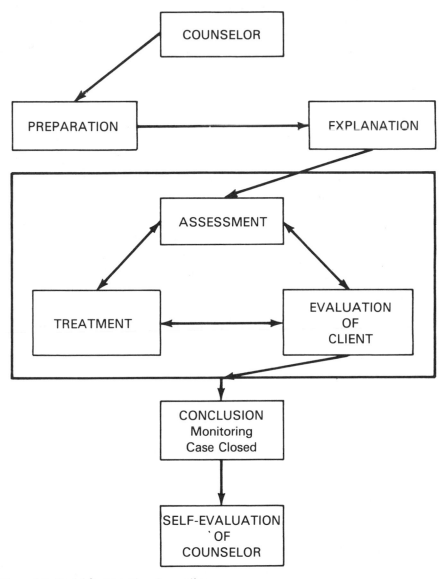

Figure 1-2 Model for Nutrition Counseling

In the treatment phase, the counselor's roles are those of expert and mutual problem solver, roles that usually can be combined only through diligent study and practice. Most novices at counseling tend to be either expert or empathizer. Neither role is bad when the two are used in combination, but singly each can be detrimental to effective counseling.

Many practitioners are familiar with the all-knowing counselor who approaches clients with an air of authority. Clients are overwhelmed by these experts' self-confidence and taken in by the appearance of wisdom. However, when clients return home, they find it very difficult to follow the diet. They tend to forget much of what was said during the counseling session and are incapable of self-direction in adhering to the new regimen. The clients' solution in such a case is to continue with old eating habits.

On the other hand, the mutual problem solvers can become so involved with the client's problems that they lose sight of the other role of information disseminators. Counselors can run into conflicts when they see a client is in error but feel that revealing the mistake may damage the individual's pride and ability to follow the diet.

"Eating fried shrimp out a few times won't matter," the counselor says. To the client on a low-cholesterol diet this may be a signal to go ahead and continue poor eating habits. Back at home, the client may comment to a family member, "The nutritionist said eating shrimp in a restaurant just a few times wouldn't hurt. Three nights a week doesn't seem too often."

In evaluating clients, counselors once again become diagnosticians. If no solution to the problem has been reached, counseling reverts to the assessment or treatment phase. In some cases the clinicians may decide to refer a client to another practitioner more experienced with the problem. In such a case the new counselor probably would start from the beginning.

In concluding the counseling session, counselors should work with clients, with possibly a few notes of wisdom, in which case the counselors become the experts again. Ending the program involves more than just closing the case. Monitoring the clients' performance in the real world is important to continued dietary adherence. This means calling to check on progress and, with the individual's permission, checking with significant others to determine how they feel the clients have progressed.

The last step involves self-evaluation of the counselors' performance. In this case the counselors become the learners, building on past experience to improve present skills.

COUNSELING SKILLS

The basic steps just discussed are a part of counseling, but the complexities go beyond what Figure 1-2 indicates. (Chapters 2 and 3 review these skills and ways to use them.)

Interviewing Skills

Basic to all counseling is a knowledge of interviewing skills. Without these, treatment cannot and will not take place.

Counseling Skills

Once clinicians have acquired this foundation, they then can learn various counseling skills to aid clients in achieving dietary goals. These skills involve assessment, treatment (including planning and implementation), and evaluation. Counseling skills integrate theories and make use of interviewing skills in assessing, treating, and evaluating the client's dietary problems.

Assessment

Assessment involves more than asking clients, "Do you have a problem?" It is a carefully thought out plan to determine areas in which problems occur.

Assessment in nutrition counseling includes ascertaining both what clients are eating and why they make certain food selections.[37] How do practitioners adequately elicit responses to both of these inquiries? The example that follows illustrates a problem that occurs particularly with weight-control clients.

A client returns for a visit following the diet instruction and reports a problem: "I just haven't lost any weight on the diet you recommended." There are several counselor responses:

1. "Did you follow all of my advice?"
2. "Well, what have you been eating?"
3. "What is your typical day like?"

These three questions indicate various levels of interviewing skills. The first question is stated in a way that immediately places clients on the defensive. They feel compelled to give a glowing picture or a multitude of excuses.

The second question focuses only on eating behaviors, disregarding totally the surrounding circumstances that may have instigated the behavior. Depending on the tone of voice, it also may make clients feel compelled to reply with what counselors want to hear.

The third question is stated sensitively and with a show of caring, characteristic of Rogerian style. It does not imply a reprimand, allows the clients time to elaborate on what actually happened, and gives the counselors the information necessary to assess the situation. It sets the stage for the Rogerian style of learning.

In work with practicing nutrition counselors, the author has found the most frequent problem during an interview to be their rush to give advice. It is important to stop and take time to assess the situation first and only then provide advice, allowing the clients to assist by describing how they expect to apply those recommendations in a true-to-life situation.

Treatment

In giving clients strategies to remedy nutrition problems or provide treatment, counselors once again must proceed slowly and involve the clients in planning and setting attainable goals. Counselors frequently decide before the interview how the problems should be solved and try to force clients into preformed molds. They do not give clients an opportunity to participate. In this phase, mutually decided goals will achieve the most success. Counselors should use this sequence of steps in setting goals:

1. Identify nutrition goals
   - Define desired nutrition behaviors [what to do]
   - Determine conditions or circumstances [where and when to do it]
   - Establish the extent or level [how much or how often to do it]

2. Identify nutrition subgoals [a subgoal for a long-term goal of eliminating snacks would be to eliminate the morning snack and determine a workable substitute behavior]
3. Establish client commitment, which includes identifying obstacles that might prevent goal attainment and listing resources needed for goal attainment.[38]

The strategy chosen to help implement these goals once again requires active listening to involve the clients in reaching solutions. Strategies are numerous and require knowledge and experience in counseling psychology. In deciding on a strategy, counselors should ask these questions:

1. Why is the client here?
2. Is the problem the client describes all or only part of the problem? [Many nutrition counselors have thrown their hands up in despair, saying, "He just isn't motivated to follow this diet." In that case the real problem may hinge on emotional stress that must be treated before nutrition counseling can take place. The client might be referred to a psychologist or other professional for help before or concurrent with the nutrition counseling session.]
3. What are the problematic nutrition behaviors and related concerns?
4. Can I describe the conditions contributing to poor nutrition adherence?
5. Am I aware of the present severity and intensity of the nutrition problem?[39]

By asking the questions above, counselors will take steps toward tailoring strategies to each individual's situation. For some clients the problem may be lack of sufficient information to follow the desired regimen. For example, a person with renal disease who follows a low-protein eating pattern routinely has elevated urine urea nitrogen levels inconsistent with diet records that show excellent compliance. A favorite entrée in her favorite restaurant is "Chicken Oscar." After requesting that the restaurant's cook slice one ounce of chicken off the actual portion, she is surprised: one ounce is much smaller than she guessed. For weeks her concept of one ounce of meat has been much greater than the actual amount. Providing enough information for the client to follow a new eating pattern is the first step.

The second step may involve solving a problem of a different nature, forgetting. A guest at a party realizes on arriving that he has no idea what ingredients are in the main dish. If before going to the party he has placed a cue on the refrigerator, "Call hostess to check on what is being served for the party tomorrow," the client can avoid a potentially awkward situation.

The third step in treating dietary problems is much more difficult. It involves diagnosing a problem involving lack of commitment to a dietary regimen. The term "lack of commitment" is not meant to reflect badly on the client but to diagnose accurately poor dietary adherence. For example, a person following a diabetic diet may decide, "I just want to be free from dietary worries for a while. Life is so complicated. I want to forget my diet and splurge." The counselor cannot say, "Fine, don't worry about it for a week," but the counselor *can* say, "What can we do to streamline your dietary efforts? Let us begin by identifying when diet is most frequently a problem." Identification may require the client to keep a diary of thoughts before and following meals that could include *all* thoughts about food—for example, "I ate that chocolate cake even though I knew it would be too high in carbohydrate after that huge dinner." If a pattern of negative thoughts seems to occur frequently at dinner time, the client needs

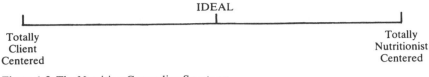

Figure 1-3 The Nutrition Counseling Spectrum

strategies to help make that meal a more positive experience.[40] By identifying a major problem time, the client may be able to work out menus in advance, elicit help from family in meal preparation on specified nights, rely on precalculated exchanges for each meal, build in time to relax before each meal, and work on more positive self-thoughts. By using the client's suggestions and combining ideas, the counselor and client can find a solution to the lack of commitment.

Evaluation

The last phase, evaluation, provides a reassessment of progress for both clients and counselors. Much of the questioning used during the assessment phase can be reused here, focusing on the desired objective and whether or not it was met. The counselors should monitor clients for a time in the real world, asking permission to check with significant others as to whether they feel the persons are doing well.

Counselor self-evaluation frequently does not take place because of time constraints. It can be very important to review what went on in an interview, then determine what made it a success and what might have improved its efficacy or quality.

COUNSELING SPECTRUM

Nutrition counselors assume a variety of roles. During the sessions some role changes take place automatically; others require a great deal of practice and effort. The role of the nutritionist falls on a spectrum such as that in Figure 1-3, including some of the positions on both ends. When counseling is totally dominated by client requests and tangential topics, little behavior change will take place. A session totally dominated by a counselor who provides only information without listening to client concerns can be equally unproductive. The ideal is a mix of client and counselor interaction.

NOTES

1. Marion Mason, Burness G. Wenberg, and P. Kay Welch, *The Dynamics of Clinical Dietetics,* 2nd ed. (New York: John Wiley and Sons, 1982), p. 49.

2. Ibid., p. 45.

3. James Trager, *Food Book* (New York: Grossman Publishers, 1970), pp. 262–263.

4. Thomas Jefferson, letter to Dr. Vine Utley, March 21, 1819, the Thomas Jefferson Memorial Foundation, Monticello, Charlottesville, Va.

5. Margaret A. Ohlson, "The Philosophy of Dietary Counseling," *Journal of the American Dietetic Association* 63 (1973): 13.

6. Lowell S. Selling and Mary Anna S. Ferraro, *The Psychology of Diet and Nutrition* (New

York: W. W. Norton & Co., 1945), pp. 164–166.

7. Allen E. Ivey, Mary Bradford Ivey, and Lynn Simek-Downing, *Counseling and Psychotherapy, Integrating Skills Theory and Practice*, 2nd ed. (Englewood Cliffs, N.J.: Prentice-Hall, 1987), p. xiv.

8. Ohlson, "Philosophy of Dietary Counseling."

9. Selling and Ferraro, *Psychology of Diet and Nutrition*, pp. 164–166.

10. Ivey, Ivey, and Simek-Downing, *Counseling and Psychotherapy*, p. xiv.

11. Buford Stefflre and Kenneth B. Matheny, *The Function of Counseling Theory* (Boston, Mass.: Houghton Mifflin Co., 1968), p. 11.

12. Maurice Lorr, "Client Perception of Therapeutic Relation," *Journal of Counseling and Clinical Psychology* 29 (1965): 148.

13. Sterling K. Gerber, *Responsive Therapy: A Systematic Approach to Counseling Skills* (New York: Human Sciences Press, Inc., 1986), p. 30.

14. Stefflre and Matheny, *The Function of Counseling Theory*, p. 11.

15. Gerber, *Responsive Therapy*, pp. 30–31.

16. Stefflre and Matheny, *Function of Counseling Theory*, p. 11.

17. Ibid., p. 12.

18. Carl R. Rogers, *Client-Centered Therapy* (Boston, Mass.: Houghton Mifflin Co., 1951), p. 487.

19. John J. Pietrofesa et al., *Counseling: Therapy Research and Practice* (Chicago, Ill.: Rand McNally College Publishing Co., 1978), pp. 71–72.

20. Ivey, Ivey, and Simek-Downing, *Counseling and Psychotherapy*, p. 429.

21. Albert Ellis, *Reason and Emotion in Psychotherapy* (New York: Lyle Stuart, 1962), p. 49.

22. Ibid., p. 28.

23. Pietrofesa et al., *Counseling: Therapy Research and Practice*, p. 77.

24. Janet T. Spence et al., *Behavioral Approaches to Therapy* (Morristown, N.J.: General Learning Press, 1976), p. 5.

25. Ivey, Ivey, and Simek-Downing, *Counseling and Psychotherapy*, p. 427.

26. Pietrofesa et al., *Counseling: Therapy Research and Practice*, pp. 80–84.

27. Ivey, Ivey, and Simek-Downing, *Counseling and Psychotherapy*, p. 430.

28. Ibid., p. 436; and Murray Bowen, *Family Therapy in Clinical Practice* (New York: Aronson, 1978), pp. 102–104.

29. Karen Glanz, "Dietitians' Effectiveness and Patient Compliance with Dietary Regimens," *Journal of the American Dietetic Association* 75 (1979): 631; and Glanz, "Nutrition Education for Risk Factor Reduction and Patient Education: A Review," *Preventive Medicine* 14 (1985): 721.

30. Glanz, "Dietitians' Effectiveness and Patient Compliance."

31. Glanz, "Nutrition Education," p. 745.

32. Maxine Hosking, "Eating Out: Salt and Hypertension," *Medical Journal of Australia* 2 (1979): 352.

33. Marshall H. Becker and Lois A. Maiman, "Strategies for Enhancing Patient Compliance," *Journal of Community Health* 6 (1980): 113–135; Zeev Ben-Sira, "Affective and Instrumental Components in Physician-Patient Relationship: An Additional Dimension of Interaction Theory," *Journal of Health and Social Behavior* 21 (1980): 170–180; Robert B. Posner, "Physician-Patient Communication," *American Journal of Medicine* 77 (1984): 59–64; M. Robin DiMatteo and D. Dante DiNicola, *Achieving Patient Compliance: The Psychology of the*

Medical Practitioner's Role (New York: Pergamon Press, 1982), p. 78; M. M. Kayvenhoven et al., "Written Simulation of Patient-Doctor Encounters," *Family Practice* 1 (1983): 25–29; Dennis C. Turk, Donald Meichenbaum, and Myles Genest, *Pain and Behavioral Medicine: A Cognitive-Behavioral Perspective* (New York: Guilford Press, 1983), pp. 182–183; Moira Stewart, "Patient Characteristics Which Are Related to the Doctor-Patient Interaction," *Family Practice* 1 (1983): 30–36; Connie L. Peck and Neville J. King, "Compliance and the Doctor-Patient Relationship," *Drugs* 30 (1985): 78–84; Gene V. Glass and Reinhold M. Kliegl, "An Apology for Research Integration in the Study of Psychotherapy," *Journal of Counseling and Clinical Psychology* 51 (1984): 28–41; Stanley B. Baker et al., "Measured Effects of Primary Prevention Strategies," *Personnel and Guidance Journal* 62 (1984): 459–464; and John T. Beck and Stanley R. Strong, "Stimulating Therapeutic Change with Interpretations," *Journal of Counseling Psychology* 29 (1982): 551–559.

34. Glanz, "Dietitians' Effectiveness and Patient Compliance"; Mason, Wenberg, and Welch, *Dynamics of Clinical Dietetics;* and Norman R. Stewart et al., *Systematic Counseling* (Englewood Cliffs, N.J.: Prentice-Hall, 1978), p. 54.

35. Mason, Wenberg, and Welch, *Dynamics of Clinical Dietetics,* pp. 108–109.

36. Ibid., pp. 124–126.

37. Ibid., pp. 110, 121.

38. Michael L. Russell, *Behavioral Counseling in Medicine* (New York: Oxford University Press, 1986), pp. 79, 116, 127; and William H. Cormier and L. Sherilyn Cormier, *Interviewing Strategies for Helpers, Fundamental Skills and Cognitive Behavioral Intervention,* 2nd ed. (Monterey, Calif.: Brooks/Cole Publishing Company, 1985), pp. 220–221.

39. Ibid., p. 296.

40. Michael J. Mahoney and Kathryn Mahoney, *Permanent Weight Control, a Solution to the Dieter's Dilemma* (New York: W. W. Norton & Co., 1976), pp. 46–48; and Michael J. Mahoney, *Self-Change, Strategies for Solving Personal Problems* (New York: W. W. Norton & Co., 1979), pp. 85–101.

Chapter 2

Interviewing Skills

Objectives for Chapter 2

1. List three characteristics necessary in performing optimum nutrition counseling.
2. Define the following three forms of nonverbal behavior: (a) kinesics, (b) paralinguistics, and (c) proxemics.
3. Apply appropriate responses to given client nonverbal behaviors.
4. Apply appropriate listening responses to given client statements.
5. Apply appropriate action responses to given client statements.
6. Apply appropriate sharing responses to given client statements.
7. Apply appropriate teaching responses to given client statements.

EFFECTIVE COUNSELOR-CLIENT RELATIONSHIPS

Interviewing skills form the foundation for nutrition counseling (Figure 2-1). To learn interviewing skills, practitioners start not by examining their clientele but by looking at themselves. What characteristics should an effective nutrition counselor possess?

Personal Characteristics of Counselors

Ivey et al. describe counseling as a process of interpersonal influence.[1] The way counselors respond to others can greatly influence how clients think and act in the future. The mere act of encouraging clients to talk as opposed to ignoring what they say may influence their lives greatly.

Gerber, in discussing the counselor's internal environment, notes that it can change from week to week and day to day. He cautions against allowing distractions, including a counselor's personal or professional problems, to interfere with a counseling interview and recommends referring a client or delaying a session until the distraction no longer competes with the counseling process.[2]

According to Russell, a good rapport between the nutrition counselor and client is essential to behavior change.[3] From the moment of initial contact, the nutrition counselor strives to develop an open, positive relationship in which the client senses the counselor's acceptance and understanding. To change their behavior, clients must feel comfortable relating intimate details of lifestyle freely to the counselor.

Cormier, Cormier and Weisser suggest a variety of personal characteristics.[4] Practitioners recognize intuitively that being understanding, conveying respect, and being

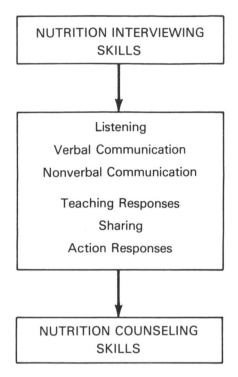

Figure 2-1 Interviewing Skills As a Foundation for Counseling

themselves help create and maintain a more positively channeled session. The way they view themselves and their priorities, values, and expectations can alter the process positively or negatively.

Cormier and Cormier focus on three problems with self-image that can result in negative consequences during an interview: competence, power, and intimacy.[5] Individuals' attitudes can involve the concept of competence. Feelings of incompetence can lead to avoidance of controversial issues in counseling sessions. Nutrition counselors may be afraid to say there are no direct or absolute answers to clients' questions. Either the counselors or the clients may regard a truthful answer such as, "The evidence is not in at this time," as a sign of incompetence, the very trait the practitioners hope to avoid.

Closely tied to feelings of incompetence are those of inadequacy, fear of failure, and fear of success. Counselors with these feelings unconsciously try to keep their negative self-images alive by using several behaviors. They may avoid positive interactions by negating positive feedback and making self-deprecating or apologetic comments. For example, an obese client who has lost weight says, "I really think you're a terrific counselor." A fearful counselor will reply, "Oh, no, I haven't done that much" instead of simply thanking the client for the compliment.

The second potential self-image problem—power—makes counselors feel both omnipotent and fearful of losing control or being weak or unresourceful. In the authoritarian role, counselors try to persuade clients to obey suggestions without question; practitioners dominate the content and direction of the interview, thinking, "I am in charge." If clients resist or do not respond, the outcome for counselors is resentment and anger. Where weak and unresourceful counselors may occupy a subordinate role, complaining, "If you would just do as I say," the powerful practitioner tends to be dictatorial and overly silent, rarely participates in the interview, and, because of this "I am mightier than thou" attitude, often loses credibility.

The third potential self-image problem focuses on feelings about intimacy. These can involve two extremes—affection and rejection. Counselors who are fearful of rejection try to elicit only positive feelings from clients, avoiding confrontation at all costs and ignoring negative cues. This type may even get involved in doing clients favors. Counselors who try to do everything for their clients may be eliminating independent problem solving. Practitioners at the opposite end of the spectrum try to ignore positive client feelings. They tend to act overly gruff and distant to avoid the closeness they fear. This type always tries to maintain the authoritarian role of "expert" to maintain distance. (Appendix A presents a counselor self-image checklist.)

How can practitioners determine whether their personal characteristics are conducive to effective counseling? Brammer stresses the importance of being able to answer these two questions: "'Who am I?' and 'What is important to me?'"[6] Other authors comment on some of the answers to these questions that may lead to more effective interviews. Loughary and Ripley cite warmth, honesty, sincerity, acceptance, self-confidence, openness, etc., as positive characteristics.[7]

Combs et al. emphasize the importance of counselors' ability to perceive from an internal rather than an external reference point.[8] Those who perceive things internally see themselves as in control of situations; those who perceive things externally see others as in charge of the situations. Combs et al. also stress the importance of looking at the world in terms of people rather than things. They describe as good counselors those who see others as able, dependable, friendly, worthy, and helpful and themselves as adequate, worthy, and trustworthy. Such practitioners view their purposes as altruistic rather than narcissistic and are concerned with larger rather than smaller meanings, being open-minded rather than single-minded, involved rather than alienated, and process oriented rather than goal oriented.

Sloane and Staples, in reviewing the effectiveness of a variety of therapies, state that successful clients rate their personal interaction with the counselor as the single most important part of the treatment.[9] Such a powerful statement is difficult to disregard.

Counselors As Growth Facilitators

One of the most crucial of all traits in nutrition counseling is the ability to facilitate growth—the art of helping clients achieve their goals and function on their own. Tyler summarizes successful growth facilitators as accepting, understanding, and sincere (congruence and genuineness).[10] The first step in setting the stage for assuming this role is to show empathy. Brammer states: "The helper sees the world the way the helpee perceives it, that is, from their internal reference."[11]

Ivey et al. identify four participants in an interview: the nutrition counselor and his or her cultural and historical background, and the client and his or her cultural and historical background.[12] For example, touching that is appropriate in many South

American cultures represents an invasion of privacy among many North Americans. Concreteness is valued highly in this culture but may be irrelevant to Asians, who communicate ideas more subtly. Counselors need to understand that the mode of being in the world differs among cultures.

Gilligan stresses the importance of differences in the way men and women think about the world. She proposes possibilities for dealing with goal-directed behaviors in males and more process-oriented and relationship-directed actions in females. Although still controversial, her ideas warrant important consideration in nutrition counseling sessions.[13]

Counselors should begin to see the world through their clients' eyes. To facilitate growth, they must be able to provide concrete and specific strategies for behavior change. (See the segments on strategies in Chapter 3, Counseling Skills.)

Facilitative Levels

Researchers have delineated growth facilitative levels that counselors assume at various points in acquiring nutrition interviewing skills.[14] The levels below illustrate a gradual progression toward a facilitative style—counselors' ability to respond appropriately to clients' problems.

Level 1: The response shows no understanding and no direction in relation to the clients' position. When they bring up a crucial personal topic, the counselors start talking about their own personal problems.

Level 2: The response shows no understanding but some direction. The counselors present only general advice: when clients express difficulty with a weight-loss strategy, the response is, "Well, don't worry about it."

Level 3: The response shows understanding but no direction. Counselors might say, "You feel afraid because you're not sure how to avoid food offers from friends."

Level 4: The response shows understanding and some direction. Counselors react to clients' deficits and proposed way of eliminating them by saying, "You feel afraid because you can't say 'no' and you want to avoid eating high-calorie foods."

Level 5: The response shows understanding and specific direction. It contains the deficit, the goal, and one explicit step for overcoming the problem and reaching the objective: "You feel afraid because you can't say 'no' and you want to avoid eating high-calorie foods. One step is to talk with friends about your attempts to lose weight. Elicit their help."

There are no perfect supercounselors who have all the characteristics to make all sessions successful. Even positive characteristics may not always enhance the interview. Beyond personal characteristics that affect the sessions are the skills that require practice. When these skills are mastered, counseling takes on the characteristics necessary to achieve behavior change.

NONVERBAL COMMUNICATION

Clients' nonverbal behavior can affect the direction of the interview. Effective counselors can use nonverbal cues as signals for unspoken feelings.[15]

Client Nonverbal Behavior

Cormier and Cormier describe three forms of client nonverbal behavior: kinesic, paralinguistic, and proxemic (Table 2-1). Kinesics include a variety of physical behaviors. Paralinguistics refers to how the client's message is delivered. Proxemics involve environmental and personal space.[16] Table 2-1 presents possible meanings associated with each behavior for each region of the body and a general category of autonomic responses. The table is designed to increase awareness of different behaviors; it is not intended to make all nutrition counselors experts on all client feelings by using an inventory to generalize meanings applicable to all such individuals. The developers of this listing (which was designed to cover diet therapy as well as psychological counseling) caution that the effect or meaning of each nonverbal behavior will vary from person to person and culture to culture.

Ivey et al. contrast nonverbal attending patterns in U.S. middle-class culture with patterns of other cultures.[17] Middle-class people tend to make direct eye contact when listening and often do so less frequently when talking; for some Blacks in the United States the pattern is directly opposite. A middle-class person in the United States leans slightly forward, with trunk facing the person, and a handshake means welcome; in certain Eskimo cultures people sit side-by-side when working on a personal issue and a handshake given by a male to a female means a sexual invitation. Middle-class people in the United States prefer varied vocal tone and moderate speech rates; many Hispanic groups prefer more extensive expressive vocal tones and rapid speech. A comfortable physical distance for U.S. middle-class persons is usually arm's length or more; in Arab and other Middle Eastern cultures 6–12 inches is preferred, a distance that makes the middle-class U.S. person uncomfortable.

Possible counselor responses to clients' nonverbal behavior are discussed below.

The Counselors' Response

Passons describes several ways of responding to nonverbal client behaviors "involving congruence, mixed messages, silence, changing cues, and refocusing for direction."[18] Nutrition counselors can use these suggestions to decide on a reply to client statements about dietary adherence.

Congruence

Are the clients' nonverbal messages congruent with the verbal ones? An example might be the individual with diabetes who comes for the first follow-up interview. With furrowed brow, the client sends this confused message to the counselor: "How do I fill in this record? I have forgotten your directions." The counselor can make a mental note of the congruence in behaviors or ask the client to explain the meaning of the nonverbal conduct: "I noticed that your brow was furrowed. What does that mean?" The response could provide information on specifically why the record was not completed. Was it too difficult? Did measuring the foods interfere with meal preparation for the family? Was the counselor's description of the information needed on the record unclear?

Table 2-1 Client Nonverbal Behavior Checklist

Nonverbal Dimensions	Behaviors	Description of Counselor-Client Interaction	Possible Effects or Meanings
Kinesics			
Eyes			
_____	Direct eye contact	Client has just shared concern with counselor. Counselor responds; client maintains eye contact.	Readiness or willingness for interpersonal communication or exchange; attentiveness
_____	Lack of sustained eye contact	Each time counselor brings up the topic of client's family, client looks away.	Withdrawal or avoidance of interpersonal exchange; or respect or deference
		Client demonstrates intermittent breaks in eye contact while conversing with counselor.	Respect or deference
		Client mentions sexual concerns, then abruptly looks away. When counselor initiates this topic, client looks away again.	Withdrawal from topic of conversation; discomfort or embarrassment; or preoccupation
_____	Lowering eyes— looking down or away	Client talks at some length about alternatives to present job situation. Pauses briefly and looks down. Then resumes speaking and eye contact with counselor.	Preoccupation
_____	Staring or fixating on person or object	Counselor has just asked client to consider consequences of a certain decision. Client is silent and gazes at a picture on the wall.	Preoccupation; possibly rigidity or uptightness; pondering; difficulty in finding an answer

Table 2-1 continued

Nonverbal Dimensions	Behaviors	Description of Counselor-Client Interaction	Possible Effects or Meanings
Eyes (cont'd)			
_____	Darting eyes or blinking rapidly—rapid eye movements; twitching brow	Client indicates desire to discuss a topic yet is hesitant. As counselor probes, client's eyes move around the room rapidly.	Excitation or anxiety; or wearing contact lenses
_____	Squinting or furrow on brow	Client has just asked counselor for advice. Counselor explains role and client squints, and furrows appear in client's brow.	Thought or perplexity; or avoidance of person or topic
		Counselor suggests possible things for client to explore in difficulties with parents. Client doesn't respond verbally; furrow in brow appears.	Avoidance of person or topic
_____	Moisture or tears	Client has just reported recent death of father; tears well up in client's eyes.	Sadness; frustration; sensitive area of concern
		Client reports real progress during past week in marital communication; eyes get moist.	Happiness
_____	Eye shifts	Counselor has just asked client to remember significant events in week; client pauses and looks away; then responds and looks back.	Processing or recalling material; or keen interest; satisfaction
_____	Pupil dilation	Client discusses spouse's sudden disinterest and pupils dilate.	Alarm; or keen interest

Table 2-1 continued

Nonverbal Dimensions	Behaviors	Description of Counselor-Client Interaction	Possible Effects or Meanings
Eyes (cont'd)		Client leans forward while counselor talks and pupils dilate.	Keen interest; satisfaction
Mouth	Smiles	Counselor has just asked client to report positive events of the week. Client smiles, then recounts some of these instances.	Positive thought, feeling, or action in content of conversation; or greeting
		Client responds with a smile to counselor's verbal greeting at beginning of interview.	Greeting
	Tight lips (pursed together)	Client has just described efforts at sticking to a difficult living arrangement. Pauses and purses lips together.	Stress or determination; anger or hostility
		Client has just expressed irritation at counselor's lateness. Client sits with lips pursed together while counselor explains the reasons.	Anger or hostility
	Lower lip quivers or biting of lip	Client starts to describe her recent experience of being laughed at by colleagues at work because she is trying hard to follow her new eating pattern. As client continues to talk, her lower lip quivers; occasionally she bites her lip.	Anxiety, sadness, or fear

Table 2-1 continued

Nonverbal Dimensions	Behaviors	Description of Counselor-Client Interaction	Possible Effects or Meanings
Mouth (cont'd)			
		Client discusses loss of parental support after a recent divorce. The problems associated with this home situation make following a new eating pattern difficult. Client bites her lip after discussing this.	Sadness
	Open mouth without speaking	Counselor has just expressed feelings about a block in the relationship. Client's mouth drops open; client says was not aware of it.	Surprise; or suppression of yawn—fatigue
		It has been a long session. As counselor talks, client's mouth parts slightly.	Suppression of yawn—fatigue
Facial Expressions			
	Eye contact with smiles	Client talks very easily and smoothly, occasionally smiling; maintains eye contact for most of session.	Happiness or comfortableness
	Eyes strained; furrow on brow; mouth tight	Client has just reported strained situation with a spouse who dislikes her efforts to cut down on fat intake. Client then sits with lips pursed together and frowns.	Anger; or concern; sadness

Table 2-1 continued

Nonverbal Dimensions	Behaviors	Description of Counselor-Client Interaction	Possible Effects or Meanings
Facial Expressions (cont'd)			
_____	Eyes rigid, mouth rigid (unanimated)	Client states: "I have nothing to say"; there is no evident expression or alertness on client's face.	Preoccupation; anxiety; fear
Head			
_____	Nodding head up and down	Client has just expressed concern over own health status and what the new eating pattern will do to improve health; counselor reflects client's feelings. Client nods head and says "That's right."	Confirmation; agreement; or listening, attending
		Client nods head during counselor explanation.	Listening; attending
_____	Shaking head from left to right	Counselor has just suggested that client's continual lateness to sessions may be an issue that needs to be discussed. Client responds with "No," and shakes head from left to right.	Disagreement; or disapproval
_____	Hanging head down, jaw down toward chest	Counselor initiates topic of termination. Client lowers head toward chest, then says "I am not ready to stop the counseling sessions."	Sadness; concern

Table 2-1 continued

Nonverbal Dimensions	Behaviors	Description of Counselor-Client Interaction	Possible Effects or Meanings
Shoulders			
_____	Shrugging	Client reports that spouse just walked out with no explanation. Client shrugs shoulders while describing this.	Uncertainty; or ambivalence
_____	Leaning forward	Client has been sitting back in the chair. Counselor discloses something personal; client leans forward and asks counselor a question about the experience.	Eagerness; attentiveness; openness to communication
_____	Slouched, stooped, rounded, or turned away from person	Client reports feeling inadequate and defeated because of snacking; slouches in chair after saying this.	Sadness or ambivalence; or lack of receptivity to interpersonal exchange
		Client reports difficulty in talking. As counselor pursues this, client slouches in chair and turns shoulders away from counselor.	Lack of receptivity to interpersonal exchange
Arms and Hands			
_____	Arms folded across chest	Counselor has just initiated conversation. Client doesn't respond verbally; sits back in chair with arms crossed against chest.	Avoidance of interpersonal exchange; or dislike
_____	Trembling and fidgety hands	Client expresses fear of weight gain; hands tremble while talking about this.	Anxiety or anger
		In a loud voice, client expresses resentment; client's hands shake while talking.	Anger

Table 2-1 continued

Nonverbal Dimensions	Behaviors	Description of Counselor-Client Interaction	Possible Effects or Meanings
Arms and Hands (cont'd)			
_____	Fist clenching of objects or holding hands tightly	Client has just come in for initial interview. Says that he or she feels uncomfortable; hands are clasped together tightly.	Anxiety or anger
		Client expresses hostility toward husband; clenches fists while talking.	Anger
_____	Arms unfolded—arms and hands gesturing in conversation	Counselor has just asked a question; client replies and gestures during reply.	Accenting or emphasizing point in conversation; or openness to interpersonal exchange
		Counselor initiates new topic. Client readily responds; arms are unfolded at this time.	Openness to interpersonal exchange
_____	Rarely gesturing, hands and arms stiff	Client arrives for initial session. Responds to counselor's questions with short answers. Arms are kept down at side.	Tension or anger
		Client has been referred; sits with arms down at side while explaining reasons for referral and irritation at being here.	Anger
Legs and Feet			
_____	Legs and feet appear comfortable and relaxed	Client's legs and feet are relaxed without excessive movement while client freely discusses personal concerns.	Openness to interpersonal exchange; relaxation

Table 2-1 continued

Nonverbal Dimensions	Behaviors	Description of Counselor-Client Interaction	Possible Effects or Meanings
Legs and Feet (cont'd)			
_____	Crossing and uncrossing legs repeatedly	Client is talking rapidly in spurts about problems; continually crosses and uncrosses legs while doing so.	Anxiety; depression
_____	Foot-tapping	Client is tapping feet during a lengthy counselor summary; client interrupts counselor to make a point.	Anxiety; impatience— wanting to make a point
_____	Legs and feet appear stiff and controlled	Client is open and relaxed while talking about job. When counselor introduces topic of marriage, client's legs become more rigid.	Uptightness or anxiety; closed to extensive interpersonal exchange
Total Body			
_____	Facing other person squarely or leaning forward	Client shares a concern and faces counselor directly while talking; continues to face counselor while counselor responds.	Openness to interpersonal communication and exchange
_____	Turning of body orientation at an angle, not directly facing person, or slouching in seat	Client indicates some difficulty in "getting in to" interview. Counselor probes for reasons; client turns body away.	Less openness to interpersonal exchange
_____	Rocking back and forth in chair or squirming in seat	Client indicates a lot of nervousness about an approaching conflict situation. Client rocks as this is discussed.	Concern; worry; anxiety
_____	Stiff—sitting erect and rigidly on edge of chair	Client indicates some uncertainty about direction of interview; sits very stiff and erect.	Tension; anxiety; concern

Table 2-1 continued

Nonverbal Dimensions	Behaviors	Description of Counselor-Client Interaction	Possible Effects or Meanings
Paralinguistics			
Voice Level and Pitch			
_____	Whispering or inaudibility	Client has been silent for a long time. Counselor probes; client responds, but in a barely audible voice.	Difficulty in disclosing
_____	Pitch changes	Client is speaking at a moderate voice level while discussing job. Then client begins to talk about unsupportive friends at work and voice pitch rises considerably.	Topics of conversation have different emotional meanings
Fluency in Speech			
_____	Stuttering, hesitations, speech errors	Client is talking rapidly about feeling uptight in certain social situations; client stutters and makes some speech errors while doing so.	Sensitivity about topic in conversation; or anxiety and discomfort
_____	Whining or lisp	Client is complaining about having a hard time losing weight; voice goes up like a whine.	Dependency or emotional emphasis
_____	Rate of speech slow, rapid, or jerky	Client begins interview talking slowly about a bad weekend. As topic shifts to client's feelings about self, client talks more rapidly	Sensitivity to topics of conversation; or topics have different emotional meanings
_____	Silence	Client comes in and counselor invites client to talk; client remains silent.	Reluctance to talk; or preoccupation
		Counselor has just asked client a question. Client pauses and thinks over a response.	Preoccupation; or desire to continue speaking after making a point; thinking about how to respond

Table 2-1 continued

Nonverbal Dimensions	Behaviors	Description of Counselor-Client Interaction	Possible Effects or Meanings
Fluency in Speech (cont'd)			
		A Chinese client talks about own family. Pauses; then resumes conversation to talk more about same subject.	Desire to continue speaking after making a point
Autonomic Responses			
_____	Clammy hands, shallow breathing, sweating, pupil dilation, paleness, blushing, rashes on neck	Client discusses the exciting prospect of having two desirable job offers. Breathing becomes faster and client's pupils dilate.	Arousal—positive (excitement, interest) or negative (anxiety, embarrassment)
		Client starts to discuss binge eating; breathing becomes shallow and red splotches appear on neck.	Anxiety, embarrassment
Proxemics			
Distance			
_____	Moves away	Counselor has just confronted client; client moves back before responding verbally.	Signal that space has been invaded; increased arousal, discomfort
_____	Moves closer	Midway through session, client moves chair toward helper.	Seeking closer interaction, more intimacy
Position in Room			
_____	Sits behind or next to an object in the room, such as table or desk	A new client comes in and sits in a chair that is distant from counselor.	Seeking protection or more space
_____	Sits near counselor without any intervening objects	A client who has been in to see counselor before sits in chair closest to counselor.	Expression of adequate comfort level

Source: From *Interviewing Strategies for Helpers,* 2nd ed., by W. H. Cormier and L. S. Cormier. Copyright ©1985, 1979 by Wadsworth Inc. Reprinted by permission of Brooks/Cole Publishing Company, Pacific Grove, California 93950.

Mixed Messages

Is there a mixed message or discrepancy between the verbal and nonverbal messages? For example, a client comes in after having followed a no-added-salt eating pattern for several weeks and states, "It's going really [pause] well. I've had [pause] very few problems," while looking down and leaning away. The nutrition counselor can deal with these discrepancies in one of three ways: (1) just to take mental note; (2) to describe the discrepancy to the client, for example, "You say the diet is really going well and that there are few problems but you were looking down and really spoke with a lot of hesitation"; (3) to reply, "I noticed you looked away and paused as you said that. What does that mean?"

Silence

Are there nonverbal behaviors with silence? Silence does not mean that nothing is happening. It can have different meanings from one culture to another.[19]

In some cultures silence denotes respect.[20] Sue and Sue point out that for the Chinese and Japanese silence means a desire to resume speaking after making a point. Once again the nutrition counselor can mentally note the silence, describe it to the client, or ask the client to explain it.

Changing Cues

Is it necessary to distract or interrupt clients by focusing on nonverbal behavior? It may be needed to change the flow of the interview because continuation of the topic may be unproductive. If clients are pouring out a lot of information or are rambling, a change in the direction of the interview may be useful. In such instances, nutrition counselors can distract clients from the verbal content by refocusing on nonverbal behavior.

For example, for unproductive content in a client's messages, a counselor might say, "Our conversation so far has been dealing with your inability to cope with your spouse's unsupportive comments about your low-protein eating pattern. Are you aware that you have been gripping the sides of your chair with your hands while you speak?"

Nutrition counselors must decide very carefully whether or not such distractions can be destructive or productive to the interview. If the change in flow makes the clients feel unable to continue to air feelings, the distraction could be detrimental. Experienced counselors probably will find that their own intuition helps in knowing when to interrupt.

Refocusing for Redirection

Are there pronounced changes in the clients' nonverbal behavior? Initially they may sit with arms crossed, then become more relaxed, with arms unfolded and hands gesturing. Once again counselors can respond either overtly or covertly. A nutrition counselor might respond to a seemingly more relaxed client by saying, "You seem more relaxed now. Do you feel less tense?"

Counselor Nonverbal Communication

The counselors' nonverbal communication can have a great impact on the relationship. Based on analogue research, Cormier and Cormier report that the nonverbal counselor behaviors that seem to be most important include expressions in the eyes and face, head nodding and smiles, body orientation and posture, some vocal cues, and physical distance between practitioners and clients.[21] Counselors can determine whether they are demonstrating desirable behaviors by asking someone to observe their nonverbal behaviors. Appendix B is a checklist a third-party observer can mark while evaluating the counselor's nonverbal behavior. One word of caution: counselors should not try to apply these behaviors to themselves in a rigid way. Inflexible conformity can increase their tension in an interview, and their nonverbal expression of that tension will be sensed and increased by clients.

VERBAL COMMUNICATION

The counselors' knowledge and command of verbal skills can play an important part in directing the interview.

Conversational Style

Beginning counselors tend to fall into a kind of conversational mode that is very comfortable for them. Such a style is typical of a friendly chat with a neighbor. As a part of this conversation they are under extreme pressure to provide an immediate solution for the client's problem.

Certain aspects of conversational style interfere with the objectives of counseling:[22]

1. Cocktail party "small talk": Responding to a client at the beginning of an interview with, "Did you see the diet recipes in today's paper?"
2. Expressions of blame, criticism, or judgments: Client: "The diet has gone badly this week." Nutrition Counselor: "I can certainly see that from this weight graph."
3. Expressions of advice offered in a preaching or self-righteous tone: "You should really learn to have more self-control with this diet," or "You really ought to lose 20 pounds."
4. Expressions of sympathy in a patronizing tone: "I really feel sorry for you. You seem to get absolutely no support from your family in following this diet," or "Now that you've told me your problems with weight loss, I'm sure I can make you feel better."
5. Threats or arguing: "You'd better follow the low-protein eating pattern for your own good," or "I think your constant rejection of my suggestions is uncalled for."
6. Rigidity or inflexibility: "There is only one right way to approach a cholesterol, fat-controlled eating pattern," or "Your suggestions won't work with a low-sodium diet."
7. Overanalyzing, overinterpreting, or intellectualizing: "I think you find being overweight enjoyable, or you would follow the diet."

8. Several questions at once: "How do you feel about following a low-cholesterol diet? Does it fit into your family life? if 'no,' why isn't it working out? Could you tell me?"
9. Extensive self-disclosure, sharing the counselor's own problems: "I've been thinking a lot about my weight loss attempts as you were talking. I, too, have had several problems. For instance...."

Each of these examples illustrates the importance of using appropriate interviewing skills during a session.

Counselor-Client Focus Identification

Once they have altered their conversational style appropriately, there are several specific ways nutrition counselors can learn to provide direction and focus for an interview. Six categories of subject focus and three areas of verbal focus, delineated by Ivey and Gluckstern, can be stated in past, present, or future time:

1. Client focused (subject is "you"): "Mrs. Jones, you feel frustrated with situations involving restaurant eating."
2. Interviewer focused (subject is "I"): "I have been thinking about your problem with lack of support at work for following this dietary regimen."
3. Other person focused (subject is "he," "she," or "they"): "Your husband appears to give you little support for following this new eating pattern."
4. Relationship of group or "we" focused (subject is "we"): "Right now we seem to be getting somewhere. Let's list some possible solutions to your problem."
5. Problem or main-theme focused (subject is a noun, such as diet, sodium, or calories). "From what you are saying, the main problem seems to be lack of time in meal preparation."
6. Culture or environment focused (subject is society, culture, or environment): "Society today seems to idealize thinness."[23]

Lavelle and Cormier and Cormier suggest three areas of focus indicated by the verb in the sentence:

1. affective focused
2. behavioral focused
3. cognitive focused.[24]

The verb "to feel" is used frequently when counselors want to focus affectively: "You are feeling very frustrated by your desire to follow the diet and your family's uncooperativeness." Behavioral focused sentences usually contain verbs such as "to do," "to act," or "to behave," as in, "What are you doing about this?" A cognitive focus is revealed by such verbs as "to think" or "to tell oneself": "What are you telling yourself when you eat the entire pie?"

The verb can be in the past, present, or future tense, which determines the time focus of the sentence. Too much focus on the past or future may indicate an avoidance of the present. An example might be this description of weight loss by one client.

"My first husband was always supportive. My second husband wants me to be small but he always tempts me with high-calorie snacks. Still, he always talks about the future when I will be thin."

This client is dwelling on both the past and the future but does not seem to recognize the importance of present goal setting.

The following examples show how verbal focusing might be used in response to a client who says: "I'm having a conflict about wanting to lose weight but have no one at home who supports me when we eat out."

1. Client-Cognitive—Present Focus: "You find yourself thinking about wanting to lose weight but also wanting to eat out with the family." In this response, the client-subject focus is reflected in "You find yourself," the cognitive focus by "thinking about," and the present time focus by the present tense of the verb "find."
2. Client-Affective—Present Focus: "You're feeling concerned about wanting to lose weight and also wanting to eat out with your family."
3. Group-Behavioral—Future Focus: "Perhaps this is an area we will explore together and see what you can do."
4. Problem-Cognitive—Present Focus: "Losing weight is not always easy. When I think about it, there are lots of obstacles to try to overcome."
5. Cultural/Environmental-Cognitive/Behavior—Past Focus: "This is a conflict many weight-loss clients have faced because of the ideas our culture has given us about what people should eat in social situations."

LISTENING RESPONSES

Listening responses are the first step in forming a repertoire of interviewing skills involving clarification, paraphrase, reflection, and summarization.[25]

Clarification

Clarification is posing a question, often after an ambiguous client message. Clarification may be used to make the previous message explicit and to confirm the accuracy of the counselor's perceptions of it. An example of incorrect use of clarification is:

> CLIENT: "I wish I didn't have to fill in those diet records. They seem so silly to me."
> COUNSELOR: "Why don't you like my diet aids?"
> CLIENT: "I like all of them and the record has been useful, but I just don't feel as though it is helping me at this point."

In the next example, a statement of clarification establishes exactly what was said without relying on assumptions and inferences that are not confirmed or explored:

> CLIENT: "I wish I didn't have to fill in those diet records. They seem so silly to me."
> COUNSELOR: "Are you saying that you don't see any purpose to filling in the diet record?"
> CLIENT: "No, I really don't. I just don't think I need them at this point."

Paraphrase

Paraphrase is a restatement or rephrasing of the client's message in the counselor's own words. For example, the client says: "I don't mind eating low-protein foods at home, but my job requires that I travel one week of every month. It is impossible to follow the diet when eating in restaurants!" In paraphrasing, counselors can:

1. restate the message to themselves
2. identify the content part of the message ("I don't mind eating low-protein foods at home," "My job requires one week of travel a month," "It is impossible to follow the diet when eating in restaurants.")
3. translate the message into their own words. ("You can follow the diet at home but have problems following it in restaurants.")

Reflection

Reflection of feelings is used to rephrase the affective part of the message. This form of listening response has three purposes: (1) to encourage expression of more feelings, (2) to help clients experience feelings more intensely so they can become aware of unresolved problems, and (3) to help clients become more aware of feelings that dominate them.

For example, a client comments: "I feel so depressed. Sometimes trying to match the foods I'm eating to insulin dosages seems useless." In reply, counselors can:

1. restate the client's message covertly
2. identify the affective part of the message ("I feel so depressed")
3. translate the clients' affect words into their own words. ("You sometimes feel frustrated with following the eating pattern for your diabetes.")

One word of caution: a reflection is more than just beginning a statement with the words "You feel. . . ." It is a reflecting back of the emotional part of the message with appropriate affect words. (Commonly used affect words are listed in Table 2-2.)

Summarization

The fourth listening response, summarization, requires extending the paraphrase and reflection responses. It is a rather complex skill that includes paying attention to both content and feelings. It also includes elements of purpose, timing, and effect of the statements (process). Brammer recommends these guidelines for summarization:

1. Attend to major topics and emotions apparent as the client speaks.
2. Summarize key ideas into broad statements.
3. Do not add new ideas.
4. Decide whether it is wise for you as a counselor to summarize or ask the client to summarize the broad themes, agreements, or plans.

Table 2-2 Commonly Used Affect Words

Happiness	Sadness	Fear	Uncertainty	Anger
Happy	Discouraged	Scared	Puzzled	Upset
Pleased	Disappointed	Anxious	Confused	Frustrated
Satisfied	Hurt	Frightened	Unsure	Bothered
Glad	Despairing	Defensive	Uncertain	Annoyed
Optimistic	Depressed	Threatened	Skeptical	Irritated
Good	Disillusioned	Afraid	Doubtful	Resentful
Relaxed	Dismayed	Tense	Undecided	Mad
Content	Pessimistic	Nervous	Bewildered	Outraged
Cheerful	Miserable	Uptight	Mistrustful	Hassled
Thrilled	Unhappy	Uneasy	Insecure	Offended
Delighted	Hopeless	Worried	Bothered	Angry
Excited	Lonely	Panicked	Disoriented	Furious

Source: From *Interviewing Strategies for Helpers,* 2nd ed., by W. H. Cormier and L. S. Cormier. Copyright © 1985, 1979 by Wadsworth Inc. Reprinted by permission of Brooks/Cole Publishing Company, Pacific Grove, California 93950.

To make this decision, counselors should review the purpose of the summarization:

1. Was it to encourage the client at the beginning of the interview?
2. Was it to bring scattered thoughts and feelings into focus?
3. Was it to close the discussion on the major theme of the interview?
4. Was it to check your understanding of the interview's progress?
5. Was it to encourage the client to explore the basic theme of the interview more carefully?
6. Was it to end the relationship with a progress summary?
7. Was it to reassure the client that the interview was progressing well?[26]

Many summarization responses include references to both cognitive and affective messages:

> CLIENT: "I want to follow the diet we discussed, but so many things pull me toward food—parties, friends, my family, etc. Above all this, though, I know I want to see my blood cholesterol come down."
>
> COUNSELOR: "You feel torn. You want to reduce your blood cholesterol level, but sometimes you feel reluctant to avoid all of the people and things pulling you toward food" (summarization of emotion), or "You know that you do want to reduce your blood cholesterol level" (summarization of contents).

ACTION RESPONSES

These listening responses deal primarily with the clients' message from their point of view. For the nutrition counseling to progress, the process must move beyond the clients' point of view to use of responses based on counselor-generated data and perceptions. These are counselor directed and are labeled active responses. They involve a combination of counselor perceptions and hypotheses, and client messages and behaviors.[27]

The purpose of active responses is to help clients recognize the need for change and positive action in solving nutrition problems. Active replies include probing, attributing, confronting, and interpreting responses.[28]

Probing

In nutrition counseling, an important part of gathering information on clients' eating patterns involves the art of probing. Probing can involve both open and closed questions.[29] Initially, it should be aimed at eliciting the most information possible. The clients should feel free to respond at length on any problem that may limit adherence to the eating pattern. The most direct way to probe is to ask open-ended questions that begin with "what," "when," "how," "where," "could," "why," or "who." Such questions require more than just "yes" or "no" responses. Their purposes can be varied:

1. to begin an interview
2. to encourage client elaboration or to obtain information
3. to elicit specific examples of clients' nutrition-related behaviors, feelings, or thoughts
4. to develop client commitment to communicate by inviting the client to talk and providing guidance toward a focused interaction.[30]

Ivey et al. indicate the questions that draw out facts. "How" questions elicit facts about the process a client goes through in maintaining an eating pattern or feelings surrounding that process, "why" questions elicit reasons for actions, and "could" questions probe into the general picture of problem eating behaviors.[31]

Once the clients have provided information adequate for assessment of the nutrition problem, counselors can help focus attention on central issues by using closed questions.[32] When the clients then have a focus on which to concentrate, open invitations to talk may be used again. In becoming skilled interviewers, counselors learn to use a balance of open and closed questions. Various types of interviews use different proportions of open and closed questions.

An example of the use of probes: The client (a 25-year-old male who is trying to follow a 300-milligram cholesterol diet) complains: "I really have problems getting my wife to cook low-cholesterol meals. She says she wants to cook the way her mother taught her. I feel really frustrated about everything."

The counselor responds with open-ended probes:

- "What else do you think or feel frustrated about?"
- "How long have you been feeling this way?"
- "When are some specific times you feel frustrated?"
- "Who are you with when you feel frustrated?"
- "What do you do when you feel frustrated?"

Counselors should keep in mind that extensive self-disclosure requests can be damaging to clients. Janis reports that seeking high self-disclosure or asking clients about material they would not usually share with other family members or friends has a detrimental effect on adherence to diet.[33] Asking clients personal questions about current and past sorrows, sex life, guilt feelings, secret longings, and similar private events can result in the clients' becoming demoralized despite the counselor's positive comments and acceptance. In contrast, moderate levels of questions about feelings that focus on strengths as well as weaknesses enhance dietary adherence.[34]

After the client has discussed at length several specific frustrating instances, the counselor can focus the interview with closed probes such as:

- "Is your wife aware that you feel frustrated in these situations?"
- "Have you spoken to your wife about these frustrating instances?"
- "Can you speak with your wife about these problem situations?"
- "Do you see any solutions to this particular frustration?"

Attributing

Attributing responses point to the clients' current potential for being successful in a designated activity. This response has several purposes:

1. to encourage the client who lacks initiative or self-confidence to do something
2. to expand the client's awareness of personal strength
3. to point out a potentially helpful client action.[35]

In deciding whether or not to use this response, counselors should focus on inferring how the client will react. Will the attributing response "reinforce the client's action-seeking behavior or the client's feelings of inadequacy?"[36] This response should be used only when there is a basis for recognizing the client's ability to pursue desired action, not simply as a pep talk to smooth over or discount true feelings of discouragement. Feelings should be reflected and clarified first. Finally, the ability or attributing response should be used when the client is ready for action but seems hesitant to jump in or initiate a step without some encouragement.

An example of an ability response:

> CLIENT (a 30-year-old woman who has tried repeatedly to lose weight): "I'm really discouraged with trying to lose weight at this point. I feel like I can't do anything right. Not only has it affected me personally but now it is affecting my family. I just don't feel I can do anything right."
> COUNSELOR: "Although you feel discouraged with weight loss right now, you still have those personal qualities you had when you lost weight before."

Confronting

Ivey et al. describe confrontation as a skill that exists only in combination with others. It may be contained in a paraphrase ("You want to see good blood sugars, but you hate watching the amount of foods you eat at parties") or a reflection of feeling ("On the one hand you are angry about having a disease that forces you to watch what you eat, but on the other hand you are grateful that following an eating pattern can improve your blood sugars") or any other skills.[37]

A confronting response can be a descriptive statement of clients' mixed messages or an identification of an alternate view or perception of something the individuals distort. There are two intended purposes behind a confronting response: to identify the client's mixed or distorted messages and to explore other ways of perceiving the client's self or situation.[38]

Confronting responses can have very powerful effects. Counselors should keep several basic rules in mind before using them:

1. Make the confronting response a description instead of a judgment or evaluation of the client's message or behavior.
2. Cite specific examples of the behavior rather than making vague inferences.
3. Prior to confronting the client, build rapport and trust.
4. Offer the confrontation when the client is most likely to accept it.
5. Do not overload the client with confrontations that make heavy demands in a short time.[39]

The timing of a confronting response is important. A confrontation should always take place at a time when clients do not feel threatened, not when it is totally unexpected. Adequate time for talking and listening should be provided in the interview.

Counselors' feelings also are important. Johnson clearly emphasizes confronting clients only if the practitioners are genuinely interested in improving the relationship,[40] never with the idea of punishing or criticizing clients. Before confronting, counselors should try to list their reasons for wanting to challenge discrepancies, distortions, or unproductive behaviors.

Johnson describes eight components of effective confrontation by counselors (Exhibit 2-1).[41]

Clients' reactions to a confrontation vary. Cormier, Cormier, and Weisser describe four types: denial, confusion, false acceptance, and genuine acceptance.[42] Egan lists specific ways clients might deny the confrontation:

1. Discredit the counselor: "How could you know when you've never had to follow a low-cholesterol diet?"
2. Persuade the counselor that his or her views are wrong or misinterpreting: "I really do want to lower my cholesterol. I try very hard. I think this diet you gave me is too high in cholesterol and fat; that's why I can't bring my blood cholesterol down."
3. Devaluate the importance of the topic: "I'm not sure this is worth all of my time. I could just take diet pills."
4. Seek support elsewhere: "I told my husband about your comment and he thinks I must accept friends' offers of food at parties."[43]

If clients seem confused about the meaning of the confrontation, the counselors may not have been specific or concise enough; or confessed lack of understanding may be a way of avoiding the impact of the confrontation.

Sometimes clients may seem to accept the confrontation. If they show a sincere desire to change behavior, their acceptance probably is genuine. However, they may

Exhibit 2-1 Components of Effective Confrontation

1. *Personal statements:* These opening statements usually begin with the pronoun "I." Included in this statement are expressions of feelings, attitudes, or opinions. Examples are:

    "I need to talk to you."

    "There is something I've been hearing over and over in our conversation that I would like to speak to you about."

    "I have been confused during this session by something you've been saying."

2. *Relationship statements:* Define your relationship with the other person. An example is:

    "Lately we've been trying to work together to come up with some possible solutions to your binge eating."

3. *Description of behavior:* A description of a specific behavior would include specific time and place of occurrence. An example is:

    "From your description, binge eating occurs on weekends during parties."

4. *Descriptions of your feelings and interpretations of the client's situation:* An example:

    "I am confused when you say that you want to stop eating at parties but you feel compelled to continue because of social pressure. There seem to be two messages here."

5. *Understanding response:* This is to be sure that what you have said is what the client has understood.

    COUNSELOR: "Do you see what I mean?" "Is this the way you see things?"

    CLIENT: "Yes."

6. *Perception check:* This is stated as a question to the client to double-check thoughts and feelings at this point.

    COUNSELOR: "How do you feel about what I am saying?"

    CLIENT: "I can see that I seem to be giving a mixed message. I want to lose weight but there are always obstacles when I go to parties. Friends always ask me to eat; I feel compelled to say "Yes."

7. *Interpretive response:* This is a paraphrase of what the client said in 5 and 6:

    "From what you have said, you seem to feel this same confusion. You want to lose weight but there is always someone pushing you to eat to be sociable."

8. *Constructive feedback:* This component of confrontation calls for working together for a solution. Alternatives are presented and weighed. The counselor, at this point, should allow the client to make suggestions on how to solve the problem:

    "Can you think of a solution?"

    "This might be one solution. What else can we come up with?"

    "I'd like to talk about it again after we've thought about it for a while."

Source: David W. Johnson, *Reaching Out: Interpersonal Effectiveness and Self-Actualization,* ©1972, p. 165. Adapted by permission of Prentice-Hall, Inc., Englewood Cliffs, New Jersey.

agree verbally with the counselors but, instead of pursuing the confrontation, may do so only to get the practitioners not to discuss the topic in the future.

There is no defined way to deal with negative reactions to a confrontation, but the Johnson components can be used to repeat the relationship statement or describe the counselor's own feelings and perceptions. The sequence might go like this:

COUNSELOR: "Both of our goals are to help eliminate binge eating at parties." (Relationship Statement)

CLIENT: "Actually I'm not sure I can ever achieve that even though I do want to lose weight." (Mixed Message)

COUNSELOR: "You say you want to lose weight but one of the major causes is too difficult to overcome." (Description of Counselor Feelings and Perceptions)

CLIENT: "No, I guess you just don't understand. You've never been in my shoes." (Discredit the Counselor)

COUNSELOR: "Because I've never been in your shoes doesn't mean we can't work on a solution together. I have had experience with many cases like yours. You seem to exhibit many qualities that show me that you can handle this problem." (Attributing Statement) "You are open about the difficulties you face and can describe specific instances where problems occur." (Attributing Statement) "Let's look at those specifics and try to come up with some solutions." (Constructive Feedback)

Ivey et al. indicate that an overly confronting, charismatic counselor can prevent client growth.[44] In a confrontation the counselor tries to point out discrepancies in attitudes, thoughts, or behaviors. Clients who come to nutrition counselors for help invariably give double messages: "I want to follow this diet, but I don't want to change my life to do it." Because almost all clients either overtly or covertly make this statement, confrontation becomes an important skill for nutrition counselors in facilitating behavior change.

Interpreting

An interpreting response is an active reply that gives a possible explanation of or association among various client behaviors. It has three intended purposes:

1. to identify the relationship between the clients' behavior and nonverbal messages
2. to examine the clients' behavior using a variety of views or different explanations
3. to help clients gain self-understanding as a basis for behavior change or action.

There are several specific ground rules.[45] Counselors must be careful about timing, and clients should demonstrate some degree of readiness for self-exploration or self-examination before an interpreting response is used. This response is best given at the beginning or middle phase of an interview so both counselors and client have sufficient time to work through the client's reaction. It is important for the counselors' interpretation to be based on the clients' actual message. Practitioners must eliminate their own biases and values. They must offer the interpretive response tentatively, using such words as, "I wonder if," "It's possible that," "Perhaps," or "Maybe." Clients should be asked whether the message is accurate.

Brammer offers these guidelines for counselors in interpreting responses:

1. Look for the clients' basic messages.
2. Paraphrase these to the clients.
3. Add your own understanding of what their messages mean (motives, defenses, needs, styles, etc.)

4. Keep the language simple and the level close to their [the clients'] message.
5. Indicate that your are offering tentative ideas.
6. Elicit the clients' reactions to your interpretations.[46]

Ivey and Authier describe the interpreting response as a part of the essence of what the clients have said (emotionally and intellectually) and as a summary that adds other relevant data.[47] An interpreting response provides the client with a new way to view the situation. Such a change in view may result in changes in thoughts and behaviors.

The following is an interpreting response:

CLIENT (an overweight middle-aged man): "I'm really discouraged with this dieting. I am at the point where I feel like I can't win. I've been to doctors and weight-loss groups. I've taken diet pills. It's at the point where I can't think straight at work because my thoughts are always on dieting. I feel very depressed."

COUNSELOR: "I wonder if you're allowing your preoccupation with weight loss to interfere with your ability to cope?" (This interpreting response makes an association between the client's desire to lose weight and resulting feelings and behavior.)

Or: "Is it possible that you're trying to find an easy, magic way to lose weight when that solution may not exist?" (This interpreting response offers a possible explanation of the client's weight-loss behaviors.)

The interpreting response can be a powerful influencer for clients who are locked into feelings of failure. It is a core skill that is vital to encouraging behavior change.

Counselors can use two sharing responses: self-disclosure and immediacy. The sharing responses involve counselor self-expression and usually content that refers to the practitioner, the client, or the emotions of either one.

Self-Disclosure

Self-disclosure is a response in which counselors verbally share information about themselves. Cormier and Cormier describe four purposes:

1. to provide an open, facilitative counseling atmosphere
2. to increase the client's perceived similarity between self and the counselor to reduce the distance resulting from role differences
3. to provide a model to assist in increasing the client's disclosure level
4. to influence the client's perceived or actual behavioral changes.[48]

There are several basic ideas to keep in mind before using self-disclosure. First, self-disclosure is a controversial interviewing skill. Cormier, Cormier, and Weisser caution that if the counselor's beliefs differ significantly from the client's on a given issue, it is probably better for the counselor to remain silent.[49]

Ivey et al. state that extensive self-disclosures take the focus away from the client and should be avoided but that moderate levels of self-disclosure help show clients how they come across to others.[50] DiMatteo and DiNicola illustrate an effective use of self-disclosure in the following example:

"Oh, I really have trouble resisting desserts too. It's tough isn't it? But I
figure it's worth it to resist them and work toward a normal weight."[51]

They note that moderate levels of self-disclosure help establish a basis for similarity
and enhance interpersonal influence. Counselors who rarely self-disclose may add to
the distance between themselves and their clients. Self-disclosing statements should
be similar in content and mood to the clients' message.[52]

Self-disclosure can be demographic, personal, positive, or negative.[53] In demographic disclosures, counselors talk about nonintimate events:

"I have had some failures in low-cholesterol meal preparation, also."

"I have not always used self-control skills to their optimum in assuring a balanced
diet."

In personal disclosures, counselors reveal more private personal events:

"Well, I don't always feel loving toward my husband (wife), especially when he (she)
is unsupportive of my efforts in meal preparation."

"I think it is very natural to want to please close friends. There are times when I've
accepted food at parties when I really didn't want it but I cared so much about the
person offering it that I couldn't say 'No.'"

In positive self-disclosure, counselors reveal positive strengths, coping skills, or
positive successful experiences:

"I'm really a task-oriented person. When I decide what must be done, I work until
the task is completed."

"It's important to be as open with my husband (wife) as possible. When he (she)
upsets me, I try to tell him (her) honestly exactly how I feel."

In negative self-disclosure, counselors provide information about personal limitations or difficult experiences:

"I also have trouble expressing opinions, I guess I am wishy-washy a lot of the time."

"Sometimes I'm also afraid to tell my husband (wife) how I really feel. Then my
frustration builds to a climax and I just explode."

Ivey and Authier list four key dimensions of self-disclosure:

1. the personal pronoun "I"
2. expression of content or feeling
3. object of the sentence (one's own experience)
4. tense of the verb in the statement (past tense is safer for both the counselor and
   client; however, present tense has more impact and is more powerful).[54]

Two examples of self-disclosure can apply to the same situation: the client is feeling
like a failure because no one seems to support the person's weight loss. The counselor
responds:

"I, too, have felt down about myself at times."

"I can remember feeling depressed when everyone seemed to take lightly something
that was important to me, like eating a favorite dish at my favorite restaurant."

Immediacy

The second sharing response, immediacy, involves counselors' reflections on a
present aspect of a thought or feeling about self, clients, or a significant relationship
issue. The verbal expression of immediacy may include the listening responses of

reflection and summation, the active responses of confrontation and interpretation, and the sharing response of self-disclosure. Examples of the three categories of immediacy are:

1. Counselor immediacy: The counselor reveals personal thoughts of immediacy at the moment they occur: "It's good to see you again;" or "I'm sorry I didn't follow that. I seem to have trouble focusing today. Let's go over that again."
2. Client immediacy: The counselor states something about the client's behavior or feeling as it occurs in the interview: "You seem uncomfortable now;" or "You're really smiling now. You must be very pleased."
3. Relationship immediacy: The counselor reveals personal feelings or thoughts about experiencing the relationship: "I'm glad that you are able to share those feelings you have about following the diet with me;" or "It makes me feel good that we've been able to resolve some of the problems with your diet."

Immediacy has two purposes: (1) it can bring covert feelings or unresolved relationship issues into the open for discussion, and (2) it can provide immediate feedback about the counselor's and client's feelings and aspects of the relationship as they occur in the session.

When making an immediacy response, counselors should (1) describe what they see as it happens, (2) reflect the "here and nowness" of the experience, and (3) reserve this response for initiating exploration of the most significant or most influential feelings or issues.

TEACHING RESPONSES

Much of nutrition counselors' work involves teaching clients how to change eating behaviors. Change means clients learn new ways to deal with themselves, others, or environmental situations. Counselors may teach new eating behaviors, new awareness of past and present ones, or new perceptions of past and present ones—or how clients can teach themselves. Three verbal responses associated with teaching and learning can give structure to what ordinarily might be haphazard teaching: instructions, verbal setting operations, and information giving.[55]

Instructions

Instructions involve one or more statements in which the counselors tell clients what eating behaviors are required, how they might occur, and allowable limits within which to perform them. When using instruction responses, counselors instruct, direct, or cue the clients to do something. Instructions may deal with what should happen within or outside the interview and can be both informing and influential. Instructions have two main purposes: (1) to influence or give cues to help clients respond in a certain way, and (2) to provide information necessary to acquire, strengthen, or eliminate a response.

After giving instructions, counselors should ascertain whether the clients really understand the directions. Clients are asked to repeat what was said to help the counselors know whether they communicated the message accurately. The counselors then exhort the clients to use the instructions.

Table 2-3 Aspects of Information Giving

Counselor's Instructions	In the Interview	Outside the Interview
What to do	"Please repeat what I have asked you to do in responding to your husband's (wife's) nonsupportiveness toward your diet. I want to be sure I am communicating the request accurately."	"Please keep a record of your thoughts before your conversations with your husband (wife)."
How to do	"When you say this, pretend that I am your husband (wife). Look at me and maintain eye contact while you say it."	"Write your thoughts down on a note card and bring them in next week."
Allowable limits	"Say it in a strong, firm voice. Don't speak in a soft, weak voice. Look at me while you say it."	"Remember to record these thoughts before, not after, you speak."

Instructions can be worded in many ways. "You should do something" is likely to put a client on the defensive—it is too demanding. More useful words are, "I'd like you to," "I'd appreciate it," or "I think it would help if." Clients are more likely to follow instructions that are linked to positive or rewarding consequences.[56]

Table 2-3 presents examples of information giving both inside and outside a nutrition counseling session.

Verbal Setting Operation

The second teaching response, the verbal setting operation, attempts to predispose someone to view a situation or an event in a certain way before it takes place. This response includes a statement describing a treatment and the potential value of counseling and/or treatment for clients. The purposes of verbal setting operations are to motivate clients to understand the purpose of and to use counseling and/or treatment.

Goldstein suggests that some initial counseling structure may prevent negative feelings in clients because they lack information about what to expect.[57] He feels that initial structuring should focus upon and clarify counselor and client role expectations. This type of structuring should be "detailed, deliberate and repeated."[58]

The following are examples of verbal setting operations:

Overview of nutrition counseling: The counselor says: "I believe it would be helpful if I first talked about what nutrition involves. We will spend some time talking together to find out first the kinds of nutrition concerns you have and what you want to do about them. Then we will work as a team to try to meet them. Sometimes I may ask you to do some things on your own outside the session."

Purpose of nutrition counseling: The counselor says: "These sessions may help you change eating behaviors to achieve weight loss. The action plans you'll carry out—with my assistance—can help you learn to eat wisely in situations that may be of concern to you."

The person's understanding of nutrition counseling can be checked by asking, "How does this fit with your expectations?"

Information Giving

Much of the nutrition counselors' responsibility involves the third teaching response—information giving. Below are specific guidelines to follow when giving information.

1. Identify information presently available to client.
2. Evaluate client's present information. Is it valid? Databased? Sufficient? Insufficient?

The following guidelines can be used in determining what information to give:

1. Identify the kind of information useful to the client.
2. Identify possible reliable sources of information.
3. Identify any preferred sequencing of information, i.e., option A before option B.

The following guidelines indicate how to deliver information:

1. Limit the amount of information given at one time.
2. Ask for and discuss client's feelings and biases about information.
3. Know when to stop giving information so action isn't avoided.
4. Wait for the client's cue of readiness for additional information after providing a large group of facts.
5. Present all relevant facts; don't protect clients from negative information.
6. Be specific, clear, detailed, concrete, and simple in communicating and giving instructions.
7. Organize the material. Information given in the first third of communication is remembered longer. The first instruction given is usually remembered the longest.
8. Provide advanced organizers (for example, "First, I will give you the reasons this diet is important. Second, I will describe the changes you need to make in the types of foods you currently eat.")
9. Repeat important information.
10. Use concrete illustrations, anecdotes, and self-disclosure to heighten the personal relevance of the material.
11. Use oral and written material together. Supplement with slides, audiotapes, videotapes, films, anatomical models, diagrams, charts, and other aids.

12. Check the client's comprehension, asking for a restatement of key features of a message.
13. Involve significant others.[59]

CHOOSING THE APPROPRIATE RESPONSE

One of the most important processes in counseling involves deciding when to use the responses just described. Steps toward determining appropriate responses include (1) identification of the purposes of the interview and of the counselor responses and (2) assessment of the effects of the selected replies and strategies on client answers and outcomes. When one response or strategy does not achieve its intended purpose, counselors can use discrimination to identify and select another that is more likely to achieve the desired results or focus.

Cormier and Cormier describe three parts of an interview that can be used in determining which responses or strategies to select:

1. Counselor identifies purposes of the interview and responses.
2. Counselor selects and implements the response.
3. Counselor determines if resulting client verbal and nonverbal responses achieve the purpose or distract from the purpose.[60]

These authors also describe a step-by-step process for counselors in conducting an effective interview:

1. Define the purpose of the interview.
2. Define the purpose of your initial response.
3. Make your initial response.
4. Identify client verbal and nonverbal responses.
5. Label those client responses as goal related or distracting.
6. Set a plan for the next response.[61]

Nutrition counselors' first step is to listen carefully to each of the client's statements. They must think about whether each is related to or distracts from the purposes of the interview. Having made this determination, counselors can select and use responses they believe will achieve the objective. If client responses are goal related, practitioners may decide that their own replies and comments are on target; however, if they note several statements that are distracting, they may need to analyze what they have been saying.

For example, one of the major goals of a counseling session may be to identify steps to help change eating behaviors in an overweight adult male. The counselor has suggested cutting down on midmorning snacking by switching from high-calorie snack foods that are low in nutrients to more low-calorie, high-nutrient foods. The client indicates that this change will not work for him. After determining that this is a distracting client response, the practitioner will need to formulate and use an alternate response—perhaps a new action step. Regardless of what that next response is, the important point is that the counselor can identify a purpose or direction, assess whether the client's answers are related to that goal, and select alternative replies with a rationale in mind. Counselors should make these assessments cognitively.

This step-by-step procedure should be used in thinking through an interview. What follows is an example of how those steps might apply in a nutrition counseling session.

Interview purpose: To listen to the client (a 26-year-old woman) describe factors contributing to her inability to lose weight over the past two years. (Details of the interview objective and the relationship between client and counselor are not included here.)

1. COUNSELOR: "According to your chart, Dr. B. sent you to see me again today. He writes here that you've been trying to lose weight and need some help in determining what factors have contributed to the lack of weight loss. Is that correct?" (The purpose of the initial response is to double-check the client's rationale for attending the interview.)

    CLIENT (fidgeting): "Well, that's true. Sometimes I think that all I have to do is to look at food and I gain weight."

Counselor thinks: She admits that she has a weight problem (indirectly). She seems to be discounting the contributing factors (distracting response). In frustration she tries to absolve herself from blame by attributing her problem to some unknown phenomenon that makes her gain weight at the very sight of food. For my next response I will check her thoughts as to her control over the weight gain.

2. COUNSELOR: "From what you have said you seem to think that your weight gain is out of your control. How well does that describe what you are thinking?"

    CLIENT: "Well, sometimes I feel that way but I suppose I do have some control."

Counselor thinks: Okay, the client is now admitting to having some control. I will focus next on areas where she may feel she has some control.

3. COUNSELOR: "What are some areas related to your weight gain that you do feel you can control?"

    CLIENT: "Well, I guess I could just stop buying groceries."

Counselor thinks: She either did not understand my question or she is feeling defensive about having to discuss situations where she might have control but doesn't exercise the option. My next response will focus on the idea of shopping and I will give her some examples using a self-disclosing response.

4. COUNSELOR: "Well, sometimes when I go shopping and I'm very hungry, I tend to buy more food and high-calorie snacks."

    CLIENT (voice pitch goes up, tone gets louder): "How would you know what it's like to go shopping and want foods you shouldn't have? You're not overweight."

Counselor thinks: My example seemed to make the client avoid the issue of contributing factors even more. She seems to have built up a great deal of frustration. Perhaps exploring her feelings about grocery buying might give me some clues. I will respond to her question and then direct the focus to her concern about buying groceries.

5. COUNSELOR: "I really can't know what it's like to be in your shoes. I can only express a situation similar to yours that I have been in. I guess buying groceries is a very important concern for you because it is tied so closely to your desire to lose weight. What feelings do you have while you're shopping?"

CLIENT (loud voice): "I feel like a child in a candy store. Here is everything I love, everything that gives me pleasure, but I am forbidden to touch any of it. Then my kids and my husband are saying, 'Oh, go on honey (or mom) buy it; we love it. We shouldn't have to suffer just because you don't have any willpower.'"

Counselor thinks: That's the most I've gotten out of her. It's the first indication that she is willing to explore the situation. It seems that one of the factors contributing to her lack of ability to lose weight is her nonsupportive husband and children. I might check this theory out further.

COUNSELOR: "Are you saying that your family really doesn't give you a lot of support in losing weight?"

CLIENT: "Yes. Being overweight is bad enough but when your own family gives you no support, losing weight is almost impossible."

Counselor thinks: The client seems to feel very strongly about this lack of family support. I will try to get at how this affects the way she feels in specific situations where nonsupport is apparent.

7. COUNSELOR: "Having your family respond negatively when you try to buy low-calorie foods and avoid high-calorie snacks seems to make you feel very frustrated. You would like them to praise your efforts. I guess having your family reject your efforts at weight loss may affect the way you see yourself, too."

CLIENT (avoids eye contact): "What do you mean?"

Counselor thinks: From the lack of eye contact and the client's verbal message, I believe either my response was unclear or she isn't ready to look at her self-image yet. I will approach this indirectly by asking her to describe some situations in which she has felt frustrated by lack of support by her family.

8. COUNSELOR: "Well, I'm not sure. Maybe you could tell me exactly what happens in a situation where your family is nonsupportive."

At this point the interview enters the area where additional counseling skills are necessary. Chapter 3 discusses those skills and how they can help nutrition counselors in formulating plans and applying strategies during interviews.

NOTES

1. Allen E. Ivey, Mary Bradford Ivey, and Lynn Simek-Downing, *Counseling and Psychotherapy: Integrating Skills, Theory and Practice,* 2nd ed. (Englewood Cliffs, N.J.: Prentice-Hall, 1987), p. 3.

2. Sterling K. Gerber, *Responsive Therapy: A Systematic Approach to Counseling Skills* (New York: Human Sciences Press, Inc., 1986), p. 30.

3. Michael L. Russell, *Behavioral Counseling in Medicine: Strategies for Modifying At-Risk Behavior* (New York: Oxford University Press, 1986), p. 37.

4. William H. Cormier, L. Sherilyn Cormier, and Roland J. Weisser, Jr., *Interviewing and Helping Skills for Health Professionals* (Belmont, Calif.: Wadsworth Health Sciences Division, 1984), pp. 41–42.

5. William H. Cormier and L. Sherilyn Cormier, *Interviewing Strategies for Helpers: Fundamental Skills and Cognitive Behavioral Interventions,* 2nd ed. (Monterey, Calif.: Brooks/Cole Publishing Co., 1985), pp. 13–14.

6. Lawrence M. Brammer, *The Helping Relationship, Process and Skills* (Englewood Cliffs, N.J.: Prentice-Hall, 1985), pp. 26–34.

7. John W. Loughary and Theresa M. Ripley, *Helping Others Help Themselves, A Guide to Counseling Skills* (New York: McGraw-Hill Book Co., 1979), pp. 23–39.

8. Arthur Wright Combs et al., *Helping Relationships* (Boston: Allyn & Bacon, 1971), pp. 10–17.

9. R. Bruce Sloane and Fred R. Staples, "Psychotherapy versus Behavior Therapy: Implications for Future Psychotherapy Research," in Janet B. W. Williams and Robert L. Spitzer, eds., *Psychotherapy Research: Where Are We and Where Should We Go?* (New York: Guilford, 1984), pp. 203–215.

10. Leona E. Tyler, *The Work of the Counselor* (New York: Appleton-Century-Crofts, Educational Division, Meredith Corporation, 1969), pp. 36–37.

11. Brammer, *Helping Relationship,* p. 36.

12. Ivey et al., *Counseling and Psychotherapy,* p. 94.

13. Carol Gilligan, *In a Different Voice* (Cambridge, Mass.: Harvard University Press, 1982), pp. 35–36.

14. Robert R. Carkhuff and Richard M. Pierce, *The Art of Helping: Trainer's Guide* (Amherst, Mass.: Human Resources Development Press, 1975), pp. 178–182.

15. Brammer, *Helping Relationship,* p. 24.

16. Cormier and Cormier, *Interviewing Strategies for Helpers: Fundamental Skills and Cognitive Behavioral Interventions,* pp. 67–78.

17. Ivey et al., *Counseling and Psychotherapy,* p. 53.

18. William R. Passons, *Gestalt Approaches in Counseling* (New York: Holt, Rinehart and Winston, 1975), pp. 103–105.

19. Helen H. Gifft, Marjorie B. Washton, and Gail G. Harrison, *Nutrition, Behavior and Change* (Englewood Cliffs, N.J.: Prentice-Hall, 1972), pp. 10–15.

20. Derald W. Sue and David Sue, "Barriers to Effective Cross-Cultural Counseling," *Journal of Counseling Psychology* 24 (1977): 427; and Stanley Feldstein and Joan Welkowitz, "A Chronography of Conversation: In Defense of an Objective Approach," in Aron W. Siegman and Stanley Feldstein, *Non-Verbal Behavior and Communication,* 2nd ed. (Hillsdale, N.J.: Lawrence Erlbaum Associates, 1987), p. 473.

21. Cormier and Cormier, *Interviewing Strategies for Helpers: Fundamental Skills and Cognitive Behavioral Interventions,* pp. 81–83.

22. William H. Cormier and L. Sherilyn Cormier, *Interviewing Strategies for Helpers: A Guide to Assessment, Treatment and Evaluation* (Monterey, Calif.: Brooks/Cole Publishing Co., 1979), p. 50; and Gerber, *Responsive Therapy,* pp. 32–33.

23. Ivey et al., *Counseling and Psychotherapy,* pp. 77–78.

24. John J. Lavelle, "Comparing the Effects of an Affective and a Behavioral Counselor Style on Client Interview Behavior," *Journal of Counseling Psychology* 24 (1977): 174; and Cormier

and Cormier, *Interviewing Strategies for Helpers: A Guide to Assessment, Treatment and Evaluation,* p. 51.

25. Brammer, *Helping Relationship,* pp. 81–83.

26. Ibid.

27. Cormier and Cormier, *Interviewing Strategies for Helpers: Fundamental Skills and Cognitive Behavioral Interventions,* p. 113.

28. Cormier and Cormier, *Interviewing Strategies for Helpers: A Guide to Assessment, Treatment and Evaluation,* p. 79.

29. Ivey et al., *Counseling and Psychotherapy,* pp. 75–76.

30. Cormier and Cormier, *Interviewing Strategies for Helpers: Fundamental Skills and Cognitive Behavioral Interventions,* p. 115.

31. Ivey et al., *Counseling and Psychotherapy,* p. 76.

32. Ibid.

33. Irvin L. Janis, "Improving Adherence to Medial Recommendations: Prescriptive Hypotheses Derived from Recent Research in Social Psychology," in Andrew Baum, Shelley E. Taylor, and Jerome E. Singer, eds., *Handbook of Psychology and Health,* vol. 4., *Social Psychology of Aspects of Health* (Hillsdale, N.J.: Erlbaum, 1984), pp. 113–148.

34. M. Robin DiMatteo and D. Dante DiNicola, *Achieving Patient Compliance: The Psychology of the Medical Practitioner's Role* (New York: Pergamon Press, 1982), p. 107.

35. Cormier and Cormier, *Interviewing Strategies for Helpers: A Guide to Assessment, Treatment and Evaluation,* p. 80.

36. Ibid., p. 81.

37. Ivey et al., *Counseling and Psychotherapy,* p. 86.

38. Cormier and Cormier, *Interviewing Strategies for Helpers: Fundamental Skills and Cognitive Behavioral Interventions,* p. 118.

39. Ibid., pp. 120–121.

40. David W. Johnson, *Reaching Out: Interpersonal Effectiveness and Self-Actualization* (Englewood Cliffs, N.J.: Prentice-Hall, 1972), pp. 159–172.

41. Ibid., p. 165.

42. Cormier, Cormier, and Weisser, *Interviewing and Helping Skills for Health Professionals,* p. 140.

43. Gerard Egan, *The Skilled Helper: A Model for Systematic Helping and Interpersonal Relating* (Monterey, Calif.: Brooks/Cole Publishing Co., 1975), pp. 169–170.

44. Ivey et al., *Counseling and Psychotherapy,* p. 86.

45. Cormier and Cormier, *Interviewing Strategies for Helpers: Fundamental Skills and Cognitive Behavioral Interventions,* p. 127.

46. Brammer, *Helping Relationship,* pp. 94–95.

47. Allen E. Ivey and Jerry Authier, *Microcounseling, Innovations in Interviewing, Counseling, Psychotherapy, and Psychoeducation* (Springfield, Ill.: Charles C. Thomas, 1978), p. 78.

48. Cormier and Cormier, *Interviewing Strategies for Helpers: Fundamental Skills and Cognitive Behavioral Interventions,* p. 29.

49. Cormier, Cormier, and Weisser, *Helping Skills for Health Professionals,* p. 41.

50. Ivey et al., *Counseling and Psychotherapy,* pp. 82–83.

51. DiMatteo and DiNicola, *Achieving Patient Compliance,* p. 107.

52. Vincenzo Giannandrea and Kevin C. Murphy, "Similarity in Self-Disclosure and Return for a Second Interview," *Journal of Counseling Psychology* 5 (1973): 547; Brenda Mann and Kevin C. Murphy, "Timing of Self-Disclosure, Reciprocity of Self-Disclosure, and Reactions to an Initial Interview," *Journal of Counseling Psychology* 23 (1976): 306; and Norman R. Simonson, "The Impact of Therapist Disclosure on Patient Disclosure," *Journal of Counseling Psychology* 23 (1976): 5.

53. Simonson, "The Impact of Therapist Disclosure," p. 3; and Mary A. Hoffman-Graff, "Interviewer Use of Positive and Negative Self-Disclosure and Interviewer-Subject Sex Pairing," *Journal of Counseling Psychology* 24 (1977): 184, 185.

54. Ivey and Authier, *Microcounseling,* p. 111.

55. Cormier and Cormier, *Interviewing Strategies for Helpers: A Guide to Assessment, Treatment and Evaluation,* p. 101.

56. Arthur Schwartz and Israel Goldiamond, *Social Casework: A Behavioral Approach* (New York: Columbia University Press, 1975), p. 30.

57. Arnold P. Goldstein, "Relationship-Enhancement Methods," in Frederick H. Kanfer and Arnold P. Goldstein, eds., *Helping People Change* (New York: Pergamon Press, 1975), p. 19.

58. Arnold P. Goldstein, *Therapist-Patient Expectations in Psychotherapy* (New York: Pergamon Press, 1962), 121.

59. Cormier and Cormier, *Interviewing Strategies for Helpers: A Guide to Assessment, Treatment and Evaluation,* p. 107; Jacqueline Dunbar, "Adhering to Medical Advice: A Review," *International Journal of Mental Health* 9 (1980): 70–87; Stephen A. Eraker, John P. Kirscht, and Marshall H. Becker, "Understanding and Improving Patient Compliance," *Annals of Internal Medicine* 100 (1984): 258–268; Ira M. Friedman and Iris F. Litt, "Promoting Adolescents: Compliance with Therapeutic Regimens," *Pediatric Clinics of North America* 33 (1986): 955–973; Howard Leventhal, Rick Zimmerman, and Mary Gutmann, "Compliance: A Self-Regulation Perspective," in W. Doyle Gentry, ed., *Handbook of Behavorial Medicine* (New York: Guilford Press, 1984), p. 377; Philip Ley, "Giving Information to Patients," in J. Richard Eiser, ed., *Social Psychology and Behavioral Medicine* (New York: Wiley, 1982), pp. 339–373; David Pendelton and John Hasler, *Doctor-Patient Communication* (London, England: Academic Press, 1983), pp. 89–92; Ted L. Rosental and Anna Downs, "Cognitive Aids in Teaching and Treating," *Advances in Behavior Research and Therapy* 1 (1985): 1–53; Irwin M. Rosenstock, "Understanding and Enhancing Patient Compliance with Diabetic Regimens," *Diabetes Care* 8 (1985): 610–616; Dennis C. Turk, Donald Meichenbaum, and Myles Genest, *Pain and Behavioral Medicine: A Cognitive-Behavioral Perspective* (New York: Guilford Press, 1983), pp. 182–183; and Dennis C. Turk, Arnold D. Holzman, and Robert D. Kerns, "Chronic Pain," in Kenneth A. Holroyd and Thomas L. Creer, eds., *Self-Management of Chronic Disease: Handbook of Clinical Interventions and Research* (Orlando, Fla.: Academic Press, 1986), p. 446.

60. Cormier and Cormier, *Interviewing Strategies for Helpers: A Guide to Assessment, Treatment and Evaluation,* p. 117.

61. Ibid., pp. 118–124.

Chapter 3

Counseling Skills

Objectives for Chapter 3

1. Explain the counseling relationship.
2. Describe the counseling process.
3. Identify four types of data necessary for adequate nutrition assessment.
4. Describe the factors involved in nutrition need specification.
5. Apply six steps in goal definition in a given nutrition counseling problem.
6. List factors influencing diet adherence.
7. List predictors of poor adherence or nonadherence.
8. Apply at least two of five modeling strategies to help in solving a given nutrition problem.
9. Apply at least three of seven strategies designed to motivate behavior change for a given nutrition problem.
10. Apply at least two self-management strategies for a given nutrition problem.
11. Describe the purposes of evaluation.
12. List the steps in evaluation.
13. List three means of monitoring the client's nutrition behavior.
14. Describe the purpose in evaluating counselor performance.

INITIAL INFORMATION

Basic counseling skills can be categorized under these topics: initial information, assessment, treatment, and evaluation. The first step is providing initial information.

Structure

Stewart and his coworkers believe that explicit structure should be provided to all new clients.[1] The point at which to provide that structure depends on the clients. Nutrition counselors should be aware of clients' feelings. If they seem anxious, unsure, hesitant, or insecure, practitioners should provide structure immediately. However, if they readily begin sharing a concern, structure would intrude on their thoughts, so counselors should introduce it later in the initial interview.

In describing the counseling process to clients, Stewart et al. recommend four aspects: purpose, responsibility, focus, and limits.[2]

Purpose

The purpose of counseling is to aid clients in coping with nutrition-related problems. Practitioners help clients develop problem-solving skills to use on conclusion of the interview.

Responsibility

Counselors' responsibility to clients is to listen to their nutrition-related concerns and observe their behavior when discussing and reviewing diet records or histories. Counselors also interact with clients to provide a safe environment to try out new behavior.

Focus

The focus of the interview is extremely important. Clients may present many concerns related to eating behavior but should be made aware that only one objective will be discussed at a time. However, before the interviews are finished, several objectives may be covered.

Limits

Nutrition counselors should make clients aware that there are limits in counseling and should report serious maladjustments to a psychologist or psychiatrist. Clients should know that the success of their counseling depends on their active participation. They also should be informed that all of the interviews will be confidential; any discussion of information with a third party would be undertaken only with their permission.

Most counseling programs require three or four visits, each of 30 to 60 minutes' duration. Interviews for evaluation and monitoring progress usually run 10 to 30 minutes. These are general guidelines. Each client is an individual, and the time required for counseling may vary depending on the problem.

ASSESSMENT

Collection of Data

As stated in Chapter 1, the assessment phase of counseling, the second step in the process, cannot be overemphasized. Mason and her coauthors describe four kinds of information collected in the assessment phase: biologic data, dietary intake data, environmental data, and behavioral data.[3]

Much of the biologic information to be collected is found in previously charted data. Medical records provide information on height and weight over time. Laboratory tests offer cues to general health status. Counselors should note specific laboratory determinations of nutrient levels and the diagnosis or specific reasons a client is seeking health care.

Extremely important to assessment is collection of dietary intake data, in which two important factors should be considered: (1) the types of nutrients consumed and (2) the appropriate quantities.[4]

Depending on the precision necessary, two methods can be used to assess the types of nutrients consumed. The *Daily Food Guide,* published by the U.S. Department of Agriculture, gives information on the food groups being consumed.[5] For more in-depth quantitative and qualitative information, diet histories are important. To analyze the data, food consumption tables can be used. Advances in technology now allow counselors to use computer programs to analyze dietary data. Chapter 5 provides additional information on this topic.

Determining the appropriateness of quantities consumed is difficult. Both the Recommended Dietary Allowances (RDA) and Canadian Dietary Standard (CDS) were developed originally to evaluate the dietary status of population groups, not to be used by nutrition counselors in evaluating individual dietary status.

Counselors should consider several factors in looking at quantities.[6] First is variation among individuals. Second is the number of repetitive food intake assessments on individual clients. Third is the validity and reliability of the instruments used to collect data. An instrument is considered valid if it truly reflects the individual's nutritional status within the limitations set, i.e., time and place. It is considered reliable if it consistently measures nutritional status given the same limitations and criteria. Many instruments developed for nutrition assessment have not been tested for either validity or reliability.

Environmental data can provide invaluable information for the assessment phase. Mason describes seven factors that may influence eating behaviors:

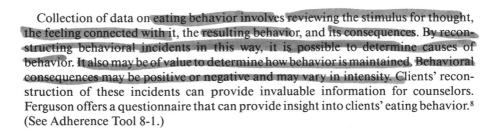

1. family status
2. occupation and income
3. education
4. ethnic orientation
5. religion
6. recreation
7. residence.[7]

Collection of data on eating behavior involves reviewing the stimulus for thought, the feeling connected with it, the resulting behavior, and its consequences. By reconstructing behavioral incidents in this way, it is possible to determine causes of behavior. It also may be of value to determine how behavior is maintained. Behavioral consequences may be positive or negative and may vary in intensity. Clients' reconstruction of these incidents can provide invaluable information for counselors. Ferguson offers a questionnaire that can provide insight into clients' eating behavior.[8] (See Adherence Tool 8-1.)

Specification of Nutrition Needs

Counselors can look at clients' situations in terms of specific problem behaviors.[9] After defining the difficulty in such terms, counselors should try to discover how the behaviors are influenced by the clients' environment. Behavior is affected by things happening within and outside oneself, by certain visible events (verbal, nonverbal, and motor responses), and by less visible events (thoughts, images, and physiological and affective states) that precede and follow many behaviors. These overt and covert happenings maintain, increase, decrease, initiate, or eliminate behavior.[10]

The ABC model of behavior identifies the relationship between the problem behavior and environmental events. In this model "B" is an example of behavior influenced by events that precede it (antecedent behavior, or "A") and follow it (consequences, or "C").[11]

Seven goals to work toward in defining a client's problems are to:

1. explain the purpose of problem definition
2. identify and select the problem concerns
3. identify the present problem behaviors
4. identify the antecedent contributing conditions
5. identify the consequent contributing conditions
6. identify problem intensity (measure or systematically count occurrences of that behavior)
7. identify the coping skills.[12]

Client and counselor should agree on the selection of dietary problems to be confronted. Related factors analyzed should include present problem behaviors, antecedent and consequent contributing conditions, problem intensity, and coping skills.

The counseling session ultimately must specify nutritional needs, cued by all of the factors just discussed. In the final analysis, clients obviously should be the central focus because they will be the primary agents of change in both their behavior and their environment.

TREATMENT PLANNING

The third major step in counseling is formulating a treatment plan, which requires seven major steps.[13]

Goal Setting

An eight-step program for selecting goals is depicted in Figure 3-1. Nutrition counselors first should identify the purpose or goals of treatment; second, ask the clients to identify what change or result is desired from counseling; and, third, determine how realistic the positive aspects of the goal might be and delineate risks in achieving the goal. An example of risk taking: an overweight husband reaches ideal weight but, because of the resulting improvement in appearance, his success produces resentment in his overweight wife, who is worried about losing his affection to someone who likes him at the new, ideal weight.

The fourth step requires decision making. The clients may decide to reconsider making a change (weight loss may not be required), the counselors may decide to refer the individuals to a counseling psychologist, for example, or they may decide to work together toward achieving the goal. At this point clients and practitioners must define in specific terms the behavioral goal, the conditions and circumstances of change, the level or extent to which it should be achieved, and the degree to which the individuals will work to attain the goal. Subgoals also can be established.

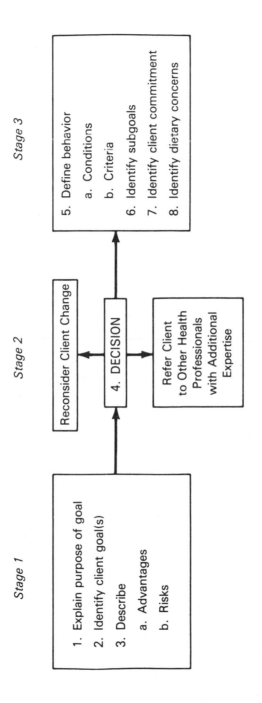

Figure 3-1 Counselor's Steps in Selecting Dietary Goals with Client. *Source:* From *Interviewing Strategies for Helpers*, 2nd ed., by W. H. Cormier and L. S. Cormier. Copyright ©1985, 1979 by Wadsworth Inc. Adapted by permission of Brooks/Cole Publishing Company, Pacific Grove, California 93950.

Goals can have these attributes:

1. They are targets which indicate where to begin and where to finish.
2. They are motivators when explicitly stated and readily attainable.
3. They are rewarding.
4. They provide for planned change.[14]

The assumption that the problem or concern will provide a goal automatically is erroneous; it is up to clients and counselors together to identify the goal.

Goals provide direction and ambition, but their achievement may be well beyond the ability of the clients and counselors. In the fifth step a behavior must be specified and incorporated into a subgoal with a focus. Target behaviors should be specific, with conditions that put limits or constraints on performance of the conduct along with minimum acceptable criteria or standards. Criteria might include a specific time during which the behavior should occur, a specific degree of performance, and a description of task accomplishment.

The sixth step involves identification of specific subgoals. For example, setting a weight loss goal of 20 pounds in a year may overwhelm many clients. A subgoal of losing one pound every two weeks is more reasonable and gives clients something to attain weekly. In the seventh step, client commitment is crucial to maintaining a dietary behavior.

Stewart et al. list three basic measures of client commitment:

1. The client has verbally agreed that the established goals are appropriate.
2. The counselor and client have discussed the costs of achieving the goal (e.g., time, money, risk, anxiety, and embarrassment).
3. The client has verbalized commitment to work with this concern.[15]

Much research has been conducted on goal setting. Some of the resulting clinical guidelines follow:

1. Client-determined, individualized, and negotiated treatment goals are most likely to be effective.
2. If necessary skills are not within the client's repertoire, then the counselor should employ easier (more readily attainable) goals. For example, in treating for weight loss monitoring behavior that leads to weight loss is more useful than graphing the more difficult weight loss itself. In this way feedback is more rapid and effective.
3. If the required skills are in the client's repertoire, then establishing more demanding rather than simpler goals is more effective. The client must perceive these goals as proximal and attainable. Bandura and Simon reported that subjects who used short-term or proximal rather than long-term or distal goals were most successful at maintenance. Attainment of treatment goals is more likely if counselors provide performance feedback.
4. There is an advantage in specifying behaviors in terms of what, when, and how to reach treatment goals.
5. Counselors must nurture client involvement and discuss a variety of treatment alternatives. By giving a client choices, a counselor reinforces a sense of personal

control. The counselor should encourage only moderate expectations of success. If expectations are too high or too low, any instances of relapse can be perceived as devastating.

6. When possible, significant others should be involved in goal setting.
7. Clients must be taught self-regulatory techniques to use in monitoring behavior. This information forms the basis for making treatment decisions and reinforcing goal achievement.[16]

Below is an example of setting a subgoal for a woman who is diagnosed with renal insufficiency following a low-protein diet:

CLIENT: "I believe my most difficult problem is eating out in restaurants." (Define inappropriate eating behavior.)

COUNSELOR: "Is there a specific time of the week when this occurs?"

CLIENT: "The worst time is Friday night, when we go to the Steak House." (Define specific conditions.)

COUNSELOR: "What do you think your goal should be?"

CLIENT: "To eat half the steak I get and take the rest home in a doggy bag." (Identify subgoal.)

COUNSELOR: "Your goal, then, is to eat only one-half of the steak you order every Friday night at the Steak House. Do you think you can achieve this?" (Identify client commitment.)

CLIENT: "Yes."

COUNSELOR: "Do you have any other concerns?" (Identify client concerns.)

CLIENT: "No, I feel good about that goal, and I know my husband will be positive."

Identifying Dietary Concerns

Although the client in the example above indicated no concerns, many clients will have several. Once goal setting is complete, identifying dietary concerns (Figure 3-2) related to an objective and its subgoals is the eighth step in the counseling process.

This stage of the process is crucial. It is the joint responsibility of both parties to identify the dietary concerns clients bring to the session—a process that takes considerable time. Dietary concerns may be related to spouse support, portion sizes, snacking, etc. To identify concerns, practitioners must maximize the use of both listening and probing skills.

From these many factors, clients and counselors must mutually identify the most immediate concern. Their selections can be based on a number of criteria, such as the immediacy or complexity of the dietary problem. Often they may select the least complex concern first as it may be the easiest to overcome.

Nutrition counselors should focus on both the content and feelings expressed in the clients' verbalization. Stewart et al. point out that the content provides the counselor with information, actions, and objects while the feeling portion can provide clues to attitudes concerning content. It is important to differentiate between content and

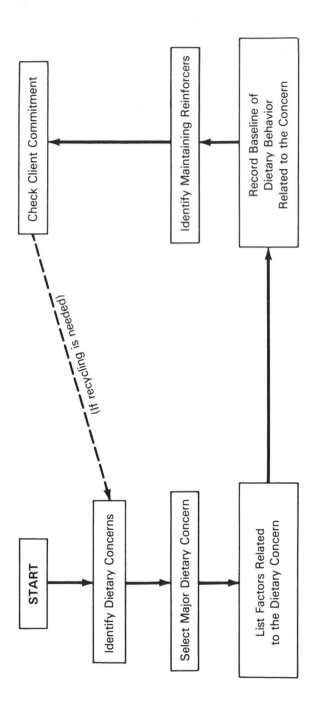

Figure 3-2 Setting Up a Process for Dealing with Client Concerns. *Source:* Norman R. Stewart et al., *Systematic Counseling,* ©1978, p. 104. Adapted by permission of Prentice-Hall, Inc., Englewood Cliffs, New Jersey.

feeling because, by focusing separately on feelings with an affective response, counselors may move clients to further self-exploration.[17]

Analysis of responses to dietary questions demonstrates that they fall into four categories: (1) response component, (2) temporal component, (3) situational component, and (4) intensity component.[18] This type of categorization can help in evaluating concerns in terms of the questions what, when, where, and how.

To identify the response facets of the problem, practitioners learn what the concern is, how it is demonstrated, and what effect it has on the client's life. It is the counselor's responsibility to describe the response in observable and measurable terms.

The temporal (timing) component of a dietary behavior can be immensely important. For this element, practitioners must be attuned to when the behavior occurs, how long it has occurred, and the sequence in which it emerges.

In the situational component counselors try to determine where or under what circumstances the problem behavior occurs.

The fourth component, intensity, emphasizes the frequency or the number of times a dietary behavior occurs and its duration. Duration means the length of time over which a given dietary behavior occurs and how long it continues each time.

Nutrition counselors often spend too little time looking at baseline dietary behaviors. Baseline data provide an assessment of behavior in terms of situation, time, frequency, and duration. Client comments can provide some information, but, ideally, counselors use a data-gathering device to shed light on the current level of the dietary concern in terms of response, time, situation, and intensity. Two useful devices are a behavioral chart (Appendix D) and a behavioral log or record (Appendix E). Usually records over one to four weeks produce adequate baseline data. This type of reporting by clients can increase the accuracy of the data, strengthen their involvement, and give them encouragement because it provides a feeling of self-control.[19]

Eventual success depends upon identification of which reinforcers promote dietary behaviors and which allow certain conduct to continue. Counselors will find it useful to list the benefits their clients derive from continuing certain behaviors that contribute to the dietary problem. If clients can identify why a behavior persists, counseling can be more effective.

At this point, the counselors can double-check their accuracy in stating the dietary problem, its components, and the reinforcers that maintain or reduce it. Clients can amend, delete, or approve the process presented in Figure 3-2. Discrepancies between what counselors say and what clients think and feel can be discussed. A review of client interpretation of the dietary concern should cover the following:

1. definition of the concern
2. response component
3. temporal component
4. situational component
5. frequency component
6. maintaining component.[20]

Helping Strategies

Helping strategies are the plans of action designed to meet the specific goals of each client. Cormier and Cormier suggest five guidelines for judging the timing for a helping strategy:

1. quality of the relationship
2. definition of the problem
3. development of desired counseling goals
4. client cues of readiness and commitment
5. collection of baseline measures.[21]

Mason et al. delineate a variety of factors necessary in selecting helping strategies. Focusing on goals is an obvious recommendation. Clients and counselors should use cues to stimulate appropriate responses and consequences that will reinforce desired behaviors. The strategy selected should help arrange more pleasant associations, with new thoughts and behaviors, and remove undesirable thoughts. The strategy should allow for trying the new behavior in an environment where it is likely to be reinforced positively.[22]

Factors Influencing Diet Adherence

In selecting helping strategies counselors should review factors that ultimately will influence client adherence to them. Four factors can be crucial to adherence: client, nutrition counselor, clinic, and regimen.[23]

The Role of the Client

The first factor involving the clients includes a variety of interview-related situations that influence adherence to a dietary pattern. Much of what takes place in a nutrition counseling session involves giving information to promote adherence. Research has shown that information recalled decreases in direct proportion to the amount given.[24] That study also shows that recall increases if information is presented over time rather than all at once. These researchers note that recall of information may be related to anxiety. Persons identified as having either high or low anxiety forget more than those with moderate anxiety; those with moderate anxiety show the best knowledge retention. Studies also have looked at fear of complications of a disease as a factor in retention of information.[25] High levels of fear promote poor dietary adherence and may lead to inadequate descriptions of nutrient intake. In the author's experience, recall improves if information is categorized and each topic is presented to a client as a unit.

Research indicates that clients who live alone show poorer adherence to their diets.[26] In selecting helping strategies, counselors should weigh this factor heavily. Asymptomatic conditions requiring preventive or supportive treatment also tend to be associated with lower adherence rates.[27]

Persons who anticipate that a diet will be easy to follow may show poor adherence when those expectations are incongruent with their experience.[28] Experience has shown that when the family expects the client will adhere to the diet, performance is better.[29]

The Role of the Counselor

According to the results of several studies, the client's satisfaction with care and with the nutrition counselor can increase adherence to diet.[30] Adherence also increases if the client sees the same counselor at each visit.[31] It seems that a personal nutrition counselor can individualize therapy more easily[32] and reduce feelings of anonymity.[33]

The Role of the Clinic

Clinic atmosphere also provides incentives for adherence to dietary strategies. A bright, well-lit room seems to be more inviting than a dark, dingy one. A minimum of waiting time also seems to increase adherence. Initial contacts are very important. The attitude of staff members in charge of routing clients to the medical staff sets the stage for client's attitudes throughout the visit.

The Role of the Regimen

The characteristics of the dietary regimen are crucial to maintaining good eating patterns. When many life changes are combined (diet, office habits, family, social functions, etc.), problems with adherence tend to increase.[34] The use of a life event inventory, including deaths in the family, retirement, and divorce, to assess life stresses may be helpful. (Chapter 7 provides information on various instruments designed to determine stressors in a persons' life.) Adherence is best when the initial dietary regimen is simple, with complexities introduced gradually. If problems arise, reassurance and inquiries about improvement can promote increased adherence. The following factors related to the regimen have been shown to affect adherence:

1. difficulty in fitting helping strategies into current life style
2. irregularity of the routine required by the helping strategies
3. difficulties with the regimen itself
4. carrying out the regimen at work or in a restaurant.[35]

The National Diet-Heart Study reported an inverse relationship between the frequency of restaurant eating and a fall in cholesterol.[36] In other words, whenever possible the regimen should be adapted to the client's life style.

Adherence Predictors

There are three possible predictors of adherence: attitudes, clinical judgment, and self-prediction.[37] Negative aspects associated with these factors, such as poor client attitudes, including predictions of low adherence, and nutritionists' preconceived negative judgments of the individuals, have been linked with future problems. However, these predictors do not identify who will fail to follow any specific regimen; to date, no single factor has been pinpointed as an accurate adherence predictor. As DiMatteo and DiNicola note, clients often feel willing to adhere, but other factors in their lives interfere with their ability to do so.[38]

Research shows that changes in beliefs are not related to alterations in long-standing diet patterns.[39] The performance of a given activity can predict subsequent adherence more clearly than can counselor attitudes or beliefs about client abilities.

The second possible predictor, the clinical judgment of the counselors as to whether adherence will be high or low, has not been shown effective in predicting compliance with a specific regimen.

Self-prediction of diet adherence has been reviewed by numerous researchers. In some cases clients were asked how well they could follow a regimen over time. Davis showed that while 77 percent of 154 new patients express a willingness to comply with their doctors' advice, only 63 percent actually exhibited compliant behavior.[40] Haynes et al. reported that, of subjects who agreed to participate in a blood pressure study, 38 of 230 did poorly in following a regimen and needed additional counseling to maintain adherence to blood pressure medication.[41]

Boczkowski et al. state that increasing clients' knowledge about their medication or disease does not increase adherence unless they are taught how to incorporate this knowledge into their treatment regimen.[42] The extent to which clients know what behaviors the regimen requires, how and when to perform them, and what to do if problems arise seems to be associated with better adherence.[43] Davis, in a blood pressure study, found that a simple interview identified half of all nonadherers.[44] However, every client should be considered a potential nonadherer because the conditions that affect compliance vary over time.

Selecting a Strategy To Promote Dietary Adherence

Once a goal has been agreed upon, counselors should consider several factors when selecting a strategy. First, the counselors should study both objective and subjective data that may indicate client motivation and willingness to participate in carrying out the strategy.

Once the strategy has been selected, counselors should list intermediate objectives to help provide some degree of early success and should review these objectives carefully with the clients to be sure they are practical and attainable. Steps necessary to achieve them should then be delineated.

The next task is to list and perform the steps (sequenced learning). This does not mean that all of the burden of performance should fall on the clients. A review of what must be done to achieve the objectives should include supporting or guiding activities by the counselors. This part of sequenced learning is the single aspect that allows for behavior change; all other functions involve planning and assessing.

Steps for a Behavior Change Plan To Promote Dietary Adherence

Stewart et al. recommend six steps for counselors to promote learning and minimize failure:

1. Divide nutrition information into manageable steps arranged in sequence.
2. Arrange for the first step in nutrition instruction to be managed with little effort.
3. Sequence the steps that follow so that the client is capable of attaining each one.
4. Attempt to make each step within the nutrition instruction small but not so easy or trivial that the client considers it worthless.
5. Involve the client in planning changes in nutrition behaviors.
6. State each step within the total nutrition instruction so that both client and counselor know what is expected and whether or not the step has been completed.[45]

Counselors have a variety of alternatives in ordering each phase. There are essentially five types of sequences:

1. natural or logical sequence
2. sequences increasing in complexity

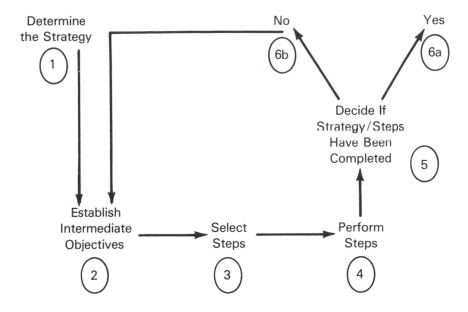

Figure 3-3 Model of Sequenced Learning. *Source:* Norman R. Stewart et al., *Systematic Counseling,* ©1978, p. 135. Reprinted by permission of Prentice-Hall, Inc., Englewood Cliffs, New Jersey.

3. sequences increasing in frequency or duration
4. sequences decreasing in frequency or duration
5. sequences increasing in anxiety-producing stimuli.[46]

In counseling situations, client anxiety can play a large part in determining eventual change in eating behaviors. The client who is to begin a difficult goal behavior change may become so anxious over failure to meet the goal that progress stops. Counselor can sequence instructional steps so that initial learning and practice occur in a nonthreatening interview, such as in clients' role-playing situations with the counselors. Following this, the counselor and client may attempt situations holding progressively more potential threat in terms of behavioral change.

For clients who are able to see the steps needed to reach their objectives, who can take the first one, and who are determined to follow the diet prescription over time, sequenced learning may be the only treatment strategy nutrition counselors need to use. Stewart et al. provide a model of sequenced learning (Figure 3-3).[47] If the steps have not been completed (step 6b on the flow chart), the process is repeated until success is achieved.

However, many clients cannot see clearly what they need to do to solve their problem. Others may have fears that inhibit learning and following the diet. Still others may find it difficult to make a continued effort to follow through. In such situations, sequenced learning is not enough—additional strategies must be selected, and the more that are available, the greater the likelihood of success.

Educational Focus To Promote Adherence

When clients do not understand the purpose of the objectives or feel that they were set solely by the nutritionist, motivation decreases. Counselors should pay particularly close attention to the difficulty and degree of challenge in each step.[48] To optimize behavior change, concrete actions to carry out the regimen, supervise practice, and individualized instructions should be listed.[49] The major emphasis in an instructional plan should be to provide information about the regimen.[50]

There are three facets to emphasize in instructing clients on an eating pattern: (1) information about the eating pattern itself, (2) the construction of the regimen around a day's activities, and (3) the rationale for its use. Providing information about the pattern itself may have limited value for future adherence,[51] but careful instruction that follows the clients' suggestions on how to fit the regimen into their daily activities should increase adherence over time[52] as well as provide the rationale for the regimen.[53] Eating habits will be even more likely to change if counselors delineate a specific sequence of concrete actions,[54] allow for supervised practice of setting up a regimen,[55] and individualize the instruction for the unique circumstances of each client's life.[56]

STRATEGY IMPLEMENTATION

After a plan for treatment of a nutrition problem has been designed, a strategy or program for implementation—a vital part of counseling—must be set. A strategy is defined as a comprehensive plan for changing a client's existing eating behavior to a desired one. The majority of the client's and counselor's time and effort is devoted to this phase. To decrease time and produce more predictable results, a practical, uncomplicated strategy should be drawn up. Cormier and Cormier present a checklist for assuring the strategy is implemented (Exhibit 3-1).[57]

Strategies for Learning New Responses

Diet strategies obviously focus on a variety of problem situations. Some aim to help clients learn new responses, others may be designed to motivate behavior change, and still others seek to promote self-directed behavior. Strategies to help promote new learning responses are modeling and simulation.

Modeling

Before presenting a model, counselors must identify clearly the response to be learned and the situational variables in which it is to occur. Stewart et al. list several uses of modeling in counseling, a procedure by which clients learn through observing and mimicking others. Modeling of a new response can increase client awareness of its performance and behavioral outcome. Individuals need to incorporate new responses into a repertoire of those already learned.[58] A second use of modeling is to demonstrate the practice of a behavior in a situation that in real life may be associated with fear, failure, anxiety, and pain.

There are several ways to set up modeling situations. When clients are their own models, they may model a behavior as it should occur, with the follow-up discussion focusing on why they cannot actualize this sort of conduct outside the counseling session. In other cases, the counselors can model a behavior if it is crucial for the

Exhibit 3-1 Checklist for Implementing a Diet Strategy

A. Verbal Set for Strategy
1. Did the nutrition counselor provide a rationale to the client about the strategy?
2. Did the counselor give an overview of the strategy?
3. Did the counselor obtain the client's willingness to try the strategy?

B. Modeling Goal Behavior
1. Were instructions about what to look for in the modeled demonstration given to the client?
2. Did the model demonstrate the goal behaviors in a coping manner?
3. Was the modeled demonstration presented in a series of sequential scenarios?
4. Did the client review or summarize the goal behaviors after the modeled demonstration?

C. Rehearsal of Goal Behaviors
1. Did the counselor review target responses before practice attempts?
2. Did the client engage in (a) covert rehearsal, (b) overt rehearsal, (c) both?
3. In initial rehearsal attempts did the counselor provide coaching and/or induction aids (e.g., dietary maintenance tools)?
4. Did the amount of coaching and induction aids decrease with practice attempts?
5. Can self-directed practice of each goal behavior be observed?
6. Was each practice attempt covered satisfactorily before moving on to another goal behavior? (Check which criteria were used in this decision):
   _____ the decision to move on was a joint one
   _____ client was able to enact the scene without feeling anxious
   _____ client was able to demonstrate target responses, as evidenced by demeanor and words
   _____ words and actions of the client were realistic to the onlooker
7. Did the counselor and client go over or arrange for a taped playback of the rehearsal?
8. Did the counselor give feedback to the client about the rehearsal? (Check whether counselor feedback included these elements):
   _____ positive reinforcer statement, a suggestion for improvement, and another positive reinforcer
   _____ the counselor encouraged each successive rehearsal attempt

D. Homework and Transfer of Training
1. Assign rehearsal homework in the client's environment?
2. Did the homework assignment include the following? (Check any that apply):
   _____ situations the client could easily initiate
   _____ graduated tasks: allow the client to gradually demonstrate the target response
   _____ a "do" statement for the client
   _____ a "quantity" statement for the client
3. Was the client given self- or other-directed assistance in carrying out homework through:
   _____ written cue cards
   _____ a trained nutrition counselor aide
4. Did the counselor instruct the client to make written self-recordings of both the strategy (homework) and the goal behaviors?
5. Did the counselor arrange for a face-to-face or telephone follow-up after the client's completion of some of the homework?

Source: From *Interviewing Strategies for Helpers,* 2nd ed., by W. H. Cormier and L. S. Cormier. Copyright ©1985, 1979 by Wadsworth Inc. Adapted by permission of Brooks/Cole Publishing Company, Pacific Grove, California 93950.

clients to learn it to solve a problem with eating behaviors. It may be helpful for clinicians to point out environmental models, asking what persons in the clients' estimation have excellent eating behaviors. These then can be used as models.

Symbolic models may also be valuable. In this approach, the model is presented through written materials, audiotapes or videotapes, films, or slide-tape exercises. An example of a symbolic model might be an actor on videotape performing an appropriate response to a friend who was offering high-calorie foods on a special holiday such as Thanksgiving or a religious feast.

Before preparing a symbolic model, practitioners should carefully consider the clients and their background. Of those who might be viewing, reading, or listening to the modeling, what are their average age, sex, ethnic origin, cultural practices, coping, mastery of the model portrayed, and concerns or problems related to nutrition? Once counselors have a good idea of the type of client who will be using the symbolic model, the goal behaviors to be modeled can be delineated. The script should include instructions, modeled dialogue, practice, written feedback, written summarization of what has been modeled, and why it is important to the individual. Finally, the script should be field tested on a sample of clients and modified on the basis of their comments and responses.[59]

Cormier and Cormier describe two additional types of modeling: covert and emotive.[60] Covert modeling requires clients to imagine a model performing desired behaviors while being instructed. One advantage of this form is its low cost: no elaborate aids are necessary. It also permits a variety of problems to be addressed. The scenes of each modeling situation can be individualized to meet the concerns of specific clients and to assist clients in practicing self-control in problem situations. With this form of modeling, clients can practice alone, an excellent alternative to live or filmed examples.

In the last form, emotive modeling, the clients focus on positive thoughts or images while imagining a discomfiting or anxiety-arousing activity or situation. By focusing on positive and pleasant images, they block embarrassing, fearful, or anxiety-provoking situations and learn ways to control responses and behavior in such settings.

Modeling seems best suited to nutritional problems that have characteristics such as these:

- The client is unaware of the response necessary to achieve an ultimate goal.
- The client is unfamiliar with the conditions that should cue a proper response.
- The client cannot foresee the reward potential of a proper response.
- The client may connect the response with a bad experience, making it unlikely that the performance will be attempted again.

Modeling provides a nonthreatening situation in which to perform a behavior. In threatening situations, individuals can establish avoidance reactions that inhibit learning a new response directly; the initial learning steps also can be nonrewarding or unpleasant. Modeling can allow the clients to learn the rewarding consequences of a behavior that they may have avoided previously.

Modeling is an excellent way to eliminate responses that may be inappropriate or used too frequently. During modeling clients can identify an undesirable eating behavior and/or replace it by one that is more appropriate. Clients who present weak but relevant cues for certain behaviors can be shown how to intensify appropriate signals and reduce inappropriate or detrimental ones; they also can learn how to discern appropriate stimuli. Modeling is useful in helping clients acquire a single response or a complex pattern of behavior.

The modeling script should reflect its content. Instructions should be given for each behavior to be demonstrated. The next part of the script should include a description of the behavior or activity to be modeled and possible dialogues of the model engaged in the activity. Following the modeling behaviors there should be opportunities for the clients to practice what they have seen. Counselors should be prepared to give clients feedback on alternatives following practice. The script should also include a summary of what has been modeled and the importance of acquiring these behaviors.

Fidelity is essential in modeling: the effective model must be as close to the real situation as possible. This fidelity must be tempered with a provision for ease of management and control of stimuli in the counseling session.

Following the modeling situation, counselors identify the relevant responses and situational cues for clients. To make this follow-up more beneficial, preorganizers or an outline to identify important elements being modeled should be provided. During the modeling, stopping the client during the action for commentary can help in explaining a response. It is sometimes helpful to prepare a script with clients so that careful thought can go into their responses. In preparing a modeling script (see Exhibit 3-2) it may be of value to exaggerate important aspects and reduce extraneous elements.

Before the modeling, the counselor can hand a typed sheet of preorganizers to the client and discuss it. While watching the modeling, the client might be asked to keep the following preorganizer questions in mind:

- What precipitated the model's response?
- What were the situational conditions and social stimuli?
- What was said?
- What was the manner of speech?
- What did the model do?
- What were the consequences of the model's response?
- How did others react?
- How did the model seem to feel about the experience?

More specific questions could be added for each individual nutrition counseling case.

Simulation

Simulation is a convenient way to provide opportunities for clients to try out responses. In modeling, clients observe and learn behaviors; in simulation, they act as participants. Simulation provides a safe environment for experiencing new responses. It is preferred to an actual situation for several reasons:[61]

- It allows individuals (clients or counselors) to cause events to happen.
- It makes it possible to compress time.
- It provides conditions that can be simplified to focus on one or two variables at a time.

Exhibit 3-2 Modeling Script

- *Instructions:* Target behavior is to eat wisely at parties.
- *Description of the Behavior:* The model is attending a graduation party where both high- and low-calorie foods are served and should use an appropriate response to an offer of high-fat foods.
- *Possible Dialogues:*
    Host: "Hey, Joe, have some of these cheese chips! They're great!"
    Guest: "No, thanks, Bob. I'm trying to avoid high-fat snacks. These fresh vegetables look perfect! Think I'll try some."
- *Discussion of Practice Alternatives*
- *Summary:* This modeled situation offered an example of how one might respond at a party to offers of inappropriate foods. Alternatives have been discussed. The actual use of this modeled behavior can assist the client in routinely following a dietary pattern, even during parties.

- It enables conditions to be controlled so that learning is managed more easily than in real-life encounters.

Stewart et al. delineate three types of simulation: (1) role playing; (2) decision-making practice, in which groups can be formed, with each member identifying with the case so individual clients then can see how the others would handle a problem; and (3) learning games.[62]

Simulations have a variety of uses in counseling. They can help in diagnosing existing or potential problems. In many cases, with clients who have no idea what is contributing to their inappropriate eating behaviors, simulation can reveal relevant aspects of the problems and stimulate the persons to recall vital elements. This strategy also permits trying alternate responses and evaluating the acquisition of new replies.[63]

Stewart et al. list seven techniques necessary to develop and use this strategy:

1. Begin by listing responses and environmental elements necessary in the simulation.
2. Carefully work as a client-counselor team to develop the situation and roles.
3. Discuss with the client the roles, situational elements, and purposes of the simulation.
4. Act out the simulation.
5. Debrief the client. Ask the client to recall experience and observations. Discuss relevant aspects of the client's performance.
6. Reenact the simulation with [the] modifications discussed following the first trial. Vary the simulation to promote the generalization of learning.

Continue the process until the objective of the simulation has been reached.[64]

Motivating Behavior Change

Some strategies for motivating behavior change are thought stopping, cognitive restructuring, reinforcement, extinction, tailoring, shaping, and contracting.

Thought Stopping

Thought stopping is useful in controlling unproductive or self-defeating thoughts and images by suppressing or eliminating these negative cognitions. Although thought stopping has been used widely and clinical case studies show encouraging results, little empirical evidence is available from controlled investigations to support the procedure. The advantages of this procedure are that it is easily administered and that clients usually understand and use it readily in a self-regulatory manner.[65]

A two-step sequence is presented for thought stopping. First, the client allows any thoughts related to eating behavior to come to mind. When the client notices a self-defeating thought, the client stops by covertly saying, "Stop!" This process is repeated until the client is able to avert self-defeating thoughts with only the covert interruption.[66]

Rimm and Masters suggest that clients think positive thoughts after the self-defeating ones are interrupted; essentially, they learn to replace negative thoughts with positive, self-directed ones following the interruption.[67] In lieu of using assertive thoughts, the clients can be asked to focus on a pleasurable or reinforcing scene or a neutral scene, such as an object in the environment.[68]

Mahoney and Mahoney suggest stopping a chain of self-defeating thoughts by replacing them with self-reinforcing ones.[69] For example, a negative monologue might go like this:

"If it weren't for my job and my family, I could lose weight."

An appropriate substitute might be:

"My schedule isn't any more hectic than anyone else's. I will be more creative in the ways I try to improve my eating habits."

Nutrition counselors can request that the clients practice this behavior at home using log sheets (Appendix F) to record the number of times they used thought stopping and the kinds of negative thoughts and positive ones that were used as replacements.[70] During the subsequent interview the log sheets should be reviewed carefully. Positive reinforcement for completing the log regardless of its content is important, particularly for positive thoughts used to replace negative ones. The counselor should work with the client in deciding on how to change negative monologues.

Cognitive Restructuring

Another very similar strategy is cognitive restructuring. This involves using coping thoughts to replace negative or self-defeating ones.[71] There is a great deal of similarity between the assertive thoughts described by Rimm and Masters[72] and the types of thoughts proposed in cognitive restructuring.

Cormier and Cormier describe six steps in cognitive restructuring during a client interview. Counselors should:

1. provide a rationale and overview of the procedure
2. identify client thoughts during problem situations.
3. introduce and practice coping thoughts
4. shift from self-defeating to coping thoughts
5. introduce and practice positive or reinforcing self-statements
6. complete homework and do follow-up.[73]

Examples of self-defeating and coping thoughts are provided in Chapters 8 through 15. Appendix G is an example of a daily record for listing use of cognitive restructuring.

Reinforcement

Reinforcement is a crucial strategy for motivating change in eating behaviors. The likelihood of an appropriate eating behavior recurring depends on the consequences. Reinforced desirable behaviors will be more likely to recur than unreinforced ones.

B. F. Skinner is credited with providing most of the basic research on the influence of reinforcement on learning.[74] A desired response can be taught through a process called shaping (discussed later in this chapter). In shaping, successive approximations of the desired response are rewarded until the new behavior is learned. Consequences of a response can increase or decrease the likelihood of its recurring.[75]

The management of reinforcement has been referred to as behavior modification. Research has shown that behavior modification is useful in eliminating inappropriate behaviors and producing goal-directed responses.[76]

Reinforcement can be used effectively in counseling by identifying the response to be reinforced, selecting the appropriate reinforcers, and having someone monitor and dispense them at the proper time. Counselors begin by identifying the responses to reinforce, then clearly describe both the behavior and the circumstances under which they are to be performed. Counselors should also affix a quantity to the reinforcement and decide which to reinforce—each occurrence of the behavior or the persistence with which clients perform a response for a period of time. A system should be set up whereby appropriate eating behaviors are reinforced immediately; however, if this is impossible, rewarding the end product of a series of such behaviors can be effective.

Reinforcement can take many forms. Social reinforcement can involve approval through verbal or nonverbal signs by a person, group, spouse, family, and/or peers. Giving clients information on past performance can be reinforcing. Arranging information on future performance in small steps that the learners can accomplish is important in helping to increase positive reinforcement.[77] In some instances tangible reinforcement is possible, such as money, clothes, etc., or valueless tokens that can be exchanged for some object or privilege related to eating behavior. Physical activities such as swimming, hiking, and skiing are extremely important reinforcers. They not only act as reward systems but also help increase caloric expenditure, firm muscles, and decrease appetite (if the exercise is strenuous). Reinforcement also can be covert or imaginal, which helps clients remain self-directed. This also is discussed later in the chapter.

All of these types of reinforcers are affected by deprivation or satiation. If there has been a period of deprivation of a reinforcer before its administration, its influence will be increased.[78] Rewards that are readily available are poor motivators.

The agents providing reinforcement can vary. Counselors, clients, or significant others in their environment all should be considered possible reinforcing agents.

Nutrition counselors should make several judgments before deciding when to reinforce clients. While clients are learning new eating behaviors, frequent rewards are most effective.[79] Each occurrence of a new behavior or each step toward it should be reinforced. During the initial learning period, rewards should be dispensed often and regularly to help clients learn to associate the appropriate eating behavior with the compensation. As progress is made, reinforcement should be administered less frequently and on a variable schedule, leading ultimately to fading. A varying number of unrewarded responses can be allowed to occur between those that are rewarded. As noted earlier, it is best to dispense the reward immediately following appropriate behavior.

Reinforcement is indicated in nutrition counseling when the following conditions exist:

- the eating behavior to be learned requires a great deal of practice before it can become a habit
- the initial learning attempts are painful
- the actual rewards that come with a new eating behavior are far off.

By using reinforcement selectively, counselors place some of the responsibility for the situation and the solution in clients' hands.

Extinction

How can nutrition counselors stop unwanted eating behaviors? A strategy called extinction offers some clues.

An unwanted behavior persists because it is reinforced. In the same way, that eating pattern gains attention, reduces anxiety, or rewards the individual. To eliminate the behavior, counselors must eliminate the reward. When withdrawal or prevention of reinforcement occurs, extinction of the behavior follows.[80] Clients can be asked to avoid certain group situations where inappropriate eating behaviors are reinforced. Another extinction method is called satiation, in which the conduct is repeated again and again, well beyond the point of fatigue. An example would be to allow the client to eat a large quantity of ice cream to reach a point of satiation. However, this is recommended only as a last resort.

The extinction strategy begins with identification of the maintaining reinforcement. When and under what circumstances the eating behavior occurs, including conditions that make it more intense or more frequent, and its immediate consequences, are recorded. Factors that appear to reduce the behavior should be noted. Clients are asked the following questions:

1. When you are eating inappropriately, what happens?
2. How do others react?
3. How do you feel?

Unwanted eating behaviors must be extinguished in the settings in which they normally occur. Implementation of extinction can be very time consuming, in part because the clients' immediate reaction may be to increase the behavior.

Tailoring

Tailoring, another strategy designed to motivate change, refers to the process of fitting the behavior to the clients' daily routine. This minimizes the number of changes the individuals must make. When using this strategy, close attention is paid to the initial baseline diet history. It often is possible to meet a dietary prescription and still arrange the eating pattern in accord with the clients' life styles and past patterns.

There are several very valid assumptions behind this strategy. First, it presumes that health behaviors are carried out in a total life context and therefore are affected directly by various aspects of daily living. It also assumes that there is no standard dietary pattern for a standard client but that each individual has unique circumstances to which the therapy must be adapted.[81]

Shaping

Shaping is a strategy that involves a gradual building of skills necessary to change a behavior. The clients proceed in steps to achieve the set criterion and gradually reach full performance.[82] For example, cholesterol intake would be reduced from 300 milligrams a day to 200 milligrams, then 100 milligrams.

The graduated approach is very similar to the shaping strategy.[83] In it, steps proceed from simple to complex behaviors and build upon one another. Important to this approach is starting at the clients' existing levels of performance. (Implementation of this approach is discussed in Chapters 8 through 15.)

Contracting

The last strategy for motivating behavior change, contracting, involves a written agreement between nutrition counselors and clients. The agreement is signed by both parties and includes the clients' agreement to carry out certain behaviors with rewards and/or punishment contingent on performance. As noted, money or other valuables sometimes are used as reinforcers. With this strategy, clients play a large role in designing their own treatment. Counselors provide advice and support while encouraging clients to plan and implement a self-managed treatment.[84]

There are several advantages to using the contracting strategy.[85] A contract in writing provides a hard-copy outline of expected behaviors.[86] Client control over treatment permits discussion of potential solutions as well as problems. The contract constitutes formal commitment to the treatment. It also provides incentive through the establishment of rewards from self or others for attaining goals.

Kanfer and Gaelick provide the following guidelines for formulating a behavioral contract:

1. Describe clearly and in detail the required behavior.
2. Set time and frequency limitations for the goal of the contract.
3. Specify positive reinforcements contingent on achievement of the required behavior.
4. Describe aversive consequences contingent on nonachievement of the required behavior.
5. Specify the method by which the contract response is observed, measured, and recorded.
6. Time the delivery of the reinforcement contingencies so that they follow the achieved behavior as closely as possible.[87]

Strategies for Becoming Self-Directed

Eventually all nutrition counselors strive to make clients self-directed. The next two strategies, decision making and self-management, help in promoting self-direction.

Nutrition counseling is merely a brief encounter in clients' lives, and its effects can be severely limited unless the individuals achieve increased control over their behavior. When clients become more self-directed, the practitioners are approaching a form of preventive counseling by preparing these persons for coping with anticipated problems on their own.

Decision Making

Clients and counselors work through the following sequence to help make decisions that facilitate change in problem eating behaviors. First, the problem is identified by the clients' answers to the following questions:

1. What is the inappropriate eating behavior?
2. What interferes with a solution?
3. When does the eating behavior occur?
4. In what situations does the eating behavior occur?
5. Under what circumstances does the eating behavior occur?
6. Under what conditions is the eating behavior most or least in variance from the recommended dietary pattern?
7. When must a decision be made or the problem eating behavior resolved?
8. How much effort is necessary to find a solution?
9. What behaviors contribute to the problem or interfere with its solution?
10. What evidence will indicate that the inappropriate eating behavior has been extinguished?[88]

Once these are answered, both values and goals must be reevaluated.[89] Not all solutions will be acceptable to clients. Their values and goals as they relate to the problem are examined so that the solution sought will be compatible with those factors. Clients might then generate a list of possible solutions or alternative courses of action. Each alternative should be evaluated in terms of time, money, effort, and advantages and disadvantages. Clients begin moving toward a solution by tentatively choosing some course of action. (It may be necessary to reexamine the decision later and select a new course.)

Several indicators can help nutrition counselors determine whether to use decision making as a strategy. First, decision making will be of value if clients are concerned about a choice to be made or an eating problem to be resolved and are unaware of alternatives. It also may benefit clients who lack the information to decide among alternatives or a method for systematically examining options and making decisions.

Decision making is an information-processing operation. The nutrition counselors' task is to help clients achieve accurate self-information and feedback. By looking at past personal experience involving specific eating behaviors, clients can discover values, interests, and abilities.

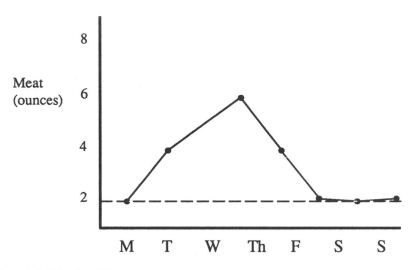

Figure 3-4 Behavioral Chart

Self-Management

Strategies for self-management involve self-monitoring, stimulus control, alternate responses, and the altering of the consequences of those responses. Self-management requires clients to alter their eating patterns on their own.

Self-Monitoring. Through self-monitoring with a food diary and intake graphs or charts, clients can learn more about their specific eating behaviors.

Self-monitoring can be very complicated or very simple. Appendix D is a simple behavioral chart that requires little effort to fill out. Figure 3-4 shows a specific problem with the amount of meat eaten at lunch. The patient makes a dot and connects the lines on the chart to denote ounces of meat eaten at lunch on certain days of the week. Appendix E allows for a more elaborate record. The patient records the number of appropriate eating behaviors and notes corresponding information about date, time, setting, and event. By listing an actual and desired behavior, the client begins to pinpoint problems with motivation. Appendix F is an example of a thought log that allows the patient to begin recording negative thoughts and replacing them with positive ones.

Role playing is another valuable way of reviewing eating patterns. Counselors and clients can record a role play and discuss it immediately, using the tape recording as an instant replay.

Self-information can come from significant others. Nutrition counselors may need to confront clients at times with information about eating habits that they may not have noticed but that those around them have. Client decision making and use of self-information are excellent motivators because they help individuals see themselves as having control over their behavior. Clients can monitor their progress even while alone; in some cases, only they can analyze thoughts about eating behavior. They can apply the decision-making strategy to future eating problems and help prevent inappropriate behaviors before they arise.

Southam and Dunbar observe that self-monitoring helps clients discover an appropriate focus for intervention, provides a baseline before treatment, helps identify antecedents and consequences of inappropriate eating behavior, assists in the adjustment of the treatment regimen, and can lead to better understanding of the disease.[90]

Self-management is crucial to the process of becoming self-directed. Counselors begin by collecting baseline information from clients' self-observation, recording relevant eating behaviors and the circumstances under which they occur, their frequency, duration, and other pertinent aspects. Clients should record this baseline information as soon as it occurs, not from memory.[91] Clients also should note the location, time, and the conditions in which the responses occur most frequently. In weight-control programs, self-monitoring may need to become a lifelong commitment.

Stimulus Control. Clients also must control the environmental stimuli associated with an eating behavior to be self-directed. All dietary behaviors are influenced by such stimuli. Situational factors can become cues that evoke or control particular behaviors.[92] By no means can clients solve all problems by avoiding situations or finding new environments.

Nutrition counselors must make clients aware that two types of eating patterns may cause problems.[93] First is the habitual behavior that is inappropriate and in need of modification. In such cases a way must be found to interrupt the normal chain of events. Cueing is one way of accomplishing this. Cues should be attention getting and associated as closely as possible with normal environmental stimuli that can evoke the response later when the special cue no longer is used. Self-cueing involves associating a response with environmental cues to effect long-term change in eating behaviors. For clients following a cholesterol-modified eating pattern, notes on the refrigerator emphasizing the use of vegetables as snack foods may serve as cues. Another example of a cue would be a written reminder on the calendar emphasizing daily exercise for clients trying to lose weight.

Many valuable cueing devices can help promote good adherence. A birthday card signed by all members of the medical staff and including a special recipe appropriate in nutrient content can help remind clients to follow their new eating pattern. A coffee mug with a special logo as a reminder to follow a new eating pattern may help a busy executive if the mug is always visible on the desk. For clients who meet milestones in following their new eating pattern, a special cake saying "Happy Anniversary" to commemorate the event may help encourage continued adherence.

A second type of eating behavior requires stimulus control for modification of conduct that is excessive or inappropriate. To control this type of conduct, the environment stimuli under which it is permitted to occur may be reduced gradually until clients perform it only in an appropriate time and place.

By gradually increasing the time spent on an appropriate eating behavior in the selected environment, the stimulus value of the setting is strengthened. The setting helps elicit the desired response. The effort is to dissociate an eating behavior from a particular stimulus by gradually eliminating the setting in which the response to be controlled tends to occur or by selecting a setting in which all responses but the controlled one are disallowed.

Interrupting response chains also can alter stimuli that elicit unwanted eating behaviors. If the chain is disrupted in its early stage, the series of inappropriate behav-

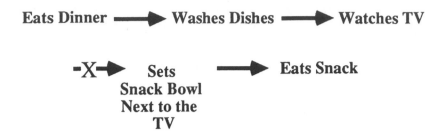

Figure 3-5 Eating Chain

iors cannot lead automatically to the terminal unwanted response. Figure 3-5 shows such a chain, with X marking the point at which it is interrupted.

Stewart et al. recommend counselors take these three steps in controlling stimuli:

1. identify elements in the eating behavior chain
2. alter conditions at one or preferably many points
3. interrupt the chain early in the sequence.[94]

Alternate Responses. In self-management clients must identify the situation in which the undesired eating behavior occurs and develop alternate patterns. Identifying the situation may involve identifying foods to be served at a special social gathering. The situation may be watching TV, taking a break at work, or binging at midnight. Counselors should help clients learn to develop alternate response patterns. Teaching clients to say "no" is a beginning: ask the client to complete a pantry survey (see Chapter 9, Adherence Tool 9-1) and substitute low-calorie foods for high-calorie foods, and work on alternate activities that exclude eating as a means of positive reinforcement.

Cueing may be necessary to remind clients to use the alternate behaviors until the new conduct becomes associated with natural environmental cues. Counselors can have clients post a list of fun nonfood activities on the refrigerator door and a list of noncaloric snack foods on the snack food cabinet door.

Altering Response Consequences. Individuals using self-rewards must learn to modify their eating behavior by monitoring their own responses and to reward reactions they see as goal directed.

In implementing self-direction, Stewart et al. recommend strategies using covert responses (thoughts, feelings, imagery, and attitudes). They suggest using thoughts as target behaviors. Clients begin by identifying desirable self-statements, monitor the frequency of positive self-thoughts, use a cue to elicit the desired ones, and finally reinforce the positive ones.[95]

In covert modeling, clients anticipate a difficult interaction and develop an imagined model of the response desired. They then rehearse covertly by imagining performing the model response in a variety of appropriate settings. When they achieve small successes, they think positive self-thoughts. This process is called covert reinforcement. Through this process, the client can begin to see a means of reward that does not necessarily involve others. An example is this goal for a person following a diabetic eating pattern:

Nutritionist's Goal
Reduce simple sugars from 35 percent
of total calories to 25 percent

Client's Goal
Reduce consumption of chocolate
candy bars from once a day to three
times a week

A further step can be labeled covert sensitization. In that process, clients link undesirable eating behaviors with an imagined aversive consequence. This is thought to be effective in reducing the actual incidence of an inappropriate response.[96] An example of covert sensitization or imagined aversive consequences follows:

Time
3:00 P.M.

Thought
"I will feel so badly if I eat this candy bar."

Focusing on self-management can lead to a self-sufficient client who knows how to assess a dietary problem and correct it.

EVALUATION

Evaluation of clients' progress by client and counselor and counselor self-evaluation provide a very important conclusion to a nutrition counseling session. Evaluation has two purposes: (1) to determine clients' progress and (2) to improve counselors' effectiveness in dealing with future clients or in further activities with present ones.[97]

Nature of Evaluation

The focus of nutrition counseling should be clients' behavior—what they actually do as a result of the process—not their feelings, attitudes, or self-concept except as these factors are affected by modifications in the individuals' eating behavior.

A review of client performance includes analyzing outcomes, determining whether or not the objectives were reached, and deciding on the need for additional counseling.[98] Some questions counselors might ask themselves are:

1. Did the client achieve the objectives as efficiently and completely as possible?
2. What have I learned from the nutrition counseling session to use in future situations?

Steps in Evaluation

Evaluation is a continuous processing of behavioral information. Counselors should begin by evaluating the accomplishment of intermediate objectives, then what the clients have done following the sessions. Evaluation strategies should be based on the clients' reports, outside sources if necessary, and clues from role-play situations.[99]

Clients should be asked to provide a record of their eating behaviors to be compared with the objectives. If the objectives were attained, counselors should decide whether further sessions are necessary by determining whether the clients are motivated enough to continue current appropriate eating behaviors on their own. Another concern or a new aspect of the same concern should be identified and the desired objective related to it. In some cases if the objective was reached there may be no need to go on.[100]

Monitoring Client Performance

Three methods of measuring clients' degree of adherence to a diet program are: client interviews, biochemical analysis, and daily records.[101]

The outcome of treatment should not be used as an indicator of how well clients are adhering to their diets. For example, weight loss should not be the only indication that clients are following a low-calorie diet. Rather, the behavior necessary to decrease food intake can be one indicator of adherence. No one completely reliable measure of adherence has yet been identified, so information must be obtained from a variety of sources.

The validity of client interviews depends on the skills of the counselors and how well they can assess behavior. Validity also depends on the clients' memory and willingness to report dietary adherence behaviors honestly. Research indicates that nonadherence is underreported. Reliability tends to improve if the clients are aware that their behavior is being assessed.[102] Overestimation of dietary intake often occurs with low consumption; underestimation is more frequent with high consumption. Specific features of the diet—calories, protein, and vitamins—also may be misreported.[103]

Biochemical assessment (through analysis of metabolic products of a dietary alteration or of the therapeutic substance itself in serum or urine) provides a more direct means of measuring adherence but tends to be inadequate over time.[104] Biochemical methods at best provide little information on the current degree of adherence, and individual variations may give misleading values.[105] The National Diet-Heart Study reports a low correlation between biochemical measures and nutritionists' ratings (.05 to .47). Such wide individual variations decrease the reliability and usefulness of biochemical assessment.[106]

Daily records as a means of assessing treatment progress have been used in behavioral weight-control programs.[107] Clients record the amount and kind of foods consumed along with the time of eating and related circumstances. The literature reports several time periods for dietary recording: an initial and final seven-day food record, two two-week food records, or a weighed food record one day a week for seven weeks and one day a month thereafter for five years.[108]

In evaluating records, counselors must keep in mind the possibility of errors in estimating portion size or omission of items.[109] One advantage of dietary records is the continuous generation of data on the behaviors under investigation. Records can provide information on erratic performance and on the origin of problems within a dietary regimen.[110] Some nutritionists find it useful to ask clients to keep food records as they maintain the diet. The process of writing down foods eaten forces clients to focus on what they are consuming and stimulates dietary adherence.

Evaluating Counselor Performance

The last step in the evaluation process pertains to counselor performance. Questions a counselor might ask include:

1. Did I help the client achieve the original objective as quickly as possible?
2. Did I use the most effective strategy?
3. Could my client have been more efficiently served by a referral source [i.e., a counseling psychologist]?
4. Were my counseling techniques appropriate for this particular client?[111]

NOTES

1. Norman R. Stewart et al., *Systemic Counseling* (Englewood Cliffs, N.J.: Prentice-Hall, 1978), pp. 95–97.

2. Ibid., pp. 97–103.

3. Marion Mason, Burness G. Wenberg, and P. Kay Welsch, *The Dynamics of Clinical Dietetics* (New York: John Wiley & Sons, 1982), pp. 181–206.

4. Ibid., pp. 182–198.

5. U.S. Department of Agriculture, Science and Education Administration, *Food: A Publication on Food and Nutrition,* Home and Garden Bulletin no. 228 (Washington, D.C., 1979).

6. Mason et al., *Dynamics,* p. 195.

7. Ibid., pp. 198–200.

8. James M. Ferguson, *Learning to Eat: Behavior Modification for Weight Control—Leader Manual* (Palo Alto, Calif.: Bull Publishing Company, 1975), Appendix—Eating Questionnaire.

9. William H. Cormier and L. Sherilyn Cormier, *Interviewing Strategies for Helpers: Fundamental Skills and Cognitive Behavioral Interventions,* 2nd ed. (Monterey, Calif.: Brooks/Cole Publishing Company, 1985), pp. 155–161.

10. Donald Meichenbaum and Dennis C. Turk, *Facilitating Treatment Adherence, A Practitioner's Guidebook* (New York: Plenum Press, 1987), p. 150.

11. Ibid., p. 151.

12. William H. Cormier and L. Sherilyn Cormier, *Interviewing Strategies for Helpers: A Guide to Assessment, Treatment and Evaluation* (Monterey, Calif.: Brooks/Cole Publishing Company, 1979), p. 140; Meichenbaum and Turk, *Facilitating Treatment Adherence,* p. 152; and Sterling K. Gerber, *Responsive Therapy, A Systematic Approach to Counseling Skills* (New York: Human Sciences Press, 1986), pp. 162–163.

13. Cormier and Cormier, *Interviewing Strategies for Helpers: A Guide to Assessment, Treatment and Evaluation,* pp. 165–166.

14. Stewart et al., *Systematic Counseling,* pp. 115–132.

15. Ibid., p. 131.

16. Daniel S. Kirschenbaum, "Proximity and Specificity of Planning: A Position Paper," *Cognitive Therapy and Research* 9 (1985): 489–506; Kirschenbaum and Randall C. Flanery, "Toward a Psychology of Behavioral Contracting," *Clinical Psychology Review* 4 (1984): 597–618; Edwin A. Locke et al., "Goal Setting and Task Performance: 1969–1980," *Psychological Bulletin* 90 (1981): 125–152; William R. Miller, "Motivation for Treatment: A Review with Special Emphasis on Alcoholism," *Psychological Bulletin* 98 (1985): 84–107; Dennis C. Turk, Peter Salovey, and Mark D. Litt, "Adherence: A Cognitive-Behavioral Perspective," in Kenneth E. Gerber and Alexis M. Nehenkis, eds., *Compliance: The Dilemma of the Chronically Ill* (New York: Springer, 1985), p. 57; Rena L. Wing et al., "Behavioral Self-Regulation in Treatment of Patients with Diabetes Mellitus," *Psychological Bulletin* 99 (1986): 78–89; and Albert Bandura and Karen M. Simon, "The Role of Proximal Intentions in Self-Regulation of Refractory Behavior," *Cognitive Therapy and Research* 1 (1977): 177–253.

17. Stewart et al., *Systematic Counseling,* pp. 115–132.

18. Ibid., pp. 106–108.

19. Ibid., pp. 109–110.

20. Ibid., pp. 111–113.

21. Cormier and Cormier, *Interviewing Strategies for Helpers: A Guide to Assessment, Treatment and Evaluation,* pp. 251–252.

22. Mason, Wenberg, and Welsch, *Dynamics,* pp. 207–209.

23. Foods and Nutrition Resource Center, *Nutrition Counseling Manual for Lipid Research Clinic Nutritionists* (Iowa City: University of Iowa Printing Service, 1980), p. 43.

24. C. R. B. Joyce et al., "Quantitative Study of Doctor-Patient Communication," *Quarterly Journal of Medicine* 38 (1969): 183–194; M. Robin DiMatteo and D. Dante DiNicola, *Achieving Patient Compliance* (New York: Pergamon Press, 1982), p. 58; and Gerber, *Responsive Therapy,* p. 30.

25. Lee Holder, "Effects of Source, Message, Audience Characteristics on Health Behavior Compliance," *Health Services Reports* 87 (1972): 843–850; Howard Leventhal, "Changing Attitudes and Habits to Reduce Risk Factors in Chronic Disease," *American Journal of Cardiology* 31 (1973): 571–580; and Leventhal, Rick Zimmerman and Mary Gutmann, "Compliance: A Self-Regulation Perspective," in W. Doyle Gentry, *Handbook of Behavioral Medicine* (New York: 1984), p. 388.

26. Morton Archer, Seymour Ringles, and George Christakis, "Social Factors Affecting Participation in a Study of Diet and Coronary Health Disease," *Journal of Health and Social Behavior* 8 (1967): 22–31.

27. Barry Blackwell, "Drug Therapy: Patient Compliance," *New England Journal of Medicine* 289 (1973): 249–252.

28. Jacqueline M. Dunbar, "Adherence to Medication Regimen: An Intervention Study with Poor Adherers" (Ph.D. diss., Stanford University, 1977), p. 13.

29. Ibid., p. 19; Dennis V. Ary, et al., "Patient Perspective on Factors Contributing to Nonadherence to Diabetes Regimen," *Diabetes Care* 9 (1986): 168–172; Tom Baronowski and Philip R. Nader, "Family Involvement in Health Behavior Change," in Dennis C. Turk and Robert D. Kerns, eds., *Health, Illness and Family* (New York: Wiley-Interscience, 1985), pp. 81–107; and Amy Herstein Gervasio, "Family Relationship and Compliance," in Kenneth E. Gerber and Alexis M. Nehenkis, eds., *Compliance: The Dilemma of the Chronically Ill* (New York: Springer, 1986), pp. 98–127.

30. Richard L. Hagen, John P. Foreyt, and Thomas W. Durham, "The Dropout Problem: Reducing Attrition in Obesity Research," *Behavior Therapy* 7 (1976): 463–471; Barbara S. Hulka et al., "Satisfaction with Medical Care in a Low Income Population," *Journal of Chronic Disease* 24 (1971): 661–673; Arnold V. Hurtado, Merwyn R. Greenlick, and Theodore J. Colombo, "Determinants of Medical Care Utilization: Failure to Keep Appointments," *Medical Care* 11 (1973): 189–198; P. R. Kaim-Caudle and G. N. Marsh, "Patient-Satisfaction Survey in General Practice," *British Medical Journal* 1 (1975): 262–264; J. A. Kincey et al., "Patient Satisfaction in General Practice," *British Medical Journal* 3 (1975): 97–98; M. Robin DiMatteo, Ron D. Hays, and Louise M. Prince, "Relationship of Physician's Nonverbal Communication Skill to Patient Satisfaction, Appointment Noncompliance, and Physician Workload," *Health Psychology* 5 (1986): 581–594; and Edward Krupkat, "The Doctor-Patient Relationship: A Social Psychological Analysis," in Robert F. Kidd and Michael J. Saks, eds., *Advances in Applied Social Psychology* (Hillsdale, N.J.: Erlbaum, 1983), pp. 19–49.

31. Joe J. Alpert, "Broken Appointments," *Pediatrics* 34 (1964): 127–132; David L. Sacket and R. Brian Haynes, eds., *Compliance with Therapeutic Regimens* (Baltimore: The Johns Hopkins University Press, 1976), pp. 40–50; Marshall H. Becker, Robert H. Drachman, and John R. Kirscht, "Predicting Mother's Compliance with Pediatric Medical Regimens," *Journal of Pediatrics* 81 (1972): 843–845; Becker and Lois A. Maiman, "Sociobehavioral Determinants of Compliance with Health and Medical Care Recommendations," *Medical Care* 13 (1975): 10–24; John R. Caldwell et al., "The Dropout Problem in Antihypertensive Treatment," *Journal of Chronic Disease* 22 (1970): 579–592; Thomas F. Garrity, "Medical Compliance and the

Clinician-Patient Relationship: A Review," *Social Science and Medicine* 15E (1981): 215–222; Ron D. Hays and M. Robin DiMatteo, "Toward a More Therapeutic Physician-Patient Relationship," in Steven W. Duck, ed., *Personal Relationships 5: Repairing Personal Relationships* (New York: Academic Press, 1984), pp. 1–20; and David Pendelton and John Hasler, *Doctor-Patient Communication* (London: Academic Press, 1983), p. 163.

32. Evan Charney, "Patient-Doctor Communication: Implications for the Clinician," *Pediatric Clinics of North America* 19 (1972): 263–279.

33. John F. Rockart and Paul B. Hofmann, "Physician and Patient Behavior Under Different Scheduling Systems in a Hospital Outpatient Department," *Medical Care* 7 (1969): 463–470.

34. Milton S. Davis and Robert L. Eichhorn, "Compliance with Medical Regimens: A Panel Study," *Journal of Health and Social Behavior* 4 (1963): 240–249; and Walter J. Johannsen, George A. Hellmuth, and Thomas Sorauf, "On Accepting Medical Recommendations: Experiences with Patients in a Cardiac Work Classification Unit," *Archives of Environmental Health* 12 (1966): 63–69.

35. Dunbar, *Medication Regimen,* pp. 19–22.

36. National Diet-Heart Study, "Final Report," *Circulation,* March 1968, Supplement 1.

37. Foods and Nutrition Resource Center, *Counseling Manual,* p. 51.

38. DiMatteo and DiNicola, *Achieving Patient Compliance,* p. 79.

39. Foods and Nutrition Resource Center, *Counseling Manual,* p. 51.

40. Milton S. Davis, "Physiologic, Psychological and Demographic Factors in Patient Compliance with Doctor's Orders," *Medical Care* 6 (1968): 115–122.

41. R. Brian Haynes et al., "Improvement of Medication Compliance in Uncontrolled Hypertension," *Lancet* 1 (1976): 1265–1268.

42. Judith A. Boczkowski, Amos Zeichner, and Niki DeSanto, "Neuroleptic Compliance Among Chronic Schizophrenic Outpatients: An Intervention Outcome Report," *Journal of Consulting and Clinical Psychology* 53 (1985): 666–671.

43. Meichenbaum and Turk, *Facilitating Treatment Adherence,* p. 112.

44. Davis, "Physiologic Factors," 115–122.

45. Stewart et al., *Systematic Counseling,* p. 136.

46. Ibid., pp. 137–138.

47. Ibid., p. 135.

48. Ibid., p. 144.

49. Foods and Nutrition Resource Center, *Counseling Manual,* pp. 64, 66, 113.

50. Southam and Dunbar, "Facilitating Patient Compliance with Medical Interventions," pp. 178–179.

51. David L. Sackett et al., "Randomized Clinical Trial of Strategies for Improving Medication on Compliance in Primary Hypertension," *Lancet* 1 (1975): 1205–1207.

52. Franklin F. Dickey, Mary E. Mattar, and Gregory M. Chudzok, "Pharmacist Counseling Increases Drug Regimen Compliance," *Hospitals* 49 (1975): 85–88; Joseph A. Linkewich, Robert B. Catalano, and Herbert L. Flack, "The Effect of Packaging and Instruction on Outpatient Compliance with Medication Regimens," *Drug Intelligence and Clinical Pharmacy* 8 (1974): 10–15; and James M. McKenney et al., "The Effect of Clinical Pharmacy Services on Patients with Essential Hypertension," *Circulation* 48 (1973): 1104–1111.

53. Irving S. Colcher and James W. Bass, "Penicillin Treatment of Streptococcal Pharyngitis: A Comparison of Schedules and the Role of Specific Counseling," *Journal of the American Medical Association* 222 (1972): 657–659.

54. Leventhal, "Changing Attitudes," 571–580.

55. Rhoda G. Bowen, Rosemary Rich, and Rozella M. Schlotfeldt, "Effects of Organized

Instruction for Patients with the Diagnosis of Diabetes Mellitus," *Nursing Research* 10 (1961): 151–159.

56. Jeanne C. Hallburg, "Teaching Patients Self-Care," *Nursing Clinics of North America* 5 (1970): 223–231; Stanley G. Rosenberg, "Patient Education Leads to Better Care for Heart Patients," *HSMHA Health Reports* 86 (1971): 793–802; Meichenbaum and Turk, "Facilitating Treatment Adherence," p. 113; Lizette Peterson and Robyn Ridley-Johnson, "Prevention of Disorders in Children," in C. Eugene Walker and Michael C. Roberts, eds., *Handbook of Clinical Child Psychology* (New York: John Wiley & Sons, 1983), pp. 1174–1197; and G. Alan Marlatt and Judith R. Gordon, *Relapse Prevention: Maintenance Strategies in the Treatment of Addictive Behaviors* (New York: Guilford Press, 1985), pp. 51–52.

57. Cormier and Cormier, *Interviewing Strategies for Helpers: A Guide to Assessment, Treatment and Evaluation,* pp. 275–276.

58. Allen E. Ivey, Mary Bradford Ivey, and Lynn Simek-Downing, *Counseling and Psychotherapy: Integrating Skills, Theory and Practice* (Englewood Cliffs, N.J.: Prentice-Hall, 1987), pp. 253–254.

59. Gerber, *Responsive Therapy,* p. 167; and Cormier and Cormier, *Interviewing Strategies for Helpers: A Guide to Assessment, Treatment and Evaluation,* pp. 278–280, 296.

60. Cormier and Cormier, *Interviewing Strategies for Helpers: A Guide to Assessment, Treatment and Evaluation,* pp. 303, 307.

61. Stewart et al., *Systematic Counseling,* p. 163.

62. Ibid., pp. 164–170.

63. Ibid., pp. 173–175.

64. Ibid., p. 176.

65. Patricia A. Wisocki and Edward Rooney, "A Comparison of Thought Stopping and Covert Sensitization Techniques in the Treatment of Smoking: A Brief Report," *Psychological Record* 24 (1974): 192.

66. Cormier and Cormier, *Interviewing Strategies for Helpers: Fundamental Skills and Cognitive Behavioral Interventions,* p. 388.

67. D. C. Rimm and J. C. Masters, *Behavior Therapy: Techniques and Empirical Findings* (New York: Academic Press, 1974), pp. 416–449.

68. John Anthony and Barry A. Edelstein, "Thought Stopping Treatment of Anxiety Attacks Due to Seizure-Related Obsessive Ruminations," *Journal of Behavior Therapy and Experimental Psychiatry* 6 (1975): 343–344; Louis Gershman, "Case Conference: A Transvestite Fantasy Treated by Thought Stopping, Covert Sensitization and Aversive Shock," *Journal of Behavior Therapy and Experimental Psychiatry* 1 (1970): 153–161; Toshiko Yamagami, "The Treatment of an Obsession by Thought Stopping," *Journal of Behavior Therapy and Experimental Psychiatry* 2 (1971): 133–135; and Joseph Wolpe, "Dealing with Resistance to Thought Stopping: A Transcript," *Journal of Behavior Therapy and Experimental Psychiatry* 2 (1971): 121–125.

69. Michael J. Mahoney and Kathryn Mahoney, *Permanent Weight Control, A Total Solution of the Dieter's Dilemma* (New York: W. W. Norton & Co., 1976), pp. 46–68.

70. Ibid., pp. 62–63, 65.

71. Michael L. Russell, *Behavioral Counseling in Medicine: Strategies for Modifying At-Risk Behavior* (New York: Oxford University Press, 1986), p. 313.

72. Rimm and Masters, *Behavior Therapy,* pp. 416–449.

73. Cormier and Cormier, *Interviewing Strategies for Helpers: Fundamental Skills and Cognitive Behavioral Interventions,* p. 405.

74. Burrhus F. Skinner, *Science and Human Behavior* (New York: The Free Press, 1965), pp. 64–66, 72–75.

75. Albert Bandura, *Principles of Behavior Modification* (New York: Holt, Rinehart &

Winston, 1969), pp. 143–148; Frederick H. Kanfer and Jeanne S. Phillips, *Learning Foundations of Behavior Therapy* (New York: John Wiley & Sons, 1970), pp. 241–368; and Mary A. Southam and Jacqueline M. Dunbar, "Facilitating Patient Compliance with Medical Interventions," in Kenneth A. Holroyd and Thomas L. Creer, eds., *Self-Management of Chronic Disease* (New York: Academic Press, 1986), pp. 163–187.

76. Leonard H. Epstein and Patricia A. Cluss, "A Behavioral Medicine Perspective on Adherence to Long-Term Medical Regimens," *Journal of Consulting and Clinical Psychology* 50 (1982): 960–971; Rena L. Wing et al., "Behavioral Self-Regulation in the Treatment of Patients with Diabetes Mellitus," *Psychological Bulletin* 99 (1986): 78–89; and Steven M. Zifferblatt, "Increasing Patient Compliance Through the Applied Analysis of Behavior," *Preventive Medicine* 4 (1975): 173–182.

77. James G. Holland and Burrhus F. Skinner, *Analysis of Behavior* (New York: McGraw-Hill Book Co., 1961), pp. 98–105, 132–136.

78. Albert Bandura, *Principles of Behavior Modification* (New York: Holt, Rinehart & Winston, 1969), pp. 182–202.

79. Holland and Skinner, *Analysis,* pp. 118–131.

80. Kelly D. Brownell et al., "Understanding and Preventing Relapse," *American Psychologist* 51 (1986): 765–782.

81. Foods and Nutrition Resource Center, *Counseling Manual,* p. 60.

82. Linda W. Craighead and W. Edward Craighead, "Implications of Persuasive Communication Research for the Modification of Self-Statements," *Cognitive Therapy and Research* 4 (1980): 117–134.

83. Marjorie E. Seybold and Daniel B. Drachman, "Gradually Increasing Doses of Prednisone in Myasthenia Gravis: Reducing the Hazards of Treatment," *New England Journal of Medicine* 290 (1974): 81–84; and Russell, *Behavioral Counseling in Medicine,* pp. 63–64.

84. Daniel S. Kirschenbaum and Randall C. Flanery, "Behavioral Contracting: Outcomes and Elements," in Michel Hersen, Richard M. Eisler, and Peter M. Miller, eds., *Progress in Behavior Modification,* vol. 15 (New York: Academic Press, 1983), pp. 217–275; and Kirschenbaum and Flanery, "Toward a Psychology of Behavioral Contracting," pp. 597–618.

85. Harold Leitenberg, ed., *Handbook of Behavior Modification and Behavior Therapy* (Englewood Cliffs, N.J.: Prentice-Hall, 1976), pp. 440–441; Penick et al., "Behavior Modification," pp. 49–55; and Thomas F. Plaut, "Doctor's Order and Patient Compliance: Letter to the Editor," *New England Journal of Medicine* 292 (1974): 435.

86. Sackett and Haynes, *Compliance,* pp. 100–109.

87. Frederick H. Kanfer and Lisa Gaelick, "Self-Management Methods," in Frederick H. Kanfer and Arnold P. Goldstein, eds., *Helping People Change,* 2d ed. (New York: Pergamon Press, 1986), p. 309.

88. Stewart et al., *Systematic Counseling,* pp. 208–209.

89. Russell, *Behavioral Counseling in Medicine,* pp. 51–52.

90. Southam and Dunbar, "Facilitating Patient Compliance with Medical Interventions," pp. 164–168.

91. Ibid., p. 127.

92. Russell, *Behavioral Counseling in Medicine,* pp. 62–63.

93. Stewart et al., *Systematic Counseling,* pp. 228–229.

94. Ibid., p. 230.

95. Ibid., p. 232.

96. Ibid., pp. 232–234.

97. Ibid., p. 238.

98. Ibid., p. 239.

99. Ibid., p. 240.

100. Ibid., pp. 240–241.

101. Foods and Nutrition Resource Center, *Counseling Manual,* p. 29.

102. Ibid., p. 30.

103. J. Patrick Madden, S. Jane Goodman, and Helen A. Guthrie, "Validity of the 24-Hour Recall," *Journal of the American Dietetic Association* 68 (1976): 143–147.

104. Foods and Nutrition Resource Center, ed., *Counseling Manual,* 30.

105. B. R. Soutter and M. C. Kennedy, "Patient Compliance Assessment in Drug Trials: Usage and Methods," *Australian and New Zealand Journal of Medicine* 4 (1974): 360–364.

106. National Diet-Heart Study, "Final Report."

107. Foods and Nutrition Resource Center, *Counseling Manual,* pp. 30–31.

108. Rose Ann L. Shorey, Bennett Sewell, and Michael O'Brien, "Efficacy of Diet and Exercises in the Reduction of Serum Cholesterol and Triglycerides in Free Living Adult Males," *American Journal of Clinical Nutrition* 29 (1976): 512–521; Sharron S. Coplin, Jean Hines, and Annette Gormican, "Outpatient Dietary Management of the Prader-Willi Syndrome," *Journal of the American Dietetic Association* 68 (1976): 330–334; and Research Committee, "Low-fat Diet in Myocardial Infarction: A Controlled Trial," *Lancet* 2 (1965): 501–504.

109. Marguerite C. Burk and Eleanor M. Pao, "Methodology for Large-Scale Surveys of Household and Individual Diets," *Home Economics Research Report,* no. 40, Agricultural Research Service, U.S. Department of Agriculture (Washington, D.C.: U.S. Government Printing Office, November 1976), pp. 39–54; Charlotte M. Young, "Dietary Methodology," in Committee on Food Consumption Patterns, Food and Nutrition Board, National Research Council, *Assessing Changing Food Consumption Patterns* (Washington, D.C.: National Academy Press, 1981), pp. 89–118.

110. Foods and Nutrition Resource Center, *Counseling Manual,* pp. 30–31.

111. Stewart et al., *Systematic Counseling,* pp. 251–253.

Tools for Nutrition Counseling

Part II covers a variety of topics designed to assist the nutrition counselor in promoting dietary adherence. In Chapter 4 Dr. Johanna Dwyer discusses assessing and monitoring dietary behaviors; Dr. Phyllis Stumbo and Ms. Sandra Powers provide insights into use of the computer in designing dietary patterns and analyzing dietary intake in Chapter 5. Chapter 6 reviews instructional planning, and Dr. John Kramer describes research on stress and methods for analyzing and managing it in Chapter 7.

Assessing and Monitoring Dietary Behaviors

Johanna T. Dwyer

Objectives for Chapter 4

1. Describe the different methods available for assessing and monitoring dietary behaviors.
2. Provide examples of their use.
3. Guide the counselor in selecting appropriate assessment and monitoring tools for clinical applications.

ASSESSMENT

Dietary assessment is the process of documenting an individual's food intake and related dietary behaviors. Its clinical objectives are to characterize current intakes to identify habitual aspects that require nutritional counseling for therapeutic, preventive, or health maintenance purposes and to contribute to the process of nutritional status assessment.

The types of information included in dietary assessment vary depending on its purpose. A description of food intake, obtained either by recall or by record keeping, is usually included. Other information may also be helpful for some purposes. In clinical situations therapeutic interventions are usually contemplated, and for these purposes additional data in hand are helpful in designing a realistic nutritional plan for the client. Such information includes any special food-related problems or habits such as allergies, intolerances, cravings, and aversions; special food likes and dislikes; and general information on food availability, including money available for food, participation in food assistance programs, food buying, cooking, storage, and preparation practices.

Importance

Dietary assessment data, when evaluated together with findings from the medical history, physical, anthropometric measurements, and biochemical indices from laboratory tests, permit an assessment of the individual's nutritional status. The assessment also provides the information necessary for any therapeutic or preventive alterations. Finally, the assessment identifies clients needing therapeutic diets, lengthy nutritional counseling, special nutritional advice, and more general nutrition information.

When To Assess

Screening

All patients need nutritional screening, and selected, high-risk patients also need nutritional assessment. Resources are never sufficient to perform detailed dietary assessments on all clients in most clinical practices. Therefore nutritionists must screen the population to identify the high-risk individuals who are most likely to have diet-related problems and who thus merit further attention. Ideally, counselors should apply agreed-upon screening criteria and pay special attention to assessing clients identified to be at high nutritional risk.

The screening process involves comparing the patient's characteristics to characteristics known to be associated with nutritional problems. Screening criteria consist of easily collected, already available information such as demographics, previous medical history, present diagnosis, and other simple, straightforward information known to characterize individuals who are at higher-than-average risk.

The most useful screening factors vary within various subgroups of the population. Exhibit 4-1 presents an example of screening criteria used to identify women at high risk who need nutritional assessment during the childbearing years. In identifying individuals with problem drinking behaviors, short questions on the frequency and amount of consumption of wine, beer, and liquor have proven useful.[1] For individuals suffering from eating disorders, questions on the frequency of binging, laxative abuse, and self-induced vomiting are useful.[2] Similar lists are available for other subgroups in the population.[3]

The data correlating these screening factors with actual nutritional problems are currently not definitive. Thus there is a good deal of room for collective judgment in some areas, and screening criteria may vary somewhat. Nevertheless, knowledge is sufficient to justify the use of screening tools. From the standpoints of efficiency, effectiveness, and fairness, the use of objective criteria still is much to be preferred to nutrition referral patterns that rely solely on the idiosyncratic and widely disparate views of individual physicians and other care providers.

Assessment

Assessment, a lengthier process than screening, includes gathering more detailed information on diet for diagnostic and intervention purposes. These data are combined with other available information from history, physicals, anthropometric measurements, and biochemical tests to determine what problem exists and how best to deal with it.

What To Assess

In most clinical situations the purpose of assessment is to identify and describe problems to deal with in treatment. To ensure that the assessment method chosen

Exhibit 4-1 Screening Criteria To Identify Women at High Risk Who Need Nutrition
Assessment during the Childbearing Years

I. Likely to need therapeutic diets
  - Deviations in maternal prepregnancy weight or pregnancy weight gain
  - Poor past obstetrical history
  - Addictions
  - Preexisting medical complications, or complications developing during gestation

II. Likely to need lengthy nutrition counseling
  - Age under 17, high parity, short interconceptional periods
  - Low income or limited food budget
  - Ethnic or language problems
  - Unusual eating habits
  - Inadequate knowledge of nutrition or food resource management
  - Poor somatic growth in previous offspring

III. Likely to need some special nutritional advice
  - Smokers who are giving up habit
  - Twin pregnancy
  - Out-of-wedlock pregnancy
  - Emotional stress or disturbance
  - Dwellers in areas where access to food is difficult

IV. All pregnant women: general nutritional advice

---

provides the information desired, the counselor needs to identify dietary characteristics of special interest.

In some situations,—for example, in describing the nutritional status of alcoholic men likely to have shortfalls in intakes of several nutrients[4]—complete records or recalls and an analysis of all the nutrients in the entire diet may be necessary. In other cases, when only a few dietary constituents are of interest, the dietary assessment can concentrate on intakes of foods that are usually major contributors of a particular nutrient. Such limited assessment proves useful in studies of the adequacy of vitamin D intake in vegan-vegetarian children and in dietary assessment of sources of fructose among children with hereditary fructose intolerance.[5] Lists of major food sources for many of the common nutrients of interest in the American diet are now available, which simplifies the development of assessment instruments targeted toward particular food constituents.[6]

While the dietary assessment usually focuses on nutrient intake, such an assessment alone may not provide the information necessary for sound treatment planning. For example, the timing of food intake may also be critical in insulin-dependent diabetics, and among compulsive overeaters mood and other situational determinants of eating may be important. Therefore counselors must take the time to think through beforehand exactly what the purpose of the assessment is.

Instruments for Dietary Assessment

Two basic types of instruments are available for assessing dietary intakes. The first type, records obtained at the time the food is eaten or shortly thereafter, involves prospective data collection after the initial dietary interview. The second type consists of retrospective records obtained at the dietary interview by recall.

Both prospective and retrospective instruments for dietary assessment have their strengths and weaknesses, and an appropriate choice depends upon one's purpose. This section describes their general characteristics and considerations to take into account in selecting between them. Recent reviews provide more details on each of these methods.[7]

Prospective Methods

Food Diaries. Clients are instructed to record in the food diary everything they eat or drink, estimating portion sizes in household measures. Individuals may be asked to keep diaries for several days at a time or only at specified times to obtain representative food intakes. The counselor then collects the diaries, examines them, clarifies any ambiguous entries or missing data, and calculates intakes of nutrients and other data of interest. The strength of food diaries is that clients record what they actually eat at the time of consumption, before they forget. The weaknesses are that diaries require a great deal of time and effort on the part of the patient, that estimating the portion sizes of many foods is difficult and thus estimated and actual quantities eaten may differ, and that clients may consciously or unconsciously alter their usual intakes while they keep diaries, distorting estimates of usual consumption. Some of these difficulties can be overcome if the counselor provides detailed instruction in advance on record keeping that stresses the need to avoid altering usual food intakes. Valid reporting is also encouraged if the counselor adopts a nonjudgmental attitude when examining the records with the patient.

Weighed Intakes. In a variation of food diaries, the client weighs on a small scale all food and drink consumed to decrease errors in the estimation of portion sizes. Chief among the method's strengths is that accuracy of estimation is high, and for this reason it is frequently used in research studies. The main difficulty is that, as accuracy increases, so does the extent to which record keeping interferes with normal life styles and usual intakes. The technique is especially difficult for people who eat out of their homes a good deal in situations where it is difficult to measure intakes. Electronic recording scales coupled with tape recorders, now available, simplify the process of obtaining weighed food intakes for research when precision is of great importance.[8] However, the cost and bother of the paraphernalia are too great for most clinical situations.

Telephone Interviews. Personal interviews are difficult to schedule and expensive. Methods are now available that use telephone interviews to report food intakes or recent food consumption immediately. The method has not as yet been proven valid for individual intakes, although it may be sufficiently precise for some research dealing with large groups of people.

Photographic Methods. In this research method the respondent photographs at a standardized distance the foods to be eaten. The strength of the method is that it minimizes writing and compares well with weighed records.[9] Its weakness is that it requires a good deal of work on the part of the client to make sure the distances are fixed for the photographs and all food consumption is recorded. Also, the interviewer must perform considerable analysis as standardized analyses are not available. Thus the method is unlikely to be used in most clinical situations.

Duplicate Portion Analysis. Sometimes counselors can collect duplicate portions of foods consumed by individuals instead of having them keep food records. The most usual procedure is to ask clients to collect duplicates and reimburse them for any costs involved. Alternatively, a trained observer can collect intakes directly. The strength of the method is that it permits the actual chemical analysis of food composites, which may be necessary if diets contain many unusual foods as staples or if tables of food composition do not usually provide the constituents of interest. The weakness of the method is that the composites are difficult to collect, messy, and costly to analyze. Also, the very process of collecting food composites may change what clients eat.

Intakes and Outputs. Another common prospective technique is to measure all food entering and leaving a client's room and to assume that the difference is what the client ate. The strengths of the method are that it places less burden on the client than does a request for diary keeping, that assessment can be done without the patient's knowledge, and that it provides more sophisticated information on food intake then simply assuming that all clients eat all the food they are served. The weaknesses are that obtaining accurate intakes and outputs is difficult in many hospitals because of conflicting pressures in clinical care, that others in the room may eat the food, and that the client may discard or hide the food (as is frequently the case in anorexia nervosa), all resulting in biased estimates of actual intake.

Retrospective Methods

24-Hour Recalls. The interviewer asks clients to recall all the foods and beverages they have consumed over the past 24 hours, often starting with the meal immediately preceding the interview. Probes and memory aids are used to ensure that recall is complete. Food models or measuring cups, spoons, and other implements to estimate portion size are used to get a rough estimate of portion sizes.

The great strengths of the 24-hour recall are that it is rapid (requiring about 30 minutes), inexpensive, and relatively well accepted by most respondents. The burden on the respondent is low; the interviewer does most of the work. Elaborate record keeping is unnecessary. Most people readily submit to the procedure, so it is relatively easy to get a representative sample of patients to cooperate in research studies. Also, the risk that individuals have changed their food consumption is less because they are not always aware that they are going to be interviewed. However, this method does not guarantee that reported intakes actually represent what the person ate; people may not wish to reveal the truth, and even over the short term people easily forget details about what they ate. Interactive computer programs now available for 24-hour recalls save time in coding and analysis.

The greatest weakness of the 24-hour recall is that it tends not to represent clients' usual intake. Several 24-hour recalls are necessary for accurate estimates of typical or usual diets. A second problem with the 24-hour recall is that it cannot be used to identify precisely individuals whose intakes are likely to be very high or low in the population.[10] That is, the fact that an individual does not meet 100 percent of the RDA on a given day does not mean that a dietary deficiency exists. A third disadvantage is that clients forget. Some individuals, such as an elderly man suffering from Alzheimer's disease, which impairs short-term memory, or a small child, may be unable to recall what they ate even after a short time. Unfortunately, clients are more likely to forget some items than to forget others, so errors in estimation of nutrient intakes may vary from one nutrient to another depending on their food sources. A fourth disadvantage is that, in contrast to record keeping, clients must tell an individual with a professional interest in nutrition what they have been eating. Many clients try to idealize their intakes, especially if they have already received dietary instructions they are supposed to be following and if they anticipate approval or disapproval. Finally, single 24-hour recalls are inappropriate in surveys of dietary adequacy or investigations of the associations between food intakes, biochemical, and other health indices; other methods covering a longer time span are more desirable.[11]

Semiquantitative and Other Food Frequency Recalls. All food frequency techniques ask the clients to describe the frequency with which they consume usual intakes of a list of various foods per day, per week, or per month, usually over several months or a year. The number and type of food items specified vary depending on the purpose of the study. Semiquantitative food frequency questionnaires also specify a portion size (either a standardized portion size or a choice of a range of sizes).

Until the 1970s food frequency questionnaires were used chiefly for gross screening of diet quality using consumption of the Basic Four, Basic Seven, or some other food grouping system as the criterion of dietary adequacy. More specialized versions were developed for the particular purposes of assessing consumption of specific foods or nutrients thought to be associated with disease risks in epidemiologic studies of particular populations.

By the late 1970s nutritionists had available several computerized dietary analysis systems that included semiquantitative food frequency questionnaires based on more elaborate food groups or concentrating on only a few nutrients, such as type and amount of fat. At that time the memory capacity of microcomputers did not usually allow for extensive food lists and large numbers of nutrients. While some of these systems were helpful for dietary analysis, validation information was not always available. Moreover, with the advent of low-cost personal computers with greatly expanded memories, more elaborate data bases and more extensive food lists became a reality and many of these systems became obsolete.

The more sophisticated and better-validated methods that became available in the mid-1980s are suitable for the general population. They differ from the earlier versions in that they have longer and more representative lists of foods that are derived from national surveys of samples of the American adult population and include the major sources of calories and several macro- and micronutrients of particular interest. Moreover, the questionnaires ask about vitamin and mineral intakes from supplements and are available in a form suitable for optical scanning for automatic scoring by computer or in an interactive form to use on personal computers. The most complete and well-validated instruments of this kind are those developed by Willett and his associates and by Block and her colleagues at the National Cancer Institute.[12]

Among the strengths of the simpler food frequency questionnaires are their simplicity, low respondent burden, low cost, and ease of administration. They can also be used as screening instruments to identify individuals whose diets place them at risk of deficiency or excess. Because certain foods are the major contributors of some food constituents, if these foods and their frequency of consumption can be established, some estimate of intakes is possible even from rather short questionnaires. For example, if only a few dozen foods contain methylxanthines, the stimulants present in coffee and tea, a food frequency questionnaire can yield rough estimates of the consumption of this substance. Specially designed, short food frequency questionnaires have been used successfully in large epidemiologic studies to assess exposure to such dietary risk factors as levels of consumption of beverages sweetened with saccharin and cyclamates and their associations with bladder cancer and alcohol consumption during pregnancy and risk of fetal alcohol syndrome.[13] Another strength of food frequency recalls is that they can describe different food consumption patterns, such as the differences in the consumption of potatoes and pasta by Irish- and Italian-Americans as well as differences in nutrient intakes. Such information may be especially useful for diet planning.

The newer semiquantitative food frequency questionnaires have a number of additional strengths. The reporting interval covers several months or a year rather than a single day, as does the 24-hour recall, so long-term habits rather than a single day's intake are more likely to be reported. They are relatively rapid and simple to administer, are well accepted by respondents, are economical to analyze, and provide information quickly if they are computerized. Some questionnaires include items that help identify seasonal differences in intakes. They provide rough estimates of intakes that may suffice when groups are being examined but are less reliable in precisely characterizing the intakes of individuals. That is, they can rank individual intakes into rough categories by quartiles but cannot provide the kind of precise intake data that are necessary for some research and clinical purposes.

Several weaknesses of food frequency questionnaires make them unsuitable for some purposes. Because both of the most popular semiquantitative food frequency questionnaires are based on the usual intakes of American adults in the 1970s, they are inappropriate for subgroups of the population with quite different food habits. For example, Chinese-Americans have very different food habits than other Americans do. The major food sources of several nutrients of their diets are also quite different, but they may not be included in questionnaires based on the general population.

Because the questionnaires were designed to tap adults' intakes, they are unsuitable for infants, children, or the very old. Also, if food consumption patterns and major food sources of the various nutrients change dramatically in the next few decades, the questionnaires will no longer describe consumption as accurately as they do now because the weightings assigned to the various foods will be wrong. Means for the nutrient contributions of food groups or of food exchange categories on these questionnaires are based on the usual mixture of foods eaten in a particular category by the population used to develop the food grouping system. If the individual surveyed chooses foods that are very different from these, the nutrient contributions to the individual's diet may be markedly different and may not be reflected in the questionnaire.

The fact that the questionnaires cannot provide quantitatively precise estimates of intakes for individuals is also a serious disadvantage for some clinical purposes requiring a great deal of quantitative precision. Nor is it not clear yet how these questionnaires assess the intakes of individuals on modified diets, such as those very low in fat and protein. Finally, the ability of such questionnaires to monitor changes in food intake over relatively short periods (such as weeks) is unknown.

Burke-Type Dietary History. The dietary history technique, often referred to as a Burke-type history in recognition of Bertha Burke, the nutritionist who first developed the technique, describes usual dietary intakes over several months or a year. The client is first asked to report all foods and beverages consumed on a usual day. Then the interview progresses to questions about the frequency and amount of consumption of these foods and others. Usually clients provide some documentation of several days' intakes in the form of food diaries; these are used to make sure oral reports include all the foods recorded on the diaries as eaten. The method also includes food models, cross-checks on food consumption, careful probing, and other techniques. The usual dietary history takes at least an hour and usually up to two hours, even when the interviewer is a highly skilled nutritionist. Some counselors use simplified versions of the dietary history that do not require food diaries.

The dietary history yields a rich and detailed description of usual food intake, its chief strength. Its weakness is that it requires highly skilled research nutritionists, that the interview is time consuming, and that it must be done face-to-face. Moreover, the reliability of the instrument is fairly low, suggesting that the method and interviewers themselves as well as the client contribute sources of variability. Analysis is usually fairly costly.

Criteria for Selecting Assessment Instruments

Why Is the Dietary Assessment Being Done?

The most important issue in selecting dietary assessment instruments is the reason for the assessment. Is it for research, clinical, or evaluation purposes? If the purpose is clinical, is the focus solely to identify problems and assist in diagnosis, or will the data also be used to formulate preventive, curative, or supportive care plans? Is diet alone the focus of analysis, or is it simply one of many factors being assessed to describe nutritional status? If other indices are being employed as well, the degree of detail required may be less than if only one or two indices of possible malnutrition are being used.

Who Is To Be Assessed?

The choice of methods is greatly influenced by whether a single individual or a group is the target of the assessment. Several references detail the specifics that are important in choosing assessment methods for large groups.[14]

What Is To Be Assessed?

The precise dietary characteristics of interest must be determined before the assessment instrument is chosen. If only a few foods or food constituents are of interest, the dietary interview can be more specific in its focus than is possible when the entire nutrient composition of the diet is the study's goal.

How Precisely Must It Be Measured?

The assessment tool must match the degree of precision needed. For some purposes qualitative statements about diet will suffice, while for others quantitative statements are necessary. The degree of quantitative precision required also needs to be established. In some cases it is enough to categorize individuals into quartiles with respect to their intakes, and semiquantitative food frequency instruments are perfectly acceptable. When very precise estimates of intakes are required to ensure that requirements are met, food records using weighing techniques may be necessary and the assessment tool will vary accordingly.

Nutritionists sometimes wrongly assume that a very high degree of quantitative precision is necessary or possible for all nutrients, when in fact it is needed only for a few dietary constituents. For example, precise estimates of intakes of certain of the amino acids are required in children suffering from phenylketonuria, but estimates of other aspects of diet do not need such precision.

Reliability

In most assessments of individuals for clinical purposes, dietary intakes must reflect typical patterns for the person because only these patterns are likely to have nutritional significance. Dietary assessment is difficult among people who have no dietary pattern. Another problem arises when an individual has a food pattern that is stable but extremely variable or unusual, as that found among shift workers. Clinicians must pay special attention in assessment to identifying these patterns, determining dietary intake for each of them, and including a suitable weighting system for developing estimates of overall diet.

Validity

Dietary assessment must measure what it purports to measure.[15] Assessment is further complicated by the fact that the very act of assessing food intake often alters the phenomenon being measured. The major threat to validity in retrospective methods of dietary assessment is forgetting, especially if forgetting is more frequent with some foods than others, which is probably true. Probes and other memory aids are often used to assist the client in remembering.[16] The greatest threat to validity in prospective studies is that people may unconsciously alter their habitual intakes to simplify recording during the observation period or to impress the nutritionist with how well they are following their diets, if they are on therapeutic regimes. This tendency can be overcome in part by careful instruction and a nonjudgmental attitude on the part of whoever does the assessment.

Validity is likely to be especially jeopardized in certain patients. Obese people often underreport their caloric intakes until they have established a rapport with their counselors. Patients suffering from anorexia nervosa and parents of some children with nonorganic failure to thrive overreport their intakes, often in a reliable but nonetheless invalid manner. Those who most commonly present threats to validity in dietary assessments include the very old, the very sick, infants and children, alcoholics, drug addicts, the confused, those who wish to please the interviewer, those whose food intakes are chaotic, and those who are disinterested or unmotivated by the dietary reporting task. Poor reports by respondents increase the difficulties of describing intakes validly and reliably.

A final aspect of validity is concurrent validity; that is, the correlation between a dietary measure and some other index such as a biochemical, clinical, or anthropometric measurement. There are several reasons for an imperfect correspondence. First, dietary assessment may be measuring deviations in nutritional status at a different and less severe level, before pathology is manifest. Second, the measurement of diet is imprecise, as are other measurements, and a certain degree of error is to be expected. Third, the quality of dietary information varies probably even more than the quality of the biochemical tests varies, thus contributing errors that decrease correlations between measurements.

Burden on the Respondent

Clinical situations often involve individuals who are ill and cannot tolerate lengthy, demanding assessment procedures. One measure of respondent burden is the time it takes to comply with assessment procedures, but the extent to which the procedure is annoying and disruptive in eating situations is also an important consideration. The longer and more onerous the interview, the more likely clients are to drop out, making the population studied unrepresentative. In research involving clinical trials of relatively well people, subjects are likely to be willing and able to tolerate the administration of more lengthy assessment tools.

Skills Required of the Respondent

The assessment methodology should be appropriate for the skills of the client, or the clinical situation should permit the client to develop these skills if they are lacking. For example, people who are blind, have difficulty writing, or are illiterate may not be able to keep food diaries. Even the literate must be carefully instructed in the keeping of food records if data are to be meaningful, and time must be set aside in the interview to do this. Obviously young children and some forgetful elderly people cannot keep food diaries or even remember their food intake to tell to the interviewer, so methods other than dietary diaries and recalls must be devised.

Skill of the Nutritionist

Some assessment methods, such as the dietary history, require a great deal of skill and previous training in the methodology on the part of the interviewer. Others, such as food frequency recalls, are relatively simple to administer. The availability and willingness of skilled personnel to perform assessments is therefore also a consideration.

Avoidance of Systematic Errors

Many people who are the most likely to be at risk of malnutrition possess other characteristics that make performing complete and representative dietary assessments very difficult. Such groups include clients who are very ill, chronic alcoholics, anorectics, bulimics, drug addicts, people with a mental handicap or Alzheimer's disease, and people who for one reason or another see themselves as standing to lose from an assessment that reflects their true intake. Their intakes from day to day may be reproducible, but they may nevertheless have systematic errors. For such groups it is important to choose an assessment method that can be validated in some other manner, for example, by simultaneous biochemical or anthropometric measurements.

The Number of Assessments Necessary

If the dietary assessment requires a great deal of quantitative precision, as is sometimes the case in research studies of individuals, it can require a surprisingly large number of interviews to obtain representative data and the desired levels of precision in estimation of nutrient intakes. Certain constituents, such as cholesterol and vitamin A intakes, that are extremely variable from day to day, may require very long observation periods.[17]

Ease of Analysis

Before the dietary assessment can be used to help the patient, it must be analyzed. Coding and analysis of nutrient intakes is extremely time consuming even in the best of circumstances and can be overwhelming when it requires a great deal of hand calculation. Fortunately a large number of computerized dietary analysis programs greatly ease the actual analysis, although coding and keying in the records can still require a good deal of time. The best way to test ease of analysis is to "walk through" the procedure with a few assessment forms.

Costs

The costs involved and one's ability to pay them must also be considered in choosing a method. The hidden costs in dietary assessment are many.[18] First are the immediately apparent costs, such as the need for forms, food models, and computer software. Second are hidden costs such as interviewer training, checking, coding, calculating and interpreting intakes, and burdens on the respondent. Also, some assessment methods are very labor intensive while others rely heavily on interactive software programs and computer-assisted interviews.

Involving the Medical Team

Because physicians are ultimately responsible for their patients' welfare, nutritionists must impress on them the importance of dietary assessment. Developments in the past decade have helped to do this, but in some situations a certain amount of marketing may still be necessary.

Inpatient Situations

During the early 1970s it became increasingly apparent that the nutritional status of hospitalized clients was not being assessed, with the result that frank malnutrition often went undetected.[19] Because this is obviously undesirable medically and because such conditions can increase lengths of hospital stays, the discovery led to a reassessment of standards of nutritional care. Today leading hospitals throughout the country have implemented routine screening and ongoing nutritional assessment for the entire duration of the patient's stay. These standards and the growing trend toward separate nutritional support services made the medical and surgical staffs in many hospitals more aware of the importance of nutritional assessment and often have led to improved practices.

However, routine assessment is still not the norm in all hospitals. For nutritionists who need to enlist support for its importance, texts are available that provide details of developing such systems and services.[20] Several professional associations, such as the American Dietetic Association, the American Society for Enteral and Parenteral

Nutrition, the American Board of Nutrition, and the American Society for Clinical Nutrition, publish journals and other materials that may help the nutritionist point out specific benefits from nutritional assessment and intervention in particular diseases and conditions.

Having nutritionists accompany physicians on rounds and attend clinical conferences can do much to raise the awareness of other providers of the need for dietary assessment, but in the end the goal is to build nutrition screening and assessment into the protocols by which all inpatients are treated. Allies in ensuring that all patients receive adequate nutritional screening and assessment are the medical, surgical, nursing, and pharmacy staffs. All these professionals need to agree on the measures used for screening and assessment, the criteria for targeting patients for more detailed assessment after screening has shown them to be at risk, and the personnel responsible for each task. Because nutritional assessment involves not only dietary assessment but medical history, physical exams, functional assessments, reviews of medications, laboratory tests, and anthropometric measurements, there is much for every member of the team to do. Nurses, because they are more likely to be involved in the actual scheduling of referrals or the calling in of consults once physicians have approved of their necessity, are especially important to involve in the screening and referral process.

Outpatient Situations

The medical team must be convinced that it is important for nutritionists to see all outpatients in need of nutrition services. One way to foster this objective and stimulate interest in the problem is jointly to develop screening criteria for nutritional risk and standards for referral of patients needing further dietary assessment. The growth of health maintenance organizations and other prepaid health care plans has led to the formulation of standardized protocols for screening, referral, assessment, and treatment of various diet-related diseases in many service settings. Screening criteria are straightforward and can be used by all members of the health care team or delegated to a single professional.

Nutritionists working on-site in the specialty clinics in the outpatient setting that generate the greatest number of referrals can informally educate other health care providers on the need for appropriate referrals. In-service presentations by nutritionists, with case examples of what assessments can do to facilitate treatment planning, are also helpful.

Formulating Behavioral Objectives

When the dietary assessment is evaluated in concert with medical history and clinical findings, anthropometric measurements, laboratory tests, and other relevant factors such as education and functional capacity, it furnishes the basis for the nutrition treatment plan. Problem-oriented medical records assist practitioners in formulating their treatment objectives in behavioral terms. Involving clients in treatment, planning enhances the likelihood of adherence. Therefore, in setting objectives for nutritional intervention practitioners must discuss and clarify treatment objectives with clients.

All too often the dietary assessment phase concentrates so much on descriptions of nutrient intakes that little or no attention is paid to the assessment of the behavioral and educational aspects of dietary behaviors. If the purpose of assessment is to bring about changes in dietary behavior, the failure to assess behavioral and educational needs can negate the entire process. Methods for performing dietary, behavioral, and educational assessments and for using the nutritional assessment as the basis for behavior change are well described in Chapter 3 and several recent texts and articles.[21]

Nutritionists who work in various specialized medical fields have developed special assessment tools that can be especially helpful for patients suffering from certain diseases and disorders.[22] Identifying learning styles, eating behaviors, aspects of psychosocial adjustment, and other dimensions may assist clients in formulating behavioral objectives for following their new eating plans.

MONITORING

Monitoring is the ongoing process of keeping watch over some aspect of diet or eating behavior with the objective of maintaining or improving some aspect of nutrition. Clinically it refers most frequently to the means of measuring the degree of adherence to a therapeutic or experimental regimen. Self-monitoring strategies are those individuals use to evaluate themselves without outside help. External monitoring strategies involve some individual or process outside of a person's own efforts to keep track of diet- and eating-related behaviors.

Importance

Nutrition counseling consists of not only assessment, or the diagnosis of diet-related problems, but intervention, monitoring, and follow-up. Once the practitioner has devised a nutrition plan tailored to the individual's problems and the patient has adopted it, both patient and therapist must find some way to keep track of progress. Long-term adherence to therapeutic diets can often reduce the need for medications and improve disease outcomes. Moreover, it has long been known that in the absence of continuous attention dietary behaviors tend to revert to old habits because individual preferences, not health considerations, are the chief factor affecting food choices. Knowledge of risk and education about beneficial dietary changes alone are not enough to ensure long-lasting dietary changes. Dietary changes involve increased cost, skill, time, and effort in food preparation, and incompatibilities with personal food likes and familial and cultural standards with respect to food.[23] Not surprisingly, these psychological and environmental barriers often overcome even the best of intentions to stick to one's eating pattern.

Self-monitoring of diet and other health indices has proven important in keeping individuals aware of where they stand, motivating or reinforcing their efforts, and ensuring that they maintain eating patterns and altered eating behaviors over the long term.[24] Other keys to improving long-term dietary adherence to therapeutic regimes include setting realistic goals, individualizing therapies, mastering skills and information needed to follow the diet, using social support systems, and systematically following up and reinforcing changes in the right direction.

Assessment

Monitoring can be helpful during dietary assessment, in the period immediately after adoption of the therapeutic regime, during the maintenance phase after clients have arrived at and are maintaining target behaviors, and when lapses have occurred and clients are striving to return to more desirable behaviors.

Monitoring is especially helpful during the dietary assessment phase in conditions such as obesity or bulimia for individuals whose overeating is caused by situational determinants.[25] By keeping records of food intake, situation, and emotions, clients can often discover maladaptive behavior patterns that they can then correct. Seeing documentation of actual behavior is also a powerful motivator for many individuals.

Intervention

At the beginning of the therapeutic diet, monitoring helps clients put new information into action by applying the new skills they have learned and obtaining immediate feedback on results. Individuals on therapeutic diets are usually "restrained eaters"; that is, they must expend effort to "keep to their diets."[26] This effort is stressful, and as time goes by stress appears to increase, which may lead to lapses in dieting behavior. Staying on the diet may contain the seeds of its own destruction.[27] The phenomenon of restrained eating has been studied most among the obese and individuals suffering from eating disorders, but it is also characteristic of those on diets for serum lipid lowering, sodium reduction, and the like. The utility of self-monitoring is that it can provide immediate reinforcement that can reward behavior and perhaps decrease the stress associated with dieting. Monitoring also continues to help in identifying situational problems in adherence during this stage of dietary change.

Maintenance

After clients have adopted the diet and made the desired short-term changes in eating habits, the difficult task of maintaining dietary change over the long run begins. Even after changes have become more or less habitual, monitoring can help motivate, provide immediate reinforcement, and provide benchmarks against which to assess progress. Monitoring also helps people who are recovering from dietary lapses.

When To Monitor

Adherence to dietary advice is an ongoing and dynamic process.[28] Thus monitoring is necessary as long as dietary behaviors must remain altered. Because many therapeutic diets are prescribed for chronic degenerative diseases and other lifelong conditions, monitoring continues to be necessary for years, if not decades.

Adoption Phase

Monitoring is useful during the period of adoption of new eating behaviors. It increases the client's awareness, evaluates progress, and improves goal setting. Combinations of external monitoring and self-monitoring are helpful in this respect. During the early stages of adoption, adherence may be excellent, but if it is due solely to external controls there is little hope that clients will sustain it over the long run when such controls are no longer present. For example, compliance with a dietary regimen in closed environments such as hospitals, live-in rehabilitation facilities, spas, and other weight reduction facilities in which the menu served conforms exactly to the therapeutic prescription may be due to the fact that clients have little or no choice over what they eat. Adherence during the adoption period may also be fostered by identification, or modeling one's dietary behavior after that of an individual with similar problems, as is common in many commercial weight-loss groups in which the instructor is a previously obese person who has successfully lost weight on a low-calorie eating plan.

Maintenance Phase

Monitoring is helpful not only when clients begin new dietary behaviors but during the maintenance period when clients are attempting to sustain these altered behaviors. Monitoring continues to help stimulate individual awareness, evaluate progress, and improve goal setting as well as assists the individual in internalizing the target dietary behaviors and in solving problems. With time and practice of new skills, adherence may become automatic and habitualized, but this rarely occurs immediately, and clients are unlikely to sustain it over the long term without paying attention to it.

New or Altered Situations. Monitoring is helpful during the maintenance phase when the individual confronts new or altered circumstances or more difficult problems such as holiday eating, eating out, and other especially difficult situations that build on elementary adherence skills developed during the adoption phase. Monitoring helps analyze dietary behaviors in these situations to develop plans for ensuring future adherence.

Recovery from Lapses. It would be idyllic for nutritionists and clients if, once eating habits and diet-related life styles were altered for the better, new practices stayed firmly in place. This is rarely the case. Dietary alterations are usually restrictive, only one part of a complex regimen, and incompatible with peer or family eating habits to some degree, and they may supersede previous eating behaviors that may not yet have been totally extinguished. Moreover, dietary alterations usually involve more rather than less difficulty than the original eating habits did in terms of buying and preparing food.[29]

Lapses from most therapeutic regimens are virtually inevitable, but automatic return to the target eating behavior is not. Monitoring can help clients recover from dietary lapses or temporary indiscretions as well as from longer periods of noncompliance or relapse to maladaptive eating habits. It builds self-awareness, encourages evaluation, and helps the individual begin again to set goals. For these reasons clients should also be monitored periodically during the maintenance phase of therapeutic regimens.

Periodic "Fine Tuning." From time to time monitoring helps bring the altered eating behaviors back to the clients' mind to reinforce appropriate behaviors.

Who Should Monitor

The care provider, the client, the client's peers, and other supportive individuals in the environment can all participate in monitoring dietary behaviors. The most important monitor is the client, who must ultimately internalize the new way of eating.

Care Providers

Routine monitoring and assessment are essential parts of managing interventions with the purpose of dietary change. Most clients find it helpful to have a health authority figure monitor and comment on their progress periodically and assist them in developing the more advanced cognitive, emotional, and behavioral skills necessary for making additional dietary changes.

Peers and Other Supportive Individuals

Peers attempting to achieve the same target dietary behaviors can also provide support and monitoring. For example, peer groups of obese patients attempting weight loss have been helpful in monitoring. Spouse monitoring and involvement in weight-loss treatment has also proven helpful.[30] Peer monitoring has long been used successfully in some addictive behaviors, such as problem drinking.[31] Peer monitoring can and often does take place in group contexts, as participants in eating behavior change groups compare their problems and progress in achieving target behaviors. The nutritionist's time is spent more effectively in many instances by combining group and individual treatment to maximize patient involvement and total contact time.[32] As nutritionists become adept at leading groups and having peers assist each other in monitoring behavior changes, participants' achievement of target dietary behaviors usually increases.[33] The additional positive effects of group monitoring on the already considerable benefits of group treatment further increase the likelihood that treatment will be successful.[34]

Self-Monitoring

Self-monitoring of dietary behaviors has proven useful in increasing awareness of habitual behaviors, evaluating progress, and facilitating goal setting.[35] Both compliance based on forced choice and copying may encourage the individual to practice the target eating behaviors. Without such practice, adherence is impossible. Monitoring by health care providers, peers, or significant others in the patient's life can also encourage adherence, but all these techniques do little good if clients view dietary control as external. The goal is for clients to internalize adherence as emanating from themselves rather than from other people or conditions in the environment. For this reason self-monitoring as well as counselor monitoring are important components of increased dietary adherence.

Admittedly, self-reports of dietary behavior are sometimes of uncertain validity, and they have been questioned on these grounds.[36] But even if validity is doubtful, self-monitoring is instructive to the patient and makes the act of eating a conscious one. Self-awareness of problem eating behaviors is likely to increase even if the monitoring records are too imprecise to be useful for research purposes. Most patients are willing to use self-monitoring instruments and to report some, even if not all, problems revealed by their use.[37] When very precise dietary data are called for, other, more objective indices of diet or outcome criteria (such as weighed dietary records or biochemical measurements) can supplement and validate these records.[38]

What To Monitor

Elements of eating behavior that are most useful to monitor vary depending on the objective of the monitoring.

Health Outcomes

For health care providers, the index that is closest to the health outcome desired is often the most useful variable to monitor. For example, to measure overall adherence and response to a lipid-lowering diet, the counselor may find it most useful to monitor fasting serum lipids monthly because changes in level are thought to be associated with dietary changes and reduction in risks of coronary artery disease.

Behavioral Antecedents

For self-monitoring purposes, it is helpful to monitor the behavioral or emotional antecedents most closely associated with target dietary behaviors. Applying self-monitoring techniques to situations that pose special difficulties to dietary adherence is especially useful. For example, to adhere to a lipid-lowering diet, the patient may find it helpful to self-monitor the type and amount of grams of fat eaten, especially in eating situations outside the home in which compliance is difficult. Such self-monitoring records also help the counselor identify and make suggestions for over-coming barriers to adherence.

Types of Instruments

Many different types of instruments are useful in monitoring various common diseases and conditions involving dietary change for prevention, treatment, or control. Below is a brief discussion of some of these indices.

Obesity

Many monitoring instruments are available for treatment of obesity.[39] Health outcome measures include changes in weight or fatness itself and in bodily circumferences of particular interest. Tools for self-monitoring of weight-related behaviors include food diaries and food exchange lists, activity diaries and activity scales to assess alterations in physical activity, and diaries of the time, place, emotions, and other circumstances surrounding eating.[40] The latter are especially popular in behavior modification programs.[41] Self-monitoring of weight itself may also be useful, but because it is too remote a consequence from the target behaviors that need to be reinforced, it is more helpful to combine it with some of the other, more immediately reinforcing indices mentioned above.

Anorexia and Bulimia

Changes in weight or body composition are usually the health indices of immediate interest in anorexia. In bulimia these changes as well as changes in frequency or severity of purging and binging are important to health.[42] Food diaries; food exchange lists; and diaries or reconstructions of the time, place, and circumstances of lapses into binging or purging behavior or both can also be helpful.[43] Bulimic episodes (sometimes referred to by patients as "pigging out"), the frequency of vomiting, the frequency of purging with laxatives or diuretics, and the experiencing of urges to overeat may also be useful in monitoring bulimic behaviors.[44]

Diabetes Mellitus

The advent of finger-prick blood sampling, urinary glucose test tapes, and other blood glucose monitoring devices has made it possible to monitor the health outcomes of diabetics more closely than was previously possible. The wider range of insulins now available, and methods for delivering insulin constantly if necessary by insulin pump, permits better control over blood sugar deviations. Dietary monitoring devices and adherence indices are also more satisfactory than they were in the past, when practitioners had available only composite indices that measured many aspects of diabetic control and that were only weakly associated with dietary adherence.[45] Self-monitoring of blood glucose is now a popular and effective means of achieving glycemic control throughout the day.[46] The associations of finger-prick monitoring with dietary compliance indices have been shown to be satisfactory.[47]

Usual blood sugar levels correlate well with many of the adverse health outcomes of diabetes mellitus, including large and small blood vessel disease and urinary tract and other infections.

Urine glucose levels were sometimes used to titrate diet, exercise, and insulin doses, but they correlate poorly with plasma glucose levels and do not permit accurate adjustment of diet and medications to blood sugar. Unfortunately, individual urine glucose responses vary even when diet composition, size, meal spacing, and insulin doses are standardized.

Long-term blood sugar levels are relatively easily measured with glycosylated hemoglobin in the blood.[48] Glycosylated hemoglobin measurements help assess long-term control of blood glucose, but they are of only limited use in diagnosing problems and suggesting ways of overcoming them. They are nonspecific in identifying the control problems experienced by the patient, so other self-monitoring devices must be used to pinpoint dietary and behavior problems.

Self–blood glucose monitoring is a much more sensitive measurement than a urine glucose level.[49] It uses a finger-prick blood sample and a reagent strip that reacts colorimetrically to an enzymatic reaction. The color intensity reflects the amount of glucose present. Daily blood glucose measurements are the method of choice for assessing overall diabetic control and determining the causes of any problems. Self–blood glucose monitoring permits clients suffering from diabetes to better titrate their diets, physical activity, and insulin doses to achieve blood sugars that are as close to normal levels as possible.[50]

Because diabetics often develop accelerated atherosclerosis, another monitoring index commonly used by physicians is serum cholesterol. Some believe that serum triglyceride levels may also be important in the special type of atherosclerosis afflicting diabetics.

For non–insulin-dependent diabetics, low-calorie diets that lead to weight loss may be sufficient to achieve satisfactory control, and the self-monitoring techniques described for obesity control may suffice.

Insulin-dependent diabetics usually require more complicated dietary modifications and more complex monitoring tools in addition to achieving desirable weight levels. Dietary self-monitoring tools for diabetics are more educationally sophisticated than they are for many other complex metabolic diseases. Diabetic exchange lists that incorporate modifications in the type and amount of carbohydrate, fat, dietary fiber, and cholesterol are available for clients to use to develop appropriate meal plans. Also available are plans of differing complexity and precision with respect to nutrients that can be tailored to individual needs for the timing of energy intakes and carbohydrate. Attempts to predict glycemic response from calculation of dietary glycemic indices fail because actual blood sugar responses vary a great deal from person to person.[51] Thus many diabetics attain optimal control by measuring representative blood sugar levels during the day. Self-monitoring of blood glucose levels with finger-prick blood samples, coupled with diet records, permits immediate feedback of the impact of dietary manipulation and suggests possible dietary adjustments. Procedures for self–blood glucose monitoring in conjunction with diet records have recently been described.[52] Clients can use the results of such monitoring to modify their diets with minimal medical supervision.[53]

Depression

Changes in weight, appetite, sleep, and mood have been used to monitor depression associated with eating disorders.[54] Decreased appetite and weight loss occur in melancholia or endogenous depression, whereas weight gain and oversleeping are common in nonendogenous depressive episodes of overeating. Weight tends to increase in seasonal mood disorders as appetite changes and sleep disorders occur.[55] Some antidepressants increase carbohydrate cravings while others have anorectic and weight-reducing effects.[56]

Pica

Blood lead levels and the monitoring of the consumption of nonfoods may help monitor health outcomes in treating pica in children.[57]

Hyperlipidemias

Changes in serum lipoproteins and apoproteins are especially good health outcome indicators for the hyperlipidemias. For monitoring dietary behaviors both the type and amount of dietary fat consumed are of interest.[58] The earliest monitoring tools were validated against serum-lipid-lowering effects in hyperlipidemic patients.[59] The use of food exchange lists that control the type and amount of fat and dietary cholesterol is common. Also popular is fat gram counting, in which clients tally the grams of fat eaten each day. Another self-monitoring tool is fat scoring systems, which are valid enough to be useful for monitoring.[60]

Kidney Disease

One easily measured index related to health outcomes in kidney disease is urinary nitrogen appearance, which is closely related to average protein intake because the nitrogen liberated during the catabolism of amino acids and protein is converted almost entirely to urea.[61] The urea nitrogen appearance rate is the sum of urinary nitrogen excretion and any accumulations of urea in the body pool measured by estimating serum urea nitrogen. Urea nitrogen appearance varies most with changes in protein (nitrogen) intake and nitrogen balance. In normal individuals urea nitrogen appearance and urea excretion are highly correlated. For example, on intakes of 40 grams of protein (or 6.4 grams of nitrogen) per day urea nitrogen appearance is approximately 4 grams per day, the remaining urea probably being degraded in the gastrointestinal tract by bacteria.[62] High values of urea nitrogen appearance indicate either that protein intakes are high or that the individual is in negative nitrogen balance and lean body mass is wasting. Low values signal unusually efficient use of ingested nitrogen, very low nitrogen intakes, or incomplete urine collections.

Other values in blood and urine, such as serum and urinary creatinine levels, urine protein, sodium, potassium, and phosphorus, may also be measured.

Among patients who are undergoing chronic ambulatory peritoneal dialysis several indices are monitored, including "dry weights" in the morning before use of the dialysis solution, the concentration of the dialysis solution, and presence or absence of infections, especially peritonitis. These records, coupled with food diaries and periodically obtained biochemical indices, make it possible to adjust the concentration and frequency of the dialysis solution and food intake to maximize health promotion.

Dietary indices that correlate well with health outcome values include special renal diet exchange lists that permit monitoring of intakes of key nutrients for the client's particular phase of illness (for example, often protein and phosphorus in chronic progressive renal disease and these plus potassium and sodium in chronic renal failure). Random 24-hour food diaries with simultaneous collection of 24-hour urines can be analyzed for urinary nitrogen and protein. Among patients with kidney disease, phosphorus levels are also important because high levels may lead to the deposition of calcium phosphate in kidney tissue.[63] In addition to dietary restriction through exchange lists, phosphorus binding agents are also employed and pill counts of their use may help assess adherence.

Hypertension

Health outcomes associated with hypertension include blood pressures taken standing, sitting, and supine by an objective observer or clients themselves with home blood pressure monitoring devices. In some circumstances the continuous monitoring of blood pressure is possible with a Doppler instrument. Weight loss is often also measured simultaneously because it is often associated with drops in blood pressure.

Helpful dietary behavior measures include tests of overnight urines for sodium with chloride strips, the monitoring of weight or weight loss, food diaries, food exchange lists, and the counting of milligrams of sodium consumed.[64]

Blood pressure is affected by many behaviors, dietary and other. The control of hypertension depends upon step care, which combines the use of several nondrug therapies, including weight control, sodium and alcohol restriction, exercise, and stress management, with a graded series of pharmacologic agents of greater potency as needed to bring blood pressure down to normal levels. Clinical treatment now centers on adherence to medication schedules, weight reduction, modifications of sodium and other cations, moderation in alcohol consumption, and, if blood cholesterol is a problem, reductions in dietary fat. The most common self-monitoring tools concentrate on measures of one or more of these behaviors. The many different behaviors that can be monitored include adherence to medication by use of pill counts or diaries, progress in weight loss, measures of urinary sodium using urine testing equipment, logs of alcohol intake, and logs of intakes of various nutrients such as sodium and potassium, which are associated with blood pressure in some individuals. The associations among these various diet-related indices and blood pressures are detailed in two recent monographs on the subject.[65] There is also some evidence that increased intakes of calcium, potassium, and magnesium may be beneficial, so intakes of these nutrients may also be monitored in experimental studies.

Criteria for Selecting Monitoring Instruments

Teachability

Monitoring provides clients with objective, nonjudgmental data that they can use to increase their awareness of dietary behaviors, evaluate progress, revise behaviors if necessary, and set further goals. Clients must thus understand what is being monitored, why it is being monitored, and what the relationship of this variable is with health promotion and disease prevention or treatment. Moreover, the procedures involved in the monitoring instrument or tool must be easily taught, even to clients with only modest intellectual or kinesthetic abilities. The instrument should tolerate error sufficiently so that it can withstand minor mistakes in application in daily life. Any written instructions should involve minimal verbiage, contain illustrations whenever possible, and be checked for readability. All monitoring instruments need to be pretested and validated in real-life situations and modified in line with findings before they are used on a wide scale. It is not enough for experts to believe the instruments are useful.

Precision

The degree to which the monitoring instrument measures what it is supposed to measure is important. First, the degree of quantitative precision required for research purposes or even for routine dietetic assessment may be much greater than that which patients need. Patients need a way of monitoring their day-to-day eating behaviors to approximate target eating behaviors more closely. For example, simplified food grouping systems such as the Basic Four or Basic Seven do not provide nutrient intake information as precisely as food records but may suffice nonetheless.

By their very nature monitoring instruments are usually imprecise. Both patients and counselors must realize that no single data point should be regarded as important. Rather, the focus of monitoring is many data points based on a representative sample of the overall eating behavior or problem situations. The profile derived from these is what is most revealing. This point is especially important to emphasize when intake of a target nutrient is being monitored. For example, the type and amount of dietary fat and cholesterol vary much more from day to day than do biochemical indices associated with their intakes.[66] Dietary cholesterol intakes require at least nine days of records to be reliable in most cases.[67] Dietary intakes are especially liable to vary from day to day, from weekday to weekend, from season to season, and in other less predictable ways. It is thus especially important to make enough observations to sample the entire range of this variation. When patients realize that many observations are necessary to obtain a fair sample of actual behavior, some of their resistance to frequent monitoring may decrease.

Specificity

Some monitoring indices, such as anthropometry, glycosylated hemoglobins, and serum lipid values, are closely associated with later health outcomes but have the disadvantage of being nonspecific. They reflect not only diet but heredity and other environmental factors that vary from person to person. For example, weight gain in a child who is suffering from failure to thrive reflects not only dietary intake but other factors influencing growth. Additional information is needed before weight gain can be used to monitor the appropriateness of feeding and eating behaviors in such a situation. For this reason infants who fail to thrive are often hospitalized to rule out other possible causes of poor growth and to permit very precise monitoring of food intake and weight gain.

Other types of monitoring instruments are quite specific, such as the use of fat gram counting for estimating the type and amount of fat consumed, but they unfortunately are somewhat more remote from the health outcome of interest. Nevertheless, they document problem dietary behaviors well with respect to intakes of this nutrient and provide data necessary for making changes.

Assuming that the instrument has been tested sufficiently to establish its validity and that it has a rather high correlation with the desired health outcome, it is helpful in choosing between monitoring instruments to include those that best reflect the behavior that needs to change. Often this is best accomplished by combining several monitoring instruments with different levels of abstraction and precision. For example, weekly counting of the type and amount of fat in daily diets combined with more detailed diet diaries and serum cholesterol indices taken every three months is a common method of monitoring clients with hyperlipidemias.

Immediacy of Feedback

Since monitoring instruments are first and foremost teaching instruments, the sooner the client can understand and act on the results of the monitoring, the better. Immediate feedback permits immediate reinforcement and helps the client achieve successively closer approximations of the target dietary behaviors without waiting for the approval or disapproval of an outside arbiter. It also puts the power for dietary change as well as the responsibility for it in the client's hands, where it belongs and where it must ultimately reside if dietary change is to be successful.

Convenience

Monitoring instruments are worthless if clients do not use them, if the data amassed are not analyzed and evaluated, and if behaviors are not modified accordingly. "User friendliness" or convenience is an essential consideration for any self-monitoring device as well as for counselor-administered tools. For example, home blood pressure monitoring devices with digital readouts are much easier for clients to use than are sphygmomanometers used in physicians' offices and are thus more likely to be acceptable to clients who must take frequent blood pressure readings. Similarly, new finger-prick tests for measuring blood sugar and serum cholesterol are much simpler than methods that rely on venepuncture, and for monitoring purposes their precision is usually satisfactory.

Cost

The costs associated with the monitoring of diet-related behaviors and indices associated with dietary adherence must also be considered in choosing a monitoring instrument. First are the outlays for paraphernalia such as instruments and biochemical tests. For example, the cost of urine testing tapes for measuring sodium levels may represent a considerable expense to some clients. Other, less obvious costs to consider include the client's time required to keep and analyze food records or diaries and the time it takes the counselor to review the records further.

Unobtrusiveness

Nobody likes to be different, including individuals attempting to alter their dietary behaviors for the better. Unobtrusive self-monitoring instruments tend to be better accepted and have a higher probability of being used than those that are not. For example, very few patients are willing to take dietetic weighing scales with them when they eat out because doing so disrupts their enjoyment of the meal and invites unwanted questions. In contrast, a small booklet or personalized food exchange list with hints for estimating portion sizes is more likely to be helpful.

Representativeness

One of the most important attributes of a monitoring instrument is that it provides a sample of representative dietary or other behavior. The very act of measurement can alter dietary behavior because it increases awareness. However, if clients use monitoring instruments only when on their best behavior, the data obtained are neither likely to be representative of dietary behavioral realities nor to help clients analyze the times eating poses particular problems. Thus monitoring instruments must sample the entire range of dietary behaviors, with special emphasis on problematic behaviors, not on "ideal" days. Most clients need to have this carefully explained since their tendency is to make diets conform to counselors' directions to please them.

Involving the Medical Team

The involvement of the entire medical team is essential in monitoring patient behavior change, reinforcing adherence to target dietary behaviors, assisting the client in overcoming barriers to greater adherence, and recovering from lapses. The degree to which health providers, in addition to the nutritionist, reinforce the dietary message enormously increases the likelihood of adherence. In addition to informal verbal communications, the medical record, preferably a problem-oriented medical record, is helpful. Also, dividing up monitoring tasks relating to nutrition-related behaviors can help, especially if the physician, nurse, pharmacist, or other caregiver points out the nutritional connections among the various indices, such as those between diet records and serum cholesterol–lowering among patients suffering from hyperlipidemia. Reviewing progress in changing dietary behaviors from the previous visit's nutrition plan and reemphasizing behavioral objectives in the new plan is another point at which all care providers can reinforce the nutritional message. All providers must communicate the same message to avoid confusing the client or falling into the trap of being manipulated by the client.

Changing Behavioral Objectives

Monitoring devices provide the feedback practitioners and patients need to assess their progress and reformulate new objectives as needs arise and circumstances change.

An excellent example of the use of monitoring devices in modifying behaviors has recently been provided for diabetes mellitus.[68] First, the combination of blood glucose data and dietary records establishes a characteristic blood glucose profile, which the client and counselor evaluate together. Profiles from self–glucose monitoring using finger pricks and diet records are also used to make changes in diet, insulin, and exercise to achieve desired levels of blood glucose control, recognize and respond to emergency situations, and help patients increase flexibility in their life styles while maintaining blood glucose control.

ENHANCING ADHERENCE

Factors Affecting Dietary Adherence

The dietary regimen for the specific disease, the client, the social environment, and the counselor all affect clients' ability to comply with dietary restrictions imposed for therapeutic purposes.

The Diet and the Disease

The availability of advice on food preparation, cookbooks, and special food products may increase diet palatability and adherence.

Client Characteristics

Client characteristics also influence adherence. All human beings like to see immediate results from their actions, and when clients who are already ill see the immediate benefits of dietary change in reduced signs and symptoms, compliance is often excellent. For example, clients who are extremely sensitive to lactose often comply well with low-lactose diets because doing so halts the flatus and diarrhea they otherwise suffer after consuming foods containing lactose. Unfortunately, most dietary therapies do not offer such immediate promise of relief. More often in diet counseling clients are ill with a disease that dietary means can control but not cure, and regardless of dietary compliance many of the signs and symptoms of the disease persist. Other clients suffer from progressive but largely asymptomatic chronic diseases. They are not simply at risk for disease; they are already suffering from it. A final group consists of those who, by virtue of their health profiles, are considered at high risk for the disease although it is not yet manifest. For patients in the last three groups, the immediate effects of adherence to medical and dietary regimens are not evident, and adherence to diet and drug therapies is usually low (see Chapter 2).[69] Denial of the disease and the usefulness of dietary measures is common among patients of these types, and dietary compliance is therefore low.[70]

Sociocultural Microenvironment

Clients' life styles and their associated sociocultural environments are potent influences on adherence to therapeutic diets. Clients who eat out frequently with others, who live alone, or who have unsupportive families are especially likely to experience difficulties.[71] Many other life style–related obstacles to compliance also exist, and social and emotional support systems can help minimize these obstacles to adherence. Assessment and self-monitoring techniques can clarify these obstacles and help the patient develop behaviors that fulfill dietary as well as social objectives more fully.

Counselor

The counselor and counseling techniques also influence adherence.[72] A personal nutrition counselor who individualizes counseling, reduces anonymity, and facilitates patient skill building helps clients become motivated and committed to dietary change as well as begin to alter their eating habits.[73]

Tailoring Counseling to Dietary Stages

Motivation and Commitment

Some, but not all, clients who are referred for therapeutic eating patterns are motivated and committed to change at the outset. If they are not, the counselor's first task is to help build commitment.

Counseling for Adoption of the Pattern

During the first few months on an eating pattern, the major counseling tasks are to provide information on food composition, skills for making food choices appropriate to the eating pattern, methods for recovering from lapses, aids for remembering to follow the diet and take medications if necessary, dietary self-monitoring tools, and information on weighing, measuring, and recording if the counselor is to monitor dietary records. In addition, anticipatory guidance is necessary to prepare dieters' inevitable slips, and ways to combat them.

With many clients counselors can achieve very striking initial changes in intakes relatively rapidly through intensive counseling that provides information and suggestions about food preparation, purchasing, cooking, and menu choice coupled with encouragement and group support.

During the adoption of the eating pattern, information about the new eating pattern, the rationale for its use, and techniques for building it into daily activities are all critical to ensuring adherence.[74] The most successful counseling for early adherence builds on a specific sequence of concrete actions required of the client.[75] It permits supervised practice in setting up the regimen and tailors assistance to the patient's unique circumstances.[76]

Maintenance Phase

After the initial diet change or adoption stage of the new eating pattern, the client faces the difficult task of maintaining new eating behaviors over the long term. Once clients have changed their eating patterns, they must preserve the new behaviors. The goal of counseling during maintenance is to develop advanced cognitive and behavioral skills for maximizing adherence and preventing dietary lapses, not simply to review previous skill development techniques. Such advanced techniques include special support and monitoring systems appropriate for both "social" dieters who thrive on social support and systems that help "loner" dieters who prefer more private styles of eating behavior change. For social dieters, techniques for enlisting family, significant other, and group support and modification of the physical environment may be especially helpful. For loners, such techniques as cognitive restructuring, self-reward, computerized menu planning, and individualized exchange lists may be more suitable. In any event, all clients need continued self-monitoring and long-term vigilance if they are to keep lapses to a minimum. Also, clients must develop alternative gratifications to substitute for dietary pleasures. Maintenance, then, confronts clients with an entirely different set of problems than does an initial dietary change.[77]

Frequently, initial dietary changes are followed by a loss of momentum in the dieter's progress. Levels of dietary change may be unsatisfactory to achieve therapeutic objectives. The most common cause of this situation is that patients cannot incorporate the dietary changes into their social and emotional lives. Counseling that not only provides information and skills but tackles problems of motivation, social, and emotional support and assists clients in incorporating eating skills into their lives helps overcome these obstacles.[78]

Many studies on such diverse dietary modifications as those to control hyperlipidemias, stroke, diabetes mellitus, and other chronic diseases testify to the efficacy of such measures and to the futility of counting on dietary advice alone to bring about even minimal lasting behavioral changes in diet. Compliance with medication schedules also depends on social and emotional support and aids that help clients deal with their social and emotional environment rather than simply providing information.[79]

Evidence shows that dietary adherence can be maintained best by increasing attention to social and emotional issues in dietary counseling. Behavioral approaches can have a synergistic effect when combined with dietary and other information.[80] The most successful strategies empower the client by forging a therapeutic alliance in which the counselor facilitates the client's development of responsibility and coping skills for maintaining dietary adherence in common life situations. A variety of techniques are available to do this, including self-monitoring and social learning. They help clients deal with the cognitive as well as the emotional and social factors that disrupt therapeutic dieting efforts and lead to lapses.[81] Special attention is given to helping clients enlist support from friends, family, and others to help them stay on the eating pattern.

The specific techniques that help the most vary from one person to the next and by the severity, type of disease, and stage of diet change the patient faces. Teaching approaches should tailor regimens and adherence aids to individuals and provide latitude for individual eating styles.

In addition to direct one-to-one assistance by a counselor, adherence can be increased in many patients by maximizing peer and family group support for the new eating behaviors.[82] Patients also need reassurance to keep up their morale during the long-term maintenance phase on therapeutic eating patterns. Combinations of group and individual support coupled with monitoring are usually more cost effective than individual counseling alone.[83]

Some patients respond best to group approaches while others prefer individual approaches, and a third group thrives on a mix of the two. Flexibility on the part of the counselor is essential. There is no perfect technique that works for everybody, and therefore the counselor should be careful to respect clients' decisions about what works best for them. When there is a clear indication that self-selected strategies are not working, clients may be amenable to other techniques.

NOTES

1. Henry L. Rosett and Lyn Weiner, *Alcohol and the Fetus: A Clinical Perspective* (New York: Oxford University Press, 1984).

2. Johanna T. Dwyer, "Nutritional Aspects of Anorexia Nervosa and Bulimia," in Steven W. Emmett, ed., *Theory and Treatment of Anorexia Nervosa and Bulimia: Biomedical, Sociocultural, and Psychological Perspectives* (New York: Brunner/Mazel Publishers, 1985), pp. 20–51.

3. Johanna T. Dwyer, Elizabeth A. Krall, and K. Anne Coleman, "The Problem of Memory in Nutritional Epidemiology Research," *Journal of the American Dietetic Association* 87 (1987): 1509–1512; and Dwyer and Thomas O'Donnell, "Nutrition," in Mark E. Molitch, ed., *Management of Medical Problems in Surgical Patients* (Philadelphia, Pa.: F. A. Davis, 1982) pp. 661–746.

4. Mary E. Farkas and Johanna T. Dwyer, "Nutrition Education Needs of Alcoholic Recovery Home Patients," *Journal of Nutrition Education* 16 (1984): 123–124.

5. Johanna T. Dwyer et al., "Risk of Nutritional Rickets Among Vegetarian Children," *American Journal of Diseases in Childhood* 133 (1979): 134–140; and Louise Bell and W. Geoffrey Sherwood, "Current Practices and Improved Recommendations for Treating Hereditary Fructose Intolerance," *Journal of the American Dietetic Association* 87 (1987): 721–730.

6. Gladys Block, Connie M. Dresser, and Anne M. Hartman, "Nutrient Sources in the American Diet: Quantitative Data from the NHANES II Survey II. Macronutrients and Fats," *American Journal of Epidemiology* 122 (1985): 27–40; and "Nutrient Sources in the American Diet: Quantitative Data from the NHANES II Survey I. Vitamins and Minerals," *American Journal of Epidemiology* 122 (1985): 13–26.

7. Shela Bingham, "The Dietary Assessment of Individuals: Methods, Accuracy, New Techniques and Recommendations," *Nutrition Abstracts and Reviews* 57 (1987): 705–742; Johanna T. Dwyer, "Assessment of Dietary Intake," in Mauria E. Shils and Vernon R. Young, *Modern Nutrition in Health and Disease* (Philadelphia, Pa.: Lea and Febiger, 1987), pp. 887–905; and Gladys Block, "A Review of Validations of Dietary Assessment Methods," *American Journal of Epidemiology* 115 (1982): 492–505.

8. Bingham, "Dietary Assessment of Individuals," pp. 705–742.

9. Ann M. Fehily and Gaynor Bird, "The Dietary Intake of Women in Caerphilly, South Wales: A Weighed and a Photographic Method Compared," *Human Nutrition: Applied Nutrition* 40A (1986): 300–307.

10. George H. Beaton, "Toward Harmonization of Dietary, Biochemical, and Clinical Assessments: The Meanings of Nutritional Status and Requirements," *Nutrition Reviews* 44 (1986): 349–358; and "What Do We Think We Are Estimating?," in Virginia Beal and M. J. Laus, eds., *Proceedings of the Symposium on Dietary Data Collection, Analysis, and Significance,* University of Massachusetts Research Bulletin No. 675 (Amherst: Massachusetts Agricultural Experiment Station, College of Food and Natural Resources, 1982), pp. 36–48.

11. National Research Council, Food and Nutrition Board, "Nutrient Adequacy: Assessment Using Food Consumption Surveys," (Washington, D.C.: National Academy Press, 1986).

12. Walter C. Willett et al., "Validation of a Dietary Questionnaire with Plasma Caratensid and Alpha Tocopherol Levels," *American Journal of Clinical Nutrition* 38 (1983): 631–639; Walter C. Willett et al., "Reproducibility and Validity of a Semiquantitative Food Frequency Questionnaire," *American Journal of Epidemiology* 122 (1985): 51–65; National Cancer Institute, Division of Cancer Prevention and Control, "Health Habits and History Questionnaire: Diet History and Other Risk Factors: Personal Computer System Packet" (Bethesda, Md.: National Institutes of Health, 1987).

13. Alan S. Morrison and Julie E. Buring, "Artificial Sweetners and Cancer of the Lower Urinary Tract," *New England Journal of Medicine* 302 (1980): 537–541; and Eileen M. Ouelette et al., "Adverse Effects on Offspring of Maternal Alcoholic Abuse During Pregnancy," *New England Journal of Medicine* 297 (1977): 528–530.

14. National Research Council, "Nutrient Adequacy"; and Human Nutrition Information Service, "Research on Survey Methodology," Administrative Report No. 382 (Beltsville, Md.: U.S. Department of Agriculture, 1987).

15. Block, "A Review of Validations."

16. Dwyer et al., "The Problem of Memory"; Elizabeth A. Krall and Johanna T. Dwyer, "Validity of a 24 Hour Recall and Food Frequency Questionnaire and a Food Diary in a Short-Term Recall Situation," *Journal of the American Dietetic Association* 87 (1987): 1374–1377; and Elizabeth A. Krall, Johanna T. Dwyer, and Anne K. Coleman, "Memory Aids for Dietary Recall," *Nutrition Research,* in press.

17. Bingham, "Dietary Assessment of Individuals," pp. 705–742.

18. Alison E. Black, "Pitfalls in Dietary Assessment," in Alan N. Howard and Ian M. Baird, eds., *Recent Advances in Clinical Nutrition* (London: John Libbey, 1981), pp. 11–32.

19. Dwyer and O'Donnell, "Nutrition," pp. 661–746.

20. John R. Caldwell et al., "The Dropout Problem in Antihypertensive Treatment," *Journal of Chronic Disease* 22 (1970): 579–592.

21. Karen Glanz, "Dietitians' Effectiveness and Patient Compliance with Dietary Regimens," *Journal of the American Dietetic Association* 74 (1979): 631–636; Glanz, "Nutrition Education for Risk Factor Reduction and Patient Education: A Review," *Preventive Medicine* 14 (1985): 721–752; and see also Chapter 3.

22. Michele L. Boutaugh, Alan L. Hull, and Wayne K. Davis, "An Examination of Diabetes Educational Diagnosis Assessment Forms," *Diabetes Educator* 7 (1982): 29–34; and Paula Hartman and Marshall H. Becker, "Noncompliance with Prescribed Regimen Among Chronic Hemodialysis Patients: A Method of Prediction and Educational Diagnosis," *Dialysis and Transplantation* 9 (1978): 978–989; Richard J. Jones et al., "A Randomized Study of Instructional Variables in Nutritional Counseling and Their Efficiency in the Treatment of Hyperlipidemia," *American Journal of Clinical Nutrition* 32 (1979): 884–904; and Kelly D. Brownell, "The Psychology and Physiology of Obesity: Implications for Screening and Treatment," *Journal of the American Dietetic Association* 84 (1984): 406–414.

23. Glanz, "Nutrition Education," pp. 721–752.

24. Matthew Cohen and Paul Zimmer, "Self Monitoring of Blood Glucose Levels in Non-Insulin Dependent Diabetes Mellitus," *Medical Journal of Australia* 2 (1983): 377–380.

25. Betty G. Kirkley, "Bulimia: Clinical Characteristics, Development, and Etiology," *Journal of the American Dietetic Association* 86 (1986): 468–475; and Kelly D. Brownell and Thomas A. Wadden, "Behavior Therapy for Obesity: Modern Approaches and Better Results," in Kelly D. Brownell and John P. Foreyt, eds., *Handbook of Eating Disorders: Physiology, Psychology, and Treatment of Obesity, Anorexia Nervosa, and Bulimia* (New York: Basic Books, 1986), pp. 180–198.

26. C. Peter Herman and Janet Polivy, "Restrained Eating," in Albert J. Stunkard, ed., *Obesity* (Philadelphia, Pa.: W. B. Saunders Co., 1980), pp. 208–225.

27. Janet Polivy and C. Peter Herman, *Breaking the Diet Habit* (New York: Basic Books, 1983); and "A Boundary Model for the Regulation of Eating," in Albert J. Stunkard and Eliot Stellar, eds., *Eating and Its Disorders* (New York: Raven Press, 1984), pp. 141–156.

28. Richard L. Ruffalo, Susan M. Garabedian-Ruffalo, and L. Gregory Pawlson, "Patient Compliance," *American Family Physician* 31 (1985): 93–100.

29. Glanz, "Nutrition Education."

30. Kelly D. Brownell and Albert J. Stunkard, "Couples Training, Pharmacotherapy, and Behavior Therapy in the Treatment of Obesity," *Archives of General Psychiatry* 38 (1981): 1224–1229.

31. G. Alan Marlatt and Judith R. Gordon, *Relapse Prevention* (New York: Guilford Press, 1983), pp. 98–115.

32. Gerald A. Bennett and Susan E. Jones, "Dropping Out of Treatment for Obesity;" *Journal of Psychosomatic Research,* 30 (1986): 567–573.

33. Robert W. Jeffrey, Rena R. Wing, and Albert J. Stunkard, "Behavioral Treatment of Obesity: The State of the Art," *Behavioral Therapy* 9 (1978): 189–199.

34. Raymond G. Kingsley and G. Terrence Wilson, "Behavior Therapy for Obesity: A Comparative Investigation of Long Term Efficacy," *Journal of Consulting and Clinical Psychology* 45 (1977): 288–298; and Albert J. Stunkard, Linda W. Craighead, and Richard O'Brien, "Controlled Trial of Behavior Therapy, Pharmacotherapy, and Their Combinations in the Treatment of Obesity," *Lancet* 2 (1980): 1045–1047.

35. Susan E. Jones, Hilary M. Owens, and Gerald A. Bennett, "Does Behavior Therapy Work for Dietitians? An Experimental Evaluation of the Effects of Three Procedures in a Weight Reduction Clinic," *Human Nutrition: Applied Nutrition* 40A (1986): 272–281; Edward E. Abramson, "A Review of Behavioral Approaches to Weight Control," *Behavior Research and Therapy* 11 (1973): 547–556; Leon Green, "Temporal and Stimulus Factors in Self Monitoring by Obese Persons," *Behavior Therapy* 9 (1978): 328–341; and William J. Fremouw and John P. Brown, "The Reactivity of Addictive Behaviors to Self Monitoring: A Functional Analysis," *Addictive Behavior* 5 (1980): 209–217.

36. Black, "Pitfalls in Dietary Assessment," pp. 11–32; and Flamingo Fidanza, "Controlled Experiments in Human Nutrition: Contemporary Problems," *Preventive Medicine* 12 (1983): 100–102.

37. Glanz, "Dietitians' Effectiveness and Patient Compliance," pp. 631–636.

38. John P. Kirscht, "Preventive Health Behavior: A Review of Research and Issues," *Health Psychology* 2 (1983): 277–301.

39. Douglas Black, "Obesity: A Report of the Royal College of Physicians," *Journal of Royal College of Physicians of London* 17 (1983): 5–64.

40. Basil M. Rifkind, "Nutrient Intakes Among Selected North American Populations in the Lipid Research Clinics Prevalence Study: Composition of Energy Intake," *American Journal of Clinical Nutrition* 41 (1985): 312–329; Ralph S. Paffenbarger et al., "Physical Activity, All Cause Mortality, and Longevity of College Alumni," *New England Journal of Medicine* 314 (1986): 605–613; and Black, "Obesity," pp. 5–6.

41. Edward M. Stricker, "Biological Basis of Hunger and Satiety: Therapeutic Implications," *Nutrition Reviews* 42 (1984): 333–340.

42. David B. Herzog and Paul M. Copeland, "Eating Disorders," *New England Journal of Medicine* 313 (1985): 295–303.

43. Dwyer, "Assessment of Dietary Intake," pp. 887–905.

44. G. Terrence Wilson, "Cognitive Behavioral and Pharmacological Therapies for Bulimia," in Brownell and Foreyt, *Handbook of Eating Disorders,* pp. 450–475.

45. Gordon H. Williams, "Quality of Life and Its Impact on Hypertensive Patients," *American Journal of Medicine* 82 (1987): 98–105.

46. Cohen and Zimmer, "Self Monitoring of Blood Glucose Levels"; and P. H. Sonksen, S. L. Judd, and C. Lowy, "Home Monitoring of Blood Glucose," *Lancet* 1 (1978): 729–732.

47. Denise Ney, Nancy Stubblefield, and Cheryl Fischer, "A Tool for Assessing Compliance with a Diet for Diabetics," *Journal of the American Dietetic Association* 82 (1983): 287–290; and Karen L. Webb et al., "Dietary Compliance Among Insulin Dependent Diabetics," *Journal of Chronic Disease* 37 (1984): 633–643.

48. Lois Jovanovic and Charles M. Peterson, "The Clinical Utility of Glycosylated Hemoglobin," *American Journal of Medicine* 70 (1981): 331–338; H. Franklin Bunn, "Nonenzymatic Glycosylation of Protein: Relevance to Diabetes," *American Journal of Medicine* 70 (1981): 325–350; and Charles M. Peterson and R. L. Jones, "Glycosylation Reactions and Reversible Sequelae of Diabetes Mellitus," in Peterson, ed., *Diabetes Management in the 80's* (New York: Praeger Publishers, 1982), pp. 12–25.

49. Michael Brownlee, "Measuring Glucose Control," in Peterson, ed., *Diabetes Management in the 1980's,* pp. 2–11; Michael L. Reeves et al., "Comparison of Methods for Blood Glucose Monitoring," *Diabetes Care* 4 (1981): 404–406; G. Raymen et al., "Comparative Accuracy of Portable Blood Glucose Monitors," *Journal of Royal College Physicians of London* 17 (1983): 183–186; and American Association of Diabetes Educators, "Position Statement on Blood Glucose Monitoring," *Diabetes Educator* 3 (1983): 1.

50. Christine A. Beebe, "Self Blood Glucose Monitoring: An Adjunct to Dietary and Insulin Management of the Patient with Diabetes," *Journal of the American Dietetic Association* 87 (1987): 61–65; and American Diabetes Association, "Consensus Statement on Self Monitoring of Blood Glucose," *Diabetes Care* 10 (1987): 95–99.

51. Thomas M. S. Wolever, et al., "Prediction of the Relative Blood Glucose Response of Mixed Meals Using the White Bread Glycemic Index," *Diabetes Care* 8 (1985): 418; Phyllis A. Crapo, *Diet and Nutrition in Diabetes: A State of the Art Review* (Washington D.C.: U.S. Department of Health and Human Services, 1983); and David J. Jenkins, "Lente Carbohydrates: A Newer Approach to the Dietary Management of Diabetes," *Diabetes Care* 5 (1982): 634–641.

52. Beebe, "Self Blood Glucose Monitoring," pp. 61–65.

53. Jay S. Skyler et al., "Algorithms for Adjustment of Insulin Dosage by Patients Who Monitor Blood Glucose," *Diabetes Care* 4 (1981): 311–318.

54. Michael Feinberg and Bernard J. Carroll, "Separation of Subtypes of Depression Using Discriminant Analyses. 1. Separation of Unipolar Endogenous Depression from Nonendogenous Depression," *British Journal of Psychiatry* 140 (1982): 384–391; Jonathan R. T. Davidson et al., "Atypical Depression," *Archives of General Psychiatry* 39 (1982): 527–534; and G. Hopkinson, "A Neurochemical Theory of Appetite and Weight Changes in Depressive States," *Acta Psychiatrica Scandinavia* 64 (1981): 217–225.

55. Norman E. Rosenthal et al., "Seasonal Affective Disorder: A Description of the Syndrome and Preliminary Findings with Light Therapy," *Archives of General Psychiatry* 41 (1984): 72–80.

56. E. S. Paykel, P. S. Mueller, and P. M. DeLaVergne, "Amytriptyline: Weight Gain and Carbohydrate Craving: A Side Effect," *British Journal of Psychiatry* 123 (1973): 501–507; C. G. Gottfries, "Influence of Depression and Antidepressants on Weight," *Acta Psychiatrica Scandinavia Supplement* 290 (1981): 353–356; and Nancy Harto-Truax et al., "Effects of Buproprion on Body Weight," *Journal of Clinical Psychiatry* 44 (1983): 183–186.

57. Darla E. Danford, "Pica and Nutrition," *Annual Review of Nutrition* 2 (1982): 303–322.

58. Diane D. Gorder et al., "Dietary Intake in the Multiple Risk Factor Intervention Trial (MRFIT): Nutrient and Food Group Changes Over 6 Years," *Journal of the American Dietetic Association* 86 (1986): 744–751.

59. Joseph T. Anderson et al., "Scoring Systems for Evaluating Dietary Pattern Effect on Serum Cholesterol," *Preventive Medicine* 8 (1979): 525–537; Patricia S. Remmell and Robert Benfari, "Assessing Dietary Adherence in the Multiple Risk Factor Intervention Trial II. Food Record Rating as an Indicator of Compliance," *Journal of the American Dietetic Association* 76 (1980): 351–360; Richard F. Heller, Hugh D. Tunstall Pedoe, and Geoffrey Rose, "A Simple Method of Assessing the Effect of Dietary Advice to Reduce Plasma Cholesterol," *Preventive Medicine* 10 (1981): 364–370; Martin D. Hyman et al., "Assessing Methods for Measuring Compliance with a Fat Controlled Diet," *American Journal of Public Health* 72 (1982): 152–160; and Patricia S. Remmell et al., "Assessing Dietary Adherence in the Multiple Risk

Factor Intervention Trial I. Use of a Dietary Monitoring Tool," *Journal of the American Dietetic Association* 76 (1980): 351–356.

60. Ardyth H. Gillespie and Charlotte E. Roderuck, "A Method for Developing a Nutrient Guide," *Home Economics Research Journal* 11 (1982): 22–28; Carol P. Ries and JoAnn L. Daehler, "Evaluation of the Nutrient Guide as a Dietary Assessment Tool," *Journal of the American Dietetic Association* 86 (1986): 228–233; and Margo Woods and Sherwood W. Gorbach, "Dietary Assessment Instruments in the Women's Health Trial," unpublished manuscript, 1987.

61. Björn Isaksson, "Urinary Nitrogen Output as a Validity Test in Dietary Studies," *American Journal of Clinical Nutrition* 33 (1980): 4–5.

62. William E. Mitch and Mackenzie Walser, "Nutritional Therapy of the Uremic Patient," in Barry Brenner and Floyd C. Rector, *The Kidney* (Philadelphia, Pa.: W. B. Saunders, 1982), pp. 1759–1790.

63. Allen C. Alfrey and Robert C. Tomford, "Phosphate and Prevention of Renal Failure," in M. M. Avram, ed., *Prevention of Kidney Disease and Long Term Survival* (New York: Plenum Press, 1982), pp. 31–38.

64. Norman M. Kaplan et al., "Two Techniques to Improve Adherence to Dietary Sodium Restriction in the Treatment of Hypertension," *Archives of Internal Medicine* 142 (1982): 1638–1641; and Efrain Reisin et al., "Effect of Weight Loss Without Salt Restriction on the Reduction of Blood Pressure in Overweight Hypertensive Patients," *New England Journal of Medicine* 198 (1978): 1–6.

65. Michael J. Horan et al., eds., *NIH Workshop on Nutrition and Hypertension: Proceedings from a Symposium* (New York: Biomedical Information Corp., 1985), pp. 1–374; and David A. McCarron, Lloyd J. Filer, and Theodore Van Itallie, eds., "Current Perspectives in Hypertension," *Hypertension* 4, Supplement 3 (1982): III-1-III-183.

66. Helen A. Guthrie and Annemarie F. Crocetti, "Variability of Nutrient Intake Over a 3 Day Period," *Journal of the American Dietetic Association* 85 (1985): 325–327; and Eleanor M. Pao, Sharon J. Mickle, and Marguerite C. Burk, "One Day and Three Day Nutrient Intakes by Individuals: Nationwide Food Consumption Survey Findings, Spring 1977," *Journal of the American Dietetic Association* 85 (1985): 313–324.

67. Edith C. White, Donald J. McNamara, and E. H. Ahrens, "Validation of a Dietary Record System for the Estimation of Daily Cholesterol Intake in Individual Outpatients," *American Journal of Clinical Nutrition* 34 (1981): 199–203.

68. American Diabetes Association, "Consensus Statement on Self-Monitoring of Blood Glucose," pp. 61–65; Beebe, "Self Blood Glucose Monitoring," pp. 95–99.

69. Barry Blackwell, "Drug Therapy: Patient Compliance," *New England Journal of Medicine* 289 (1973): 249–252; and Ruffalo et al., "Patient Compliance," pp. 128–135 and Chapter 2.

70. Milton S. Davis and Robert L. Eichhorn, "Compliance with Medical Regimens: A Panel Study," *Journal of Health and Social Behavior* 4 (1963): 240–249; and Walter J. Johannsen, George A. Hellmuth, and Thomas Sorauf, "On Accepting Medical Recommendations: Experience with Patients in a Cardiac Work Classification Unit," *Archives of Environmental Health* 12 (1966): 63–69.

71. Morton Archer, Seymour Rinzler, and George Christakis, "Social Factors Affecting Participation in a Study of Diets and Coronary Heart Disease," *Journal of Health and Social Behavior* 8 (1967): 22–31; and Jacqueline M. Dunbar, "Adherence to Medication Regimen: An Intervention Study With Poor Adherers," Ph.D. diss, Stanford University, 1977, p. 13.

72. See Chapter 3.

73. Norman R. Stewart et al., *Systematic Counseling* (Englewood Cliffs, N.J.: Prentice-Hall, 1978), pp. 95–97; William H. Cormier and L. Sherilyn Cormier, *Interviewing Strategies for Helpers: A Guide to Assessment, Treatment and Evaluation* (Monterey, Calif.: Brooks/Cole Publishing Co., 1979), pp. 128–131; Richard L. Hagen, John P. Foreyt, and Thomas W.

Durham, "The Dropout Problem: Reducing Attrition in Obesity Research," *Behavior Therapy* 7 (1976): 463–471; Barbara S. Hulka et al., "Satisfaction with Medical Care in a Low Income Population," *Journal of Chronic Disease* 24 (1971): 661–673; R. Brian Haynes, D. Wayne Taylor, and David L. Sackett, *Compliance in Health Care* (Baltimore, Md.: Johns Hopkins University Press, 1979), pp. 121–143; Marshall H. Becker and Lois A. Maiman, "Sociobehavioral Determinants of Compliance with Health and Medical Care Recommendations," *Medical Care* 13 (1975): 10–24; Caldwell et al., "Dropout Problem," pp. 579–592; Evan Charney, "Patient Doctor Communication: Implications for the Clinician," *Pediatric Clinics of North America* 19 (1972): 263–279; and John F. Rockart and Paul B. Hofmann, "Physician and Patient Behavior Under Different Scheduling Systems in a Hospital Outpatient Department," *Medical Care* 7 (1969): 463–470.

74. Sackett, *Compliance in Health Care*, pp. 121–143; Franklin F. Dickey, Mary E. Mattar, and Gregory M. Chudzik, "Pharmacy Counseling Increases Drug Regimen Compliance," *Hospitals* 49 (1975): 85–88; Joseph A. Linkewich, Robert B. Catalano, and Herbert L. Flack, "The Effect of Packaging and Instruction on Outpatient Compliance with Medication Regimens," *Drug Intelligence and Clinical Pharmacy* 8 (1973): 10–15; James M. McKenney et al., "The Effect of Clinical Pharmacy Services on Patients with Essential Hypertension," *Circulation* 48 (1973): 1104–1111; and Irving S. Colcher and James W. Bass, "Penicillin Treatment of Streptococcal Pharyngitis: A Comparison of Schedules and the Role of Specific Counseling," *Journal of the American Medical Association* 222 (1972): 657–659.

75. Howard Leventhal, "Changing Attitudes and Habits to Reduce Risk Factors in Chronic Disease," *American Journal of Cardiology* 31 (1973): 571–580.

76. Rhoda G. Bowen, Rosemary Rich, and Rozella M. Schlotfeldt, "Effects of Organized Instruction for Patients With the Diagnosis of Diabetes Mellitus," *Nursing Research* 10 (1961): 151–159; Jeanne C. Hallburg, "Teaching Patients Self Care," *Nursing Clinics of North America* 5 (1970): 223–231; and Stanley G. Rosenberg, "Patient Education Leads to Better Care for Heart Patients," *HSMHA Health Reports* 86 (1971): 793–802.

77. Marlatt and Gordon, *Relapse Prevention*, pp. 19–30.

78. Brownell and Wadden, "Behavior Therapy for Obesity"; and R.C. Benfari, E. Eaker, and J.G. Stoll, "Behavioral Interventions and Compliance to Treatment Regimens," *Annual Review of Public Health* 2 (1981): 431–474.

79. R. Brian Haynes, "Determinants of Compliance: The Disease and the Mechanics of Treatment," in Haynes, Taylor, and Sackett, *Compliance in Health Care*, pp. 49–62.

80. James A. Blumenthal and Robert M. Levenson, "Behavioral Approaches to Secondary Prevention of Coronary Heart Disease," *Circulation Supplement* 76 (1987): I-130–I-137.

81. Kelly D. Brownell et al., "Understanding and Preventing Relapse," *American Psychologist* 41 (1986): 765–782.

82. Michael G. Perri et al., "Effect of a Multicomponent Maintenance Program on Long Term Weight Loss," *Journal of Consulting and Clinical Psychology* 52 (1984): 480–481; Brownell and Stunkard, "Couples Training," p. 1224; and Marlatt and Gordon, *Relapse Prevention*, pp. 19–30.

83. Bennett, "Dropping Out of Treatment for Obesity," pp. 567–573; Jeffrey, Wing, and Stunkard, "Behavioral Treatment of Obesity," pp. 189–199; Kingsley and Wilson, "Behavior Therapy for Obesity," pp. 228–298; and Stunkard, Craighead, and O'Brien, "Controlled Trial of Behavior Therapy," pp. 1045–1047.

Computer Assisted Nutrition Counseling

Sandra N. Powers and Phyllis J. Stumbo

Objectives for Chapter 5

1. Describe characteristics of computer software useful in nutrition counseling.
2. Discuss the selection and use of nutrient data base software for diet and nutrient calculations.
3. Apply spreadsheet and graphic functions to nutrition counseling situations.

Microcomputers are now commonplace both in the health care setting and in the homes of health professionals and their clients. Nutrition counselors use this powerful resource to promote efficiency and precision in gathering and reporting nutritional data. Traditionally, nutrition counselors have used microcomputers to calculate diets, menus, and recipes, but they should also consider using microcomputers to facilitate dietary compliance. As technology advances and software choices increase and improve, the potential for expanded use of the computer for nutrition counseling becomes more attractive and feasible.

The nutrition counselor can use the computer as an information processor, educational tool, feedback provider, and simulator. With nutritional analysis software, the computer acts as an information processor by calculating the nutrient content of foods. The computer can assist in teaching dietary modification and encouraging change in eating habits. Prescribing and teaching an eating pattern involves much more than handing someone printed guidelines and a sample menu, an all-too-frequent scenario in busy clinical practices. Heavy client loads and other time constraints leave many nutrition counselors with enough time only to explain the printed dietary guidelines, thus leaving the client to translate the guidelines into foods to eat.

Ideally, the dietitian or nutrition counselor should have time to evaluate an individual's usual intake before explaining and teaching the new eating pattern. Obtaining a history of usual intake might include a 24-hour dietary recall and quantified food frequency. By having a computer at the work site, nutrition counselors can obtain and assess dietary history information more efficiently and accurately. Menu planning requires considerable knowledge of nutrition, skill, and time, especially when several nutritional parameters are controlled simultaneously. Menus designed to meet a diet prescription and tailored to an individual's needs are an excellent educational tool and can be planned more efficiently and accurately with a computer.

The use of a computer during the counseling session for nutritional calculation and menu planning provides for immediate feedback and the opportunity to simulate eating situations by asking "what if" questions. Computer-generated graphics, a component of some applicable software packages, can help identify and solve problems as well as be an attractive means of education and monitoring compliance.

CHOOSING APPROPRIATE SOFTWARE FOR NUTRITION COUNSELING

Nutrition counselors most commonly use software applications to calculate the nutrient composition of a food record (diet diary), 24-hour dietary recall, menu, or recipe. This type of software, often referred to as a stand-alone program, is dedicated to a single purpose and usually does not require modification or programming.

Another type of software for nutrition counselors is the spreadsheet. Computerized spreadsheets can be designed to perform some of the same functions as stand-alone nutrient analysis programs do. The U.S. Department of Agriculture's (USDA) nutrient data bases are available on floppy diskettes that are compatible with several spreadsheet programs, resulting in a nutrient data base that interfaces with spreadsheet software.[1] Computerized spreadsheets can be designed to develop meal patterns, plan menus, and calculate diet records, especially within select and limited nutrient parameters.

Performing nutritional calculations on a spreadsheet is similar to doing so by hand but requires less time and is more accurate. Counselors may need considerable practice to become proficient in using either a stand-alone nutrient analysis program or designing applications to use with spreadsheet software. Features such as help screens, templates, and interactive tutorials, which are components of advanced software programs, decrease learning time but usually increase software cost. Since stand-alone and spreadsheet software differ in their flexibility, functionality, and cost, buyers should carefully consider the software features required for nutrition counseling before investing in software.

Stand-alone Nutritional Analysis Software for Nutritional Counseling

Factors to consider when selecting stand-alone nutrient analysis software are the program's cost, functionality, and data base. Talking with other software users, reviewing product literature, reading published reviews, observing demonstrations, and trying a variety of programs help counselors identify software that meets specific needs.

Cost

Cost is usually a major consideration although it does not necessarily indicate how well the software performs or meets the user's needs. The initial cost of software development is usually high, but the cost of reproducing the finished product is low; therefore, popular software usually becomes less expensive with time. The purchase price usually increases when revisions are made to upgrade the product, increase power and sophistication, or make the product more competitive. The cost of nutritional analysis software can range from $10 to several thousand dollars. Some stand-alone programs sell for under $100, and purchasing them should be considered in much the same way as purchasing a good book: one need not be limited to only one program.

A brief description of a few inexpensive programs will help counselors evaluate their usefulness. Public domain programs are the least expensive. The Idaho Extension Services' $10 program is a good example of a high-quality product developed with public money. With 324 foods based on USDA food values, the program is a "no frills" purchase option with a good data base and good programming. The data base is USDA's; nutrient values in the data base are complete. The printout from the program lists in a set format the foods selected and displays the totals for each meal and for the entire day in a bar graph (see Figure 5-1), conveniently comparing the caloric value and nutrient content with the RDA. A meal is considered a good source of a nutrient if the bar for that nutrient is as long as or longer than the calorie bar. This graphic representation of nutrient density helps illustrate nutritional adequacy. The program is useful for general nutrition education and uncomplicated weight loss but lacks important details needed for counseling for modified diets.

Another low-cost option is Nutrition Wizard, from the Center for Science in the Public Interest. This program has a standard printout, is easy to use, and it features a component that supports calculating nutrients in a recipe and entering a serving onto the data base.

The two programs above are mentioned for two reasons. First, they are inexpensive and may prove useful, and second, they illustrate differences between programs. The Idaho program does not generate nutrient data for individual foods, which limits its suitability for some applications. Nutrition Wizard does not accept food amounts entered in gram weight, which limits its usefulness in other applications. A single program is not likely to provide for every possible need. For some applications counselors may want to develop reporting forms that support their preferred teaching style and objectives and copy information generated by computer onto these forms. Ideally, counselors should determine their educational needs and choose a computer program that supports these goals rather than choosing a program first and then tailoring counseling sessions to the computer program.

Many programs cost more than the examples given, up to 7,500 dollars. Some of the added cost is due to more elaborate programming options, such as help screens and customized printouts, but customer service is probably the most expensive aspect of nutrition software. Frequent data base updates and telephone and personal support require a staff that is paid from product sales or rental profits.

Many nutrient analysis programs become out-of-date in a few years because of changes in the nature of the food supply, the frequent appearance of new products, and new eating trends. When investing in higher-priced software, counselors should expect the software company to provide periodic upgrading, a guarantee, and computer support (answering questions and solving problems). Less expensive software should also carry a guarantee, but the owner should be content with the design and data base and not expect updates or ongoing support. As the less expensive software becomes obsolete, the owner should replace it with a newer product. Whatever the cost, the level of satisfaction is largely determined by the software's functionality and versatility, the quality of the data base, and the ability to meet counselor needs.

Some of the characteristics that make nutrient analysis software suitable for nutritional counseling are often found in higher-priced software. A computer system used

```
University of Idaho          Idaho Diet Analysis              Ver 4.0 070486
==============================================================================

                            - Total Bar Graph -

   Nutrient      Amount     % RDA   0  10  20  30  40  50  60  70  80  90 100 %
  -----------   ----------  -------  !---+---+---+---+---+---+---+---+---+---+---!
  Calories .:    1545.7     86.1 %  |**********************************         |
  Protein ..:      76.2 G  182.2 %  |**************************************** |+
  Vitamin A :    7281.0 IU 182.0 %  |**************************************** |+
  Vitamin C :     106.2 Mg 177.1 %  |**************************************** |+
  Thiamin ..:       0.9 Mg  89.0 %  |************************************      |
  Riboflavin:       1.7 Mg 138.5 %  |**************************************** |+
  Niacin ...:      16.8 Mg 128.8 %  |**************************************** |+
  Calcium ..:     611.7 Mg  76.5 %  |******************************            |
  Iron .....:      10.5 Mg 105.3 %  |**************************************** |+
  Vitamin B6:       2.4 Mg 121.6 %  |**************************************** |+
  Magnesium :     357.2 Mg 119.1 %  |**************************************** |+

                     - Recommended Daily Allowances -

                        Nutrient      Amount
                       -----------   ----------
                       Calories* :    1795.0
                       Protein* .:      41.8 G
                       Vitamin A :    4000.0 IU
                       Vitamin C :      60.0 Mg
                       Thiamin ..:       1.0 Mg
                       Riboflavin:       1.2 Mg
                       Niacin ...:      13.0 Mg
                       Calcium ..:     800.0 Mg
                       Iron .....:      10.0 Mg
                       Vitamin B6:       2.0 Mg
                       Magnesium :     300.0 Mg

              * Based on weight, age and energy requirements.

               - Fat, Protein and Carbohydrate Requirements -

                         Per cent of calories  Per cent of calories
               Nutrient     for balanced diet       in your diet
              ----------  --------------------  --------------------
               Protein    No less than 12-14 %          22 %
                 Fat      No more than 30-35 %          24 %
             Carbohydrate        Remainder              54 %

==============================================================================
```

Figure 5-1 Sample Output from Idaho Extension Service Computer Program

during a counseling session needs to be fast, efficient, and user-friendly, features that usually increase the price.

Functionality

Functionality is a term used to describe such features as ease of entering and correcting data, method and type of calculations, screen format and prompts, command choices, and printed format. Software characteristics that are helpful for nutritional counseling include (1) user-friendliness, (2) food name or key word entry, (3) adequate number of portion size options, (4) ability to calculate a series of diet records or menus, (5) ability to view on-screen the entered foods along with the nutrient values, (6) availability of an ongoing summary of nutrient calculations, (7) the ability to edit and modify easily, (8) attractive and readable hard copy, and (9) a graphics component. The best way to evaluate functionality and determine the characteristics that satisfy counseling goals is to try the software. Many companies give prospective buyers an opportunity to use the software before purchase or provide names of current users. A large holding of commercial nutritional analysis programs is housed in the National Library of Agriculture in Beltsville, Maryland, and with an appointment users can review the software on the premises. Table 5-1 lists some of the nutritional analysis software available at the library along with the suggested purchase price. A complete set of current holdings is available from the library.[2] Catalogs and directories of nutrition software can be found at most universities, libraries, and bookstores.

Programs vary in their ease of use. Most programs require reading a manual to get started while others provide extensive help screens and elaborate prompts. The latter programs are sometimes described as user-friendly because their design makes them easy to use without requiring the user to study a manual. Many counseling situations need a user-friendly program.

The method by which users enter food information into the computer also indicates ease of use. Data can be entered by a food code or number, key word, food name, or a combination of these methods. Entry by a food code or number involves searching for a food item in a manual and entering into the computer the food code or number related to the item. This process can be tedious and time consuming, but food codes or numbers can be an expedient method when the user is calculating a series of diet records or menus, especially if the user or coder is familiar with the manual and codes. Entry by key word, food name, or on-screen food code search is more user-friendly and is preferred in counseling situations, especially for menu planning and entering diet histories. Key word entry often requires two steps: (1) typing or selecting of a food group name, such as milk, and (2) selection of an appropriate item from a list displayed, such as 2 percent fat milk. Entry by food name usually requires entering the food name just as it is listed in the data base, sometimes making it difficult to find foods by name if the user enters a wrong word or incorrect spelling. For example, a user may try several times to select a hamburger bun, not knowing it is listed as a roll rather than as a bun in the data base. A few programs accept entry of a partial food name (such as "oran"), which usually results in the appearance of a list of food items (all food names with "oran") on-screen from which to select. When the food name is more complete and specific, the food list is usually shorter. This method of food name entry, which is becoming more common, has its advantages in nutrition counseling. Software packages should include a table that lists the foods in the data base or give the user the capability to look at or print such a table. A directory of the contents of the data base also helps in determining how many types of a food item are included in the data base, such as how many margarines. The user may never need a printed version of the food table, especially if the program offers other ways to examine the data base, but the software should provide some method for studying the data base.

The method and types of calculations performed are important indicators of functionality. For nutrient analysis, calculations depend on portion or serving size. The software should provide several choices, such as fluid ounce, cup, and spoon measures and weights for ounce and gram. Some programs allow entry of imprecise yet common portion sizes, such as "piece," "slice," or "serving." While this feature

Available for Preview at the National Agriculture Library, Beltsville, MD

	Cost ($)	Source	Address
...l	349	Soft Bite, Inc.	PO Box 1484, East Lansing, MI 48823
Computrition	1995	Computrition, Inc. Suite 201	21049 Devonshire St Chatsworth, CA 91311
Datadiet Nutrient Analysis	375	IPC Software Suite 747	5 Town and Country Vilag San Jose, CA 95128-2026
Diet Analyzer System	995	CBORD Group, Inc. Suite 300, The Commons	First Bank Bldg Ithaca, NY 14850
Dietary Assessment System	195	Softech Computing Co.	264 Morris Street Pawaukee, WI 53072
Dietician	59	Dietware	PO Box 503 Spring, TX 77373
Diets-Diet Intake Evaluation and Tabulation System	50	R. Michael Jenkins Kent State University	School of Fam & Consumer Studies Kent, OH 44242
Eat for Health	25	Genesee Intermediate School District	2413 West Maple Flint, MI 48507
Eat Smart	20	Pillsbury Company, Consumer Public Rel.	M/S 3286, Pillsbury Ctr Minneapolis, MN 55402
Eating Machine	50	Muse Software	
Eats II	125	Penn State University Nutrition Education Ctr	Benedict House University Park, PA 16802
Evrydiet: A Nutrition and Diet Guide	60	Evryware	131 Clay Street New Haven, CT 06513
Fast Food Micro-guide	49	The Learning Seed	330 Telser Road Lake Zurich, IL 60047
Food Processor II (Demo disc only)	250	ESHA Research	PO Box 13028 Salem, OR 97309
Fooday Diet Assess	35	Extend Univ of MN	475 Coffey Hall, 1420 Eckles Ave St. Paul, MN 55108
Health Appraisal-Nutrition Evaluation	200	Computerized Health Appraisals	13705 SE 142nd Street Clackamas, OR 97105
Health-Aide	80	Knossos, Inc.	422 Redwood Ave. Corte Madera, CA 94925
Idaho Diet Analysis	10	University of Idaho, Agriculture Communication Center	Cooperative Extension 111 Ag Science Moscow, ID 83843
IFT's Calcaloric	975	DFM Software Sys, Inc	4812 W. Ninth St. Des Moines, IA 50315
In Shape! (includes exercise analysis)	95	DEG Software Suite 150	11999 Katy Freeway Houston, TX 77079
Nutra Comp	275	Programs "R" Us Suite F-301	199 W El Camino Rd Encinitas, CA 92024
Nutranal	250	S and N Services	4659 E Amherst Avenue Denver, CO 80222
Nutri-Calc PC	145	CAMDE Corp Suite 331	4435 S. Rural Road Tempe, AZ 85282

Table 5-1 (continued)

Program Name	Cost ($)	Source	Address
Nutri-Data (NourishChec)	195	Meridian Educ Corp	608 E Locust St Bloomington, IL 61701
Nutri-pak	40	MicroComp, Inc. The Computer Store	2015 NW Circle Blvd Corvallis, OR 97330
Nutri-Tally	125	Nutrition Counseling Suite 100	221 Seventh Street, N Columbus, MS 39701
Nutrichec	60	D Thurman and W Parkey	Oral Roberts Univ Tulsa, OK 74171
Nutrient Analysis	40	Exar Communications, Inc.	267B McClean Avenue Staten Island, NY 10305
Nutrient Analysis System	199	Dietary Data Analysis	PO Box 26 Hamburg, NJ 07419
Nutriplan	75	MicroMedx	187 Gardiners Ave Levitton, NY 11756
Nutriplanner & Nutripract. 4000	1250	Practorcare Corp. Suite 2F	10951 Sorrento Valley Rd San Diego, CA 92121
Nutriquest II	695	Capitol Systems Group, Inc.	11301 Rockville Pike Kensington, MD 20895
Nutrition Design	120	Nutrition Design	3406 SW Chintimini Ave Corvallis, OR 97333
Nutrition Wizard	100	Center for Science in the Public Interest	1755 S Street, NW Washington, DC 20009
Nutrition, Volume I	46	Minnesota Educational Computing Corp	3490 Lexington Ave, N St Paul, MN 55126-8097
Nutritionist II	295	N-Squared Computing	5318 Forest Ridge Rd Silverton, OR 97381
Nutritionist III	495		
Recipe: Nutritional Analysis Program	Free	Jo Anne Barton, Extension Specialist	322 Wallace Hall VA Tech, Blacksburg, VA 24061
The Dine System	170	DineSystems, Inc	724 Robin Road West Amherst, NY 14228
What Did You Eat Yesterday?	59	The Learning Seed	330 Telser Road Lake Zurich, IL 60047
You are what you eat	42	Marshware	PO Box 8082 Shawnee Mission, KS 66208

may sometimes be useful, the user must know the true serving size used for the calculations. A screen format that displays serving or portion size options for each food item selected allows greater understanding of the data base as well as more efficient and accurate entry of data. The ability to calculate average totals for a series of food records or menus, a feature found in most software, is needed for many counseling situations.

Several programs allow the user to view the foods, nutrient values, and summary of the calculations on-screen before printing the results on paper, a desirable feature for nutrition counseling. By reviewing data on-screen, users can discover mistakes and correct them before printing. Some programs allow editing as soon as mistakes are made while others require users to enter all data before correcting or modifying previous entries. The ability to edit and modify as mistakes are made is essential in using the computer for nutritional counseling.

The time it takes a program to calculate a menu or recipe is a good basis for comparing software. To calculate a test menu, consider a simple breakfast such as orange juice, cereal, egg, toast, milk, and coffee—foods that should be included in all programs. A more effective comparison is to calculate a meal that includes a few unusual or combination foods, like chicken salad, quiche, or a taco. Calculation of sample menus containing simple and combination foods is an excellent way to evaluate software for ease of use, speed, and quality of the data base as well as suitability for counseling.

A useful and outstanding feature found in some of the newer stand-alone software is dynamic nutrient displays. The screen displays the food names and portion size along with the nutrient values for each item while giving a running total of user-selected nutrients. As all nutrients cannot fit on the screen at the same time, a select feature allows the user to choose the nutrient(s) to appear on screen and a scroll feature lets the user view all nutrients. The totals are recalculated as foods and amounts are added, deleted, or changed. This feature may add to the purchase price, but some nutrition counselors consider it essential to counseling needs. Only a few companies offer this feature, which makes menu planning easy, fun, and efficient.[3]

The printout design, an important aspect of functionality, should be clear and attractive, with a readable format. The quality of the printed page depends partly on the quality of the paper and printer. When selecting software, users should consider the printed format in relation to counseling needs. Format is especially important if the printout is to be given to the client for teaching purposes. In some nutrient analysis programs the printout includes only the summary (totals of the nutrients), not the nutrient composition of individual foods that comprise the diet, menu, or recipe. For some purposes, the totals for all nutrients may be sufficient, but in most counseling it is important to know how individual foods contribute to the total diet, so nutrients for each food item should appear on the printed copy. Another desirable feature for education and counseling is for the user to be able to select the nutrients that appear on the printout. A printout with more than 50 nutrients often overwhelms clients and can sometimes lead to misinterpretation of data. The option to print only a few key nutrients is desirable.

Many nutritional analysis programs have a graphics component. During teaching and counseling, a simple graph or histogram can create a long-remembered picture. Graphics are useful to compare nutrient intake over time or to compare intake of a selected nutrient with a dietary goal. Displaying nutrient values in graphic form seems to be more meaningful and can have a greater impact than a list or table of nutrient values.

Another important consideration is the data base. The quality of the data base influences the validity of the calculations produced. When evaluating a data base in relation to needs, users should consider the size of the data base (number of food items and nutrients), the completeness of the data, and the speed at which the software runs.

DATA BASE CONSIDERATIONS FOR NUTRITION COUNSELING

Stand-alone programs come with their own data bases. Nutritionists who use a spreadsheet to develop their own applications must select or create an appropriate data base for the spreadsheet program. The brief discussion of data base characteristics that follows will help the nutrition counselor choose a data base or evaluate programs with their own data bases.

Characteristics of Nutrient Data Bases

Data base construction and verification are complex topics. Developers and users of data bases meet annually to discuss issues and share information, and proceedings from these conferences are published. A few are available for purchase from the National Technical Information Service.[4]

Important points about data bases for nutrition counselors to consider are:

1. Are the nutrient data complete?
2. Are foods on the data base named in a consistent and familiar manner?
3. Are desired nutrients provided?

A brief discussion of these three points will serve as an overview to data base selection. Readers interested in a more extensive discussion of this topic are referred to proceedings from the annual data bank conferences mentioned above.

Are the Nutrient Data Complete?

The USDA compiles and distributes comprehensive nutrient values for American foods. Data bases distributed as part of stand-alone programs are created from these basic nutrient values plus values for brand-name foods.

The addition of brand-name products has two effects on a data base. First, it makes locating desired foods easier for inexperienced users. USDA data sets employ generic food descriptors such as "sandwich cookie" rather than "Oreo" or other brand names, a practice that reduces the number of nutrient profiles needed to describe the food supply. Including values for individual brand-name products on a nutrient data base creates the possibility of listing 500,000 or more individual foods. In practice commercial data bases that list brand-name products choose representative ones, usually nationally advertised products, to keep the data base manageable.

The second effect of adding brand-name products to a data base is that it usually makes the data base more "sparse" or incomplete. When USDA develops a generic food category, it estimates values for all nutrients so the data base is complete. If foods are listed by brand name, the data base usually includes only nutrient values provided by the food company. Typically, brand-name foods provide limited nutrient information, often only calories, carbohydrate, protein, and fat. Therefore, when the data base is used to evaluate food records containing brand-name items, the values of nutrients such as calcium, zinc, and vitamin B-6 may be listed as zero even though the food may be a good source of these nutrients. This sparseness is a problem with many types of data bases, including nutrient data bases. At least one data base developer has created generic food categories to be used along with a thesaurus of brand names.[5] For example, this scheme develops three cookie profiles, low-fat, medium-fat, and high-fat, and a brand-name list on which each individual cookie is labeled with one of the generic codes. This system has the advantage of keeping the data base small, while providing brand-name-specific nutrient profiles. In general, however, users must balance the convenience of brand-name specificity with the sparseness of brand-name nutrient profiles. If the nutrition counselor understands the limitations of the data base, the convenience of specifying products by brand name can be helpful.

Assessing the completeness of nutrient data bases that accompany commercial programs is difficult because information about sparseness is often not made public. When nutritionists demand brand-name specificity, they by necessity sacrifice data completeness. Nutrient information is more accurate in a data base chosen for completeness rather than size. A data base with 5,000 or 10,000 foods, only 4,000 with complete nutrient profiles, is no more accurate than one with 1,000 or 2,000 foods with complete nutrient profiles. Information on nutrients such as zinc and fiber is typically incomplete on data bases with numerous brand-name entries.

An understanding of the three data bases USDA produces for public use will help the nutrition counselor understand other data bases. The first, which provides data published in a consumer booklet called "Home and Garden Bulletin No. 72" (commonly referred to as "Bulletin 72"),[6] has 910 food items and complete data for 19 food components. Measurements are given in household units to make it easy to evaluate home-type meals. The second data base, called the "Standard Reference Data Base" ("Standard Reference"), provides information on 21 components for more than 4,000 foods.[7] Nutrients for 100-gram portions and the weight of one or two typical serving sizes are given. A third data base, developed by USDA for its own use in conducting surveys of food consumption, is called the "Continuing Survey for Individual Intakes" ("CSFII").[8] It gives complete nutrient data for 30 food components. Bulletin 72 and Standard Reference are available on diskette for users interested in developing their own applications on the microcomputer. Commercial programs select data from one or all of these data bases to create others.

Are Foods Named in a Consistent and Familiar Manner?

Users locate foods on a data base either by number or name. Several descriptors may be needed to select a specific food. For example, the world "milk" is not sufficient to specify chocolate milk with 0.5 percent butterfat. Commercial programs often provide a "search" function that permits users to ask for "milk" and view a list of types of milk from which to select the appropriate item. Home and Garden Bulletin No. 72 database includes only the most common form of most foods, which makes it easy to use. For example, it includes only cow's milk because it is the most common product in use, but the Standard Reference data base includes goat, buffalo, and sheep milk as well. The Standard Reference data base is intended for users who will develop the data base further. Names are abbreviated to include all pertinent data. One entry for round steak on Standard Reference is "BEEF RD L+F RAW," which refers to raw beef round with both lean and fat. A data base builder would need to give the entry a more natural name because the name *BEEF* is not unique (there are about 100 Beef entries) and *RD* is not a natural abbreviation for round steak. Bulletin 72 is easier to use since it requires less refinement.

Developing orderly and natural food descriptors is an important aspect of data base development. Evaluating nutrient data bases is difficult with a cursory review of a computer program, but the organization of the data base is one aspect of the program that makes it easy or difficult to use.

Are Desired Nutrients Provided?

The micronutrient content of all foods or forms of foods eaten in the United States has not been determined, yet the counselor may need information on many nutrients. A desirable data base has complete data and reasonably comprehensive food selections. The needs of clinicians and researchers differ, and data bases that support the work of these two groups also differ. Researchers may require data bases with nutrient values that are available for only a few foods and will plan test diets designed from these foods. However, the counselor, who is concerned with spontaneously ingested foods, needs to have nutrient values for a wide variety of foods. If copper values are available for only 15 percent of the foods in a client's diet, summing these few values grossly underestimates the diet's true composition. For this reason the counselor must select a complete data base. Data bases commonly include nutrients for which only limited data are available.

The data base created by USDA for their continuing survey is complete for all nutrients for which reasonably accurate data are available for most American foods. Table 5-2 lists the nutrients included on the CSFII data base, those for which data bases usually provide complete data. Users should carefully evaluate the completeness of any data base but should be especially critical of the completeness of data on nutrients not included in the survey data base since complete data for these nutrients are generally not available from USDA. The CSFII data base is not designed for consumer use and may not be available for use with spreadsheet software applications. However, some commercial software producers use data from the CSFII data base.

Interpretation of Nutrient Data

Almost as important as the quality and quantity of the nutrient data base is the interpretation of the data for counseling. The nutrition counselor is responsible for translating the nutrition data into helpful and meaningful information for the client. A computer printout of the nutritional calculations may appear precise, but counselors should interpret them cautiously because, as already discussed, the nutrient data base may not be complete. Missing nutrient values in a data base affect the accuracy and interpretation of the nutrient calculations.

The nutrient calculations are only as good as the accuracy of the input data, which usually consist of a food intake record (diet diary or diet record), 24-hour dietary recall, recipe, or planned menu and provide both qualitative and quantitive information. The type as well as the amount of food is important. In recording food intake, estimation of portion size is critical. Instructing clients in reading food labels and weighing and measuring food is a common method of improving the accuracy of recorded or estimated intake. Measuring spoons and cups, food models, and a ruler help clients estimate portion sizes for a dietary recall and quantified food frequency. The use of weights listed on prepackaged items or food labels improves the likelihood of accuracy because most prepackaged foods are subject to strict quality control. The descriptions should be as complete as possible and include information such as brand name, variety, and method of preparation. The more specific the description, the greater the chance of selecting the appropriate foods for analysis.

Table 5-2 Nutrients Included in USDA Surveys

Water (percent)
Food energy (kilocalories)
Protein (grams)
Total fat (grams)
Total saturated fatty acids (grams)
Total monounsaturated fatty acids (grams)
Total polyunsaturated fatty acids (grams)
Cholesterol (milligrams)
Carbohydrate (grams)
Total dietary fiber (grams)
Alcohol (grams)
Vitamin A (International Units)
Vitamin A (Retinol Equivalents)
Carotenes (Retinol Equivalents)
Vitamin E (alpha-tocopherol equivalents in milligrams)
Ascorbic acid (milligrams)
Thiamin (milligrams)
Riboflavin (milligrams)
Niacin (milligrams)
Vitamin B6 (milligrams)
Folacin (micrograms)
Vitamin B12 (micrograms)
Calcium (milligrams)
Phosphorus (milligrams)
Magnesium (milligrams)
Iron (milligrams)
Zinc (milligrams)
Copper (milligrams)
Sodium (milligrams)
Potassium (milligrams)

SPREADSHEET APPLICATIONS FOR NUTRITION COUNSELING

Spreadsheet software can easily be adapted to nutrition counseling. While most spreadsheet software is easy to use and requires no programming skills, the user does have to know and use a series of commands. This type of software is ideal for tasks that require repetitive, time-consuming calculations and organization of data, such as developing individualized diet patterns,[9] planning menus tailored to meet a diet prescription as well as individual preferences,[10] and analyzing select and limited nutrients from diet records.

Spreadsheets are composed of intersecting rows (horizontal) and columns (vertical) to organize text or numbers. The lines forming the rows and columns are not visible on the screen but are tracked by numbered rows and lettered columns. The intersection of a row and a column on the computerized spreadsheet is known as a cell. Cell size can be adjusted by widening or narrowing the column size. A cell can contain text, numbers, formulas, or numeric functions. The user can see only a small portion of the spreadsheet at one time but can view the entire spreadsheet by scrolling the screen. Most popular spreadsheet software programs have at least 256 columns and 8,000 rows.

Designing a spreadsheet on a computer is much like designing one by hand. The primary advantages of using spreadsheet software instead of the manual method are increased speed, increased accuracy, and the ability to modify the data easily while the computer automatically recalculates numbers. With simple computer commands the user can not only adjust the width of some or all of the columns but can move, copy, delete, or insert columns and rows of data.

Spreadsheet software for nutrition counseling cannot be evaluated in the same way as stand-alone software because of the distinct differences among the programs. Because the use of spreadsheets for nutrition counseling is relatively new, users must first understand the difference between stand-alone nutrient analysis software and spreadsheet software, the way computerized spreadsheets work, and the effective use of spreadsheets for nutrition counseling.

Differences between Stand-alone Software and Spreadsheet Software for Nutrition Counseling

The most obvious difference between stand-alone nutrient analysis software and spreadsheet software is that spreadsheet software does not come with a data base (although data bases designed for spreadsheet use can be purchased) while stand-alone software does. To calculate nutrients with a spreadsheet, the user must enter foods and nutrients manually. Appropriate formulas, such as a formula that commands the computer to add a range (column or row) of cell numbers, are entered into the spreadsheet to obtain the desired calculations.

Exhibit 5-1 shows a spreadsheet for calculating the sodium content of a diet record using exchange values. The spreadsheet has been designed with formulas inserted to permit automatic calculations in the "Total" rows as nutrient values are entered. Unlike in stand-alone nutrient analysis software, the user must enter the foods and nutrient values. Even though this may be a slow process, entering food names and nutrient values of choice has advantages. With stand-alone nutrient software, the user must accept the food names and nutrient values as they appear in the data base. Food names in a data base are often descriptive to facilitate the selection of the most appropriate food item, such as "orange juice, canned, unsweetened," versus entering "orange juice" into the appropriate column of the spreadsheet. Clients may understand a printout with the food name "orange juice" more quickly, especially if specificity is not critical. With a spreadsheet, the user can select nutrient values based on the specific needs. If more exact or specific nutrient values are needed, they can be taken from accepted references such as the USDA nutrient composition tables or from the client's educational material or an exchange list. The spreadsheet approach to nutrient calculations allows individualization of client education through the use of food names and nutrients specific to client needs.

Another difference between stand-alone nutrient analysis software and spreadsheet software is functionality. Spreadsheet software is not dedicated to one function but can be used for multiple purposes. This flexibility is an advantage in nutritional counseling because the software package can meet the specific educational and counseling needs of most patient populations as well as such administrative functions as accounting and record keeping.

Exhibit 5-1 Spreadsheet for Calculating the Sodium Content of a Diet Record

```
--------------------------------------------------------------
MENU #1 - SODIUM CONTROLLED DIET
--------------------------------------------------------------
                                       SODIUM
FOOD                       AMOUNT       EXCHANGE VALUE

orange juice               1/2 cup              0
whole wheat toast          1 slice            150
margarine                  1 tsp.              50
coffee                     8 oz.                0
                                        ---------------
Total for breakfast                         200 MG


sandwich:
    whole wheat bread      2 slices           300
    bologna                1 slice 1/8"       400
    mustard                2 tsp.             150
apple                      1 medium             0
skim milk                  1 cup              125
                                        ---------------
Total for lunch                             975 MG

chopped steak              3 ounces            75
baked potato               1 medium             0
steamed broccoli           1 cup                0
dinner roll                1 regular          200
margarine                  2 tsp.             100
skim milk                  1 cup              125
                                        ---------------
Total for dinner                            500 MG

TOTAL FOR THE DAY                          1675 MG

--------------------------------------------------------------
```

Source: "Sodium Controlled Diet Plan," Nashville District Dietetic Association, 1980.

Spreadsheet software is inexpensive, especially considering its many purposes. Quality spreadsheet software can range in price from $75 to $500. Some spreadsheet software is integrated with other application type software, such as data base management, graphics, and word processing, making the software package applicable to multiple situations at a price well below that of many stand-alone nutrient analysis programs.

The Design and Use of Electronic Spreadsheets

After the user becomes familiar with the basic spreadsheet commands, the next step is to design the spreadsheet. It is best first to draft the spreadsheet on paper, deciding on the title, column and row headings, column width, and placement and type of formulas.

A basic process for designing a spreadsheet follows, using as an example the design of a spreadsheet to keep track of types and frequency of diet instructions given each month in an outpatient clinic (see Exhibit 5-2).

1. Design the spreadsheet on paper.
2. In the upper left-hand side of the screen, type the title of the spreadsheet and other identifying data, ignoring the column and row format.
3. Adjust the column width to accommodate the length of the names of the diet

Exhibit 5-2 Spreadsheet for an Out-Patient Nutrition Clinic

```
----------------------------------------------------------------
Monthly Record of Types and Frequency of Diet Instructions
----------------------------------------------------------------
Type of Instruction:       Week 1   Week 2   Week 3   Week 4   TOTALS

Diabetic                      2        2        1        1        6
Sodium Controlled             2        3        5        3       13
Fat Controlled                0        0        1        1        2
Calorie Controlled            1        3        5        5       14
                                                                  0
Diabetic Sodium Controlled    3        1        1        2        7
Diabetic Fat Controlled       1        0        0        0        1
Diabetic Calorie Controlled   4        3        4        1       12
Sodium Fat Controlled         0        1        0        1        2
Sodium Calorie Controlled     3        2        3        4       12
Calorie Fat Controlled        0        0        0        1        1

Other


----------------------------------------------------------------
Totals per week:             16       15       20       19       70

----------------------------------------------------------------
```

instruction types. The default setting for column width is usually 9 characters; for this example the column should be widened to 25 characters.

4. Head columns with week numbers (Week 1, Week 2, and so on) and make a "Totals" column that contains formulas that add the numbers in the rows of cells for types of diet instructions.
5. Make a row on the spreadsheet to enter formulas that add the numbers in the "Week" columns.
6. Insert a formula to obtain the total number of instructions for the month.
7. Enter the types of diet instructions and the number given each week. As the numbers are entered, the "total" rows and columns are automatically calculated.

A spreadsheet that is designed for a specific purpose, such as the one described above, but that can be used repeatedly is known as a template. Creating a template requires an initial investment of time, but once created, the template can save significant time.

Once the spreadsheet has been completed for one month, a hard copy can be printed. The spreadsheet can be used for additional monthly records in several ways. The numbers for each week for each type of instruction can be erased and new numbers entered, or the old numbers can be overwritten with new numbers. The first spreadsheet can be used as a template and then imported into new and different spreadsheets. Another way to reuse the spreadsheet template is to copy the first spreadsheet.

Designing Spreadsheets for Nutrition Counseling

Diet Patterns Using Exchanges

Nutrition counselors commonly use exchange lists and exchange values to facilitate the client's transition from diet prescription to menu planning and as a tool in

Table 5-3 Nutrient Data Base for Meal Patterns

Exchange	Carbohydrate	Protein	Fat
	(g)	*(g)*	*(g)*
Bread/Starch	15	3	
Meat, High Fat		7	8
Meat, Med Fat		7	5
Meat, Low Fat		7	3
Vegetable	5	2	
Fruit	15		
Milk, Whole	12	8	8
Milk, Lowfat	12	8	5
Milk, Skim	12	8	0
Fat			5

teaching nutrient values. Table 5-3 shows the exchange lists for the diabetic diet,[11] which probably represents the smallest nutrient data base in common use. Exchange lists are nothing more than simplified nutrient data bases with foods grouped by similar nutrient content. The nutrient values for an exchange group are usually determined either by averaging the specific nutrient content of the food items within an exchange group, using a mean or median value, or by adjusting portion sizes to permit common nutrient content. The value is then rounded off to simplify nutrient calculations and to make it easier to remember the nutrient content of the exchange group. Exchange lists, while lacking the specificity of comprehensive data bases, are nonetheless excellent tools for educating, assessing, and monitoring. Exchange lists can be considered the client's nutrient data base, enabling the client to focus only on the nutrient values pertinent to dietary goals and prescription.

One of the quickest and easiest ways a nutrition counselor can use an electronic spreadsheet is to create individualized diet patterns using the "exchange" data base. The repetitive calculations required to develop an individualized diet pattern make it a suitable spreadsheet application.

Exhibit 5-3 shows a spreadsheet designed to calculate a diabetic diet pattern. The user enters formulas into appropriate cells to calculate the total number of calories and grams of carbohydrate, protein, and fat based on the number of exchanges entered into the "Number of Exchanges" column. Formulas are also entered into the "Totals" row to calculate the total number of calories and grams of carbohydrate, protein, and fat in the diet pattern. The formulas to calculate the percent of calories from carbohydrate, protein, and fat are entered, and the values are thus automatically recalculated as numbers are entered into the "Number of Exchanges" column.

The advantage of creating diet patterns with an electronic spreadsheet is the time saved in calculations. Usually time constraints permit the counselor to develop one diet pattern per client by hand. Electronic spreadsheets permit calculation and design of an individualized diet pattern within seconds, with the added potential to create numerous patterns to meet individual preferences as well as fall within acceptable diet prescription range. Counselors can create new patterns (see Exhibit 5-3, Pattern 2) by changing the number and kind of exchanges while the computer recalculates the totals until the target prescription is reached.

Exhibit 5-3 Spreadsheet Design for Calculating a Diabetic Diet Pattern

Diet Pattern #1

EXCHANGE GROUP	NUMBER OF EXCHANGES	CARBOHYDRATE (grams)	PROTEIN (grams)	FAT (grams)	CALORIES (grams)
Starch/Bread	4	60	12	0	320
Meat					
Lean	0		0	0	0
Medium-Fat	3		21	15	225
High-Fat			0	0	0
Vegetable	8	40	16		200
Fruit	8	130			480
Milk					
Skim		0	0		0
Low-Fat	0	0	0	0	0
Whole	1	12	8	8	150
Fat	5			25	225
Totals:		232	57	48	1600
Percent of Total Calories:		58%	14%	27%	

Diet Pattern #2

EXCHANGE GROUP	NUMBER OF EXCHANGES	CARBOHYDRATE (grams)	PROTEIN (grams)	FAT (grams)	CALORIES (grams)
Starch/Bread	4	60	12	0	320
Meat					
Lean	1		7	3	55
Medium-Fat	3		21	15	225
High-Fat			0	0	0
Vegetable	8	40	16		200
Fruit	8	120			480
Milk					
Skim		0	0		0
Low-Fat	0	0	0	0	0
Whole	1	12	8	8	150
Fat	4			20	180
Totals:		232	64	46	1610
Percent of Total Calories:		58%	16%	26%	

Source: The Exhange Lists are the basis of a meal planning system designed by a committee of the American Diabetes Association and the American Dietetic Association. While designed primarily for people with diabetes and others who must follow special diets, the Exchange Lists are based on principles of good nutrition that apply to everyone. ©1986 American Diabetes Association, Inc., American Dietetic Association.

Most stand-alone nutrient analysis software programs use a more precise nutrient value instead of an exchange nutrient value. The ability to use exchanges and exchange values to develop diet patterns and plan menus is valuable in teaching dietary modification, especially if the process can be computerized with a spreadsheet. Spreadsheets can be designed to accommodate any number or type of exchange lists, thereby increasing the potential application for nutrition counseling.

Menu Planning

Creating a menu planning template is similar to creating a template for meal pattern development. The user enters identifying data, heads or labels the columns and rows, and enters the formulas.

Exhibit 5-4 gives an example of a menu planning template for a renal diet. Once the user has created the template, it can be saved as a file and then imported to other spreadsheets. When the user is ready to formulate a new menu, the template can easily be modified to accommodate the needs of another client and diet prescription.

Exhibit 5-4 Spreadsheet Design for a Renal Diet Menu

```
-----------------------------------------------------------------------------------------------
Menu #1    .

FOOD                AMOUNT  FOOD        NUMBER OF     HIGH      LOW      SODIUM  POTASSIUM  PHOSPHOROUS  CALORIES
                            EXCHANGE    EXCHANGES   QUALITY   QUALITY    (MG)     (MG)        (MG)
                            GROUP                   PROTEIN   PROTEIN
                                                     (GM)      (GM)
-----------------------------------------------------------------------------------------------
Breakfast:



    Totals for Breakfast:                  -------------------------------------------------------
                                                0         0         0        0          0         0
Lunch:



    Totals for Lunch:                      -------------------------------------------------------
                                                0         0         0        0          0         0
Dinner:



    Totals for Dinner:                     -------------------------------------------------------
                                                0         0         0        0          0         0
                                           =======================================================
TOTALS FOR THE DAY:                             0         0         0        0          0         0
    mEq Potassium                                                           0


Diet Prescription:
```

Source: "Your Renal Diet," Nashville District Dietetic Association, 1980.

After the template is created, foods with associated nutrient values can be entered and the program automatically calculates the totals. The spreadsheet's ability to recalculate the totals as nutrient values are entered or changed makes menu planning with computerized spreadsheets efficient and accurate. This feature is valuable when counselors change the type and amount of food to permit the controlled nutrients to fall within the diet prescription range.

Once the counselor has planned a menu that satisfies the diet prescription as well as individual preferences, the menu can be saved, copied to another area of the spreadsheet, and modified to create a new menu. The menu in Exhibit 5-5 was copied to another area of the spreadsheet, where a few foods and amounts were changed, thus creating a new menu within minutes. Portion sizes and types of foods can be adjusted to allow totals to fall within diet prescription ranges as shown in Exhibit 5-6.

There are many advantages to designing an individualized spreadsheet for menu planning. Food items can easily be deleted, inserted, and modified to create new menus. The menus in Exhibits 5-5 and 5-6 incorporate foods that are traditionally omitted on some restricted renal diets, such as salt, bacon, potatoes, and grapefruit juice. Because of the ease of making changes on an electronic spreadsheet, and by considering the entire day's menu and knowing the nutrient content of the food items, the counselor can easily adjust types and amounts of foods to incorporate a few

Exhibit 5-5 Spreadsheet Design for a Renal Diet Menu

Menu #1

FOOD	AMOUNT	FOOD EXCHANGE GROUP	NUMBER OF EXCHANGES	HIGH QUALITY PROTEIN (GM)	LOW QUALITY PROTEIN (GM)	SODIUM (MG)	POTASSIUM (MG)	PHOSPHOROUS (MG)	CALORIES
Breakfast:									
Apple Juice	1 cup	Fruit I	2	0	0	0	250	20	230
Egg, fried with	2 medium	Meat	2	14	0	100	80	200	160
Margarine	1 tsp.	Fat	1	0	0	50	0	0	35
Bacon, fried	1 strip	Fat	1	2	0	75	20	20	45
White Bread,									
toasted	2 slices	Bread	2	0	4	300	60	40	130
Margarine	2 tsp.	Fat	2	0	0	100	0	0	70
Jelly	1 tbsp.	Free	as desired						
Totals for Breakfast:				16	4	625	410	280	670
Lunch:									
Green Beans*	1/2 cup	Vegetable I	1	0	1	0	100	20	15
Cooked Cabbage*	1/2 cup	Vegetable I	1	0	1	0	110	10	15
Cooked Carrots*	1/2 cup	Vegetable I	1	0	1	50	170	20	25
Margarine to									
season	1 tbsp.	Fat	3	0	0	150	0	0	105
Strawberries									
sweetened	1/2 cup	Fruit I	1	0	0.5	0	140	20	140
Lemonade	1 cup	Fruit I	1	0	0	0	40	0	110
Totals for Lunch:				0	3.5	200	560	70	410
Dinner:									
Baked Chicken	3 oz.	Meat	3	21	0	75	360	240	135
Mushrooms,	1/2 cup	Vegetable I	1	0	1	0	130	30	15
sauteed in									
margarine	1 tbsp.	Fat	3	0	0	150	0	0	105
Asparagus*	1/2 cup	Vegetable II	1	0	2	0	130	40	15
Margarine	2 tsp.	Fat	2	0	0	100	0	0	70
Iced Tea	1 cup	Free	as desired						
Sugar	1 tbsp.	Free	as desired						
Sherbet	1 cup	Dessert	2	3	0	100	40	20	260
Totals for Dinner:				24	3	425	660	330	600
*Fresh, cooked, no added salt									
TOTALS FOR THE DAY:				40	10.5	1250	1630	680	1680
mEq Potassium							42		
Add 1/4 tsp. salt to increase sodium						600			
Total sodium:						1850			
Diet Prescription:				38-42	10-15	1500-2000	40-50	350-700	>1500

Source: "Your Renal Diet," Nashville District Dietetic Association, 1980.

favorite foods. The counselor can also take advantage of the spreadsheet to teach clients how to plan and incorporate favorite foods without exceeding prescribed nutrient levels. Using the nutrient values pertinent to the clients' diet prescription helps the client and counselor focus only on the nutrients that need control.

Exhibit 5-6 Spreadsheet Design for a Renal Diet Menu

Menu #2

FOOD	AMOUNT	FOOD EXCHANGE GROUP	NUMBER OF EXCHANGES	HIGH QUALITY PROTEIN (GM)	LOW QUALITY PROTEIN (GM)	SODIUM (MG)	POTASSIUM (MG)	PHOSPHOROUS (MG)	CALORIES
Breakfast:									
Grapefruit Juice	1/2 cup	Fruit II	1	0	0.5	0	205	20	65
Egg, fried with	1 medium	Meat	1	7	0	50	40	100	80
Margarine	1 tsp.	Fat	1	0	0	50	0	0	35
Bacon, fried	2 strips	Fat	2	4	0	150	40	40	90
White Bread,									
toasted	1 slice	Bread	1	0	2	150	30	20	65
Margarine	1 tsp.	Fat	1	0	0	50	0	0	35
Jelly	2 tsp.	Free	as desired						
Totals for Breakfast:				11	2.5	450	315	180	370
Lunch:									
Green Beans*	1/2 cup	Vegetable I	1	0	1	0	100	20	15
Yellow Squash*	1/2 cup	Vegetable I	1	0	1	0	130	20	15
Margarine to									
season	1 tbsp.	Fat	3	0	0	150	0	0	105
Dinner Roll	1 medium	Bread	1	0	2	200	30	20	85
Margarine	1 tsp.	Fat	1	0	0	50	0	0	35
Apple Pie	1/8 pie	Dessert	1	0	2.5	350	100	25	300
Milk	1 cup	Milk	1	8	0	125	350	230	160
Totals for Lunch:				8	6.5	875	710	315	715
Dinner:									
Roast Beef	3 oz.	Meat	3	21	0	75	210	120	195
Mashed Potatoes*	1/4 cup	Vegetable II	.5	0	1	0	205	30	40
Margarine	2 tsp.	Fat	2	0	0	100	0	0	70
Mushrooms,	1/2 cup	Vegetable I	1	0	1	0	130	30	15
sauteed in									
Margarine	1 tbsp.	Fat	3	0	0	150	0	0	105
Iced Tea	1 cup	Free	as desired						
Sugar	1 tbsp.	Free	as desired						
Sherbet	1/2 cup	Dessert	1	1.5	0	50	20	10	130
Totals for Dinner:				22.5	2	375	565	190	555
*Fresh, cooked, no added salt									
TOTALS FOR THE DAY:				41.5	11	1700	1590	685	1640
mEq Potassium							41		
Diet Prescription:				38-42	10-15	1500-2000	40-50	350-700	>1500

Source: "Your Renal Diet," Nashville District Dietetic Association, 1980.

Programming with Spreadsheet Software

Writing macros that automatically calculate nutrient amounts for the number and type of exchanges used can save time in planning diets with exchanges, such as the diabetic diet. A macro is a miniprogram that consists of a series of commands executed with a few keystrokes. Macros enable the user to take shortcuts. For the experienced spreadsheet user, writing and using macros can automate many repetitive spreadsheet functions.

Dietary Intake Assessment

Spreadsheets can also be used to assess specific nutrient intake during counseling. Instead of recording the 24-hour recall on paper, the counselor can enter foods and amounts directly into the spreadsheet, using a template similar to the one for menu planning. Spreadsheet history taking does not produce a nutrient analysis, as standalone software does. The user must enter pertinent nutrient values, preferably those limited to the nutrients being controlled in the diet prescription. The nutrient values used in the client's educational material are usually easy and appropriate to use, thus creating a data base to use for teaching the client as well as assessing the client's intake. Assessment of dietary intake with this data base during a counseling session provides the client with feedback on the nutrients being controlled in the diet prescription. If the calculations of the 24-hour recall do not fall within the diet prescription range, the nutrition counselor and client can then modify the diet recall to meet the diet prescription, thus providing the client with an example of a menu that leads to dietary compliance.

USING THE COMPUTER TO FACILITATE DIETARY COMPLIANCE

Much has been written about the use of computers in health care education.[12] The educational advantages of computer technology include:

1. self-paced instruction
2. active learning
3. mastery of learning
4. individualized evaluation
5. prompt reinforcement
6. entertaining instruction
7. opportunity for testing ideas.[13]

Many of these advantages can facilitate dietary compliance in counseling. For example, menu planning and diet pattern development with the client's involvement provide a setting for active learning, prompt reinforcement, creative individualized instruction, and testing of new ideas. Traditionally dietitians have had very little time to plan patient menus because of the time involved in manually preparing individualized menus. With a computer and appropriate software, the counselor and client can work together to create menus the client will follow.

Diet Records

Computer analysis of food intake with careful interpretation provides valuable information for both counselor and client. The nutrition counselor can effectively use the results from several nutritional calculations to estimate usual intake, identify trends in eating, help monitor dietary change, facilitate goal setting, and provide feedback. The computer facilitates a more precise, more efficient dietary assessment.

Menu Planning

Just as many nutrition counselors have electronic spreadsheets available, many clients know how to use them, too. Teaching clients to calculate and plan individualized menus on an computerized spreadsheet during counseling sessions may improve compliance, as clients may actually follow self-planned menus better than those planned by the dietitian. When the client takes an active part in menu planning and incorporating favorite foods into the menus while still staying within the target prescription level, compliance may actually increase.

Simulation

A computer interactive counseling session with the client and counselor present can teach by means of "what if" questions and simulation. An example is a sodium-controlled menu that includes fast food, usually forbidden on such a diet, and incorporates lower-sodium foods for the remainder of the day. Many fast food chains publish nutrient analysis information that is available for entry into the spreadsheet and is often included in stand-alone nutrient analysis software data bases. Menus can be planned by adjusting the type and amount of foods to incorporate the desired selection yet stay within the diet prescription.

Another example is to plan a menu by simulating a client eating at a favorite restaurant. Both counselor and client can estimate the caloric content of the restaurant meal and plan the rest of the day's menu to stay within the desired calorie level.

Teaching and counseling with the computer can decrease the time it takes to assess and plan intake while providing more accurate data. Computers can help identify problems as well as develop solutions.

Computer Graphics for Nutrition Education and Counseling

Graphics have long been a popular and powerful business tool. With computers at the work site and graphics software, nutrition counselors can create innovative and individualized graphs to use for education and counseling. Graphs are useful because they draw attention to important numerical information, provide a quick way to analyze and interpret data, and show trends and relationships with much greater impact than a series of numbers. Most useful in nutrition education and counseling are bar (either side by side or stacked), line, and pie graphs. Bar graphs are probably the easiest type to understand, which is why they are considered a business standard. Figures 5-2, 5-3, and 5-4 provide examples of how to use bar graphs for education and counseling.

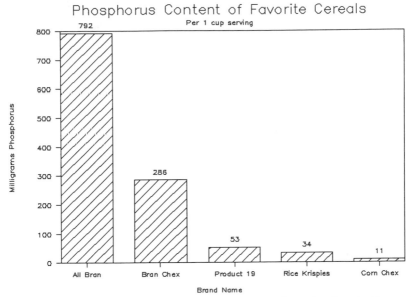

Figure 5-2 Bar Graph Representing Phosphorus Content of Favorite Cereals. *Source: Food Values of Portions Commonly Used,* 14th ed., by J. A. Pennington and H. N. Church, Harper & Row Publishers, © 1985.

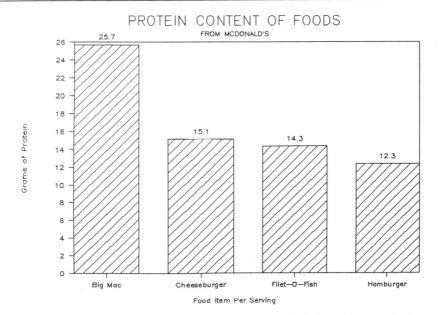

Figure 5-3 Bar Graph Representing the Protein Content of Foods from McDonald's Restaurants. *Source: Food Values of Portions Commonly Used,* 14th ed., by J. A. Pennington and H. N. Church, Harper & Row Publishers, © 1985.

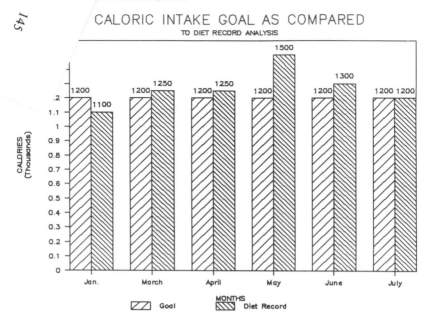

Figure 5-4 Double Bar Graph Representing Caloric Intake Goal As Compared to Diet Record Analysis

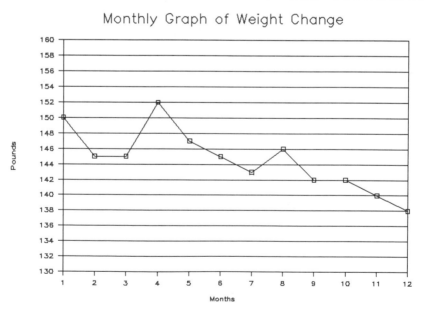

Figure 5-5 Line Graph Representing a Monthly Graph of Weight Change

Figure 5-2 is a bar graph that explains the phosphorus content of a client's favorite cereal. When a client exceeds the prescribed phosphorus level, the nutrition counselor can evaluate intake to identify sources of excess phosphorus and create a graph that illustrates the problem as well as a possible solution. A bar graph that focuses on the individual problem is much more impressive than a generic list of foods with phosphorus content. Bar graphs such as the one shown allow the client to take an active part in selecting an appropriate substitute.

Figure 5-3 shows a graph designed to illustrate the protein content of popular fast foods. A graph of this type is appropriate for someone who is having trouble following a protein-controlled diet. Being aware that the client likes to eat lunch at fast food restaurants, the counselor can select appropriate foods, graph the protein content, and generate a meaningful graph to clarify the concept.

Figure 5-4 shows double bar graphs comparing planned and actual caloric intake that the counselor can create after analyzing a series of diet records.

Line graphs are a convenient tool for monitoring changes in anthropometric measurements, nutrient intake, laboratory values with nutritional implications such as blood glucose measurements and blood pressure. Figure 5-5 is an example of a weight graph.

Pie graphs are useful in comparing data that relate parts to a whole. Figure 5-6 is a pie graph illustrating the percentage of calories from protein, carbohydrate, and fat in the sample menu shown in Exhibit 5-3. Similar graphs are meaningful for people following diabetic, fat-controlled, and weight-control diets.

A stacked bar graph is shown in Figure 5-7, which displays the fat, carbohydrate, and protein content of entries taken from a series of diet records. Graphs of this type illustrate trends and help assess long-term compliance.

Designing and generating an individualized graph may appear complex. Creating graphs requires planning, but counselors can use an effective format repeatedly to illustrate new points. Graphic software packages differ in how easy they are to learn, but the results of selecting software and learning the commands are well worth the time invested. Graphic software packages can be purchased as stand-alone programs or as part of integrated software—programs that combine several functions such as graphics, word processing, data base management, and spreadsheets. Users who need more advanced and enhanced features usually purchase stand-alone graphics software. Integrated packages usually offer less sophisticated graphic features than do stand-alone software programs, but they have the advantage of creating a picture from data already entered into another part of the program. Popular, easy-to-use integrated graphics packages include *Enable, Framework, 1-2-3, Symphony, Quatro,* and *Excel.*[14]

Computer graphics can be used in several ways during a counseling session. Before the interview, the counselor can print a hard copy of a graph to use during the counseling session. Another approach is to create and save the graph, then load the graph file just before or during the interview to view on the screen. With experience, counselors can create graphs within minutes with graphics software.

The advantage of computer-generated graphics in nutrition education and counseling is that they allow counselors to focus on individual needs. Graphs are particularly useful for clients with chronic diseases who are followed on a long-term basis. Once counselors are skillful in designing and generating graphs, the possibilities and creative uses are numerous. Computer graphs can be generated much more quickly

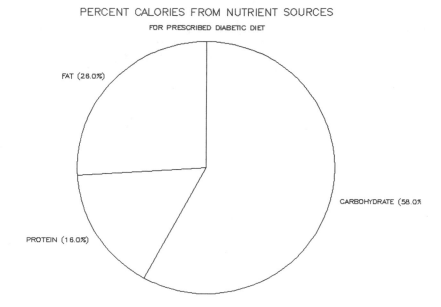

Figure 5-6 Pie Graph Representing Percent of Calories from Nutrient Sources for a Prescribed Diabetic Diet

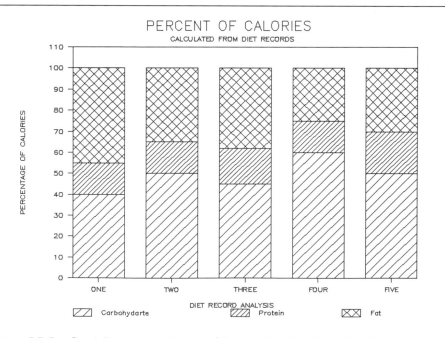

Figure 5-7 Bar Graph Representing Percent of Calories Calculated from Diet Records

than hand-generated graphs, and competence and experience significantly reduce the time needed. In addition, computer graphics can be fun and impressive, and provide the counselor with a creative outlet.

Computer-assisted counseling should become more common as the price of computers decreases and counselors become more proficient in their use. The potential for creative, individualized education and counseling is great, and nutrition counselors should take advantage of the computer to reach counseling goals.

NOTES

1. National Technical Information Service (NTIS), "Listing of Data Files on Floppy Diskette" (Springfield, Va.: U.S. Department of Commerce, May 1988), p. 1, PR-771-1.

2. "Microcomputer Software Collection," Food and Nutrition Information Center (Beltsville, Md.: National Agriculture Library, April 1988).

3. CBORD Diet Analyzer (Ithaca, N.Y.: The CBORD Group, Inc., 1985); and Nutripractor 4000 and Dietvalue (San Diego, Calif.: Practorcare Corporation).

4. *Proceedings of the 10th National Nutrient Data Bank Conference,* 1985, available from NTIS, U.S. Department of Commerce, 5285 Port Royal Road, Springfield, VA 22161. (8th Conference Proceedings also available from NTIS.)

5. Nutrition Coding Center, 2829 University Avenue, SE, Minneapolis, MN 55414.

6. *Nutritive Value of Foods,* USDA Home and Garden Bulletin No. 72 (Washington, D.C.: U.S. Department of Agriculture, 1986).

7. "Computerized Nutrient Data Set: Nutrient Data Base for Standard Reference," Release 6 (Springfield, Va.: NTIS, U.S. Department of Commerce, 1987).

8. "Nutrient Data Base for Individual Food Intake Surveys," Release 2 (Springfield, Va.: NTIS, U.S. Department of Commerce, 1987).

9. Karen Eckhoff, "Use of Electronic Spreadsheet Software for Exchange Calculations," in Directions for Action Annual Meeting Abstracts (Chicago, Ill.: American Dietetic Association, 1985), p. 50.

10. Sandra Powers, "Microcomputers in Clinical Trial for Dietary Management" (Abstract), *Controlled Clinical Trials* 7 (1986): 34.

11. *Exchange Lists for Meal Planning* (Chicago, Ill.: American Dietetic Association, 1986).

12. Warren Morrisett, "More on Patient Education: Use of Microcomputer," *Diabetes Care* 7 (1984): 105; Diane M. Billings, "Advantages and Disadvantages of Computer Assisted Instruction," *Dimensions of Critical Care Nursing* 5 (1986): 356–362; Moon S. Chen et al., "Microcomputer-Based Patient Education Programs for Family Practice," *Journal of Family Practice* 18 (1984): 149–150; Lynda B. M. Ellis et al., "Health Education Using Microcomputers," *Preventive Medicine* 11 (1982): 212–224; and Virginia G. Sinclair, "The Computer as Partner in Health Care Instruction," *Computers in Nursing* 3 (1985): 212–216.

13. Sinclair, "The Computer as Partner in Health Care Instruction," p. 214.

14. Cheryl L. Goldberg and Gerard Kunkel, "Graphics Software on Display," *PC Magazine* 6, No. 5 (March 10, 1987): 124–125.

Chapter 6

Designing Instructional Plans

Objectives for Chapter 6

1. List the reasons for using instructional plans in nutrition counseling.
2. List the three steps necessary in instructional planning.
3. Describe research relative to the advantages of objectives in learning and achievement.

Much of nutrition counselors' work in helping clients adhere to a dietary pattern initially involves planning to cover basic concepts in each counseling session. Presenting concepts step-by-step can help increase the probability that a client can retain an idea and transfer it to an actual situation.[1] Instructional plans for sessions requiring lengthy dietary instruction are of benefit for the following reasons: (1) they allow the nutritionist to separate parts of a complicated dietary pattern into manageable components, (2) they provide for more organized counseling sessions, and (3) they ensure that the nutrition counselor covers all necessary information with the client.

Instructional plans for the initial phases of dietary instruction do not have to be complicated or involved but must be detailed enough to cover a topic adequately. They provide the nutrition counselor with a map of the direction of the instructional counseling sessions, ways of achieving optimum client understanding, and criteria to assess how well the client achieves objectives.[2]

Designing an instructional plan involves three steps: (1) identifying the objective(s) for the session, (2) listing teaching steps, and (3) selecting materials and activities.

OBJECTIVES

Objectives form the apex of each instructional plan. They set the stage for what will be taught and how it will be taught. Performance objectives permit clients to direct their learning toward the specific behaviors they must master to follow an eating pattern for long periods of time. Objectives allow clients to evaluate themselves because they can compare their performance against a specific criterion and feel more in control of their lives and less dependent on the nutritionist. Objectives can encourage clients to progress at their own rate. In some cases they may learn more rapidly because expectations and requirements are clearly defined.

Mager is credited with producing the classic set of instructions on writing objectives.[3] An objective is described simply as "a description of a pattern of behavior

Table 6-1 List of Contrasting Words

Words Open to Many Interpretations	Words Open to Fewer Interpretations
to know	to write
to understand	to identify
to really understand	to solve
to grasp the significance of	to list
to appreciate	to compare

(performance) we want the learner to be able to demonstrate."[4] Mager suggests writing such descriptions with three components:

1. the actions clients will be taking when they have achieved the objective (for example, to eat three ounces of meat a day or to reduce milk intake from eight to four ounces)
2. the relevant conditions under which the clients will be acting ("with the aid of an exchange list")
3. how well the clients must perform the action ("on six out of seven days in a week").

The action must be that which the dietary pattern requires clients to do, because only in this way can the counselor assess their skill in applying dietary concepts to everyday situations. To say that clients "understand how to apply the concept of an exchange list to selecting foods" is unclear. The word "understand" can be interpreted in a variety of ways. However, to say that clients can "write" or "state orally" is much clearer. The counselor can observe these actions and infer clients' capabilities from the achievements they can demonstrate. Glaser offers a list of contrasting words to illustrate this point (Table 6-1).[5] In summary, Mager's first suggestion for writing objectives is to take a statement of goal, such as "understand how to apply the concept of an exchange," and reword it to describe what clients will be doing when they have achieved the goal, such as "write the equivalent of ½ cup of potatoes in terms of an exchange."

For an objective to be effective, it must contain a description of the conditions imposed on clients when they perform the action—that is, the tools clients will possess when trying to practice a skill, such as "describe foods in terms of exchanges using a list of commonly used foods and specified amounts." Kibler et al. offer three suggestions for determining the conditions under which clients will be expected to demonstrate achievement:[6]

1. Specify the information (exchange list), tools (measuring utensils), equipment (calculator), source materials (tables with food values), and anything else that will be available to clients to help them perform the eating behavior required in the objective.
2. Specify the information, tools, equipment, source materials, and anything else that clients cannot use when demonstrating knowledge of the eating behavior. For example, you may want the client to know how to evaluate a restaurant meal by looking at a plate of food and estimating the number and type of exchanges without weighing or measuring with a scale.

3. List as many of the actual conditions (eating in restaurants, social dining, parties, camping trips, and other social activities) as possible under which clients might be expected to demonstrate the eating behavior in a real-life setting, and try to include as many of them in the objective as possible.

The final component of Mager-type objectives, a statement of how well clients must perform the action, is the performance standard that measures whether clients have mastered the objective. Some examples for nutritionists are "to identify the exchange group for four out of five foods correctly"; "to write the number of exchanges for four out of five foods correctly given a list of foods with amounts"; "to take at least 90 percent of a dietary supplement within a month after being given a pill box to serve as a reminder." Kibler et al. have provided some examples of various types of performance standards.[7] The list is not exhaustive, but it should help counselors understand alternative forms for the component:

- *Minimum Number:* "must list four steps," "write all ten exchanges with specified amounts of protein and kilocalories," "distinguish three main foods which are high in phosphorus."
- *Percent or Proportion:* "calculate the exchanges for 10 commonly used foods with an accuracy rate of 90%," "take 90% of the iron sulfate supplements prescribed over a one month period."
- *Limitation of Departure from Fixed Standard:* "calculate the protein intake of two sample menus to within 10% of the diet prescription (using exchanges or counting grams of protein)."[8]

TEACHING STEPS

The second part of an instructional plan includes the steps in teaching a concept of dietary change. The accomplishment of an objective results from the combined efforts of the client and the nutritionist in completing steps toward maximum learning. According to Gagné et al., the following teaching steps assist in improving client learning:

1. Gain attention.
2. Inform the client of the objective.
3. Stimulate recall of prerequisite information.
4. Present the stimulus material.
5. Provide learning guidance.
6. Elicit the performance.
7. Provide feedback about performance correctness.
8. Assess the performance.
9. Enhance retention and transfer.[9]

Gaining Attention

A key to gaining the client's attention is to direct the counseling sessions toward the individual experiences of each client. A session might begin with a discussion of the client's feelings about beginning a new eating pattern. When the session focuses on the client's feelings about or past experiences with diets, the counselor centers the client's attention on eating habits. A counseling session that begins with the basic concept of exchanges without the counselor's first gaining the client's trust and involvement will end with little success.

Maintaining the client's attention may require other techniques. Having an outline of what will take place during the session and checking off topics as they are covered can help hold the client's attention.

Filmmakers apply a variety of techniques to gain, focus, and maintain attention, including cartoon-like characters, unusual voices, and exaggerated actions or sounds. Pop-in arrows or stars call attention to specific parts of a visual display, and sound narration may aid in identifying parts of an unfamiliar piece of equipment, such as a scale for weighing foods. Counselors can use these ideas in designing handouts—for example, by adding a humorous cartoon to a long discussion of low-cholesterol eating or using a slide-tape show to describe the tedious details of a diet, with a taped voice to add variety to the instruction.

A note of caution: frequently counselors use slide-tape shows with audiotapes or videotapes to the exclusion of an interpreter, the nutritionist. This can be very detrimental to the learning process and to the client-nutritionist relationship. Video and audio presentations should be accompanied by the nutritionist with whom the client is working. If questions arise, the nutritionist can give the client immediate feedback. It is a mistake to use the video or audio presentation as a form of "client-sitting."

Reviewing Objectives

A second teaching step is to let clients know where the session is headed. For some clients a discussion of objectives is appropriate: for others different terminology, such as "Let's talk about where we are going during this hour," may be wise.

There are many ways to make objectives clear to the client:

1. Make the objectives as simple as possible.
2. Be sure the objective is phrased in language the client can understand.
3. Be prepared to say or write the objective in a variety of ways if the client appears not to understand it as first presented.
4. Demonstrate how to perform the objective.
5. Show examples of correct practice so the client knows exactly how to perform correctly. These might include a videotape of someone eating correctly in a restaurant or a written example of how to convert one-half cup of corn to a number of exchanges.
6. Allow the client to practice the behavior delineated in the objective.

Stimulating Recall

A third teaching step is to stimulate recall of prerequisite learning. In this step the nutritionist tries to elicit information the clients have learned in the past that might help or hinder the learning process. For example, clients who are just beginning a low-protein eating pattern may have difficulty with the exchange system because they have followed a low-calorie, low-cholesterol, low-fat dietary regimen in the past. Some of the past learning may be helpful in teaching new concepts; other concepts learned well in the past may make the new exchange pattern very difficult. Helping the clients to recall past learning is both valuable for their understanding and helpful to the nutritionist in designing materials for dietary instruction.

Presenting the Stimulus

Presenting the stimulus material is the fourth step. In work with clients the stimulus might be the idea of weighing and measuring if portioning is important to maximizing dietary adherence. The idea of food portions can be presented in either too simplistic or too tedious a manner; a middle-of-the-road policy is best. First, decide on the importance of client-generated self-information. Will this information be used for data in the eventual analysis of a study? Will this information be used for a general idea of how well the client is doing with the diet? The purpose of the data collection dictates how much detail the client must provide and how extensive the instruction on the topic of portioning must be.

Having determined the degree of detail, the nutritionist can begin to design the stimulus material. If the material is lengthy and detailed, a great deal of attention should be given to graphics—drawings of dimensions, of the appropriate ways to weigh items on a scale, and of ways to measure leftovers. Audiovisual descriptions of measuring also help. Coleman and coworkers have developed an excellent audiovisual presentation of two women weighing and measuring a lunch.[10]

If portioning instruction requires less detail, simple descriptions of how to measure liquid and solid foods included on the diet diary are sufficient, along with verbal descriptions of how to portion. If measuring utensils are available, demonstrations of weighing and measuring during the client counseling sessions are helpful.

Providing Learning Guidance

The next step involves the way the nutritionist presents information. Research has shown that learning increases under certain conditions.[11] Learning in lists of paired associates, such as pairing an exchange amount with an amount of food, is most likely to require learning a small number of pairs at a time. Research findings suggest that as the number of pairs increases, the time to learn increases disproportionately. Practice of a relatively small number, such as five to ten pairs, is more economical than practicing 100 at a time. This indicates that it is best to present one food group or a portion of a food group at a time when presenting an exchange list.

A second finding is that learning and recall are aided when information is preceded by an outline or an advance organizer to help the client organize the information in a meaningful way. Learning can also be facilitated if the presentations include periodic review or summary statements. Time should be allowed for the counselor to pause, ask questions for the client to answer either overtly or covertly, and give feedback on the correct response. Giving the client time to respond may be the best single condition for learning when the information is more technical than novel. The more difficult the message, the more important the client response and the feedback from the nutritionist. Research also indicates that when more than mere recall is needed and application of information is necessary, examples are very important. The more tailored the examples are to each client's situation, the greater the likelihood that client will use the information.

Briggs and Gagné provide suggestions for determining the best kind of guidance for various types of learning outcome.[12] In teaching nutrition-related knowledge, counselors rely most heavily on four types of learning outcome: discrimination, rules, problem solving, and facts. An example of discrimination is to identify the differences between diabetic exchange groups. An illustration of rules is the nutrient data that form each exchange category ("A bread exchange equals 15 grams of carbohydrate and 2 grams of protein. All foods in this category equal approximately this amount of carbohydrate and this amount of protein."). Problem solving is the major learning outcome with which nutritionists must deal ("How will Mr. Doe select from the exchange list when eating out in a restaurant?"). The last learning outcome involves memorization of facts ("How much saturated fat is in a 28-gram slice of bologna?").

How can counselors guide clients to optimize learning? As for discrimination, counselors can begin by pointing out the distinctive features of each exchange category, such as the number of grams of carbohydrate in each exchange group. For the next learning outcome category, listing rules, the counselor can show how each food within an exchange group equals the amount of grams of protein, etc., for that category. The third type of learning outcome, problem solving, requires the nutritionist to give a minimum of guidance or cues to allow the learner to select and apply rules. The counselor might give clients a list of foods with amounts and ask them to tell the proportion of the bread exchange each represents. The last learning outcome, providing facts, requires the nutritionist to provide guidance by placing related facts into a meaningful context. An example would be to give a client the cholesterol content of all items on a list of favorite foods.

Eliciting the Performance

The sixth teaching step is eliciting client performance. Practice materials to take home or work on during a nutrition session can be very helpful. They might require clients to list the nutrients of importance in each exchange group, calculate the number of exchanges in a recipe, or make a menu of foods often eaten that include all exchanges for the day. Although self-report forms such as the diet diary may provide information that the client has modified to include only what the nutritionist wishes to see, they can be very enlightening as a means of indicating adherence to diet in daily situations. One way of helping to avoid falsification of the diet diary is always to praise the act of completing the diary and not to use it as a means of passing judgment on the client's abilities. It can be a tool that allows the client and nutritionist mutually to resolve problem behaviors.

Providing Feedback

As the case of feedback on the diet diary indicates, the nutritionist must acknowledge the client's effort to record dietary information and follow a diet daily. When providing feedback, the counselor should promote the concept of mutual problem solving.

Assessing Performance

The seventh step in teaching is assessing performance. The data received from clients on dietary intake are important to an evaluation of both the clients' efforts and the nutritionist's expertise in facilitating that effort.

Studies by Locke and coworkers indicate that specific and challenging objectives lead to higher performance than do easy objectives, "do your best" objectives, or no objectives.[13] Objectives affect performance by directing attention, mobilizing effort, increasing persistence, and motivating strategy development. (See Parts III and IV for more lengthy discussions on performance assessment.)

Enhancing Retention and Transfer

The last teaching step is enhancing retention and transfer. The ultimate goal of the nutritionist is for the client to be able to recall information about an eating pattern and apply it to many situations. Nutritionists can enhance this process by having clients practice the appropriate behaviors in a mock setting (modeling). Clients can bring in menus from favorite restaurants, discuss selections on the menu, and decide which are appropriate for the new eating pattern. Preliminary discussions like this can be very helpful in setting the stage for appropriate behaviors during difficult situations like eating in restaurants.

Teaching steps are critical to client learning. When designing instructional plans, nutritionists must clearly understand how to apply teaching steps to individual clients' life styles.

MATERIALS AND ACTIVITIES

An extremely important part of an instructional plan is the list of materials and activities that facilitate meeting objectives and maximize learning. Briggs and Gagné list 12 categories of educational media:[14]

1. verbal
2. visual
3. recordings
4. slides
5. motion pictures
6. television
7. exhibits (bulletin board displays)
8. trips to food manufacturing places
9. food demonstrations
10. role playing
11. contrived experiences (modeling and simulation)
12. direct purposeful experiences.

Table 6-2 is a general instructional plan that includes examples of some of these forms of media. This instructional plan was set up for a diabetic eating pattern. The tools described in this section are the Adherence Tools in Chapter 10.

CONCLUSION

An instructional plan should help provide structure for the initial sessions of a dietary interview. It need not be followed to the letter if the client's educational level dictates otherwise. Some instructional plans suggest times for each session, which may lengthen or shorten depending on the rate at which each client proceeds. Some clients with a great deal of mathematical ability move quickly through a session involving calculations of exchange portions; others may move very slowly and need remedial work on certain sections.

Instructional plans are not necessary for every session a client attends. Some sessions may be devoted to impromptu discussions of feelings and involve little

Table 6-2 Instructional Plan

Concepts of Basic Nutrition

Objectives	Teaching Steps	Materials and Activities
1. Review concepts, including carbohydrate, protein, fat, polyunsaturated/saturated fat ratio, and calorie control, as they relate to the diabetic eating pattern.	Stress the importance of all nutrients in a diabetic diet. Discuss interrelationship of fat, carbohydrate, and protein in the body. Describe diet prescription. Stress the need to attain and maintain desirable body weight. Explain rationale for carbohydrate and fat modification. List calorie-containing nutrients.	Use slides to describe the relationship of fat, carbohydrate, and protein.
2. Identify major nutrients needed by the body.	Explain the function of vitamins A, C, and D, calcium, riboflavin, niacin, thiamine, and iron.	
3. Review carbohydrate metabolism.	Describe the rate of absorption of foods high in: 1. Fiber 2. Complex carbohydrate 3. Simple carbohydrate 4. Protein 5. Fat	Use a graph to show peaking curves for various nutrients.
	Identify the reality of using combinations of nutrients. Discuss effect on blood sugars.	Use a graph indicating combinations of nutrients.

Table 6-2 continued

Effects of Nutrients on Blood Sugars, Exchanges, and Their Use in Meal Planning

Lesson 2
Day 2
Visit 1

Objectives	Teaching Steps	Materials and Activities
1. State the effects of carbohydrate and protein on blood sugars.	Research shows carbohydrate and protein (animal) to have an effect on blood sugars.	Review diet history with participant. Ask participant to make a list of three typical days' meals.
2. Describe six major exchange groups.	Review exchanges within each food category. State six major food groups. List food groups containing high amounts of carbohydrate, protein, and fat.	Credit Card Exchange Pattern[1] and Exchange Booklet[2]
3. Use exchanges in meal planning.	Discuss how to set up a menu using exchanges.	Plan a typical day's diet with the participant using the exchange booklet. Exchange Booklet[2]
4. Review portion sizes within the six exchange categories.	Stress portion sizes to stay within exchanges.	Show videotape. (Available from Dr. Phyllis Stumbo, Clinical Research Center, University of Iowa Hospitals, Iowa City, Iowa 52242.)

[1]The Credit Card Exchange Pattern is a credit card-sized piece of paper which has been laminated. It includes the exchange pattern for each meal and snacks. It can be carried in a wallet or coin purse for quick review when the client eats away from home.
[2]This is a booklet which includes the client's pattern and exchange categories with foods listed and amounts.

Table 6-2 continued

TAG and Recipe Calculations

Lesson 3
Day 3
Visit 1

Objectives	Teaching Steps	Materials and Activities
1. Describe the Total Available Glucose (TAG) system.	Count carbohydrate and use a conversion factor for protein.	Write the TAG for each exchange group. "TAG" (Adherence Tool 10-8)
2. Practice identifying exchanges and TAG.	Identify the steps necessary to describe a food in terms of TAG and exchanges.	Practice describing a list of foods as exchanges or TAG. "Practice with Exchanges and TAG" (Adherence Tool 10-7)
3. Plan meals using TAG.	Identify exchanges and TAG for each meal on an individualized meal plan.	Ask participant to identify exchanges and TAG for the three typical days' meals developed on Day 2. Ask participant to prepare a grocery list for these three typical days. Exchange Booklet and "TAG for Mixed Food" (Adherence Tool 10-13) "Calculating TAG" (Adherence Tool 10-14)
4. Calculate exchanges and TAG for recipes.	Identify exchanges for individual ingredients. Determine exchanges per serving. Incorporate these recipes into the above individualized meal plan.	Ask participant to practice: 1. calculating exchanges for individual ingredients 2. totaling the exchanges 3. determining exchanges per serving. Ask participant to incorporate correctly the recipes for which exchanges have been calculated into the menu Recipe Calculation Worksheets: "Chicken Soup," "Chocolate Cookies," "Chicken Almond Oriental" (Adherence Tools 10-9–11)

Table 6-2 continued

Applying Dietary Concepts and Experience with Dining Out

Lesson 4
Day 4
Visit 1

Objectives	Teaching Steps	Materials and Activities
1. Discuss weighing foods.	Point out differences in weights of various-sized apples.	Using a food scale, weigh fresh fruits showing variations in weight depending on size.
	Point out differences in raw versus cooked weight of products.	Using a food scale, weigh raw and cooked macaroni showing variations in weight.
	Calculate grams of carbohydrate for various weights of a food using ratio and proportion.	Ask participant to calculate grams of carbohydrate using ratio and proportion.
		Food Scale and "Weighing and Measuring" (Adherence Tool 10-12)
2. Discuss food labeling.	Identify calories, carbohydrates, protein, and fat amounts from a label. List ingredients from greatest to smallest amount. Determine exchanges and TAG in this product. Create a balanced meal using this product.	Finish the labeling worksheet. "Worksheet for Food Labeling" (Adherence Tool 10-16)

3. Discuss ways of handling problem situations.	Point out restaurant menu items for those places the participant frequents using the "Fast Food Facts" booklet. Stress ways of counting convenience foods using "Convenience Food Facts."	Ask the participant to plan a meal using "Fast Food Facts." Visit the restaurant, allowing the participant to bolus or inject with insulin prior to going. Ask the participant to select some frequently used convenience foods using "Convenience Food Facts." After selection, ask the participant to show how he or she would use them in a meal. "Fast Food Facts"* "Convenience Food Facts"*
4. Describe the relationship of alcohol to diabetes.	Alcohol may lower blood sugars. Stress the problems with alcohol and dulled senses.	
5. Explain how to adjust food intake for altered meal times.	Stress consistency and regularity of mealtimes. Emphasize leaving at least three hours between meals.	Demonstrate how to make correct adjustments in meal patterns using the "Fast Food Facts" and "Convenience Food Facts" booklets. "Fast Food Facts"* "Convenience Food Facts"* Optional: "Food Values of Portions Commonly Used"**

Table 6-2 continued

Review of Fat, Cholesterol, and Sodium in Foods

Lesson 5
Day 5
Visit 2

Objectives	Teaching Steps	Materials and Activities
1. Review diet.	Review dietary pattern and TAG.	Ask participant to state exchanges and TAG for each meal.
2. Discuss types of fats in foods.	Discuss the differences in animal and vegetable fat.	Ask participant to describe highly saturated foods which are currently eaten. Ask the participant to identify three foods high in saturated fat and three foods high in polyunsaturated fat.
	Describe the properties of saturated and polyunsaturated fat, i.e., saturated fats are solid at room temperature and polyunsaturated fats are liquid at room temperature.	"P/S Ratio of Various Fats and Oils" (Adherence Tool 9-10)
	Discuss the polyunsaturated and saturated fats in various oils, nuts, and seeds.	
	Identify animal and vegetable products high in saturated fat.	
	Identify foods high in polyunsaturated fat.	
3. Discuss the cholesterol content of foods.	State the differences in cholesterol content of foods.	Ask participant to list four foods high in cholesterol.
	Identify animal products high in cholesterol.	
4. Discuss low-sodium foods.	Identify low- and high-sodium foods.	Ask participant to list four high-sodium foods and four low-sodium substitutes.

Table 6-2 continued

Alcohol and Diabetes

Instructional Plan 6
Day 6
Visit 3

Objectives	Teaching Steps	Materials and Activities
1. Review diet.	Review the dietary pattern and TAG.	Ask the participant to state exchanges and TAG for each meal.
2. Discuss the carbohydrate and alcoholic content of favorite drinks (optional if the participant does not drink alcoholic beverages).	Stress the importance of acknowledging problems associated with drinking alcohol: 1. Dulled senses 2. Low blood sugar 3. Increases in dietary carbohydrate 4. Increases in total daily calories.	Demonstrate for the participant additions of carbohydrate and calories when consuming alcohol. "Alcoholic Beverages"*

Problem Situations Involving Your Eating Pattern

Lesson 7
Day 7
Visit 4

Objectives	Teaching Steps	Materials and Activities
1. Review TAG.	Use slides to demonstrate and review use of TAG. Stress consistency and timing of boluses.	Use a slide-tape show to review TAG, consistency, and bolus timing (see Chapter 10).
2. Discuss problem situations involving the eating pattern.	Review problematic situations: 1. Holidays 2. Eating in: • restaurants • friend's home 3. Snacking 4. Others	Ask the participant to provide solutions to the problems.

Table 6-2 continued

High Fat Foods and Weight Gain

Lesson 8
Day 8
Visit 5

Objectives	Teaching Steps	Materials and Activities
1. Discuss fat as related to weight gain and carbohydrate.	Discuss keys to good dietary control: 1. dietary fat and weight gain 2. saturated fat and coronary heart disease.	Use slides to show variations in dietary fat and resulting weight gain. Use slides to stress the importance of limiting saturated fat (see Chapter 10).
2. Review eating pattern.	Discuss exchange pattern and TAG.	Ask participant to state the exchange pattern and TAG for each meal.

Monitoring Timing of Food and Insulin

Lesson 9
Day 9
Visit 6

Objectives	Teaching Steps	Materials and Activities
1. Discuss monitoring, three meals a day, amount of insulin to cover a meal, and timing.	Stress the importance of monitoring. Review the importance of eating three meals a day. Describe use of insulin to cover snacks and potential problems. Review the timing of a bolus when a snack is high in fiber and fat.	Use slides to demonstrate blood sugars and intake that lead to lack of control. The slides stress: • three meals a day • bolusing insufficiently for snacks • changing timing for snacks/meal boluses (see Chapter 10). "Fiber"**

*International Diabetes Center, Park Nicollet Medical Foundation, 5000 West 39th Street, Minneapolis, Minnesota 55416.
**Jean A. T. Pennington and Helen Nichols Church, *Bowes and Church's Food Values of Portions Commonly Used*, 14th ed. (New York: Harper and Row, 1985).

dissemination of information. In the latter stages of nutrition counseling, once didactic information has been covered, unstructured sessions with topics dictated by the client seem to work best. Instructional plans are most useful if they help organize and define how to teach information during initial nutrition counseling sessions.

NOTES

1. Robert M. Gagné, Leslie J. Briggs, and Walter W. Wagner, *Principles of Instructional Design,* 3rd ed. (New York, New York: Holt, Rinehart & Winston, 1988), p. 223; and Leslie J. Briggs, ed., *Instructional Design: Principles and Applications* (Englewood Cliffs, N.J.: Educational Technology Publications, 1977), p. 213.

2. Robert F. Mager, *Developing Attitude Toward Learning* (Palo Alto, Calif.: Fearon Publishers, 1968), pp. 3, 21, 69.

3. Robert F. Mager, *Preparing Objectives for Programmed Instruction* (San Francisco: Fearon Publishers, 1961), pp. 1–53; and *Preparing Instructional Objectives,* 2nd ed. (Belmont, Calif.: Pitman Management and Training, 1984), p. 21.

4. Mager, *Preparing Instructional Objectives,* p. 3.

5. Robert Glaser, ed., *Teaching, Machines and Programmed Learning, II* (Washington, D.C.: National Education Association of the United States, 1965), pp. 21–65.

6. Robert J. Kibler et al., *Objectives for Instruction and Evaluation* (Boston: Allyn & Bacon, Inc., 1974), p. 38.

7. Ibid., p. 39.

8. Ibid.

9. Gagné et al., *Principles of Instructional Design,* p. 12.

10. Laura Coleman, Joanne Csaplar, Johanna Dwyer, Carole Palmer, and Molly Holland, "Weighing and Measuring in Women's Health Trial," videotape, 1986.

11. Briggs, *Instructional Design,* p. 206.

12. Ibid., pp. 209–211; Gagné et al., *Principles of Instructional Design,* pp. 249–252.

13. Edwin A. Locke et al., "Goal Setting and Task Performance: 1969–1980," *Psychological Bulletin* 90 (1981): 125–152.

14. Briggs, *Instructional Design,* p. 226; Gagné et al., *Principles of Instructional Design,* pp. 206–207.

Chapter 7

Stress: An Overview

John R. Kramer

Objectives for Chapter 7

1. Identify instruments used to measure stress.
2. Discuss the relationship between stress, illness, and adherence.
3. Describe approaches to stress management and adherence.

The word "stress" has several meanings. It can signify emphasis, as in spoken language or music. Physicists use the term to describe strain exerted by physical forces on objects such as metal, sometimes causing the objects to become deformed. This chapter focuses on processes that strain people, often with adverse consequences.

Nutrition counselors can benefit from a familiarity with stress because it is very much a part of their professional activities. A number of their clients have chronic disorders and high levels of accompanying stress. Dietary indiscretions are more frequent when individuals are under stress. In addition, nutritional regimens can themselves cause stress, especially if they are complex or inconvenient.

This chapter is designed to serve as an introduction to stress. Both the assessment and management of stress are difficult endeavors that should not be attempted without the active collaboration of experienced health professionals. The first section of the chapter presents two research approaches as illustrations of different ways to study stress and a discussion of ways to measure stress in clients. In the second section, general considerations of the relationship between stress and illness are discussed. The third section illustrates these points with the example of diabetes. The final section surveys different techniques of stress management. A list of Suggested Readings organized by topic ends the chapter.

THE CONCEPTUALIZATION AND MEASUREMENT OF STRESS

Stress is a word that is used frequently among health professionals and their clients. A nutrition counselor might, for instance, hear "family stress" offered as an explanation for failure to maintain an eating pattern. Despite its popularity, or perhaps because of it, there is disagreement about exactly what the term means. Part of the problem stems from the fact that stress has been studied by individuals from different disciplines, such as sociology, medicine, and psychology. Each has its own perspective and terminology, and there is very little collaborative research that integrates these points of view.

The most general notion is that stress is an aversive event or condition that affects thoughts, emotions, behavior, and/or physiological functioning. The event or condition can be physical (malnutrition) and/or psychological (severe conflict among family members). Research on stress has tended to focus on several different parts of the process. These include (a) the *events* that trigger stress (extreme cold, family conflict), (b) the organism's interpretation or *perception* of the event (threatening), and (c) the organism's *physiological response* (rapid heartbeat, increased adrenaline). Some authors prefer to use the term "stressors" when referring to triggering events and "stress responses" when describing the physiological, mental, and behavioral reactions to these events. Over extended periods of time, the two can become intertwined as stress responses themselves become stressors (see "Stress and Illness: General Considerations" below and "Conceptualization of Stress" in the Suggested Readings).

Two major research approaches illustrate differences in the way stress has been studied. One emphasizes physiological stress responses, and the other focuses on events that cause stress and their subjective impact. Because of space limitations, human studies will be emphasized more than animal investigations.

Physiological Studies

Hans Selye was one of the first researchers to study systematically the physiological mechanisms of stress. In his pioneering laboratory investigations, which began in the 1930s, Selye noted that the pattern of animals' responses to a broad range of noxious physical stimuli, including extreme temperature, infection, and trauma, was quite similar. Among other changes, he observed the enlargement of the adrenal glands, secretion of corticoids such as cortisol and aldosterone, increased output of growth hormone by the pituitary, and elevation of catecholamine levels. A sufficiently long and intense stressor produced three distinct stages, which he labeled alarm, resistance, and exhaustion. Although he recognized the existence of both stress responses ("the nonspecific result of any demand upon the body") and stressors ("agents or demands which evoke the patterned response"),[1] Selye's work focused largely on the former.

More recent research has modified Selye's observations. It is now known, for instance, that biological responses to stressors are more widespread than originally assumed and include the sympathoadrenomedullary system, the hypothalamic-pituitary-adrenocortical system, endogenous opiates, and the immune system (see "Physiological Measures of Stress" and "Stress and Illness" in the Suggested Readings).

Selye's premise that all stressors elicit the same pattern of responses has been challenged by a number of studies. Two major types of investigations have been conducted with humans. In laboratory studies, subjects have been asked to perform difficult mental tasks (arithmetic problems) or expose themselves to unpleasant physical stimuli (immersion of a hand in ice water). In field studies, individuals have been monitored before, during, and after anxiety-producing and dangerous activities like examinations and car racing.

Differences among Individuals

The results of these investigations have led to two major modifications of Selye's observations. First, it is now known that individuals differ in both the intensity and pattern of physiological responses. These differences are far from absolute, however, and there is considerable overlap between the responses of one person and those of another.[2]

Individual variations in stress responses are probably due to both biology and experience. Much of the research has centered on biology. For instance, the size of cardiovascular responses to laboratory stressors correlates significantly in identical twins, sometimes more so than in fraternal twins. These and other studies suggest that the intensity of certain stress responses is moderately heritable.[3]

Sex and age are two other biological influences on individual stress physiology. Women tend to exhibit smaller neuroendocrine response to stressors than men, for instance; in two studies, rises in adrenaline levels following exams and venipuncture were smaller in females than in males. Age also may affect stress responses; for instance, the magnitude of vascular and norepinephrine responses to cold stress has been found to increase with age.[4]

Differences among Stressors

Physiological stress responses vary not only with the individual but also with the type of stressor. For instance, evidence suggests that mentally stressful tasks cause a greater rise in adrenaline than do physically stressful tasks. Some authors have proposed the existence of at least two major patterns of stress responses. The first, sometimes referred to as a "fight or flight" response, is triggered by physically dangerous situations and characterized by muscular vasodilation and increases in muscular activity, cardiac output, adrenaline, cortisol, and prolactin. The second reaction pattern, triggered by situations that require alertness or vigilance, is characterized by muscular vasoconstriction, decreased muscular activity, and increases in males' levels of testosterone.[5] There is also evidence that the degree to which a person responds adaptively to a stressor is associated with different physiological patterns.[6] Clearly, Selye's original conception of a uniform pattern of physiological responses to all stressors was oversimplified.

Self-Report Studies

In contrast to investigations that focus on physiological reactions to stressors, a second line of research has centered on events that trigger stress and on people's perception of these events. Studies in this area take place outside of the laboratory and use questionnaires and interviews, although sometimes physiological measures are added.[7] Unlike the laboratory investigations, these field studies are correlational rather than experimental, and it is more difficult to interpret their findings in terms of cause and effect. A major appeal of this approach, however, is that it allows the study of more realistic stressors and of the long-term effects of stress. Four main areas of inquiry are discussed below: life events, daily hassles, the perception of stress, and social support.

Life Events

Both clinical observation and systematic research suggest that adverse situations may cause or intensify mental and physical problems. Holmes and colleagues, beginning in the 1950s, designed some of the first questionnaires by identifying events in people's lives that appeared to occur around the time they became ill; most of these events involved change or adjustment of some sort ("son or daughter leaving home; change in residence").[8]

The Social Readjustment Rating Scale (SRRS) was incorporated in many studies during the 1970s, and early results looked promising. Investigators found that individuals with high scores on this scale (indicating a relatively large amount of change) were more likely than people with low scores to exhibit or to develop medical, behavioral, and psychiatric problems, including a wide range of conditions like sudden cardiac death, arthritis, obstetric complications, poor school performance, depression, suicide, and schizophrenia.[9] As findings accumulated, however, initial enthusiasm was tempered by the realization that SRRS scores predicted such problems only modestly at best.

A number of explanations have been offered for this disappointing performance. One is that the SRRS estimates the change necessitated by each event with group ratings rather than the judgment of the particular person who completes the form. Research indicates that the amount of adjustment required by a particular event varies from individual to individual.[10] The item "pregnancy" is likely to have a different impact on an unwed adolescent than on a married woman who is planning a family.

The pregnancy example illustrates a second problem: the SRRS does not discriminate between conditions that are viewed as positive and negative. In a number of studies, negatively rated events were found to predict impaired functioning or illness better than do positively rated events, and the SRRS may be diluting its ability to measure stress by mixing them together.[11]

Partly in response to problems with the SRRS, other life events questionnaires have appeared in the literature. One of these, the Life Experiences Survey, is discussed along with the SRRS below under "The Use of Instruments To Measure Stress." Issues in life events measurement are covered at greater length under "Self-Report Measures of Stress" in the Suggested Readings.

Daily Hassles

Major life events do not occur daily. Some authors argue that they cause stress primarily through more minor daily occurrences. For instance, the loss of a job, a major life event, may cause problems primarily because of its daily consequences, such as a reduced standard of living and fears about the future.

Scales have been developed to measure these events, typically referred to as hassles. Lazarus and colleagues developed one of the first instruments, the Hassles Scale, to measure "the irritating, frustrating, distressing demands" that have occurred within a recent time period.[12] A number of the items on the Hassles Scale and life events scales are quite similar, but the Hassles Scale also contains other kinds of items, such as minor environmental events ("misplacing things") and thoughts and emotions ("thoughts about death"). At first glance, some of these items appear to be reactions to stressors rather than stressors. It can be argued, however, that behaviors or thoughts may originally be reactions to a stressor and later become stressors themselves. For example, the loss of a friend might lead to overeating. This behavior, initially a reaction to the loss, might turn into a stressor itself, contributing to a poor self-image, anxiety, and excess weight.

In some studies, the Hassles Scale or similar measures have predicted mental and physical problems more powerfully than have life events measures.[13] Hassles scales are not necessarily substitutes for life events scales, however; there is some evidence that the two types of measures provide the most useful information when used in combination.[14]

Most of the life events and hassles research has been conducted in a way that makes the findings difficult to interpret for individuals. In a typical study, a group of subjects completes only one or two stress instruments and one health symptom measure, such as a physical or mental health checklist (based on one point or the average of a few points in time). A correlation is then computed that estimates the extent to which individuals with high stress scores exhibit more mental and physical problems than do individuals with low stress scores at one point.

These group studies often obtain significant associations between stress and symptoms, but the results do not indicate whether, for a particular individual, *changes* in stressors are associated with changes in health over time. This is an important clinical question for nutrition counselors who see clients with chronic disorders. To determine the relationship between changes in stress and changes in health status, it is necessary to collect measures of stressors and symptoms repeatedly from the same people. Some of the laboratory studies of stress described earlier have used this method; for example, repeated measures of blood pressure have been collected during and following mental arithmetic problems over the course of 10 or 20 minutes. In contrast to laboratory research, studies of live events and daily hassles have not usually collected repeated measures. One reason is that long time spans are required—days, weeks, or months—a time-consuming and expensive process.

A few investigators have measured life events and hassles in the same subjects over time. Their results suggest that there is some relationship between the occurrence of stressors and subsequent physical and mental symptoms, but that the relationship varies from individual to individual. Delongis et al., for example, examined 75 adults for six months and had them complete an abbreviated version of the Hassles Scale on several consecutive days each month, as well as daily measures of mood and physical symptoms.[15] About one-third of the subjects displayed a strong correlation between high hassles scores and physical symptoms on the same day or the following day. Another third of the subjects exhibited few or no associations between hassles and physical symptoms, and the remaining third exhibited correlations in the opposite direction—that is, more hassles were associated with fewer physical symptoms. Other investigators who have examined the relationship between stress and symptoms over time have also reported a diversity of patterns.[16] Until additional studies of this nature are conducted, knowledge about the relationship between stressful events and illness for individuals over time will remain vague. (Further discussion of this issue is found in "Stress and Illness: General Considerations" below.)

Perception of Stress and Characteristics of Events

Life events and hassles scales do not merely register the occurrence of events. They also incorporate an event's perceived impact, like the amount of adjustment entailed (SRRS) or its severity (the Hassles Scale).

Perception and Stress. Perceptions are part of almost every stress scale because they help determine the degree to which an event causes stress. Individuals differ in their reactions to events not only physiologically but perceptually as well. One client might view a new eating pattern as a burden, while another client might consider it a positive challenge. The eating pattern is more likely to cause stress in the first case than in the second.

Lazarus and colleagues believe that stress results when individuals (a) think that a situation threatens their well-being and (b) judge that resources for coping with it are inadequate to meet the challenge.[17] High blood pressure would be perceived as threatening by people who (a) considered hypertension to be dangerous and (b) did not think diet or medication would enable them to lower their blood pressure. Other individuals with equally severe hypertension who did not believe in the associated health risks would be less likely to appraise the situation as threatening because, in their view, their well-being was not at stake. People with high blood pressure who were convinced of the risks but also believed that diet and/or medication would reduce these risks would also be less likely to see the situation as threatening because they would judge the available resources as adequate to meet the challenge.

Thus stress is likely to occur when people perceive that a situation threatens something important that they cannot adequately protect. The greater its importance and the more imminent and severe the threat, the more likely the person will experience stress.[18]

Characteristics of Stressful Events. Individual biology, personality, and experience probably play a role in the appraisal process. Some aspects of the events themselves also make them more likely to be viewed as threatening. One characteristic is the degree to which *pain* or *danger* is involved. Much of the stress research involves situations in which one or both are present; immersion of a hand in ice water and the Three Mile Island incident are instances of painful and dangerous situations that have been investigated.

An event that is new or *novel* may also elicit stress. For instance, in a study of parachute jumping, increases in cortisol levels were greatest during the first few trials and diminished as the task became more familiar to the subjects.[19] Novelty is closely related to change, which, as mentioned above, is a key element of stress in life events scales. The other extreme, lack of change, can also create stress; individuals whose lives are made monotonous because of retirement attest to this. Similarly, an eating pattern which has a narrow range of foods may be stressful to clients.

Events that occur *unpredictably* sometimes are associated with stress.[20] Lack of predictability also includes events that are expected to occur but do not. An overweight individual who diets but does not lose the anticipated amount of weight may undergo stress.

Events that are *uncontrollable* tend to be stressful.[21] In one study, subjects were divided into two groups, those who could reduce the duration of electric shock by responding quickly to a warning signal and those who could not. Even though all subjects received the same amount of shock, the first group exhibited smaller galvanic skin responses (an index of stress) before and during the shock than the second group.[22] Similarly clients who cannot control their food supply easily—when, for example, their job forces them to eat at restaurants frequently—are more likely to experience stress in attempting to adhere to a prescribed eating pattern.

In the absence of real control, even the belief that one has control may reduce stress. Glass and Singer exposed two groups of subjects to a very loud, unpleasant noise.

Members of one group were told they could terminate the sound with a button but were asked not to press it; the second group did not have this option. Nobody in the first group actually ever pushed the button, and both groups heard the same amount of noise. On a subsequent proofreading task, however, the first group detected significantly more errors.[23] One interpretation is that the belief they had control over the noise enabled members of the first group to withstand it better.

The qualities just described are not entirely independent. Events that are difficult to predict also tend to be difficult to control, for instance. Novelty, unpredictability, and lack of control may together indicate how *uncertain* a situation is. Presumably, the more uncertain, the more stressful events are.[24] Scales that measure these characteristics are discussed in the section on the use of instruments to measure stress.

Social Support

The stress of an event depends not only on certain characteristics and individual perceptions, but also on the availability of social support. The literature on social support suggests that friends and family reduce the impact of distressing events, although the findings have not been entirely uniform, due in part to incomplete definitions of social support. In many early studies researchers measured social support simply by counting the number of friends and family members available to a given individual. This approach did not take into account the nature or quality of such contacts. Their quality is important because a person who knows a large number of people only superficially might receive less support than an individual with a few close friends. It is now recognized that, in adequately measuring the effects of social support, the kinds of relationships available may be more important than the number of friends.

An example of this can be found in the work of Cutrona and Russell, who have investigated the relationship between various types of social support and stress. Their studies incorporated a scale that measures several dimensions of social support (see "The Use of Instruments To Measure Stress" below). Consistent with much of the literature, these researchers found that people with high overall levels of social support exhibited fewer physical and psychological problems in the aftermath of stress.[25] For instance, in a study of adolescent and adult new mothers, those with low levels of support were more likely to exhibit depression than were those with high levels of support.

The types of support most strongly associated with protection from depression were different in the two age groups. Support from friends was one of the best predictors of lower depression scores for adolescent mothers, whereas availability of guidance appeared to be more important for adult mothers. There was also evidence that the most effective kinds of support varied with the type of stress. Among the adult mothers, availability of guidance most powerfully correlated with reduced depression two weeks after delivery; however, eight weeks after delivery, the availability of friends with shared interests most powerfully correlated with reduced depression. The new mothers might have been intimidated by lack of knowledge at two weeks and therefore might have benefited most from guidance at that time. Six weeks later, however, the predominant stress might have changed to that of isolation from others and might have been most effectively offset by support from friends.

The relationships between social support and stress are complex. The type of support that is most strongly associated with protection from stress varies with a person's age as well as with the kind of stress. The amount of stress may also be a factor; some investigators have found that social support best counteracts stress when levels are low,[26] although others have found social support to be effective in high-stress situations like Three Mile Island.[27] The majority of researchers in this area have not followed subjects over time. Thus the extent to which changes in stress follow changes in social support is largely unknown. (Further discussion of these issues can be found in the "Social Support" section of the Suggested Readings.)

The Use of Instruments To Measure Stress

Stress instruments can be used in two major ways: (1) to determine the degree to which a new client is under stress and (2) to trace changes in stress through repeated administration to the same client.

The first signs of stress may take a number of forms. Clients may (a) state that they feel a lot of stress; (b) exhibit unusually frequent or severe negative emotions (such as frustration, anger, anxiety, and depression); and/or (c) suggest by tone of voice, manner of speech, sighing, or other behaviors that stress is present. Since none of these behavioral and verbal indicators is well standardized, it is appropriate to follow up such informal cues with validated questionnaires, interviews, and/or physiological measures.[28]

An important first principle is to use more than one method of assessment. Stress is a multilevel phenomenon, and no single measure can capture this complexity adequately.[29] Furthermore, every instrument has imperfections, and the use of several measures decreases the chance that the flaws of any one will result in an inaccurate assessment.

A second way to reduce the probability of errors is to use the measures more than once. Misleading scores caused by technical problems in physiological measures or the overhasty completion of questionnaires are more likely to be detected by subsequent measures that reveal them to be out of range for a particular client. These two principles will be restated more specifically in the discussion of physiological and self-report measures that follows.

Physiological Measures

Physiological measures of stress can be divided into two major categories. *Psychophysiological* measures include such responses as heart rate, blood pressure, and galvanic skin response. They are used in research and in clinical settings for biofeedback training (see "Stress Management" below). *Biochemical* measures include hormones and neurotransmitters like adrenaline and cortisol and are used primarily in research.

Physiological measures should be collected by trained individuals because of the measures' sensitivity to error. Small deviations in procedures may lead to erroneous readings. For instance, arm size can affect blood pressure measurement, and the manner in which biochemical assays are handled and stored may lessen their accuracy. An additional problem is that certain measures display cyclic variation. Cortisol, for instance, tends to be higher in the morning and lower in the evening among adults. Other factors, such as diet, medication, and phase of menstrual cycle can affect readings and make interpretation difficult.[30]

One solution to the instability of these measurements is repetition. With repeated measurement one can establish a baseline for each individual and try to screen out fluctuations not caused by stress. More than one measure is desirable, since they are not interchangeable—there is no single central physiological indicator of stress. Thus the use of a finger thermometer on one or two occasions to assess levels of stress is likely to be misleading.

Practitioners should not rely entirely on physiological indicators to measure stress, for they do not reveal specific events or thoughts that have initiated or exacerbated the process. Talking with clients informally can shed considerable light on the sources of stress, but the counselor should also obtain more systematic and complete information with standardized instruments.

Self-Report Measures of Stress

Questionnaires, often in the form of rating scales, are the most common way to measure stress, primarily because they require less time. Because interviews are more detailed and complete, some authors argue that they are worth the extra effort. Paykel, for example, who designed the Interview for Recent Life Events, provides evidence that subjects recall events more consistently and accurately with this interview than with life events scales.[31] Paykel's instrument takes between 30 and 90 minutes to administer, probably too long for many clinics. Because rating scales will probably be used in most settings, counselors should approach problems with clarity by making sure that the client understands all instructions. Answers that are unclear or suggest major problems should be discussed in detail.

It is important to choose instruments that are well designed and researched. Scales printed in popular magazines are not recommended because usually little information about their validity and few guidelines for their use are available. In contrast, scales published in research journals must pass minimum standards of reliability and validity and contain more detailed instructions. The measures discussed earlier in this chapter and described in more detail below have all been drawn from journals. An individual who is experienced in psychometric assessment should help select, administer, and interpret these measures.

Life Events. Major life events can be measured by instruments like the SRRS. It contains 43 items, each with a Life Change Unit score to indicate the degree of adjustment a particular event entails compared with a standard, marriage. "Death of spouse," for instance, is equivalent to 100 Life Change Units, whereas "minor violations of the law" has a value of 11. An individual's total score consists of the number of Life Change Units accrued over a specified time period (typically, the previous 6 or 12 months).

Another frequently used instrument is the Life Experiences Survey (LES), a 47-item rating scale on which subjects record events that have taken place over the previous 6 to 12 months.[32] Many of the items in the LES are similar to those in the SRRS, but their impact is rated differently. Each event on the LES is rated on a seven-point scale that ranges from "extremely positive" to "extremely negative." Thus the degree of impact is determined by the subject rather than by group ratings. The Negative Change Score, the sum of all negative ratings, is used most frequently; the Positive Change Score and Total Change Score, computed in parallel fashion, have been found to predict stress-related disorders less consistently. The LES is more useful than the SRRS for therapy because it includes information about clients' individual perception of each event. (Other life events measures are referenced in "Self-Report Measures of Stress" in the Suggested Readings.)

Hassles. Life events scales should be supplemented with a hassles measure because it offers additional information. The two types of scales in combination may predict stress-related outcomes more powerfully than either measure alone.[33] In addition, hassles are more likely to provide ideas for treatment than are major life events.[34] It is difficult to "treat" a life event like the death of a client's spouse, but the daily hassles that result from it, such as less regular meals, are more amenable to intervention.

The Hassles Scale consists of 117 items that have occurred within a recent time period, usually one month.[35] Some examples are "misplacing or losing things," "inconsiderate smokers," and "thoughts about death." Subjects indicate which events have taken place and rate their severity on a three-point scale. Two scores are usually computed, frequency (total number of hassles checked) and severity (sum of severity ratings); the latter score usually correlates with stress-related outcome more powerfully than the first.

Perceived Stress. A measure of perceived stress can provide a third source of information about a client's perception and interpretation of the environment. Such scales do not detail specific events, but instead emphasize feelings about and reactions to them. Cohen and his associates have developed the Perceived Stress Scale (PSS) to assess to what extent individuals view their lives as unpredictable, out of control, and overwhelming.[36] The PSS comes in both a 14-item and an abbreviated 4-item version. Subjects are asked to indicate, for instance, "In the last month, how often have you felt that you were unable to control the important things in your life?" and ". . . how often have you been upset because of something that happened unexpectedly?" Subjects respond on a five-point scale, which ranges from "very often" to "never," and the ratings are summed across all items to form a total stress score. Other measures of this type are available, but the PSS has one of the broadest research bases.[37] A measure of perceived stress gives the client an opportunity to report problems that may not appear on life events or hassles scales; some individuals report very little stress when confronted with a list of life events or hassles but indicate considerable stress on a perceived stress measure for that same time period.

Social Support. Social support is related to stress protection as well as better adherence to health care regimens such as weight reduction programs, although this conclusion is not firmly established.[38]

An example of a multidimensional approach to measuring social support can be found in the Social Provisions Scale of Cutrona and Russell.[39] Their instrument contains 24 items with which the rater indicates the availability of social support on four-point scales ranging from "completely true" to "not at all." Social support is grouped into six categories: *attachment* ("I feel a strong emotional bond with at least one other person"), *social integration* ("I feel part of a group of people who share my attitudes and beliefs"), *reassurance of worth* ("I have relationships where my competence and skill are recognized"), *opportunity for nurturance* ("I feel personally responsible for the well-being of another individual"), *reliable alliance* ("There are people I can count on in an emergency"), and *guidance* ("There is someone I could talk to about important decisions in my life").

Like physiological measures, rating scales are prone to error, and more confidence can be placed in them if they are used with a particular client more than once. In addition, periodic repetition of these scales is necessary to determine if changes in stress are followed by changes in clients' functioning. Because the amount of time required to complete them is not great, scales can be given repeatedly without undue inconvenience. As part of a research project, ten adults with high school or college educations completed the LES, the Hassles Scale, and the PSS. Total administration time averaged 15 minutes for all three scales, with a range of 8 to 27 minutes.

With repeated measurements, a life events scale need be administered only a few times a year because major events do not occur or change very often. Accuracy is optimal when the period of time that the client has to recall is six months or less.[40] Measures of hassles and perceived stress can be administered more frequently if desired; they typically require the client to rate the previous month. Social support scales can be repeated if major changes in support are suspected (such as following a divorce or a move to a new location).

The scales described in this chapter have been designed for general use. More specialized instruments exist for clients who work in a particular environment or who suffer from a specific disorder. Kanner, for instance, has designed the Diabetes Hassles Scale by modifying the original Hassles Scale and incorporating problems that are specific to diabetes.[41] In theory, such scales should pinpoint better the stressors that are most likely to occur in a given kind of client. One disadvantage of these measures is that they may be less thoroughly researched than more general stress instruments. Table 7-1 provides a summary of instruments to measure stress.

STRESS AND ILLNESS: GENERAL CONSIDERATIONS

Clinical experience supports the notion that stress and disease are connected. It is generally believed that certain forms of ulcers, hypertension, and migraine headaches are "stress-related." Stress has also been implicated in a variety of mental disorders, and a special category, "post-traumatic stress disorder" has been designated for individuals who manifest psychiatric disturbance as a result of exposure to war and other extreme conditions.[42] Unfortunately, precisely how stress contributes to illness remains a mystery. Hinkle states the problem as follows:

> That the relation of people to their society and to the people around them can influence the incidence, the prevalence, the course, and the mortality of diseases seems clear enough. The questions at issue are the questions of when they do so, under what circumstances, by what mechanisms, and to what extent. Precise answers to these questions will not be forthcoming without a great deal of scientific effort.[43]

Stress might contribute to physical and mental problems in two main ways. First, the presence of stress could cause or help cause a disorder. People often recall an unpleasant event that occurred shortly before a disease began. This anecdotal evidence can be misleading, however, and more systematic data are necessary to demonstrate an association between the two.

A second way that stress could contribute to disorders is by making them worse. Stress might, for example, cause an obese client to gain more weight or become more resistant to treatment. The possibility that stress could adversely affect an existing condition has important implications for clients with chronic disorders. When long-term clients experience stress, it may worsen their illness or their compliance with dietary and other health regimens.

Table 7-1 Self-Report Stress Instruments Discussed in the Chapter

Instrument	What the Scale Measures	Comments
Social Readjustment Rating Scale (SRRS)	Major life events	Uses group ratings No negative/positive rating Ratings cover several months
Life Experiences Survey (LES)	Major life events	Uses individual ratings Negative/positive ratings Ratings cover several months
Hassles Scale	Everyday events Emotions & thoughts	Ratings cover one month Best used with major events measure
Perceived Stress Scale (PSS)	Perceptions of recent past as unpredictable, uncontrollable, and overwhelming	Ratings cover one month Best used with major events and/or hassles measure
Social Provisions Scale	Six categories of social support	Should be repeated if support structure changes

Stress may make a disorder worse in two ways: through physiological mechanisms and through changes in behavior. Thus hypertensive clients might experience higher blood pressure under stress because (a) it contributed to their high blood pressure directly (physiologically) and (b) they took worse care of themselves by drinking more alcohol, eating more high-fat and high-sodium foods, and neglecting their medication.

Stress and disease most likely augment each other, especially when long timespans are involved.[44] For instance, anorexia might initially be partly a response to stressors like family conflict. Later on the illness itself might cause further stress by increasing the conflict. Thus each may increase the other, and the distinction between stressor and stress response may blur. Although these complex interactions seem plausible and square with clinical experience, they have rarely been documented because so few researchers have measured stress and illness over time.

STRESS AND ILLNESS: THE EXAMPLE OF DIABETES

This section is devoted to studies of the relationship between stress and diabetes, which will provide an illustration of the issues involved. Background information about diabetes is provided in Chapter 10. Investigations of stress in relation to other physical illness (such as heart disease and ulcers) and mental disorders (such as schizophrenia, depression, and post-traumatic stress syndrome) are listed in the Suggested Readings under "Stress and Illness."

Stress As a Cause of Diabetes

Although much of the research on stress and diabetes has dealt with the effects of stress on people who already have the disease, some investigations have addressed the possibility that stress might be a cause of diabetes. One source of evidence has come from case reports in which individuals with diabetes became diabetic after a traumatic event or period. Also, in some group studies individuals with diabetes have reported a history of more stress (such as family losses) than have individuals without diabetes.[45] Since these investigations rely on the recollection of sometimes distant events, distortions of memory are a potential problem. Moreover, not all investigators find evidence of greater stress among diabetics prior to their diagnosis.[46]

Although there is little direct evidence that stress causes either Type I or Type II diabetes, physiological data suggest that it may be a contributing factor in both disorders. Type I diabetes appears to be triggered by an autoimmune reaction to viruses in which the body attacks and destroys its own insulin-producing cells. Stress, because it affects the immune system, might influence its response to a virus and increase the likelihood of Type I diabetes. Experimental evidence on Type II diabetes suggests that heightened sympathetic nervous system sensitivity underlies some of its mechanisms. Because stress is intimately connected with sympathetic arousal, it may play an important role in the initiation or course of the disease.[47]

Stress As an Influence on Diabetic Control

This section and the following review evidence of the relationships between psychological stress, blood sugar control, and compliance among diabetics. The main measures of compliance discussed are dietary behaviors, because of their relevance to the nutrition counselor. Blood glucose and hemoglobin A_{1c}, a measure of blood sugar averaged over several weeks, are the primary measures of control. Laboratory and field studies are reviewed in turn.

Laboratory Studies

Stressors are capable of influencing blood sugar control physiologically. Studies of nondiabetic subjects have shown that blood glucose may rise in conjunction with stressors like parachute jumping.[48] These elevations are probably the result of hormones such as cortisol and epinephrine, which increase during stress and also affect glucose control.[49]

Among people who have diabetes, stressful physical conditions are known to influence the regulation of blood sugar. A cold, for example, can raise glucose levels and make their control more difficult. Laboratory investigations of psychological stressors have revealed a variety of reactions. In some studies, stressors have been followed by a rise in blood glucose. Baker and colleagues interviewed a preadolescent girl with Type I diabetes and deliberately discussed a topic that was a source of stress to her, as indicated by increases in corticoids, growth hormone, and epinephrine. Blood glucose levels rose considerably during the interview and for an hour afterwards.[50]

Other laboratory investigators have reported different findings. Carter and associates stressed 21 subjects with Type I diabetes by having them play the Pacman video game competitively. Blood glucose values went down rather than up in most individuals, although not to a statistically significant degree. In another study by the same researchers, 14 Type-I diabetics were given mental arithmetic to do for 20 minutes. Some subjects displayed a rise in blood sugar, others exhibited a fall, and still others showed no change at all. These individual differences were moderately consistent when the same procedures were repeated 12 weeks later.[51]

There are two major reasons laboratory studies have not revealed a consistent response pattern to psychological stressors. One is that the studies have not always been conducted properly or consistently. Some of the early investigators did not ascertain whether the subjects actually perceived the stressors as unpleasant. In addition, results from these early studies were not always tested statistically.[52] The timing of blood sugar readings has not been standardized, and a study in which timing was systematically varied indicated that it can alter results considerably.[53] Finally, subjects' blood sugar levels before exposure to the stressors were not always taken into account, an important consideration because prior levels bear on the amount of change that subsequently takes place.[54]

A second reason for the varied findings is that the blood sugar changes found in response to laboratory stressors may actually differ among subjects. That is, some diabetics may characteristically respond to stress with a rise in blood sugar, while others may respond to stress with a decline in blood sugar or with no change at all. One factor related to these individual differences is personality. Stabler and colleagues tested 13 diabetic children with a challenging video game accompanied by a loud timer and feedback that they weren't performing as well as expected.[55] The children had been previously classified as exhibiting either primarily Type A or Type B behavior on the basis of teacher ratings. Type A behavior is associated with extremes of competitiveness, aggression, and impatience and Type B behavior is associated with the relative absence of such characteristics.[56] In 5 of the 6 children classified as Type A, blood sugar went up during the video game. In 7 of the 8 children classified as Type B, however, blood sugars went down during the game. (See also "Stress and Personality" in the Suggested Readings.)

Field Studies

Laboratory findings suggest that stressors can produce short-term changes in blood sugar levels under controlled conditions. Field studies have also been conducted with stress questionnaires to determine whether this also holds true for stressors outside of the laboratory. Some investigators have reported small positive associations between stress scores and blood sugar values. Frenzel et al. for example, measured hemoglobin A_{1c} in 39 diabetic subjects, mostly Type I, and asked them to complete the Hassles Scale and the PSS.[57] The latter exhibited a significant but small positive correlation with hemoglobin A_{1c}. In similar fashion, several other researchers have obtained modest positive correlations between stress scales and blood sugar levels. The subjects in these studies who had the highest stress scores tended to have the highest average blood sugar levels.[58] Not every study has generated significant results, however.[59]

Stress As an Influence on Adherence

Data from field studies suggest that stress is associated not only with glucose control but also with self-care behaviors—that is, adherence with the diabetes regimen. In Frenzel et al.'s investigation, subjects kept track of their insulin injections and blood glucose testing, and most subjects monitored their food intake with a three-day diet record.[60] Scores on the Hassles Scale and PSS moderately correlated with the extent of calorie deviations, defined as the average daily difference between calories prescribed and calories consumed. However, deviations from recommended exchanges and meal times did not correlate with stress scores. In a second study, Hanson and associates investigated 39 adolescents at a diabetes camp.[61] Counselors unobtrusively monitored each subject's meals on hand-held charts and recorded the amount of food consumed. A nutrition counselor then calculated the caloric equivalents of each meal, and dietary adherence was expressed as the ratio of calories consumed to calories prescribed. This adherence measure correlated moderately with two hassles measures, again indicating an association between stress and dietary nonadherence. Schafer et al. found that stressful family interactions predicted low compliance with diet in Type I diabetics.[62] However, as with Frenzel et al.'s study, not every measure of dietary adherence in his studies correlated with family stress.

The data generated by field studies reviewed thus far suggest that at least part of the association between stress and blood sugar control may be due to a link between stress and the deterioration of dietary and other self-care behaviors. Part of stressors' effect on blood sugar, however, appears to be physiological and relatively independent of behavioral changes.[63]

One problem with these field investigations is that the measures used to assess adherence are sometimes quite vague and of dubious validity. In one study, for instance, dietary adherence was measured simply by asking patients the percentage of time during the previous three months that they remembered exceeding recommended caloric intake.[64] Also, most field investigations suffer from a drawback discussed earlier in this chapter—they do not indicate how changes in stressors are related to changes in compliance and blood sugar within individuals over time. The laboratory studies suggest that some diabetic individuals experience a drop, others a rise, and still others no change in blood sugars when exposed to stressors for several minutes. Whether this also occurs with chronic stressors over longer periods of time has yet to be determined.

Treatment of Stress in Diabetes

Because stress may increase blood sugar levels in some diabetics, lowering stress might reverse these effects. Several investigators have examined the effects of relaxation training, biofeedback, and other stress-reduction techniques (see "Stress Management"). The findings indicate that therapy sometimes leads to an improvement in glucose control. For example, Lammers et al. collected pretreatment blood sugar levels (Period 1) from four Type I diabetics, then gave them relaxation training (Period 2), withdrew treatment (Period 3), and later reinstated it (Period 4).[65] In comparisons of periods of no treatment (1 and 3) and periods of treatment (2 and 4), two of the four subjects showed decreases in daily blood glucose levels, although not all differences were significant. A more recent study is generally consistent with these findings.[66] Twenty-four patients with Type I diabetes were given either stress inoculation training (see "Stress Management") or no treatment for 5 weeks. Subjects in the experimental group exhibited a significant drop in hemoglobin A_{1c} between the 1st and 18th week of the study, whereas control subjects did not. The results were based on group statistics, and not every trained individual displayed this pattern. In addition, average blood sugars went up before they went down; hemoglobin A_{1c} was actually higher 5 weeks into the study than it was at the beginning.

Research by Surwit and Feinglos suggests that relaxation training may be more effective with Type II than with Type I diabetics. The investigators first trained six adults with Type II diabetes in relaxation and biofeedback techniques for five days; another group of six diabetics received no training.[67] Diabetic control was measured by a glucose tolerance test at the beginning of the study and one week later. Subjects in the relaxation group significantly improved on the glucose tolerance test; control subjects did not show any improvement.

In a subsequent study, ten adults with Type I diabetes followed a similar program of biofeedback-assisted relaxation.[68] No significant differences were found between the experimental and untrained subjects on glucose tolerance tests one week later or on hemoglobin A_{1c} after six weeks of daily relaxation practice.

Even if relaxation training does not reliably lower average blood glucose levels or improve glucose tolerance in Type I diabetics, it may still prove beneficial. In a study by Landis et al., five adults with Type I diabetes were given biofeedback training for several months.[69] As in Surwit and Feinglos' study, average daily blood glucose levels did not change significantly. However, the *range* of values decreased with training. That is, relaxation training reduced the frequency of extremely high and extremely low blood glucose levels. This finding, if replicated in other studies, could have important health implications, as both very high and very low blood sugar can be dangerous.

The literature reviewed above suggests that relaxation training can be useful for certain clients with diabetes. However, not all individuals respond to these procedures in the same way. The effects of training depend to some degree on the type of diabetes. In addition, other factors, such as personality, may play a role. Clinical experience suggests that some patients overreact to relaxation procedures with dangerously low sugar levels. Clearly, stress reduction is not appropriate for all clients and its effects should be carefully monitored.

STRESS MANAGEMENT

This section presents general issues in stress management and surveys a variety of approaches and techniques. The following material is not a "how-to" manual, and the reader is discouraged from using it to conduct therapy without the assistance of an experienced clinician. In addition, clients should not expect to treat themselves merely by reading self-help articles or books. Their effectiveness is often untested, readers often fail to follow through over extended periods, and in some instances such material may actually harm individuals.[70] Ethel Roskies, a noted stress researcher, examined four self-help stress books and concluded, "There is not a single one of these stress management guides that I can honestly recommend. . . . The two books presenting an array of stress management techniques are too vague or complex to be used on a do-it-yourself basis, and the two single-technique manuals are simplistic."[71]

Common Objectives and Underlying Mechanisms

Borkovec et al. and Cameron and Meichenbaum list several major objectives of stress management.[72] The first is to reduce daily tension levels and promote a sense of well-being in individuals who are functioning without much stress. Second, counselors can train clients to prepare for anticipated stressors by providing them with cognitive and behavioral skills; this approach is exemplified by the Lamaze childbirth program and by programs that prepare patients for surgery.[73] Third, stress management can be used to help individuals tolerate difficult situations, probably the most common application. Finally, these techniques can help people recover from distressing episodes more rapidly and completely by minimizing their aftereffects.

Although a considerable variety of stress management techniques are used to achieve the above objectives, they may all do so by activating the same physiological mechanisms. All of these techniques appear to reverse partially the physiological processes associated with stress. For example, cortisol, heart rate, blood pressure, and aldosterone have been found to decrease with autogenic training, progressive muscle relaxation, and biofeedback. These changes suggest that a decrease in sympathetic nervous system activity, a reduction in adrenocortical axis functions, and/or an increase in parasympathetic activity is taking place, the opposite of what is found in stress responses.[74] However, these findings do not occur in every study or in every client within a study. It should not be surprising that the physiological effects of stress reduction vary among individuals, as the physiology of stress itself varies from person to person.

General Approaches and Orientations

Problem-focused versus Emotion-focused. There are two major approaches to stress reduction. The first is to change one's environment—alter the stressor or reduce exposure to it—and the second is to change one's responses to the environment—alter reactions to a stressor. These two orientations are sometimes referred to, respectively, as problem focused and emotion or appraisal focused. "Emotion focused" is used broadly here to include techniques that modify a person's emotional, physiological, and cognitive reactions to stressors. Relaxation training and medication are examples of techniques that are largely emotion focused, designed to change the way a person responds to a stressor. Assertion training and time management are more problem focused, aimed toward modifying an environmental stressor (such as friends who persistently offer high-calorie foods, or a difficult work load). These two approaches are complementary rather than mutually exclusive, and most therapists teach clients to use both.

Emotion-focused and problem-focused strategies characterize not only techniques that are taught in therapy, but also techniques that people use on their own without training. The latter, sometimes referred to as coping style, consists of a blend of strategies that an individual characteristically uses when confronting stress, although it is not known how consistently.[75] Researchers have categorized coping styles in a number of different ways (such as problem versus emotion focused; approach versus avoidance),[76] and, as with all aspects of stress research, there is no final consensus on how best to measure it. Coping style can become an issue when teaching stress management techniques. The therapist may have to work within narrow limits if clients are rigid about the approaches they will consider because of their habitual coping styles. For example, an obese client may prefer to deal with stress by eating and exercising. If the nutrition counselor attempts to teach this individual to eat more balanced meals without addressing this desire to exercise, the client may resist treatment.

Group versus Individual Orientation. Although stress management techniques are often taught in individual therapy sessions, a number can be learned in group settings. Stress sometimes creates a sense of isolation, and the comradeship of working with others on shared problems may alleviate this feeling. Group sessions can also provide opportunities to perfect new techniques with role playing and feedback, which is especially useful for clients confronting the stress provided by long-term medical regimens. In a study by Kaplan and colleagues, a group of adolescents with diabetes identified social situations that made it difficult for them to comply with their diet and other parts of their regimen.[77] The subjects practiced skills (such as assertively refusing inappropriate food) for three weeks in group sessions with videotape to help them resist pressure from peers. Compared with subjects who received only medical information, the first group had significantly lower average blood sugars four months later, suggesting that dietary and other compliance had improved.

Specific Techniques

Different stress management approaches may have similar physiological effects, such as a decrease in sympathetic nervous system arousal, but they differ considerably in orientation and technique, as the survey below illustrates. The particular method chosen is based on the expertise and preferences of the therapist and the needs of the client.

Hypnosis, Relaxation, Meditation, and Biofeedback. All the methods in this section are used to train individuals to relax more deeply and to reduce their reactivity to stressors. They are considered together because of their similar techniques, mechanisms, and effects. Some of the common elements are:

- a quiet environment
- assumption of a reclining posture
- closed eyes
- deep, even breathing
- a stimulus to help concentration (such as a sound or image).[78]

Hypnosis, developed by the Austrian physician Mesmer, was used in surgery to reduce pain before chemical anesthetics became available in the 19th century. Hypnosis includes suggestions of sleepiness and relaxation as well as statements that encourage changes in behavior during or after the trance. It is rarely employed simply to relax an individual; usually other goals are involved, like altering perceptions (body image) or behavior (overeating).[79]

Progressive Muscle Relaxation (PMR) was developed by Jacobson in the 1920s. The client is taught to tense a series of muscle groups for several seconds and then relax them. Usually a therapist provides the initial training and periodic follow-up sessions. The client practices at home between sessions, often with audiotapes.[80]

Autogenic training was developed in Germany by Schultz at about the same time Jacobson was investigating PMR in the United States.[81] Instead of tensing muscle groups, the client listens to a series of statements, similar to hypnosis, that combine imagery with suggestions of peace and deep relaxation ("my mind is calm and quiet; my hands, my arms, and my shoulders feel heavy, relaxed, and comfortable").

Benson's *Respiratory One* Method and *Transcendental Meditation* (TM) are similar in procedure.[82] Both emphasize a short sound or word that is repeated silently in conjunction with controlled breathing. Proponents of TM maintain that the sound must be carefully tailored to each individual, whereas Benson believes that this is not necessary. Others forms of meditation, mostly based on Eastern religious traditions, also have been used but are less common in the West.

Biofeedback, developed in the early 1960s, consists of presenting subjects with readings of biological functions of which they are normally not aware. Heart rate, blood pressure, forehead muscle activity, and finger temperature are among the more common processes measured. Feedback can be in the form of a visual signal (a meter) or an auditory signal (a tone that varies in pitch). With practice, some individuals learn to exert control over the signals and, therefore, the functions they represent. Biofeedback is sometimes used in conjunction with other procedures (such as autogenic training).

With the possible exception of meditation, the techniques described above cause similar physiological changes.[83] These techniques also overlap considerably in their clinical effects. Controlled investigations of relaxation training, hypnosis, and biofeedback find them reasonably effective in alleviating stress-related disorders such as migraine headaches, asthma, insomnia, Raynaud's disease, and hypertension.[84] It is unclear whether one technique is superior to another in treating a specific condition; some reviewers find little evidence for this, while others argue that particular methods work best for particular disorders.[85]

Relaxation, meditation, and biofeedback have also been shown to reduce the reactivity of heart rate and blood pressure to stressors. However, the literature consists primarily of short-term laboratory demonstrations rather than long-term clinical trials. In addition, not all individuals or all studies show this response to training, and studies that have compared the abilities of different methods to reduce cardiovascular reactivity to stressors have failed to identify one particular technique as consistently superior.[86] There is also evidence that a subject's confidence in a particular technique plays a role in its effectiveness, and future investigators will have to show that these techniques include active ingredients that are separate from these effects of expectation alone.

Relaxation, meditation, and biofeedback are best conducted by an experienced health professional. This increases the probability that the client will learn the techniques properly and continue to practice them on a regular basis. The health professional should be familiar not only with the technical aspects of a procedure but also with its interpersonal ramifications. For example, clients sometimes undergo emotional distress (such as sudden crying or fears) during relaxation, and the instructor should have the expertise to help the client interpret and cope with these occurrences.

Exercise. Considerable enthusiasm has been generated over the potential benefits of exercise. However, the research has sometimes been based on comparisons between individuals who voluntarily chose to exercise and those who did not, making the results difficult to interpret because people in the two groups may have been different in a number of ways (in motivation and personality, for example). A second problem is that people who begin exercise regimens also make other positive changes in their lifestyle at the same time (change diet or meet new people), and the effects of these additional changes have generally not been separated from the effects of exercise itself.[87]

Exercise has been credited with improving morale, depression, and anxiety, but few systematic studies of its psychological effects exist.[88] The effects of exercise on physiological responses to stressors are better established. There is evidence that exercise reduces the degree or duration of heart rate increases to stress,[89] although other investigators disagree.[90] Aerobically fit subjects also respond to physical stress with less extreme blood pressure and fewer hormonal changes than do unfit individuals, but these differences as well have not appeared in every investigation.[91]

If exercise is incorporated as a part of stress management, a person trained in this area (such as a physical therapist) should establish an exercise regimen tailored to the particular client's abilities and goals. Subjects are more likely to comply if they are responsible to an individual who monitors them carefully. This is an important consideration because about half of the subjects who begin an exercise program drop out within a few months.[92]

Medication. Drugs are sometimes prescribed to help control stress as part of treatment for psychiatric disorders. Amitriptyline and other tricyclic antidepressants, for instance, have been used to calm depressed patients as well as improve their mood.

Medication also has been prescribed for stress management in individuals who are not psychiatrically disturbed. The benzodiazepines (for example, Valium and Librium) are among the more popular agents of this type. They are most effective for internal symptoms of stress (such as anxiety). As with all pharmacological agents, this class of drugs may produce side effects like weight gain, drowsiness, and heightened emotionality.[93]

Beta blockers (such as Propranalol) are a family of drugs that are especially suited for the control of physiological and behavioral responses to stressors (such as rapid heart beats and tremors).[94] Beta blockers have been used to help manage anxiety in athletes and other public performers. In a study of stage musicians, for example, Neftel gave subjects either placebo or the beta blocker atenolol.[95] Experimental subjects' pulse rates decreased relative to those on placebo. Independent ratings of the performance also indicated that the drug did not impair the quality of their playing.

Dietary Modification. Evidence suggests that caffeine and salt increase responsiveness to stressors. (See Chapters 9 and 12 for discussion of long-term consequences of caffeine and salt.)

Caffeine is contained in a number of foods, beverages, and prescription and over-the-counter medications. Because some individuals increase their use of coffee when they are experiencing stress, its potential to intensify reactions to stress is especially important.[96] A study conducted in 1979 suggests that 80 percent of adults in the United States drink coffee, most between one and three cups daily. Heavy use (defined as more than five cups or 525 milligrams per day) is found most frequently among middle-aged males.[97]

Caffeine's effects on physiology include an increase or a decrease in heart rate as well as a rise in blood pressure, cardiac output, epinephrine, and free fatty acids. These changes (with the exception of heart rate decreases) suggest that caffeine augments sympathetic nervous system activity.[98] Tolerance for caffeine varies considerably among individuals. Daily consumption in excess of six to nine milligrams per kilogram of body weight generally leads to physical dependence, characterized by physical and psychological symptoms (irritability, tiredness, and headaches) when caffeine is withdrawn.[99]

Most investigations of caffeine have been conducted in laboratories. In general, systolic and diastolic blood pressure responses to laboratory stressors (such as mental arithmetic) have been greater when subjects drink coffee than when they drink placebo. Individuals with a family history of heart trouble are especially likely to display this effect.[100]

Caffeine studies are limited in two ways. First, they usually do not consider coffee habits and tolerance to caffeine. The effects of subjects' having more coffee or less coffee than they are used to are therefore confused with the effects of caffeine itself. Second, stressors are usually laboratory stimuli rather than real-world events. A study by Pincomb et al. attempted to minimize both of these drawbacks.[101] The authors examined 20 male medical students, excluding infrequent coffee drinkers, during

finals week and during a week where no exams were given. Subjects were administered either 3.3. milligrams per kilogram of body weight of caffeine or placebo. Physiological measures taken at the beginning of each day and 40 minutes after drinking
coffee revealed that heart rate and systolic blood pressure were higher during exam
week than during the week of no exams, as might be expected. In addition, caffeine
decreased heart rate, increased diastolic and systolic blood pressure, and increased
cortisol and serum cholesterol levels. The effects of exams and caffeine on systolic
blood pressure were additive, and in combination they doubled the number of
subjects in the borderline hypertensive range. This investigation suggests that
caffeine amplifies the effects of psychological stressors on cardiovascular functioning
in some individuals. The nutrition counselor should keep these points in mind with
clients who (a) are undergoing stress, (b) display risk factors such as a family history of
cardiac problems, and (c) are judged to be consuming excessive amounts of coffee or
other sources of caffeine.

Data on the relationship between salt and reactivity to stressors among humans are
highly complex. Individual responses to dietary sodium vary considerably because of
differences in heredity and environment. In some subjects high salt intake is associated with increases in blood pressure; in other individuals, however, no response or
even the opposite pattern of reactions occurs.[102]

Sodium, like caffeine, increases sympathetic nervous system activity.[103] Investigators have demonstrated that salt intake increases reactivity to physical stressors (such
as norepinephrine infusion),[104] and there is evidence that reducing salt intake may
decrease such reactivity. In a study of medical students, Skrabel and colleagues examined cardiovascular responses to a physical and a mental stressor—norepinephrine
infusion and mental arithmetic.[105] Subjects who decreased their sodium intake to a
moderate degree and also increased their potassium intake over two weeks had
decreased blood pressure reactions to the stressors, but the diet also caused greater
heart rate reactivity. Another investigator reported reduced blood pressure and heart
rate responses to stress with restricted salt intake, but only among subjects whose
parents were hypertensive.[106] These complex data illustrate the need for more human
studies of sodium and stress reactivity. When confronted with a client who (a) shows
evidence of stress, (b) has a high salt intake, and (c) displays risk factors like borderline
hypertension or a family history of hypertension, the nutrition counselor may wish to
consider salt restriction on a trial basis.

Cognitive-Behavioral Therapy. This approach incorporates many of the techniques
described earlier. A cognitive-behavioral orientation, by definition, is an attempt to
change both the way clients perceive their environment and the way they behave. Just
as stress is measured more comprehensively with multiple than with single instruments, it is often better treated by multiple-technique than by single-technique
methods.[107]

Cameron and Meichenbaum's Stress Inoculation Training (SIT) procedures illustrate this approach.[108] Three phases are involved, but they are not always strictly
sequential since there is some back-and-forth movement among them.

In the first phase, therapist and client "collect data" about perceptions and behaviors. The purpose of this process is to help individuals think more scientifically about
themselves and the people with whom they interact. This process may challenge some
of the clients' most strongly held beliefs. Thus an adolescent with diabetes might be
convinced that friends won't like her unless she eats snacks with them. The therapist
could suggest that she test this notion by sticking to the dietary regimen and observing

friends' reactions or by asking friends how her regimen affects them. The client is thus taught to appraise herself and the environment more accurately by routinely testing hypotheses and revising them as evidence dictates.

In the second phase, the therapist teaches the client to behave in ways that decrease stress and increase the likelihood of achieving goals. Sometimes an individual lacks a skill and must acquire it. In other cases the person has the skill but is reluctant to use it because of inhibitions or misconceptions about its usefulness. Behaviors that are taught or encouraged in this phase may be problem focused or emotion focused. The adolescent with diabetes described above might be taught to refuse sweets assertively by practicing different ways to say no. In addition to this problem-focused approach, she might also be taught emotion-focused relaxation skills to reduce her anxiety when friends tease or harass her for not eating with them.

In the final phase of SIT, the client and therapist rehearse and implement the newly acquired skills. Initially, rehearsal may take place in a safe, controlled environment like the therapist's office. For example, the diabetic teenager who wishes to refuse snacks from friends might first practice by having the therapist offer her candy. Gradually, more realistic situations are rehearsed until the adolescent can perform the desired behaviors in their natural environment—among friends and family. Note the blend of approaches employed with this fictitious client: revising attitudes and hypotheses, relaxation training, assertion training, and behavioral rehearsal.

A high probability of success must be associated with each trial so that the client has a sense of effectiveness or self-efficacy. Theory and research suggest that individuals who believe they can accomplish a goal are in fact more likely to do so.[109] Table 7-2 includes a list of stress management techniques that summarizes the above discussion.

Stress Management and Compliance

Compliance is related to stress, and like stress, it is a complex topic. (See the "Patient Compliance" section of Suggested Readings.) A client who adheres to one part of a regimen (such as testing insulin) may not adhere to a different part (such as timing meals properly).[110] Even if one considers one area of self-care, such as nutrition, the various behaviors it subsumes do not always correlate highly with each other. Thus a diabetic child who adheres to recommended calories may not wait the proper amount of time between insulin injections and eating; a second child might display the opposite pattern of compliance.[111]

Compliance with an eating pattern is related to the amount of stress a client is experiencing. Some of this stress may stem from the eating pattern itself; the more complex a pattern is, the less likely an individual will adhere to it completely. Eating patterns that have to be followed for a long time also tend to elicit lower rates of adherence. Credibility is important; to the extent that nutritional recommendations are perceived as ineffective, a client is less likely to follow them. Finally, the cost of a regimen to clients, in terms of money, time, inconvenience, and embarrassment, may cause them to abandon it, even if it works.[112] The dietary characteristics associated with reduced compliance—complexity, difficulty, lack of perceived effectiveness, and cost—are features one might associate with any stressful event.

By reducing the stress associated with a dietary regimen, the nutrition counselor may be able to increase a client's adherence to it. Two aspects of stress, control and

Table 7-2 Stress Management Techniques

Technique	Primary Purpose
Hypnosis	Reduce physiological/cognitive stress responses
	Change behavior
Relaxation/Meditation/Biofeedback	Reduce physiological/cognitive stress response
Exercise	Decrease cardiovascular reactivity to stress
	Increase sense of well-being
Medication	Control emotion (e.g., anxiety) and behavioral (e.g., tremors) manifestations of stress
Dietary Modification (caffeine, salt)	Reduce physiological responsiveness to stressful events
Cognitive-Behavioral Therapy, e.g.: testing and revision of thoughts/-attitudes	Reduce unrealistic negative perceptions
Assertion training and Time management	Reduce stressful events by changing behavior
Relaxation training	Reduce physiological/cognitive stress response

information, are mentioned here as examples. Clients with a chronic disease may feel less stressed by a dietary regimen that gives them a sense of control and choice over food items. Some clients, however, are not capable of control or do not wish to assume it. In the research cited earlier on control, a small percentage of subjects actively displayed *more* stress when they had control than when they did not. In addition, in some situations most subjects prefer not to have control. In a reaction-time study, for instance, subjects were paired and told that one of them must respond quickly to a signal to avoid shock for both of them. Subjects who believed the partner could respond more quickly than they generally preferred to give the partner responsibility; individuals who believed they were faster than their partners preferred to keep control over the reaction task themselves.[113] Similarly, if a client believes the nutrition counselor is far better suited to making dietary decisions, then specific guidelines from the dietitian and a limited number of choices may reduce stress and bolster compliance. It may take a certain amount of trial and error to determine what blend of authoritative advice and collaboration works best for a specific client.

The point about control also holds true for information. In some circumstances, providing clients with abundant information about their regimen (such as physiological reasons why a particular eating pattern is best for them) may lessen stress and increase adherence,[114] but this is not universally true. In a study of oral surgery patients, subjects were classified as those who preferred a lot of information and those who coped by avoiding information.[115] They were then given either a problem-focused intervention or an emotion-focused intervention for their upcoming surgery. Better adjustment to the surgery and lower pain ratings occurred among individuals whose information-seeking styles matched the program they were given. That is, the problem-focused approach worked best with individuals who preferred information, and the emotion-focused approach worked best with individuals who avoided information. Subjects who avoided information were *more* distressed when they were offered a lot of information in the problem-focused program. Thus, as discussed earlier, counselors need to consider clients' coping styles when determining how much and at what rate to communicate information about their health regimens.

Brownell and associates have devised a series of cognitive-behavioral procedures aimed specifically at the problem of relapse and noncompliance.[116] Relapse is viewed as a part of most treatments rather than as an unusual occurrence caused by a poor therapist or poorly motivated client. The focus of their program is to prevent a single deviation from treatment, like going off a diet for one day, from snowballing into a total abandonment of therapy. Clients are taught to identify situations that increase the risk of noncompliance. For example, eating out and negative emotions (boredom or anger) may set the stage for inappropriate eating. Rehearsing such situations and utilizing cognitive and behavioral strategies may minimize the impact of such situations when they occur. Other components of this approach include (a) screening individuals at the beginning of treatment and admitting those who appear most highly motivated, (b) writing behavioral contracts to increase compliance, and (c) encouraging the maintenance of therapeutic gains with social support and the continued monitoring of problem behaviors. There is limited but encouraging evidence that this approach can improve adherence to stress management regimens such as exercise.[117]

CONCLUSION

The definition of stress is complex. Stressors can be physical or psychological; they range from annoying thoughts to major life events. Stress may last for a few minutes or persist over long periods of time; its consequences may be minor or serious. Stressors, stress responses, and consequences of stress are often difficult to untangle because they enhance each other in a reverberating fashion over time.

Stress is an interaction between client and environment; it occurs when a particular event strikes a particular vulnerability in an individual. The best known personal characteristics include biological predispositions, perceptions, and personality. Qualities of events that contribute to stress include pain, danger, novelty, lack of predictability, and lack of control. Characteristics of the general environment are also important. The availability of strong social support, for example, may lessen the stressfulness of events, whereas the simultaneous occurrence of several adverse conditions may increase their impact.

The term stress is misleading in the sense that many unrelated phenomena share the same name. The processes that are set in motion by exposure to extreme cold are not the same as those that result from marital conflict, although they probably share certain features. Despite the fact that stress is not a precisely defined or unitary phenomenon, it remains an important issue for the nutrition counselor. Clients with chronic diseases are prone to its influence, and their compliance with dietary regimens may suffer during stressful periods. The regimen itself needs to be viewed as a potential source of stress, especially when it places complex demands on a client.

It is hoped that this chapter has provided a starting point from which the nutrition counselor may pursue more information. A list of Suggested Readings, organized by topic, follows to assist this search.

NOTES

1. Hans Selye, "History and Present Status of the Stress Concept," in Leo Goldberger and Schlomo Breznitz, eds., *Handbook of Stress: Theoretical and Clinical Aspects* (New York: The Free Press, 1982), pp. 7, 14.

2. David S. Krantz, Stephen B. Manuck, and Rena R. Wing, "Psychological Stressors and Task Variables as Elicitors of Reactivity," in Karen A. Matthews et al., eds., *Handbook of Stress, Reactivity, and Cardiovascular Disease* (New York: John Wiley & Sons, 1986), pp. 95–99.

3. Richard J. Rose, "Familial Influences on Cardiovascular Reactivity to Stress," in Matthews et al., eds., *Handbook of Stress*, pp. 259–272; and Timothy W. Smith et al., "Blood Pressure Reactivity in Adult Male Twins," *Health Psychology* 6 (1987): 209–220.

4. Laurence O. Watkins and Elaine Eaker, "Population and Demographic Influences on Reactivity," in Matthews et al., eds., *Handbook of Stress*, pp. 234–240.

5. Redford B. Williams, Jr., "Patterns of Reactivity and Stress," in Ibid., pp. 109–125; and Neil Schneiderman and Philip M. McCabe, "Biobehavioral Responses to Stressors," in Tiffany M. Field, Philip M. McCabe, and Neil Schneiderman, eds., *Stress and Coping* (Hillsdale, N.J.: Lawrence Erlbaum Associates, 1985), pp. 14–16.

6. Sandra W. Elwood, H. Bruce Ferguson, and J. Thakar, "Catecholamine Response of Children in a Naturally Occurring Stressor Situation," *Journal of Human Stress* 12 (Winter 1986): 154–161.

7. Klaus A. Neftel et al., "Stage Fright in Musicians: A Model Illustrating the Effect of Beta Blockers," *Psychosomatic Medicine* 44 (1982): 461–469.

8. Thomas H. Holmes and Richard H. Rahe, "The Social Readjustment Rating Scale," *Journal of Psychosomatic Research* 11 (1967): 213–218.

9. George L. Engel, "Sudden and Rapid Death During Psychological Stress: Folklore or Folk Wisdom?" *Annals of Internal Medicine* 74 (1971): 771–782; Richard L. Gorsuch and Martha K. Key, "Abnormalities of Pregnancy as a Function of Anxiety and Life Stress," *Psychosomatic Medicine* 36 (1974): 352–362; Thomas H. Holmes and Minoru Masuda, "Life Change and Illness Susceptibility," in Barbara S. Dohrenwend and Bruce P. Dohrenwend, eds., *Stressful Life Events: Their Nature and Effects* (New York: John Wiley & Sons, 1974), pp. 45–72; and James E. Barrett, Robert M. Rose, and Gerald L. Klerman, eds., *Stress and Mental Disorder* (New York: Raven Press, 1979).

10. Daniel P. Mueller, Daniel W. Edwards, and Richard M. Yarvis, "Stressful Life Events and Psychiatric Symptomatology: Change as Undesirability," *Journal of Health and Social Behavior* 18 (1977): 307–317. There is still controversy over the advantages of group versus individual ratings.

11. Amiram Vinokur and Melvin L. Selzer, "Desirable Versus Undesirable Life Events: Their Relationship to Stress and Mental Distress," *Journal of Personality and Social Psychology* 32 (1975): 329–337; D. G. Byrne and H. M. Whyte, "Life Events and Myocardial Infarction Revisited: The Role of Measures of Individual Impact," *Psychosomatic Medicine* 42 (1980): 1–10; and Antonette M. Zeiss, "Aversiveness Versus Change in the Assessment of Life Stress," *Journal of Psychosomatic Research* 24 (1980): 15–19.

12. Allen D. Kanner et al., "Comparison of Two Modes of Stress Measurement: Daily Hassles and Uplifts Versus Major Life Events," *Journal of Behavioral Medicine* 4 (1981): 3.

13. Anita DeLongis et al., "Relationship of Daily Hassles, Uplifts, and Major Life Events to Health Status," *Health Psychology* 1 (1982): 119–136; and Ibid., pp. 18–19.

14. Scott Monroe, "Major and Minor Life Events as Predictors of Psychological Distress: Further Issues and Findings," *Journal of Behavioral Medicine* 6 (1983): 189–205.

15. Anita DeLongis, Susan Folkman, and Richard S. Lazarus, "Hassles, Health, and Mood: A Prospective Study with Repeated Daily Assessments," *Journal of Personality and Social Psychology*, in press.

16. See Igor Grant et al., "Life Events and Symptoms: Fourier Analysis of Time Series from a Three-Year Prospective Inquiry," *Archives of General Psychiatry* 39 (1982): 598–605.

17. For a more detailed account, see Susan Folkman, Catherine Schaefer, and Richard S. Lazarus, "Cognitive Processes as Mediators of Stress and Coping," in Vernon Hamilton and David M. Warburton, eds., *Human Stress and Cognition* (Chichester, U.K.: John Wiley & Sons,

1979), pp. 265–298; see also Richard S. Lazarus and Susan Folkman, *Stress, Appraisal, and Coping* (New York: Springer Publishing Co., 1984).

18. Randolf J. Paterson and Richard W. J. Neufeld, "Clear Danger: Situational Determinants of the Appraisal of Threat," *Psychological Bulletin* 101 (1987): 404–416.

19. Seymour Levine, "Cortisol Changes Following Repeated Experiences with Parachute Training," in Holger Ursin, Eivind Baade, and Seymour Levine, eds., *Psychobiology of Stress: A Study of Coping Men* (New York: Academic Press, 1978), pp. 51–56.

20. Lawrence S. Gaines, Barry D. Smith, and Brett E. Skolnick, "Psychological Differentiation, Event Uncertainty, and Heart Rate," *Journal of Human Stress* 3 (September 1977): 11–25.

21. Suzanne M. Miller, "Why Having Control Reduces Stress: If I Can Stop the Roller Coaster, I Don't Want to Get Off," in Judy Garber and Martin E. P. Seligman, eds., *Human Helplessness* (New York: Academic Press, 1980), pp. 71–95.

22. James H. Greer, Gerald C. Davison, and Robert I. Gatchel, "Reduction of Stress in Humans through Nonveridical Perceived Control of Aversive Stimulation," *Journal of Personality and Social Psychology* 16 (1970): 731–738.

23. David C. Glass and Jerome E. Singer, *Urban Stress: Experiments on Noise and Social Stressors* (New York: Academic Press, 1972), pp. 64–69.

24. David V. Perkins, "The Assessment of Stress Using Life Events Scales," in Goldberger and Breznitz, eds., *Handbook of Stress*, p. 324; Miller, "Why Having Control Reduces Stress," pp. 72–75; and Folkman, Schaefer, and Lazarus, "Cognitive Processes," pp. 276–282.

25. Carolyn E. Cutrona, "Social Support and Stress in the Transition to Parenthood," *Journal of Abnormal Psychology* 93 (1984): 378–390; and Cutrona and Daniel W. Russell, "The Provisions of Social Relationships and Adaptation to Stress," in W. H. Jones and D. Perlman, eds., *Advances in Personal Relationships,* vol I (Greenwich, Conn: JAI Press, 1987), pp. 37–67.

26. Cutrona, "Social Support and Stress," p. 384.

27. Raymond Fleming et al., "Mediating Influences of Social Support on Stress at Three Mile Island," *Journal of Human Stress* 8 (1982): 14–22.

28. See Donald P. Spence, "Verbal Indicators of Stress," in Goldberger and Breznitz, eds., *Handbook of Stress,* pp. 295–305.

29. Lee J. Cronbach and Paul E. Meehl, "Construct Validity in Psychological Tests," in Herbert Feigl and Michael Scriven, eds., *Minnesota Studies in the Philosophy of Science:* vol. I. *The Foundations of Science and Concepts of Psychology and Psychoanalysis* (Minneapolis: University of Minnesota Press, 1955), pp. 174–204.

30. David S. Goldstein, "Biochemical Indices of Cardiovascular Reactivity," in Matthews et al., eds., *Handbook of Stress*, pp. 187–190; and Seymour Levine and Christopher L. Coe, "The Use and Abuse of Cortisol as a Measure of Stress," in Field, McCabe, and Schneiderman, eds., *Stress and Coping*, pp. 149–158.

31. Eugene S. Paykel, "Methodological Aspects of Life Events Research," *Journal of Psychosomatic Research* 22 (1983): 342–343.

32. Irwin G. Sarason, James H. Johnson, and Judith M. Siegel, "Assessing the Impact of Life Changes: Development of the Life Experiences Survey," *Journal of Consulting and Clinical Psychology* 46 (1978): 932–946.

33. Monroe, "Major and Minor Life Events."

34. DeLongis et al., "Relationships," pp. 133–134.

35. Kanner et al., "Comparison of Two Modes of Stress Measurement," p. 3.

36. Sheldon Cohen, Tom Kamarck, and Robin Mermelstein, "A Global Measure of Perceived Stress," *Journal of Health and Social Behavior* 24 (1983): 385–396.

37. Margaret W. Linn, "A Global Assessment of Recent Stress (GARS) Scale," *International Journal of Psychiatry in Medicine* 15 (1985–86): 47–59.

38. Kelly D. Brownell et al., "Understanding and Preventing Relapse," *American Psychologist* 41 (July 1986): 771; and Rona L. Levy, "Social Support and Compliance: Salient Methodological Problems in Compliance Research," *Journal of Compliance in Health Care* 1 (1986): 189–198.

39. Cutrona and Russell, "The Provisions of Social Relationships."

40. C. David Jenkins, Michael W. Hurst, and Robert M. Rose, "Life Changes: Do People Really Remember?" *Archives of General Psychiatry* 36 (1979): 379–384.

41. Allen D. Kanner, personal communication, 1987.

42. *Diagnostic and Statistical Manual of Mental Disorders* (Washington, D.C.: American Psychiatric Association, 1987), pp. 247–251.

43. Lawrence E. Hinkle, "The Concept of 'Stress' in the Biological and Social Sciences," *Science, Medicine and Man* 1 (1973): 47.

44. Richard A. Depue and Scott M. Monroe, "Conceptualization and Measurement of Human Disorder in Life Stress Research: The Problem of Chronic Disturbance," *Psychological Bulletin* 99 (1986): 45–47.

45. For example, Stefan D. Stein and Edward Charles, "Emotional Factors in Juvenile Diabetes Mellitus: A Study of Early Life Experiences of Adolescent Diabetics," *American Journal of Psychiatry* 128 (1971): 700–704.

46. Michael F. Koch and George D. Molnar, "Psychiatric Aspects of Patients with Unstable Diabetes Mellitus," *Psychosomatic Medicine* 36 (1974): 57–68.

47. Richard S. Surwit and Mark N. Feinglos, "Stress and Autonomic Nervous System in Type II Diabetes: A Hypothesis," *Diabetes Care* 11 (January 1988): 83–85.

48. Rolf Eide and Anna Atteras, "Blood Glucose," in Ursin, Baade, and Levine, eds., *Psychobiology of Stress*, pp. 99–103.

49. Harry Shamoon, Vijay R. Soman, and Robert S. Sherwin, "The Influence of Acute Physiological Increments of Cortisol on Fuel Metabolism and Insulin Binding to Monocytes in Normal Humans," *Journal of Clinical Endocrinology and Metabolism* 50 (1980): 495–501; Vijay R. Soman, Harry Shamoon, and Robert S. Sherwin, "Effects of Physiological Infusion of Epinephrine in Normal Humans: Relationship between the Metabolic Response and B-Adrenergic Binding," *Journal of Clinical Endocrinology and Metabolism* 50 (1980): 294–297; and P. Barglow et al., "Stress and Metabolic Control in Diabetes: Psychosomatic Evidence and Evaluation of Methods," *Psychosomatic Medicine* 46 (1984): 129–132.

50. Lester Baker et al., "Beta Adrenergic Blockade and Juvenile Diabetes: Acute Studies and Long-Term Therapeutic Trial," *Journal of Pediatrics* 75 (1969): 19–29.

51. William R. Carter et al., "Effect of Stress on Blood Glucose in IDDM," *Diabetes Care* 8 (July–August 1985): 411–412.

52. Patrick Lustman, Robert Carney, and Henry Amado, "Acute Stress and Metabolism in Diabetes," *Diabetes Care* 4 (November–December 1981): 658–659.

53. Rena R. Wing et al., "Psychologic Stress and Blood Glucose Levels in Nondiabetic Subjects," *Psychosomatic Medicine* 47 (November–December 1985): 558–564.

54. Carter et al., "Effect of Stress on Blood Glucose."

55. B. Stabler et al., "Differential Glycemic Response to Stress in Type A and Type B Individuals with IDDM," *Diabetes Care* 9 (September–October 1986): 550–552.

56. Ray H. Rosenman and Margaret A. Chesney, "Type A Behavior Pattern: Its Relationship to Coronary Heart Disease and its Modification by Behavioral and Pharmacological Approaches," in Michael R. Zales, ed., *Stress in Health and Disease* (New York: Brunner/Mazel, 1985), pp. 208–210.

57. Mary P. Frenzel et al., "The Relationship of Stress and Coping to Regimen Adherence and Glycemic Control of Diabetes," *Journal of Social and Clinical Psychology,* in press.

58. Stephanie L. Hanson and James W. Pichert, "Perceived Stress and Diabetes Control in Adolescents," *Health Psychology* 5 (1986): 439–452; Daniel J. Cox et al., "The Relationship between Psychological Stress and Insulin-Dependent Diabetic Blood Glucose Control: Preliminary Investigations," *Health Psychology* 3 (1984): 63–75; Mark Peyrot, personal communication, 1986; Cindy L. Hanson, Scott W. Henggeler, and George A. Burghen, "Model of Associations Between Psychosocial Variables and Health-Outcome Measures of Adolescents with IDDM," *Diabetes Care* 10 (November–December 1987): 752–758; and Hanson, Henggeler, and Burghen, "Social Competence and Parental Support as Mediators of the Link between Stress and Metabolic Control in Adolescents with Insulin-Dependent Diabetes Mellitus," *Journal of Consulting and Clinical Psychology* 55 (1987): 529–533.

59. Daniel J. Cox, L. K. Berke, and S. Bobbit, "Psychological Stress: Adherence, Social Support and Type II Control," *Diabetes* 33 (1984): 100A.

60. Nedra K. Christensen et al., "Quantitative Assessment of Dietary Adherence with Patients with Insulin-Dependent Diabetes Mellitus," *Diabetes Care* 6 (May–June 1983): 245–250.

61. Hanson and Pichert, "Perceived Stress and Diabetes Control."

62. Lorraine C. Schafer et al., "Adherence to IDDM Regimens: Relationship to Psychological Variables and Metabolic Control," *Diabetes Care* 6 (September–October 1983): 493–498; and Schafer, Kevin D. McCaul, and Russell E. Glasgow, "Supportive and Nonsupportive Family Behaviors: Relationships to Adherence and Metabolic Control in Persons with Type I Diabetes," *Diabetes Care* 9 (March–April 1986): 179–185.

63. Hanson and Pichert, "Perceived Stress," pp. 447–448; Cox et al., "Relationship," pp. 68–69; Mark F. Peyrot and J. F. McMurray, "Behavioral and Psychophysiological Effects of Stress on Glucose Control," *Diabetes* 35 (May 1986): 21A; Hanson, Henggeler, and Burghen, "Model of Associations"; and Hanson, Henggeler, and Burghen, "Social Competence and Parental Support."

64. W. Wilson et al., "Psychological Predictors of Self-Care Behaviors (Compliance) and Glycemic Control in Non-Insulin-Dependent Diabetes Mellitus," *Diabetes Care* 9 (November–December 1986): 616–617.

65. Craig A. Lammers, Bruce D. Naliboff, and Alvin J. Straatmeyer, "The Effects of Progressive Relaxation on Stress and Diabetic Control," *Behaviour Research and Therapy* 22 (1984): 641–650.

66. Kevin V. Amory, Barry H. Ginsberg, and Eric T. Hillerbrand, "The Effect of Stress Inoculation Training Procedures on the Control of Blood Glucose and Stress Levels in Individuals with Diabetes Mellitus," unpublished manuscript, 1987.

67. Richard S. Surwit and Mark N. Feinglos, "The Effects of Relaxation on Glucose Tolerance in Non-Insulin-Dependent Diabetes," *Diabetes Care* 6 (March–April 1983): 176–179.

68. Mark N. Feinglos, Priscilla Hastedt, and Richard S. Surwit, "Effects of Relaxation Therapy on Patients with Type I Diabetes Mellitus," *Diabetes Care* 10 (January–February 1987): 72–75.

69. Bernard Landis et al., "Effect of Stress Reduction on Daily Glucose Range in Previously Stabilized Insulin-dependent Diabetic Patients," *Diabetes Care* 8 (November–December 1985): 624–626.

70. Gerald Rosen, "Self-Help Treatment Books and the Commercialization of Psychotherapy," *American Psychologist* 42 (1987): 46–51.

71. Ethel Roskies, "Stress Management: Averting the Evil Eye," in Alan Monat and Richard S. Lazarus, eds., *Stress and Coping* (New York: Columbia University Press, 1985), p. 377.

72. Thomas D. Borkovec, M. C. Johnson, and D. L. Block, "Evaluating Experimental Designs in Relaxation Training," in Robert L. Woolfolk and Paul M. Lehrer, eds., *Principles and Practice of Stress Management* (New York: Guilford Press, 1984), pp. 397–398; and Roy Cameron and Don Meichenbaum, "The Nature of Effective Coping and the Treatment of Stress

Related Problems: A Cognitive-Behavioral Perspective," in Goldberger and Breznitz, eds., *Handbook of Stress*, p. 698.

73. Judith K. Wells et al., "Presurgical Anxiety and Postsurgical Pain and Adjustment: Effects of a Stress Inoculation Procedure," *Journal of Consulting and Clinical Psychology* 54 (1986): 831–835.

74. Richard S. Surwit, "Pharmacologic and Behavioral Modulators of Cardiovascular Reactivity: An Overview," in Matthews et al., eds., *Handbook of Stress*, pp. 395–398.

75. Rudolf H. Moos and Andrew G. Billings, "Conceptualizing and Measuring Coping Resources and Processes," in Goldberger and Breznitz, eds., *Handbook of Stress*, pp. 212–230.

76. Susan Roth and Lawrence J. Cohen, "Approach, Avoidance, and Coping with Stress," *American Psychologist* 41 (July 1986): 813–819.

77. Robert M. Kaplan, Michele W. Chadwick, and Leslie E. Schimmel, "Social Learning Intervention to Promote Metabolic Control in Type I Diabetes Mellitus: Pilot Experiment Results." *Diabetes Care* 8 (March–April 1985): 152–155.

78. Michael Feuerstein, Elise E. Labbe, and Andrzej R. Kuczmierczyk, *Health Psychology: A Psychobiological Perspective* (New York: Plenum, 1986), p. 189.

79. A review of this technique can be found in Theodore X. Barber, "Hypnosis, Deep Relaxation, and Active Relaxation: Data, Theory, and Clinical Applications," in Woolfolk and Lehrer, eds., *Principles and Practice of Stress Management*, pp. 142–187.

80. Douglas A. Bernstein and Thomas D. Borkovec, *Progressive Relaxation Training: A Manual for the Helping Professions* (Champaign, Ill.: Research Press, 1973); and F. J. McCuigan, "Progressive Relaxation: Origins, Principles, and Clinical Applications," in Woolfolk and Lehrer, eds., *Principles and Practice of Stress Management*, pp. 12–42.

81. Elmore Green et al., "Autogenic Feedback Training," *Psychotherapy & Psychosomatics* 25 (1975): 88–98.

82. Herbert Benson, *The Relaxation Response* (New York: William Morrow, 1975).

83. Rolf G. Jacob and Margaret A. Chesney, "Psychological and Behavioral Methods to Reduce Cardiovascular Reactivity," in Matthews et al., eds., *Handbook of Stress*, pp. 423–427.

84. See Steven Fahrion et al., "Biobehavioral Treatment of Essential Hypertension: A Group Outcome Study," *Biofeedback and Self-Regulation* 11 (1986): 257–277.

85. Surwit, "Pharmacologic and Behavioral Modulators," pp. 387–394; and Paul M. Lehrer and Robert L. Woolfolk, "Are Stress Reduction Techniques Interchangeable, or Do They Have Specific Effects?: A Review of the Comparative Empirical Literature," in Woolfolk and Lehrer, eds., *Principles and Practice of Stress Management*, pp. 404–477.

86. A good review of this topic is contained in Jacob and Chesney, "Psychological and Behavioral Methods."

87. Joel E. Dimsdale, Bruce S. Alpert, and Neil Schneiderman, "Exercise as a Modulator of Cardiovascular Reactivity," in Matthews et al., eds., *Handbook of Stress*, pp. 369, 377.

88. Ibid., pp. 366–371.

89. David Sinyor et al., "Aerobic Fitness Level and Reactivity to Psychological Stress: Physiological, Biochemical, and Subjective Measures," *Psychosomatic Medicine* 45 (1983): 205–217.

90. John Jamieson and Norman Lavoie, "Type A Behavior, Aerobic Power, and Cardiovascular Recovery from a Psychological Stressor," *Health Psychology* 6 (1987): 361–371.

91. Francois Peronnet et al., "Plasma Norepinephrine Response to Exercise before and after Training in Humans," *Journal of Applied Physiology: Respiratory Environmental and Exercise Physiology* 51 (1981): 812–815; and Peter Seraganian et al., "Failure to Alter Psychophysiological Reactivity in Type A Men with Physical Exercise or Stress Management Programs," *Psychology and Health* 1 (1987): 195–213.

92. Rodney K. Dishman, "Prediction of Adherence to Habitual Physical Activity," in Francis J. Nagle and Henry J. Montoye, eds., *Exercise in Health and Disease* (Springfield, Ill.: Charles C Thomas, 1981), p. 260.

93. M. Lader, "Pharmacological Methods," in Woolfolk and Lehrer, eds., *Principles and Practice of Stress Management,* pp. 312–323.

94. "Beta Adrenergic Blockers for Anxiety," *Medical Letter* 26 (1984): 61–63.

95. Neftel et al., "Stage Fright in Musicians."

96. Terry L. Conway et al., "Occupational Stress and Variation in Cigarette, Coffee, and Alcohol Consumption," *Journal of Health and Social Behavior* 22 (1981): 155–165.

97. Gordon S. Bonham and Paul E. Leaverton, "Use Habits Among Adults of Cigarettes, Coffee, Aspirin, and Sleeping Pills," *Vital and Health Statistics,* Series 10, No. 31, DHEW Publication No. PHS 80-1599 (Washington, D.C.: U.S. Government Printing Office, 1980).

98. David Shapiro, James D. Lane, and James P. Henry, "Caffeine, Cardiovascular Reactivity, and Cardiovascular Disease," in Matthews et al., eds., *Handbook of Stress,* pp. 312–318.

99. R. M. Gilbert et al., "Caffeine Content of Beverages as Consumed," *Canadian Medical Association Journal* 114 (1976): 205–208.

100. Shapiro, Lane, and Henry, "Caffeine, Cardiovascular Reactivity, and Cardiovascular Disease," pp. 318–321.

101. Gwendolyn A. Pincomb et al., "Caffeine Enhances the Physiological Response to Occupational Stress in Medical Students," *Health Psychology* 6 (1987): 101–112.

102. Bonita Falkner and Kathleen C. Light, "The Interactive Effects of Stress and Dietary Sodium on Cardiovascular Reactivity," in Matthews et al., eds., *Handbook of Stress,* pp. 329–332.

103. M. Gary Nicholls et al., "Plasma Norepinephrine Variations with Dietary Sodium Intake," *Hypertension* 2 (1980): 29–32.

104. See Lara I. Rankin et al., "Sodium Intake Alters the Effects of Norepinephrine on Blood Pressure," *Hypertension* 3 (1981): 650–656.

105. F. Skrabel, J. Auboeck, and H. Hortnaegl, "Low Sodium–High Potassium Diet for Prevention of Hypertension: Probable Mechanisms of Action," *Lancet* 2 (October 24, 1981): 895–900.

106. Bonita Falkner, Gaddo Onesti, and Evangelos Angelakos, "Effect of Salt Loading on the Cardiovascular Response to Stress in Adolescents," *Hypertension* 3 (1981, Supplement II): 195–199.

107. Leonard I. Pearlin and Carmi Schooler, "The Structure of Coping," *Journal of Health and Social Behavior* 19 (1978): 2–21.

108. Cameron and Meichenbaum, "The Nature of Effective Coping," pp. 695–710.

109. Albert Bandura, "Self-Efficacy: Toward a Unifying Theory of Behavior Change," *Psychological Review* 84 (1977): 191–215; and "Self-Efficacy in Human Agency," *American Psychologist* 37 (1982): 122–147.

110. Russell E. Glasgow, Willetta Wilson, and Kevin D. McCaul, "Regimen Adherence: A Problematic Construct in Diabetes Research," *Diabetes Care* 8 (May–June 1985): 300–301; and Glasgow, McCaul, and Lorraine C. Schafer, "Self-Care Behaviors and Glycemic Control in Type I Diabetes," *Journal of Chronic Diseases* 40 (1987): 399–412.

111. Suzanne Bennett Johnson et al., "Assessing Daily Management in Childhood Diabetes," *Health Psychology* 5 (1986): 552–557.

112. M. Robin DiMatteo and D. Dante DiNicola, *Achieving Patient Compliance* (New York: Pergamon Press, 1982), pp. 127–138.

113. Miller, "Why Having Control Reduces Stress," pp. 88–95.

114. Wells et al., "Presurgical Anxiety."

115. Michael F. Martelli et al., "Stress Management in the Health Care Setting: Matching Interventions with Patient Coping Styles," *Journal of Consulting and Clinical Psychology* 55 (1987): 201–207.

116. Brownell et al., "Understanding and Preventing Relapse," pp. 765–782.

117. Marc Belisle, Ethel Roskies, and Jean-Michel Levesque, "Improving Adherence to Physical Activity," *Health Psychology* 6 (1987): 159–172.

SUGGESTED READINGS

General References

Baum, Andrew, and Singer, Jerome, eds. *Handbook of Psychology and Health.* Vol. 5, *Stress.* Hillsdale, N.J.: Lawrence Erlbaum Associates, 1987.

Feuerstein, Michael; Labbe, Elise E.; and Kuczmierczyk, Andrzej R. *Health Psychology: A Psychobiological Perspective,* pp. 95–236. New York: Plenum Press, 1986.

Field, Tiffany M.; McCabe, Philip M.; and Schneiderman, Neil, eds. *Stress and Coping.* Hillsdale, N.J.: Lawrence Erlbaum Associates, 1985.

Fleming, Raymond; Baum, Andrew; and Singer, Jerome E. "Toward an Integrative Approach to the Study of Stress." *Journal of Personality and Social Psychology* 46 (1984): 939–949.

Goldberger, Leo, and Breznitz, Schlomo, eds. *Handbook of Stress: Theoretical and Clinical Aspects.* New York: Free Press, 1982.

Health Psychology (journal). Hillsdale, N.J.: Lawrence Erlbaum Associates.

Journal of Human Stress. Washington, D.C.: Heldref Publications.

Matthews, Karen A. et al., eds. *Handbook of Stress, Reactivity, and Cardiovascular Disease.* New York: John Wiley & Sons, 1986.

Monat, Alan, and Lazarus, Richard S., eds. *Stress and Coping.* 2d ed. New York: Columbia University Press, 1985.

Psychology and Health (journal). London: Harwood Academic Publishers.

Psychosomatic Medicine (journal). New York: Elsevier Publishing.

Conceptualization of Stress

Eisdorfer, Carl. "The Conceptualization of Stress and a Model for Further Study." In *Stress in Health and Disease,* edited by Michael R. Zales. New York: Brunner/Mazel, 1985.

Engel, Bernard T. "Stress is a Noun! No, a Verb! No, an Adjective!" In *Stress and Coping,* edited by Tiffany M. Field, Philip M. McCabe, and Neil Schneiderman. Hillsdale, N.J.: Lawrence Erlbaum Associates, 1985.

Hinkle, Lawrence E. "The concept of 'Stress' in the Biological and Social Sciences." *Science, Medicine, and Man* 1 (1973): 31–48.

Weiner, Herbert. "The Concept of Stress in the Light of Studies on Disasters, Unemployment, and Loss: A Critical Analysis." In *Stress in Health and Disease. See* Eisdorfer.

Physiological Measures of Stress

Baum, Andrew; Grunberg, Neil E.; and Singer, Jerome E. "The Use of Psychological and Neuroendocrinological Measurements in the Study of Stress." *Health Psychology* 1 (1982): 217–236.

Goldstein, David S., and McDonald, Robert H. "Biochemical Indices of Cardiovascular Reactivity." In *Handbook of Stress, Reactivity, and Cardiovascular Disease,* edited by Karen A. Matthews et al. New York: John Wiley & Sons, 1986.

Schneiderman, Neil, and McCabe, Philip M. "Biobehavioral Responses to Stressors." In *Stress and Coping,* edited by Tiffany M. Field, Philip M. McCabe, and Neil Schneiderman. Hillsdale, N.J.: Lawrence Erlbaum Associates, 1985.

Self-Report Measures of Stress

Cohen, Sheldon; Kamarck, Tom; and Mermelstein, Robin. "A Global Measure of Perceived Stress." *Journal of Health and Social Behavior* 24 (1983): 385–396.

Depue, Richard A., and Monroe, Scott M. "Conceptualization and Measurement of Human Disorder in Life Stress Research: The Problem of Chronic Disturbance." *Psychological Bulletin* 99 (1986): 36–51.

Derogatis, Leonard R. "Self-Report Measures of Stress." In *Handbook of Stress: Theoretical and Clinical Aspects,* edited by Leo Goldberger and Schlomo Breznitz. New York: The Free Press, 1982.

Dohrenwend, Bruce P., and Shrout, Patrick E. "'Hassles' in the Conceptualization and Measurement of Life Stress Variables." *American Psychologist* 40 (July 1985): 780–785.

Holmes, Thomas H., and Rahe, Richard H. "The Social Readjustment Rating Scale." *Journal of Psychosomatic Research* 11 (1967): 213–218.

Kanner, Allen D. et al. "Comparison of Two Modes of Stress Measurement: Daily Hassles and Uplifts Versus Major Life Events." *Journal of Behavioral Medicine* 4 (1981): 1–39.

Lazarus, Richard S. et al. "Stress and Adaptational Outcomes: The Problem of Confounded Measures." *American Psychologist* 40 (1985): 770–779.

Lewinsohn, Peter M. et al. "The Unpleasant Events Schule: A Scale for the Measurement of Aversive Events." *Journal of Clinical Psychology* 41 (July 1985): 483–498.

Linn, Margaret. "A Global Assessment of Recent Stress (GARS) Scale." *International Journal of Psychiatry in Medicine* 15 (1985–86): 47–59.

Linn, Margaret. "Modifiers and Perceived Stress Scale." *Journal of Consulting and Clinical Psychology* 54 (1986): 507–513.

Perkins, David V. "The Assessment of Stress Using Life Events Scales." In *Handbook of Stress: Theoretical and Clinical Aspects. See* Derogatis.

Sarason, Irwin G.; Johnson, James H.; and Siegel, Judith M. "Assessing the Impact of Life Changes: Development of the Life Experiences Survey." *Journal of Consulting and Clinical Psychology* 46 (1978): 932–946.

Social Support

Cohen, Sheldon, and Syme, S. Leonard, eds. *Social Support and Health.* Orlando, Fla.: Academic Press, 1985.

Cutrona, Carolyn, and Russell, Daniel. "The Provisions of Social Relationships and Adaptation to Stress." In *Advances in Personal Relationships,* vol I. Edited by W. H. Jones and D. Perlman. Greenwich, Conn.: JAI Press, 1987.

Heitzmann, Carma A., and Kaplan, Robert M. "Assessment of Methods for Measuring Social Support." *Health Psychology* 7 (1988): 75–109.

Kobasa, Suzanne C. et al. "Effectiveness of Hardiness, Exercise and Social Support as Resources against Illness." *Journal of Psychosomatic Research* 29 (1985): 525–533.

Sarason, Irwin, and Sarason, Barbara, eds. *Social Support: Theory, Research, and Applications.* Boston: Martinus Nijhoff Publishers, 1985.

Schradle, Susan, and Dougher, Michael. "Social Support as a Mediator of Stress: Theoretical and Empirical Issues." *Clinical Psychology Review* 5 (1985): 641–661.

Stress and Personality

Allen, Michael T. et al. "Type A Behavior Pattern, Parental History of Hypertension, and Cardiovascular Reactivity in College Males." *Health Psychology* 6 (1987): 113–130.

Holahan, Charles J., and Moos, Rudolf H. "Personality, Coping, and Family Resources in Stress Resistance: A Longitudinal Analysis." *Journal of Personality and Social Psychology* 51 (1986): 389–395.

Lundberg, Ulf. "Stress and Type A Behavior in Children." *Journal of the American Academy of Child Psychiatry* 25 (1986): 771–778.

Rosenman, Ray H., and Chesney, Margaret A. "Type A Behavior Pattern: Its Relationship to Coronary Heart Disease and its Modification by Behavioral and Pharmacological Approaches." In *Stress in Health and Disease,* edited by Michael R. Zales. New York: Brunner/ Mazel, 1985.

Stress and Illness

Anderson, David E. "Behavioral Stress and Experimental Hypertension." In *Stress and Coping,* edited by Tiffany M. Field, Philip M. McCabe, and Neil Schneiderman. Hillsdale, N.J.: Lawrence Erlbaum Associates, 1985.

Antoni, Michael H. "Neuroendocrine Influences in Psychoimmunology and Neoplasia: A Review." *Psychology and Health* 1 (1987): 3–24.

Blaney, Paul H. "Stress and Depression in Adults: A Critical Review." In *Stress and Coping. See* Anderson.

Campbell, Priscilla A. "Effects of Stress on the Immune Response." In *Stress and Coping. See* Anderson.

Davidson, Laura M., and Baum, A. "Chronic Stress and Posttraumatic Stress Disorders." *Journal of Consulting and Clinical Psychology* 54 (1986): 303–308.

Kasl, Stan V., and Cooper, Cary L., eds. *Stress and Health: Issues in Research Methodology.* New York: John Wiley & Sons, 1987.

Kiecolt-Glaser, Janice K., and Glaser, Ronald. "Psychosocial Moderators of Immune Function." *Annals of Behavioral Medicine* 9 (1987): 16–20.

Rabkin, Judith G. "Stress and Psychiatric Disorders." In *Handbook of Stress: Theoretical and Clinical Aspects,* edited by Leo Goldberger and Schlomo Breznitz. New York: The Free Press, 1982.

Roskies, Ethel et al. "The Montreal Type A Intervention Project: Major Findings." *Health Psychology* 5 (1986): 45–69.

Stein, Marvin, and Schleifer, Steven J. "Frontiers of Stress Research: Stress and Immunity." In *Stress in Health and Disease,* edited by Michael R. Zales. New York: Brunner/Mazel, 1985.

Stone, Arthur A.; Reed, Bruce R.; and Neale, John M. "Changes in Daily Event Frequency Precede Episodes of Physical Symptoms." *Journal of Human Stress* 13 (Summer 1987): 70–74.

Weiss, Jay M. "Neurochemical Mechanisms Underlying Stress-Induced Depression." In *Stress and Coping. See* Anderson.

Stress Medicine (journal). Sussex, England: John Wiley & Sons.

Stress Management

Benson, Herbert, *The Relaxation Response.* New York: William Morrow, 1975.

Benson, Herbert. *Beyond the Relaxation Response.* New York: Berkeley Publishers, 1985.

Bernstein, Douglas A., and Borkovec, Thomas D. *Progressive Relaxation Training: A Manual for the Helping Professions.* Champaign, Ill.: Research Press, 1973.

Biofeedback and Self Regulation (journal). New York: Plenum Publishing Corp.

Dimsdale, Joel E.; Alpert, Bruce S.; and Schneiderman, Neil. "Exercise as a Modulator of Cardiovascular Reactivity." In *Handbook of Stress, Reactivity, and Cardiovascular Disease,* edited by Karen A. Matthews et al. New York: John Wiley & Sons, 1986.

Domar, Alice D.; Noe, Joel M.; and Benson, Herbert. "The Preoperative Use of the Relaxation Response with Ambulatory Surgery Patients." *Journal of Human Stress* 13 (Fall 1987): 101–107.

Jacob, Rolf G., and Chesney, Margaret A. "Psychological and Behavioral Methods to Reduce Cardiovascular Reactivity." In *Handbook of Stress, Reactivity, and Cardiovascular Disease. See* Dimsdale.

Meichenbaum, Donald. *Stress Inoculation Training.* New York: Pergamon Press, 1985.

Meichenbaum, Donald, and Jaremko, Matthew, eds. *Stress Reduction and Prevention.* New York: Plenum Press, 1983.

Shapiro, Alvin P.; Krantz, David S.; and Grim, Clarence E. "Pharmacologic Agents as Modulators of Stress." In *Handbook of Stress, Reactivity, and Cardiovascular Disease. See* Dimsdale.

Surwit, Richard S. "Pharmacologic and Behavioral Modulators of Cardiovascular Reactivity: An Overview." In *Handbook of Stress, Reactivity, and Cardiovascular Disease.* See Dimsdale.

Woolfolk, Robert L., and Lehrer, Paul M. *Principles and Practice of Stress Management.* New York: Guilford Press, 1984.

Patient Compliance

Davidson, Park. "Therapeutic Compliance." *Canadian Psychological Review* 17 (1976): 247–259.

DiMatteo, M. Robin, and DiNicola, D. Dante. *Achieving Patient Compliance.* New York: Pergamon Press, 1982.

Dunbar, Jacqueline M., and Stunkard, Albert J. "Adherence to Diet and Drug Regimen." In *Nutrition, Lipids, and Coronary Heart Disease,* edited by Robert L. Levy et al. New York: Raven Press, 1979.

Haynes, R. Brian. "Improving Patient Compliance: An Empirical View." In *Adherence, Compliance, and Generalization in Behavioral Medicine,* edited by R. Stuart. New York: Brunner/ Mazel, 1982.

Journal of Compliance in Health Care. New York: Springer Publishing Co.

Meichenbaum, Donald, and Turk, Dennis C. *Facilitating Treatment Adherence: A Practitioner's Guidebook.* New York: Plenum Press, 1987.

Suedfeld, Peter. "Environmental Factors Influencing Maintenance of Lifestyle Change." In *Adherence, Compliance, and Generalization in Behavioral Medicine. See* Haynes.

Ziffenblatt, Steven M. "Increasing Patient Compliance through the Applied Analysis of Behavior." *Preventive Medicine* 4 (1975): 173–182.

Application of Interviewing and Counseling Skills

Part III discusses problems in eating behaviors that are associated with certain prescribed dietary patterns involving modifications in calories, fat, cholesterol, carbohydrates, protein, and sodium. Each chapter begins with a review of research on the association between nutrients and the disease, followed by a discussion of research on compliance with an eating pattern in which specified nutrients are restricted. Suggestions follow for assessing individual behaviors that are inappropriate to the prescribed eating pattern. Treatment of such behaviors is then analyzed in terms of strategies to combat lack of knowledge, forgetfulness, and lack of commitment.

Strategies to deal with clients' lack of knowledge are both informational and behavioral. Informational strategies focus on imparting facts on the regimen. Behavioral strategies include many ways to change behavior by identifying information in terms of the antecedents and consequences of target behaviors without necessarily intervening directly with respect to nutrition or health knowledge and attitudes. Suggestions for modifying these antecedents and consequences are proposed as steps toward behavior change. Strategies to solve problems of forgetfulness include behavioral techniques such as cueing.

Clients who seem to be less committed to dietary change may benefit from strategies designed to intervene directly to change their attitudes. These strategies focus on persuasion through engaging relevant motivations or increasing clients' readiness to change by affecting their attitudes. Behavioral strategies are frequently coupled with these motivational strategies to increase commitment to a modified eating pattern.

The counselor must individualize all of these elements for each client and some may be inappropriate for some individuals. Discussion of suggested assessment and treatment strategies for specific dietary patterns should be encouraged if this book is used as a classroom text because there are many ways to solve each problem.

Chapters 8 through 15 provide examples of three types of adherence tools: (1) those that can be used as monitoring devices to determine how well clients are adhering to their dietary patterns, (2) those that supplement the basic dietary instruction, and (3) those that function as cueing devices. Each tool:

Exhibit III-1 Qualitative Rating of Counselor's Helping Style

	Rarely	Occasionally	Undecided	Often	Almost Always
1. Did the nutrition counselor appear to be comfortable with the client and with the subject areas discussed?					
2. Did the counselor avoid imposing values on the client?					
3. Did the counselor remain objective?					
4. Did the counselor focus on the client, not just on the procedure of providing a diet instruction?					
5. Were the counselor's skills spontaneous and nonmechanical?					
6. How would you describe the likelihood of the client's returning to this nutrition counselor again?					
Comments from Rater or Client					

Source: From *Interviewing Strategies for Helpers,* 2nd ed., by W. H. Cormier and L. S. Cormier. Copyright © 1985, 1979 by Wadsworth Inc. Adapted by permission of Brooks/Cole Publishing Company, Pacific Grove, California 93950.

1. has a goal or an objective
2. gains the client's attention
3. is concise and to the point
4. allows for individual differences in eating habits.

Health professionals who do not have formal training in dietetics should work closely with a registered dietitian in recommending changes for modified regimens. For example, the modified eating pattern for clients with renal insufficiency (Chapter 11) includes changes in many nutrients. Registered dietitians trained in the field should be consulted.

Exhibits III-1 and III-2 are qualitative and quantitative evaluations of interviewing styles to use during practice sessions in which peers or clients evaluate the counselor's progress with counseling skills or as a check that counselors have acquired basic skills before beginning Part III.

The qualitative scoring (Exhibit III-1) involves a subjective judgment by a rater or by the client (or both) about aspects of the counselor's style. After observing the interview for each of the six items, the rater or client checks the box for items that represent the appropriate judgment about the counselor for most of the interview.

Exhibit III-2 Quantitative Rating of Counselors

Nutrition Counselor Statement No.	Verbal Responses															Nonverbal Behavior											Para-linguistics	
	Listening				Action				Sharing		Teaching					Eyes		Face		Body								
	Clarification	Paraphrase	Reflection of Feeling	Summarization	Probe	Ability Potential	Confrontation	Interpretation	Self-Disclosure	Immediacy	Instructions	Verbal Setting Operation	Information Giving	Initiates Eye Contact	Breaks Eye Contact	Head Nods	Smiles	Body Facing Client	Body Turned Away	Body Leaning Forward	Body Leaning Backward	Body Relaxed	Body Tense	Completed Sentences	Broken Sentences, Speech Errors			
1																												
2																												
3																												
4																												
5																												
6																												
7																												
8																												
9																												
10																												
Total																												

Source: From *Interviewing Strategies for Helpers,* 2nd ed., by W. H. Cormier and L. S. Cormier. Copyright © 1985, 1979 by Wadsworth Inc. Adapted by permission of Brooks/Cole Publishing Company, Pacific Grove, California 93950.

Comments can be added at the bottom of the rating sheets. The quantitative scoring (Exhibit III-2) involves counting certain of the counselor's verbal and nonverbal responses. For each statement by the counselor, the client or rater indicates the type of verbal and nonverbal response. At the end of the interview, the responses associated with each category are tallied.

The following chapters give examples of nutrition as a means of preventing disease and/or its complications, and ways to use counseling skills to promote adherence to new eating patterns. Each new eating pattern focuses on disease prevention and long-term maintenance as opposed to brief therapeutic symptom management.

Chapter 8

Nutrition Counseling in Treatment of Obesity

Objectives for Chapter 8

1. Identify common inappropriate behaviors associated with weight gain or overeating.
2. Identify steps in assessing individual eating behaviors.
3. Identify strategies to treat inappropriate eating behaviors contributing to weight gain.
4. Generate appropriate strategies to counsel overweight clients to control eating patterns.
5. Recommend certain dietary adherence tools for weight-loss clients.

Obesity, one of the most common medical disorders in this country,[1] is an important disorder because of its association with many common diseases that enhance morbidity and mortality.

THEORIES AND FACTS ABOUT NUTRITION AND OBESITY

Assessment of the obese client requires both clinical and laboratory techniques. Obesity may be associated with high blood pressure, diabetes, and, in some people, coronary heart disease, as well as endocrine, hypothalamic, and genetic disorders.[2] The major diseases associated with obesity (high blood pressure, diabetes, and coronary heart disease) and their nutritional associations are discussed in Chapters 9, 10, and 12; the text does not discuss other associated etiologic classifications such as endocrine, hypothalamic, and genetic disorders.

Government authorities such as the U.S. Food and Nutrition Board's Committee on Recommended Dietary Allowances and the Canadian Ministry of Health and Welfare have published recommended energy intakes for various groups by age and sex.[3] The energy RDA meets the needs of an average person. (As indicated previously, RDAs do not necessarily apply to individuals, but, because they are the sole reference for calorie needs, they will be used here to address the needs of an average person.) An energy deficit of 3,500 calories is necessary for the loss of a pound of body fat. This means that with a deficit of 500 calories per day, a pound of weight will be lost each week. Whitney and Hamilton found that the loss of more than two pounds of body fat a week rarely can be maintained and cautioned that a diet supplying less than 1,200 calories per day can be made adequate in vitamins and minerals only with great difficulty.[4]

To promote adequate nutrition, counselors must pay attention to nutrient levels. For adults, the RDAs are .8 grams protein per kilogram of body weight per day.[5] For a 70-kilogram man, that would be 56 grams of protein per day, and for a 55-kilogram woman, 44 grams.

There is a considerable difference of opinion as to whether carbohydrates or fats should be reduced in an energy-restricted diet. Significant weight reductions on carbohydrate-free diets probably result from loss of water bound to glycogen. Without carbohydrates in the diet, the body uses stored glycogen to maintain normal blood glucose levels. The water with its electrolytes that are bound to the glycogen is excreted by the kidneys.

An energy-restricted diet should provide vitamins and minerals at least equivalent to the RDAs. If calorie intake is very restricted, vitamin and mineral supplements may be needed.

The alcohol content of the diet should be assessed carefully at baseline, particularly because clients tend to underestimate consumption. One gram of alcohol provides seven calories. Beer and wine contain carbohydrates that also contribute calories. The calories from alcoholic beverages may be the difference between losing and gaining weight.

Water and other nonnutritive fluids are not restricted unless there are heart or kidney complications.

ADHERENCE WITH WEIGHT LOSS PROGRAMS

Much has been written about the dismal results for weight loss and the high rate of recidivism among those who achieve short-term weight reduction.[6] Two recent reports suggest that the success rates in clinical populations may be much smaller than in the general public, which includes many people who treat themselves. Schachter's investigation of "self-cure" showed that 62.5 percent of the 40 people in the sample who tried to lose weight were successful in losing weight and keeping it off.[7] In a Minnesota survey, approximately one-third of those who reported having been overweight said that they had successfully reduced.[8] Possibly reported failure rates for organized weight-loss programs are inflated because many people who drop out of a treatment program turn up in other programs, where they may later be counted as dropouts again. Another explanation for the discrepancies between these studies and clinical findings is that only those who have already failed at managing their weight themselves seek professional treatment. Also, therapists may communicate the intractability of the overweight condition, thus advancing a self-fulfilling prophecy for their clients.[9] In any case, data on the success of self-prescribed weight loss diets are limited, and further study is needed.

The medical team has many options available for weight loss management. Before selecting a strategy, practitioners should analyze numerous methods. In weight loss programs, unlike other areas of dietary change, practitioners have a great deal of research from which to draw conclusions. In the 1970s much was written on treatments based on behavior modification and their effectiveness as compared with traditional dietary methods based on short-term evaluation.[10] Although weight losses resulting from behavior modification treatment strategies are statistically different from control group losses, these changes are small and not clinically significant, especially for grossly overweight persons.

Few long-term follow-up evaluations are available for dietary, medical, or behavior modification programs. However, 12-month and longer evaluations of behavior modification programs began to appear in the literature in the late 1970s. In a self-controlled behavioral program, Hall et al. found short-term weight losses but they were not maintained over time.[11] Other studies have shown similar results.[12] Data from Stuart provide a single exception to these studies.[13] Using two key elements, individual behavior modification sessions coupled with booster sessions throughout the follow-up, he found an average weight loss of 32 lbs. for eight patients at 12 months.

Miller and Sims evaluated components of a weight loss program to compare the successful client with the unsuccessful one.[14] Initially, stimulus control and contingency management (contracts) were found useful, but they were not significantly related to long-term success. This finding was corroborated in reports by Brownell and Stunkard and Jeffrey, Wing, and Stunkard[15] suggesting that techniques necessary for weight maintenance may be quite different from those needed for short-term weight loss.

The majority of successful clients over a 12-month period used (1) cognitive restructuring techniques (positive self-thoughts), (2) exercise, (3) social skills (assertiveness skills), and (4) eating style changes.[16] Other recent studies corroborate the importance of the first three of these procedures. Mahoney and Mahoney report that changes in perfectionistic standards, negative beliefs, and self-defeating private monologues are important to success in a 12-month weight control program.[17]

Stalons, Johnson, and Christ found physical activity to be an influential factor in weight loss after one year.[18] The exact reason for the influence of exercise on weight control, which deserves further study, may be direct (caloric expenditure) or indirect (enhanced feelings of psychological well-being).

Many studies have stressed the importance of social support in weight loss maintenance. Mahoney and Mahoney reported a high correlation between weight loss and family support in a two-year follow-up study.[19] In a more controlled study Brownell and coworkers evaluated the involvement of spouses in the weight loss program.[20] Subjects whose spouses were trained to be supportive showed three times the weight loss of clients whose spouses were not trained. Clients were also taught the interpersonal skills, such as assertiveness, that are necessary for requesting appropriate support from others.

Research on eating style is contradictory.[21] Researchers have compared duration of eating, size of mouthfuls, time between bites, and chewing time of obese and nonobese individuals, but it is unclear whether these groups differ in these dimensions. Some researchers suggest that the "nonobese" eating style may be important in controlling food intake because it increases awareness of satiety cues and enhances feelings of self-efficacy and self-control.[22]

More research is needed in the form of controlled clinical trials (the Miller and Sims research was not in this category). Even though social skills training, exercise, and cognitive restructuring appear to influence long-term success, other forms of behavioral therapy should not be totally discounted. Indeed, combinations of behavioral techniques are provided below as examples of ways to deal with lack of commitment.

There are a variety of general techniques to facilitate weight loss. Coates reviews various psychological strategies, and Booth provides a list of various methods, both psychological and nonpsychological, for treating overweight persons:[23]

1. calorie counting
2. behavior modification
3. self-help groups, such as TOPS (Takes Off Pounds Sensibly), Weight Watchers, and Overeaters Anonymous
4. jejunoileal and gastric bypass surgery
5. drugs to increase metabolic rate and suppress appetite
6. popular "lose pounds quick" diets.

Van Itallie et al. carefully review the problems associated with the last three methods listed.[24] A variety of behavior modification methods are discussed in the remainder of this chapter.

INAPPROPRIATE EATING BEHAVIORS

The following thoughts are frequently associated with weight gain:

- "I deserve it."
- "It's just no use. I have no willpower."
- "I'm bored."
- "I'm off that rotten diet now."

Each of these can have a direct bearing on the individual's propensity to gain weight. Nutrition counselors must be aware of a variety of thought processes as well as overt eating behaviors before trying to assess the major problem. It is important to try to identify antecedents and consequences of inappropriate eating behaviors.

Many present or future clients begin thinking about weight loss in terms of going on and off diets: "I go on a diet to lose weight. Usually I can't stand the diet. I just wait until I lose 10 or 15 pounds and then go back to eating those really good foods I'm accustomed to." This particular syndrome frequently is associated with alternating increases and decreases in weight.

Nutrition counselors might consider generally trying to avoid the term "diet" in their instructions to describe a means toward weight loss. The rationale is that along with the word "diet" the two negative words "going off" tend to follow.

Many clients will suggest that food is a kind of reward: "When I finish the housework (or reach the 3 P.M. break at my job) I feel like I deserve a reward, so I just go to the refrigerator (or vending machines or cafeteria). Right there in front of me are all the rewards I need. I really deserve to eat in payment for my hard work."

Signals or cues to eat are everywhere. Counselors should study each client's environment and note specific cues that trigger inappropriate eating behaviors. At home, candy near the television set can trigger snacking responses that might not occur otherwise. TV commercials may provide a stimulus to go to the kitchen for potato chips, candy bars, beverages, etc.

Many clients will admit that boredom can cause inappropriate eating behaviors: "I eat because there is nothing else to do." Counselors can suggest many substitutes for eating to eliminate boredom and possibly increase activity. In some cases hobbies can serve as substitutes for eating, such as doing needlework or polishing shoes instead of snacking while watching TV.

Some inappropriate behaviors involve rapid eating. It appears that the client is saying, "How fast can I clear this plate?" Along with this is the inability to listen when the body provides signals of fullness or satiety. Booth states that satiety may cease to originate solely from gastric motility and distention or a physiological state and that the power of suggestion also may play a large role in providing signals of fullness.[25]

In the eating chain syndrome as described by Ferguson, activities can be used to break up patterns that lead to inappropriate behaviors.[26] He says that eating occurs at one end of a chain of responses. If the counselor works backward from the terminal behavior of eating, events or cues in the environment that started the chain of events leading to it can be identified.

Much of what goes on in the client's head, such as negative thoughts, can trigger inappropriate eating behaviors. The client who is thinking, "I'm really a rotten person for eating that piece of candy. It's no use. I might as well eat until I'm stuffed," probably will overeat out of despair. Mahoney and Mahoney describe the reversal of this process as "cognitive ecology."[27] By substituting positive thoughts for negative ones, clients can develop a built-in self-reward system.[28]

In some cases lack of exercise can be a problem. Some clients may complain, "I just don't feel like moving." Studies have shown that weight loss plus exercise can be beneficial.[29] In fact, more fat tissue is reduced as opposed to muscle tissue if exercise programs are included with lowered caloric intake.

In general, inappropriate eating behaviors and lack of exercise may contribute to weight gain. The first step in achieving weight loss is to identify accurately the inappropriate eating behaviors.

ASSESSMENT OF EATING BEHAVIORS

The nutrition counselor's next task is assessment of clients' eating behaviors. The first step is to try to identify the general problem from the many that may surface in a general interview. In reality, overweight clients may not want to lose weight but appear at a counseling session because their spouse or doctor has sent them. In some cases the major problem may be psychological and referral to a specialist in that field may be the best course of action.[30]

If referral does not seem necessary, the next step is data collection. Six factors related to weight gain data should be emphasized:

1. eating patterns
2. food quantities
3. food quality
4. activity levels
5. food-related thoughts
6. food-related cues.

Exhibit 8-1 presents instructions and a form to use in gathering information in each of these categories, and Exhibit 8-2 is a sample already filled out. Adherence Tool 8-1 is a questionnaire for clients to fill out, and a simplified monitoring device for use with goal attainment is provided in Adherence Tool 8-2.

Other authors also discuss the vital importance of assessment for obese clients. Brownell states that these categories are important to cover:[31]

Exhibit 8-1 Data Collection Chart

Instructions for Filling Out the Food Diary
Time: Starting time for a meal or snack
Minutes spent eating: Length of the eating episode in minutes
M/S: meal or snack: Indicate type of eating by the appropriate letter, "M" or "S"
H: Hunger on a scale of 0 to 3, with 0 = no hunger, 3 = extreme hunger
Body position:
  1. walking
  2. standing
  3. sitting
  4. lying down
Activity while eating: Record any activity you carry out while eating, such as watching
  television, reading, function in a workplace, or sweeping the floor.
Location of eating: Record each place you eat, such as your car, workplace, kitchen table,
  living room couch, or bed.
Food type and quantity: Indicate the content of your meal or snack by kind of food and
  quantity. Choose units of measurement that you will be able to reproduce from week
  to week. Accuracy is not as important as consistency.
Eating with whom: Indicate with whom you are eating or whether you are eating that
  meal or snack alone.
Feelings before and during eating: Record your feelings or mood immediately before (B)
  or while (W) eating. Typical feelings are angry, bored, confused, depressed, frustrated,
  sad, etc.
Minutes spent exercising today: Record the total number of minutes you spent exercising,
  followed by the type of exercise—walking, jogging, running, riding a bicycle or a horse,
  dancing, skiing, swimming, bowling, etc.

Day of Week_____   Name_____

Time	Minutes Spent Eating	M/S	H	Body Position	Activity While Eating	Location of Eating	Food Type and Quantity	Eating With Whom	Feeling Before (B) and while (W) Eating	Minutes Spent Exercising Today
6:00										
11:00										
4:00										

H: Degree of Hunger (0 = None. 3 = Maximum)
Body Position: 1 = Walking. 2 = Siting. 4= Lying Down
(B): Before
(W): While
Source: Adapted from *Habits Not Diets* by J. M. Ferguson, pp. 13–14, with permission of Bull
Publishing Company, © 1976.

Exhibit 8-2 Example of a Completed Food Diary Form

SAMPLE

Day of Week   MONDAY   Name   R.S.T.

Time	Minutes Spent Eating	M/S	H	Body Position	Activity While Eating	Location of Eating	Food Type and Quantity	Eating With Whom	Feeling Before (B) and while (W) Eating	Minutes Spent Exercising Today
6:00 7:20-30	10 min	M	0	3	PAPER	KITCHEN	8oz. Coffee	WIFE	HAPPY	40 minutes
8:15-20	5 min	S	0	2	TALKING	WORK	1 cup cereal 4oz wholemilk 1 cal e doughnut 8oz coffee	FRIENDS	TIRED (B)	WALKING
10:30-?	5 min	S	1	1	WALKING	HALL	1 cake doughnut	ALONE	LATE (W)	
11:00 12:30	1 min	S	2	2	WORK	DESK	1-1.5oz Snickers	ALONE	LATE (W)	
3:30-3:40	10 min	M	3	3	READING	RESTAURANT	1-8oz Coke 3oz ckd. hamburger patty 1 Hamb. Bun	ALONE	TIRED (B)	
4:00 5:30-6:00	30 min.	S	3	3	Paper TV	L.R.	1oz SCOTCH 1/4 cup peanuts	FAMILY	TIRED (B)	
6:00-7:00	1 hour	M	2	3	TV	D.R.	Beef TV Dinner 1 cup ice Cream	FAMILY	ANGRY (B)	
9:00 10:30-10:45	15 min	S	0	2	TV	LR.	1/2 cup ice Cream	WIFE	BORED (B)	

M/S: Meal or Snack
H: Degree of Hunger (0 = None, 3 = Maximum)
Body Position: 1 = Walking, 2 = Standing, 3 = Sitting, 4 = Lying Down
(B): Before
(W): While

Source: Adapted from *Habits Not Diets* by J. M. Ferguson, pp. 13–14, with permission of Bull Publishing Company, © 1976.

1. physiology
2. eating behaviors
3. physical activity
4. psychological and social adjustment.

Physiological factors can include an assessment of cell size and number. In assessing physical status, several categories should be considered: endocrine, hypothalamic, cardiopulmonary, orthopedic, genetic, weight, and family history. Bray and

Teague provide an algorithm for the medical assessment of obese clients and delineate the steps necessary in diagnosing medical problems of an obese client.[32]

In the physiological analysis, counselors also should be concerned about body fat, which can be assessed through a variety of tests. The one most commonly used is skinfold thickness, using a caliper. Body fat is an indicator of physical status. Appendix C provides information on physiological measures of nutritional status.

Assessing eating behaviors is very important to eventual treatment. The most frequently used assessment method is a diet record. This can provide details on food preferences, eating style, environmental cues to eating, and amounts eaten.

Physical activity is an important component in any weight-loss program. Counselors should check on exercise during both working and nonworking hours. Equally important is psychological and social functioning. Psychological functioning can include positive and negative monologues as described earlier; social functioning deals with responses by spouse, children, coworkers, or friends to weight loss and eating behaviors.

TREATMENT STRATEGIES

The treatment strategies described here deal with the following three problems: lack of knowledge, forgetfulness and lack of commitment.

Strategies To Deal with Lack of Knowledge

At baseline, the client needs a clear understanding of information pertinent to weight gain. Adherence Tool 8-1 elicits information on current eating disorders. Baseline data should be compared with information collected during strategy implementation. Adherence Tool 8-3 provides suggestions on facilitating weight loss.

Strategies to combat inappropriate eating behaviors follow. One is substitution of non-food-related activities. With this method, it is necessary to work with the clients in developing a list of enjoyable activities, particularly those requiring substantial expenditure of energy. The information obtained in the Data Collection Chart (Exhibit 8-1) can suggest a starting point.

It is preferable to select activities that fit into the clients' daily routine, based on their suggestions as to which ones would work best. This is a time when counselors' listening skills and encouragement for clients can generate solutions that will lead to optimum results. Instead of eating, clients can turn to substitute activities such as those in Exhibit 8-3.

Interposing time between eating episodes is a second method for diminishing the urge. This strategy may require the use of a cooking timer, alarm clock, etc. Clients are asked to delay a snack for a certain number of minutes. Gradually they will be able to increase the time between the urge to snack and the actual act of eating to 10 or 15 minutes. During this interlude they should be encouraged to perform some other activity. They usually are amazed at how well this strategy curbs their appetites.

The third strategy is cue elimination. Exhibit 8-1 can help in determining which cues lead to improper eating. For example, by looking at a rough house plan and identifying where eating episodes are occurring, clients can set up roadblocks to those cues. Many clients will find their snacking locations show up in clusters around the television set, favorite chairs, or in the kitchen by the refrigerator or sink (or the cafeteria or vending machines at work). They may be shocked to find they eat in more places than they believed.

Exhibit 8-3 Activity Substitutes for Eating

Clients can resort to numerous activities as alternates to overeating. They can:
- Rearrange furniture
- Spend extra time with a friend
- Play cards or a game with someone—chess, Monopoly, bridge, etc.
- Go to a movie, play, or concert
- Do something for charity
- Go to a museum
- Take a quiet walk
- Take a long, leisurely bubble bath
- Balance their checkbook
- Write a letter
- Make a phone call to a friend or relative
- Wash their hair
- Start a garden
- Do home repairs
- Write a creative poem or story
- Do some sewing or creative stitchery
- Do a crossword puzzle
- Go jogging
- Play golf
- Join a softball team
- Jump rope
- Take up weight lifting
- Go hiking
- Take up, or increase participation in, a sport.

Ferguson has designed an exercise to help eliminate eating cues:[33]

1. Ask the clients to select a specific room in the house in which all eating should occur. This place should be regarded as relatively comfortable. They also should designate eating places away from home, such as in a restaurant, cafeteria, lunchroom, or by vending machines. They should be cautioned to avoid eating while working to break the chain of association between eating and other activities. It could be suggested that every designated eating place be special. If clients must eat while working, if at all feasible a place mat and silverware should be set, with a real (not plastic) cup for coffee or tea. At home, candlelight, flowers, and attractive plates and silverware can make the designated place "special."
2. Ask the clients to change their usual eating place at the table. If, for example, it is the head, they should move to one side; if at the side, change with someone on the other side. The rationale is to break long-standing cues at the table.
3. Ask the clients to separate eating from other activities—to avoid combining eating with telephone conversations, watching TV, reading, working, etc. The emphasis should be on food with others and on making eating enjoyable by focusing on the taste and texture of the ingredients.
4. Ask clients to remove food from all places (particularly visible ones) except appropriate storage areas in the kitchen and to keep stored food out of sight by placing it in cupboards, in opaque containers, or in the refrigerator.
5. Suggest that clients keep fresh fruits and vegetables for snacks in attractive containers.

6. Request that clients remove serving containers from the table during mealtimes.

Once nutrition counselors have helped clients eliminate cues, the strategy can turn to decreasing serving size slowly. The use of smaller plates and smaller portions will decrease total caloric consumption. Nouvelle cuisine, with its very small portions arranged artistically in the center of large plates, is an attractive alternative. The foods need not involve fancy French cooking; the regular "menu" can simply be restaged in a fancier setting at no additional cost.

Many of these strategies involve getting help from spouse, family, and/or friends. Clients should be told to explain the strategies to anyone seen regularly. Closest friends' understanding of the program rationale can provide moral support. Through teaching others, clients may grasp strategies more clearly.

Strategies To Deal with Forgetfulness

At social events people may unknowingly forget to follow a diet. A note on the refrigerator can remind the client of an upcoming event, "Don't forget to plan for Jan's party." Planning may involve calling the hostess on the phone to obtain a list of party foods to be served.

This same idea can help clients plan for problem times such as eating out, weddings, or anniversaries. The cues should be simple and visible, such as "Remember your restaurant engagement Friday at noon!" posted on the bathroom mirror.

Many problems occur when people act spontaneously and either unknowingly or by choice fall into old habits. By providing memory cues, planning ahead can give clients the time they need to avoid situations that lead to an inappropriate eating behavior.

Strategies To Deal with Lack of Commitment

When clients know what is causing inappropriate behaviors and have used memory joggers without success, they may be entering a phase in which altering their life style to make changes in body size no longer seems important. At this point a review of the client's initial list of reasons for wanting to lose weight may be valuable in identifying why commitment is waning.

In some cases negative thoughts result from repeated indiscretions, which leads to another strategy, positive thinking. Appendix E gives examples of ways in which record keeping can help uncover negative thoughts associated with inappropriate eating behaviors. Getting clients to see how often negative thoughts force excessive food consumption can be a first step to weight control. This change from negative to positive thinking is an activity in which clients are very much in charge. Counselors can provide examples of thoughts such as: "I'm such a failure. I can't do anything right. I might as well give up. Who cares if I stuff myself with this cake?"

This negative monologue can be transformed to more positive thinking: "I ate one piece of cake, and even though it is high in calories I can stop with that one piece. I'm really feeling good about being able to stop without going ahead and eating the entire cake." From that point on, the clients can formulate positive self-thoughts to replace their negative ones.

For most people, increasing exercise in combination with decreasing calories is helpful. Exhibit 8-1 is used to determine baseline activity levels. Many of the suggestions listed as substitutes for eating in Exhibit 8-3 involve an increase in activity.

Exhibit 8-4 Diet Maintenance Data Collection

Day of Week _____ Name _____

Time	M/S	H	Food Type and Quantity	Minutes Spent Exercising and Type of Exercise
6:00 a.m.				
11.00 a.m.				
4:00 p.m.				
9:00 p.m.				

M/S: Meal or Snack
H: Degree of Hunger (0 = none; 3 = maximum)

Source: Adapted from *Habits Not Diets* by J. M. Ferguson, p. 87, with permission of Bull Publishing Company, © 1976.

Counselors should encourage clients to enroll in exercise programs but caution them to check with a physician first.

Client progress is evaluated by comparing current and past data, as in Exhibit 8-4. Clients can be asked to extend a strategy, possibly by increasing negative-to-positive thought transformations. If a strategy is not working, it should be revised. For example, if finding a designated eating place at work poses problems, the nutrition counselor may need to discuss other means of cue elimination—using a place mat, plate, and silverware. In some cases, a new strategy may be appropriate. If clients find it impossible to substitute noneating activities for routine snacking, it may be necessary first to work to eliminate negative monologues, then add other activities as monologues are transformed to a more positive mode.

Facilitating the desire for commitment may require more intensive counselor-client interaction. This may involve periodic phone calls set up to assess compliance with behaviors identified in a contract such as the one shown in Exhibit 8-5.

Although individual counseling is important and is effective initially in tailoring the diet, group sessions can be very helpful in facilitating maintenance of a low-calorie eating pattern. Groups provide support, ideas, chastisement, and concern. They can be very potent factors in achieving behavior change.

The following are some basic group process guidelines:

1. Ask open questions to begin sessions and start conversations on successes or failures with weight loss.
2. Use the group members as a source for problem-solving ideas.

Exhibit 8-5 Sample Contract

"I will reward myself each day for avoiding a high-calorie snack from 8:00 A.M. to 12:00 noon. I will avoid those foods I frequently use:

> 3 doughnuts or
> 2 Hostess Twinkies or
> 24 chocolate drops.

I will substitute instead low-calorie foods from home:

> 5 saltine crackers with low calorie jelly
> or sugar-free gum or
> 5 pretzel sticks.

If I accomplish this goal in three out of five working days, I will reward myself with one of the following:

> 1. shopping spree
> 2. visit to my best friend who lives 20 miles away
> 3. a night out at the theater.

If I do not achieve the above goal, I will receive no rewards.
Every Friday at 10:00 A.M. (nutrition counselor) will call to check on my progress."

> Patient _____
> Friend or Spouse _____
> Nutritionist _____

3. Place yourself, the counselor, in the role of facilitator.
4. Make eye contact with less verbal class members to draw them out.
5. Use more positive group members to keep other group members' more negative thoughts at a minimum.
6. Use basic interviewing and counseling skills.

The group process is more a matter of skill mastery than concept memorization. To gain skill in this area, counselors should request to observe a Weight Watchers meeting. Any group process–oriented meeting that requires members' active participation is helpful.

In summary, nutrition counseling for weight loss requires a knowledge of cues which promote overeating, suggestions for planning ahead and behavioral strategies to increase commitment to dietary change.

Client Eating Questionnaire for Low-Calorie Eating Patterns in Treating Obesity*

The following questionnaire has been designed to efficiently collect patient information in clinical weight control programs. It has several functions.

Initially, it is a useful screening device or test of motivation. Individuals who will not take time to fill it out probably will not take time to participate fully in the behavioral weight control program.

Secondly, the answers to these questions can be of great use to the therapist during the initial interviews and later during the weight control lessons. The weight history allows him or her to systematically look at the clients' own views of their weight problems, and at some of the environmental influences they feel are important to their weight problems. The history of past attempts to lose weight, the lengths of time they have stayed in weight loss programs, and the reasons for past failure can all be useful during the 20 weeks of this program. Also, their report of mood changes during previous periods of weight loss can help you anticipate and deal with problems that might arise during treatment.

A brief medical history is included to give you a basis for referral. For example, if someone indicates he or she is a diabetic, and does not have a physician, you might suggest contacting a doctor before the weight control program begins. Similarly, if someone indicates a history of heart disease, you may want to check with that person's physician before dealing with increased activity and exercise.

The questions about social and family history provide additional information that is of use medically: for example, the cause of parental death and the family weight history.

In most states the information contained in this questionnaire is confidential. Without *written* approval from the clients, this information cannot be divulged to interested individuals, physicians, insurance companies, or law enforcement agencies.

---

*Adapted from *Learning To Eat, Behavior Modification for Weight Control* by J.M. Ferguson with permission of Bull Publishing Company, © 1975.

Name:_____ Sex: M F Age:____ Birthdate:_____

Address:_____ Home phone:_____

_____ Office phone:_____

WEIGHT HISTORY:

1. Your present weight _____ Height _____

2. Describe your present weight (circle one)

| very | slightly | about |
| overweight | overweight | average |

3. Are you dissatisfied with the way you look at this weight? (circle one)

Completely   Very
  Satisfied   Satisfied   Neutral   Dissatisfied   Dissatisfied

4. At what weight have you *felt* your best or do you think you would feel your best?

_____

5. How much weight would you like to lose? _____

6. Do you feel your weight affects your daily activities?

   No effect   Some effect   Often interferes   Extreme effect

7. Why do you want to lose weight at this time?_____

_____

8. What are the attitudes of the following people about your attempt(s) to lose weight?

	Negative (They disapprove or are resentful)	*Indifferent* (They don't care or don't help)	*Positive* (They encourage me and are understanding)
Husband			
Wife			
Children			
Parents			
Employer			
Friends			

9. Do these attitudes affect your weight loss or gain?   Yes   No
   If yes, please describe: _____

_____

_____

10. Indicate on the following table the periods in your life when you have been overweight. *Where appropriate,* list your maximum weight for each period and number of pounds you were overweight. Briefly describe any methods you used to lose weight in that five-year period, e.g., diet, shots, pills. Also list any significant life events you feel were related to either your weight gain or loss, e.g., college tests, marriage, pregnancies, illness.

Age	Maximum Weight	Pounds Overweight	Methods Used to Lose Weight	Significant Events Related to Weight Change
Birth				
0–5				
5–10				
10–15				
15–20				
20–25				
25–30				
30–35				
35–40				
40–45				
45–50				
50–55				
55–60				
60–65				

11. How *physically* active are you? (circle one)

    Very active   Active   Average   Inactive   Very inactive

12. What do you do for physical exercise and how often do you do it?

ACTIVITY (for example, swimming, jogging, dancing)	FREQUENCY (daily, weekly, monthly)

13. A number of different ways of losing weight are listed below. Please indicate which methods you have used by filling the appropriate blanks.

	Ages Used	Number of Times Used	Maximum Weight Lost	Comments: Length of Time Weight Loss Maintained; Success; Difficulties
TOPS (Take Off Pounds Sensibly)				
Weight Watchers				
Pills				
Supervised Diet				
Unsupervised Diet				
Starvation				
Behavior Modification				
Psychotherapy				
Hypnosis				
Other				

14. Which method did you use for the longest period of time? _____

15. Have you had a major mood change during or after a significant weight loss? Indicate any mood changes on the following checklist.

	Not at all	A little bit	Moderately	Quite a bit	Extremely
a. Depressed, sad, feeling down, unhappy, the blues.					
b. Anxious, nervous, restless, or uptight all the time.					
c. Physically weak.					
d. Elated or happy.					
e. Easily irritated, annoyed, or angry.					
f. Fatigued, worn out, tired all the time.					
g. A lack of self-confidence.					

16. What usually goes wrong with your weight loss programs?_____

_____

_____

_____

MEDICAL HISTORY:

17. When did you last have a complete physical examination? _____

18. Who is your current doctor? _____

19. What medical problems do you have at the present time? _____

_____

_____

20. What medications or drugs do you take regularly? _____

_____

_____

21. List any medications, drugs or foods you are allergic to. _____

_____

_____

22. List any hospitalizations or operations. Indicate how old you were at each hospital admission.

Age   Reason for hospitalizations

_____   _____

_____   _____

23. List any serious illnesses you have had which have not required hospitalization. Indicate how old you were during each illness.

      Age   Illness

_____   _____

_____   _____

_____   _____

_____   _____

24. Describe any of your medical problems that are complicated by excess weight.

_____

_____

_____

_____

_____

25. How much alcohol do you usually drink per week? _____

26. List any psychiatric contact, individual counseling, or marital counseling that you have had or are now having.

      Age   Reason for contact and type of therapy

_____   _____

_____   _____

_____   _____

_____   _____

SOCIAL HISTORY:

27. Circle the last year of school attended:

      1 2 3 4 5 6 7 8   9 10 11 12   1 2 3 4   M.A. Ph.D.
        Grade School   High School   College

     Other _____

28. Describe your present occupation _____

_____

29. How long have you worked for your present employer? _____

30. Present marital status (circle one):

     single   married   divorced   widowed   separated   engaged

31. Answer the following questions for each marriage:

    Dates of marriages   _____   _____   _____

    Dates of terminations   _____   _____   _____

    Reason (death, divorce, etc.)   _____   _____   _____

    Number of children   _____   _____   _____

32. Spouse's Age _____ Weight _____ Height _____

33. Describe your spouse's occupation _____

34. Describe your spouse's weight (circle one):

very overweight	slightly overweight	about average	slightly underweight	very underweight

35. List your children's ages, sex, heights, weights, and circle whether they are over-weight, average, or underweight. Include any children from previous marriages, whether they are living with you or not.

Age	Sex	Weight	Height	Overweight			Underweight	
___	___	_____	_____	very	slightly	average	slightly	very
___	___	_____	_____	very	slightly	average	slightly	very
___	___	_____	_____	very	slightly	average	slightly	very
___	___	_____	_____	very	slightly	average	slightly	very
___	___	_____	_____	very	slightly	average	slightly	very

36. Who lives at home with you? _____

FAMILY HISTORY:

37. Is your father living?   Yes   No   Father's age now, or age at and cause of death _____

38. Is your mother living?   Yes   No   Mother's age now, or age at and cause of death _____

39. Describe your father's occupation _____

40. Describe your mother's occupation _____

41. Describe your father's weight while you were growing up (circle one).

very overweight	slightly overweight	about average	slightly underweight	very underweight

42. Describe your mother's weight while you were growing up (circle one).

very	slightly	about	slightly	very
overweight	overweight	average	underweight	underweight

43. List your brothers' and sisters' ages, sex, present weights, heights, and circle whether they are overweight, average, or underweight.

Age	Sex	Weight	Height	Overweight			Underweight	
——	——	————	————	very	slightly	average	slightly	very
——	——	————	————	very	slightly	average	slightly	very
——	——	————	————	very	slightly	average	slightly	very
——	——	————	————	very	slightly	average	slightly	very
——	——	————	————	very	slightly	average	slightly	very

44. Please add any additional information you feel may be relevant to your weight problem. This includes interactions with your family and friends that might sabotage a weight-loss program, and additional family or social history that you feel might help us understand your weight problem.

_____

_____

_____

_____

_____

_____

_____

_____

Adherence Tool 8-2 Monitoring Device

Goal Attainment Chart

Date _____

Suggestions:

Goal: _____

Number of times I will achieve this goal: _____

Behavior Monitored: _____

	Days						
	1	2	3	4	5	6	7

If Did→ ✩
If Did Not→ ✓

Number of ✩s = _____
Number of ✓s = _____

Source: Courtesy of Nancy L. Schwartz, R.D.

Adherence Tool 8-3 Informational and Cueing Device

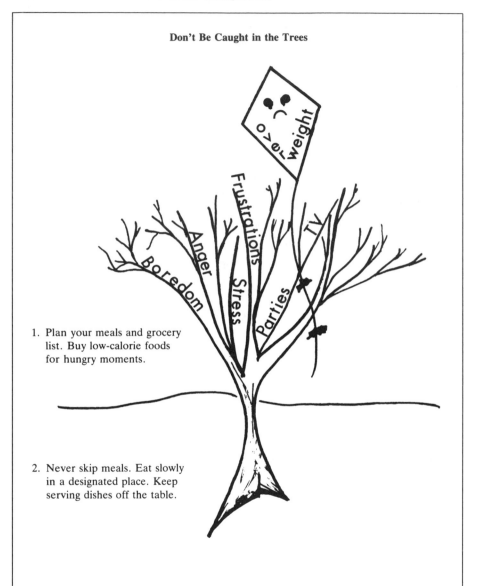

Don't Be Caught in the Trees

1. Plan your meals and grocery list. Buy low-calorie foods for hungry moments.

2. Never skip meals. Eat slowly in a designated place. Keep serving dishes off the table.

Adherence Tool 8-3 continued

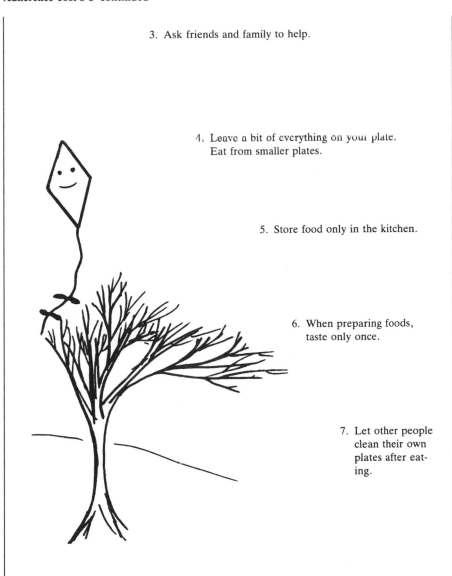

3. Ask friends and family to help.

4. Leave a bit of everything on your plate. Eat from smaller plates.

5. Store food only in the kitchen.

6. When preparing foods, taste only once.

7. Let other people clean their own plates after eating.

Review of Chapter 8
(Answers in Appendix I)

1. In the following examples, identify the inappropriate eating behaviors associated with weight gain:

   "I have followed this diet so religiously. I'm really proud of myself. The agony of passing up cocktails and opting for the diet drink at a party, the embarrassment of refusing my friend's seven-layer torte, the pain of refusing the birthday cake my kids made especially for me, and on and on. Those days are behind me now. I lost 20 pounds and now I'm home free."

   What syndrome is this sort of thinking leading to? _____

   "What is wrong with me? Don't I have any willpower? I look like a fat slob and yet I continue to eat. I'm just a hopeless case."

   What syndrome does this sort of self-talk tell you as a counselor that the client is struggling with? _____

2. List three steps in assessing individual eating behaviors.
   a. _____
   b. _____
   c. _____

3. List six strategies that might be used to facilitate weight loss in the following two clients.

   Jan, a 30-year-old female, is nearly 20 pounds overweight. She is very upset over this and has tried many ways toward quick and easy weight control—diet pills, fasting, fad diets, etc. Jan has a family of four and works from 8 A.M. to 5 P.M. at a dress shop. She prepares breakfast for her family each morning, eats at a cafeteria for lunch, and fixes dinner for the family each evening. Her major problem, she indicates, is evening snacking.

   Dan, a 40-year-old male, is 30 pounds overweight. He frequently is depressed over his weight and has tried many lose-weight-quick treatments. All have failed. He lives alone and works nights on a line in a factory. He sleeps during the day and eats all of his meals away from home.

   a. _____
   b. _____
   c. _____
   d. _____
   e. _____
   f. _____

4. Describe one situation in which you would use one or more of those six strategies. Indicate your rationale. _____
   _____
   _____
   _____

NOTES

1. George A. Bray and R. J. Teague, "An Algorithm for the Medical Evaluation of Obese Patients," in George A. Bray, ed., *Obesity* (Philadelphia, Pa.: W. B. Saunders Co., 1980), pp. 240–248.

2. Ibid.; Kelly D. Brownell and Albert J. Stunkard, "Differential Changes in Plasma High Density Lipoprotein Cholesterol in Obese Men and Women," *Archives of Internal Medicine* 141 (1981): 1142–1146; and Bo Larson, Per Björntrop, and Gosta Tibblin, "The Health Consequences of Moderate Obesity," *International Journal of Obesity* 5 (1981): 97–116.

3. Food and Nutrition Board, *Recommended Dietary Allowances,* 9th ed. (Washington, D.C.: National Academy of Sciences, National Research Council, 1980), p. 46.

4. Eleanor Noss Whitney and Eva May Nunnelley Hamilton, *Understanding Nutrition* (St. Paul, Minn.: West Publishing Co., 1981), p. 248.

5. Food and Nutrition Board, *Recommended Dietary Allowances,* p. 46.

6. Kelly D. Brownell, "The Psychology and Physiology of Obesity: Implications for Screening and Treatment," *Journal of the American Dietetic Association* 84 (1984): 406–414.

7. S. Schachter, "Recidivism and Self-Cure of Smoking and Obesity," *American Psychologist* 84 (1982): 436–444.

8. Robert W. Jeffrey et al., "Prevalence of Overweight and Weight Loss Behavior in a Metropolitan Adult Population: The Minnesota Heart Survey Experience," *American Journal of Public Health* 74 (1984): 349–352.

9. Schachter, "Recidivism and Self-Cure."

10. D. Balfour Jeffrey, "Treatment Evaluation Issues in Research on Addictive Behaviors," *Addictive Behaviors* 1 (1975): 23–26; Gloria R. Leon, "Current Directions in the Treatment of Obesity," *Psychological Bulletin* 83 (1976): 557–578; and Albert J. Stunkard, "From Explanation to Action in Psychosomatic Medicine: The Case of Obesity," *Psychosomatic Medicine* 37 (1975): 195–236.

11. Sharon M. Hall et al., "Permanence of Two Self-Managed Treatments of Overweight in University and Community Population," *Journal of Consulting Clinical Psychology* 42 (1974): 781–786.

12. William M. Beneke and Barbara K. Paulsen, "Long Term Efficacy of a Behavior Modification Weight Loss Program: A Comparison of Two Follow-up Maintenance Strategies," *Behavior Therapy* 10 (1978): 8–13; Robert W. Jeffrey, Rena R. Wing, and Albert J. Stunkard, "Behavioral Treatment of Obesity: The State of the Art in 1976," *Behavior Therapy* 9 (1978): 189–199; Raymond G. Kingsley and G. Terence Wilson, "Behavior Therapy for Obesity: A Comparative Investigation of Long Term Efficacy," *Journal of Consulting and Clinical Psychology* 45 (1977): 288–298.

13. Richard B. Stuart, "Behavior Control of Overeating," *Behaviour Research and Therapy* 5 (1967): 357–365.

14. Peter M. Miller and Karen L. Sims, "Evaluation and Component Analysis of a Comprehensive Weight Control Program," *International Journal of Obesity* 5 (1981): 57–65.

15. Kelly D. Brownell and Albert J. Stunkard, "Behavior Therapy and Behavior Change: Uncertainties in Programs for Weight Control," *Behaviour Research and Therapy* 16 (1978): 301; and Jeffrey, Wing, and Stunkard, "Behavioral Treatment of Obesity."

16. Miller and Sims, "Evaluation and Component Analysis."

17. Michael J. Mahoney and Kathryn Mahoney, "Treatment of Obesity: A Clinical Exploration," in Ben J. Williams, Sander Martin, and John P. Foreyt, eds., *Obesity: Behavioral Approaches to Dietary Management* (New York: Brunner/Mazel, 1976), pp. 30–39.

18. Peter M. Stalones, Jr., William G. Johnson, and Maryann Christ, "Behavior Modification

for Obesity: The Evaluation of Exercise, Contingency Management and Program Adherence," *Journal of Consulting Clinical Psychologists* 46 (1978): 463–469.

19. Mahoney and Mahoney, "Treatment of Obesity."

20. Kelly D. Brownell et al., "The Effect of Couples Training and Partner Cooperativeness in the Behavioral Treatment of Obesity," *Behaviour Research and Therapy* 16 (1978): 323–333.

21. Michael J. Mahoney, "The Obese Eating Style: Bites, Beliefs and Behavior Modification," *Addictive Behaviors* 1 (1975): 47–53; and Nancy Adams et al., "The Eating Style of Obese and Non-Obese Women," *Behaviour Research and Therapy* 16 (1978): 225–232.

22. Beneke and Paulsen, "Long Term Efficacy."

23. Thomas J. Coates, "Eating—A Psychological Dilemma," *Journal of Nutrition Education* 13 (1981) (Supplement): S34–S48; and David A. Booth, "Acquired Behavior Controlling Energy Input and Output," in Albert J. Stunkard, ed., *Obesity* (Philadelphia, Pa.: W. B. Saunders Co., 1980), p. 102.

24. Theodore B. Van Itallie, "Dietary Approaches to the Treatment of Obesity," in Albert J. Stunkard, ed., *Obesity* (Philadelphia: W. B. Saunders Co., 1980, pp. 249–261; George A. Bray, "Jejunoileal Bypass, Jaw Wiring, and Vagotomy for Massive Obesity," in Albert J. Stunkard, ed., *Obesity* (Philadelphia: W. B. Saunders Co., 1980, pp. 369–387; and John E. Blundell, "Pharmacological Adjustment of the Mechanisms Underlying Feeding and Obesity," in Albert J. Stunkard, ed., *Obesity* (Philadelphia: W. B. Saunders Co., 1980), pp. 182–207.

25. Booth, "Acquired Behavior."

26. James M. Ferguson, *Habits Not Diets* (Palo Alto, Calif.: Bull Publishing Co., 1976), p. 65.

27. Michael J. Mahoney and Kathryn Mahoney, *Permanent Weight Control* (New York: W. W. Norton & Co., 1976), pp. 46–68.

28. M. Robin DiMatteo and D. Dante DeNicola, "Achieving Patient Compliance: The Psychology of the Medical Practitioner's Role" (New York: Pergamon Press, 1982), pp. 236–237.

29. Rosy Woo, John S. Garrow, and Fi Xavier Pi-Sunyer, "Effect of Exercise on Spontaneous Calorie Intake," *American Journal of Clinical Nutrition* 36 (1982): 470–484; and James O'Hill et al., "Effects of Exercise and Food Restriction on Body Composition," *American Journal of Clinical Nutrition* 46 (1987): 622–630.

30. Michael L. Russell, *Behavioral Counseling in Medicine: Strategies for Modifying at Risk Behavior* (New York: Oxford University Press, 1986), pp. 306–315.

31. Kelly D. Brownell, "Assessment of Eating Disorders," in David Barlow, ed., *Behavioral Assessment of Adult Disorders* (New York: The Guilford Press, 1981), pp. 366–374.

32. George Bray and R. J. Teague, "An Algorithm for the Medical Evaluation of Obese Patients," Bray, ed., *Obesity*, pp. 240–248.

33. Ferguson, *Habits*, pp. 31–32.

Chapter 9

Nutrition Counseling in Prevention and Treatment of Coronary Heart Disease

Objectives for Chapter 9

1. Identify common dietary misconceptions about fat- and cholesterol-modified patterns that lead to inappropriate eating behaviors.
2. Identify common dietary excesses that contribute to inappropriate eating behaviors associated with diets low in fat and cholesterol.
3. Identify specific nutrients that should be emphasized in assessing a baseline eating pattern before providing dietary instruction.
4. Identify strategies to treat inappropriate behaviors associated with fat- and cholesterol-modified eating patterns.
5. Generate strategies to deal with clients following low-fat and low-cholesterol eating patterns.
6. Recommend dietary adherence tools for clients on fat- and cholesterol-modified eating patterns.

In 1984 the National Institutes of Health sponsored a Consensus Development Conference (CDC) on Lowering Blood Cholesterol to Prevent Heart Disease. The purpose of "consensus development" was to narrow the gap between the health research community, practicing physicians, and the public. The 14-member consensus panel recommended the following:[1]

1. In high-risk persons (with values above the 90th percentile for total blood cholesterol [see Table 9-1]) treatment should be dietary under the guidance of a physician, dietitian, or other health professional. If dietary restrictions do not result in lower blood cholesterol, appropriate drugs should be added to the treatment regimen.
2. Adults with moderate-risk blood cholesterol levels (values between the 75th and 90th percentiles for total blood cholesterol [see Table 9-1]) should be treated intensively with diet. Only a small percentage of this group will require drugs.

Table 9-1 Mean Serum Cholesterol Levels of Men and Women, SEM, Age-Adjusted Values, Selected Percentiles, Number of Examined Persons, and Estimated Population, by Race and Age: United States, 1978–1980

Race, Age, y	No. of Persons Examined	Estimated Population in Thousands	Mean	SEM	Percentile*								
					5th	10th	15th	25th	50th	75th	85th	90th	95th
Men													
All races†													
20–74	5604	63611	211	1.2	144	156	165	179	206	239	258	271	291
20–24	676	9331	180	1.7	129	136	145	155	176	202	215	227	246
25–34	1067	15895	199	1.5	141	152	159	172	194	220	240	254	275
35–44	745	11367	217	2.0	153	166	173	187	215	244	262	275	293
45–54	690	11114	227	1.8	159	176	182	197	223	255	271	283	303
55–64	1227	9607	229	1.8	164	176	184	198	225	254	277	288	307
65–74	1199	6297	221	1.8	153	167	175	191	217	249	265	279	301
White													
20–74	4883	55808	211	1.2	145	157	166	179	207	239	258	271	291
20–24	581	8052	180	1.8	131	138	146	155	176	202	216	229	244
25–34	901	13864	199	1.7	144	153	161	172	194	220	239	254	273
35–44	653	9808	217	1.8	153	166	173	187	214	244	260	272	291
45–54	617	9865	227	1.8	160	177	181	198	222	254	271	283	303
55–64	1086	8642	230	2.0	164	178	185	199	225	255	278	289	307
65–74	1045	5576	222	2.0	153	167	175	191	217	250	266	281	301
Black													
20–74	607	6102	208	2.5	133	146	156	171	200	238	260	273	301
20–24	79	1043	171	3.7†	...†	128	134	149	170	193	210	211	...†
25–34	139	1546	199	4.1†	129	136	144	163	192	226	248	259	301
35–44	70	1112	218	8.3†	...†	156	168	176	202	238	275	283	...†
45–54	62	1044	229	7.1†	...†	174	184	195	232	261	268	279	...†
55–64	129	801	223	4.8†	157	168	172	183	218	254	271	299	312
65–74	128	555	217	4.2	149	163	173	183	216	244	261	277	299

Table 9-1 continued

Race, Age, y	No. of Persons Examined	Estimated Population in Thousands	Mean	SEM	Percentile*								
					5th	10th	15th	25th	50th	75th	85th	90th	95th
Age-adjusted values													
All races,													
20-74	...	...	211	1.1	...	...	...	...	...	...	...	...	...
White,													
20-74	...	...	211	1.1	...	...	...	...	...	...	...	...	...
Black,													
20-74	...	...	209	2.5	...	...	...	...	...	...	...	...	...
Women													
All races†													
20-74	6260	69994	215	1.2	143	156	166	179	210	245	266	282	305
20-24	738	9994	184	1.9	132	140	145	157	180	204	216	230	250
25-34	1170	16856	192	1.4	135	145	154	164	188	215	233	243	263
35-44	844	12284	207	1.8	147	158	164	177	202	231	248	260	276
45-54	763	11918	232	2.2	164	178	188	199	228	257	275	290	306
55-64	1329	10743	249	2.0	180	193	203	215	242	277	299	314	336
65-74	1416	8198	246	1.6	173	189	198	214	241	274	295	309	327
White													
20-74	5418	60785	216	1.3	143	156	166	179	210	246	267	282	305
20-24	624	8408	184	2.1	133	140	147	159	181	204	215	230	249
25-34	1000	14494	192	1.5	135	145	153	164	188	215	235	244	261
35-44	726	10584	207	1.9	147	157	164	177	203	231	248	259	277
45-54	647	10369	232	2.6	166	179	188	199	228	257	274	290	308
55-64	1176	9601	249	1.7	180	193	203	215	244	277	298	312	330
65-74	1245	7329	246	1.7	174	190	199	214	242	275	296	309	328

Table 9-1 continued

Race, Age, y	No. of Persons Examined	Estimated Population in Thousands	Mean	SEM	Percentile*								
					5th	10th	15th	25th	50th	75th	85th	90th	95th
Women con't													
Black													
20-74	729	7579	212	3.1	140	154	166	176	205	237	263	279	308
20-24	94	1304	185	4.9†	...†	136	144	156	178	204	220	237	...†
25-34	145	1953	191	4.1†	129	144	156	167	190	212	226	235	267
35-44	103	1415	206	4.5†	143	158	170	175	194	233	254	274	279
45-54	100	1215	230	7.2†	150	172	181	200	226	263	277	291	306
55-64	135	959	251	8.0†	178	185	198	211	233	280	318	336	345
65-74	152	733	243	4.2	173	189	198	211	237	269	290	308	323
Age-adjusted values													
All races,													
20-74	...	...	215	1.2	...	...	...	...	...	...	...	...	...
White,													
20-74	...	...	215	1.2	...	...	...	...	...	...	...	...	...
Black,													
20-74	...	...	214	2.7	...	...	...	...	...	...	...	...	...

*Serum cholesterol values are given in milligrams per deciliter. To convert values to millimoles per liter, multiply by 0.02586.

†Includes data for races not shown separately.

Source: Data taken from "Total Serum Cholesterol Levels of Adults 20-74 Years of Age: United States, 1976–1980, Vital and Health Statistics" by National Center for Health Statistics, Ser. II, No. 236, Department of Health and Human Services publication, PHS 86–1686, U.S. Government Printing Office, May 1986.

3. All Americans (with the exception of children under two years) should adopt a diet containing 30 percent of total calories from fat, less than 10 percent of calories from saturated fat, less than 10 percent from polyunsaturated fat, and 10 percent of calories from monounsaturated fat. Cholesterol should be reduced to 250 to 300 milligrams (100 milligrams of cholesterol per 1,000 calories) or less per day. (The American Academy of Pediatrics does *not* endorse this recommendation, preferring to leave percentages of fat unspecified for children.)
4. Intake of total calories should be that which maintains ideal body weight. The panel recommended a program of moderate exercise.
5. In individuals with elevated blood cholesterol levels, special attention should be given to the management of other risk factors (hypertension, cigarette smoking, diabetes, and physical activity).

The panel stated that these recommendations paralleled those of the American Heart Association and the Inter-Society Commission for Heart Disease Resources.[2] The statements indicate a major trend toward diet intervention as a first-line therapy for treatment and prevention of coronary heart disease. The CDC has provided nutritionists with goals to achieve using the many counseling strategies discussed in Chapters 1–7. This chapter shows how counseling on a special low-cholesterol, fat-modified eating pattern can help prevent coronary disease.

Good basic nutrition should play a primary role in devising a fat-modified diet pattern. The Food and Nutrition Board has not established an RDA for fat.[3] It does recommend that adequate lipids be incorporated into the diet to provide the body with essential fatty acids and carriers of fat-soluble vitamins. Ingesting 15 to 25 grams of fat per day normally meets this requirement.

Studies in both humans and animals have shown that the necessary requirement for essential fatty acids is fulfilled when 1 to 2 percent of the total caloric intake is provided by linoleic acid.[4] A diet of 1,500 calories should provide 1.5 to 3.0 grams of linoleic acid. This is accomplished easily by using vegetable oils in cooking and salad dressing. Corn, soy, and cottonseed oils each contain 6 to 8 grams of linoleic acid per tablespoon, mayonnaise 6 grams, and margarines from 1 to 5 grams.

The United Nations Committee on Dietary Allowances also places a maximum limit on the amount of polyunsaturated fat consumed in a day. The committee recommends not exceeding 10 percent of dietary calories as polyunsaturated fat.[5] Counselors should begin decreasing saturated fat in clients' diets, thereby automatically increasing the ratio of polyunsaturated to saturated fat (P/S ratio) of the diet. A diet modifying fat and cholesterol should not be started by increasing polyunsaturated fat without first decreasing saturated fat.

THEORIES AND FACTS ABOUT NUTRITION AND CORONARY HEART DISEASE

Eating large amounts of cholesterol and fat can cause an elevation in various lipid-carrying particles in our blood, a condition called hyperlipidemia. Hyperlipoproteinemia is a more specific term used to define the class or classes of plasma lipoproteins that are elevated.

There is clinical interest in hyperlipoproteinemia because of its close association with coronary heart disease. Although the etiology of coronary heart disease involves a multitude of factors, epidemiological studies have conclusively shown that hypercholesterolemia is a major risk factor for coronary heart disease.[6] Many of these studies use a single value of cholesterol at the time of entry into the study. However, multiple measurements of plasma cholesterol concentrations increase their power to identify premature risk for coronary heart disease.[7]

Research on Lipoproteins

Although total plasma cholesterol serves as an indicator of coronary heart disease, identifying the risk associated with specific particles that carry cholesterol provides even greater diagnostic information. The transport of cholesterol in lipoprotein particles is discussed below.

Before insoluble cholesterol is transported out of the liver cell into the plasma, it must be solubilized by special mechanisms. The liver has developed the capacity to "package" cholesterol into macromolecular complexes in which specific proteins, called apoproteins, interact with phospholipids to bring lipids into soluble form. The resultant particles are called lipoproteins. They contain lipids in their core with unesterified cholesterol (free cholesterol or FC), phopholipids (PL), and apoproteins (aP) in their membranelike coats.

The major lipoprotein secreted by the liver is very low-density lipoprotein (VLDL). Newly secreted VLDL contains triglyceride (TG) in its core. Immediately upon entrance into plasma, the basic structure of VLDL begins to alter. First, it acquires more cholesterol esters (CE) in the core. High-density lipoprotein (HDL) appears to transfer CE directly into VLDL, which is altered by lipolypsis of triglyceride through the action of lipoprotein lipase. As hydrolysis proceeds, free fatty acids (FFA) are released, the size of VLDL is reduced, and density increases, resulting in a new category of lipoprotein, designated intermediate-density lipoprotein (IDL). IDL appears to be transformed to a lipoprotein of lower density, low-density lipoprotein (LDL). In tissues culture studies, when lipoproteins are added to media cells can derive most of their cholesterol from uptake of these IDL particles. Figure 9-1 illustrates schematically the mechanisms for cholesterol transport.

Stein and Glomset propose that HDL may protect against atherosclerosis by promoting removal of cholesterol from the tissues.[8] In this case it would transport cholesterol from peripheral tissues to the liver. A second mechanism by which HDL might potentially protect against atherosclerosis is by competing with the uptake of LDL by the cells in the arterial wall.

The normal limits for lipoproteins are described below (expressed in milligrams per 100 milliliters). Table 9-2 contains mean cholesterol levels for persons 20 to 74 years of age.

Research on Cholesterol and Fatty Acids and Their Effect on Lipoproteins

Research has shown that dietary cholesterol is related to morbidity and mortality from coronary heart disease.[9] A number of investigators have examined the effect of various fatty acids on lipoprotein levels. All have concluded that a significant portion of the saturated fatty acids should be removed to lower total cholesterol significantly. The investigations have raised questions about what source of energy should replace the saturated fatty acids, with the three major candidates being carbohydrate, polyunsaturated fatty acids, and monounsaturated fatty acids.

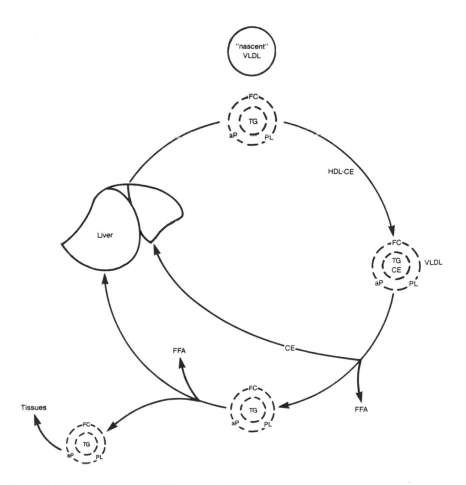

Figure 9-1 Plasma Transport of Cholesterol

A series of recent studies has compared the effects of these three replacements on lipoprotein levels, with Shepherd, Grundy, and Mensink and Katan the prominent investigators in this area. Considered together, Shepherd et al.'s studies suggest that diets very high in polyunsaturated fatty acids (P/S = 4.0) compared with a high–saturated fatty acid diet (P/S = 0.25) may lower LDL and HDL cholesterol proportionately.[10] Studies by Matthson and Grundy suggest that a high–polyunsaturated fatty acid diet (40 percent of calories from safflower oil) compared with a high–saturated fatty acid diet (40 percent of calories from lard) produces a lower LDL and HDL level with a greater effect on LDL.[11] Mensink and Katan and Grundy, in comparing a high-monounsaturated (40 percent of total calories from fat, P/S = 2.0) with a high-carbohydrate diet (20 percent of calories from fat, P/S = 1.0), showed that the high-carbohydrate diet lowered total cholesterol, LDL, and HDL.[12] These data

Table 9-2 Calculated Levels of Serum Low-Density Lipoprotein (LDL) Cholesterol* for Persons† 20 to 74 Years of Age Fasting 12 Hours or More, by Sex and Age: Means and Selected Percentiles, United States, 1976–1980

Sex, Age, y	No. of Persons Examined	Estimated Population in Thousands	Mean	SD	Selected Percentiles								
					5th	10th	15th	25th	50th	75th	85th	90th	95th
Men													
20-74	1037	21262	140	39	80	92	100	113	136	164	181	194	208
20-24	72	1852	109	36	..‡	70	74	88	104	129	149	154	..‡
25-34	174	5186	128	33	76	87	94	108	128	148	161	171	189
35-44	130	3866	145	40	81	96	105	116	138	176	192	203	206
45-54	106	3543	150	36	99	103	112	119	146	171	189	195	211
55-64	267	3943	148	39	84	101	108	118	147	171	191	206	217
65-74	288	2872	149	40	87	105	109	120	144	174	188	199	217
Women													
20-74	1246	27102	141	43	81	91	98	110	136	164	186	199	220
20-24	105	3325	114	33	69	74	83	94	106	136	149	155	179
25-34	194	5517	121	33	72	83	90	98	116	139	154	166	187
35-44	166	4800	129	34	78	90	97	107	126	150	163	171	191
45-54	168	5155	157	45	94	104	116	125	156	184	200	213	226
55-64	282	4644	159	42	101	113	118	129	150	188	205	219	237
65-74	331	3661	162	44	98	109	122	135	158	186	207	226	245

*Serum LDL Cholesterol = Serum Total Cholesterol − HDL Cholesterol − (Triglycerides/5). Persons with a serum triglyceride value greater than 400 mg/dL were excluded.

†Includes other races in addition to black and white.

‡Sample size insufficient to produce statistically reliable results.

Source: Data taken from "Total Serum Cholesterol Levels of Adults 20-74 Years of Age: United States, 1976–1980, Vital and Health Statistics" by National Center for Health Statistics, Ser. II, No. 236, Department of Health and Human Services publication, PHS 86–1686, U.S. Government Printing Office, May 1986.

suggest that a high–monounsaturated fatty acid diet may maintain HDL levels better than a high-carbohydrate diet does.

An important element of the studies described above is that they were performed in inpatient or outpatient clinical research units; participants were given food or liquid diets. No investigator compared the three replacement nutrients (polyunsaturated fat, monounsaturated fat, or carbohydrate) in the same series of study subjects. A final limitation is that the studies compared very large changes in dietary fatty acid composition, without any gradations.

Fish oils (omega-3 fatty acids) are also being researched. The major change in lipoprotein levels in subjects taking fish oil capsules was in triglycerides.[13] Some research showed decreased changes in platelet aggregation in participants who were given fish oil supplements.[14] More definitive research on larger numbers of people is necessary to prove these hypotheses.

RESEARCH ON COMPLIANCE WITH EATING PATTERNS LOW IN FAT AND CHOLESTEROL

Ten studies aimed at changing dietary habits to include low-cholesterol, fat-modified eating patterns are summarized below.

In the Multiple Risk Factor Intervention Trial (MRFIT), intervention focused on the subjects' developing lifelong shopping, cooking, and eating patterns rather than specifying a structured diet.[15] Individual nutrition counseling with periodic monitoring resulted in significant cholesterol reductions, though risk also declined in the control group.[16] A comprehensive community health-promotion program in North Karelia, Finland, yielded significant reductions in cholesterol in comparison with a reference county where no intervention was implemented.[17] However, the North Karelia Project's design precluded knowledge of which aspects of the health education program instigated the change.

In an evaluation of nutrition education for persons with postmyocardial infarction, Karvetti found significant improvements with both lecture-discussion and food-preparation demonstration strategies. Though neither approach was significantly more effective for stimulating behavior change, this study pointed out the possible importance of organized nutrition education programs for persons with coronary heart disease.[18] Several studies have compared the use of educational materials and mass media with interventions augmented by personal contact or counseling by a health professional.[19] In each instance, educational programs that included interpersonal methods were more successful.

Several of the programs designed for delivery to groups have engaged social support. For example, family participation improved the magnitude of cholesterol reductions in Witschi et al.'s subjects, though they did not maintain the reductions after the intervention was discontinued.[20] In fact, it has been found repeatedly that improved eating habits and reduced lipid levels do not persist when an intervention is not sustained.[21] Bruno et al. were able to attain high continuous participation rates (81 percent) in a worksite program that included six monthly maintenance meetings.[22] The achievement of long-term benefits from dietary interventions on lipids requires further development of booster sessions, self-monitoring techniques, and reinforcement techniques. Glanz summarizes the elements needed to maintain dietary compliance to low-cholesterol, fat-modified diets: enlist social support, maintain periodic contact, encourage self-monitoring, and provide feedback about adherence.[23]

INAPPROPRIATE EATING BEHAVIORS

False information about eating patterns modified for fat and cholesterol can lead to inappropriate eating behaviors.

A common problem many clients face is use of commercial products. Keeping abreast of information on new fat-containing products must be a continuing effort by both nutrition counselors and their clients. Clients and counselors can develop and use a shopping guide to determine whether new products are low or high in fat, as in Exhibit 9-1. This information is based on labels; more specific data can be obtained by writing to the manufacturers.

A frequent problem is the mistaken idea that all vegetable oils are low in saturated fat. A client might exclaim joyously: "This palm oil listed on the label is probably okay on my diet since it is vegetable oil." Unfortunately, palm oil is highly saturated. Another misconception is that eggs alone cause elevated cholesterol levels. A client might state: "As long as I cut out eggs in my diet, I don't need to worry." In fact, foods low in cholesterol and high in saturated fat, such as palm oil and coconut oil, also elevate serum cholesterol.

Some clients feel that certain foods possess strange powers to eliminate cholesterol and therefore lower its concentration in the blood. They see single foods as a panacea. A client might claim: "I eat large amounts of fruits and vegetables so I don't worry about my cholesterol intake." The total diet must be considered when assessing fat and cholesterol intake. Single foods do not eliminate the effect of fat and cholesterol in the diet.

Still another erroneous idea is that total fat content does not really matter. As long as a high-fat item is cholesterol free, clients may believe mistakenly that it can be eaten in unlimited quantities. A client might state proudly: "I eat large amounts of peanut butter because it is cholesterol free." This statement is true, but large quantities of fat elevate the caloric level of the diet and can lead to weight gain.

These misconceptions are by no means the only ones that clients voice. They are, however, very common sources of problem eating behaviors. Nutrition counselors see only a small sampling of daily eating behaviors, so if self-report methods like diet diaries are used, it is possible that clients can consume commercial products containing saturated fat without detection for long periods of time.

Clients following fat- and cholesterol-modified eating patterns must wrestle with problems of excess much as clients on weight-control diets do. Social pressures can lead clients to eat something they know increases cholesterol, with the familiar alibi: "I just couldn't stop with one bite of that cheesecake at the party last night." These eating patterns also may mean a drastic reduction in the amounts of foods clients are accustomed to eating. They may comment: "No one can live on this small amount of meat."

Inappropriate eating behaviors may be a direct result of childhood excesses. The stalwart farmer may declare: "I grew up eating three eggs every morning."

Manufacturers have come to the aid of clients who must follow fat-modified diets by providing either "filled" products or nearly fat-free substitutes. The "filled" products are those that may, for example, have animal fat removed and a polyunsaturated fat added. Others may have all animal fat removed, with no polyunsaturated fat replacement. This can leave the product virtually fat free. Unfortunately, in many cases clients anticipate that these new products will be identical in taste to the originals, so frustration and even anger may result when those expectations are not met. In

Exhibit 9-1 Shoppers' Guide to Low Cholesterol

Date: _____

Breads
Acceptable
Sourdough Toast (Wasa)
The following mixes, prepared with home fat:
   Honey French Sourdough Bread Mix (Goldrush)
   Wheatberry Sourdough Bread Mix (Goldrush)
   Bran and Buttermilk Sourdough Bread Mix (Goldrush)
   Sourdough Pancake and Waffle Mix: Whole Wheat, Honey, Buttermilk varieties
   (Goldrush)
   Buttermilk Pancake Mix (Martha White)

Cereals
Acceptable
Back to Nature (Organic Milling Co.)
   Almond Crisp   No added fat
   Raisin Bran Crunch   No added fat
To be avoided (too high in total fat and
contain saturated fat)
Golden Harvest (Natural Sales Co.):   Fat (gms/100 gms)
   Apple Bran   24.7—soybean oil, coconut
   Old Fashioned Granola   14.1—soybean oil, coconut
   Premier Granola   21.2—soybean oil, coconut

Sauces, Seasonings, Gravies
Acceptable
Picanto Sauce (Tostitos)   No fat
Snacks
(Relatively high in fat; Use only _____ *)
For use with discretion
   Potato Chips, regular and barbecue   Approx. 40% fat—liquid cottonseed oil
     flavor (Charles Chips)
   Natural Flavor Potato Chips (Health   Approx. 40% fat—safflower oil
     Valley)
   Natural Flavor Bran Corn Chips   Approx. 37% fat—safflower oil
Miscellaneous
To be avoided (Too high in total fat and contain saturated fat)
                         Fat (gms/100 gms)
   On-Yos Salad Topping (General Mills)   37—partially hydrogenated vegetable oil
                                (soybean, palm, cottonseed)
   Nut-Os Salad Topping (General Mills)   31—vegetable oil (coconut, cottonseed,
                                sunflower seed, peanut, soybean)

_____
*The amount specified will depend on the particular diet prescription for each client.

desperation, they may revert to old eating habits, including products high in animal fat.

Clients equate excesses with the prevention of medical problems: "I use large amounts of oil and margarines extremely high in polyunsaturated fat because I know polyunsaturated fat lowers cholesterol." These inappropriate eating behaviors can lead to excess, unwanted calories. Clients must learn first to examine ways to reduce saturated fats.

ASSESSMENT OF EATING BEHAVIORS

As in counseling on other eating patterns, knowledge of what the client is currently eating is extremely important. By learning how strict the client's present diet is, the nutrition counselor can tailor dietary intake to lower blood cholesterol. For example, learning that a client currently consumes 600 milligrams of cholesterol a day through a semiquantified food frequency may mean that a prescription of 200 milligrams of cholesterol per day with a P/S ratio of 1.0 will lower blood cholesterol dramatically. In contrast, for a client whose intake is 200 milligrams of cholesterol per day, an eating pattern containing 100 milligrams of cholesterol per day with a P/S ratio of 1.0 may be necessary to lower blood cholesterol.

Ideally, a seven-day record along with a quantified food frequency gives excellent information on current dietary patterns. Five crucial components of the eating pattern should be assessed: (1) cholesterol, (2) saturated fat, (3) polyunsaturated fat, (4) monounsaturated fat, and (5) total dietary fat. When time is short Exhibit 9-2 may serve as a quick means of getting a rough estimate of fat and cholesterol intake. The list can be increased or abbreviated depending on the information needed in formulating a dietary pattern. The review of the dietary data should indicate where a major problem is occurring—cholesterol content, saturated fat content, or both. Identification of where the major excess lies will lead to a plan for dietary change focused on strategies to help eliminate the inappropriate patterns.

If counselors use the short food frequency monitor in Exhibit 9-2 but inadequacies in the overall nutritional quality of the diet are in question, clients might fill out a more detailed, all-inclusive food frequency record to assess the nutrient content of their diet. Adherence Tool 9-1 is a questionnaire that focuses on food preparation and food patterns, with an emphasis on fat and cholesterol intake.

The fat-related misinformation spread by the media makes it important to assess the amount of misinformation a client currently has, for example, by asking, "Is this statement true or false? All vegetable oil helps lower cholesterol." An instrument with a variety of short true-or-false questions could serve as a basis for discussions of misinformation. Adherence Tool 9-2, Facts or Misfacts, is a short, fun way to discuss misconceptions about the low-cholesterol, fat-controlled eating pattern. This tool should not be used as a test but as a way of opening a discussion about incorrect ideas the media may have promoted.

As with other eating patterns, assessment of adherence to the low-cholesterol, fat-controlled eating pattern is important. It may involve seven-day diet records or very simple check-off systems, as in Adherence Tool 9-3. Just a "✓" in the box would indicate adherence with the recommendation of 2 ounces of meat at lunch. Analysis of dietary intake from diet diaries can provide valuable information on adherence. Adherence Tools 9-4 and 9-5 provide graphs that illustrate the client's level of dietary adherence.

A survey of food items in the kitchen can reveal inappropriate cueing that triggers inappropriate eating behaviors. Adherence Tool 9-6 is an example of a monitoring device that helps identify foods high in fat that are in the client's kitchen. Clients write down the food and check the column corresponding to the type of fat present in the largest quantity.

Exhibit 9-2 Fat and Cholesterol Intake Monitor

Name _____   Visit No. _____   Date _____

	Amount	Cholesterol (mg.)	Total Fat (gm.)	Saturated Fat (gm.)	Polyun- saturated Fat (gm.)	Monoun- saturated Fat (gm.)	Minimum Significant Amount
Eggs							½ mo
Bacon							4 strips/mo
Sausage							2 oz/mo
Meat Lunch							
Dinner							
Luncheon Meat							See sausage
Shrimp							2 oz/mo
Liver, Pork, or Beef							3 oz/6 mo
Liver, Chicken							1 oz/2 mo
Gravy							1 cup/mo
Milk, whole____							½ cup/wk
2%____							1 cup/wk
Cheese _____							1 oz/2 wks
Cottage Cheese							½ cup/2 wks
Cream—Light, Sour							1 tb/wk
Heavy							1 tb/mo
Half and Half							1 tb/wk
Nondairy Creamer							1 tb/wk
Ice Cream							½ cup/mo
Ice Milk							1 cup/mo
Butter							1 tsp/2 wks
Margarine (as spread)							
Oil (in cooking)							1 tsp/wk
Salad Dressing							1 tsp/wk

Exhibit 9-2 continued

	Amount	Cholesterol (mg.)	Total Fat (gm.)	Saturated Fat (gm.)	Polyunsaturated Fat (gm.)	Monounsaturated Fat (gm.)	Minimum Significant Amount
*Breaded Fried Foods							1 tb/wk
*Fried Potatoes							1 tsp/wk
*Baked Products							1 tsp/wk
*Snack Foods							1 sv/mo
Chocolate							½ oz/wk
Peanut Butter							1 tb/wk
Nuts							4 tb/mo
Total							

Polyunsaturated fat ÷ saturated fat (P/S) = _____

*For use in calculating:

	Yields
3–4" diameter pancakes	1 tsp. fat
1 fried egg	1 tsp. fat
1 tbsp. of salad dressing	1½ tsp. fat
1 oz. pan fried meat, fish and poultry	½ tsp. fat
1 oz. breaded and fried meat, fish and poultry	1 tsp. fat

	Yields
15 pieces of French fried potatoes (1½"×½"×½")	2 tsp. fat
½ cup pan fried potatoes	2 tsp. fat
cake with frosting (1 piece, 2"×3"×2")	3 tsp. fat
pie (1 piece, 1/7th of 9")	4 tsp. fat
cookies (4 pieces, 3" diam.)	3 tsp. fat
doughnuts and sweet rolls (1 piece, 4" diam.)	2 tsp. fat
crackers and chips (excluding low-fat crackers) (12 pieces)	3 tsp. fat

Source: Courtesy of Joan Bickel, Karen Smith, Linda G. Snetselaar, and Laura Vailas.

TREATMENT STRATEGIES

Treatment strategies involve three aspects of compliance: lack of knowledge, forgetfulness, and lack of commitment.

Strategies To Deal with Lack of Knowledge

Meal planning is one way to avoid last-minute decisions and to ensure that clients consistently adhere to the basics of a low-cholesterol, fat-modified diet. Adherence Tool 9-7 provides a format for planning menus. Showing clients how to select foods low in cholesterol and fat is crucial to their eventual success, and counselors should indicate the total cholesterol, saturated fat, polyunsaturated fat, and monounsaturated fat in the original high-cholesterol, high-fat eating pattern. It can then be compared with one that includes preferred foods but follows a prescription low in cholesterol and fat. Adherence Tool 9-8 is a short list of suggestions for use when dining out, and Adherence Tool 9-9 provides examples of meals eaten at home and in restaurants that are both high and low in cholesterol and fat. Adherence Tool 9-10 shows ranges of P/S ratios for various fats and oils.

With a clear description of the problem, counselors can begin tailoring the diet to specific client needs. Tailoring involves more than just adapting a standard low-cholesterol, fat-modified diet instruction sheet; a major element is calculating a pattern compatible with the prescription and the client's previous daily eating behavior. A hypothetical example of how tailoring might work in one situation follows:

Mrs. S. eats seven eggs each week and six ounces of meat a day, drinks only skim milk, and uses four teaspoons of margarine (soft, tub, nondiet) with approximately two teaspoons of Mazola oil. She loves eggs and has eaten only high-fat meats such as bologna, salami, beef weiners, etc. Based on her blood values and past health history, the dietary prescription agreed upon by the medical team is 200 milligrams of cholesterol, P/S ratio (polyunsaturated fat divided by saturated fat) of 1.0, and total fat 20–25 percent of total calories.

Table 9-3 offers a possible dietary pattern designed to incorporate this basic information and still meet the prescription. The table shows how to design a regimen designed to give success initially because it is tailored to past eating habits. Clients should be cautioned that there always will be compromises and changes necessary to meet a specific prescription. Clients should tailor other elements of the diet while working it into their life style. For example, an alteration in Mrs. S.'s diet may involve eliminating some of the seven eggs she eats each week. She may need to experiment with low-fat breakfast items such as cereal and English muffins.

Once clients and counselors agree on the pattern, instruction on the diet can begin. This consists of planned steps, beginning with tasks accomplished most easily, and working up to the more difficult ones, a process called staging the diet instruction. For example, Mrs. S. is not a dairy product lover and eats high-fat dairy products only occasionally. Her program would begin by working to eliminate all such products and on arranging substitutes. The next step would be changing the amounts and types of meats eaten. Finally, eggs are her "first love" and it will be difficult to eliminate them or to work in alternate foods. Each of these three changes can be accomplished gradually during separate interviews or telephone conversations. Either way, time should be allowed for the clients to experiment with ideas in daily life before moving on to more difficult changes.

Table 9-3 Example of a Tailoring Pattern

	Cholesterol*	Total Fat†	Saturated Fat†	Polyun- saturated Fat†	Monoun- saturated Fat†
3 eggs/week	117	2.39	.72	.31	1.36
4 oz. meat/day	119	15.90	9.00	1.12	5.78
0 dairy (fat)	—	—	—	—	—
3 teaspoons Fleischmann's tub margarine/day		7.56	1.32	2.94	3.30
3 teaspoons Mazola oil/day	___	13.62	1.74	7.98	.97
Total	236	39.47	12.78	12.35	14.34
(% of 1,500 calories)		(24%)	(8%)	(7%)	(9%)

*Figures are calculated to the nearest whole number.
†Figures are calculated to the nearest hundredth.

Lack of knowledge or confusion from past learning can play a major part in the client's ability to lower blood cholesterol. For example, a man who is asked to lose weight may initially switch from foods that provide polyunsaturated fat to those lower in calories, such as from regular French dressing to low-calorie, fat-free French dressing and from large amounts of margarine to small amounts of diet margarine (which is lower in polyunsaturated fat per teaspoon than regular margarine). The result may be an elevation in blood cholesterol due to a lowering of polyunsaturated fat intake. Several diet diaries may be needed to identify this type of information. The change to small amounts of regular dressing and regular margarine can help in lowering blood cholesterol.

In addition to lack of knowledge, counselors should address misconceptions. A few were covered earlier in this chapter. Others include comments that:

- "All beef should be avoided because it is too high in saturated fat." New breeding methods have resulted in low fat beef cuts that can be used in moderation.
- "All pork is forbidden on low-cholesterol diets." In reality, lean pork is lower in saturated fat than is beef.
- "If I fry commercial pork sausage until it's brown, all of the fat is removed." It is impossible to remove all fat from high-fat meats such as pork sausage.
- "I use a lot of nondairy powdered whipped toppings because they contain coconut oil rather than dairy fat." Coconut oil is a highly saturated vegetable oil so clients should avoid consuming it in large quantities.

To help clear up misconceptions, counselors can provide a list of commercial and noncommercial foods such as that in Exhibit 9-1.

Counselors can build a resource file of manufactured food products through letters like that in Exhibit 9-3. The letters should be concise, to the point and specific as to the types of information requested; in this case, the only interest is fat content. In some instances, additional information on, for example, carbohydrates or protein can be requested.

Exhibit 9-3 First Step in Building a Resource File

August 11, 1988

Bonnell Soup Company
1000 East Main Street
Anytown, U.S. 99999

Dear Sirs:

Since we are involved in counseling many hundreds of patients on cholesterol and fat-modified diets, we often need the assistance of food manufacturers. Determining the exact composition of products allows us to incorporate them into diets, where otherwise they might be prohibited.

Would you please send us your latest figures on the levels of cholesterol, monounsaturated, polyunsaturated, and saturated fatty acids in your Italian Spaghetti with Meatballs? Figures on a per-weight basis are most useful to us.

We would appreciate this information at your earliest possible convenience. Thank you for your help and cooperation.

Sincerely yours,

John Smith, R.D., M.S.
Research Nutritionist

While information on manufactured products is valuable, clients also need to know how to alter old eating habits on social occasions. In the past, food was considered a symbol of gratitude, love, and celebration on special occasions—associations that can make changing old eating habits at such events very unpleasant or difficult. Telephoning the hostess prior to a social function can help in determining which foods would be best to eat and can aid in avoiding major deviations from the diet prescription.

Strategies To Deal with Forgetfulness

Reminders to eat low-cholesterol, fat-modified foods can take the form of a change in the types of foods clients keep in the refrigerator. Substituting low-fat cheeses and dips for high-fat can serve as a cueing device always to eat appropriately. A reminder on the cupboard door saying, "Don't forget to eat low-fat foods!" can also serve as a cueing device. Notes on the refrigerator to remind the client to call the hostess before a party are valuable cues, too.

Clients for whom diet alone is not enough to bring blood cholesterol levels to within normal range may need to take medications like cholestyramine, a powder that acts as a bile acid sequestrant and thus helps lower blood cholesterol. Clients taking cholestyramine may need reminders or cueing devices. Calendars that indicate when medication is taken can also serve as reminders to take it. Adherence Tool 9-3 provides examples of a one-month and a one-week calendar. This tool can be used to find patterns in the day and time in a week clients forget to take medication. For example, Friday lunches may preclude taking medication, resulting in missed doses. A note on the refrigerator saying, "Don't forget to take your noon dose of cholestyramine on Friday" may help. The monthly calendar might be used to observe whether this strategy increases adherence.

Strategies To Deal with Lack of Commitment

Frequent expressions of waning commitment include: "I have more difficulty eating in restaurants than I used to," or "I miss all the 'good' food I used to eat," or "I'm tired of low-fat foods." Responding to these comments with more than information requires careful assessment of the actual problem. Why is commitment declining? Changes in clients' lives can lead to declines in adherence. Is the family in financial hardship? If the family is in danger of losing financial stability, that problem will become a priority. The family that goes through the turmoil of divorce, marriage, remarriage, the addition of a new family member, or the death of a close relative may be at risk for declining adherence and lack of commitment to the medical regimen. Other adherence problems may stem from losing a job or starting a new job.

As with other diets, some rule relaxation may be necessary for a time to help the client through the difficulties of the change. Exhibit 9-4 is a contract that provides an example of how to deal with this type of problem.

Positive monologues can be important in increasing adherence when commitment is low. By assessing thought processes before and following eating, counselors can observe negative monologues and teach clients to change them to positive monologues. Appropriate improvements in adherence may result. For example, the client who eats a small piece of cheddar cheese may say, "That's it. I blew the diet. It is no use! I just can't stay on this diet. I give up!" With this comment the client may go into a binge that includes eating three more pieces of cheese. A change from negative to positive might have resulted in this: "I had one small piece of cheese. I know that it is high in saturated fat. I will only have this one piece. I feel great that I was able to stop with this one piece. I will be careful the rest of the day and can still be within the limits of my diet." Most positive thinking involves positive self-rewards. This type of self-rewarding system can be embellished with positive reinforcement from others.

Exhibit 9-4 Contract

"I will not take my cholestyramine for the two days that I am in divorce court (January 21–22, 1987). On January 23 I will begin to take the full dose of medication again and will reward myself by going to a movie on that night. The nutrition counselor will contact me on January 24 at 7:00 p.m. to check on reestablishing the medication regimen.

If I do not take the full dose of medication on January 23, I forfeit the reward of going to a movie.

Patient _____

Nutrition Counselor _____

MD _____

The support of the family or significant other is crucial to adherence. Many members of a family may become upset if eating habits must focus on lowering saturated fat. This negative attitude may have an equally negative effect on client adherence. Changes in eating behavior can be made easier if clients can make clear to friends and relatives why the new pattern is necessary. For example, clients can explain that cutting down on cholesterol and saturated fats can help prevent coronary heart disease. Such a rationale can encourage helping others who are hosting parties to serve foods that are low in cholesterol and saturated fat. On their own, clients will find that a positive step is to learn to avoid foods that are high in fat and/or cholesterol and to limit their intake to those that are lower in these elements. Exhibit 9-5 shows a food list that allows for holiday treats.

Families can do much to help clients adhere to a fat-modified diet. Nutrition counselors might involve family members in sessions in which the clients are taught food preparation and receive dietary recommendations. However, too much family involvement can pose problems. For example, a quiet hyperlipidemic teenager may have a mother who volunteers all information and allows no verbal contact between client and counselor. The counselor may decide to see the client alone for parts of the interview or use subtle extinction techniques and nonverbal (i.e., no eye contact) gestures to curb too much involvement by the mother. The counselor might state at the beginning of the interview, "Mrs. J., during today's session I would like to find out from your son what his eating habits are at school. When he has finished, I will ask you to help him in describing eating habits at home." It is important to keep good eye contact with the son to encourage his responses rather than his mother's.

Counselors should instruct the client's friends and other family members (if possible) on how to provide positive reinforcement as a way to improve the individuals' adherence to a fat-modified diet. The following is a checklist family members might use for positive reinforcement techniques. They should:

- Praise efforts at decreasing serving sizes of meat, cheese, eggs, and other high-fat, high-cholesterol products.
- Avoid teasing or tempting with high-fat, high-cholesterol foods.
- Record the number of positive and negative comments they make about the diet and try to increase the positive and decrease the negative ones.
- Avoid referring to low-cholesterol fat-modified foods as "different" or "strange."

In summary, facilitating adherence to low-cholesterol, fat-modified eating patterns requires clients to have a thorough knowledge of the fat and cholesterol content of foods. Along with increasing clients' knowledge, the counselor must facilitate adherence by providing suggestions for more appropriate cueing devices. Lack of commitment to this eating pattern can cause lapses in dietary adherence. The nutrition counselor has many behavioral strategies available to increase commitment to dietary change.

Exhibit 9-5 Watch the Lights for Eating at Parties

Go Ahead!		**Proceed Slowly!**	**Stop!**
Finger Foods		*Meat Appetizers*	Chicken livers
Carrot sticks	Tomatoes	Shrimp	
Celery sticks	Mush-	Crab	Hors d'oeuvres wrapped in
Cauliflower	rooms	Chicken and ham salad	bacon
Radishes	Pickles	Sweet and sour pork	Cocktail wieners and
Lettuce	Arti-	Fish	sausages
Cabbage	chokes		Braunschweiger
	Avocado	*Party Munchies*	Chopped liver, liver
Sauces and		Potato chips	pâté
Spreads	*Fruits*	Cheese nibbles	
Cocktail sauce	All kinds:	Corn chips	Cheese and chocolate
Sweet and sours	Fresh	Party crackers	fondues (unless you can
Peanut butter	Frozen		stop at one bite)
	Canned	*Dips and Nibbles*	
Low-Fat		(Use only skim milk	Chocolate candies
Munchies		the rest of the day)	
Pretzels	Oyster	Low-fat yogurt dips	Commercial snacks
Rye crisps	crackers		containing high-fat crust
Saltines	Graham	*Pizza Hors D'Oeuvres*	(eggrolls, tarts, etc.)
Popcorn, no	crackers		
butter	Melba toast	*Fruit Breads and Cakes*	Cream cheese appetizers
Bread, white,	Bread sticks		
rye and			Sour cream dips
pumpernickel	*Nuts*		
	Peanuts		
Candy	Pecans		
Gumdrops	Brazil nuts		
Hard candies	Almonds		
Peanut brittle	Cashews		
Beverages			
Soft drinks			
Fruit punches			
Alcoholic			
beverages			
(without egg			
or cream)			

Source: Courtesy of Karen Smith and Linda G. Snetselaar.

Client Eating Questionnaire for Cholesterol- and Fat-Controlled Eating Patterns[*][1]

The following questionnaire has been designed to efficiently collect patient information in clinical nutrition programs. It has several functions.

Initially, it is a useful screening device or test of motivation. Individuals who may not take time to fill it out probably won't take time to participate fully in the behavioral diet and cholesterol modification program.

Secondly, the answers to these questions can be of great use to the therapist during the initial interviews and later during the nutrition lessons. The weight history allows a systematic look at the clients' own views of their weight problems (if there are any), and at some of the environmental influences they feel are important to their eating habits. The history of past attempts to make changes in eating patterns, the lengths of time they have stayed in dietary modification programs, and the reasons for past failure can all be useful. Also, their report of mood changes during previous periods of dieting can help you anticipate and deal with problems that might arise during treatment.

The questions about social and family history provide additional information that is of use medically: for example, the cause of parental death and the family weight history.

In most states the information contained in this questionnaire is confidential. Without *written* approval from the clients, this information cannot be divulged to interested individuals, physicians, insurance companies, or law enforcement agencies.

---

*Adapted from *Learning To Eat: Behavior Modification for Weight Control* by J.M. Ferguson with permission of Bull Publishing Company, © 1975.

Questions 50–56 are reprinted from "Food Preparation Questionnaire" with permission of Nutrition Coordinating Center, University of Minnesota.

251

Name:_____ Sex: M F   Age:____ Birthdate:_____

Address:_____ Home phone:_____

_____ Office phone:_____

WEIGHT HISTORY:

1. Indicate on the following table the periods in your life when you have been overweight. *If you have never been overweight, skip to question 15.* Where appropriate, list your maximum weight for each period and number of pounds you were overweight. Briefly describe any methods you used to lose weight in that five-year period, e.g., diet, shots, pills. Also list any significant life events you feel were related to either your weight gain or loss, e.g., college tests, marriage, pregnancies, illness.

Age	Maximum Weight	Pounds Overweight	Methods Used to Lose Weight	Significant Events Related to Weight Change
Birth				
0–5				
5–10				
10–15				
15–20				
20–25				
25–30				
30–35				
35–40				
40–45				

Age	Maximum Weight	Pounds Overweight	Methods Used to Lose Weight	Significant Events Related to Weight Change
45–50				
50–55				
55–60				
60–65				

2. Your present weight _____ Height _____

3. Describe your present weight (circle one)

very overweight	slightly overweight	about average

4. Are you dissatisfied with the way you look at this weight? (circle one)

Completely Satisfied	Satisfied	Neutral	Dissatisfied	Very Dissatisfied

5. At what weight have you *felt* your best or do you think you would feel your best?

_____

6. How much weight would you like to lose? _____

7. Do you feel your weight affects your daily activities?

No effect   Some effect   Often interferes   Extreme effect

8. Why do you want to lose weight at this time?_____

_____

9. What are the attitudes of the following people about your attempt(s) to lose weight?

	Negative (They disapprove or are resentful)	*Indifferent* (They don't care or don't help)	*Positive* (They encourage me and are understanding)
Husband			
Wife			
Children			
Parents			
Employer			
Friends			

10. Do these attitudes affect your weight loss or gain?   Yes   No
    If yes, please describe: _____
    _____
    _____

11. A number of different ways of losing weight are listed below. Please indicate which methods you have used by filling the appropriate blanks.

	Ages Used	Number of Times Used	Maximum Weight Lost	Comments: Length of Time Weight Loss Maintained; Success; Difficulties
TOPS (Take Off Pounds Sensibly)				
Weight Watchers				
Pills				
Supervised Diet				
Unsupervised Diet				
Starvation				
Behavior Modification				
Psychotherapy				
Hypnosis				
Other				

12. Which method did you use for the longest period of time? _____

_____

13. Have you had a major mood change during or after a significant weight loss? Indicate any mood changes on the following checklist.

	Not at all	A little bit	Moderately	Quite a bit	Extremely
a. Depressed, sad, feeling down, unhappy, the blues.	_	_____	_____	_____	_____
b. Anxious, nervous, restless, or uptight all the time.	_____	_____	_____	_____	_____
c. Physically weak.	_____	_____	_____	_____	_____
d. Elated or happy.	_____	_____	_____	_____	_____
e. Easily irritated, annoyed, or angry.	_____	_____	_____	_____	_____
f. Fatigued, worn out, tired all the time.	_____	_____	_____	_____	_____
g. A lack of self-confidence.	_____	_____	_____	_____	_____

14. What usually goes wrong with your weight loss programs? _____

_____

_____

_____

15. How *physically* active are you? (circle one)

   Very active   Active   Average   Inactive   Very inactive

16. What do you do for physical exercise and how often do you do it?

ACTIVITY (for example, swimming, jogging, dancing)	FREQUENCY (daily, weekly, monthly)

MEDICAL HISTORY:

17. When did you last have a complete physical examination? _____

18. Who is your current doctor? _____

19. What medical problems do you have at the present time? _____

_____

_____

20. What medications, vitamins or mineral preparations or drugs do you take regularly? _____

_____

_____

Attach label if available.

21. List any medications, drugs or food you are allergic to: _____

_____

_____

22. List any hospitalizations or operations. Indicate how old you were at each hospital admission.

      Age   Reason for hospitalizations

_____   _____

_____   _____

23. List any serious illnesses you have had which have not required hospitalization. Indicate how old you were during each illness.

      Age   Illness

_____   _____

_____   _____

_____   _____

_____   _____

24. Describe any of your medical problems that are complicated by excess weight.

_____

_____

_____

_____

_____

25. How much alcohol do you usually drink per week? _____

26. List any psychiatric contact, individual counseling, or marital counseling that you have had or are now having.

      Age   Reason for contact and type of therapy

_____   _____

_____   _____

_____   _____

_____   _____

SOCIAL HISTORY:

27. Circle the last year of school attended:

     1 2 3 4 5 6 7 8   9 10 11 12   1 2 3 4   M.A.   Ph.D.
     Grade School   High School   College
     Other _____

28. Describe your present occupation _____   _____

    _____

29. How long have your worked for your present employer? _____

30. Present marital status (circle one):

     single   married   divorced   widowed   separated   engaged

31. Answer the following questions for each marriage:

     Dates of marriages   _____   _____   _____
     Dates of termination   _____   _____   _____
     Reason (death, divorce, etc.) _____   _____   _____
     Number of children   _____   _____   _____

32. Spouse's Age _____ Weight _____ Height _____

33. Describe your spouse's occupation _____

    _____

34. Describe your spouse's weight (circle one)

     very   slightly   about   slightly   very
     overweight   overweight   average   underweight   underweight

35. List your children's ages, sex, heights, weights, and circle whether they are over-weight, average, or underweight. Include any children from previous marriages, whether they are living with you or not.

Age	Sex	Weight	Height	Overweight			Underweight	
____	____	_____	_____	very	slightly	average	slightly	very
____	____	_____	_____	very	slightly	average	slightly	very
____	____	_____	_____	very	slightly	average	slightly	very
____	____	_____	_____	very	slightly	average	slightly	very
____	____	_____	_____	very	slightly	average	slightly	very

36. Who lives at home with you? _____

FAMILY HISTORY:

37. Is your father living? Yes   No   Father's age now, or age at and cause of death

    _____

    _____

38. Is your mother living?   Yes   No   Mother's age now, or age at and cause of death _____

_____

39. Describe your father's occupation _____

40. Describe your mother's occupation _____

41. Describe your father's weight while you were growing up (circle one). If you have never been overweight, skip to question 50.

| very overweight | slightly overweight | about average | slightly underweight | very underweight |

42. Describe your mother's weight while you were growing up (circle one).

| very overweight | slightly overweight | about average | slightly underweight | very underweight |

43. List your brothers' and sisters' ages, sex, present weights, heights, and circle whether they are overweight, average, or underweight.

Age	Sex	Weight	Height	Overweight			Underweight	
___	___	_____	_____	very	slightly	average	slightly	very
___	___	_____	_____	very	slightly	average	slightly	very
___	___	_____	_____	very	slightly	average	slightly	very
___	___	_____	_____	very	slightly	average	slightly	very
___	___	_____	_____	very	slightly	average	slightly	very

44. Please add any additional information you feel may be relevant to your current eating habits. This includes interactions with your family and friends that might sabotage a dietary modification program, and additional family or social history that you feel might help us understand your dietary habits.

_____

_____

_____

_____

_____

_____

_____

_____

FOOD PREPARATION HABITS:

45. Do you salt your food at the table? (circle one)

        always   occasionally   never

46. If you add salt, how would your rate yourself in terms of amount of salt added at the table? (circle one)

      light   moderate   heavy

47. Do you use a salt substitute at the table such as Lite, Lo-Salt, or No-salt? (circle one)

      always   occasionally   never

If used, specify brand name: _____

48. Do you regularly use other salt seasonings at the table such as Accent, onion salt, or garlic salt? (circle one)

      Yes   No
      Specify kind(s): _____

49. Check whether salt or salt substitute is usually added in *preparing* the following foods:

	salt	salt substitute	seasoning salts	none
Pasta, such as noodles, macaroni	[ ]	[ ]	[ ]	[ ]
Rice	[ ]	[ ]	[ ]	[ ]
Potatoes	[ ]	[ ]	[ ]	[ ]
Other vegetables	[ ]	[ ]	[ ]	[ ]
Meat	[ ]	[ ]	[ ]	[ ]
Fruit	[ ]	[ ]	[ ]	[ ]
Other (e.g., coffee)	[ ]	[ ]	[ ]	[ ]
specify _____	[ ]	[ ]	[ ]	[ ]
_____	[ ]	[ ]	[ ]	[ ]

If salt substitute, specify kind/brand _____

50. Are the following table and cooking fats used (circle one)?

    Butter   yes → Specify: regular
                    no   unsalted
    Margarine   yes → Specify: regular
                    no   unsalted

Specify brand(s):

_____	stick	tub	diet	spread
_____	stick	tub	diet	spread
_____	stick	tub	diet	spread

Vegetable oil (such as corn, soy, safflower, sunflower, etc.) (circle one)

yes →   Specify types and/or brands used:
no   _____
          _____

Spray shortening (such as Pam) (circle one)

yes →   Specify brand:

no   _____

Solid shortening (such as Crisco, Spry, Fluffo, etc.) (circle one)

yes →   Specify types and/or brands used:

no   _____
                          _____

Other cooking fats (such as lard, bacon drippings, salt pork, poultry fat, etc.) (circle one)

yes →   Specify _____

no   _____

51. Check the fat most often used in preparing each of the following foods:

	Butter	Margarine	Spray shortening	Oil, such as Wesson, Mazola	Vegetable shortening such as Crisco, Fluffo, Spry	Bacon fat	Lard	Chicken fat	Beef suet	None
Eggs, fried	[ ]	[ ]	[ ]	[ ]	[ ]	[ ]	[ ]	[ ]	[ ]	[ ]
Eggs, scrambled	[ ]	[ ]	[ ]	[ ]	[ ]	[ ]	[ ]	[ ]	[ ]	[ ]
French toast	[ ]	[ ]	[ ]	[ ]	[ ]	[ ]	[ ]	[ ]	[ ]	[ ]
Cornbread	[ ]	[ ]	[ ]	[ ]	[ ]	[ ]	[ ]	[ ]	[ ]	[ ]
Potatoes, mashed	[ ]	[ ]	[ ]	[ ]	[ ]	[ ]	[ ]	[ ]	[ ]	[ ]
Potatoes, french fried	[ ]	[ ]	[ ]	[ ]	[ ]	[ ]	[ ]	[ ]	[ ]	[ ]
Potatoes, pan fried	[ ]	[ ]	[ ]	[ ]	[ ]	[ ]	[ ]	[ ]	[ ]	[ ]
Greens	[ ]	[ ]	[ ]	[ ]	[ ]	[ ]	[ ]	[ ]	[ ]	[ ]
Other vegetables	[ ]	[ ]	[ ]	[ ]	[ ]	[ ]	[ ]	[ ]	[ ]	[ ]
White beans, pinto	[ ]	[ ]	[ ]	[ ]	[ ]	[ ]	[ ]	[ ]	[ ]	[ ]
Gravy	[ ]	[ ]	[ ]	[ ]	[ ]	[ ]	[ ]	[ ]	[ ]	[ ]
White sauce	[ ]	[ ]	[ ]	[ ]	[ ]	[ ]	[ ]	[ ]	[ ]	[ ]
Pie crust	[ ]	[ ]	[ ]	[ ]	[ ]	[ ]	[ ]	[ ]	[ ]	[ ]

52. Indicate the most *usual* method of preparing each of the following. If you fry any of them, comment on whether the item is dipped in flour or batter or breaded before frying and what fat is used for frying. Also check whether gravy is prepared.

ITEM	METHOD OF COOKING such as pan frying, broiling, deep frying	KIND OF FAT USED (if any)
Hamburger		
Steaks		
Chops		
Poultry		
Fish		
Shellfish (shrimp, etc.)		
Liver		
Other, specify		

53. Do you use gravy on meats? (circle one)

    Yes   No

54. If you prepare gravies, do you usually use (circle one):   cornstarch   flour
    Is the liquid usually (circle one): milk   water   other, specify: _____

55. Indicate how much fat is usually trimmed from the meat before cooking or eating (circle one):

    trim most   trim some   usually don't trim

56. Check the salad dressing *most often* used with the following salads: (Specify brand)

	Mayonnaise-type such as Miracle Whip, Spin Blend	Regular mayonnaise such as Hellmann's, Kraft	Imitation mayonnaise such as Bright Day	Weight Watchers' Mayonnaise	Other—specify as French, Italian, Ranch-style, etc. Also specify creamy, clear, lo-cal, etc.
Potato salad					
Cole slaw					
Tossed salad					
Macaroni salad					
Other (specify)					

Adherence Tool 9-2 Monitoring Device

Fat Facts or Misfacts		
	true	false
1. All vegetable oil helps lower cholesterol.	_____	_____
2. Saturated fat is found only in animal products.	_____	_____
3. Hydrogenation is a beneficial process that makes fat less saturated.	_____	_____
4. Cholesterol is found in some peanut butter.	_____	_____
5. Cholesterol is found in all animal products.	_____	_____
6. All foods that are high in saturated fat are also high in cholesterol.	_____	_____

Adherence Tool 9-3 Monitoring Device
One-Month Calendar

One-Month

Sun.	Mon.	Tues.	Wed.	Thur.	Fri.	Sat.
1	2	3	4	5	6	7
8	9	10	11	12	13	14
15	16	17	18	19	20	21
22	23	24	25	26	27	
28	29	30	31	1	2	3

month of _____ 19 _____   If you have any questions, please call: _____

One-Week

NAME: _____

ATTN: _____   THANK YOU!

Adherence Tool 9-4 Monitoring Device
Graphs of Dietary Intake of Sterols and Fats

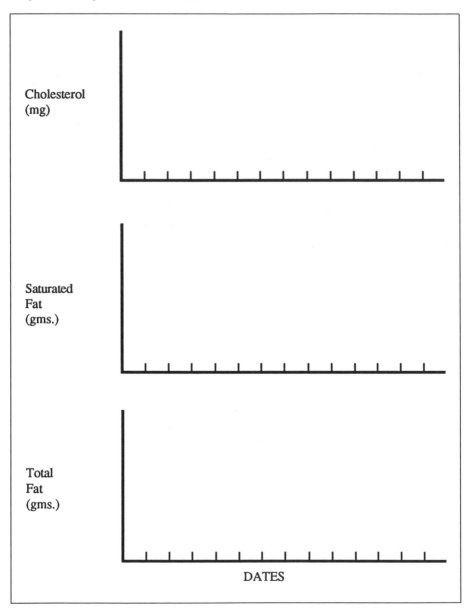

Adherence Tool 9-5 Monitoring Device
Graphs of Serum Lipid Values

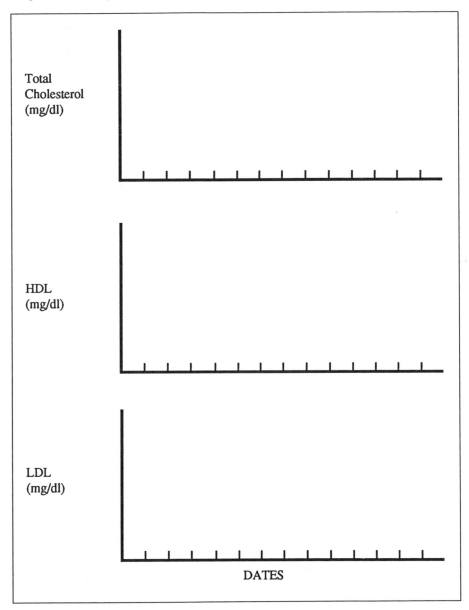

Adherence Tool 9-6 Monitoring Device

	Pantry Survey		
Food	Saturated Fat (Hydrogenated Vegetable Fat)	Polyun- saturated Fat	Monoun- saturated Fat

Adherence Tool 9-7 Informational Device

	Day 1	Day 2	Day 3
Client Meal Planning Chart Meal planning can help you in keeping your fat and cholesterol intake low. Before your next visit, plan three days of meals in which you have avoided foods high in fat and cholesterol.			
Breakfast:			
Snack:			
Lunch:			
Snack:			
Dinner:			
Snack:			

Adherence Tool 9-8 Informational Device

Tips for Dining in Restaurants

Select from the following suggestions:

Appetizers

Clear soup (bouillon, fat-free consomme). Fruits or vegetables, juices, seafood cocktail (except shrimp), oysters, or clams on the half-shell. (Be sure to count the seafood as part of your meat allowance).

Salads

Lettuce and other vegetables, fruits, fruit and cottage cheese (use as part of milk allowance), gelatin. Use lemon juice, vinegar, vinegar and oil, French dressing, or mayonnaise as your dressing.

Entree

Baked, broiled, or roasted fish, poultry, lean meat, cottage cheese.

Vegetables

All vegetables prepared without butter, meat fat, or cream sauce.

Potatoes and Substitutes

Baked or broiled without dressing, mashed if made without butter, plain rice, macaroni, or spaghetti.

Desserts

Fresh or canned fruits, fruit compotes, sherbert, gelatin, unfrosted angel food cake.

Beverages

Coffee or tea (without cream), carbonated beverages, fruit juices, milk (as allowed), and alcoholic beverages (unless not allowed because of medical problems).

Breakfast Cereals

All cereals without coconut, served with allowed milk.

Miscellaneous

Nuts (except walnuts and filberts), honey, jam, syrup, hard candy, marshmallows, gumdrops, hard fruit drops, jellybeans, mints (no chocolate or bon bons), condiments, and seasoning, as allowed.

Avoid

Combination dishes, fried or creamed foods, foods made with whole milk products, butter, cheese, or gravy. Do not eat pastries (sweet rolls, pies, cakes, cookies, doughnuts, waffles), fatty meats (bacon, sausage, luncheon meats), cream soups, or potato or corn chips.

Inquire about the fat and other ingredients used in menu items. Then give specific instructions regarding the methods of preparation of your selection.

Adherence Tool 9-9 Informational Device
Comparing High-Cholesterol, Low-Fat Menus with Low-Cholesterol, Low-Fat Menus

Adherence Tool 9-9A High-Cholesterol, High-Fat Menu (at Home)

Breakfast 1

Egg (1)
Bacon (2 strips)
Toast (2 slices)
Blue Bonnet Stick Margarine (2 teaspoons)
Milk, Whole (8 ounces)
Orange Juice (4 ounces)

Lunch 1

Bologna (1 ounce)
Bread (2 slices)
Mayonnaise (1 tablespoon)
Blue Bonnet Stick Margarine (2 teaspoons)
Potato Chips (1 cup)
Mr. Goodbar (1 bar)
Milk, whole (8 ounces)

Dinner 1

Roast Beef (5 ounces)
Mashed Potatoes (½ cup)
Corn (½ cup)
Bread (2 slices)
Blue Bonnet Stick Margarine (6 teaspoons)
Cherry Cobbler (1 cup)
Ice Cream (½ cup)
Milk, whole (8 ounces)

Adherence Tool 9-9B High-Cholesterol, High-Fat Menu (at Home)

Breakfast 1

	Amount	Cholesterol (mg.)	Total Fat (gm.)	Saturated Fat (gm.)	Polyunsaturated Fat (gm.)	Monounsaturated Fat (gm.)	P/S Ratio
Egg	1	274	5.58	1.68	.73	3.17	
Bacon	2 strips	11	6.24	2.20	.74	3.30	
Toast	2 slices	—	—	—	—	—	
Blue Bonnet Stick Margarine	2 tsp.	—	7.54	1.46	2.16	3.92	
Milk, whole	8 oz.	34	8.15	5.08	.29	2.78	
Orange juice	4 oz.	—	—	—	—	—	
TOTAL		319	27.51	10.42	3.92	13.17	.38

Lunch 1

	Amount	Cholesterol (mg.)	Total Fat (gm.)	Saturated Fat (gm.)	Polyunsaturated Fat (gm.)	Monounsaturated Fat (gm.)	P/S Ratio
Bologna	1 slice (23 gm)	13	6.52	2.68	.24	3.60	
Bread	2 slices	—	—	—	—	—	
Mayonnaise	1 tbsp.	8	10.96	1.19	7.59	2.18	
Blue Bonnet Stick Margarine	2 tsp.	—	7.54	1.46	2.16	3.92	
Potato Chips	1 cup	8	8.60	3.42	1.02	4.16	
Mr. Goodbar	1 bar	5	11.90	6.00	2.00	3.90	
Milk, whole	8 oz.	34	8.15	5.08	.29	2.78	
TOTAL		68	53.67	19.83	13.30	20.54	.67

Adherence Tool 9-9B continued

Dinner 1

	Amount	Choles-terol (mg.)	Total Fat (gm.)	Saturated Fat (gm.)	Polyun-saturated Fat (gm.)	Monoun-saturated Fat (gm.)	P/S Ratio
Roast Beef (medium fat)	5 oz.	130	21.10	9.15	5.50	6.45	
Mashed Potatoes*	½ cup	—	—	—	—	—	
Corn*	½ cup	—	—	—	—	—	
Bread	2 slices	—	—	—	—	—	
Blue Bonnet Stick Margarine	6 tsp.	—	22.62	4.38	6.48	11.76	
Cherry Cobbler*	1 cup	—	—	—	—	—	
Ice Cream	½ cup	30	7.16	4.46	.27	2.43	
Milk, whole	8 oz.	34	8.15	5.08	.29	2.78	
TOTAL		194	59.03	23.07	12.54	23.42	.54

*Fat used in these recipes was figured into the amount of Blue Bonnet margarine.

Total Daily Intake

	Choles-terol (mg.)	Total Fat (gm.)	Saturated Fat (gm.)	Polyun-saturated Fat (gm.)	Monoun-saturated Fat (gm.)	P/S Ratio
Diet 1	581	140.21	53.32	29.76	57.13	.56
Percent of 2,770 Calories		46%	17%	10%	19%	
Recommendations	200	25%	8.3%	8.3%	8.3%	1.00

Adherence Tool 9-9C High-Cholesterol, High-Fat Menu (in a Restaurant)

Breakfast 2

Egg McMuffin (1)
Orange Juice (4 ounces)
Milk, whole (8 ounces)

Lunch 2

Big Mac (1)
Fries (regular)
Milk, whole (8 ounces)
Apple Pie (1)

Dinner 2

Tenderloin (1)
Fries (regular)
Milk, whole (8 ounces)

Adherence Tool 9-9D High-Cholesterol, High-Fat (in a Restaurant)

Breakfast 2

	Amount	Choles-terol (mg.)	Total Fat (gm.)	Saturated Fat (gm.)	Polyun-saturated Fat (gm.)	Monoun-saturated Fat (gm.)	P/S Ratio
Egg McMuffin	1	277	8.59	2.57	.97	5.05	
Orange Juice	4 oz.	—	—	—	—	—	
Milk, whole	8 oz.	34	8.15	5.08	.29	2.78	
TOTAL		311	16.74	7.65	1.26	7.83	.16

Lunch 2

	Amount	Choles-terol (mg.)	Total Fat (gm.)	Saturated Fat (gm.)	Polyun-saturated Fat (gm.)	Monoun-saturated Fat (gm.)	P/S Ratio
Big Mac	1	90	27.14	7.17	7.59	12.38	
Fries, regular	1	12	12.90	5.13	1.53	6.24	
Milk, whole	8 oz.	34	8.15	5.08	.29	2.78	
Apple Pie	1	12	12.90	5.13	1.53	6.24	
TOTAL		148	61.09	22.51	10.94	27.64	.49

Adherence Tool 9-9D continued

Dinner 2

	Amount	Cholesterol (mg.)	Total Fat (gm.)	Saturated Fat (gm.)	Polyunsaturated Fat (gm.)	Monounsaturated Fat (gm.)	P/S Ratio
Tenderloin	1	90	24.99	6.42	5.55	13.02	
Fries, regular	1	12	12.90	5.13	1.53	6.24	
Milk, whole	8 oz.	34	8.15	5.08	.29	2.78	
TOTAL		136	46.04	16.63	7.37	22.04	.44

Total Daily Intake

	Cholesterol (mg.)	Total Fat (gm.)	Saturated Fat (gm.)	Polyunsaturated Fat (gm.)	Monounsaturated Fat (gm.)	P/S Ratio
Diet 2	595	123.87	46.79	19.57	57.51	.42
Percent of 2,500 Calories		45%	17%	7%	21%	—
Recommendations	200	25%	8.3%	8.3%	8.3%	1.00

Adherence Tool 9-9E Low-Cholesterol, Low-Fat Menu (at Home)

Breakfast 3

English Muffin (1)
Canadian Bacon (1 ounce)
Milk, skim (8 ounces)
Fleischmann's Tub Margarine (2 teaspoons)
Orange Juice (4 ounces)

Lunch 3

Turkey (1 ounce)
Bread (2 slices)
Miracle Whip (1 teaspoon)
Chips (½ cup)
Zucchini Cake (1 serving)
Milk, skim (8 ounces)

Dinner 3

Fish (5 ounces)
Mashed Potatoes (½ cup)
Corn (½ cup)
Tossed Salad (1 cup)
Dressing (1 tablespoon)
Fleischmann's Tub Margarine (1 teaspoon)
Sherbert (½ cup)
Milk, skim (8 ounces)

Adherence Tool 9-9F Low-Cholesterol, Low-Fat (at Home)

Breakfast 3

	Amount	Cholesterol (mg.)	Total Fat (gm.)	Saturated Fat (gm.)	Polyunsaturated Fat (gm.)	Monounsaturated Fat (gm.)	P/S Ratio
English Muffin	1	—	—	—			
Canadian Bacon	1 oz.	25	2.84	.87	.28	1.69	
Milk, Skim	8 oz.	5	.44	.29	.02	.13	
Fleischmann's Tub Margarine	2 tsp.	—	7.56	1.32	2.94	3.30	
Orange Juice	4 oz.	—	—	—	—	—	
TOTAL		30	10.84	2.48	3.24	5.12	1.3

Lunch 3

	Amount	Cholesterol (mg.)	Total Fat (gm.)	Saturated Fat (gm.)	Polyunsaturated Fat (gm.)	Monounsaturated Fat (gm.)	P/S Ratio
Turkey	1 oz.	22	1.10	.33	.26	.51	
Bread	2 slices	—	—	—	—	—	
Miracle Whip	1 tsp.	1	1.63	.24	.88	.51	
Chips	½ cup	—	4.67	.59	2.72	1.36	
Zucchini Cake	1 sv.	—	4.67	.59	2.72	1.36	
Milk, Skim	8 oz.	5	.44	.29	.02	.13	
TOTAL		28	12.51	2.04	6.60	3.87	3.2

Adherence Tool 9-9F continued

Dinner 3

	Amount	Cholesterol (mg.)	Total Fat (gm.)	Saturated Fat (gm.)	Polyunsaturated Fat (gm.)	Monounsaturated Fat (gm.)	P/S Ratio
Fish (6%)	5 oz.	113	5.70	1.50	1.32	2.88	
Mashed Potatoes	½ cup	—	3.78	.69	1.68	1.41	
Corn	½ cup	—	3.78	.69	1.68	1.41	
Tossed Salad	1 cup	—	—	—	—	—	
Dressing	1 tbsp.	—	4.67	.61	1.87	2.19	
Fleischmann's Tub Margarine	1 tsp.	—	3.78	.69	1.68	1.41	
Sherbet	½ cup	—	—	—	—	—	
Milk, Skim	8 oz.	5	.24	.14	.00	.10	
TOTAL		118	21.95	4.32	8.23	9.40	1.90

Total Daily Intake

	Cholesterol (mg.)	Total Fat (gm.)	Saturated Fat (gm.)	Polyunsaturated Fat (gm.)	Monounsaturated Fat (gm.)	P/S Ratio
Diet 3	176	46.07	8.95	18.97	18.15	2.11
Percent of 1,923 Calories		21%	4%	9%	8%	
Recommendations	200	25%	8.3%	8.3%	8.3%	1.00

Adherence Tool 9-9G Low-Cholesterol, Low-Fat Menu (in a Restaurant)

Breakfast 4

Raspberry Danish (1)
Orange Juice (4 ounces)
Milk, skim (8 ounces)

Lunch 4

Big Mac (1)
Orange Drink (12 ounces)
Strawberry Sundae (1)

Dinner 4

Broiled Cod (13 ounces)
Baked Potato (1)
Tossed Salad (2 cups)
Dressing (1 tablespoon)
Fleischmann's Tub Margarine (2 teaspoons)
Fresh Fruit Compote (1 cup)
Milk, skim (8 ounces)

Adherence Tool 9-9H Low-Cholesterol, Low-Fat (in a Restaurant)

Breakfast 4

	Amount	Choles-terol (mg.)	Total Fat (gm.)	Saturated Fat (gm.)	Polyun-saturated Fat (gm.)	Monoun-saturated Fat (gm.)	P/S Ratio
Raspberry Danish	1	27	15.90	3.11	1.10	11.69	
Orange Juice	4 oz.	—	—	—	—	—	
Milk, Skim	8 oz.	5	.44	.29	.02	.13	
TOTAL		32	16.34	3.40	1.12	11.82	.33

Lunch 4

	Amount	Choles-terol (mg.)	Total Fat (gm.)	Saturated Fat (gm.)	Polyun-saturated Fat (gm.)	Monoun-saturated Fat (gm.)	P/S Ratio
Big Mac	1	90	27.14	7.17	7.59	12.38	
Orange Drink	12 oz.	—	—	—	—	—	
Strawberry Sundae	1	25	8.70	3.18	1.11	4.41	
TOTAL		115	35.84	10.35	8.70	16.79	.84

Adherence Tool 9-9H continued

Dinner 4

	Amount	Choles-terol (mg.)	Total Fat (gm.)	Saturated Fat (gm.)	Polyun-saturated Fat (gm.)	Monoun-saturated Fat (gm.)	P/S Ratio
Broiled Cod (6 %)	3 oz.	68	3.84	.87	1.26	1.71	
Baked Potato	1	—	—	—	—	—	
Tossed Salad	2 cups	—	—	—	—	—	
Dressing	1 tbsp.	—	4.54	.71	2.60	1.23	
Flesichmann's Tub Margarine	2 tsps.	—	7.56	1.32	2.94	3.30	
Fresh Fruit Compote	1 cup	—	—	—	—	—	
Milk, Skim	8 oz.	5	.44	.29	.02	.13	
TOTAL		73	16.38	3.19	6.82	6.37	2.14

Total Daily Intake

	Choles-terol (mg.)	Total Fat (gm.)	Saturated Fat (gm.)	Polyun-saturated Fat (gm.)	Monoun-saturated Fat (gm.)	P/S Ratio
Diet 4	220	68.56	16.94	16.64	34.98	.98
Percent of 2,455 Calories		25%	6%	6%	13%	
Recommendations	200	25%	8.3%	8.3%	8.3%	1.00

Adherence Tool 9-10 Informational Device P/S Ratios of Various Fats and Oils

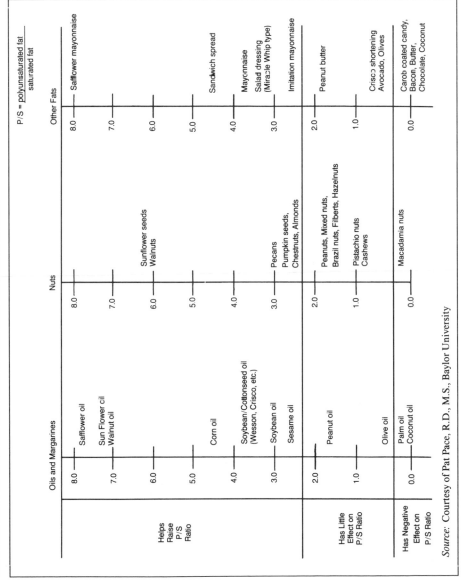

$P/S = \dfrac{\text{polyunsaturated fat}}{\text{saturated fat}}$

Oils and Margarines

8.0	Safflower oil
7.0	Sun Flower oil / Walnut oil
6.0	
5.0	
4.0	Corn oil / Soybean/Cottonseed oil (Wesson, Crisco, etc.)
3.0	Soybean oil / Sesame oil
2.0	Peanut oil
1.0	Olive oil
0.0	Palm oil / Coconut oil

Nuts

8.0	
7.0	
6.0	Sunflower seeds / Walnuts
5.0	
4.0	
3.0	Pecans / Pumpkin seeds, Chestnuts, Almonds
2.0	Peanuts, Mixed nuts, Brazil nuts, Filberts, Hazelnuts
1.0	Pistachio nuts / Cashews
0.0	Macadamia nuts

Other Fats

8.0	Safflower mayonnaise
7.0	
6.0	
5.0	Sandwich spread
4.0	Mayonnaise / Salad dressing (Miracle Whip type)
3.0	Imitation mayonnaise
2.0	Peanut butter
1.0	Crisco shortening / Avocado, Olives
0.0	Carob coated candy, Bacon, Butter, Chocolate, Coconut

Helps Raise P/S Ratio

Has Little Effect on P/S Ratio

Has Negative Effect on P/S Ratio

Source: Courtesy of Pat Pace, R.D., M.S., Baylor University

Review of Chapter 9
(Answers in Appendix I)

1. List six dietary misconceptions and excesses related to low-cholesterol and fat-modified eating patterns that lead to inappropriate eating behaviors.

   a. _____

   _____

   b. _____

   _____

   c. _____

   _____

   d. _____

   _____

   e. _____

   _____

   f. _____

   _____

2. List three of five specific dietary components of a baseline diet that must be assessed before instructing a client on a fat-modified diet.

   a. _____

   _____

   b. _____

   _____

   c. _____

   _____

3. List three strategies that might help the client follow a fat- and cholesterol-controlled eating pattern.

   a. _____

   _____

   b. _____

   _____

   c. _____

   _____

4. The following is an exercise (based on data collected using Exhibit 9-3) to help you apply the ideas just discussed.

   Jim is a 48-year-old mailman who eats all meals at home except for social occasions, in which he participates frequently. He loves meat and rarely eats eggs or dairy products. Tailor an eating pattern to his needs and explain two counseling strategies that might be used to help his dietary adherence on social occasions. The dietary prescription is 200 milligrams of cholesterol with a P/S ratio of 1.0 and 20 percent of the calories coming from fat.

	Choles-terol	Total Fat	Saturated Fat	Polyun-saturated Fat	Mono-unsaturated Fat
___ eggs/week	—	—	—	—	—
___ ounces meat/day	—		—	—	—
___ ounces whole milk/day	—	—	—	—	—
___ _____					
margarine/day	—	—	—	—	—
___ _____					
oil/day	—	—	—	—	—
Total	—	—	—	—	—
(% of 2,400 calories)		(___%)		(___%)	(___%)

P/S ___

Strategies:_____

NOTES

1. Consensus Development Panel, "Lowering Blood Cholesterol to Prevent Heart Disease," *Journal of the American Medical Association* 253 (1985): 2080–2086; and Nancy D. Ernst, "NIH Consensus Development Conference on Lowering Blood Cholesterol to Prevent Heart Disease: Implications for Dietitians," *Journal of the American Dietetic Association* 85 (1985): 586–588.

2. American Heart Association, *Diet and Coronary Heart Disease* (Dallas: 1978); and Inter-Society Commission for Heart Disease Resources, "Optimal Resources for Primary Prevention of Atherosclerotic Disease," *Circulation* 70 (1984): 190A.

3. National Research Council, Food and Nutrition Board, *Recommended Dietary Allowances,* 9th ed. (Washington, D.C.: National Academy of Sciences, 1980), p. 33.

4. A. E. Hansen et al., "Role of Linoleic Acid in Infant Feeding: Clinical and Chemical Study of 428 Infants Fed on Milk Mixtures Varying in Kind and Amount of Fat," *Pediatrics* 31 (1963, Supplement): 171–192; and Ralph T. Holman, W. O. Caster, and Hilda F. Wiese, "The Essential Fatty Acid Requirement of Infants and the Assessment of Their Dietary Intake of Linoleic by Serum Fatty Acid Analysis," *American Journal of Clinical Nutrition* 14 (1964): 70.

5. National Research Council, Food and Nutrition Board, *Recommended Allowances,* p. 36; and FAO Expert Committee, *Dietary Fats and Oils in Human Nutrition,* FAO Food and Nutrition Paper No. 3 (Rome: United Nations Food and Agriculture Organization), 1980.

6. William B. Kannel and Tavia Gordon, eds., "The Framingham Study: The Epidemiological Investigation of Cardiovascular Disease," Publication NIH 76-1083 (U.S. Department of Health, Education and Welfare, 1976); and Jeremiah Stamler, *Lectures on Preventive Cardiology* (New York: Grune & Stratton, 1967), pp. 10–27.

7. Ibid.

8. John A. Glomset, "The Plasma Lecithin: Cholesterol Acyltransferase Reaction," *Journal of Lipid Research* 9 (1968): 155–157; O. Stein and Y. Stein, "The Removal of Cholesterol from Landschutz Ascites Cells by High-Density Apolipoprotein," *Biochimica and Biophysica Acta* 326 (1973): 232–244; and Y. Stein et al., "The Removal of Cholesterol from Aortic Smooth

Muscle Cells in Culture and Landschutz Ascites Cells by Fractions of Human High Density Apolipoprotein," *Biochimica and Biophysica Acta* 380 (1975): 106–118.

9. Sonya L. Connor and William E. Connor, "The Importance of Dietary Cholesterol in Coronary Heart Disease," *Preventive Medicine* 12 (1983): 115–123.

10. James Shepherd et al., "Effects of Saturated and Polyunsaturated Fat Diets on the Chemical Composition and Metabolism of Low Density Lipoproteins in Man," *Journal of Lipid Research* 21 (1980): 91–99; Shepherd et al., "Effects of Dietary-Fat Saturation on the Composition of Very-Low Density Lipoproteins and on the Metabolism of Their Major Apoprotein B," *Biochemical Society Transactions* 6 (1978): 779–780; Shepherd et al., "Effects of Dietary Polyunsaturated Fat on the Properties of High Density Lipoproteins and the Metabolism of Apolipoprotein A-I," *Journal of Clinical Investigation* 61 (1978): 1582–1592; and Henry J. Pownall et al., "Effect of Saturated and Polyunsaturated Fat Diets on the Composition and Structure of Human Low Density Lipoproteins," *Atherosclerosis* 36 (1980): 299–314.

11. Gloria T. Vega et al., "Influence of Polyunsaturated Fats on Composition of Plasma Lipoproteins and Apolipoproteins," *Journal of Lipid Research* 23 (1982): 811–822; and Fred Mattson and Scott M. Grundy, "Comparison of Effects of Dietary Saturated, Monounsaturated and Polyunsaturated Fatty Acids on Plasma Lipids and Lipoproteins in Man," *Journal of Lipid Research* 26 (1985): 194–202.

12. Ronald P. Mensink and Martin B. Katan, "Effects of Monounsaturated Fatty Acids Versus Complex Carbohydrates on High-Density Lipoproteins in Healthy Men and Women," *Lancet* 1 (1987): 122–124; and Scott M. Grundy, "Comparison of Monounsaturated Fatty Acids and Carbohydrates for Lowering Plasma Cholesterol," *New England Journal of Medicine* 314 (1986): 745–748.

13. William S. Harris et al., "The Mechanism of the Hypotriglyceridemic Effect of Dietary Omega-3 Fatty Acids in Man," *Clinical Research* 32 (1984): 560A (abstract); and Harris et al., "Dietary Omega-3 Fatty Acids Prevent Carbohydrate-Induced Hypertriglyceridemia," *Metabolism* 3 (1984): 1016–1019.

14. C. R. M. Hay, R. Saynor, and A. P. Durber, "Effect of Fish Oil and Platelet Kinetics in Patients with Ischemic Heart Disease," *Lancet* 1 (1982): 1269–1272; and Aizan Hirai et al., "Eicosapentaenoic Acid and Platelet Function in Japanese," *Lancet* 2 (1980): 1132–1133.

15. Arlene W. Caggiula et al., "The Multiple Risk Factor Intervention Trial (MRFIT). VI. Intervention on Blood Lipids," *Preventive Medicine* 10 (1981): 443–475; and Therese A. Dolecek, "A Long-term Nutrition Intervention Experience: Lipid Responses and Dietary Adherence Patterns in the Multiple Risk Factor Intervention Trial," *Journal of the American Dietetic Association* 86 (1986): 752–798.

16. Multiple Risk Factor Intervention Trial Research Group, "Multiple Risk Factor Intervention Trial: Risk Factor Changes and Mortality Results," *Journal of the American Medical Association* 248 (1982): 1465–1477.

17. Alfred McAlister et al., "Theory and Action for Health Promotion: Illustrations from the North Karelia Project," *American Journal of Public Health* 72 (1982): 43–50.

18. Ritra-Liisa L. Karvetti, "Effects of Nutrition Education," *Journal of the American Dietetic Association* 79 (1981): 660–667.

19. Ann C. Buller, "Improving Dietary Education for Patients with Hyperlipidemia," *Journal of the American Dietetic Association* 72 (1978): 277–281; Richard F. Heller, Hugh D. Tunstall-Pedoe, and Geofrey Rose, "A Simple Method of Assessing the Effect of Dietary Advice to Reduce Plasma Cholesterol," *Preventive Medicine* 10 (1981): 364–370; and Michael P. Stern et al., "Results of a Two-Year Health Education Campaign on Dietary Behavior," *Circulation* 54 (1976): 826–833.

20. Jella C. Witschi et al., "Family Cooperation and Effectiveness in a Cholesterol-Lowering Diet," *Journal of the American Dietetic Association* 72 (1978): 384–389.

21. Rebecca S. Reeves et al., "Effects of a Low Cholesterol Eating Plan on Plasma Lipids: Results of a Three-Year Community Study," *American Journal of Public Health* 73 (1983): 873–877; Stern et al., "Results"; Curtis S. Wilbur et al., "The Long Term Results of Short Term Lipid Therapy," unpublished manuscript, 1979; and Witschi et al., "Family Cooperation and Effectiveness."

22. Robert Bruno et al., "Randomized Controlled Trial of a Nonpharmacological Cholesterol Reduction Program at the Worksite," *Preventive Medicine* 12 (1983): 523–532.

23. Karen Glanz, "Nutrition Education for Risk Factor Reduction and Patient Education: A Review," *Preventive Medicine* 14 (1985): 721–752.

Nutrition Counseling in Treatment of Diabetes

Objectives for Chapter 10

1. Identify factors that contribute to common inappropriate behaviors associated with carbohydrate-, protein-, and fat-controlled eating patterns.
2. Identify specific nutrients to emphasize in assessing a baseline eating pattern before providing dietary instruction.
3. Identify strategies to help combat inappropriate eating behaviors.
4. Generate strategies to deal with clients following carbohydrate-, protein-, and fat-controlled eating patterns.
5. Recommend dietary adherence tools for clients on carbohydrate-, protein-, and fat-controlled eating patterns.

Providing appropriate eating patterns for clients with diabetes can be a challenge. All factors of the diet—both amounts and content—must be carefully controlled, yet the client must be allowed a reasonable selection of foods. This chapter is designed to provide potential solutions to problems encountered in working with these clients.

The American Dietetic Association's *Handbook of Clinical Dietetics* lists the purposes of eating patterns for individuals with diabetes as follows:

1. "To attain and maintain ideal body weight,
2. to meet individual needs for essential nutrients,
3. to facilitate normal growth and development . . .,
4. to minimize glycosuria and maintain serum glucose levels as close to physiological levels as possible . . . , and
5. to reduce elevated serum lipids . . . ."[1]

Diet for treatment of diabetes falls into two categories based on whether the client has insulin-dependent diabetes or non-insulin-dependent diabetes.

Information is provided on theories and facts related to persons with non-insulin- and insulin-dependent diabetes. The effects of specific nutrients, sweeteners, alcohol, and exercise on blood glucose levels are described. Methods and means of managing diabetes through glucose monitoring, insulin regimens, and dietary intervention are reviewed. Adherence to diabetic eating patterns is covered in a section describing research in this area. Also included are eating behaviors which are inappropriate for optimum compliance with diabetic eating patterns. Methods for assessing eating patterns prior to instruction on a diabetic dietary recommendation are described. Treatment strategies including lack of knowledge related to general dietary modifications that affect blood glucose levels and lack of knowledge regarding fat intake and weight gain are discussed. Strategies designed to deal with forgetfulness and lack of commitment are provided.

THEORIES AND FACTS ABOUT NUTRITION AND NON-INSULIN-DEPENDENT DIABETES

The non-insulin-dependent diabetic person is usually obese and has peripheral resistance to insulin. The treatment of choice is caloric restriction and weight loss, which results in decreased insulin resistance and reduced and normalized blood glucose levels. The single most important goal in managing the obese non-insulin-diabetic person is to achieve and maintain desirable body weight by reducing total energy intake to levels below energy expenditure. With the loss of weight, blood glucose levels normalize.

The macronutrient composition of the diet for the non-insulin-dependent person is less important than for the person with insulin-dependent diabetes. For weight reduction, the diet should be adequate in nutrients but restricted in calories. For persons on diets very low in calories and suboptimal in micronutrients a vitamin and mineral supplement is appropriate. For persons who cannot adhere to a weight-loss diet, insulin or oral agents may be necessary to lower blood glucose levels. Such persons are usually insulin insensitive and respond poorly to exogenous insulin. The oral agents function in two ways to lower blood glucose levels: they increase insulin release from the beta cells and potentiate the peripheral effect of insulin. Of the four oral agents, tolbutamide (Orinase) and acteohexamide are the weaker oral agents; and tolazamide (Tolinase) and chorpropamide (Diabinese) are the more potent agents.

The sulfonylurea compounds all circulate bound to plasma albumin and are metabolized in the liver and then excreted by the kidneys. Some of the metabolites produced in the liver also have hypoglycemic effects. The presence of hepatic or renal disease is a contraindication for the use of oral agents. In the Type I insulin-dependent person, they are absolutely contraindicated. For these drugs to be effective, the patient must be able to produce endogenous insulin.

In the obese, non-insulin-dependent person treated with oral agents, regularity of meals and the relationship of meals to physical activity are important. Irregular exercise and eating patterns can lead to periods of severe hypoglycemia. In the obese person with diabetes not receiving insulin or oral glucose-lowering agents, regularity of meals and the relationships of meals to physical activity are less important than decreased caloric, but otherwise nutritionally adequate, intake. Problems associating alcohol intake and oral glucose-lowering agents are discussed under the section, "Alcohol."

THEORIES AND FACTS ABOUT NUTRITION AND INSULIN-DEPENDENT DIABETES

Insulin-dependent persons have complete beta cell failure, cannot produce insulin, are prone to ketoacidosis, and require exogenous insulin. Therapy revolves around insulin, diet, and exercise.

The insulin-dependent person lives at a time when research is flourishing. Diet is known to be important in controlling plasma glucose abnormalities and preventing hypoglycemia.[2] Whether normalized blood sugars play a role in preventing or delaying the development of neuropathy, microvascular disease, or atherosclerosis is uncertain. The National Institute of Diabetes, Digestive and Kidney Diseases, a part of the National Institutes of Health, has funded a clinical trial to help answer the unresolved question: Does normalizing blood sugars in the Type I diabetic person decrease the incidence of diabetic complications such as neuropathy, eye disease, and renal disease?

Even though research in the area of complications is lacking, effective insulin treatment to avoid extremely high and low blood glucose levels requires a standardized daily regimen of food intake. Several factors in dietary control are important: (1) timing of meals, (2) dietary composition, (3) caloric intake, and (4) level and regularity of physical activity.

Even if a client is following an intensive regimen in which each meal is covered with regular insulin or a more standard regimen of one or two shots of insulin a day, timing and regularity of meals are important. Practitioners should view each person as an individual, taking life style, physical activity, and insulin administration into consideration. They should stress a regular eating and exercise pattern as a goal for clients receiving insulin. Inconsistency in meals or exercise makes regulation of insulin doses difficult and can frequently lead to highs and lows in blood sugars.

Controversy exists with regard to the best dietary prescription in terms of nutrient percentages. The American Dietetic Association recommends the following nutrient distribution:

1. 12–20 percent of total energy intake from high biological value protein
2. 50–60 percent of total energy intake from carbohydrate (glucose and glucose-containing disaccharides, sucrose and lactose, are restricted)
3. 20–38 percent of total energy intake from fat (with less than 10 percent of calories from saturated fat, up to 10 percent of calories from polyunsaturated fat, and the remainder of fat from monounsaturated fatty acids).[3]

These recommendations are general, flexible requirements. The major goal should be to normalize blood sugars with glycosylated hemoglobin (HbA_{1c}) in the normal range. (See Table 10-1 and "Blood Glucose Monitoring" below for a detailed discussion of HbA_{1c}.) Doing so may mean using nutrient percentages of energy intake that vary slightly from the above recommendation. If blood sugars and other biological data are within the normal range, the diet is helping achieve the ultimate goal.

Effects of Specific Nutrients, Sweeteners, Alcohol, and Exercise on Blood Glucose Levels

Carbohydrates

Digestible Carbohydrate. Traditionally, dietary recommendations focused on use of complex carbohydrate and minimization of simple carbohydrate, assuming that the latter was absorbed rapidly and thus produced swings in blood glucose.[4] Subsequent studies demonstrated significantly different blood glucose and insulin responses to different types of simple and complex carbohydrates.[5]

Table 10-1 Values for Glycosylated Hemoglobin

Excellent	$<6\%$
Good	$6-9\%$
Poor	$>10\%$

Simple sugars include two groups of carbohydrates: monosaccharides and disaccharides. In nutrition the monosaccharides of most importance are the six-carbon sugars glucose, fructose, and galactose. Glucose, also known as dextrose or corn sugar, is present in sweet fruits such as berries, grapes, pears, and oranges and in certain vegetables, notably corn and carrots. Relatively large amounts occur in honey as well. Dextrose from corn syrup is often used commercially as a sweetener in prepared foods. Fructose, also called levulose or fruit sugar, is also found in most fruits and vegetables. Galactose is not found free in foods, although it is a major constituent of the principal carbohydrate in milk, lactose.

Disaccharides are formed when two monosaccharides are chemically bonded together. When glucose and fructose are bonded, sucrose, or table sugar, results. It is found in most fruits and vegetables and is a major component of brown sugar, maple sugar, and molasses. Many processed foods are sweetened with sucrose. When glucose and galactose are bonded, the disaccharide lactose results. Lactose, the only significant carbohydrate of animal origin, is found in milk and milk products. Maltose is another important disaccharide that results when two identical glucose units bond. Maltose is found in germinating seeds, some breakfast cereals, and fermented products, such as beer.

The term polysaccharide denotes the combination of a number of monosaccharides. They are often referred to as complex carbohydrates, as contrasted with the simple carbohydrates, mono- and disaccharides. Most polysaccharides of plant origin are commonly known as starches, of which there are several types. Different carbohydrate-containing foods, for example, corn, wheat, and apples, have different starches, each genetically determined. For example, amylose is a plant starch in which hundreds of glocose units are combined to form one long, straight chain. Amylopectin is another plant starch, also composed solely of glucose units, but arranged in branched chains. Various plants contain both amylose and amylopectin, although in different proportions.

The most abundant polysaccharide (and probably the most common organic molecule on earth) is cellulose, a component of plant cell walls. The body cannot digest cellulose because the human digestive system does not have the capacity to break the cellulose linkage structure. The amylose structure, however, is readily digested. Small structural distinctions, then, make the difference in how each molecule behaves and is utilized.

The one animal polysaccharide, glycogen, is not present in the food supply to an appreciable extent. Although it is stored as an energy source in some animal tissue (muscle and liver), it disappears with the death of the animal, leaving only negligible amounts in such foods as liver and fresh shellfish. The significance of glycogen for humans is its manufacture by the body during the course of glucose metabolism.[6]

During digestion, even large molecules of carbohydrate, such as starch, are eventually hydrolyzed to monosaccharides. Through enzymatic activity and chemical

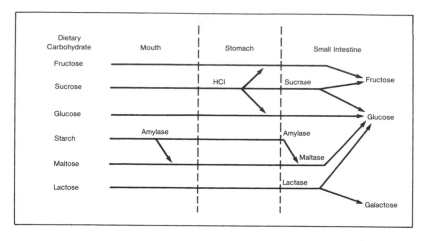

Figure 10-1 Schematic Diagram of Carbohydrate Digestion. *Source:* P. A. Kreutler, *Nutrition in Perspective,* 2nd ed., © 1987, p. 33. Reprinted by permission of Prentice-Hall, Inc., Englewood Cliffs, New Jersey.

activity involving gastric acid, dietary carbohydrate is converted to the three monosaccharides (Figure 10-1).

Although much research is still necessary to explain fully how complex carbohydrates affect diabetic control, research has provided some very interesting ideas. Studies point to the following factors in the relationship of complex carbohydrates and their effect on blood glucose values:

1. nature of the starch
2. protein-starch interaction
3. antinutrients other than fiber
4. physical form
   a. cooking method
   b. particle size (blending, grinding, etc.).

Crapo and coworkers studied the glycemic and insulin responses to a group of carbohydrate-containing foods, including bread, rice, potato, and corn, of normal and glucose-intolerant volunteers. Their findings indicated that the differences in responses to these foods are related to differences in the digestibility of starches.[7] Studies have also shown that amylopectin can be digested more quickly than amylase, a result that relates to the chemical structure of each. The glucose chains of amylose are bound by hydrogen bonds, making them less available for amylitic attack than amylopectin, which has many branched chains of glucose.[8] Indeed, raw legume starch (high in amylose) is less digestible than cornstarch in rats.[9]

An interaction between the protein and starch in food may also influence the digestibility and blood glucose response to the starch. Anderson found that removing protein from flour increased its digestibility.[10]

In addition to the starch and protein components of foods, antinutrients (natural enzyme inhibitors, lectins, phytates, and tannins) may affect starch digestibility and the blood glucose response. Enzyme inhibitors and lectins were shown to produce hypoglycemia and decreased growth in rats.[11] Furthermore, antinutrients may inhibit starch digestion in the gastrointestinal tract.[12]

The physical form of complex carbohydrates also affects blood glucose responses. A greater rise in blood glucose was reported after consumption of cooked as opposed to raw starches. Raw plant foods were shown to produce lower blood glucose responses than did cooked plant foods.[13] Researchers have also begun to look at moist and dry heat methods of cooking. Jenkins found that drying cooked red lentils in a warm oven for 12 hours resulted in significantly enhanced glycemic response and rate of in vitro digestion as compared with lentils boiled 20 minutes.[14]

The size of the starch particle is also important in starch digestibility. Digestibility increased when beans were ground first and then cooked as opposed to when they were cooked first and then ground.[15] O'Dea and others found that the blood glucose response to whole apples increased when apples were blended to a purée or when the juice was extracted.[16]

Oettlé and coworkers showed that eating sugary, manufactured snacks (chocolate-coated candy bars and cola drinks) versus whole food snacks (raisins and peanuts, bananas and peanuts) that were similar in fat and total calories resulted in plasma glucose levels that tended to rise higher and fall lower.[17] These findings suggest that foods and drinks with added fiber-depleted sugars stress and sometimes overwhelm homeostatic mechanisms and that the physical state of the food influences the insulin response to it. In general, it appears that the more processed a food is, the higher the blood glucose response it produces.

Indigestible Carbohydrate. There has been considerable interest in the 1980s in the possibility that increasing the dietary fiber content of the diabetic eating pattern may improve diabetic control. Fiber, carbohydrate that is not hydrolyzed by human digestive enzymes, consists of plant cell walls composed mostly of three polysaccharides: (1) cellulose, (2) pectic substances, (3) hemicellulose, as well as (4) noncarbohydrate lignin. Fiber is a component of plant foods only; it is not found in foods of animal origin.

It is important to draw a clear distinction between the effects of purified fiber added to a diet and fiber naturally present in food. In general, the viscous, water-soluble fibers, such as guar and pectin (purified fiber), have been most effective in flattening postprandial glycemia in normal and diabetic volunteers[18] and reducing urinary glucose loss in diabetic subjects.[19] Part of this action may stem from the ability of these fibers to slow gastric emptying[20] and reduce the rate of small intestinal absorption,[21] possibly by increasing the thickness of the unstirred water layer immediately adjacent to the small intestinal absorptive surface. Fiber naturally occurring in foods may reduce the rate of small intestinal digestion by impeding the penetration of the food by digestive enzymes, as may viscous forms of fiber. However, disruption of the normal relationship of starch and fiber, as in the milling of wheat products, may greatly reduce any effect the fiber might have on postprandial glycemia.

Concerns have been raised about the vitamin and mineral status of people who change from an habitually low-fiber diet to a diet of higher fiber content. Studies of vitamin and mineral status in adult subjects on high-fiber diets have not found evidence of deficiency, but populations at greatest risk—children, pregnant women, and the elderly—have not been evaluated. Use of high-fiber diets in these groups should be approached with caution. Use of high-fiber diets in persons with gastroparesis is contraindicated.

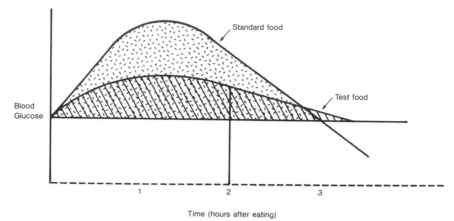

Time (hours after eating)

Figure 10-2 Glycemic Index Response Curves. A glycemic index compares the area under the blood glucose response curve for a specified period of time and for equivalent carbohydrate portions of test foods to that of a standard food. *Source:* Reprinted from *Handbook of Diabetes Nutritional Management* by M.A. Powers, p. 209, Aspen Publishers, Inc., © 1987.

Classifying Carbohydrates Using the Glycemic Index. As stated earlier, studies have shown variations in blood sugars when specific foods within the categories of simple and complex carbohydrate were tested for postingestion blood glucose excursions. Jenkins and his colleagues provided one method of classifying foods according to their effect on blood glucose levels.[22] This approach compares differences in the areas under the blood glucose response curve for equivalent carbohydrate-containing portions of test foods with that of a standard food and expresses them as a percentage of the standard food:

$$\text{Glycemic Index} = \frac{\text{Area under Curve of Test Food}}{\text{Area under Curve of Standard Food}} \times 100.$$

Figure 10-2 shows the two curves indicated in the equation. With this method of food classification, the higher the glycemic index of a food, the higher a person's blood glucose levels are expected to rise after eating that food. Research indicates that when the total diet is assessed, the glycemic or blood glucose differences between foods may be lessened to such a degree that clinically significant effects cannot be seen.[23] There is no consensus on this issue. Prospective clinical investigations are needed to clarify the benefit of specific eating patterns based on glycemic response.

Experiments have demonstrated variations in glycemic responses to different starchy foods. Early studies found that potatoes elicited a blood glucose response similar to that of an equivalent amount of glucose, whereas rice elicited a much flatter glycemic response.[24] As mentioned earlier, subsequent studies demonstrated that the food form is important. Further studies conducted on a large number of foods found differences in the two-hour glucose response areas to different foods ranging from 98 percent to 15 percent of their glucose equivalents.[25]

As a class, legumes are the foods that produce the flattest glycemic response,[26] which is thought to be due to the slow release of carbohydrate during digestion rather than to slowed carbohydrate absorption.

In vitro studies to evaluate the digestibility of different foods using human diges- tive juices found that some starchy foods released their products of carbohydrate digestion more slowly than did other starchy foods.[27] There is a positive relationship between the rate of digestion of foods and the glycemic responses elicited by the foods in both nondiabetic and diabetic people. These studies emphasized the likely impor- tance of gastrointestinal events in determining glycemic response. Nevertheless, as stated earlier, foods contain many components that may alter their digestibility, such as fiber, enzyme inhibitors, lectins, tannins, phytates, sugars, fats, proteins, and starches. Protein-starch interactions, cooking procedures, or the structure of food (ground or whole) also can alter digestibility. At present there is no chemical analysis that can predict with certainty the physiological response to a food. In addition, little is known about nutrient-nutrient interactions that may affect glycemic response. Total dietary fiber analysis cannot tell enough because the physical state and types of the fiber within the food and the interaction of fiber with other nutrients can affect the expected response.

While the state-of-the-art for dietary recommendations does not permit clear recommendations, broad generalizations may be justified. All starchy foods should not be considered to elicit similar postprandial glycemic responses. Indeed, the type of carbohydrate used in the diabetic diet may eventually be found to be a more impor- tant variable than the total amount of carbohydrate. At this time it seems reasonable that emphasizing carbohydrates of leguminous origin could be considered an aid in controlling postprandial glycemic responses. As with any change in the diet, however, the addition of other foods (such as fats) to provide palatability must be considered. Any change in the diet creates counterchange; therefore, counselors must always consider the total diet and its appropriateness for an individual.

Fat

The fat content of the diet is important from two standpoints. First, diabetic persons have a two to three times greater incidence of atherosclerosis and risk of death from cardiovascular disease than do nondiabetic persons.[28] Lower saturated fat, cholesterol, and total fat may help avoid coronary complications. Second, a study by O'Dea in Type II diabetes showed that the coingestion of fat with a carbohydrate meal reduced the postprandial glucose response to carbohydrate load but had no effect on insulin response.[29] The mechanism of action is poorly understood. One possibility is that glucose absorption from the small intestine is delayed because of the fat-induced delay in gastric emptying.

Although fat has been associated with decreased gastric emptying, the addition of fat to a carbohydrate load does not necessarily alter its effect on blood glucose levels.[30] Studies on the effect of fat on blood glucose levels showed varying responses. One showed that fat has no impact on digestion rates or blood glucose responses.[31] Others found a reduction in postprandial blood glucose responses when a saturated fat (butter) was eaten with carbohydrate, without an associated decrease in insulin response.[32] One study showed no significant changes in acute postprandial glucose responses and insulin levels when subjects ingested amounts of fat smaller than those described in the studies above. However, the subjects demonstrated a large impair- ment of carbohydrate tolerance following a standard meal eaten four hours after the high-fat breakfast.[33] The exact mechanism behind this effect is unclear. Ferrannini and his coworkers demonstrated an inhibition of insulin-stimulated glucose utilization when plasma-free fatty acids were elevated.[34]

Protein

Protein is also important in the diabetic person's diet. Approximately 58 percent of animal protein intake may eventually be converted to glucose, but at a much slower rate than carbohydrate.[35] High-protein diets have been recommended for the treatment of diabetes and may be associated with beneficial effects in some people with diabetes, but these diets have not yet been investigated scientifically. Concern about high-protein diets seems to center on the increased fat and cholesterol content that accompanies such diets unless food choices are made carefully. High-protein diets are contraindicated in diabetic patients with renal disease in predialysis states.

Addition of protein to a carbohydrate load can decrease its blood glucose effect.[36] The nature of the protein ingested also influences blood glucose and insulin responses to a meal.[37]

Salt

One study indicated an increase in postprandial plasma glucose and insulin when salt was added to test meals of lentils or white bread,[38] possibly because of an accelerating effect of salt on digestion or absorption.

Calories

The caloric content of the diet is very important, as the majority of persons with insulin-dependent diabetes initially lose a significant amount of weight. A diet must be adequate in calories for normal growth and development in pediatric age groups and for desirable body weight in adults. In the pregnant diabetic individual, caloric intake must be adjusted for normal growth and development of the fetus.

Sweeteners

Many alternatives are open to diabetic persons who want to use non-glucose-containing sweeteners. Two classes of sweeteners available are nutritive (fructose, sorbitol, xylitol, and aspartame) and nonnutritive (saccharin). Nutritive sweeteners have a caloric value that must be considered in the diabetic diet.

Fructose. Fructose is a common monosaccharide found in its free form in honey and fruit. Recent technical advances have made pure crystalline fructose available for clinical and commercial use. This form of fructose has a much smaller effect on blood glucose level in both controlled diabetic and nondiabetic people than does glucose, sucrose, or even some complex carbohydrates, although it can result in blood glucose increases in those who are poorly controlled. Short-term studies indicate no need for well-controlled diabetic persons to avoid the moderate use of crystalline fructose (defined as less than 75 grams per day),[39] but long-term studies of the effectiveness and safety of fructose have not been reported.

Fructose contains as many calories as sucrose, so persons concerned with their weight should use it with discretion. Crystalline fructose should be calculated as carbohydrate calories if more than 20 calories are eaten at one time, because of the slight rise in blood glucose that results with ingestion. Fructose should not be viewed as a low-calorie sweetener.[40]

Sorbitol and Xylitol. The polyalcohols, sorbitol and xylitol, seem to have relatively small effects on blood glucose and insulin levels in well-controlled diabetes but can be associated with osmotic diarrhea when ingested in amounts greater than 30 to 50 grams.[41] Recent evidence suggests an etiologic role of sorbitol in diabetic neuropathy, and some caution in its use may be wise.[42]

Xylitol is thought to be tolerated to a greater degree than is sorbitol or mannitol. Salminen and coworkers found that three of six healthy volunteers who consumed 30 grams of xylitol as a solution had complaints.[43] Investigations in rats show adaptation to xylitol with no diarrhea. Although the United States and the World Health Organization (WHO) have not specified daily intakes, the WHO has recommended that adults who take xylitol for the first time not exceed 30 grams per day and that eventually they may tolerate 200 to 300 grams per day.[44]

Aspartame. Aspartame (L-aspartame-L-phenylalanine methyl ester) is the newest member of the sweetener family, approved for use by the Food and Drug Administration (FDA) in 1981. It is a dipeptide of aspartic acid and phenylalanine that has a sweet taste without any metallic or chemical aftertaste. Since it is 120 to 280 times sweeter than sugar, depending on the food system in which it is used, it can dramatically reduce calories in some products. It is considered a nutritive substance, not an artificial sweetener, because its components occur naturally in foods, and it is metabolized in the body in the same way as the naturally occurring amino acids. It cannot be used in baking, frying, or broiling because prolonged heat causes a breakdown of the molecule and loss of sweetness. Consequently, it will not fill all sweetener needs. The daily intake considered acceptable for aspartame is 50 milligrams per kilogram of body weight in the United States and 40 milligrams in Canada; the WHO has set 40 milligrams per kilogram as the acceptable daily intake.[45] While aspartame's extreme sweetness makes its caloric contribution to a product negligible, for powdered table use it is packaged with a lactose buffer whose calories (four calories for the equivalent sweetness of one teaspoon of sugar) must be considered. In addition, persons with the hereditary disease phenylketonuria (PKU) must avoid aspartame.

Saccharin. Partly because of a possible ban on saccharin, an active search has continued for a nonnutritive sweetener that is completely satisfactory. None of the new sugar substitutes being investigated has yet passed all the tests required for FDA approval. After the ban on cyclamates in 1969, saccharin became the only nonnutritive sweetener used in the United States. In 1977 the FDA proposed bans on saccharin, but in the same year a moratorium was mandated, and it has been extended separately in 1979, 1981, 1983, and 1985.[46] Saccharin is 300 to 400 times sweeter than sucrose and has essentially no caloric value, but it has a bitter aftertaste that is objectionable to some people. In its powdered form, it is usually packaged with a dextrose or lactose buffer whose calories (approximately four calories for the equivalent sweetness of two teaspoons of sugar) must be considered. Users can calculate their intake using product labels, and compare it with recommended intakes. The United States and the WHO recommend not exceeding 1 gram of saccharin per day. The WHO recommendation is 2.5 milligrams per kilogram of body weight.[47]

While none of the sweeteners can be recommended without reservation, they are all alternatives that people with diabetes can use judiciously with an understanding of their drawbacks.

Alcohol

In the past diabetic persons were advised to avoid alcohol; however, research has demonstrated that alcohol, when consumed in moderate amounts (no more than 6 percent of total calories per day), does not lead to deterioration in diabetic control.[48] Many diabetologists now feel that reasonable amounts of alcohol are not contraindicated in diabetes. When alcohol is allowed in the diet, several factors need to be considered.

First, alcohol increases the rate of tolbutamide metabolism, and counselors need to follow clients receiving this drug and ingesting alcohol closely for irregularities in response to drug treatment and make adjustments as necessary. Clients using chlorpropamide (Diabinese) may have a disulfiram or antabuselike reaction (flushing, palpitations) with alcohol ingestion.[49] Because the effects of alcohol are as bad for people with diabetes as they are for others, an intoxicated diabetic person is probably less competent to administer insulin or other hypoglycemic agents or to time and plan meals appropriately. In addition, alcohol intoxication can mask the symptoms of hypoglycemia and impede appropriate treatment. Another potential metabolic consequence of alcohol ingestion is elevated plasma triglyceride levels.[50] Because diabetes is associated with an increased incidence of hypertriglycericemia, counselors should consider the effect of alcohol on plasma triglyceride levels in the dietary therapy of any diabetic client. It would seem prudent to curtail alcohol ingestion significantly in clients with preexisting elevations of plasma triglyceride. The caloric content of the alcohol must be considered and included in the diabetic meal plan if it is to be consumed. Finally, alcohol intake may cause hypoglycemia because alcohol dehydrogenase inhibits gluconeogenesis in the liver.[51]

In summary, persons with diabetes obviously should avoid alcohol abuse, as should any other person. Counselors should explain the specific risks for people with diabetes, especially for clients who are being treated with glucose-lowering agents. Moderate ingestion of alcohol is the key for diabetic individuals, with caution regarding its effect on caloric balance, control of plasma triglyceride levels, and reduced reaction time.

Exercise

Exercise can play a major part in altering insulin levels. The nutrition counselor must be prepared to view changes in blood glucose levels as a function of variations in diet and exercise. Changes in hormone levels and sickness can alter blood glucose levels independent of diet and exercise.

The questions about nutritional issues that are still unanswered make it impossible to quantify definitively the ideal macronutrient content of the diabetic diet. It is the nutrition counselor's responsibility to review dietary intake and look at corresponding blood sugars to determine possible alterations in matching insulin and diet for future occasions. The field is developing rapidly and, as new facts have emerged from research, nutritional recommendations have been revised. As research advances continue to be made, new data will help to define the components of the optimal diet.

Management of Diabetes

To manage diabetes, counselors must understand blood glucose testing, insulin types and their effect on blood glucose levels, and management schemes both traditional and intensive.

Blood Glucose Monitoring

For the insulin-dependent person, home blood glucose monitoring has almost completely replaced urine glucose determinations. Urine values depend on the renal threshold for glucose, which is generally 180 milligrams per deciliter (mg/dl) or higher. Thus a negative urine may not reflect normal blood glucose levels.[52] Methods are now available for accurate and convenient self-measurement of blood glucose. In one, a small drop of blood is obtained from the finger with a device called an autolet and placed on a plastic strip (Chemstrip or Dextrostick). An enzymatic reaction takes place to cause the strip to change color, indicating the amount of glucose in the blood. The stick is read through comparison with a color chart or by a machine, the glucometer. Thorough instruction in monitoring is crucial and should be given by trained medical personnel. Home blood glucose monitoring that is completed incorrectly may not reflect actual blood glucose levels.

Monitoring blood glucose levels requires measurement in the fasting state and then two or three hours after breakfast, lunch, and dinner. The fasting blood glucose level is a guide to the effectiveness of overnight control of diabetes. The postprandial blood glucose values show how well insulin matches the foods eaten at meals. The goal is to prevent hyperglycemia and hypoglycemia after a meal. When multiple injections of regular insulin are given, it is preferable to measure blood glucose levels before each meal (30 minutes before a meal at approximately the time of an injection or a bolus) rather than two hours after a meal. For patients who are willing, measurement 30 minutes before a meal and 2 hours following may give information that helps in normalizing blood glucose levels. Changes in insulin regimens are based on these blood glucose determinations, usually on a pattern of blood sugars over a period of days (3 days).

In addition to blood glucose monitoring, the measurement of glycosylated hemoglobin indicates the degree of long-term control of diabetes. Glucose in the blood reacts with free amino groups in proteins in a stable and irreversible nonenzymatic process called glycosylation. Thus glucose is attached to the protein for the life of the protein. Hemoglobin, one of several proteins exhibiting glycosylation, has a lifespan of 100 to 120 days. The percentage of glycosylated hemoglobin in the blood reflects the time-averaged blood glucose levels from the preceding two to three months.[53]

Acceptable glycosylated hemoglobin values and blood glucose values vary with the individual client and the desires of the diabetologist or physician managing the client's care. In general a glycosylated hemoglobin level above 10 percent is considered high and requires adjustments to bring clients into better control.[54] Research indicates that fasting values of blood glucose greater than 145 mg/dl as a weekly average result in glycosylated hemoglobin levels higher than 14.5 percent. Jovanovic and Petersen indicated that a glycosylated hemoglobin level of 5.15 percent is considered normal.[55] Table 10-1 above indicates ranges for glycosylated hemoglobin.

Beebe identified normal blood glucose levels for various times of the day: during a fasting state, 80–120 mg/dl; before meals, 80–120 mg/dl; one hour after a meal, less than 180 mg/dl; and two hours after a meal, less than 160 mg/dl.[56] These numbers represent optimum values and may not be realistic for all clients with diabetes.

In insulin-dependent persons, it is important to determine the presence of ketones in the urine. When blood glucose levels are out of control or when clients are acutely ill, ketone bodies can be important early warning signs of impending diabetic ketoacidosis. On sick days, it is important for clients to take insulin, test their blood glucose frequently, test their urine for ketones, and try to eat their usual amount of carbohydrate, divided into smaller meals and snacks. If blood glucose levels rise above 250 mg/dl, all of the usual amount of carbohydrate is not necessary. Frequent fluid intake is also recommended.

Types of Insulin

Diet and insulin must be matched closely to achieve normalized blood glucose levels. The insulin preparations available today fall into three categories:

1. *Short-acting insulins* peak in three to four hours and last six to eight hours. Included in this category are regular and semilente insulin.
2. *Intermediate-acting insulins* peak 8 to 10 hours after injection and last 18 to 24 hours. NPH (neutral-protamine Hagedorn) and lente are intermediate-acting insulins.
3. *Long-acting insulins* peak 14 to 16 hours after injection and have some effect for up to 36 hours. Prolamine zinc (PZI) and ultralente are long-acting insulins.

Examples of three commonly used insulin regimens follow.[57]

Mixed-Insulin Dosage Regimen. In this regimen both short-acting (usually regular) and intermediate-acting insulin are given in a single injection. Ideally the client on this regimen has available a short-acting insulin to eliminate hyperglycemia in the morning and an intermediate-acting insulin to provide blood glucose control throughout the rest of the day and night.

Split-Insulin Dosage Regimen. In this two-dose regimen, one dose is administered before breakfast to control daytime blood glucose and one at supper to control hyper-glycemia at night. This regimen is useful for the client for whom one injection does not last throughout the day. Usually both morning and evening doses consist of an intermediate-acting insulin. If hyperglycemia is a problem only in the evening, a regular insulin may be substituted for an intermediate.

Split- and Mixed-Insulin Dosage Regimen. This regimen requires two insulin injections, each consisting of both short-acting and intermediate-acting insulin. Each component of insulin has a peak action time during one particular period of the day that also includes one major meal. Activity and any hypoglycemic episodes during a given time period should correspond to the insulin component and meals during that period.

New advances in treatment of the insulin-dependent person have changed some of the concepts often taught in the past. The constant-infusion insulin pump has provided the dietitian with a wealth of flexibility in dietary recommendations, a flexibility that can prove disastrous if not used appropriately. Timing of meals, dietary composition, caloric content of the diet, and physical activity are immensely important to the successful use of a constant-infusion insulin pump. Teamwork among physician, nurse, and dietitian is crucial to success.

Regular insulin is used in the constant-infusion insulin pump, which is attached to the abdomen subcutaneously with a needle. From a syringe attached to the pump, insulin flows through tubing to the needle injection site. The pump is a kind of computer that, when programmed, allows insulin to enter the body much as the pancreas slowly maintains a constant insulin level throughout the day. The pump also allows the client to increase the amount of insulin in a bolus at each meal, which also mimics the normally functioning pancreas. A basal dose of insulin is programmed into the computer-like pump to provide a constant, small dose of regular insulin at all times. Meals are covered by bolusing or pushing a button on the pump with the appropriate number (shown in a window) that coincides with the correct units of regular insulin to match a meal.

Multiple daily injections, or MDI, therapy is similar to the pump concept in that regular insulin is injected via syringe to cover each meal. Basal needs are usually met with NPH, frequently given at supper or bedtime for overnight control, or with one to two injections of ultralente insulin given before breakfast or before both breakfast and supper.

Dietary Intervention

Both the pump and MDI therapy require the use of a dietary exchange pattern, which should be based upon individual needs and preferences (i.e., for cardiovascular problems, American Heart Association's recommendations as discussed in Chapter 9 may be necessary). The one shown in Adherence Tool 10-6 includes only items preferred by one particular client. Each food is placed in a category with items that have approximately equivalent carbohydrate, protein, and fat contents. For persons on the pump or MDI, an additional step that allows more flexibility without sacrificing accuracy is the Total Available Glucose (TAG) system.[58] This system is based on research described by Munro and Allison in their classic text, *Mammalian Protein Metabolism,* Volume I, in which they present discussions of the gluconeogenic properties of certain proteins.[59] The amino acids that are definitely gluconeogenic are those that are rapidly degraded to intermediates of glycolysis of the tricarboxylic acid cycle. Amino acids that give irregular results when administered in a large single dose are relatively slowly degraded, either because of the low activity of the enzymes of intermediary metabolism or because of the slow absorption. The high yield of glucose on feeding proteins indicates that the conversion of protein to carbohydrate in dogs can be maximal. Munro and Allison identify amino acids as rapidly gluconeogenic, variably gluconeogenic, and nongluconeogenic.

Lusk showed in 1928 that meat protein yields 58 grams of glucose per 100 grams of protein metabolized.[60] He also studied the gluconeogenic effects of casein, whose amino acid composition is similar to that of mixed meat protein. The calculated maximum yield of casein is 57 grams of glucose per 100 grams of protein. This idea has resulted in the use of a fixed number (Total Available Glucose) for each meal as a way of controlling blood sugars. The number is derived from calculations with exact figures of carbohydrate and animal protein, found in *Food Values of Portions Commonly Used.*[61] For example, cooked beef cubed steak weighs 3 1/2 ounces (100 grams), contains 0.0 grams of carbohydrate, 28.6 grams of animal protein, and 14.4 grams of fat. To calculate TAG, the following formula is used: 0.0 grams of carbohydrate plus (28.6 grams of animal protein × 0.58) equals TAG. The conversion factor for animal protein is that discovered in Lusk's animal studies. Total Available Glucose is a value that approximates the amount of ingested glucose that will be available for cell use. Research by Lusk also showed that about 10 percent of fat is converted to carbohydrate. Some nutritionists add in this value for a total TAG calculation.[62] In an attempt to simplify calculations, this value, usually low if diets include 30 to 35 percent of calories from fat, is not used here. By giving each meal a total figure

Table 10-2 1986 ADA-ADA Exchange List Calculation Guide

Exchange List	Carbohydrate (g)	Protein (g)	Fat (g)	Calories (g)
Starch/Bread	15	3	Trace*	80
Meat, lean	—	7	3	55
Meat, medium-fat	—	7	5	75
Meat, high-fat	—	7	8	100
Vegetable	5	2	—	25
Fruit	15	—	—	60
Milk, skim	12	8	Trace*	90
Milk, low-fat	12	8	5	120
Milk, whole	12	8	8	150
Fat	—	—	5	45

*One gram of fat can be used for calculation purposes.

Source: Reprinted from *Exchange Lists for Meal Planning*, p. 5, with permission of The American Diabetes Association Inc. and The American Dietetic Association, © 1986.

for TAG, individuals can vary intake without going over the recommended grams of TAG. TAG for each exchange is as follows:

- 1 Fruit Exchange = 15 grams of TAG
- 1 Meat Exchange = 4 grams of TAG
- 1 Vegetable Exchange = 5 grams of TAG
- 1 Bread Exchange = 15 grams of TAG
- 1 Milk Exchange = 17 grams of TAG

Table 10-2 shows calories, carbohydrate, protein, and fat values for each exchange. Exhibit 10-1 shows exchange groups with amounts of food equivalent to one exchange.

There are several guidelines to follow to cover intake (TAG) with insulin. One unit of regular insulin covers approximately 10 to 15 grams of TAG. Each individual will find that one unit of regular insulin covers a number of grams of TAG that is unique to that person. For one person, one unit of insulin may cover 11 grams of TAG, with normal blood glucose values resulting. For a second person one unit of regular insulin will cover 9 grams of TAG. For each person the ratio of TAG to insulin depends on the time of day and physical activity. The ratio may be different at breakfast than at lunch or supper.

As a general rule of thumb, a person with diabetes should wait 30 minutes before eating a meal after bolusing or injecting regular insulin. Table 10-3 is a rough guide for changing timing if a meal changes dramatically from the usual diet in terms of fat, fiber, or simple sugar content.

Extreme accuracy in weighing and measuring food is important, as is consistency in timing meals to ensure that a meal is eaten 30 minutes after regular insulin is taken. The types of foods eaten may play a part in timing injections or boluses of regular insulin.

Exhibit 10-1 Exchange Lists for Meal Planning

STARCH/BREAD LIST

Each item in this list contains approximately 15 grams of carbohydrate, 3 grams of protein, a trace of fat, and 80 calories. Whole grain products average about 2 grams of fiber per serving. Some foods are higher in fiber.

Those foods that contain 3 or more grams of fiber per serving are identified with the fiber symbol*.

You can choose your starch exchanges from any of the items on this list. If you want to eat a starch food that is not on the list, the general rule is that:

- ½ cup of cereal, grain or pasta is one serving
- 1 ounce of a bread product is one serving.

Your dietitian can help you be more exact.

Cereals/Grains/Pasta

*Bran cereals, concentrated	⅓ cup
*Bran cereals, flaked (such as Bran Buds,® All Bran®)	½ cup
Bulgur (cooked)	½ cup
Cooked cereals	½ cup
Cornmeal (dry)	2½ Tbsp.
Grapenuts	3 Tbsp.
Grits (cooked)	½ cup
Other ready-to-eat unsweetened cereals	¾ cup
Pasta (cooked)	½ cup
Puffed cereal	1½ cup
Rice, white or brown (cooked)	⅓ cup
Shredded wheat	½ cup
*Wheat germ	3 Tbsp.

Dried Beans/Peas/Lentils

*Beans and peas (cooked) (such as kidney, white, split, blackeye)	⅓ cup
*Lentils (cooked)	⅓ cup
*Baked beans	¼ cup

Starchy Vegetables

*Corn	½ cup
*Corn on cob, 6 in. long	1
*Lima beans	½ cup
*Peas, green (canned or frozen)	½ cup
*Plantain	½ cup
Potato, baked	1 small (3 oz.)

Note: *indicates 3 g or more of fiber
** indicates foods that have 400 mg or more of sodium if more than 1 or 2 servings are eaten
† indicates 400 mg or more of sodium

Exhibit 10-1 continued

Potato, mashed	½ cup
*Squash, winter (acorn, butternut)	¾ cup
Yam, sweet potato, plain	⅓ cup

Bread

Bagel	½ (1 oz.)
Bread sticks, crisp, 4 in. long × ½ in.	2 (⅔ oz.)
Croutons, low fat	1 cup
English muffin	½
Frankfurter or hamburger bun	½ (1 oz.)
Pita, 6 in. across	½
Plain roll, small	1 (1 oz.)
Raisin, unfrosted	1 slice (1 oz.)
Rye, pumpernickel	1 slice (1 oz.)
Tortilla, 6 in. across	1
White (including French, Italian)	1 slice (1 oz.)
Whole wheat	1 slice (1 oz.)

Crackers/Snacks

Animal crackers	8
Graham crackers, 2½ in. square	3
Matzoth	¾ oz.
Melba toast	5 slices
Oyster crackers	24
Popcorn (popped, no fat added)	3 cups
Pretzels	¾ oz.
Rye crisp, 2 in. × 3½ in.	4
Saltine-type crackers	6
Whole wheat crackers, no fat added (crisp breads, such as Finn®, Kavli®, Wasa®)	2–4 slices (¾ oz.)

Starch Foods Prepared with Fat
(Count as 1 starch/bread serving, plus 1 fat serving.)

Biscuit, 2½ in. across	1
Chow mein noodles	½ cup
Corn bread, 2 in. cube	1 (2 oz.)
Cracker, round butter type	6
French fried potatoes, 2 in. to 3½ in. long	10 (1½ oz.)
Muffin, plain, small	1
Pancake, 4 in. across	2
Stuffing, bread (prepared)	¼ cup
Taco shell, 6 in. across	2

Exhibit 10-1 continued

Waffle, 4½ in. square	1
Whole wheat crackers, fat added (such as Triscuits®)	4–6 (1 oz.)

MEAT LIST

Each serving of meat and substitutes on this list contains about 7 grams of protein. The amount of fat and number of calories vary, depending on what kind of meat or substitute you choose. The list is divided into three parts based on the amount of fat and calories: lean meat, medium-fat meat, and high-fat meat. One ounce (one meat exchange) of each of these includes:

	Carbohydrate *(grams)*	Protein *(grams)*	Fat *(grams)*	Calories
Lean	0	7	3	55
Medium-Fat	0	7	5	75
High-Fat	0	7	8	100

You are encouraged to use more lean and medium-fat meat, poultry, and fish in your meal plan. This will help decrease your fat intake, which may help decrease your risk for heart disease. The items from the high-fat group are high in saturated fat, cholesterol, and calories. You should limit your choices from the high-fat group to three (3) times per week. Meat and substitutes do not contribute any fiber to your meal plan.

Those foods containing 400 mg or more of sodium are identified with the symbol †.

TIPS

1. Bake, roast, broil, grill, or boil these foods rather than frying them with added fat.
2. Use a nonstick pan spray or a nonstick pan to brown or fry these foods.
3. Trim off visible fat before and after cooking.
4. Do not add flour, bread crumbs, coating mixes, or fat to these foods when preparing them.
5. Weigh meat after removing bones and fat, and after cooking. Three ounces of cooked meat is about equal to 4 ounces of raw meat. Some examples of meat portions are:
   2 ounces meat (2 meat exchanges) =
   1 small chicken leg or thigh
   ½ cup cottage cheese or tuna
   3 ounces meat (3 meat exchanges) =
   1 medium pork chop
   1 small hamburger
   ½ of a whole chicken breast
   1 unbreaded fish fillet
   cooked meat, about the size of a deck of cards
6. Restaurants usually serve prime cuts of meat, which are high in fat and calories.

Lean Meat and Substitutes
(One exchange is equal to any one of the following items.)

Beef:	USDA Good or	1 oz.
	Choice grades of lean beef, such as round, sirloin, and flank steak; tenderloin; and chipped beef†	

Exhibit 10-1 continued

Pork:	Lean pork, such as fresh ham; canned, cured or boiled ham†; Canadian bacon†, tenderloin	1 oz.
Veal:	All cuts are lean except for veal cutlets (ground or cubed). Examples of lean veal are chops and roasts	1 oz.
Poultry:	Chicken, turkey, Cornish hen (without skin)	1 oz.
Fish:	All fresh and frozen fish	1 oz.
	Crab, lobster, scallops, shrimp, clams (fresh or canned in water†)	2 oz.
	Oysters	6 medium
	Tuna† (canned in water)	¼ cup
	Herring (uncreamed or smoked)	1 oz.
	Sardines (canned)	2 medium
Wild Game:	Venison, rabbit, squirrel	1 oz.
	Pheasant, duck, goose (without skin)	1 oz.
Cheese:	Any cottage cheese	¼ cup
	Grated parmesan	2 Tbsp.
	Diet cheeses† (with less than 55 calories per ounce)	1 oz.
Other:	95% fat-free luncheon meat	1 oz.
	Egg whites	3 whites
	Eggs substitutes with less than 55 calories per ¼ cup	¼ cup

Medium-Fat Meat and Substitutes
(One exchange is equal to any one of the following items.)

Beef:	Most beef products fall into this category. Examples are: all ground beef, roast (rib, chuck, rump), steak (cubed, Porterhouse, T-bone), and meatloaf	1 oz.
Pork:	Most pork products fall into this category. Examples are: chops, loin roast, Boston butt, cutlets	1 oz.
Lamb:	Most lamb products fall into this category. Examples are: chops, leg, and roast.	1 oz.
Veal:	Cutlet (ground or cubed, unbreaded)	1 oz.
Poultry:	Chicken (with skin), domestic duck or goose (well-drained of fat), ground turkey	1 oz.
Fish:	Tuna† (canned in oil and drained)	¼ cup
	Salmon† (canned)	¼ cup

Exhibit 10-1 continued

Cheese:	Skim or part-skim milk cheeses, such as:	
	Ricotta	¼ cup
	Mozzarella	1 oz.
	Diet cheeses† (with 56-80 calories per ounce)	1 oz.
Other:	86% fat-free luncheon meat†	1 oz.
	Egg (high in cholesterol, limit to 3 per week)	1
	Egg substitutes with 56–80 calories per ¼ cup	¼ cup
	Tofu (2½ in. × 2¾ in. × 1 in.)	4 oz.
	Liver, heart, kidney, sweetbreads (high in cholesterol)	1 oz.

High-Fat Meat and Substitutes

   Remember, these items are high in saturated fat, cholesterol, and calories, and should be used only three (3) times per week. *(One exchange is equal to any one of the following items.)*

Beef:	Most USDA Prime cuts of beef, such as ribs, corned beef†	1 oz.
Pork:	Spareribs, ground pork, pork sausage† (patty or link)	1 oz.
Lamb:	Patties (ground lamb)	1 oz.
Fish:	Any fried fish product	1 oz.
Cheese:	All regular cheeses†, such as American, Blue, Cheddar, Monterey, Swiss	1 oz.
Other:	Luncheon meat†, such as bologna, salami, pimento loaf	1 oz.
	Sausage†, such as Polish, Italian, or smoked	1 oz.
	Knockwurst	1 oz.
	Bratwurst†	1 oz.
	Frankfurter† (turkey or chicken)	1 frank (10/lb.)
	Peanut butter (contains unsaturated fat)	1 Tbsp.

Count as one high-fat meat plus one fat exchange:

	Frankfurter† (beef, pork, or combination)	1 frank (10/lb.)

VEGETABLE LIST*

   Each vegetable serving on this list contains about 5 grams of carbohydrate, 2 grams of protein, and 25 calories. Vegetables contain 2–3 grams of dietary fiber. Vegetables that

Exhibit 10-1 continued

contain 400 mg of sodium per serving are identified with a † symbol, and those containing 3 or more grams of fiber per serving are indicated with an * symbol.

Vegetables are a good source of vitamins and minerals. Fresh and frozen vegetables have more vitamins and less added salt. Rinsing canned vegetables will remove much of the salt.

Unless otherwise noted, the serving size for vegetables (one vegetable exchange) is:
½ cup of cooked vegetables or vegetable juice
1 cup of raw vegetables

Artichoke (½ medium)	Mushrooms, cooked
Asparagus	Okra
Beans (green, wax, Italian)	Onions
Bean sprouts	Pea pods
Beets	Peppers (green)
Broccoli	Rutabaga
Brussels sprouts	Sauerkraut†
Cabbage, cooked	Spinach, cooked
Carrots	Summer squash (crookneck)
Cauliflower	Tomato (one large)
Eggplant	Tomato/vegetable juice†
Greens (collard, mustard, turnip)	Turnips
Kohlrabi	Water chestnuts
Leeks	Zucchini, cooked

Starchy vegetables such as corn, peas, and potatoes are found on the Starch/Bread List.

For free vegetables, see Free Food List.

FRUIT LIST
Each item on this list contains about 15 grams of carbohydrate and 60 calories. Fresh, frozen, and dry fruits have about 2 grams of fiber per serving. Fruits that have 3 or more grams of fiber per serving have a * symbol. Fruit juices contain very little dietary fiber.

The carbohydrate and calorie contents for a fruit serving are based on the usual serving of the most commonly eaten fruits. Use fresh fruits or fruits frozen or canned without sugar added. Whole fruit is more filling than fruit juice and may be a better choice for those who are trying to lose weight. Unless otherwise noted, the serving size for one fruit serving is:
½ cup of fresh fruit or fruit juice
¼ cup of dried fruit

Fresh, Frozen, and Unsweetened Canned Fruit

Apple (raw, 2 in. across)	1 apple
Applesauce (unsweetened)	½ cup
Apricots (medium, raw) or	4 apricots
Apricots (canned)	½ cup, or 4 halves
Banana (9 in. long)	½ banana
*Blackberries (raw)	¾ cup
*Blueberries (raw)	¾ cup

Exhibit 10-1 continued

Cantaloupe (5 in. across)	⅓ melon
(cubes)	1 cup
Cherries (large, raw)	12 cherries
Cherries (canned)	½ cup
Figs (raw, 2 in. across)	2 figs
Fruit cocktail (canned)	½ cup
Grapefruit (medium)	½ grapefruit
Grapefruit (segments)	¾ cup
Grapes (small)	15 grapes
Honeydew melon (medium)	⅛ melon
(cubes)	1 cup
Kiwi (large)	1 kiwi
Mandarin oranges	¾ cup
Mango (small)	½ mango
*Nectarine (2½ in. across)	1 nectarine
Orange (2½ in. across)	1 orange
Papaya	1 cup
Peach (2¾ in. across)	1 peach, or ¾ cup
Peaches (canned)	½ cup, or 2 halves
Pear	½ large, or 1 small
Pears (canned)	½ cup, or 2 halves
Persimmon (medium, native)	2 persimmons
Pineapple (raw)	¾ cup
Pineapple (canned)	⅓ cup
Plum (raw, 2 in. across)	2 plums
*Pomegranate	½ pomegranate
*Raspberries (raw)	1 cup
*Strawberries (raw, whole)	1¼ cup
Tangerine (2½ in. across)	2 tangerines
Watermelon (cubes)	1¼ cup

Dried Fruit

*Apples	4 rings
*Apricots	7 halves
Dates	2½ medium
*Figs	1½
*Prunes	3 medium
Raisins	2 Tbsp.

Fruit Juice

Apple juice/cider	½ cup
Cranberry juice cocktail	⅓ cup
Grapefruit juice	½ cup
Grape juice	⅓ cup
Orange juice	½ cup
Pineapple juice	½ cup
Prune juice	⅓ cup

Exhibit 10-1 continued

MILK LIST

Each serving of milk or milk products on this list contains about 12 grams of carbohydrate and 8 grams of protein. The amount of fat in milk is measured in percent (%) of butterfat. The calories vary, depending on what kind of milk you choose. The list is divided into three parts based on the amount of fat and calories: skim/very lowfat milk, lowfat milk, and whole milk. One serving (one milk exchange) of each of these includes:

	Carbohydrate (grams)	Protein (grams)	Fat (grams)	Calories
Skim/ Very Lowfat	12	8	trace	90
Lowfat	12	8	5	120
Whole	12	8	8	150

Milk is the body's main source of calcium, the mineral needed for growth and repair of bones. Yogurt is also a good source of calcium. Yogurt and many dry or powdered milk products have different amounts of fat. If you have questions about a particular item, read the label to find out the fat and calorie content.

Milk is good to drink, but it can also be added to cereal, and to other foods. Many tasty dishes such as sugar-free pudding are made with milk (see the Combination Foods list). Add life to plain yogurt by adding one of your fruit servings to it.

Skim and Very Lowfat Milk

skim milk	1 cup
½% milk	1 cup
1% milk	1 cup
lowfat buttermilk	1 cup
evaporated skim milk	½ cup
dry nonfat milk	⅓ cup
plain nonfat yogurt	8 oz.

Lowfat Milk

2% milk	1 cup
plain lowfat yogurt (with added nonfat milk solids)	8 oz.

Whole Milk

The whole milk group has much more fat per serving than the skim and low fat groups. Whole milk has more than 3¼% butterfat. Try to limit your choices from the whole milk groups as much as possible.

whole milk	1 cup
evaporated whole milk	½ cup
whole plain yogurt	8 oz.

FAT LIST

Each serving on the fat list contains about 5 grams of fat and 45 calories.

The foods on the fat list contain mostly fat, although some items may also contain a small amount of protein. All fats are high in calories and should be carefully measured. Everyone should modify fat intake by eating unsaturated fats instead of saturated fats.

Exhibit 10-1 continued

The sodium content of these foods varies widely. Check the label for sodium information. Foods that have 400 mg or more of sodium if more than 1 or 2 servings are eaten are indicated with a ** symbol.

Unsaturated Fats

Avocado	⅛ medium
Margarine	1 tsp.
**Margarine, diet	1 Tbsp.
Mayonnaise	1 tsp.
**Mayonnaise, reduced-calorie	1 Tbsp.
Nuts and Seeds:	
Almonds, dry roasted	6 whole
Cashews, dry roasted	1 Tbsp.
Pecans	2 whole
Peanuts	20 small or 10 large
Walnuts	2 whole
Other nuts	1 Tbsp.
Seeds, pine nuts, sunflower (without shells)	1 Tbsp.
Pumpkin seeds	2 tsp.
Oil (corn, cottonseed, safflower, soybean, sunflower, olive, peanut)	1 tsp.
**Olives	10 small or 5 large
Salad dressing, mayonnaise-type	2 tsp.
Salad dressing, mayonnaise-type, reduced-calorie	1 Tbsp.
**Salad dressing (all varieties)	1 Tbsp.
†Salad dressing, reduced-calorie	2 Tbsp.

(Two tablespoons of low-calorie salad dressing is a free food.)

Saturated Fats

Butter	1 tsp.
**Bacon	1 slice
Chitterlings	½ ounce
Coconut, shredded	2 Tbsp.
Coffee whitener, liquid	2 Tbsp.
Coffee whitener, powder	4 tsp.
Cream (light, coffee, table)	2 Tbsp.
Cream, sour	2 Tbsp.
Cream (heavy, whipping)	1 Tbsp.
Cream cheese	1 Tbsp.
**Salt pork	¼ ounce

FREE FOODS

A *free food* is any food or drink that contains less than 20 calories per serving. You can eat as much as you want of those items that have no serving size specified. You may eat two or three servings per day of those items that have a specific serving size. Be sure to spread them out through the day.

Exhibit 10-1 continued

Drinks:
Bouillon† or broth
   without fat
Bouillon, low-sodium
Carbonated drinks,
   sugar-free
Carbonated water
Club soda
Cocoa powder,
   unsweetened (1
   Tbsp.)
Coffee / Tea
Drink mixes, sugar-
   free
Tonic water, sugar-
   free

Nonstick pan spray

Fruit:
Cranberries,
   unsweetened (½ cup)
Rhubarb,
   unsweetened (½ cup)

Vegetables:
(raw, 1 cup)
Cabbage
Celery
Chinese cabbage*
Cucumber
Green onion
Hot peppers
Mushrooms
Radishes
Zucchini*

Salad greens:
Endive
Escarole
Lettuce
Romaine
Spinach

Sweet substitutes:
Candy, hard, sugar-
   free
Gelatin, sugar-free
Gum, sugar-free
Jam / Jelly, sugar-
   free (2 tsp.)
Pancake syrup,
   sugar-free (1–2
   Tbsp.)
Sugar substitutes
   (saccharin,
   aspartame)
Whipped topping (2
   Tbsp.)

Condiments:
Catsup (1 Tbsp.)
Mustard
Horseradish
Pickles†, dill,
   unsweetened
Salad dressing, low-
   calorie (2 Tbsp.)
Taco sauce (1 Tbsp.)
Vinegar

Seasonings can be very helpful in making food taste better. Be careful of how much sodium you use. Read the label, and choose those seasonings that do not contain sodium or salt.

Basil (fresh)
Celery seeds
Chili powder
Chives
Cinnamon
Curry
Dill
Flavoring extracts
   almonds, walnut,
   peppermint, butter,
   lemon, etc.)

Lemon juice
Lemon pepper
Lime
Lime juice
Mint
Onion powder
Oregano
Paprika (vanilla,
Pepper
Pimento
Spices

Exhibit 10-1 continued

Garlic	Soy sauce†
Garlic powder	Soy sauce, low sodium ("lite")
Herbs	Wine, used in
Hot pepper sauce	cooking (¼ cup)
Lemon	Worcestershire sauce

COMBINATION FOODS

Much of the food we eat is mixed together in various combinations. These combination foods do not fit into only one exchange list. It can be quite hard to tell what is in a certain casserole dish or baked food item. This is a list of average values for some typical combination foods. This list will help you fit these foods into your meal plan. Ask your dietitian for information about any other foods you'd like to eat. The *American Diabetes Association/American Dietetic Association Family Cookbooks* and the *American Diabetes Association Holiday Cookbook* have many recipes and further information about many foods, including combination foods. Check your library or local bookstore.

Food	Amount	Exchanges
Casseroles, homemade	1 cup (8 oz.)	2 starch, 2 medium-fat meat, 1 fat
Cheese pizza†, thin crust	¼ of 15 oz. or ¼ of 10'	2 starch, 1 medium-fat meat, 1 fat
Chili with beans*,† (commercial)	1 cup (8 oz.)	2 starch, 2 medium-fat meat, 2 fat
Chow mein*,† (without noodles or rice)	2 cups (16 oz.)	1 starch, 2 vegetable, 2 lean meat
Macaroni and cheese†	1 cup (8 oz.)	2 starch, 1 medium-fat meat, 2 fat
Soup:		
Bean*,†	1 cup (8 oz.)	1 starch, 1 vegetable, 1 lean meat
Chunky, all varieties†	10¾ oz. can	1 starch, 1 vegetable, 1 medium-fat meat
Cream† (made with water)	1 cup (8 oz.)	1 starch, 1 fat
Vegetable† or broth-type†	1 cup (8 oz.	1 starch

Exhibit 10-1 continued

Food	Amount	Exchanges
Spaghetti and meatballs† (canned)	1 cup (8 oz.)	2 starch, 1 medium-fat meat, 1 fat
Sugar-free pudding (made with skim milk)	½ cup	1 starch

If beans are used as a meat substitute:

Dried beans*, peas*, lentils*	1 cup (cooked)	2 starch, 1 lean meat

FOODS FOR OCCASIONAL USE

Moderate amounts of some foods can be used in your meal plan, in spite of their sugar or fat content, as long as you can maintain blood-glucose control. The following list includes average exchange values for some of these foods. Because they are concentrated sources of carbohydrate, you will notice that the portion sizes are very small. Check with your dietitian for advice on how often and when you can eat them.

Food	Amount	Exchanges
Angel food cake	1/12 cake	2 starch
Cake, no icing	1/12 cake, or a 3″ square	2 starch, 2 fat
Cookies	2 small (1 3/4″ across)	1 starch, 1 fat
Frozen fruit yogurt	⅓ cup	1 starch
Gingersnaps	3	1 starch
Granola	¼ cup	1 starch, 1 fat
Granola bars	1 small	1 starch, 1 fat
Ice cream, any flavor	½ cup	1 starch, 2 fat
Ice milk, any flavor	½ cup	1 starch, 1 fat
Sherbet, any flavor	¼ cup	1 starch
Snack chips†, all varieties	1 oz.	1 starch, 2 fat
Vanilla wafers	6 small	1 starch

Source: The Exchange Lists are the basis of a meal planning system designed by a committee of the American Diabetes Association and the American Dietetic Association. While designed primarily for people with diabetes and others who must follow special diets, the Exchange Lists are based on principles of good nutrition that apply to everyone. © 1986 American Diabetes Association, Inc., American Dietetic Association. Reprinted from *Handbook of Diabetes Nutritional Management* by M.A. Powers, pp. 155–163, Aspen Publishers, Inc., © 1987.

Table 10-3 Timing Boluses To Cover Snacks or Meals That Are Very High in Fiber, Fat, or Simple Sugars As Compared with Usual Snacks or Meals

Time of Bolus	Usual Meal	High in Fiber	High in Fat	High in Simple Sugars
15 Minutes		X	X	
30 Minutes	X			
45 Minutes				X

There are several cautions in using TAG. This value does not take into consideration the fat or vegetable protein calories contributed by the diet. Clients may be consuming a diet very high in calories but have normal blood glucose levels. Even though TAG can allow for flexibility, it is very important to follow an exchange pattern as a guide for making food selections along with counting TAG. If body weight increases (which occurs frequently with persons on the pump or MDI), the limit for fat intake in the exchange pattern can be reemphasized or altered to help with weight loss. TAG can also be used without an adequate nutrient intake and still achieve optimal blood sugars. In combination with the TAG system, the exchange system ensures more adequate nutrient intake.

One last qualifying statement is important. Munro and Allison stated that, while it is possible to determine whether an amino acid can cause a net increase of carbohydrate, it cannot be predicted whether this gluconeogenic effect is significant.[63] TAG in combination with a standard exchange system can result in good blood glucose control in compliant persons.

In summary, there are basically five ways of controlling blood sugars in the Type I diabetic person. All involve diet and insulin. The first regimen, mixed-insulin dosage regimen, is depicted in Figure 10-3. The second regimen, split-insulin dosage regimen, is represented in Figure 10-4. The third regimen, the split-mixed dosage regimen, is represented in Figure 10-5.

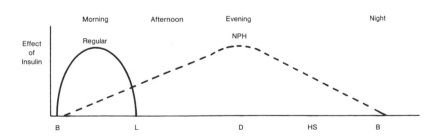

Figure 10-3 Schematic Representation of Mealtimes and Mixed-Insulin Dosage Regimen

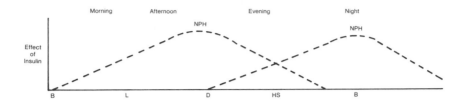

Figure 10-4 Schematic Representation of Mealtimes and Split-Insulin Dosage Regimen

The fourth is the constant-infusion insulin pump. The pump's effect might schematically be shown as seen in Figure 10-6. The amount of insulin given to cover each meal varies for each individual. It takes time and constant supervision by a physician to find the right match of insulin for TAG to achieve normal blood glucose levels. For example, at breakfast three units of regular insulin may be given to cover 45 grams of TAG, equivalent to one unit of insulin for every 15 grams of TAG (45 grams TAG ÷ 3 units of regular insulin = 15 grams of TAG/1 unit of regular insulin). If this client were to plan an increase in food intake at this meal to 60 grams of TAG or an increase of 15 grams over the recommended TAG, one extra unit of insulin will be needed.

At lunch this client boluses two units of regular insulin for every 66 grams of TAG, which equals one unit of insulin for every 33 grams of TAG (66 grams of TAG ÷ 2 units of regular insulin = 33 grams of TAG/1 unit of regular insulin). If the client planned to eat only 33 grams of TAG at lunch, a bolus of one unit of insulin would cover the decreased intake.

At dinner nine units of regular insulin are given to cover 81 grams of TAG, or one unit of insulin for every 9 grams of TAG (81 grams of TAG ÷ 9 units of regular insulin = 9 grams of TAG/1 unit of regular insulin). If 47 grams of TAG were planned for dinner, this client could bolus with 5.2 units of regular insulin (47 grams of TAG ÷ 9 grams of TAG/1 unit of regular insulin = 5.2 units of insulin).

The fifth regimen, Multiple Daily Injections, might schematically be shown as seen in Figure 10-7.

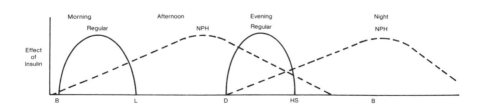

Figure 10-5 Schematic Representation of Mealtimes and Split- and Mixed-Insulin Dosage Regimen

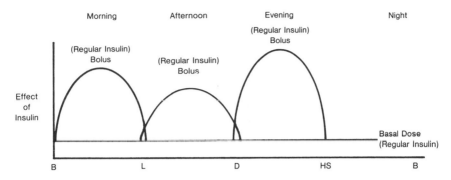

Figure 10-6 Schematic Representation of Mealtimes and Their Correspondence with Insulin Delivered by the Constant-Infusion Insulin Pump

These figures show that the number of meals varies with each regimen. Both pump and MDI therapy show three meals a day with a possible evening snack that may or may not be covered with regular insulin. Some MDI therapies include a mid-morning snack to help avoid mid-morning reactions. Caloric intake for the day is designed to maintain ideal weight. The diet must be constant from day to day and distributed properly throughout the day to coincide with the client's insulin regimen. Most mixed- and split-dose insulin regimens require the client to eat three meals, along with a midmorning snack, a midafternoon snack, and a late bedtime snack to prevent hypoglycemia.

The remainder of this chapter is devoted to dietary adherence research, inappropriate eating behaviors and counseling strategies to overcome them in the insulin-dependent diabetic person. Strategies for promoting weight loss in the non-insulin-dependent person are covered in Chapter 8.

RESEARCH ON ADHERENCE WITH EATING PATTERNS CONTROLLED FOR CARBOHYDRATE, PROTEIN, AND FAT

Adherence to a prescribed dietary plan is one of the most important aspects of diabetes management and perhaps the most difficult for clients to learn or with which to comply. Research has shown that many clients do not understand or follow their diabetic diet regimens.[64] As a solution to this problem, clinicians are beginning to advocate highly individualized, flexible approaches to diet management that can accommodate individuals' eating habits and preferences.[65]

A number of studies have examined correlates of diabetic diet noncompliance, including knowledge, health values, and social and cultural factors.[66] None of these studies provides a clear, unified direction for diabetic nutrition education, but when reviewed in combination, they emphasize the need for comprehensive interventions that include social support, promotion of self-care and active participation, and

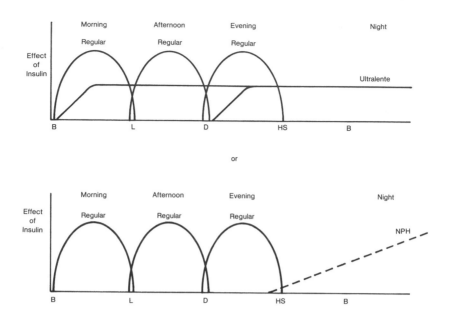

Figure 10-7 Schematic Representation of Mealtimes and Multiple Daily Injections

emphasis on how (not only why) to follow the dietary eating pattern.[67] Because of the complexity of the optimal educational approach, few studies have rigorously evaluated the effectiveness of strategies to improve dietary adherence among clients with diabetes.

Wiensier et al. achieved excellent compliance with an individualized diet prescription, frequent follow-up and feedback, and social support in a controlled trial of an experimental diabetic diet.[68] However, controlled educational experiments have been few. One found that a group program was more effective than individual bedside teaching.[69] Another demonstrated that a programmed learning unit that reduced the amount of professional time needed resulted in knowledge increases comparable to those achieved after a longer individual counseling session.[70] Dunn et al. found that a comprehensive program resulted in knowledge gains.[71] The Webb et al. study of a multimethod group program demonstrated the program's effects in improving adherence to the carbohydrate and fat composition of the diet, as well as glycemic control.[72]

Because of the generally accepted comprehensive approach to diabetes education, along with the complex self-care regimens prescribed for clients with diabetes, it is unlikely that research can tell nutritionists exactly which educational strategies contribute the most to diet adherence. Self-monitoring of blood glucose is a relatively new technology that has been found acceptable to clients and effective for improving glycemic control.[73] Unfortunately, the investigators of this strategy did not collect dietary data to discern the behavioral effects of self-monitoring; nor did they employ a control group receiving similar management without glucose self-monitoring.

Several implications for practice emerge from the studies reviewed here and the published commentaries of clinicians. Most important, dietary adherence is best when the diet is tailored to the individual client. The education plan should also be tailored, as seen in Slowie's case studies.[74] Comprehensive educational diagnosis tools have been developed, and validated knowledge tests toward this end are available.[75] Computerized dietary analysis with simple recommendations as part of a printout can provide both assessment and feedback.[76]

Social support from family members as well as other clients with diabetes is important in facilitating life-style changes.[77] Schwartz et al. found a higher percentage of abnormal blood glucose control measures (fasting blood glucose values and HbA_{1c}) in individuals with many recent life events. These researchers felt that social support may help in decreasing the individual's isolation and in dealing with life events, with resulting improved control.[78] Frequent follow-up, feedback (including glucose self-monitoring), and behavioral methods such as contingency contracting and self-reinforcement can improve outcomes.[79] A large number of print and audiovisual instructional aids are available through health agencies, the American Diabetes Association, and commercial sources. Educational materials must be appropriate for the comprehension level of program participants; a mismatch can impede understanding of the regimen.[80] A simplified glycemic index to characterize foods in diabetic diets has potential for assisting clients to apply dietary information for better glycemic control.[81]

Research on compliance with accuracy in describing food portions showed that persons with diabetes underestimated chicken portions (i.e., ate portions that were larger than estimated) by an average of 30 to 40 percent and underestimated rice portions (i.e., ate portions that were smaller than estimated) by an average of 25 to 35 percent.[82] In another study, clients with diabetes (24 insulin-dependent and 184 non-insulin-dependent) were asked what factors contributed to nonadherence to their diabetic regimens. Standardized questions revealed few differences between Type I and Type II participants on either levels of reported adherence or reasons for nonadherence. Subjects reported adhering least well to dietary and physical activity components of the regimen. Open-ended questions revealed that the most common reasons for dietary nonadherence were the situational factors of eating out at restaurants and inappropriate food offers from others. These researchers suggested that diabetes education programs should inform clients of high-risk situations and provide training in covert modeling and behavioral rehearsal to enhance assertive skills.[83]

INAPPROPRIATE EATING BEHAVIORS

Most persons with insulin-dependent diabetes complain about the lack of spontaneity in their new eating patterns. The joy of eating seems to rely partially on the element of surprise, but one very important way to normalize blood sugars is to keep the eating pattern consistent from day to day. This is one of the most difficult dilemmas facing the client with insulin-dependent diabetes. Without consistency in the eating pattern, changes in insulin dosages are difficult and dangerous.

A second common problem involves social eating. The major problem is knowing how to count foods with unknown ingredients. Secondary, but also important, is the ability to avoid large quantities of foods that elevate blood glucose levels. As do clients on many eating patterns, the insulin-dependent person initially finds the diet new and exciting. Adherence to diet and blood glucose levels are excellent. With time, the newness of the diet wears off and the desire to be "like everyone else" becomes greater than the desire to achieve good control or normalized blood glucose levels.

ASSESSMENT OF EATING BEHAVIORS

A thorough initial assessment is crucial to future dietary success. Assessing the client's prior experience with dieting and on diabetic eating patterns is very important. Many persons with Type I diabetes have followed weight-loss diets in the past, even though one of their initial symptoms of diabetes is weight loss. Some younger diabetic persons may have never followed a diet. If this is the case, setting the stage for successful adherence to diet is crucial.

Carefully assessing daily eating patterns is important. Time may not allow for food record collection, but a thorough diet history or quantified food frequency may provide enough information on past eating habits. Counselors should attend to variations in eating patterns. For example, a clue to potential problems with weekend blood sugars is dietary patterns that are very different from weekday patterns.

The diet history can also give the counselor a good impression of nutrient intake. Many persons, particularly teenagers, may be eating diets low in calcium, iron, or vitamin A and C. Fat intake may be high, with a large portion coming from saturated fat. Cholesterol intake may also be high. In addition to a quantified food frequency or diet history, the Client Eating Questionnaire for Calorie Restricted Eating Patterns, Adherence Tool 8-1 in Chapter 8, may be useful in identifying past and present weight loss and resulting dietary behaviors. Once the client begins the new eating pattern, food records can be very helpful. The food record in Adherence Tool 10-1 might be used in assessing adherence to the new eating pattern.

Throughout the initial assessment phase, family support is crucial to eventual success. For adolescents, positive support without overbearing dictation of rules is important. For older clients, positive support from spouse or significant others should be assessed.

Prior knowledge about foods is also important. Some persons who are newly diagnosed may have a variety of misconceptions about a diabetic eating pattern. "I can no longer eat carbohydrates," is one common fallacy. Counselors should determine whether the client has followed a previous diet with an exchange pattern that might conflict with the new diabetic exchange pattern. Some concepts learned in Weight Watchers may no longer apply. Some clients may begin using only commercial foods labeled "dietetic." Counselors should assess each client's understanding of what is eliminated in "dietetic" products. Frequently fat, not carbohydrate, is reduced, leaving a product that may be high in simple sugars.

Once a client is instructed on the new eating pattern, frequent and consistent assessment of adherence to the pattern is important. This may involve diet records, 24-hour recalls on the phone, if possible, for one week, or short diet records requiring simple check-off systems, such as Adherence Tool 10-2. This tool can be used to help clients monitor and avoid snacking if it is not a part of the recommended regimen.

Tracking eating behaviors with a graph may be helpful. If the recommendation for TAG is 40 at breakfast, 40 at lunch, and 60 at dinner, graphing intake over one month's time may be helpful. Adherence Tool 10-3 shows an example of a graph in which TAG for breakfast is represented by a line. One heavy line drawn to connect dots denoting TAG at breakfast represent the desired TAG for this meal.

Dietary nonadherence will be reflected in biochemical data such as blood glucose and glycosylated hemoglobin levels. Graphing these two parameters can help showing trends. For example, drawing a graph of weekly blood sugar and glycosylated hemoglobin levels once every three months will show bad weeks and good weeks (see Adherence Tools 10-4A and 10-4B). Adherence Tool 10-5 allows the client to make a "✓" when boluses are 30 minutes prior to a meal. Assessing what might have happened to cause changes in blood sugars may be the first step to changes in adherence.

TREATMENT STRATEGIES

Problems with following diabetic eating patterns fall into three categories: lack of knowledge, forgetfulness, and lack of commitment. This chapter provides suggestions for strategies to use in dealing with lack of knowledge and cueing devices to help solve problems of forgetting. Lack of commitment, the most difficult problem to solve, is obvious from repeated highs and lows in blood sugars, elevated glycosylated hemoglobins, or both, in spite of information given to help correct the situation.

Strategies To Deal with Lack of Knowledge

Lack of Knowledge Related to General Dietary Modifications Which Affect Blood Glucose

To begin a nutrition counseling session appropriately, counselors need to provide the client with adequate information. In Figure 6-1, there is an example of a instructional plan designed to provide information on a diabetic eating pattern, including one week of intensive dietary counseling, possibly a one-week hospital stay, while the client is beginning the new diet pattern. Additional information is given in subsequent visits one month apart. Note that information is given in small amounts, with practice time included in each session to allow the client to complete exercises with the nutrition counselor. This valuable practice is a way of setting the stage for behaviors that will be required in daily life.

Tailoring is once again very important to diet adherence (see Adherence Tool 10-6). Ideally each client should receive a diet pattern that fits the individual's life style. Chapter 5 describes how to use the computer in creating an individual exchange list and dietary pattern. For the person with diabetes, this type of tailoring makes for less work in learning many food items, provides greater detail, and can stimulate learning because it creates a feeling of ownership.

In teaching the concept of TAG, counselors should use concrete and tailored examples (see Exhibit 10-2). Adherence Tools 10-7 and 10-8 provide practice and tips on using TAG. Adherence Tools 10-9 to 10-11 help the client practice calculating TAG and exchanges in recipes. In applying TAG clients need a basic understanding of weighing and measuring (see Adherence Tool 10-12). For clients who want to take home information about TAG, Adherence Tools 10-13 and 10-14 are helpful. Written as well as verbal advice is important.

Meal planning is also extremely important. Adherence Tool 10-15 provides practice in planning a menu using a new eating pattern.

Counselors should emphasize the importance of knowing what commercial products contain. Adherence Tool 10-16 provides practice in reading labels.

Exhibit 10-2 Teaching TAG

---

1. Give an example:

Exchange	TAG
2 Fruit	= 30
1 Bread	= 15
1 Meat	= 4
1 Fat	= 0
	49 = TAG at breakfast

2. Describe clearly what the client can eat:

Breakfast	Breakfast TAG	
	Carbohydrate (grams) +	Animal Protein (grams) × .58
1 large apple	30.0	—
(197 grams)	—	
1 slice of bread	11.7	—
1 teaspoon margarine	—	—
1 ounce Canadian bacon	—	+ (5.6 grams × 0.58 = 3.3)
	41.7	+ 3.3 = 45.0 grams of TAG

The same example can be used with exchanges only:

Breakfast	Breakfast Exchanges
1 large apple	2 Fruit
1 slice of bread	1 Bread
1 teaspoon margarine	1 Fat
1 ounce Canadian bacon	1 Meat

If clients frequently eat in restaurants, counselors should select the menus to a few favorite places, calculate TAG for a meal, have the client bolus, and actually visit the restaurant with the client. If problems arise, the counselor can guide the client through the meal.

After presenting crucial information in a way that tailors the eating pattern to each person, counselors must stage changes in eating habits to coincide with recommendations. As happens with other eating patterns, clients can find it difficult to follow all dietary restrictions as a package immediately. Counselors should focus on the least difficult problem first while asking clients to continue to follow all restrictions to the greatest degree possible, always working closely with clients and letting them decide which problem is the least difficult.

An example of this type of staging with information follows:

> CLIENT: "I think learning the specific amounts of foods in each of these exchange categories will be difficult."
> NUTRITION COUNSELOR: "Let's begin slowly, taking each category one week at a time. Continue to look up amounts for the categories you must follow, but learn amounts of your favorite foods in one category by reviewing them daily over a one-week period."
> CLIENT: "That sounds more manageable!"

Lack of Knowledge Related to Fat Intake and Weight Gain

Lack of knowledge about foods can make a crucial difference in weight gain for insulin-dependent persons. Many clients are upset by the initial and frequently steady

Table 10-4 Recommended and Actual Fat Consumption before Instruction*

Breakfast	Recommended Breakfast Pattern			
	Carbohydrate (gm.)	Protein (gm.)	Fat (gm.)	TAG
1 Meat	—	7	5	4
2 Bread	30	4	—	30
3 Fat	—	—	15	—
2 Fruit	30	—	—	30
	60	11	20	64

464 kilocalories
3.86 grams saturated fat
5.19 grams polyunsaturated fat

Breakfast	Actual High-Fat Breakfast			
	Carbohydrate (gm.)	Protein (gm.)	Fat (gm.)	TAG
1 ounce sausage (28 grams)	0.5	4.0	8.1	2.8
2 muffins (40 grams)	32.0	6.2	8.0	32.0
4 teaspoons margarine	—	—	16.4	—
1 large apple (197 grams)	30.0	0.4	0.7	30.0
	62.5	10.6	33.2	64.8

591 kilocalories
14.40 grams saturated fat
2.68 grams polyunsaturated fat

*Food values taken from Jean A. T. Pennington and Helen Nichols Church, *Bowes and Church's Food Values of Portions Commonly Used* (New York: Harper and Row, 1985).

weight gain that results when blood glucose levels normalize because calories, no longer being lost in the urine, are used for energy and, eventually, weight gain. Many clients misuse the idea that fat contributes little to elevations in blood glucose. If fat is "free," they think, it may be used to "add to" meals when a TAG limit or exchange pattern is "used up" in a day.

Table 10-4 illustrates the case of one client whose blood glucose levels were normal on the average but whose fat intake was causing significant climbs in weight based on monthly determinations. The diet was checked very carefully to determine where caloric intake might be contributing to weight gain. This client is doing everything requested in terms of following exchanges and TAG for breakfast. Blood glucose levels are normal, but unfortunately weight and blood cholesterol levels are up because the breakfast eaten contains 127 more calories than the recommended meal. Blood low-density lipoprotein cholesterol is up, mainly because of the extremely high intake

Table 10-5 Recommended and Actual Fat Consumption after Instruction*

Breakfast	Recommended Breakfast Pattern			
	Carbohydrate (gm.)	Protein (gm.)	Fat (gm.)	TAG
1 Meat	—	7	5	4
2 Bread	30	4	—	30
3 Fat	—	—	15	—
2 Fruit	30	—	—	30
	60	11	20	64

464 kilocalories
3.86 grams saturated fat
5.19 grams polyunsaturated fat

Breakfast	Actual Low-Fat Breakfast			
	Carbohydrate (gm.)	Protein (gm.)	Fat (gm.)	TAG
1 ounce Canadian bacon (28 grams)	—	5.6	2.00	3.2
1 English muffin (57 grams)	26.2	4.5	1.10	26.2
3 teaspoons margarine	—	—	11.34	—.
1 large apple (197 grams)	30.0	0.4	0.70	30.0
	56.2	10.5	15.14	59.4

403 kilocalories
2.67 grams saturated fat
5.14 grams polyunsaturated fat

*See Table 10-4.

of saturated fat (the recommended amount of saturated fat is 3.86 grams; actual consumption is up to 14.40 grams).

Following in-depth dietary instruction on the fat and saturated fat content of certain foods, this client can alter intake to reduce weight and blood cholesterol levels. Table 10-5 indicates recommended intake and actual intake after instruction. The figures show that TAG is actually a bit low in the low-fat meal. A suggestion might be to add 4.6 grams of carbohydrate, or approximately 5 grams (1/3 fruit exchange).

Table 10-6 compares nutrient intake for the recommended high- and low-fat diets. It clearly illustrates how careful instruction on fat content of foods can minimize eventual problems with weight gain and increases in low-density lipoprotein cholesterol.

Table 10-6 Comparison of Recommended versus High- and Low-Fat Diets

Nutrients (gm.)	Recommended Diet	High-Fat Diet	Low-Fat Diet
Carbohydrate	60.00	62.5	56.2
Protein	11.00	10.60	10.50
Fat	20.00	33.20	15.14
Saturated Fat	3.86	14.40	2.67
Polyunsaturated Fat	5.19	2.68	5.14
Kilocalories	464	591	403

Figure 10-8 shows two weight graphs for a client. One indicates an increase in weight following high fat intake. The second shows how weight comes down with a change in the fat content of the diet.

Clear instructions on monitoring blood glucose levels is essential to eventually determining dietary problems. A client who is not monitoring appropriately or is guessing at blood glucose levels can be counseled to increase or decrease insulin and dietary intake inappropriately.

For persons on the constant-infusion insulin pump, eating three meals a day is very important. Snacking can lead to problems, as Exhibit 10-3 shows. This example illustrates several rules. First, clients on the constant infusion pump must limit meals to three a day or at least keep three hours between meals. Second, timing boluses is extremely important. In most cases 30 minutes before eating clients should give an injection or punch in a bolus on the pump. The blood glucose of 60 at 5:00 P.M. indicates a timing problem: insufficient time (five minutes) between bolus and snack. The candy bar caused a rise in blood glucose before the regular insulin could have an effect. By the time the insulin peaked, the effect of the candy bar was gone, resulting in low blood glucose. Third, it is important to cover snacks with adequate amounts of regular insulin. Exhibit 10-3 shows insufficient amounts of insulin given to cover both snacks. In this case assume that one unit of insulin covers every 10 grams of TAG.

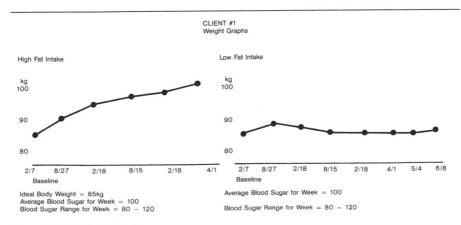

Figure 10-8 Weight Graphs

Exhibit 10-3 Meal, Blood Glucose, and Insulin Diary

Blood Glucose Levels	Actual Intake			
	Breakfast (10:30 A.M.) Nothing Eaten			
Pre-Lunch (10:30 A.M.) Blood Glucose = 100 mg/dl Recommended Insulin Given				
	Lunch (11:00 A.M.) Recommended Pattern Followed			
Pre-Afternoon Snack (2:55 P.M.) No Blood Glucose Taken Insulin Given = 2 Units Regular Insulin				
	Afternoon Snack (3:00 P.M.) 2-ounce Snicker's Candy Bar			
	Carbohy- drate	Protein	Fat	Kilocalories
	33.0	6.0	13.0	270
Pre-Dinner (5:00 P.M.) Blood Glucose = 60 mg/dl Took glucose tablet				
	Dinner (5:30 P.M.) Recommended Dietary Pattern Followed			
Pre-Bedtime Snack (9:45 P.M.) No Blood Glucose Taken Insulin Given =1 Unit Regular Insulin				
	Bedtime Snack (10:00 P.M.) Popped Corn (6 cups) + 5 tablespoons margarine			
	Carbohy- drate	Protein	Fat	Kilocalories
	64.2	10.8	34.2	607.8

(Remember, in reality the ratio of insulin to TAG varies for different times of day and different persons.) The bedtime snack was very high in fat and fiber. Timing was changed to allow for high fat and fiber intake, but the bolus for the bedtime snack did not sufficiently cover TAG (assuming one unit of insulin for every 10 grams of TAG, one unit of insulin will not cover 64 grams of TAG). Some clients may not need to cover bedtime snacks with regular insulin, but the client in Exhibit 10-3 has very high nighttime blood sugars if regular insulin is not used to cover the snack.

Data from Table 10-3 are a rough guide for timing boluses on the constant-infusion insulin pump. These times are helpful when covering a snack (if necessary) that is very different in fat and/or fiber content from the usual snack. Changing the timing of a bolus may help to allow for increased digestion time, such as 15 minutes instead of 30 minutes for popped corn with a large amount of fat. In addition, allowing three hours between meals can prevent one bolus of regular insulin from affecting the bolus that follows. The data in Table 10-7 illustrate this idea. In this example the regular insulin bolus for breakfast peaks too close to the peak of the lunch bolus, resulting in a reac-

Table 10-7 Timing Boluses

Blood Glucose Levels	Actual Intake
Prebreakfast (9:30 A.M.) Blood Glucose = 100 Recommended Insulin Given	
	Breakfast (10:00 A.M.) Recommended Pattern Followed
Pre-Lunch (11:00 A.M.) Blood Glucose = 285 Extra Dose of Regular Insulin Given	
	Lunch (11:30 A.M.) Recommended Pattern Followed
Postlunch (12:30 P.M.) Blood Glucose = 45 (REACTION) Treated with Glucose Tablets	

tion at 12:30 P.M. The prelunch blood glucose is actually postprandial breakfast glucose. Because the prelunch blood glucose is high, extra insulin is given to adjust for it and bring blood glucose levels down. With extra insulin for lunch and less than three hours between breakfast and lunch, the regular insulin peaks are too close, resulting in hypoglycemia.

In summary, many of the difficulties encountered by clients with Type I diabetes can be eliminated through monitoring (via diary) and thus identifying problems contributing to poor adherence. Basic early instruction on diet is crucial. Tailoring the regimen helps eliminate certain problems with later backsliding. For example, although fat intake may be of minor significance in altering blood glucose values, it is important to eventual weight gain. Information about fat is important. Three basic rules for clients on the constant infusion pump or MDI are also important. First, limit meals to three a day and/or allow 3 hours between meals. Second, bolus or inject insulin 30 minutes prior to eating. Third, cover diet intake with adequate amounts of insulin.

Strategies To Deal with Forgetfulness

Cueing devices can help persons with insulin-dependent diabetes remember to bolus or inject insulin on time. Reminders on the refrigerator to give insulin 30 minutes before eating are important. If a morning or evening dose is a problem, signs on the mirror in the bathroom can cue clients.

A simple calendar requiring check marks can help the client who constantly forgets to bolus or inject insulin 30 minutes before a meal. Adherence Tool 10-5 is an example of a monthly monitoring device that, if placed in a visible area and used as a daily recording device, could serve as a cue. The same calendar might serve as a reminder of problems for clients who eat in restaurants frequently. A star might remind clients to plan for a restaurant meal by calling the restaurant to find out what is on the menu and ask questions to determine what is in a recipe. By planning ahead, clients can select food appropriately with little effort while in the restaurant. Most people can save favorite restaurant menus and calculate exchange or TAG values for favorite selections. Extra care and effort initially can make eating in restaurants more enjoyable.

Strategies To Deal with Lack of Commitment

Most insulin-dependent persons enter periods of low commitment to keeping blood glucose levels normal. This can be evidenced in a variety of ways. One is "bouncing" blood glucose levels that have a roller coaster appearance when graphed. Another is relatively good blood glucose levels with high glycosylated hemoglobin levels. This may indicate problems with high blood sugars at night, but it can also signal fabricated glucose values. A third clue to lack of commitment is the client who comes in saying, "I just want to have one day where I don't have to worry about blood glucose levels, fingersticks, diet, and exercise."

A problem with lack of commitment is not solved with recipes, information on the nutrient content of a commercial product, or more telephone contact without appropriate intervention. The following dialogue illustrates one possible initial approach to dealing with lack of commitment. Strategies include open questions to identify the problem, paraphrasing empathy, and contracting.

> CLIENT: "I just want to have one day without diabetes, without fingersticks, and without dietary calculations. Living with diabetes is not like other tasks in life. You can't say, 'I worked hard and now I am finished. I did a good job.' Diabetes is forever!"
>
> NUTRITION COUNSELOR: "You have thought about this for a long time. Can you describe why you feel this way now and initially you seemed to be more enthusiastic?" (Open Question)
>
> CLIENT: "When you first have diabetes, it's fun and exciting. You feel better for the first time in a long while. You feel in control. You are given responsibility for diet and fingersticks and exercise."
>
> NUTRITION COUNSELOR: "You're sort of in a honeymoon phase." (Paraphrase)
>
> CLIENT: "Yes, exactly. But things change. Your friends get tired of hearing about how well you are doing. They don't give you as much positive reinforcement for your labor. In fact they seem to get tired of hearing you talk about your disease and how well you are doing. Without this support you get tired of doing everything well."
>
> NUTRITION COUNSELOR: "So you need to have some kind of reward for your efforts but your friends don't always come through." (Paraphrase and Empathy)
>
> CLIENT: "Yes."
>
> NUTRITION COUNSELOR: "Let's try to list a few ways that you can provide positive reinforcement for yourself. What things in your life really make you feel good?"
>
> CLIENT: "Well, I like to read. I love to watch MTV. I like eating pizzas."
>
> NUTRITION COUNSELOR: "Great, let's set up a contract. Whenever you have blood sugars on three consecutive preprandial sticks between 100 and 130 in a day, you can reward yourself with one of these fun things. We will even figure out how to count pizza. I can help by calling the restaurant. Let's write the contract." (See Exhibit 10-4.)

As with other diets, lack of commitment may be a direct result of a change in life events. Clients who go through a divorce may blame their preoccupation with diabetes care, resulting in changes in the care taken to follow a dietary regimen.

Exhibit 10-4 Contract

"I will reward myself each day for preprandial blood sugars between 100 and 130 on three consecutive occasions in a day. The following things will be used as rewards:
1. Going to the library for a good novel
2. Watching MTV
3. Eating three slices of a Pizza Hut Canadian Bacon Pizza containing approximately 63 grams of TAG.

If my blood sugars are not between 100 and 130 preprandially, I will not receive any of the above three rewards.
   (*Nutrition counselor*) will call me each Friday at 10:00 A.M. at work to check on my progress."
Patient ⎯⎯⎯⎯⎯⎯⎯⎯⎯⎯⎯⎯⎯⎯⎯⎯⎯⎯⎯⎯⎯⎯⎯⎯⎯
Nutrition Counselor ⎯⎯⎯⎯⎯⎯⎯⎯⎯⎯⎯⎯⎯⎯⎯⎯⎯⎯⎯⎯

Significant family changes such as marriage or remarriage, birth of a child, or death of a close relative can have devastating effects on blood sugars. In one family the husband, Mr. X, was on an insulin pump. His father died of complications of the disease. Following his death, the client's wife began looking at the disease differently. She felt that she should not have married someone with a disease so devastating and was concerned about her children eventually being diagnosed with diabetes. For several months Mr. X's blood glucose values were uncontrolled and his attitude toward his care was very casual. His wife finally sought psychiatric care, and Mr. X's dietary adherence began to improve.

Job-related changes can also affect blood glucose values. The loss of a job and beginning of a new one can cause schedule changes that make lunch hours less predictable or stimulate snacking. One woman who began baby sitting in her home snacked every time the children ate. Her blood glucose values were very high and occasionally low from insulin boluses taken too close together. Another woman moved from a secretarial position to a job in a bakery. Everyone snacked on doughnut holes at 10:00 A.M., and she joined the group. Loss of a job can make matters other than diabetes care a higher priority.

The insulin-dependent person who is diagnosed with another disease, such as heart disease, may become very discouraged. One man stated, "I am too young to have to worry about both diabetes and heart disease." Frequently another illness may require added dietary restrictions that complicate the regimen and make it more difficult to follow, adding stress to an already complicated life situation.

One of the positive aspects of normalized blood glucose levels, good adherence, is fewer symptoms. When a client can connect diet with positive, healthful feelings there is a great deal of incentive to work hard for good dietary adherence. Reminding clients how well they felt while they were following the new eating pattern strictly may be enough to change lack of commitment to enthusiasm. In some cases planning a one-week menu may help the client cut back on dietary calculations and worry just before a meal. After planning the menu with the nutrition counselor on several occasions, clients may begin planning on their own, allowing for more spontaneity and fewer calculations for the rest of the week.

Counselors can involve family members in helping with diet by asking them to reinforce positively good dietary behaviors. They might even participate in signing a contract. With the client, the counselor can make a list of stressful events that take place in one week and ask the family to assist in making certain times of the day less stressful. The children might help with laundry or pack a sack lunch.

In some cases constructive confrontation may be beneficial to increasing dietary commitment.

> NUTRITION COUNSELOR: "I really thought we were doing well in working together on dietary problems. (Personal Relationship Statement) I see your glycosylated hemoglobin has gone up one whole point. Your diet records also show an increase in snacking." (Description of Behavior)
>
> CLIENT: "I know I just don't have any motivation. I really want to do well."
>
> NUTRITION COUNSELOR: "You seem to be saying two things: (1) you want to do well, and (2) you just don't care. (Description of Feelings and Interpretation of Client's Situation) Am I right?"
>
> CLIENT: "Yes." (Understanding Response)
>
> NUTRITION COUNSELOR: "How do you feel about what I am saying?" (Perception Check)
>
> CLIENT: "I'm trying to do two things, and I feel like a failure all the time. Sometimes I just say I might as well give up, and I do. I don't check my blood sugars or I check them at times when I know they are good and write those numbers down. Then I just throw my hands up in despair and say what's the use and start snacking."
>
> NUTRITION COUNSELOR: "Good, you seem to be able to talk about exactly what you are feeling and that's pretty low sometimes. (Interpretive Response and Constructive Feedback) Would you be willing to do a diary of your thoughts?"
>
> CLIENT: "What's that?"
>
> NUTRITION COUNSELOR: "It's not difficult. Just record what you think in a few sentences every time you eat. Use this form (Appendix G). We will talk about your thought diary when you come to the next visit."
>
> CLIENT: "I will try to record before and after each meal, but may miss on weekends."
>
> NUTRITION COUNSELOR: "Record as often as you can. This is to help you. I do not want it to become a burden."

At the next visit the discussion could revolve around how to replace negative thoughts with positive thoughts, such as "I only ate one small cracker. I won't eat any more. I'm doing great today."

Strategies to deal with lack of commitment are very important to a client's long-term success with a diabetic regimen. Identifying changes in life events can signal eventual problems. Strategies to deal with these changes include identifying positive support persons and appropriate use of constructive confrontation.

Adherence Tool 10-1 Monitoring Device

		No. of Exchanges	Type of Foods and Amount
One-Day Food Record			
Name_____			
Breakfast	1. Bread		
	2. Fruit		
	3. Milk		
	4. Meat		
	5. Fat		
Midmorning	1. Bread		
	2. Fruit		
	3. Milk		
	4. Meat		
	5. Fat		
Lunch	1. Bread		
	2. Fruit		
	3. Veg. A		
	4. Veg. B		
	5. Milk		
	6. Meat		
	7. Fat		
Midafternoon	1. Bread		
	2. Fruit		
	3. Milk		
	4. Meat		
	5. Fat		
Dinner	1. Bread		
	2. Fruit		
	3. Veg. A		
	4. Veg. B		
	5. Milk		
	6. Meat		
	7. Fat		
Bedtime	1. Bread		
	2. Fruit		
	3. Milk		
	4. Meat		
	5. Fat		

Adherence Tool 10-2 Monitoring Device

One-Week Check-off System To Identify Morning Snacking Problems

Monday

_____

Tuesday

_____

Wednesday

_____

Thursday

_____

Friday

_____

Saturday

_____

Sunday

  + = Had a snack
  * = Avoided a snack

Adherence Tool 10-3 Monitoring Device

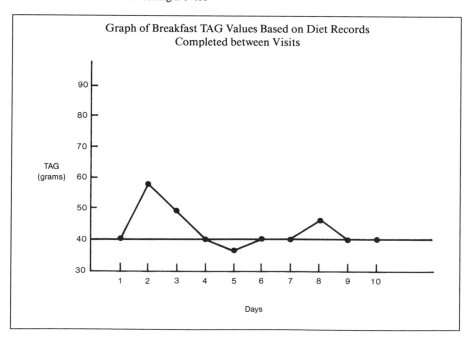

Graph of Breakfast TAG Values Based on Diet Records
Completed between Visits

Adherence Tool 10-4A Monitoring Device

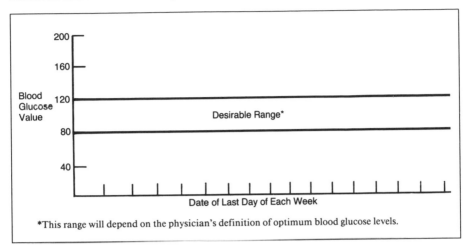

*This range will depend on the physician's definition of optimum blood glucose levels.

Adherence Tool 10-4B Monitoring Device

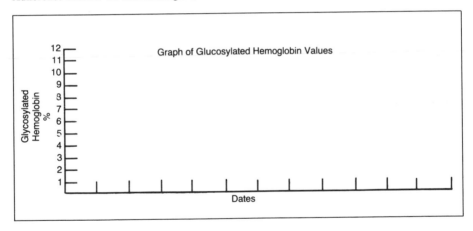

Adherence Tool 10-5 Monitoring Device

Monthly Check-off System for Premeal Insulin Injections

One-Month

Sun.	Mon.	Tues.	Wed.	Thur.	Fri.	Sat.

month of _____ 19 _____   If you have any questions, please call: _____

Adherence Tool 10-6 Informational Device

Individualized Exchanges for Meal Planning

Starch/Bread List
Cereals/Grains and Pasta
  Grapenuts, 3 tablespoons
Starch Vegetable
  Corn, ½ cup
  Potato, baked, 1 small (3 ounces)
Bread
  Whole wheat bread, 1 slice (1 ounce)
Meat List
  Lean Meats, 1 ounce
    Beef sirloin, 1 ounce
    Canned ham, 1 ounce
    Chicken, 1 ounce
    Tuna, 1 ounce
    Cottage cheese, ¼ cup
Vegetable List
  Cooked vegetables, ½ cup
  Raw vegetables, 1 cup
Fruit List
  Apple, raw, 2 inches across, 1
  Banana (9 inches long), ½
  Pear, large, ½
  Raisins, 2 tablespoons
  Orange juice, ½ cup
Milk List
  2% Milk, 1 cup
Fat List
  Margarine, 1 teaspoon
  Reduced-calorie mayonnaise, 1 tablespoon

Adherence Tool 10-7 Informational Device

Practice with Exchanges and Total Available Glucose (TAG)
Determine the exchanges and TAG for each of the following foods:

	Exchanges	TAG
Corn, ½ cup		
Orange juice, 6 ounces		
Poached egg, 1		
Chicken, 3 ounces		
Pork chop, 2 ounces		
Tuna fish, ½ cup		
Green beans, ¾ cup		
Saltine crackers, 6		
Party crackers (Triscuits), 5		
Graham crackers, 3		
Skim milk, 8 ounces		
Whole milk, 8 ounces		
Peanut butter, 2 tablespoons		
Italian dressing, 1 tablespoon		
Wheat bread, 2 slices		
Mayonnaise, 1 tablespoon		
Grape juice, ⅔ cup		
Grapes, 15		
Watermelon, 1¼ cup		
Small olives, 10		
Stick pretzels, ¾ ounces		
Dry nonfat milk, ⅓ cup		
Baked beans, ½ cup		
French fries, 10 (3½ inches long)		
Muffin, 1, small plain		
Bacon, 2 slices		
American cheese, 1 ounce		
Bran Buds®, ½ cup		
Oatmeal, 1 cup		
Plain nonfat yogurt, 1 cup		
Ice cream, ½ cup		
Sherbet, ½ cup		

Adherence Tool 10-7 continued

List the amount of carbohydrate, protein, fat, and kilocalories in the following exchange groups:

Exchange	Carbo-hydrate (grams)	Protein (grams)	Fat (grams)	Kilocalories (grams)	TAG
Bread					
Milk (skim)					
Fat					
Vegetable					
Meat					
Fruit					

Source: Courtesy of Sydne K. Carlson.

Adherence Tool 10-8 Informational Device

"TAG"

TAG = Carbohydrate (CHO) (gms.) + [Animal Protein (PRO) (gms.) × .58]

	CHO	Animal + PRO (.58)	= TAG
1 Fruit Exchange	= 15 gms.	+ 0	= 15
1 Meat Exchange	= 0	+ 7 gms. (.58)	= 4
1 Milk Exchange	= 12 gms	+ 8 gms. (.58)	= 17
1 Break Exchange	= 15 gms.	+ 0	= 15
1 Vegetable Exchange	= 5 gms.	+ 0	= 5

The number that results from this formula can be used to determine what each of your meals might include.

Counting *Total Available Glucose* (TAG) is a way of assuring consistency in diet from day to day. We count carbohydrate because we know it tends to raise blood sugars. Animal proteins also raise blood sugar levels because they are eventually converted to carbohydrate by our bodies. Fat does not raise blood sugar levels because very little of it is converted to carbohydrate. We do try to keep fat intake low enough to prevent increases in weight and also consider the type of fat you eat to be sure it is optimum for possible prevention of coronary heart disease.

Adherence Tool 10-9 Informational Device

Worksheet for Calculating Exchanges and Total Available Glucose (TAG) in a Recipe
Chocolate Cookies

1¾ cups flour	1 egg
½ teaspoon baking soda	⅓ cup buttermilk
½ teaspoon salt	1 teaspoon vanilla
½ cup butter or margarine	2 ounces melted unsweetened chocolate
1 cup white sugar	½ cup chopped walnuts

Ingredients:	Fruit	Veg	Bread	Meat	Fat	Milk	TAG
1¾ cups flour							
½ teaspoon baking soda							
½ teaspoon salt							
½ cup butter or margarine							
1 cup white sugar							
1 egg							
⅓ cup buttermilk							
1 teaspoon vanilla							
2 ounces melted chocolate							
½ cup walnuts							

Total Exchanges: Bread_____Fruit_____
Meat_____Vegetable_____
Fat_____Milk_____
TAG_____

Exchanges per Serving_____
TAG per Serving_____

Directions: Indicate what portion of an exchange each ingredient contains. Divide by the number of servings for each ingredient to obtain total exchanges and exchanges per serving. Use Pennington and Church to calculate TAG for each ingredient and per serving.

Source: Courtesy of Sydne K. Carlson.

Adherence Tool 10-10 Informational Device

Worksheet for Calculating Exchanges and Total Available Glucose (TAG) in a Recipe

Chicken Soup

12 ounces cooked chicken (weigh after removing from bone)

⅓ cup rice, uncooked	½ teaspoon salt
½ cup diced celery	⅛ teaspoon pepper
½ cup carrots, chopped	½ teaspoon celery salt
¼ cup diced onion	4 cups water

Ingredients:	Fruit	Veg	Bread	Meat	Fat	Milk	TAG
12 ounces chicken							
⅓ cup rice, uncooked							
½ cup diced celery							
½ cup carrots, chopped							
¼ cup diced onion							
½ teaspoon salt							
⅛ teaspoon pepper							
½ teaspoon celery salt							
4 cups water							

Total Exchanges: Bread_____Fruit_____

Meat_____Vegetable_____

Fat_____Milk_____

TAG_____

Exchanges per Serving_____

TAG per Serving_____

Source: Courtesy of Sydne K. Carlson.

Adherence Tool 10-11 Informational Device

Worksheet for Calculating Exchanges and Total Available Glucose (TAG) in a Recipe Chicken Almond Oriental 4–6 Servings							
Ingredients:	Fruit	Veg	Bread	Meat	Fat	Milk	TAG
1 pound chicken breast without bone and skin							
1½ cups broccoli cut into 1″ pieces							
½ cup blanched almonds							
1 teaspoon cornstarch							
½ teaspoon sugar							
2 Tablespoons soy sauce							
2 Tablespoons dry sherry							
1 medium onion, cut into thin wedges							
½ cup water chestnuts, thinly sliced							
½ cup bamboo shoots							
Total Exchanges:							
Exchanges per Serving:							
TAG per Serving:							

Source: Sydne K. Carlson.

Adherence Tool 10-12 Informational Device

Weighing and Measuring

STANDARD:	Weight	Carbo-hydrate	Protein	Fat
Apple, raw, 1 medium, with skin (without core)	138 grams	21.1	0.3	0.5

ACTUAL:

Your apple weighs 200 grams (without core).

$$\frac{\text{Weight of Standard}}{\text{Carbohydrate (gms.) of Standard}} = \frac{\text{Weight of Actual}}{?\ \text{Carbohydrate (gms.) in Actual}}$$

$$\frac{138}{21.1} = \frac{200}{X}$$

$$138X = 200 \times 21.1$$

$$X = \frac{200 \times 21.1}{138}$$

$$X = 30.6 \text{ gms. of Carbohydrate in your actual serving.}$$

Adherence Tool 10-13 Informational Device

Total Available Glucose (TAG) for Mixed Food

1. Philly Sandwich

	Carbo-hydrate	Protein	Fat
	45 grams	28 grams	24 grams

2. How much of the 28 grams of protein is vegetable protein?
   How many bread exchanges are in 45 grams of carbohydrate?
   45/15 grams carbohydrate in each exchange = 3 bread exchanges.
   Protein = 3 grams in 1 bread exchange.
   $3 \times 3 = 9$ grams vegetable protein.
3. Subtract grams of vegetable protein from grams of total protein to get grams of animal protein.
   $28 - 9 = 19$ grams of animal protein
4. Use TAG formula:

TAG	= Carbohydrate grams + (Animal Protein $\times$ .58)
TAG	= $45 + (19 \times .58$ grams)
TAG	= $45 + 11.02$
TAG	= 56.02 grams
TAG	= 56 grams

Adherence Tool 10-14 Informational Device

Calculating Total Available Glucose (TAG)

1. Look for food value in Pennington and Church.*
                    Standard Value: <u>3 oz. Meat</u>
                                        21 gms. Protein
2. Determine (by weighing) your meat portion.
                            <u>2 oz. Meat</u>
                                x
3. Calculate the ratio and proportion.
                    <u>3 oz.</u>   = <u>2 oz.</u>
                    21 grams Protein   x
                            3x   = 2 × 21
                            3x   = 42
                            x   = 14 grams Protein
4. Calculate TAG = grams Protein ×.58.
                    TAG   = 14 × .58
                    TAG   = 8.12 grams
5. Add this TAG to total Carbohydrate in rest of meal.

*Jean A.T. Pennington and Helen Bowes Church, *Bowes and Church's Food Values of Portions Commonly Used* (New York: Harper & Row, 1985).

Adherence Tool 10-15 Informational Device

Menu Planner

Meal 1

_____
_____
_____
_____
_____

Nutrition Guide		
	Rec.*	Act.**
Meat		
Milk		
Fruit & Vegetable		
Bread & Cereal		

Meal 2

_____
_____
_____
_____
_____

Meal 3

_____
_____
_____
_____
_____

Snacks

_____
_____
_____
_____
_____
_____

Source: Courtesy of Nancy L. Schwartz, R.D.   *Rec. = Recommended amounts
**Act. = Actual amounts

Adherence Tool 10-16 Informational Device

Worksheet for Food Labeling

1. Select a label and obtain the following information:
   Product name _____
   Serving size _____
   Number of servings per container _____
   Calories _____
   Protein (gms.) _____
   Carbohydrates (gms.) _____
   Fat (gms.) _____
   Ingredients _____
   _____
   _____
   _____

2. From the information listed above, calculate the exchanges and TAG contained in this product.

3. On the back of this page, use this product with other foods to create a balanced meal (breakfast, lunch, or dinner), using your meal pattern.

Review of Chapter 10
(Answers in Appendix I)

1. List three factors that are commonly associated with carbohydrate-modified diets and lead to inappropriate eating behaviors:
   a. _____
   b. _____
   c. _____

2. List two nutrients to emphasize in collecting baseline information on diets for persons with diabetes.
   a. _____
   b. _____

3. Identify four strategies to help combat inappropriate eating behaviors when working with clients on new diabetic eating patterns:

a. _____

b. _____

c. _____

d. _____

4. The following describes a problem situation with a client who has been instructed on a diabetic diet. Identify a strategy that might help solve this client's problem and explain your reason for selecting it.

> Mr. J. has been placed on a diabetic diet. During nutrition assessment you found that he has most difficulty with afternoon snacks. At his company during break, everyone eats frosted cupcakes, candy bars, or jellybeans. (a) What further questions would you ask to elicit more information? (b) What strategies would you use to help alleviate the problem? (c) Why did you choose these strategies?

a. _____

b. _____

c. _____

NOTES

1. American Dietetic Association, *Handbook of Clinical Dietetics* (New Haven, Conn.: Yale University Press, 1981), p. F3.

2. Roland L. Wiensier et al., "High and Low Carbohydrate Diets in Diabetes Mellitus," *Annals of Internal Medicine* 80 (1974): 332–341; Committee of Food and Nutrition, American Diabetes Association, "Principles of Nutrition and Dietary Recommendations for Patients with Diabetes Mellitus," *Diabetes* 20 (1971): 633–634; John D. Brunzell et al., "Improved Glucose Tolerance and High Carbohydrate Diets with High Carbohydrate Feeding in Mild Diabetes," *New England Journal of Medicine* 284 (1971): 521–524; Roger L. Lerner et al., "Mechanism of Improved Glucose Tolerance on High Carbohydrate Diets in Normal and Mild Diabetes," *Diabetes* 20 (1971): 342; and Pincus Taft, "Diet in Management of Diabetes. Why Restrict Carbohydrate?" *Medical Journal of Australia* 1 (1976): 838–840.

3. American Dietetic Association, *Handbook*, p. F6.

4. Phyllis A. Crapo, Gerald Reaven, and Jerrold Olefsky, "Plasma Glucose and Insulin Responses to Orally Administered Simple and Complex Carbohydrates," *Diabetes* 25 (1976): 741–747; and James W. Anderson and Kyleen Ward, "Long Term Effects of High Carbohydrate, High Fiber Diets on Glucose and Lipid Metabolism. A Preliminary Report on Patients with Diabetes," *Diabetes Care* 1 (1978): 77–82.

5. Phyllis A. Crapo, "Carbohydrate," in Margaret A. Powers, ed., *Handbook of Diabetes Nutritional Management* (Rockville, Md.: Aspen Publishers, Inc., 1987), p. 206.

6. Ibid., pp. 22–25, 28, 285–286.

7. Crapo, Reaven, and Olefsky, "Plasma Glucose and Insulin Response." Ann Coulson et al., "Effect of Source of Dietary Carbohydrate on Plasma Glucose and Insulin Responses to Test Meals in Normal Subjects," *American Journal of Clinical Nutrition* 33 (1980): 1279–1282; Phyllis A. Crapo et al., "Postprandial Hormonal Responses to Different Types of Complex Carbohydrate in Individuals with Impaired Glucose Tolerance," *American Journal of Clinical Nutrition* 33 (1980): 1723–1728; and Ann Coulson et al., "Effect of Differences in Sources of Dietary Carbohydrate on Plasma Glucose and Insulin Responses to Meals in Patients with Impaired Carbohydrate Tolerance," *American Journal of Clinical Nutrition* 34 (1981): 2716–2720.

8. Rudolph M. Sandstedt et al., "The Digestibility of High Amylose Corn Starches. The Apparent Effect of the ae Gene on Susceptibility to Amylose Action," *Cereal Chemistry* 39 (1962): 123–131.

9. P. Geervani and F. Theophilus, "Influence of Legume Starches on Protein Nutrition and Availability of Lysine and Methionine to Albino Rats," *Journal of Food Science* 46 (1981): 817–828; and Kantha S. Shurpalekar, O.E. Sundaravalli, and M. Narayana Rao, "In-vitro and In-vivo Digestibility of Legume Carbohydrate," *Nutrition Reports International* 19 (1979): 111–117.

10. Isabel H. Anderson, Allen S. Levine, and Michael D. Levitt, "Incomplete Absorption of the Carbohydrate in All-Purpose Wheat Flour," *New England Journal of Medicine* 304 (1981): 891–892.

11. Donald E. Bowman, "Amylase Inhibitor of Navy Beans," *Science* 102 (1945): 358–359; D. Wynne Griffiths, "The Inhibition of Digestive Enzymes by Extracts of Field Beans," *Journal of Science and Food Agriculture* 30 (1979): 458–462; H.F. Hintz, D.E. Hogue, and L. Krook, "Toxicity of Red Kidney Beans (Phaseolus vulgaris) in the Rat," *Journal of Nutrition* 93 (1967): 77–86; Werner G. Jaffé and Clara L. Vega Lette, "Heat Labile Growth Inhibitory Factors in Beans (Phaseolus vulgaris)," *Journal of Nutrition* 94 (1968): 203–210; and M.L. Kakade and R.J. Evans, "Growth Inhibition of Rats Fed Raw Navy Beans (Phaseolus vulgaris)," *Journal of Nutrition* 90 (1961): 191–198.

12. W. Puls and U. Keup, "Influence of an α-Amylase Inhibitor (BAY d 7791) on Blood Glucose, Serum Insulin and NEFA in Starch Loading Tests in Rats, Dogs and Man," *Diabetologia* 9 (1973): 97–101; I. Hillebrand et al., "The Effect of the α-Glucosidase Inhibitor Bay g 5421 (Acarbose) on Meal Stimulated Elevations of Circulating Glucose, Insulin and Triglyceride Levels in Man," *Research in Experimental Medicine* 175 (1979): 81–86; Penny Snow and Kerin O'Dea, "Factors Affecting the Rate of Hydrolysis in Starch in Food," *American Journal of Clinical Nutrition* 34 (1981): 2721–2727; and Jane H. Yoon, Lilian V. Thompson, and David J.A. Jenkins, "The Effects of Phytic Acid on In Vitro Rate of Starch Digestibility and Blood Glucose Response," *American Journal of Clinical Nutrition* 38 (1983): 835–842.

13. P. Collings, C. Williams, and I. Macdonald, "Effect of Cooking on Serum Glucose and Insulin Responses to Starch," *British Medical Journal* 282 (1981): 1032; John M. Douglas, "Raw Diet and Insulin Requirement," *Annals of Internal Medicine* 82 (1975): 61–62; and David L. Horwitz and Linda Slowie, "Raw Diet and Diabetes Mellitus," *Annals of Internal Medicine* 82 (1975): 853–854.

14. David J.A. Jenkins et al., "Effect of Processing on Digestibility and the Blood Glucose Response: A Study of Lentils," *American Journal of Clinical Nutrition* 36 (1982): 1093–1101.

15. Ibid.

16. Kerin O'Dea, Paul J. Nestel, and Lynne Antonoff, "Physical Factors Influencing Post-Prandial Glucose and Insulin Responses to Starch," *American Journal of Clinical Nutrition* 33 (1980): 760–765; Greg Collier and Kerin O'Dea, "Effects of Physical Form of Carbohydrate on the Postprandial Glucose, Insulin and Gastric Inhibitory Polypeptide Response in Type 2 Diabetes," *American Journal of Clinical Nutrition* 36 (1982): 10–14; and G.B. Haber et al., "Depletion and Disruption of Dietary Fiber. Effect on Satiety, Plasma-Glucose and Serum Insulin," *Lancet* 2 (1977): 679–682.

17. G. Julien Oettlé, Pauline M. Emmett, and Kenneth W. Heaton, "Glucose and Insulin Responses to Manufactured and Whole-Food Snacks," *American Journal of Clinical Nutrition* 45 (1987): 86–91.

18. David J.A. Jenkins et al., "Decrease in Post-Prandial Insulin and Glucose Concentration by Guar and Pectin," *Annals of Internal Medicine* 86 (1977): 20–23; Joan G. Potter et al., "Effect of Test Meals of Varying Dietary Fiber Content on Plasma Insulin and Glucose Response," *American Journal of Clinical Nutrition* 34 (1981): 328–334; David J.A. Jenkins et al., "Unabsorbable Carbohydrate and Diabetes; Decreased Post-Prandial Hyperglycemia," *Lancet* 2 (1976): 172–174; and David J.A. Jenkins et al., "Effect of Guar Crisp Bread with Cereal Prod-

ucts and Leguminous Seeds on Blood Glucose Concentrations of Diabetics," *British Medical Journal* 281 (1980): 1248–1250.

19. James W. Anderson, "High Carbohydrate, High Fiber Diets for Patients with Diabetes," in Rafael A. Camerini-Davalos and Bernard Hanover, eds., *Treatment of Early Diabetes* (New York: Plenum Press, 1979), pp. 263–272; Anderson and Wen-Ju Lin Chen, "Plant Fiber Carbohydrate and Lipid Metabolism," *American Journal of Clinical Nutrition* 32 (1979): 346–363; Anderson and Ward, "Long-Term Effects"; Anderson and Ward, "High Carbohydrate, High Fiber Diets for Insulin Treated Men with Diabetes Mellitus," *American Journal of Clinical Nutrition* 32 (1979): 2312–2321; David J.A. Jenkins et al., "Treatment of Diabetes with Guar Gum," *Lancet* 2 (1977): 779–780; Tae G. Kiehm, Anderson, and Ward, "Beneficial Effects of High Carbohydrate, High Fiber Diets in Hyperglycemic Men," *American Journal of Clinical Nutrition* 29 (1976): 895–899; Perla M. Miranda and David L. Horwitz, "High Fiber Diets in the Treatment of Diabetes Mellitus," *Annals of Internal Medicine* 88 (1978): 482–486; A. Rivellese et al., "Effect of Dietary Fiber on Glucose Control and Serum Lipoproteins in Diabetic Patients," *Lancet* 2 (1980): 447–450; and H.C.R. Simpson et al., "A High Carbohydrate Leguminous Fibre Diet Improves All Aspects of Diabetic Control," *Lancet* 1 (1981): 1–5.

20. Stephen Holt et al., "Effect of Gel Fibre on Gastric Emptying and Absorption of Glucose and Paracetamol," *Lancet* 1 (1979): 636–639; A.R. Leeds et al., "Pectin and Gastric Emptying in the Dumping Syndrome," *Proceedings of the Nutrition Society,* 37 (1978): 23A (Abstract); Leeds et al., "Pectin and the Dumping Syndrome: Reduction of Symptoms and Plasma Volume Changes," *Lancet* 1 (1981): 1075–1078; and Rodney H. Taylor, "Gastric Emptying, Fiber and Absorption," *Lancet* 1 (1979): 872.

21. B. Elsenhans et al., "The Influence of Carbohydrate Gelling Agents on Rat Intestinal Transport of Monosaccharides and Neutral Amino Acids In-Vitro," *Clinical Science* 59 (1980): 373–380; and I.T. Johnson and J.M. Gee, "Inhibitory Effect of Guar Gum on the Intestinal Absorption of Glucose In-Vitro," *Proceedings of the Nutrition Society* 39 (1980): 52A (Abstract).

22. David J. Jenkins et al., "Glycemic Index of Foods: A Physiological Basis for Carbohydrate Exchange," *American Journal of Clinical Nutrition* 34 (1981): 362–366.

23. Crapo, "Carbohydrate," p. 206.

24. Jenkins et al., "Glycemic Index of Foods"; Jenkins et al., "Rate of Digestion of Foods and Post-Prandial Glycaemia in Normal and Diabetic Subjects," *British Medical Journal* 281 (1980): 14; Jenkins, "Lente Carbohydrates: A Newer Approach to the Dietary Management of Diabetes," *Diabetes Care* 5 (1982): 634; Claire B. Hollenbeck et al., "The Effects of Variations in Percent of Naturally Occurring Complex and Simple Carbohydrates on Plasma Glucose and Insulin Response in Individuals with Non-Insulin Dependent Diabetes Mellitus," *Diabetes* 34 (1985): 151; Phyllis A. Crapo, Gerald H. Reaven, and Jerrold Olefsky, "Post-Prandial Plasma Glucose and Insulin Receptors to Different Complex Carbohydrates," *Diabetes* 26 (1977): 1178–1183; and Crapo et al., "Post-Prandial Hormone Responses to Different Types of Complex Carbohydrate in Individuals with Impaired Glucose Tolerance," *American Journal of Clinical Nutrition* 33 (1980): 1723.

25. Jenkins et al., "Glycemic Index of Foods"; Jenkins et al., "Rate of Digestion"; and Jenkins, "Lente Carbohydrates."

26. Jenkins et al., "Glycemic Index of Foods"; and David J.A. Jenkins et al., "Exceptionally Low Blood Glucose Response to Dried Beans: Comparison with Other Carbohydrate Foods," *British Medical Journal* 281 (1980): 578–580.

27. David J.A. Jenkins et al., "Relationship Between the Rate of Digestion of Foods and Post-Prandial Glycaemia," *Diabetologia* 22 (1982): 450–455.

28. George Steiner, "Diabetes and Atherosclerosis," *Diabetes* 30 (Supplement 2) (1981): 1–7; Christopher D. Saudek and Nancy L. Young, "Cholesterol Metabolism in Diabetes Mellitus: The Role of Diet," *Diabetes* (Supplement 2) 30 (1981): 76–81; Ronald B. Goldberg, "Lipid Disorders on Diabetes," *Diabetes Care* 4 (1981): 561–572; Fredrick L. Dunn et al., "The Effect of Diabetic Control on Very Low-Density Lipoprotein-Triglyceride Metabolism in Patients with

Type II Diabetes Mellitus and Marked Hypertriglyceridemia," *Metabolism Clinical and Experimental* 33 (1984): 117–123; Om P. Ganda, "Pathogenesis of Macrovascular Disease in the Human Diabetic," *Diabetes* 29 (1980): 931–942; and James W. Anderson, "Hyperlipidemia and Diabetes: Nutrition Considerations" in Lois Jovanovic and Charles M. Peterson, eds., *Nutrition and Diabetes* (New York: Alan R. Liss, 1985), pp. 133–159.

29. O'Dea, Nestel, and Antionoff, "Physical Factors."

30. David A. Jenkins et al., "Diabetic Diets, High Carbohydrate Combined with High Fiber," *American Journal of Clinical Nutrition* 33 (1980): 1729–1733.

31. Susan Wong, Kathy Traianedes, and Kerin O'Dea, "Factors Affecting the Rate of Hydrolysis of Starch in Legume," *American Journal of Clinical Nutrition* 42 (1985): 38–43.

32. Gregory Collier and Kerin O'Dea, "The Effect of Co-Ingestion of Fat on the Glucose, Insulin, and Gastric Inhibitory Polypeptide Responses to Carbohydrate and Protein," *American Journal of Clinical Nutrition* 37 (1983): 941–944; and Collier and O'Dea, "The Effect of Co-Ingestion of Fat on the Metabolic Responses to Slowly and Rapidly Absorbed Carbohydrates," *Diabetologia* 26 (1984): 50–54.

33. Gregory R. Collier, Thomas M.S. Wolever, and David A. Jenkins, "Concurrent Ingestion of Fat and Reduction in Starch Content Impairs Carbohydrate Tolerance to Subsequent Meals," *American Journal of Clinical Nutrition* 45 (1987): 963–969.

34. Eleuterio Ferrannini et al., "Effect of Fatty Acids on Glucose Production and Utilization in Man," *Journal of Clinical Investigation* 72 (1983): 1737–1747.

35. Hamish N. Munro and James B. Allison, *Mammalian Protein Metabolism,* volume I (New York: Academic Press, 1964), pp. 162–170.

36. David J.A. Jenkins, "Diabetic Diets: High Carbohydrate Combined with High Fiber." *American Journal of Clinical Nutrition* 33 (1980): 1729–1733.

37. Christian Villaume, et al., "Effect of Exchange of Ham for Boiled Egg on Plasma Glucose and Insulin Responses to Breakfast in Normal Subjects," *Diabetes Care* 9 (1986): 46–49.

38. Anne W. Thorburn, Jennie C. Brand, and A. Stewart Truswell, "Salt and the Glycaemic Response," *British Medical Journal* 292 (1986): 1697–1699.

39. C. P. Lamar, "Comparative Oral Glucose and Fructose Tolerance Test in Normal Subject and in Diabetic Patients," *Journal of Florida Medical Association* 46 (1959): 180–186; and Gertraud Schauberger et al., "Exchange of Carbohydrates According to the Effect on Blood Glucose," *Diabetes* 26 (Supplement 1) (1977): 415.

40. Margaret A. Powers and Dawn C. Laine, "Sweeteners," in *Handbook of Diabetes Nutritional Management,* p. 289.

41. Jerrold M. Olefsky and Phyllis Crapo, "Fructose, Xylitol, and Sorbitol," *Diabetes Care* 3 (1980): 390–393.

42. Mark E. Molitch, "Complications of Diabetes Mellitus," in Margaret A. Powers, ed., *Handbook of Diabetes Nutritional Management* (Rockville, MD: Aspen Publishers, 1987), p. 35.

43. S. Salminen, E. Salminen, and V. Marks, "The Effects of Xylitol on the Secretion of Insulin and Gastric Inhibitory Polypeptide in Man and Rats," *Diabetologia* 22 (1982): 480–482.

44. "Alternatives to Cane and Beet Sugar," *Food Technology* 40 (1986): 116.

45. Joint FAO/WHO Expert Committee on Food Additives, *Evaluation of Certain Food Additives,* Technical Report Series 683 (Geneva: World Health Organization, 1982).

46. American Diabetes Association, "Saccharin," *Diabetes Care* 2 (1979): 380.

47. Joint FAO/WHO Expert Committee on Food Additives, *Evaluation of Certain Food Additives.*

48. Janet McDonald, "Alcohol and Diabetes," *Diabetes Care* 3 (1980): 629–637; and Kelly M. West, "Diabetes Mellitus," in Howard A. Schnieder, Carl E. Anderson, and David B. Coursin, eds., *Nutritional Support of Medical Practice* (Hagerstown, Md.: Harper & Row, 1977), pp. 278–296.

49. "Alcohol-Drug Interactions," *FDA Drug Bulletin* 9 (1979): 10–12.

50. Henry Ginsberg et al., "Moderate Ethanol Ingestion and Plasma Triglyceride Levels—A Study in Normal and Hypertriglyceridemic Persons," *Annals of Internal Medicine* 80 (1974): 143–149; and Linda V. VanHorn, "Lipids," in *Handbook of Diabetes Nutritional Management*, p. 260.

51. Karmeen D. Kulkarni, "Altering the Basic Meal Plan," in *Handbook of Diabetes Nutritional Management*, p. 176.

52. H. Franklin Bunn, "Nonenzymatic Glycosylation of Protein: Relevance to Diabetes," *American Journal of Medicine* 70 (1981): 325; and Lois Jovanovic and Charles M. Peterson, "The Clinical Utility of Glycosylated Hemoglobin," *American Journal of Medicine* 70 (1981): 331–338.

53. Jovanovic and Peterson, "Clinical Utility"; H. Franklin Bunn, "Nonenzymatic Glycosylation of Protein: Relevance to Diabetes," *American Journal of Medicine* 70 (1981): 325; Jovanovic and Peterson, "Hemoglobin A_{Ic}—The Key to Diabetic Control," *Laboratory Medicine for the Practicing Physician* (July–August 1978): 11; and Peterson and Robert L. Jones, "Glycosylation Reactions and Reversible Sequelae of Diabetes Mellitus," in Charles M. Peterson, ed., *Diabetes Management in the 80's* (New York: Praeger Pubs., 1982): 12–25.

54. Jovanovic and Peterson, "Clinical Utility"; and Petersen et al., "Feasibility of Improved Blood Glucose Control in Patients with Insulin-Dependent Diabetes Mellitus," *Diabetes Care* 2 (1979): 329–335.

55. Jovanovic and Peterson, "Clinical Utility," pp. 332, 333.

56. Christine A. Beebe, "Self Blood Glucose Monitoring: An Adjunct to Dietary and Insulin Management of the Patient with Diabetes," *American Dietetic Association Journal* 87 (1987): 63.

57. Jay S. Skyler et al., "Instructing Patients in Making Alterations in Insulin Dosage," *Diabetes Care* 2 (1979): 40–41.

58. Mary Joan Oexmann, *Total Available Glucose, Diabetic Food System* (Charleston, S.C.: Medical University of South Carolina Printing Service, 1987).

59. Munro and Allison, *Mammalian Protein Metabolism*, pp. 162–264.

60. Graham Lusk, *The Elements of the Science of Nutrition* (Philadelphia, Pa.: W.B. Saunders Co., 1928), pp. 206–209.

61. Jean A.T. Pennington and Helen Nichols Church, *Bowes and Church's Food Values of Portions Commonly Used* (New York: Harper & Row, 1985).

62. Oexmann, *Total Available Glucose.*

63. Munro and Allison, *Mammalian Protein Metabolism*, p. 164.

64. Sarah C. Stulb, "The Diabetes Supplement of the National Health Survey. IV. The Patient's Knowledge of Food Exchanges," *Journal of the American Dietetic Association* 52 (1968): 391–393; William M. Holland, "The Diabetes Supplement of the National Health Survey. III. The Patient Reports on His Diet," *Journal of the American Dietetic Association* 52 (1968): 387–390; and Kelly M. West, "Diet Therapy of Diabetes: An Analysis of Failure," *Annals of Internal Medicine* 79 (1973):425–534.

65. John W. Ensinck and Edwin L. Bierman, "Dietary Management of Diabetes Mellitus," *Annual Review of Medicine* 30 (1979): 155–170; and Frank Q. Nuttall, "Diet and the Diabetic Patient," *Diabetes Care* 6 (1983): 197–207.

66. Julia D. Watkins et al., "A Study of Diabetes Patients at Home," *American Journal of Public Health* 57 (1967): 452–459; Brenda A. Broussard, Mary A. Bass, and M. Yvonne Jackson, "Reasons for Diabetic Diet Noncompliance Among Cherokee Indians," *Journal of Nutrition Education* 14 (1982): 56–57; and Elizabeth A. Schlenk and Laura K. Hart, "Relationship Between Health Locus of Control, Health Values and Social Support and Compliance of Persons with Diabetes Mellitus," *Diabetes Care* 7 (1984): 566–574.

67. Leslie Eckerling and Mary B. Kohrs, "Research on Compliance with Diabetic Regimens: Applications to Practice," *Journal of the American Dietetic Association* 84 (1984): 805–809.

68. Roland L. Wiensier et al., "Diet Therapy of Diabetes: Description of a Successful Methodologic Approach to Gaining Adherence," *Diabetes* 23 (1974): 639–673.

69. Jean Hassell and Eva Medved, "Group/Audiovisual Instruction for Patients with Diabetes," *Journal of the American Dietetic Association* 66 (1975): 465–470.

70. Gwen S. Tani and Jean H. Hankin, "A Self-Learning Unit for Patients with Diabetes," *Journal of the American Dietetic Association* 58 (1971): 331–335.

71. Stewart M. Dunn et al., "Development of the Diabetes Knowledge Scales: Forms DKNA, DKNB, and DKNC," *Diabetes Care* 7 (1984): 36–41.

72. Karen I. Webb et al., "Dietary Compliance Among Insulin-Dependent Diabetics," *Journal of Chronic Disease* 37 (1984): 633–643.

73. P.H. Sonksen, S.S. Judd, and C. Lowry, "Home Monitoring of Blood Glucose," *Lancet* 1 (1978): 727–732; S. Walford et al., "Self-Monitoring of Blood Glucose," *Lancet* 1 (1978): 732–735; and Matthew Cohen and Paul Zimmet, "Self-Monitoring of Blood Glucose Levels in Non-Insulin-Dependent Diabetes Mellitus," *Medical Journal of Australia* 2 (1983): 377–381.

74. Linda A. Slowie, "Patient Learning—Segments from Case Histories," *Journal of the American Dietetic Association* 58 (1971): 563–567.

75. M. Boutaugh, A. Hall, and W. Davis, "An Examination of Diabetes Educational Diagnosis Assessment Forms," *Diabetes Educator* 7 (1982): 29–34; Dunn et al., "Development of the Diabetes Knowledge Scales"; and George E. Hess and Wayne K. Davis, "The Validation of a Diabetes Patient Knowledge Test," *Diabetes Care* 6 (1983): 591–596.

76. Webb et al., "Dietary Compliance."

77. Randee Jae Shenkel et al., "Importance of 'Significant Others' in Predicting Cooperation with Diabetic Regimen," *International Journal of Psychiatry in Medicine* 15 (1985): 149–155.

78. Lee S. Schwartz et al., "The Role of Recent Life Events and Social Support in the Control of Diabetes Mellitus," *General Hospital Psychiatry* 8 (1986): 212–216.

79. Michael A. Bush, "Compliance, Education, and Diabetes Control," *Mount Sinai Journal of Medicine* 54 (1987): 221–227; Rena R. Wing et al., "Behavioral Self-Regulation in the Treatment of Patients with Diabetes Mellitus," *Psychological Bulletin* 99 (1986): 78–89; and D.K. McColloush et al., "Influence of Imaginative Teaching on Diet on Compliance and Metabolic Control in Insulin Dependent Diabetes," *British Medical Journal* 287 (1983): 1858–1861.

80. Belinda McNeal et al., "Comprehension Assessment of Diabetes Education Program Participants," *Diabetes Care* 7 (1984): 232–235.

81. Jenkins et al., "Glycemic Index of Foods."

82. Stephen R. Rapp et al., "Food Portion Size Estimation by Men with Type II Diabetes," *The Journal of the American Dietetic Association* 86 (1986): 249–251.

83. Dennis V. Ary et al., "Patient Perspective on Factors Contributing to Nonadherence to Diabetes Regimens," *Diabetes Care* 9 (1986): 168–172; Karen Glanz, "Nutrition Education for Risk Factor Reduction and Patient Education: A Review," *Preventive Medicine* 14 (1985): 721–752.

Chapter 11

Nutrition Counseling in Treatment of Renal Disease

Objectives for Chapter 11

1. Identify factors that lead to inappropriate eating behaviors associated with protein-modified regimens.
2. Identify specific nutrients that should be emphasized in assessing a baseline eating pattern before providing dietary instruction.
3. Identify strategies to treat inappropriate eating behaviors associated with low-protein patterns.
4. Generate strategies to use in facilitating problem solving for clients who are following a protein-modified eating pattern.
5. Recommend dietary adherence tools for clients on protein-modified eating patterns.

This chapter provides guidance for the dietitian involved in working on possible prevention of dialysis or predialysis therapy for the person diagnosed with chronic renal insufficiency. Current facts and theories are discussed as researched by some of the foremost nephrologists in the world. The ideas presented correspond to those discussed in the American Dietetic Association's *Handbook of Clinical Dietetics*. In "Controlled Protein, Potassium, and Sodium Diets," the purpose of the low-protein eating pattern is described as follows:

1. "To achieve and maintain adequate nutritional status."
2. "To lighten the work of a diseased kidney by reducing the urea, uric acid, creatinine, and electrolytes (especially potassium, sodium, and phosphorus) that must be excreted."
3. "To replace substances, e.g., protein and sodium, that are lost to the body in abnormal amounts because of impaired renal function."[1]

Some of the information in this chapter involves new theories that are currently being researched. The focus remains on the outpatient in a predialysis state.

348

THEORIES AND FACTS ABOUT NUTRITION AND CHRONIC RENAL FAILURE

In the 1980s there has been a flurry of interest in diet and renal disease. Many nephrologists are now looking to low-protein diets as a means of halting deterioration of renal function. The worsening of renal function seems to occur independently of the associated disease when renal function is less than 25 milliliters per minute of glomerular filtration.[2] Assuming that urea requires renal work to be excreted, Addis proposed a low-protein diet as a way to decrease the workload of surviving nephrons.[3]

Two hypotheses have been proposed to explain this phenomenon. In 1978 Ibels et al. theorized that hyperphosphatemia was responsible for renal function deterioration,[4] and in 1982 Brenner et al. developed the glomerular hyperfiltration theory. The Brenner hypothesis suggests that a low-protein diet halts the progression of chronic renal insufficiency in two ways: (1) by preventing the increase in glomerular plasma flow and (2) by preventing high capillary pressures.[5] Accompanying proteinuria and structural alterations of epithelial cells seem to be less severe when predialysis persons are placed on low-protein diets.[6] In the absence of a low-protein diet, glomerular hyperfiltration continues. As the function of sclerosing glomeruli is lost, less severely affected glomeruli undergo further compensatory hyperfiltration with subsequent injury. This process favors progression of kidney damage and eventual total loss of glomeruli and renal function.

More research is needed to show that the hyperfiltration theory is the major link between excessive dietary protein intake and glomerular pathology. Although it seems clear from animal studies that excessive dietary protein accelerates functional deterioration in chronic renal disease,[7] the mechanisms by which a low-protein diet retards progression have not been clarified. Several nephrologists in Europe have used diets for long periods in persons with different degrees of chronic renal failure with varied success.[8] Guidelines must be established, and more information is required on the extent of protein restriction necessary to obtain maximal effects on the progression of renal disease without impairing growth and/or producing prolonged negative nitrogen balance and malnutrition.[9] More information is also needed on how difficult it is for a client to follow a low-protein diet. The National Institute of Diabetes, Digestive and Kidney Diseases, a part of the National Institutes of Health, is currently funding a clinical trial to help answer unresolved issues surrounding low-protein intake and chronic renal insufficiency.

The principle of reducing dietary protein and maximizing the biological quality of protein intake in predialysis clients has been generally accepted for decades. These measures increase the efficiency with which nitrogen is used for synthesis and reduce the ingested quantities of total nitrogen, nonprotein nitrogen, potassium, phosphorus, and sulfur. This results in a reduction of the requirements for excretion of urea, uric acid, potassium, phosphate, sulfate, and acid and decreases the tendency of such persons to develop azotemia, acidosis, hyperkalemia, and hyperphosphatemia with their consequences.

The levels of dietary protein recommended for persons suffering from chronic renal failure to maintain nitrogen balance are controversial. Unlike persons with normal renal function, a person who is renal insufficient requires more protein because of the altered metabolism associated with uremia, which may promote protein catabolism. Most obvious are proteinuria and occult gastrointestinal bleeding. These problems increase protein requirements not only because blood proteins may not be completely reabsorbed, but also because they cannot be resynthesized with complete efficiency. Hormonal disturbances such as hyperglucagonemia and carbohydrate intolerance in uremic persons may increase protein requirements.[10] On the other hand, the reduced rates of excretion of nonurea urinary nitrogen components mentioned above reduce nitrogen requirements. Even though urea nitrogen reutilization is questioned, nitrogen balance can be maintained in some uremic persons on very low intakes.[11]

The estimated safe allowance for protein intake in persons without proteinuria or occult blood loss has been controversial. The many studies that have addressed this issue were reviewed by the Joint Food and Agriculture Organization/World Health Organization Expert Committee on energy and protein requirements, which recommended 0.55 gram of protein per kilogram of body weight to maintain positive nitrogen balance.[12]

The consensus among nephrologists seems to be that 0.57 gram per kilogram of protein (40 grams per 70 kilograms), predominantly of high biological value, is adequate to maintain nitrogen balance in the absence of substantial proteinuria or occult blood loss.[13] Research indicates that nitrogen balance in persons with chronic renal failure can be maintained by giving 0.55 to 0.60 gram of protein per kilogram per day and a minimum of 35 kilocalories per kilogram per day.[14] In this study positive nitrogen balance depended directly on caloric intake. Use of protein in uremia also depended in part on the biological value of protein. The literature indicates a range for intake of protein of high biological value from 70 percent to 75 percent.[15]

Experimental diets currently being tested use ketoacid amino-acid packets plus a very low protein diet (15–30 grams per day) or amino-acid tablet supplements combined with the same very low protein diet. More information on their effectiveness will be forthcoming following completion of the Modification of Diet in Renal Disease study funded by the National Institutes of Health. Preliminary data from small metabolic studies are presented below.

Work by Mitch and Walser has pointed to the use of diets very low in protein (0.29–0.43 gram per kilogram per day) with the addition of ketoacid amino-acid supplements.[16] The advantage of this diet is that much more variety is possible in the choice of foods when protein quality (percentage of protein of high biological value) is not restricted, making such diets more acceptable to many clients than diets containing 40 grams of protein (0.60 gram per kilogram per day), predominantly of high biological value.[17] The disadvantage is that the lower-protein eating pattern is essentially vegetarian including no meat or dairy products.

Since the first step in the major metabolic pathway of four of the essential amino acids (valine, leucine, isoleucine, phenylalanine) is reversible transamination to the corresponding alpha-ketoacid, it is not surprising that these ketoacids can serve as dietary substitutes for the corresponding amino acids. Furthermore, essential amino acids for which transamination is a minor but recognized pathway of metabolism (methionine, tryptophan, and histidine) can also be replaced in the diet by their corresponding keto-analogs. Lysine and threonine do not undergo transamination and therefore cannot be replaced by their keto-analogs.[18]

The ketoacid amino-acid supplement can be taken in powder form in juices three times a day with meals. Although fruit juices are usually recommended, the flavor of the ketoacid and amino-acid mixture is similar to concentrated beef broth and seems more acceptable to some patients in vegetable juices. One drawback to using vegetable juices is their protein content, which may be prohibitive on very restricted

Table 11-1 Amino-Acid Supplement Doses

Amino Acid	Dose per Tablet (milligrams)	Daily Dose for a 70-Kilogram Standard Weight Person (grams)
Histidine	45	1.26
Isoleucine	60	1.68
Leucine	90	2.52
Lysine acetate, equivalent to lysine	65	1.82
Methionine	90	2.52
Phenylalanine	70	1.96
Threonine	65	1.82
Tryptophan	25	.40
Tyrosine	75	2.10
Valine	135	3.78
	720	20.16

research diets. The flavor of the powder is objectionable to most patients, and experimentation is necessary before an ideal beverage is chosen. For some clients, sorbets or ices camouflage the taste. The ketoacid and amino-acid mixture is very unstable and requires refrigeration at all times to maximize preservation.

A commercial amino-acid supplement has been used.[19] (See Table 11-1.) The formulation of these supplements considers the altered amino acid and protein metabolism that results during chronic renal failure.[20] There are reductions in serum concentrations of albumin, transferrin, and plasma concentrations of valine, leucine, isoleucine, lysine, and tryptophan. The conversion of phenylalanine to tyrosine is impaired,[21] indicating a need for an increase in tyrosine and a decrease in phenylalanine. Histidine, which cannot be transaminated, acts as an essential amino acid.[22] Excess histidine increases serum phenylalanine levels and should therefore be avoided. Excess methionine and other sulfur-containing amino acids should be avoided because they delay the repletion process.[23]

The role of serum phosphate in the progression of renal disease is also controversial.[24] Walser has found excellent clinical results with dietary phosphorus restrictions in persons with modest protein restrictions (40 grams).[25] Phosphorus was reduced by restricting intake of milk, milk products, cheese, cola beverages, and instant powdered beverages to bring the level of phosphorus down to approximately 600 milligrams, approximately one-half the usual daily intake.

As an alternative to diet, aluminum salts, for example, AluCaps and Alternage, are frequently given to reduce the intestinal absorption of dietary phosphorus. Walser cautioned against using only aluminum salts in the treatment of hyperphosphatemia[26] because their effect on phosphorus absorption is less than theoretically indicated (130 milligrams of phosphorus per gram of dry gel).[27] In practice, only a portion of dietary phosphorus exists as or is absorbed as inorganic phosphate. Walser indicated that the absorption of phosphorus from phosphopeptides, nucleic acids, phospholipids, and other organic phosphates may not be susceptible to inhibition by aluminum and stressed that one should not attempt to reduce serum phosphorus without also reducing dietary phosphorus.[28]

Early in the course of renal failure, intestinal calcium absorption is reduced before serum vitamin D levels fall.[29] Later vitamin D deficiency further aggravates this problem. Both azotemia and acidosis independently increase renal excretion of calcium.[30] Calcium balance is usually negative in uremic persons unless calcium supplementation is prescribed.[31] Hypocalcemia depends on both calcium deficiency and hyperphosphatemia. Serum calcium approaches normal as serum phosphate falls during administration of aluminum salts.[32] Calcium carbonate can also be used as a phosphate binder when taken with meals.

Research shows that calcium supplements in the presence of hyperphosphatemia may aggravate renal insufficiency by allowing the deposition of calcium and phosphate in the kidney. In two studies, when serum calcium times the phosphorus product increased during calcium carbonate treatment, serum creatinine also rose.[33] This change occurred only a few weeks following calcium carbonate administration, and therefore probably did not result from the natural progression of the disease. More research is necessary to answer this question unequivocally. With this in mind Walser recommended reducing serum phosphate with diet, if necessary by giving short-term aluminum salts, before giving calcium supplements.

Nutritionists should be aware of sodium, potassium, and acid-base balance. Persons with renal insufficiency suffer from uremic acidosis, a condition caused by accumulation of phosphate, sulfate, and organic acids, impaired ammonia excretion, and renal bicarbonate wastage. The degree of renal bicarbonate wastage is variable; therefore, the requirement for sodium bicarbonate also varies from 0 to as much as 14 milliequivalents per kilogram of body weight.

Decreasing dietary protein results in some improvement in acidosis because the major source of acid in acid-ash diets is dietary protein (particularly its sulfur content). Treating acidosis is important for several reasons:

1. prevention of dissolution of bone salt
2. reduction in symptoms associated with decreased pH (which usually are not apparent until serum bicarbonate is 16 millimoles or lower)
3. prevention of the protein catabolic effect of acidosis. An alkaline-ash diet, comprised mostly of fruits and vegetables, may help but is rather monotonous.

Chronic uremic persons differ markedly from normal persons in their ability to vary renal excretion of sodium. They excrete a large, relatively fixed fraction of filtered sodium.

Various techniques have been developed to determine an optimal level of dietary sodium in a given client. Generally the sodium bicarbonate requirement should be assessed first, because it affects the level of sodium chloride to be given. Ideally 24-hour sodium output should be determined first. Providing an amount of sodium chloride equal to this quantity (in milliequivalents) minus the sodium bicarbonate intake will then maintain sodium balance.

Diuretics are indicated in most cases of moderate or severe renal failure.[34] When the diuretic is administered chronically, the same extracellular fluid volume may be maintained with higher salt intake, making the diet less difficult to follow.

Potassium balance in the chronic uremic client is less of a problem than sodium balance. However, hyperkalemia is quite common in more advanced stages of renal disease. Modest reductions in high-potassium foods such as tomatoes, bananas, potatoes, and oranges can be effective. A small number of persons with renal failure may exhibit a tendency toward hypokalemia. Increasing foods high in potassium and or potassium supplements is recommended for them.

A few clients may develop hyponatremia, especially those on severely sodium-restricted intakes or those with congestive heart failure. Water intake must be restricted to correct and prevent hyponatremia.

Vitamin and mineral levels must be assessed in the chronically uremic client. Supplements of B vitamins and vitamin C are indicated. Serum levels of vitamin A and of retinol-binding protein are commonly elevated.[35] Because these substances are normally cleared by the kidney, vitamin A should not be given. Zinc concentrations are low in plasma leucocytes and hair of uremic persons, so supplementation is recommended.[36]

In summary, the client with chronic renal failure requires careful, consistent nutrition monitoring through blood and urine values. Low-protein, low-phosphorus diets are experimental and require semimonthly to monthly nutritional monitoring. Safety has not been adequately evaluated with the very low protein diets for long-term use.

RESEARCH ON ADHERENCE WITH EATING PATTERNS IN TREATMENT OF RENAL DISEASE

Treatment for chronic renal failure involves major adjustments and stress for clients. Although compliance with renal diets can be easily monitored with laboratory tests, many physiological factors can modify the results of these tests. For persons who are losing weight because calorie intake on low-protein diets tends to be low, loss of muscle mass may contribute to urinary nitrogen, which is used as a marker for dietary compliance. There is much to learn about urinary nitrogen and the possible effect of chronic renal disease on that biological marker. In many cases very compliant persons whose intake by self-report may look excellent are classified as noncompliant on analysis of urinary nitrogen. Estimates of noncompliance with hemodialysis regimens have ranged from 5 percent to 50 percent or more.[37] Compliance of home dialysis clients is apparently not much better than that among clients receiving treatment at a dialysis center.[38] Manley and Sweeney argue that compliance scales may be overly strict, so that the resulting conclusions regarding good and poor adherence must be subject to question.[39]

With the exception of Blackburn's descriptive report of compliance following individual instruction and encouragement of use of personal food preferences,[40] only three small intervention studies have been published that tested behavioral strategies relative to dietary compliance. Token economy systems, behavioral contingency contracting, and self-monitoring of weight gain were effective in all three studies.[41]

Further study of behavioral approaches to improve the client's dietary adherence to protein- and phosphorus-modified regimens is needed. Because of the powerful impact of renal disease on the client's life, dietary instruction is most effective when the meal preparer is included and family support is enlisted. Last, research shows a generalized decrease in dietary compliance as the time on dialysis increases.[42] Efforts to include reinforcements in client education are helpful.

INAPPROPRIATE EATING BEHAVIORS

The chronically renal-insufficient person seen as an outpatient requires a great deal of assistance in dietary adherence. The regimen for a predialysis client is extremely complicated and requires extra time and assistance from the dietitian. The exchange lists alone can be overwhelming for many clients who have followed other diets in the past. A low-calorie diet in principle contrasts directly with the renal diet, so a person who has followed low-calorie diets in the past will have some difficulty in readjusting to the new principles of the renal diet. For example, on a low-calorie diet fat and pure carbohydrate foods are discouraged, but on a low-protein diet they are encouraged. With reduction in protein, an increase in calories through fat and carbohydrate is essential. Weight maintenance is important.

A family member who is diabetic may influence a renal client to avoid foods high in simple sugars. The renal client may have difficulty accepting the idea that simple sugars are necessary on a low-protein diet to maintain adequate caloric intake.

As most clients on many other eating patterns, clients must struggle with social pressures that are multiplied by the large number of restrictions. Clients may drop out of social affairs to avoid the embarrassment of having to explain their health problems. "Everything in my life has changed!" is a common exclamation. Old eating habits are replaced by a constant preoccupation with restriction. The tradition of enjoying all food is replaced by a feeling that meals are never spontaneous but always associated with "don'ts." For clients with a protein restriction, eating can become only a means of existence instead of a means of recreation.

On a protein- and phosphorus-restricted diet, usual foods may be replaced by low-protein and low-phosphorus foods that are less moist, have an aftertaste, and are lower in fiber (due to the phosphorus restriction). The result is less enjoyment in taste and texture sensations, and frequently an initial side-effect is constipation because of the reduction in fiber. These negative associations with the protein-restricted diet can lead to inappropriate eating behaviors.

ASSESSMENT OF EATING BEHAVIORS

Early assessment of the chronically renal insufficient client is crucial to dietary success. Identification of potential problems is important. Because many of these clients suffer from uremic symptoms, signs of depression may be more frequent than in the normal population. Prior to instruction on an involved eating pattern, some clients may require psychological counseling. It is important to look for predictors of adherence, especially in clients for whom the dietary and medication regimens are very complicated. A person is required to decrease protein and phosphorus intake drastically, sometimes reducing meat to 1 ounce per day and milk to one half cup per day. Along with the diet there are many medications that must be taken daily, for example, multivitamins, calcium, iron, blood pressure regulators, keto- or amino-acid supplements.

Identifying the support of others is crucial. Support by a spouse or significant other may signal excellent future adherence. Lack of support signals poor adherence.

The assessment of the person with renal insufficiency also requires close attention to personal indicators. For example, before instituting a low-protein eating regimen, counselors should identify past dietary behaviors. Has the patient tried without success in the past to follow a low-calorie diet? Good past performance is an indicator of future success with a new eating pattern. Initial assessment might include eliciting a list of reasons the client wants to follow the new eating pattern and take medications. Later, when commitment wanes, a review of the reasons and circumstances in the client's life that have altered commitment can improve adherence.

The counselor should provide an opportunity for the client to try out behaviors before actually starting a regimen. For example, holding a special event for clients centered around a holiday buffet can give them an opportunity to try some foods they might like to serve during the holiday season. Vegetable fettuccine made with low-protein pasta and nondairy creamer along with black forest cake prepared with low-protein flour and without eggs are examples of festive low-protein dishes clients may wish to serve.

Careful, detailed assessments of dietary intake should include the protein content of the diet along with other baseline information on dietary phosphorus, potassium, sodium, calcium, and magnesium. Intake assessment might include several diet records (three a month for three months) and diet recalls (once a month for three months). In addition, a food frequency or diet history may be valuable. The questionnaire in Adherence Tool 11-1 can provide valuable information on past eating habits. Once the client is placed on the new eating pattern, Adherence Tool 11-2 might be used to monitor intake.

An assessment of medication-taking habits is also important. Many renal clients have taken blood pressure medications. Potential problems with taking medications at certain times of day may be apparent from a description of past habits.

Before providing information about a new eating pattern, the counselor needs to assess the client's knowledge of diets. What information does the client presently have concerning dietary exchange patterns? What impact will these patterns have on learning a new dietary exchange list? What basic principles taught in relation to past diets may no longer be true? For example, a client who has followed low-calorie diets in the past may have difficulty switching to a totally new exchange list in which foods are categorized based on protein content rather than calories. The idea of limiting high-carbohydrate, high-fat foods is no longer valid. It is extremely difficult to assure a client that on a low-protein diet it is not only good but mandatory to eat high-carbohydrate, high-fat foods on a daily basis for adequate caloric intake.

Assessment of adherence to a low-protein regimen may involve medication counting, review of urine urea nitrogens, a corresponding estimated protein intake,* and a review of laboratory serum and urine values. Adherence Tool 11-3 includes a worksheet to help calculate percent adherence to medications or packets. Adherence Tool 11-4 is an accompanying list of adherence rates at each visit that serves as a monitoring device for clients and clinicians. Graphs can also be used to track diet adherence (Adherence Tool 11-5).

It is extremely important to track serum and urine laboratory values for clients on low-protein eating patterns. The laboratory data can help determine how well the client is adhering to diet and medication. Adherence Tool 11-6 includes space for recording laboratory values and corresponding normal ranges for each chemistry value.

---

*Equation: $6.25 \times$ [Urine Urea Nitrogen $+ (0.31 \times$ Standard Body Weight) + Urine Protein] $-$ $X =$ Estimated Protein Intake (grams per kilogram).

If urine protein is greater than 5, add it into this equation. If it is less than 5, set urine protein equal to 0. X equals 0 if clients are not on ketoacid amino-acid supplements or if they are not on Aminess. For patients on Aminess, $X = 2.16 \times$ (Standard Body Weight/10) $\times 0.122$. For patients on ketoacid amino-acid supplements, $X = 2.8 \times$ (Standard Body Weight/10) $\times 0.097$. Standard body weight is rounded to the nearest 10.

TREATMENT STRATEGIES

Problems with low-protein eating patterns fall into the three categories mentioned for other diets: lack of knowledge, forgetfulness, and lack of commitment. As with all dietary regimens, lack of knowledge can be easily remedied. Cueing devices can provide help when forgetting is a problem. Lack of commitment is probably the most difficult problem to solve.

Strategies To Deal with Lack of Knowledge

Before dealing with problems involving lack of knowledge, counselors have at their disposal large quantities of information to present to the client in a variety of ways. The most potent strategy to solve lack of knowledge is tailoring. The ideal situation for tailoring allows for an individual dietary pattern (see Chapter 5 for use of the computer in planning an individual pattern) and an individualized exchange list for each person. The pattern shows exchanges with amounts tailored to each client's preferred eating style, such as X ounces or grams of meat, X servings of vegetables, X servings of fruits, X servings of milk, and so on. The tailored exchange list includes only foods the client eats; all others are eliminated from the list. The tailored list is preferred over one general list for the following reasons:

1. A tailored list can be very short and thus less cumbersome. Fewer items mean less work for the person learning the list.
2. It allows for much greater detail. With fewer items, more information can be included for each item, such as protein, phosphorus, and calories, automatically giving the person using the list more information about the eating pattern.
3. It stimulates learning because it can create a feeling of ownership.

Along with individualizing exchanges, individualized menu planning with active client participation can be an aid to later adherence.

Once counselors have presented individualized crucial information to each client, they must stage changes in eating habits to coincide with the recommended dietary components. At this point counselors should avoid creating the impression that they are the "experts" and in sole control. Too often counselors present forms, lists, and other documents in a way that leaves clients feeling totally removed from the process of change. They begin to regard themselves as unwilling objects to be moved, shaped, and molded by the counselors. The goal during the sessions should be to shape the eating patterns with clients as they continue to follow the dietary prescription.

Staging or setting priorities for the components of a diet with several restrictions, all of which clients must follow as a package, can be difficult. In this case, staging allows clients to solve one problem at a time while continuing to follow all restrictions to the best of their ability. Once again, clients must be very actively involved in the developmental process. In choosing which problems to work on first, counselors should consider several factors:

- Which problem, if solved, will allow the most success? Initial success can be very important to continued improvement in dietary adherence.
- Which problem is the most difficult and inhibiting from the standpoint of dietary adherence? The counselor and client may need to deal first with a very

large problem that precludes following the diet. A client who refuses to comply with any recommendations may need to be seen by a psychologist or psychiatrist before any instruction on a dietary regimen.

- Which problems will be moderately difficult to solve? Counselors should focus first on the easiest problems to solve, then rank the more difficult problems and discuss each separately. The ultimate choice should be a product of client-counselor teamwork.

In dealing with a client on a low-protein eating pattern, staging learning can be very important. Counselors should begin by focusing on selecting appropriate amounts of food from an exchange group high in protein, choosing a group less preferred by the client so that cutting back is not impossible. The counselor should try to ensure success. The area listed as most difficult should be the last. Waiting makes it possible to use the idea of attribution to facilitate adherence to a more difficult problem. For example, the counselor might say, "You have done so well in eating the required amounts of food in the milk category (Attribution). You should eventually do well in cutting back on meat." Staging may also take the form of menu planning to initially provide direct guidance in dietary adherence. As time passes, the client will become comfortable assuming personal responsibility for menu planning.

Lack of knowledge can often be the major problem in a variety of issues. One of clients' most commonly voiced concerns is social eating, which includes eating at friends' homes and in restaurants. Tracking adherence to diets and medications shows major decreases in group adherence rates during holidays such as Hanukkah and Christmas and during vacation periods. These times involve accelerated social eating.

Initial assistance in this area can be informational. Counselors can involve clients by asking them to plan a menu (Adherence Tool 11-7). Adherence Tools 11-8 and 11-9 provide practice in learning exchanges and modifying recipes, and listing favorite low-protein foods. During the holidays, counselors can help clients adhere to the eating pattern by giving information as shown in Adherence Tool 11-10. This tool was designed to allow a client who has used up all exchanges for breakfast, lunch, and dinner to select foods spontaneously at a late-night party. It shows many "free" items in terms of protein content, allows a few lower-protein foods, and says "stop" to many high-protein foods. Adherence Tool 11-11 is a birthday card that includes a recipe for a low-protein birthday cake. When signed by all clinical staff, the card becomes an important reminder and aid in following the new eating pattern at a difficult time.

Restaurant eating can be very difficult for clients following a low-protein eating pattern. It is important to provide adequate information so clients can follow the diet when eating out. A file of menus for the client's favorite restaurant is extremely valuable. Counselors can ask clients to plan a day's menu that includes eating out. It is helpful to call the restaurant before using a menu and elicit as much information as possible on serving sizes. By giving clients enough information, counselors can make restaurant eating much less difficult.

Eating at home when following restricted protein eating patterns can be easier if the client has access to low-protein products that provide added calories. Adherence Tool 11-12 provides space to identify low-protein products along with company names. These products make it possible to include a greater amount of some high-protein foods. For example, by eating low-protein bread which has minimal protein content, more protein can come from meat products rather than regular bread products.

Lack of knowledge may be evidenced by the lack of ability to identify circumstances preceding and following a behavior. For example, if snacking in the evening seems to be a behavior that pushes protein intake over the recommended amount, examining events leading to that behavior may help determine how to modify it. The chain of events might be as follows: Eat dinner, wash dishes, watch TV (Antecedents), eat snack of cheese and crackers (Behavior), tell myself how bad I've been, feel depressed, eat a peanut butter sandwich (Consequences).

Identifying the ABC's of behavior (antecedents, behavior, and consequences) makes a variety of solutions available. First, the counselor can determine how important regular, as opposed to low-protein, crackers are. It is very easy to suggest low-protein crackers and jelly as an alternative to regular crackers and cheese. If this change is too drastic, a compromise might be a mixture of mayonnaise and very small amounts of cheese (0.2 ounces), mixed and microwaved, on low-protein crackers. The positive self-reinforcement that replaces the negative reinforcement indicated in the above chain will probably make the additional peanut butter sandwich less tempting. By saying, "This is great! I can eat this snack without increasing my protein intake significantly," the client can eliminate the feelings of depression and subsequent eating.

The more self-management through self-reinforcement a counselor can help the client achieve, the greater the likelihood of dietary success.

Strategies To Deal with Forgetfulness

Cueing devices can be very helpful in avoiding problems of forgetting. A note on the refrigerator saying, "Eat two slices of low-protein bread with margarine today" may help keep protein low and calories high. Placing hard candy in jars throughout the house can cue the client to eat adequate calories without added protein.

Forgetting is most often a problem in dealing with medication. Pill boxes with sections for each day's doses (morning, noon, evening, and before bed) are useful. If placed in visible areas, such as the kitchen table or counter, they can serve as prompts to taking medication (see Adherence Tool 11-13).

For medications used in research studies like ketoacids, which are in packet not bulk form, a medication dispenser (see Adherence Tool 11-14) with sections for each day of the week and three times of day can help remind the client to take all packets. The dispenser must go into the refrigerator and have rounded edges for easy cleaning. A dishwasher-safe dispenser might be helpful. Dispensers serve as monitoring devices as well. They alert the client to problem times of the day: "Lunch is always a hard time for me. There are always pills left in my pill dispenser at lunch."

During vacation times, a postcard (Adherence Tool 11-15) with cues to remind the client to take medications during the trip can help avoid poor adherence. Some clients may not prefer a postcard. They may wish to have a sealed letter instead. Calendars (Adherence Tool 11-16) can help document times when clients forget to take medication. Recording the amount of medication taken at each time of day can help clients see when they miss medications, and the recording may be a cue to improve adherence.

Strategies To Deal with Lack of Commitment

On a low-protein regimen with many restrictions, almost every client inevitably faces periods when commitment wanes. The degree is directly related to the number of adherence predictors identified during the initial assessment. Counselors should watch persons prone to depression for more frequent periods of decreased commitment to diet and adherence to medication. Lack of support or constant negative reinforcement by a spouse or significant other may set the stage for more frequent and longer periods of decreased commitment. Clients who have tried in vain to follow an eating pattern in the past will probably experience like periods of poor adherence to the low-protein eating pattern.

The first indication of reduced commitment may be a comment such as, "I'm tired of taking medications and following this strict diet." Assuming the counselor has provided enough information about the diet and the medication regimen and has offered cueing devices that the client is using, this comment indicates:

1. First, that more dietary information will probably only aggravate the situation. The client is not looking for more information at this point.
2. Second, that failing to remember to take the medication and follow the diet is not the major problem. Offering more cueing devices will only make the client angry because as a counselor you are not listening to what the client is saying.

At this point, the skills of listening discussed in Chapter 3 become very important. The counselor may either alienate the client by giving short, uninsightful answers such as "You just need to use more low-protein products," or, more positively, retrieve a potential nonadherer and improve adherence at the same time. The dialog that follows illustrates one way to begin approaching the person who lacks commitment:

> CLIENT: "I'm really tired of following this diet and taking all those medications."
> NUTRITION COUNSELOR: "When you say you are 'tired,' what specifically do you mean?"
> CLIENT: "I have lost the desire to fight. I look at my pill dispenser and notice that I should take a noon dose, but I don't have the desire to do it. So I don't. I have started eating a second serving of meat at night."
> NUTRITION COUNSELOR: "You were so committed when we started. I remember you listed several reasons for wanting to do well. I have the list here:
> 1. "I don't want my disease to get worse."
> 2. "I want to feel better."
> 3. "I want to succeed."
> CLIENT: "Yes, I remember, but many things have changed since then. I lost my job. My husband was laid off. It is hard to succeed or even see a reason to succeed if your future looks so bleak. We have so many financial problems that the diet and taking my medications have taken a back seat."

In many cases lack of commitment may mean that other stressful life events have taken priority over adhering to an eating pattern or medication regimen. One of the most positive aspects in maintaining adherence to the low-protein regimen is that in the predialysis client it can result in uremic symptoms that are less severe. During life events when the stress factor is temporary, a short time of reducing requirements until life events stabilize may be necessary. For example, if a client is going through a divorce, the counselor can help the client identify the most difficult time period and arrange a way of decreasing monitoring during that time, or set up a contract (Adherence Tool 11-17). The client can agree to monitor medication and dietary intake for one meal with a calendar every other week and try to do well without monitoring during the other weeks.

In some cases a client may adhere poorly to diet for a few days when eating at home is impossible. Once again, a contract (Adherence Tool 11-18) can avoid monumental indiscretions and create controlled ones. Instead of following a pattern of 0.6 gram per kilogram of protein, for a time the diet might be 0.7 gram per kilogram of protein. This process of relaxing the rules can help in times of crisis and serve as a way of staging back to the original prescription—from 0.7 grams per kilogram of protein to 0.65 grams per kilogram and finally back to 0.6 grams per kilogram. The contract written during this period should clearly indicate the times during which the rules will be relaxed and state exactly what relaxing the rules will change. The contract should make it very clear that the rules will be relaxed only while the client is recovering from an experience that precludes following the diet. The counselor should stress that the ultimate goal is to follow the diet 100 percent of the time.

At certain points constructive confrontation may be necessary:

> NUTRITION COUNSELOR: "I've enjoyed working with you over the past few weeks and I really thought you were making progress. (Personal and Relationship Statements). As I review your urine urea nitrogen levels, it is evident that you have not been following your low-protein eating pattern. Your diet records also show an increase in protein intake." (Description of Behavior)
>
> CLIENT: "I really want to do well, but particularly during breaks at work I just can't resist."
>
> NUTRITION COUNSELOR: "I am confused when you say you want to do well but your behavior during breaks shows that you actually do the opposite. There seem to be two messages. (Description of Feelings and Interpretation of Client's Situation) Do you understand what I mean?"
>
> CLIENT: "Yes." (Understanding Response)
>
> NUTRITION COUNSELOR: "How do you feel about what I am saying?" (Perception Check)
>
> CLIENT: "I am giving a mixed message. You are right, but it is so hard to say 'no' to my friends."
>
> NUTRITION COUNSELOR: "You seem to feel confused. You want to follow the diet, but the urgings of friends during breaks push you into eating more protein that you would like. (Interpretive Response) Can we come up with a solution?" (Constructive Feedback)

For the client with little support from a spouse or significant other, several alternatives are valuable. One is to identify another support person—a friend, daughter, sister, brother, cousin, or someone on a similar diet who is doing well. A second alternative is to train the spouse to give positive reinforcement. For example, the counselor can provide many examples of positive reinforcement during a counseling session when a husband and wife are present. A third alternative is to help clients with self-reinforcement. Counselors can ask clients to record thoughts about eating and help the client turn negative to positive thoughts during the next counseling session.

For example, a client might write, "I ate the cottage cheese and I know it is increasing my protein intake beyond what is recommended. I might as well give up." A more positive way to approach the situation is to say, "I ate more protein at this meal than I should have but tonight at supper I can keep the amount of protein down by eating a small lettuce salad, toasted low-protein bread and margarine, 7-Up, low-protein jello, and two low-protein cookies. I don't have to go over my protein allowance just because I have a problem with one meal." Adherence Tool 11-19 is a form on which to record both positive and negative monologues.

In summary, major problems with adherence to new eating patterns and supplementary medications involve information regarding the protein content of foods and means of applying this knowledge to specific situations. Cueing devices can be helpful in altering events to take medications and follow low-protein eating patterns. The most difficult problem involving lack of commitment might be approached with strategies such as self-monitoring, contracting, reinforcement, and positive thinking.

Adherence Tool 11-1 Monitoring Device

Client Eating Questionnaire for Protein-restricted Eating Patterns

Name: _____

Address: _____

_____

Sex: M _____ F _____

Birthdate: _____

Home Phone: _____

Office Phone: _____

Doctor's name: _____

Anthropometry:
Elbow Breadth _____
Frame Size _____
Standard Body Weight _____ (Use Metropolitan Life Insurance Tables)

Weight History:

1. Your present weight _____ height _____

2. Describe your present weight. (circle one)

| Very Overweight | Slightly Overweight | Above Average | Average | Slightly Underweight |

3. Are you dissatisfied with the way you look at this weight? (circle one)

| Completely Satisfied | Satisfied | Neutral | Dissatisfied | Very Dissatisfied |

4. What do you do for physical exercise and how often do you do it?

ACTIVITY	FREQUENCY
(for example swimming,	(daily, weekly, monthly)
jogging and dancing)	

_____

_____

_____

_____

PAST DIETS:
(If you have never followed a special diet, skip to question 12.)

5. Have you followed a low-protein diet in the past? _____ If "yes," what was the number of grams of protein eaten per day? _____ When did you start this diet? _____ Are you still following it? _____

6. How would you describe your ability to follow the diet? (circle one)

Excellent   Good   Fair   Poor

7. What were or are the attitudes of the following people about your attempts to follow the low-protein diet? (Place an X in the appropriate box.)

	Negative (They disapprove or are resentful.)	Indifferent (They don't care or don't help.)	Positive (They encourage me and are understanding.)
Husband			
Wife			
Children			
Parents			
Employer			
Friends			

8. Did or do these attitudes affect your ability to follow the low-protein diet? _____ . If "yes," please describe: _____

_____

_____

_____

_____

9. What other diets have you followed in the past or are you currently following? (Circle as many as apply.)
   High-calorie
   Low-cholesterol, low-fat
   Low-calorie
   Low-salt
   Diabetic
   Low-potassium
   High-potassium
   Low-phosphorus
   Other _____

   _____

   _____

10. What special products did you use or are you currently using?
    Low-protein products
    Low-salt products
    Sugar-free products
    Other _____

11. Have you had a major mood change while or after following a special diet? Indicate any mood changes on the following checklist.

	No Change	A Little Change	Moderate Change	A Lot of Change	Extreme Change
A. Depressed, sad, feeling down, unhappy, the blues					
B. Anxious, nervous, restless, or uptight all the time					
C. Physically weak					
D. Elated or happy					
E. Easily irritated, annoyed, or angry					
F. Fatigued, worn out, tired all the time					
G. A lack of self-confidence					

MEDICAL HISTORY:

12. What was the date of your last physical exam? _____

13. Other than your kidney disease, do you currently have other medical problems?
    _____

14. What medications or drugs do you take regularly? _____
    _____
    _____
    _____
    _____

15. List any medications, drugs or food to which you are allergic:
    _____
    _____
    _____

16. List any hospitalizations or operations. Indicate how old you were at each
    hospital admission.
    <pre>   Age   Reason for hospitalization</pre>
    _____
    _____
    _____
    _____
    _____

17. List any serious illnesses you have had that have not required hospitalization.
    Indicate how old you were during each illness.
    <pre>   Age   Illness</pre>
    _____
    _____
    _____
    _____
    _____

18. How much alcohol do you usually drink in a week? _____ oz.

19. List any psychiatric contact, individual counseling, or marital counseling that
    you have had or are now having.
    <pre>   Age   Reason for contact and type of therapy</pre>
    _____
    _____
    _____

20. List any recurring symptoms you are currently experiencing, vomiting, diarrhea, constipation, weak feeling, etc.

_____

_____

_____

_____

SOCIAL HISTORY:

21. Circle the last year of school attended:

    1 2 3 4 5 6 7 8   9 10 11 12   1 2 3 4   MA/MS PhD/MD
    grade school   high school   college

22. Describe your present occupation: _____

_____

(If self-employed, skip to question #24.)

23. How long have you worked for your present employer?

_____

24. Present marital status (circle one):

    single   engaged   married   divorced   widowed   separated

25. Describe spouse's occupation: _____

_____

_____

26. Who lives at home with you?

_____

_____

_____

_____

FAMILY HISTORY:

27. Is your father living? Yes _____ No _____
Father's age now, or age at and cause of death: _____

_____

_____

28. Is your mother living? Yes _____ No _____
Mother's age now, or age at and cause of death: _____

_____

_____

29. Please add any additional information you feel may be relevant to your dietary success. This includes interactions with your family and friends that might sabotage your ability to follow a low-protein diet and additional family or social history that you feel might help us understand problems you will encounter with eating low-protein meals.

Adherence Tool 11-2 Monitoring Device

Daily Record of Foods Containing Protein			
Time	*Protein-Containing Food*	*Amount*	*Source*

Adherence Tool 11-3 Monitoring Device

Calculating Adherence

Last visit date _____

Last visit number _____

Start counting for next visit adherence on   (date)

_____

                         (a.m., p.m., or bedtime dose)

_____

Number of days since last visit _____

Number of prescribed pills (packets) per day _____

   a. Number of pills (packets) issued since last visit _____

   b. Returned by client this visit _____

   c. Left at home or accidentally destroyed _____

   d. Not taken (b + c) _____

   e. Subject has taken since last visit (a–d) _____

   f. Should have taken _____

   g. Percent adherence to nearest whole number _____

      (a/f × 100)

   h. Number of days missed (f − e) / number of pills (packets) _____

Since your last visit, have you stopped taking your study medicine for any reason?

_____

Since your last visit, have you changed the dose of study medicine for any reason?

_____

_____

Adherence Tool 11-4 Monitoring Device

Record of Adherence Percentages	
(Medication)	(Dosage)
Date	Percent Adherence

Adherence Tool 11-5 Monitoring Device

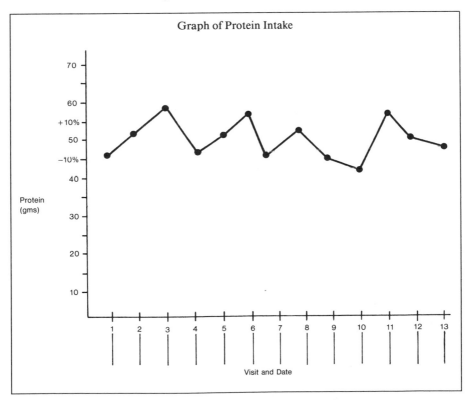

Graph of Protein Intake

Adherence Tool 11-6 Monitoring Device

Laboratory Data

Name: _____

Hospital Number: _____

Diagnosis: _____

Visit Date Normal Values							
Serum Values							
Total Protein							
Albumin							
Transferrin							
Urea Nitrogen Appearance (UNA)							
Creatinine							
Sodium							
Potassium							
Chloride							
Bicarbonate							
Calcium							
Phosphorus							
Magnesium							
Iron							
Glucose							
White Blood Cells							
Hemoglobin							
Hematocrit							
Urine Values							
Protein							
Creatinine							
Phosphorus							
pH							
Glucose							

Adherence Tool 11-7 Informational Device

Client Diet Basics and One-Day Menu

My diet should contain _____ grams of protein per day.
Examples of foods containing all essential amino acids:

Meats	Fish	Milk
Poultry	Eggs	Cheese

Examples of foods lacking one or more essential amino acids:

Breads	Fruits	Cereals
Vegetables	Gelatin	

Essential amino acids are:

Histidine	Threonine
Isoleucine	Tryptophan
Leucine	Valine
Lysine	

Plan one day's menu using protein-containing foods:

Breakfast	*Lunch*	*Dinner*	*Snacks*

Adherence Tool 11-8 Informational Device

Exchange Practice for Your Low-Protein Eating Pattern

Please write in the amount of protein coming from the food in the list and its exchange amount.

Food	Amount of Protein	Amount of Phosphorus	Exchange*
¼ cup corn			
½ cup ice cream			
8 ounces grape juice			
1 ounce hard candy			
4 saltine crackers			
⅛ of or 7″ of apple pie			
¾ cup applesauce			
¼ cup mashed potatoes			
28 grams lean roast beef			
28 grams lean ham			
56 grams frankfurters			
28 grams cheddar cheese			
¼ cup yogurt			

*Only the amount of protein may be important if exchanges are unnecessary.

Adherence Tool 11-9 Informational Device

Recipe Modifications for Your Low-Protein Diet
(Title of Recipe)

Ingredients	Amount	Grams of Protein	Milligrams of Phosphorus	Calories

Total Protein _____ grams
Animal Protein _____ grams
Total Phosphorus _____ milligrams
Calories _____
Exchanges _____
_____
_____

Adherence Tool 11-10 Informational Device

Holiday Eating

Christmas Goodies
That Are "Go"
Candy Canes
Lollipops
Cut Rock (Prim Rose brand)
Mint Filled Straws (Prim
Rose brand)
Holiday Mints (Brachs)
Yule Mints (Brachs)
Christmas Jellies (Brachs)
Cinnamon Santas (Brachs)
Starlight Mints (Brachs)
Jelly Wreaths and Trees
(Brachs)
Ribbon Candy (Brachs)
Pastel Mints (Richardson)
Gumdrops (Brachs)
Lifesavers
Hard Candy
Spice Drop Candy (Sweets
and Treats Candy Shop at
Old Capitol Mall, Iowa
City)
Christmas Gummy Bear
(Sweets and Treats)
Mini Fruit Balls (Sweets and
Treats)
Rock Candy (Sweets and
Treats)
Fruit Flavored Ices (Baskin
Robbins)
Orange Ice (Sealtest)
Carbonated Beverages
Apple Juice, Apple Cider
Cranberry Juice
Wine
Whiskey (mixed with water)
Candied Apricots, Cherries,
Citron, Lemons, Oranges

Use Caution with These
Raw Vegetables:
Carrot Sticks (not more
than 4 [3″] sticks)
Celery sticks (not
more than 3 [3″]
sticks)
Broccoli (not more than
1 florette)
Cherry Tomato (not
more than 1 small)
Radishes (not more
than 5 small)
Mushrooms (not more
than 2 tablespoons)
Fruits:
Kumquat, raw (not
more than 1 average)
Apple, raw (not more
than ½ large)
Cranberry-Orange
Relish (not more than
¼ cup)
Pear, raw with skin (not
more than ½
medium)
Pineapple, raw, cubed
(not more than ¼ cup)
Potato Chips (not more
than ¼ cup)
Mayonnaise Dips (not
more than 1 tablespoon)
Salad Dressing Dips (i.e.,
Miracle Whip) (not
more than 2
tablespoons)

Stop!
Sour Cream Dips
Chocolate Candies
Fudge
Meat and Cheese
Appetizers and
Snacks
Nuts
Peanut Brittle
Cheese Spreads
Ice Cream
Munchies: Pretzels,
Crackers, Popcorn,
Melba Toast, Bread
Sticks, Potato Chips,
(over ¼ cup), Cheese
Curls, Corn Chips

Source: Courtesy of Lisa Brooks.

Adherence Tool 11-11 Informational Device

Birthday Card

[Insert Recipe Here]   Happy
                                        Birthday

                                        Linda Barry
                                        John Max
                                        Larry Joe
                                        Amy

Chocolate Cake

Number of Servings 12   Recipe makes 1 12-inch by 8-inch cake

1 cup margarine   ¼ teaspoon salt
½ cup cocoa   2 teaspoons vanilla extract
2 cups granulated sugar   ¾ cup chopped walnuts
4 teaspoons egg replacer mixed with   1 cup miniature marshmallows
   8 tablespoons water
1½ cups low-protein baking mix

1. Microwave margarine and cocoa in 2½-quart glass casserole dish at high for 2 minutes.
2. Stir in sugar.
3. Add eggs and beat well.
4. Blend in flour, salt, vanilla, and nuts.
5. Pour batter into a 12-inch by 8-inch glass baking dish.
6. Microwave at high 10 to 11 minutes; rotate dish ½ turn after 5 minutes.
7. Leave cake in pan, spread miniature marshmallows over warm cake.
8. Top with fudge frosting.

Fudge Frosting

½ cup margarine   1 pound box powdered sugar
⅓ cup Rich's liquid coffee creamer   dash of salt
2 tablespoons cocoa   1 teaspoon vanilla extract

1. Microwave margerine, Rich's liquid coffee creamer, and cocoa in a 2-quart glass casserole dish at high for 2 minutes.
2. Stir in sugar, salt, and vanilla.
3. Spread on warm cake.

Adherence Tool 11-11 continued

Note: Do not freeze.

Protein	3.4 grams	Serving Size: 1/12 cake
HBV* Protein	0.3 gram	Serving Weight: 130 grams
LBV** Protein	3.1 grams	
Calories	625	
Phosphorus	104 milligrams	

*HBV = High Biological Value
**LBV = Low Biological Value

Adherence Tool 11-12 Informational Device

Low-Protein Foods for Your Diet	
Item Description	Company

Adherence Tool 11-13 Cueing Device

Pill Box

	M	T	W	T	F	S	S
Morning							
Noon							
Evening							
Bed							

Adherence Tool 11-14 Cueing Device

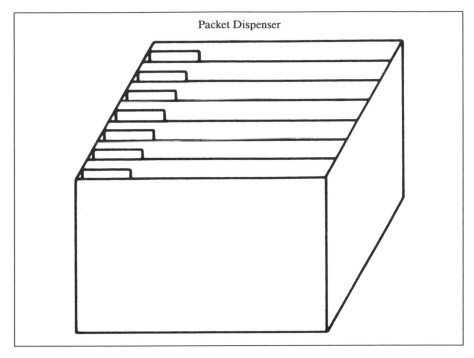

Packet Dispenser

Adherence Tool 11-15 Cueing Device

Vacation Postcard

Your travel checklist

Have you

Yes	No	
☐	☐	Temporarily cancelled the newspaper
☐	☐	Put a stop on mail delivery
☐	☐	Locked all doors and windows
☐	☐	Counted your medication pills packets and added ones in case you stay longer than planned
☐	☐	Packed your favorite medication shaker and mixer
☐	☐	Obtained a medication letter for customs clearance if traveling abroad
☐	☐	Checked and fueled your car, if driving
☐	☐	Left your destination phone number with a friend
☐	☐	Confirmed all reservations

Adherence Tool 11-16 Cueing Device

Calendars

One-Month

Sun.	Mon.	Tues.	Wed.	Thur.	Fri.	Sat.

month of _____ 19 _____   If you have any questions, please call: _____

One-Week

NAME: _____

ATTN: _____   THANK YOU!

Adherence Tool 11-17 Reinstituting Commitment

Contract I

During the week of January 2 (January 2–9) I agree to limit my monitoring of medication to every other day. For all other weeks in the month of January, I will monitor daily. I will record the exact amount of medication I take at breakfast, lunch, and dinner on the calendar provided. Each evening, I will allow myself to watch TV, call my friend, or read a book if I have been successful in recording for that week. If I fail to achieve this goal on designated weeks (all of those other than the week of January 2) I will not allow myself to engage in any of these behaviors. I will not reinforce during the week of January 2.

I understand that this break in my monitoring will be only temporary. Once life is back to normal (following the week of January 2) I will return to my old routine on January 10.

_____ Client

_____ Spouse/Parent/Friend

_____ Nutrition Counselor

_____ Physician

Adherence Tool 11-18 Reinstituting Commitment

Contract II

During the week of February 3 (February 3–9) I agree to limit my dietary intake to the new and temporary exchange list (.7 grams per kilogram of protein per day) provided by my dietitian. Each day that I successfully follow this exchange pattern, I will reward myself by reading a book, going shopping, or visiting my cousin. If I do not follow the diet on a day, I will not allow myself to engage in any of these behaviors.

I recognize that this change in diet is temporary. On February 10 I will return to an intermediate dietary exchange pattern (.65 grams per kilogram of protein per day). On February 17 I will return to my old exchange pattern (.6 grams per kilogram of protein per day).

_____ Client

_____ Spouse/Parent/Friend

_____ Nutrition Counselor

_____ Physician

Adherence Tool 11-19 Reinstituting Commitment

Record of Monologues		
Time	Food Eaten	Thoughts

Review of Chapter 11
(Answers in Appendix I)

1. List four factors associated with inappropriate eating behaviors when following a protein-modified eating pattern:

   a. _____

   b. _____

   c. _____

   d. _____

2. Identify five possible nutrients that should be identified as to baseline intake:

   a. _____

   b. _____

   c. _____

   d. _____

   e. _____

3. List four strategies to treat inappropriate eating behaviors associated with protein-modified patterns:

   a. _____

   b. _____

   c. _____

   d. _____

4. The following is an exercise to help in applying the ideas just discussed:

   John is a 31-year-old minister who eats all of his meals at home except for a few social gatherings. His major problem is his wife's reluctance to help him modify his diet because she feels there are too many restrictions. Explain what you would do, and why, to change the wife's feelings about the diet. (Don't presume the significant other's behavior will change.)

_____

_____

_____

_____

_____

_____

_____

_____

_____

_____

_____

NOTES

1. American Dietetic Association, *Handbook of Clinical Dietetics* (New Haven, Conn: Yale University Press, 1981), pp. C9–C22.

2. Barry M. Brenner, Timothy W. Meyer, and Thomas H. Hostetter, "Dietary Protein Intake and the Progressive Nature of Kidney Disease," *New England Journal of Medicine* 307 (1982): 652–659.

3. Thomas Addis, "The Ratio Between the Urea Content of the Urine and the Blood After the Administration of Large Quantities of Urea: An Approximate Index of the Quantity of Actively Functioning Kidney Tissue," *Journal of Urology* 1 (1917): 263–287; and *Glomerular Nephritis: Diagnosis and Treatment* (New York: Macmillan, 1948).

4. Lloyd S. Ibels et al., "Preservation of Function in Experimental Renal Disease by Dietary Phosphate Restriction," *New England Journal of Medicine* 298 (1978): 122–126.

5. Brenner, Meyer, and Hostetter, "Dietary Protein."

6. Thomas H. Hostetter et al., "Hyperfiltration in Remnant Nephrons: A Potentially Adverse Response to Renal Ablation," *American Journal of Physiology* 241 (1981): F83–F93; and Jean L. Olson et al., "Altered Glomerular Permeability and Progressive Sclerosis Following Ablation of Renal Mass," *Kidney International* 22 (1982): 112–126.

7. Hostetter et al., "Hyperfiltration in Remnant Nephrons"; Olson, "Altered Glomerular Permeability"; Isidro Salusky et al., "Prolonged Renal Survival and Stunting with Protein-Deficient Diets in Experimental Uremia," *Journal of Laboratory Clinical Medicine* 97 (1981): 21–30; Lee E. Farr and Joseph E. Smadel, "The Effect of Dietary Protein on the Course of

Nephrotoxic Nephritis in Rats," *Journal of Experimental Medicine* 70 (1939): 615–627; and Peter S. Friend et al., "Dietary Restrictions Early and Late: Effects on the Nephropathy of the NZB x NZW Mouse," *Laboratory Investigation* 38 (1978): 629–632.

8. Carmelo Giordano, "Prolongation of Survival for a Decade or More by Low Protein Diet," in Carmelo Giordano and Eli A. Friedman, eds., *Pathobiology of Patients Treated for 10 Years or More* (Milan: Wichtig Editore Srl, 1981), p. 100; and Giuseppe Maschio et al., "Effects of Dietary Protein and Phosphorus Restriction on the Progression of Early Renal Failure," *Kidney International* 22 (1982): 371–376.

9. Saulo Klahr, John Buerkert, and Mabel L. Purkerson, "Role of Dietary Factors in the Progression of Chronic Renal Disease," *Kidney International* 24 (1983): 579–587.

10. Gordon L. Bilbrey et al., "Hyperglucagonemia of Renal Failure," *Journal of Clinical Investigation* 53 (1974): 841–847; and Ralph A. DeFronzo and Anders Alvestrand, "Glucose Intolerance in Uremia: Site and Mechanism," *American Journal of Clinical Nutrition* 33 (1980): 1438–1445.

11. C. Giordano, M. Pluvio, and R. Esposito, "Urea Index and Nitrogen Balance in Uremic Patients on Minimal Nitrogen Intakes," *Clinical Nephrology* 3 (1975): 168–171.

12. Report of a Joint FAO/WHO Ad Hoc Expert Committee, *Energy and Protein Requirements* (Geneva: World Health Organization, 1973), p. 55.

13. Joel D. Kopple, "Nutritional Therapy in Kidney Failure," *Nutrition Review* 39 (1981): 193–206.

14. Joel D. Kopple, J.K. Shaib, and F. Monteon, "Energy Expenditure in Chronic Renal Failure and Hemodialysis Patients" (Abstract), *American Journal of Nephrology* (1983): 50A.

15. American Dietetic Association, *Handbook of Clinical Dietetics*, pp. C9, C16; and S. R. Acchiardo, L. W. Moore, and S. Cockrell, "Does Low Protein Diet Halt the Progression of Renal Insufficiency?" *Clinical Nephrology* 25 (1986): 289–294.

16. William E. Mitch et al., "The Effect of a Keto Acid-Amino Acid Supplement to a Restricted Diet on the Progression of Chronic Renal Failure," *The New England Journal of Medicine* 311 (1984): 623–629; Mitch, Elias Abras, and Mackenzie Walser, "Long-term Effects of a New Ketoacid-Amino Acid Supplement in Patients with Chronic Renal Failure," *Kidney International* 22 (1982): 48–53; and Walser, Mitch, and Abras, "Supplements Containing Amino Acids and Keto Acids in the Treatment of Chronic Uremia," *Kidney International* 24 (1983): S285–S289.

17. Dieter Kampf, Hans-Ch. Fischer, and Michael Kessel, "Efficacy of an Unselected Protein Diet (25 grams) with Minor Oral Supply of Essential Amino Acids and Keto Analogues Compared with a Selective Protein Diet (40 grams) in Chronic Renal Failure," *American Journal of Clinical Nutrition* 33 (1980): 1673–1677.

18. Mackenzie Walser, "Nutrition in Renal Failure," *Annals of the Review of Nutrition* 3 (1983): 133–134.

19. Mitch et al., "The Effect of a Keto Acid-Amino Acid Supplement," p. 623.

20. Joel D. Kopple et al., "Amino Acid and Protein Metabolism in Renal Failure," *American Journal of Clinical Nutrition* 31 (1978): 1532–1540; and C. Giordano, N. G. DeSanto, and M. Pluvio, "Nitrogen Balance in Uremic Patients on Different Amino Acid and Keto Acid Formulation—A Proposed Reference Pattern," *American Journal of Clinical Nutrition* 31 (1978): 1797–1801.

21. Michael R. Jones, Joel D. Kopple, and Marian E. Swendseid, "Phenylalanine Metabolism in Uremic and Normal Man," *Kidney International* 14 (1978): 169–179.

22. P. Fürst et al., "Principles of Essential Amino Acid Therapy in Uremia," *American Journal of Clinical Nutrition* 31 (1978): 1744–1755; and Joel D. Kopple and Marian E. Swendseid, "Evidence that Histidine is an Essential Amino Acid in Normal and Chronically Uremic Man," *Journal of Clinical Investigation* 55 (1975): 881–891.

23. Giordano, DeSanto, and Pluvio, "Nitrogen Balance."

24. Ibels et al., "Preservation of Function"; and Robert C. Tomford et al., "Effect of Thyroparathyroidectomy and Parathyroidectomy on Renal Function and Nephrotic Syndrome in Rat Nephrotoxic Serum Nephritis," *Journal of Clinical Investigation* 68 (1981): 655–664.

25. Walser, "Nutrition in Renal Failure," pp. 125–154.

26. Ibid.

27. Robert E. Sparks et al., "Maximizing Phosphate Capacity of Aluminum-Based Gels," *Kidney International* 13 (1978) (Supplement 8): S160–162.

28. Walser, "Nutrition in Renal Failure," p. 140.

29. Jack W. Coburn et al., "Intestinal Absorption of Calcium, Magnesium, and Phosphorus in Chronic Renal Insufficiency" in David S. David, ed., *Calcium Metabolism in Renal Failure and Nephronlithiasis* (New York: John Wiley & Sons, 1977), pp. 77–109.

30. Claudio C. Marone et al., "Acidosis and Renal Calcium Excretion in Experimental Chronic Renal Failure," *Nephron* 28 (1981): 294–296.

31. Coburn et al., *Calcium Metabolism in Renal Failure and Nephronlithiasis,* p. 402.

32. Th. Friis, S. Hahnemann, and E. Weeke, "Serum Calcium and Serum Phosphorus in Uraemia During Administration of Sodium Phytate and Aluminum Hydroxide," *Acta Medica Scandinavica* 183 (1968): 497–505.

33. G. M. Berlyne, "Calcium Carbonate Treatment of Uremic Acidosis," *Israel Journal of Medical Science* 7 (1971): 1235–1239; and Dwight L. Makoff et al., "Chronic Calcium Carbonate Therapy in Uremia," *Archives of International Medicine* 123 (1969): 15–21.

34. Gary T. Wollam et al., "Diuretic Potency of Combined Hydrochlorothiazide and Furosemide Therapy in Patients with Azotemia," *American Journal of Medicine* 72 (1982): 929–938.

35. Frank Rees Smith and DeWitt S. Goodman, "The Effects of Diseases in Liver, Thyroid and Kidneys on Transport of Vitamin A in Human Plasma," *Journal of Clinical Investigation* 50 (1971): 2426–2436.

36. S. Mahajan et al., "Zinc Metabolism and Taste Acuity in Renal Transplant Recipients," *Clinical Research* 30 (1982): 246A (Abstract).

37. Harry S. Abram, Gordon L. Moore, and Frederic B. Westervelt, "Suicidal Behavior in Chronic Hemodialysis Patients," *American Journal of Psychiatry* 127 (1971): 1199–1204; Sue L. Blackburn, "Dietary Compliance of Chronic Hemodialysis Patients," *Journal of the American Dietetic Association* 70 (1977): 31–37; A. Kaplan De-Nour and J. W. Czaczkes, "Personality Factors in Chronic Hemodialysis Patients Causing Noncompliance with Medical Regimen," *Psychosomatic Medicine* 34 (1972): 333–344; and Eileen J. Shea et al., "Hemodialysis for Chronic Renal Failure. IV. Psychological Considerations," *Annals of Internal Medicine* 62 (1964): 558–564.

38. Susan H. Witenberg et al., "Evaluation of Compliance in Home and Center Hemodialysis Patients," *Health Psychology* 2 (1983): 227–237.

39. Myrl Manley and John Sweeney, "Assessment of Compliance in Hemodialysis Adaptation," *Journal of Psychosomatic Research* 30 (1986): 153–161.

40. Blackburn, "Dietary Compliance."

41. M. Rae Barnes, "Token Economy Control of Fluid Overload in a Patient Receiving Hemodialysis," *Journal of Behavioral Therapy in Experimental Psychiatry* 7 (1976): 305–306; Robert R. Hart, "Utilization of a Token Economy Within a Chronic Dialysis Unit," *Journal of Consulting Clinical Psychology* 47 (1979): 646–648; and Terence M. Keane, Donald M. Prue, and Frank L. Collins, "Behavioral Contracting to Improve Dietary Compliance in Chronic Renal Dialysis Patients," *Journal of Behavioral Therapy in Experimental Psychiatry* 12 (1981): 63–76.

42. Blackburn, "Dietary Compliance."

Chapter 12

Nutrition Counseling in Treatment of Hypertension

Objectives for Chapter 12

1. Identify factors that lead to inappropriate eating behaviors associated with sodium-modified regimens.
2. Identify important steps in the assessment of a baseline diet for clients following a sodium-modified eating pattern.
3. Identify strategies to treat inappropriate eating behaviors associated with sodium-modified patterns.
4. Generate strategies to use in facilitating problem solving for clients who are following sodium-modified patterns.
5. Recommend dietary adherence tools for clients on sodium-modified eating patterns.

Research on treating hypertension has focused primarily on the use of pharmacological agents. A report submitted by the Joint National Committee on Detection, Evaluation and Treatment of High Blood Pressure indicates that use of these agents must be balanced against the potential long-term adverse effects of drug treatment.[1] For persons with moderate to severe hypertension, the benefits of drug treatment outweigh the risks, but in milder levels of hypertension (diastolic blood pressure of 90–104 millimeters of mercury [mm Hg]) the benefits may not be compelling, according to the Joint National Committee.

The many options for nonpharmacological treatment of mild hypertension are an excellent addition to drug therapy for moderately to severely hypertensive patients. Three nonpharmacological approaches to treating hypertension are supported by sufficient scientific research to warrant recommendation by the 1984 Joint National Committee on Detection, Evaluation and Treatment of High Blood Pressure: weight control, alcohol restriction, and sodium restriction.[2] These forms of therapy may control blood pressure independently of drugs in the mildly hypertensive person and may make possible a reduction in the number and dosage of prescribed pharmacological agents for those with more severe hypertension.

Table 12-1 Blood Pressure Levels*

Diastolic Blood Pressure (millimeters of mercury)	Category
<85	Normal Blood Pressure
85–89	High Normal Blood Pressure
90–104	Mild Hypertension
105–114	Moderate Hypertension
>115	Severe Hypertension

Systolic Blood Pressure When Diastolic Blood Pressure Is <90 Millimeters of Mercury (millimeters of mercury)	Category
<140 mm Hg	Normal Blood Pressure
140–159 mm Hg	Borderline Isolated Systolic Hypertension
>160 mm Hg	Isolated Systolic Hypertension

*Borderline isolated systolic hypertension or isolated systolic hypertension takes precedence over a classification of high normal blood pressure when both occur in the same person. A classification of high normal blood pressure takes precedence over a classification of normal blood pressure when both occur in the same person.

Source: "Hypertension Prevalence and the Status of Awareness, Treatment, and Control in the United States" by Subcommittee on Definition and Prevalence of the 1984 Joint National Committee in *Hypertension,* Vol. 7, pp. 457–468, American Heart Association, Inc., ©1985.

THEORIES AND FACTS ABOUT NUTRITION AND HYPERTENSION

The Joint National Committee on Detection, Evaluation and Treatment of High Blood Pressure recommends the classification scheme in Table 12-1 for blood pressure levels.

Research on Weight Control

Epidemiological Research Relating Body Weight and Blood Pressure

A compelling body of evidence relates obesity to hypertension.[3] Many studies in epidemiology have shown the relationship of body weight and arterial pressure in both hypertensive and normotensive persons.[4] In smaller studies body weight and blood pressure have also been correlated in children and adolescents.[5] In adults relative body weight, body weight change over time, and skinfold thickness have been directly related to blood pressure levels and to subsequent rate of development of hypertension.[6] In addition, the risk of normotensive persons' later becoming hypertensive is related to the degree of overweight. Several additional studies have documented the importance of weight gain in subsequent development of hypertension.[7]

This research shows that obesity is an important coexisting and compounding problem in hypertensive disease. In young persons weight gain is a predisposing factor for later development of hypertension. In affluent cultures an increase in body weight with age may be a determinant of age-related rise in arterial pressure, which is common in these populations. Although hypertension is caused by various mechanisms, research indicates that one cause may be associated with obesity.

Mechanisms Explaining the Association between Hypertension and Obesity

Some of the mechanisms that have been proposed to explain the association between hypertension and obesity are (1) expanded blood volume, (2) elevated cardiac output associated with the volume expansion, (3) associated increased dietary sodium intake and increased vascular responsiveness to the sodium, and (4) increased adrenergic participation in obesity-related hypertension.[8] Since plasma volume does not seem to be contracted in obesity-related hypertension,[9] a volume overload seems to be added to an already increased left ventricular afterload. The dual load may account for the increased cardiovascular risk associated with obesity-hypertension. Dahl, Silver, and Christie suggested that hypertension occurs in obese persons sensitive to a high sodium intake associated with long-term calorie excess.[10] Several subsequent studies have shown the opposite.[11] Significant weight loss in the absence of a sodium-restricted diet resulted in either no fall in pressure or a smaller fall than when sodium was restricted,[12] but later research showed that weight loss lowered blood pressure without a restriction on sodium intake.[13]

Several investigators have suggested increased adrenergic participation in obese-hypertensive persons in whom plasma norepinephrine levels decreased with blood pressure. With associated negative salt and water balances, and presumably a contracted plasma volume, plasm renin activity failed to increase.[14] These researchers attributed altered adrenergic activity to the obesity-related hypertensive state.[15]

Methodological problems exist in much of the current research assessing the mechanisms that may explain the correlation between obesity and hypertension. The major problem is accuracy in determining the degree of obesity. Relative body weight has been the most common measure used, but it does not distinguish between large muscle mass and excessive body weight. The best method for determining lean body mass is underwater weighing, a cumbersome method that may deter volunteer participation. Skinfold thicknesses are easier but have not been assessed adequately over a wide range of degrees of obesity.[16]

Metabolic Research Relating Body Weight and Blood Pressure

Research provides a variety of evidence that weight reduction induced by calorie restriction lowers blood pressure. Experimental starvation studies have shown falls in systolic pressure from 104 mm Hg to 93 mm Hg and diastolic pressures from 70 mm Hg to 63 mm Hg. All subjects were normotensive. With refeeding, blood pressure values returned to prestarvation levels.[17]

Research correlating changes in blood pressure in hypertensive persons with changes in weight began in the 1920s. Rose showed that weight reduction resulted in lower pressures,[18] and later many researchers reported falls in blood pressure with weight loss.[19] One study, however, did not demonstrate a fall in blood pressure with weight reduction.[20] One Israeli study showed no difference in blood pressure pre- and post-weight loss when dietary sodium was controlled by adding supplementary sodium.[21] Long-term follow-up has shown that when persons regained lost weight, blood pressure rose to pretreatment levels.[22]

Several studies have shown that, in compliant persons with high blood pressure, weight reduction correlated closely with decreases in both systolic and diastolic pressures. One study showed that decreases in pressure correlated with the severity of pretreatment blood pressure.[23]

Clinical Trials Relating Body Weight and Blood Pressure

In the Chicago Coronary Prevention Evaluation Program, a considerable decrease in body weight was associated with decreases in pressure, heart rate, and serum cholesterol.[24] A later Israeli study indicated that most obese hypertensive persons achieved normal pressure when they lost only half of their excess weight, even though they remained very obese.[25] Achieving ideal body weight was not crucial to reducing blood pressure, and the pressure fall persisted as long as the decreased body weight was maintained. The Dusseldorf Obesity study showed that, for hypertensive persons not receiving antihypertensive medication over four and one-half years, the pressure fall was greatest in those who lost 12 kilograms.[26] In another study, the decrease in blood pressure in subjects who lost weight was associated with contraction of plasma volume and a decline in cardiac output, which in turn was related to slower heart rate and decreases in plasma cholesterol, uric acid, and blood glucose.[27]

Conclusion

Basic conclusions from these studies follow:

1. Increased body mass is clearly related to elevated blood pressure.
2. Decreases in blood pressure can be expected when weight is reduced.
3. Cardiovascular morbidity and mortality will decrease even if pressure does not, and for persons on antihypertensive drugs the number and/or dosage of these agents may be reduced.
4. These associations do not explain why blood pressure is not elevated in all obese persons or why pressures do not decline in all obese hypertensives who lose weight.

The 1984 Joint National Committee on Detection, Evaluation, and Treatment of High Blood Pressure makes the following recommendations:

1. Weight reduction is recommended for all obese persons with hypertension. Antihypertensive drugs are recommended if pressure is not controlled by weight loss in persons with milder degrees of hypertension.
2. For persons with severe hypertension, weight loss is not a substitute for initiating antihypertensive drug treatment.[28]

Research on Dietary Sodium Restriction

A second nonpharmacological method for controlling high blood pressure is restricting dietary sodium. Only a few well-controlled studies have examined the effects of moderate sodium restriction in persons with mild hypertension. All were short-term and involved a small number of subjects. The results of these studies were mixed. In a study by MacGregor et al. mean blood pressure was significantly lower in subjects on a low-sodium than on a high-sodium intake.[29] Results of a similar study by Watt et al. showed no difference in pressures of subjects on high- and low-sodium intake.[30] An interesting finding in this study was that pressures were significantly lower in both groups during the control period on unrestricted salt intake. A third study conducted by Richards et al. showed no difference in pressures between subjects on the high-sodium and low-sodium regimens.[31]

In a larger but less well controlled study, compliance with diet based on urinary sodium excretion showed a mean value of 197 milliequivalents during a control period, with a decrease in urinary sodium excretion to 70 milliequivalents in the sodium-restricted period. The mean blood pressure results from the control period to the sodium-restricted period were 121 and 119 mm Hg, respectively.[32] Parfrey et al. found that blood pressures fell 8 mm Hg with a change from a five-day regimen of 350 milliequivalents of sodium to a five-day regimen of 10 milliequivalents of sodium.[33] Silman et al. showed a blood pressure decline in both the control and experimental groups.[34] Mean daily urinary sodium excretion varied from 159 milliequivalents in the control group to 117 milliequivalents in the low-sodium (experimental) group. This study was hampered by many confounding variables that were not controlled statistically. For example, the control group received exercise, weight reduction, and relaxation training, interventions that may have altered their pressures.

Beard et al. conducted a similar study.[35] Even drastic reductions in sodium intake and corresponding reductions in urinary sodium excretion from 150 to 37 milliequivalents resulted in no differences in blood pressures between groups. However, groups on both high- and low-sodium intakes demonstrated significant declines in blood pressure, and persons on low-sodium diets were able to discontinue or greatly reduce their antihypertensive medications. This was not true for the control group.

Persons whose blood pressures increase with high sodium intake and decrease with low sodium intake have been termed a salt-sensitive subset with essential hypertension.[36] Recently published data from the Dietary Intervention Study in Hypertension show that reducing dietary sodium in those whose hypertension has been under control for five years doubles the success of reducing drug therapy.[37] Because no long-term trials have measured pressure reduction in the general population, the generalizability of a moderately restricted sodium diet and its long-term effect on the entire hypertensive population are not known. The 1984 Joint National Committee on Detection, Evaluation and Treatment of High Blood Pressure recommends this method of treating hypertension on a trial basis in most persons with hypertension because moderate sodium restriction (less than 2 grams per day*) apparently causes no harm.[38]

Research on Alcohol

A third important nonpharmacological method of helping to lower blood pressure is reduction in alcohol consumption. Epidemiological surveys have shown that consuming more than 60 to 80 grams (1-1/2 to 2 ounces) of alcohol per day is associated with a significantly higher prevalence of hypertension.[39] In one study 51.5

---

*To convert milliequivalents (mEq) to milligrams (mg) of sodium: one milliequivalent of sodium is 23 milligrams, the gram-atomic weight. A diet prescription of 40 milliequivalents of sodium equals 920 milligrams of sodium (23 mg × 40 mEq = 920 mg). Sodium chloride contains 39.3 percent sodium. This means that 10 grams of salt contain 3.93 grams of sodium (10 × 0.393 = 3.93 grams).

percent of clients who consumed more than 80 grams of alcohol per day had hypertension (blood pressure greater than 140/90 mm Hg) on admission to a hospital.[40] Following elimination of alcohol, systolic and diastolic pressures decreased; only 9 percent remained hypertensive. Those who abstained from alcohol over time remained normotensive; most of those who reverted back to drinking also reverted to previous elevated levels of blood pressure.

Although these studies point to the importance of abstinence from the standpoint of hypertension, almost all epidemiological evidence has shown lower morbidity and mortality from coronary heart disease in people who consume one to two ounces of ethanol per day compared with those who do not drink.[41] Thus alcohol may protect against coronary heart disease while causing myocardial damage and hypertension.[42]

The 1984 Joint National Committee on Detection, Evaluation and Treatment of High Blood Pressure makes the following recommendations about alcohol:

1. Alcohol intake should be assessed in all persons with hypertension.
2. Because it is often difficult to achieve normal blood pressures in persons with high alcohol intake, a reduction to 2 ounces per day is recommended (2 ounces of 100-proof whiskey, 8 ounces of wine, or 24 ounces of beer, each of which contains 1 ounce of alcohol). If blood pressures are still high, abstinence is advised.
3. No change is necessary for persons who consume 2 ounces of alcohol or less per day.[43]

Research on Potassium

The trials of dietary potassium supplementation in clients with mild essential hypertension have not been convincing. No data are available on short-term or long-term compliance or on the risks and the effects of potassium, and equally important, long-term effects on blood pressure remain unknown.[44]

Research on Calcium, Magnesium, and Trace Elements

An increasing body of knowledge emanating from epidemiological studies, clinical research, and animal studies suggests that dietary calcium influences blood pressure. Because of the complexities of calcium's role in the regulation of pressure and in the pathogenesis of hypertension, the fragile nature of some of the epidemiologically documented inverse associations between dietary calcium and blood pressure, and the paucity of data collected on hypertensive clients receiving oral calcium supplements, it seems premature to recommend to the public or to hypertensive clients in particular changes in their intake of dietary calcium or in the use of calcium supplements. The preliminary data suggest that if augmenting dietary calcium or using supplements is good for clients with hypertension, it is probably good only for yet undefined subsets. Additionally, data are insufficient to ascertain the hazards of exposing entire populations of either normotensive or hypertensive people to increasing amounts of dietary calcium or supplemental calcium in pill form. Before such precise recommendations can be made, more information is needed about the basic mechanisms by which calcium affects blood pressure, both to establish which clients are most likely to benefit by increasing their intake of dietary or supplemental calcium and to determine the optimal doses.[45]

Recommendations about the increasing dietary sources of magnesium or magnesium supplements are also premature until more is known about the role of magnesium in blood pressure regulation and hypertension. Moreover, no firm data suggest that any of the trace elements play a major role in the pathogenesis of hypertension, at least not in a significant number of hypertensive persons.[46]

In conclusion, three methods of treatment—weight control, sodium restriction, and alcohol restriction—are recommended for management of hypertension. Evidence is too meager to justify recommendations about other nutrients in relation to hypertension. The research behind recommendations for low-calorie, low-sodium diets adds strength to the overall objective of reducing high blood pressure. The following sections provide examples of inappropriate eating behaviors, methods of assessing those behaviors, and strategies for dealing with problems of lack of knowledge, forgetfulness, and lack of commitment to low-sodium methods of altering high blood pressure. Indeed, persons who are hypertensive at ideal body weight may require only the low-sodium diet to normalize blood pressure. Suggestions for weight loss are covered in Chapter 8.

The third nonpharmacological method of treating high blood pressure—reduction in alcohol consumption—can be as easy as asking the client to reduce intake. On the other hand, the process may be difficult and require referral to a program like Alcoholics Anonymous. This chapter does not deal with this aspect of treatment.

RESEARCH ON ADHERENCE TO EATING PATTERNS IN TREATMENT OF HYPERTENSION

Steckel and Swain found contingency contracting effective in reducing weight in a hypertensive client population.[47] Further, a feasibility test for the Dietary Intervention Study of Hypertension showed that interventions for weight reduction and sodium-potassium modification among hypertensives can be relatively independent,[48] implying that a hypertension education program could be divided into these components or that these interventions could be used separately.

Monitoring of and feedback on urinary sodium levels resulted in successful sodium reductions in studies by Kaplan et al. and Nugent et al.[49] The simplification of urine sodium estimation procedures through use of overnight instead of 24-hour urine samples and immediate feedback by analysis using chloride titrator strips are important advances in the practicality of these monitoring techniques.

Hovell et al. stressed the importance of regular monitoring of both behavioral (pill counts) and physiological outcome (blood pressure) data to avoid accidentally blaming clients for inadequate therapeutic response.[50] Indeed, a client may be an excellent adherer but show little physiological response if treatment is inappropriate or inadequate. Evers and associates suggested that the primary cause of dietary noncompliance may be inadequate dietary counseling.[51] Nurses trained by the medical director, a physician, counseled 489 subjects, who received information on the causes and results of hypertension and the elimination of salt at the table and in cooking, and discussed lists of high-sodium foods and substitutes. The 512 subjects in the control group were treated by family physicians in their usual manner, which generally included advice to restrict salt usage but no intensive dietary counseling or extra assistance. The failure to note differences in the two groups in this study was attributed to a lack of nutrition counseling as described by Tillotson, Winston, and Hall and others.[52] Evers also stated that the counseling sessions involved only the client; yet family support has been found to be important in successful adherence to dietary regimens.[53]

A study in Finland showed favorable results when cooperation between physician and client improved.[54] Physicians began providing information on hypertension, both orally and in writing, that emphasized the importance of adherence to treatment. Clients also received a blood pressure follow-up card on which the blood pressure reading and the precise time of the next appointment were recorded. Clients who missed their appointments were sent a new invitation.

Miller, Weinberger, and Cohen stressed the importance of clients' believing that the benefits of hypertensive treatment outweigh the adverse effects.[55] Many clients believe that taking medicine should make them feel better. Since hypertension is an asymptomatic illness, the client does not obtain symptom relief from the medication or diet.

Kerr stated that in chronic health care situations such as hypertension, a belief in shared control or cooperation between clients and health providers lays the groundwork for optimum treatment outcomes.[56] This finding suggests that other, internal and powerful characteristics may interact in the best interests of the client. Shared responsibility in control of hypertension may be critical to increasing adherence in the client with uncontrolled hypertension.

Schlundt, McDonel, and Langford and Cohen described components of a structured behavior modification program: (1) self-monitoring of sodium and/or calorie intake, (2) nutrient and behavior goal setting, (3) structured problem solving, and (4) skill training.[57] Prevention of relapse should be addressed in the context of emotional, social, and environmental forces that impinge upon the individual's behavior. Elements in the relapse prevention program include (1) introducing the client to the concept of high-risk situations and assessing previous coping strategies; (2) including skill training and behavior rehearsal to increase the client's coping skills in response to negative emotions, interpersonal conflict, and social pressure; (3) enhancing motivation through an emphasis on the long-term consequences of engaging in prohibited behaviors; (4) teaching clients how to cope cognitively and behaviorally with slips; (5) tailoring the rules of a low-sodium–weight-loss eating pattern to the individual's unique situation; (6) teaching strategies for minimizing high-risk situations; and (7) teaching clients to seek and enhance the social support available for following an antihypertensive eating pattern. Schlundt and coworkers also stressed the importance of follow-up contact after completion of the initial program and recommended individual counseling, group meetings, telephone contact, and regular mail contact for at least the first three to six months,[58] the time the majority of relapses occur.[59]

INAPPROPRIATE EATING BEHAVIORS

Diets modified in sodium content may be extremely difficult for most clients with whom nutrition counselors must deal. Salt is used as a flavoring agent in nearly every food. Altering such dietary habits means drastic changes for most clients.

Counselors frequently hear the complaint, "I really miss familiar flavors" or "Everything I eat tastes like sawdust." For unconscious salters (those who salt without tasting), the true flavors of foods may never have come through. They can gradually discover the natural flavors in foods through treatments suggested in this chapter.

The new eating pattern limits their food options because most commercial products are very high in sodium. With the trend toward prepackaged commercial meals

Exhibit 12-1 Sodium Intake Information

Food	Amount		Time	Place	Who Present
	In Cooking	At Table			

and other products, clients on a low-sodium regimen are left with fewer choices. This limitation has led to many alterations in old eating habits. Clients not only must change what they usually eat but also must become accustomed to a new and foreign range of food flavors.

The food industry, in an effort to assist these persons, has developed a variety of low-salt products. However, these generate comments such as, "You expect me to eat this low-sodium soup? It's terrible." Another complaint is that some salt substitutes leave a bitter aftertaste. Objections to commercial low-sodium products constitute a recurring problem for nutrition counselors.

ASSESSMENT OF EATING BEHAVIORS

For clients who must follow a low-sodium diet, a baseline assessment is crucial. Such regimens require changes in many foods individuals routinely and even unconsciously consume. Identifying when, where, with whom, and how much sodium is consumed can be of great benefit in helping to reduce salt intake patterns. The format in Exhibit 12-1 can be used to collect baseline data.

In collecting this information the clients are self-monitoring their sodium intake. Before using the form, clients should be asked simply to observe their general behaviors involving sodium consumption, i.e., salting before tasting. They should be told which basic foods are high in sodium.

During the baseline data collection clients begin counting sodium intake occurrences, along with collecting related information indicated in the form. These guidelines can be of help:

1. The form must be portable and readily available for recording.
2. Clients must be familiar enough with high-sodium foods to record all occurrences of the target behavior (sodium intake).
3. Clients should record the data as the behaviors occur.
4. Clients always should keep written records—memory is not adequate for baseline data collection.[60]

During this period, some changes in behavior may occur automatically and make the nutrition counselors' job that much easier. Unfortunately, not all clients respond with behavior changes during this time, and some need guidance in the treatment phase. Counselors also should emphasize to clients that treatment interventions should begin after, not before, the baseline data collection.

One important factor during data collection is clients' increasing awareness of and attention to sodium intake. For example, during a meal they may become conscious of salting food before tasting. They also should elicit help from friends and family. There are many ways family members can delicately and supportively word their attempts to point out excessive use of sodium.

Clients should never allow recordkeeping to become a punishment, so counselors must help find ways to reinforce this function positively.

Clients should be aware of how important the baseline data are in identifying types of foods, amounts, and related factors—information that will improve their adherence to the dietary pattern. At this point they might well ask, "How long should I keep baseline data?" The reply depends on several factors:

1. The data collection should continue for at least one week, since the intake of sodium occurs daily.
2. It is best to gather data for two weeks if an initial review reveals large variations in sodium intake from one day to the next.
3. Data should be recorded for a long enough time to provide a good estimate of when in a day the largest amounts of sodium are consumed.
4. Data gathering can end when clients and counselors are satisfied that the records show the actual patterns and frequencies of sodium intake.[61]

Clients also may wonder when they will know a stable baseline has been reached. Watson and Tharp provide the following guidelines:

1. It is rare to get a stable baseline in less than one week. It generally should run at least one "normal" week and should go beyond three or four weeks only rarely.
2. The greater the variation from day to day, the longer it will take to get a stable baseline.
3. Clients should be asked to be sure the period during which the data were gathered is representative of their usual life style.[62]

In helping clients fill out the recording form, counselors should ask:

1. Are the categories to be recorded defined specifically?
2. Are both sodium intakes and related factors recorded?
3. Will the form always be present during times of food consumption?
4. Is the format simple and not punishing or intimidating?
5. Is it possible to reinforce the recordkeeping positively?[63]

Questions that focus on sodium intake are provided in Adherence Tool 9-1. These questions might also be used to supplement the client eating questionnaire (Adherence Tool 8-1) which addresses the issue of weight control.

The Food Diary Form in Exhibit 8-1 can identify a wealth of information related to eventual treatment. Assessment based on this form can lead to identification of causes of weight gain and of strategies to achieve and maintain ideal body weight.

TREATMENT STRATEGIES

The treatment strategies that follow are organized around three topics—lack of knowledge, forgetfulness, and lack of commitment.

Strategies To Deal with Lack of Knowledge

Initially, providing adequate information for the client who wishes to follow a low-sodium diet is crucial. Before recommending treatment strategies, counselors should identify a general problem to solve first. Along with the statement of that problem, inappropriate regular eating patterns should be identified. Clients should be asked to help discover possible solutions, with the counselors providing expertise by drawing from the strategies described next.

Tailoring and staging strategies help focus the dietary pattern on the clients' special needs. Behavior change is necessary for social occasions and for the routine alterations in eating style that the regimen requires.

Most nutrition counselors provide lists of standard do's and don'ts for low-sodium eating patterns. These do not allow for individualizing eating patterns to meet each client's needs. The counselors should tailor the eating pattern to the clients, first by carefully studying the baseline information. Attention must be paid not only to consumption of sodium but also to other factors associated with its intake. If clients have a favorite high-sodium food, the counselors can discuss how it might be incorporated to meet a 2,000-milligram sodium limit, cautioning that other foods containing sodium may have to be eliminated or reduced. Compromises as to the amount of the favorite foods allowed should be discussed as well.

In tailoring, the counselors should point out which foods on the diet record qualify for the sodium-restricted eating pattern. Foods the clients routinely eat and like should be discussed and the reasons for full acceptance, curtailment, or elimination explained. Any and all positive aspects of the low-sodium eating pattern should be emphasized.

Staging the diet can be crucial in maintaining adherence over time. It is very tempting for counselors to hand clients a list of foods high in sodium and send them on their way complaining that they never will be able to follow the diet. In beginning the staging process there are two simple rules: (1) it can never begin too low and (2) the steps upward can never be too small. As the interviews progress, these rules should be individualized for each client. If the sessions move too slowly, the counselors can move up a step or discuss fewer steps. This type of staging helps clients feel that changes are easy and, therefore, that their chances for success are increased. Staging also can help in analysis of the component parts of these situations.

An alternative to this approach is to stage the dietary restrictions for sodium, with the clients slowly adjusting to sets of restrictions. One way is to start with the group of foods easiest to begin using in low-sodium form, enabling clients to succeed with the initial group. The baseline data can be used to prepare lists in consultation with clients.

A common experience in following staging schedules is the plateau. Week after week clients may make excellent progress, then suddenly stop. Moving up through all the previous steps may have seemed so easy, but now a new one—the same size as all the rest—seems very difficult. The easiest way to continue to progress is to subdivide the difficult step. If this does not help, the counselors should try increasing reinforcement.

Many clients confide to practitioners that they are guilty of cheating—taking the reinforcers even though they have not achieved a particular step. In such cases, the counselors must redesign the staged schedule so clients can be reinforced at a level they find achievable.

Some clients complain that they are losing the willpower to follow the low-sodium diet. They may experience this in two ways: If they cannot get started, counselors and clients may not have set the initial step low enough. This can be resolved by moving to a lower step. If they have started but insist that they see no progress, smaller steps are necessary.

In changing eating behaviors counselors must review with clients the sequence antecedent-behavior-consequence. The counselors begin to identify antecedents (events that precede a behavior) by asking the clients to think about the following questions as they relate to an eating occurrence:

1. What were the physical circumstances? (i.e., was the client surrounded by large tables of food?)
2. What was the social setting?
3. What was the behavior of others?
4. What did you think or say to yourself?[64]

The client should be asked to collect data on these antecedents.

One tactic in changing eating behaviors is to lengthen the chain of events before partaking of a desired item such as high-sodium cheese. By pausing before eating, immediate gratification is delayed and the behavior eventually may not occur at all. It also may be possible to interrupt the chain by identifying an early link; a discontinuance or prolonged pause at that point may prevent the inappropriate behavior. The events also may be scrambled so that the eventual behavior is never reached.

Another strategy is to provide good substitutions for salt—other flavoring agents such as spices, herbs, fruit juices, etc.—as proposed in Table 12-2. Adherence Tool 12-1 provides a brief guide to low-sodium meal planning and space to practice applying the ideas. The average sodium content of all spices is less than 1 milligram

Table 12-2 Chart of Spices That Can Substitute for Salt

Spice	APPETIZER	SOUP	MEAT & EGGS	FISH & POULTRY	SAUCES	VEGETABLES	SALAD & DRESSING	DESSERTS
Allspice	Cocktail Meatballs	Pot Au Feu	Hamsteak	Oyster Stew	Barbecue	Eggplant Creole	Cottage Cheese Dressing	Apple Tapioca Pudding
Basil	Cheese Stuffed Celery	Manhattan Clam Chowder	Ragout of Beef	Shrimp Creole	Spaghetti	Stewed Tomatoes	Russian Dressing	
Bay Leaf	Pickled Beets	Vegetable Soup	Lamb Stew	Simmered Chicken	Bordelaise	Boiled New Potatoes	Tomato Juice Dressing	
Caraway Seed	Mild Cheese Spreads		Sauerbraten		Beef a la Mode Sauce	Cabbage Wedges		
Cinnamon	Cranberry Juice	Fruit Soup	Pork Chops	Sweet and Sour Fish	Butter Sauce for Squash	Sweet Potato Croquettes	Stewed Fruit Salad	Chocolate Pudding
Cayenne	Deviled Eggs	Oyster Stew	Barbecued Beef	Poached Salmon Hollandaise	Bearnaise	Cooked Greens	Tuna Fish Salad	
Celery Salt and Seed	Ham Spread (Salt)	Cream of Celery (Seed)	Meat Loaf (Seed)	Chicken Croquettes (Salt)	Celery Sauce (Seed)	Cauliflower (Salt)	Cole Slaw (Seed)	
Chervil	Fish Dips	Cream Soup	Omelet	Chicken Saute	Vegetable Sauce	Peas Francaise	Caesar Salad	
Chili Powder	Seafood Cocktail Sauce	Pepper Pot	Chilli con Carne	Arroz con Pollo	Meat Gravy	Corn Mexicali	Chili French Dressing	
Cloves	Fruit Punch	Mulligatawney	Boiled Tongue	Baked Fish	Sauce Madeira	Candied Sweet Potatoes		Stewed Pears
Curry Powder	Curried Shrimp	Cream of Mushroom	Curry of Lamb	Chicken Hash	Orientale or Indienne	Creamed Vegetables	Curried Mayonaise	
Dill Seed	Cottage Cheese	Split Pea	Grilled Lamb Steak	Drawn Butter for Shellfish	Dill Sauce for Fish or Chicken	Peas and Carrots	Sour Cream Dressing	
Garlic Salt or Powder	Clam Dip	Vegetable Soup	Roast Lamb	Bouillabaisse	Garlic Butter	Eggs and Tomato Casserole	Tomato and Cucumber Salad	
Ginger	Broiled Grapefruit	Bean Soup	Dust lightly over Steak	Roast Chicken	Cocktail	Buttered Beets	Cream Dressing for Ginger Pears	Stewed Dried Fruits

	Quiche Lorraine	Petite Marmite	Veal Fricassee	Fish Stew	Creole	Succotash	Fruit Salad	Cottage Pudding
Mace								
Marjoram	Fruit Punch Cup	Onion Soup	Roast Lamb	Salmon Loaf	Brown	Eggplant	Mixed Green Salad	
Mint	Fruit Cup	Sprinkle over Split Pea	Veal Roast	Cold Fish	Lamb	Green Peas	Cottage Cheese Salad	Ambrosia
Mustard *Powdered Dry*	Ham Spread	Lobster Bisque	Virginia Ham	Deviled Crab	Cream Sauce for Fish	Baked Beans	Egg Salad	Gingerbread Cookies
Nutmeg	Chopped Oysters	Cream DuBarry	Salisbury Steak	Southern Fried Chicken	Mushroom	Glazed Carrots	Sweet Salad Dressing	Sprinkle over Vanilla Ice Cream
Onion *Powder, Salt, Flakes, and Instant Minced Onion*	Avocado Spread (Powder)	Consommes (Flakes)	Meat Loaf (Instant Minced Onion)	Fried Shrimp (Salt)	Tomato (Powder)	Broiled Tomatoes (Salt)	Vinaigrette Dressing (Instant Minced Onion)	
Oregano	Sharp Cheese Spread	Beef Soup	Swiss Steak	Court Bouillon	Spaghetti	Boiled Onions	Sea Food	
Paprika	Creamed Seafood	Creamed Soup	Hungarian Goulash	Oven Fried Chicken	Paprika Cream	Baked Potato	Cole Slaw	
Parsley *Flakes*	Cheese Balls	Cream of Asparagus	Irish Lamb Stew	Broiled Mackerel	Chasseur	French Fried Potatoes	Tossed Green Salad	
Rosemary	Deviled Eggs	Mock Turtle	Lamb Loaf	Chicken a la King	Cheese	Sauteed Mushrooms	Meat Salad	
Sage	Cheese Spreads	Consomme	Cold Roast Beef	Poultry Stuffing	Duck	Brussels Sprouts	Herbed French Dressing	
Savory	Liver Paste	Lentil Soup	Scrambled Eggs	Chicken Loaf	Fish	Beets	Red Kidney Bean Salad	
Tarragon	Mushrooms a la Greque	Snap Bean Soup	Marinated Lamb or Beef	Lobster	Green	Buttered Broccoli	Chicken Salad	
Thyme	Artichokes	Clam Chowder	Use sparingly in Fricassees	Poultry Stuffing	Bordelaise	Lightly on Sauteed Mushrooms	Tomato Aspic	

Source: Reprinted from *How To Stay on a Low-Calorie, Low-Sodium Diet* with permission of the American Spice Trade Association. ©1980.

Table 12-3 Sodium Content of Spices

Spice	Milligrams/ teaspoon	Spice	Milligrams/ teaspoon
Allspice	1.4		
Basil Leaves	0.4	Nutmeg	0.2
Bay Leaves	0.3	Onion Powder	0.8
Caraway Seed	0.4	Oregano	0.3
Cardamon Seed	0.2	Paprika	0.4
Celery Seed	4.1	Parsley Flakes	5.9
Cinnamon	0.2	Pepper, Black	0.2
Cloves	4.2	Pepper, Chili	0.2
Coriander Seed	0.3	Pepper, Red	0.2
Cumin Seed	2.6	Pepper, White	0.2
Curry Powder	1.0	Poppy Seed	0.2
Dill Seed	0.2	Rosemary Leaves	0.5
Fennel Seed	1.9	Sage	0.1
Garlic Powder	0.1	Savory	0.3
Ginger	0.5	Sesame Seed	0.6
Mace	1.3	Tarragon	1.0
Marjoram	1.3	Thyme	1.2
Mustard Powder	0.1	Turmeric	0.2

Source: Reprinted from *Low-Sodium Spice Tips* with permission of the American Spice Trade Association, ©1980.

per teaspoon. The spice highest in sodium is parsley flakes, which contain not quite 6 milligrams per teaspoon. In comparison, one gram of salt contains 2,300 milligrams of sodium. Adherence Tool 12-2 provides information on the natural sodium content of foods.

The importance of reading labels carefully should be stressed because some spices are prepared in combination with salt. Anyone on a low-sodium diet should avoid the spice-salt combination products. Table 12-3 indicates the sodium content of spices prepared without salt.

Strategies To Deal with Forgetfulness

Calendars may serve as reminders to take blood pressure medications. Adherence Tool 11-16 (Cueing device) provides a sample. For clients who must take medication, a lack of change in pressures results from forgetting to take medications. The calendar in Adherence Tool 11-16 provides a means of checking on days or on times of day when patients find it most difficult to take medications. The calendar can also function as a cueing device to remind the client to take medication.

Another type of calendar (Adherence Tool 12-3) may also be used to record when a client eats a high-sodium meal. If lunch has been targeted as a difficult meal, marking a "X" on days when lunch was high in sodium lets the counselor and the client know on what days the client needs special help in changing habits. The calendar helps remind the client, "I must watch Monday lunches." By planning ahead, the client may not slip into old high-sodium eating habits.

Strategies To Deal with Lack of Commitment

Frequently model adherers to diet revert to old habits. They tire of always choosing low-sodium meals and decide to "live a little." In some cases this period of lack of commitment is short lived and may end after one or two days. Indeed, a client who can limit indiscretions to a two-day period should be commended. But others may have difficulty working back to appropriate eating habits and need assistance in renewing commitment.

Social occasions can present special problems. Clients can begin to learn to cope with such situations by collecting data on what types of reinforcers maintain their eating of high-sodium foods during social events. The same reinforcer that maintains an undesired eating behavior can be used to strengthen appropriate conduct. For example:

> CLIENT at a party: "Boy, do those salty chips look good. But I know that they aren't on my diet. Over here, though, are some fresh vegetables. They look just as good and are on my diet. I feel really good about myself after eating them and I haven't cheated on my diet."

A list of positive reinforcers may help clients maintain a low-sodium diet. Watson and Tharp provide a set of questions clients might be asked when making a list of positive reinforcers:

1. What kinds of low-sodium foods do you like to eat?
2. What are your major interests?
3. What are your hobbies?
4. What people do you like to be with?
5. What do you like to do with these people?
6. What do you do for fun, for enjoyment?
7. What do you do to relax?
8. What do you do to get away from it all?
9. What makes you feel good?
10. What would be a nice present to receive?
11. What kinds of things are important to you?
12. What would you buy if you had an extra five dollars? Ten dollars? Fifty dollars?
13. What behaviors do you perform every day?
14. Are there any behaviors that you usually perform instead of the target behavior?
15. What would you hate to lose?
16. Of the things you do every day, what would you hate to give up?[65]

Counselors can construct additional questions. Determining the best reinforcers will depend upon each individual client. Before choosing a reinforcer, counselors should consider how closely the consequence meets a client's needs and desires. The reinforcer must be manageable from the client's point of view and must be contingent on performance of the desired behavior—eating low-sodium foods. The reinforcer should be strong enough to help in changing behavior.

The next step in helping to alter behavior is to set up a contract (Exhibit 12-2, for a woman client) that should specify stages of the change in eating habits, kinds of reinforcers to be gained at each step, and self-agreement to make gaining those reinforcers contingent on changing eating behavior involving high-sodium foods.[66]

Exhibit 12-2 Contract for a Sodium-Modified Diet

I agree to carry out each of the following steps and supply each reinforcer listed as each step is achieved:

Steps	Reinforcer
1. Eliminate salting before tasting	Read a new cookbook
2. Slowly eat unsalted foods to allow detection of true flavors	Buy a new scarf
3. Add new spices to foods in place of salt	Buy a new pair of shoes

Signed: _____

Cosigned (counselor): _____

Date: _____

Ideally, a contract should be written and signed and should specify each detail of dietary change. Each element of this intervention plan should be very specific. A plan—a written contract—will help clients in those inevitable moments of weakness.

Reinforcers should fall within the realm of possibility or be readily accessible. They also should be potent. For example, buying clothes is not a potent reinforcer if the client does not enjoy doing it. The clients should be told to use "intuition" or estimate potency. The counselors' own data, collected during intervention, can indicate whether or not the chosen reinforcer is sufficiently powerful. A desired eating behavior should be reinforced immediately after the clients have performed it. The longer reinforcement is delayed, the less effective it will be.

If immediate reinforcement is impossible, token reinforcers can be appropriate. A token is a symbolic reinforcer because it can be converted into real reinforcement. Tokens include money, poker chips, gold stars, checkmarks, and ticket punches. A point system also can be used (this one is for a woman client; reinforcers for men and youngsters will vary):

One token . . . . one new blouse
Two tokens . . . . two new blouses
Three tokens . . . . a new dress
Four tokens . . . . a new suit

Reinforcements can be increased as a new eating behavior becomes more frequent. This provides additional incentives for continuing self-modification.

One particular reinforcer should not be overused or clients will become satiated by it. In other words, a specific reward loses its reinforcing quality through overrepetition.

A reinforcer that punishes someone else should not be used. For example, if a married woman client uses money to buy a dress as a reinforcer, the counselor must be sure the husband is in agreement.

The discussion and dispensing of reinforcers can and should involve the family directly. If the family members are aware of potent reinforcers, they can help dispense them at opportune times.

In summary, treatment strategies for low-sodium eating patterns involve tailoring and staging with calendars as a means of dealing with forgetting. To deal with a lack of commitment, it is important to make a list of self-reinforcers, use contracting, and use token economics.

Adherence Tool 12-1 Informational Device

Spices for Low-Sodium Diets

Spices for Use with Meats:

Dill seed for fish or chicken sauces
Garlic powder for bouillabaisse
Ginger for roast chicken
Mace for fish stew
Marjoram for salmon loaf

Mint for veal or lamb roast
Mustard for cream sauce on fish
Nutmeg for southern fried chicken
Oregano for Swiss steak
Rosemary for chicken à la king
Savory for chicken loaf
Tarragon for marinated beef
Thyme for clam chowder

Spices for Use with Vegetables:

Allspice for eggplant creole
Basil for stewed tomatoes
Bay leaf for boiled new potatoes
Caraway seed for cabbage wedges
Cinnamon for sweet potatoes
Celery seed for cauliflower
Chili powder for Mexican-style corn

Cloves for candied sweet potatoes
Curry for creamed vegetables
Dill seed for peas and carrots
Garlic for stewed tomatoes
Ginger for beets
Mace for succotash
Mint for green peas
Powdered dry mustard for baked beans
Nutmeg for glazed carrots
Rosemary for sauteed mushrooms
Sage for Brussels sprouts
Savory for beets
Tarragon for broccoli
Thyme lightly on sauteed mushrooms

Plan menus for three meals. The menus should be low in sodium and should use the spices suggested above. Choose spices you think you and your family would enjoy.

BREAKFAST	LUNCH	DINNER

Adherence Tool 12-2 Informational Device

Estimated Natural Sodium Content of Foods

A rough guide follows for the natural sodium content of foods that are grown or produced and processed without the addition of sodium.

8 oz. milk	=	120 mg. of sodium
1 oz. meat	=	25 mg. of sodium
1 egg	=	70 mg. of sodium
½ cup vegetable	=	9 mg. of sodium
½ cup fruit	=	2 mg. of sodium
1 slice of bread	=	5 mg. of sodium
1 teaspoon of fat	=	0 mg. of sodium

Source: Nutrition in Health and Disease by H.S. Mitchell et al., p. 430, J.B. Lippincott Company, ©1976.

Adherence Tool 12-3 Monitoring Device

Daily Food Record with Emphasis on Sodium Intake

Time	Food Eaten	Amount	Low in Na+*	Moderate in Na+*	High in Na+*

*Place an X in the column to indicate whether the food is high, moderate, or low in sodium.

Review of Chapter 12
(Answers in Appendix I)

1. List four factors that lead to inappropriate eating behaviors associated with sodium-modified patterns.

   a. _____

   b. _____

   c. _____

   d. _____

2. Identify three important steps in the assessment of a baseline diet for clients following a low-sodium regimen.

   a. _____

   _____

   b. _____

   _____

   c. _____

3. List four strategies to use in treating problems associated with eating patterns low in sodium.

   a. _____

   _____

   b. _____

   _____

   c. _____

   _____

   d. _____

4. Mrs. B. is 40 years old and has just been placed on a low-sodium diet. She has collected baseline information. She says she has tried and failed to follow a low-sodium diet previously. She loves cheese and cold cuts. What other facts would be beneficial to know? Based on hypothetical answers to those facts, what strategies would you recommend to solve her problems with low-sodium eating patterns? Explain why you would use these strategies.

   _____

   _____

   _____

   _____

   _____

   _____

   _____

NOTES

1. "1984 Report of the Joint National Committee on Detection, Evaluation, and Treatment of High Blood Pressure," *Archives of Internal Medicine* 144 (1984): 1045–1057.

2. Subcommittee on Nonpharmacological Therapy of the 1984 Joint National Committee on Detection, Evaluation and Treatment of High Blood Pressure, "Nonpharmacological Approaches to the Control of High Blood Pressure," *Hypertension* 8 (1986): 444–467.

3. "Health Implications of Obesity: National Institutes of Health Consensus Development," *Annals of Internal Medicine* 103 (1985): 977–1077; Edward D. Frohlich et al., "The Problems of Obesity and Hypertension, *Hypertension* 5 (1983): Suppl. III-71–III-78; Lot B. Page, Albert Damon, and Robert C. Moellering, "Antecedents of Cardiovascular Disease of Six Solomon Island Societies," *Circulation* 49 (1974): 1132–1146; and Benjamin N. Chiang, Lawrence V. Perlman, and Frederick H. Epstein, "Overweight and Hypertension," *Circulation* 39 (1969): 403–421.

4. I.A.M. Prior et al., "Sodium Intake and Blood Pressure in Two Polynesian Populations," *New England Journal of Medicine* 279 (1968): 515–520; H.M. Whyte, "Body Build and Blood Pressure of Men in Australia and New Guinea," *Australian Journal of Experimental Biology and Medical Science* 41 (1963): 395–404; G.V. Mann et al., "Cardiovascular Disease in the Masai," *Journal of Atherosclerosis Research* 4 (1964): 289–312; C.R. Lowe, "Arterial Pressure, Physique and Occupation," *British Journal of Preventive and Social Medicine* 18 (1964): 115–124; Frederick H. Epstein et al., "Prevalence of Chronic Disease and Distribution of Selected Physiological Variables in a Total Community, Tecumseh, Michigan," *American Journal of Epidemiology* 81 (1965): 307–323; and S. Padmavati and Savitri Gupta, "Blood Pressure Studies in Rural and Urban Groups in Delhi," *Circulation* 19 (1959): 395–405.

5. Antonie W. Voors et al., "Body Height and Body Mass as Determinants of Basal Blood Pressure in Children: The Bogalusa Heart Study," *American Journal of Epidemiology* 106 (1977): 101–108; and John A. Morrison et al., "Studies of Blood Pressure in School Children (Ages 6–19) and Their Parents in an Integrated Suburban School District," *American Journal of Epidemiology* 111 (1980): 156–165.

6. William B. Kannel et al., "Relation of Adiposity to Blood Pressure and Development of Hypertension: The Framingham Study," *Annals of Internal Medicine* 67 (1967): 48–59.

7. Ralph S. Paffenbarger, Jr., Melvyn C. Thorne, and Alvin L. Wing, "Chronic Disease in Former College Students: VII. Characteristics in Youth Predisposing to Hypertension in Later Years," *American Journal of Epidemiology* 88 (1968): 25–32; Albert Oberman et al., "Trends in Systolic Blood Pressure in the Thousand Aviator Cohort Over a Twenty-four-year Period," *Circulation* 36 (1967): 812–822; Arnold L. Johnson et al., "Influence of Race, Sex and Weight on Blood Pressure Behavior in Young Adults," *American Journal of Cardiology* 35 (1975): 523–530; and Siegfried Heyden et al., "Elevated Blood Pressure Levels in Adolescents, Evans County, GA: Seven-Year Follow-Up of 30 Patients and 30 Controls," *Journal of the American Medical Association* 209 (1969): 1683–1689.

8. Subcommittee on Nonpharmacological Therapy of the 1984 Joint National Committee on Detection, Evaluation and Treatment of High Blood Pressure, "Nonpharmacological Approaches," p. 445.

9. James K. Alexander, "Obesity and the Circulation," *Modern Concepts in Cardiovascular Disease* 32 (1963): 799–803; H. Malcom Whyte, "Behind the Adipose Curtain: Studies in Australia and New Guinea Relating to Obesity and Coronary Heart Disease," *American Journal of Cardiology* 15 (1965): 66–80; Franz H. Messerli et al., "Obesity and Essential Hypertension: Hemodynamics, Intravascular Volume, and Plasma Renin Activity," *Archives of Internal Medicine* 141 (1981): 81–85; and Efrain Reisin et al., "Cardiovascular Changes After Weight Reduction in Obesity Hypertension," *Annals of Internal Medicine* 98 (1983): 315–319.

10. Lewis Dahl, Lawrence Silver, and Robert Christie, "Role of Salt in Fall of Blood Pressure Accompanying Reduction of Obesity," *New England Journal of Medicine* 258 (1958): 1186–1192.

11. Melbourne F. Hovel, "The Experimental Evidence for Weight Loss Treatment of Essential Hypertension: A Critical Review," *American Journal of Public Health* 72 (1982): 359–368; and Efrain Reisin et al., "Effect of Weight Loss Without Salt Restriction on the Reduction of Blood Pressure in Overweight Hypertensive Patients," *New England Journal of Medicine* 298 (1981): 1–10.

12. Dahl, Silver, and Christie, "Role of Salt in Fall of Blood Pressure."

13. James K. Alexander, "Obesity and the Circulation," *Modern Concepts in Cardiovascular Disease* 32 (1963): 799–803; Reisin et al., "Effect of Weight Loss Without Salt Restriction"; and Morton H. Maxwell et al., "Blood Pressure Changes in Obese Hypertensive Subjects During Rapid Weight Loss: Comparison of Restricted Versus Unchanged Salt Intake," *Archives of Internal Medicine* 144 (1984): 1581–1584.

14. Michael L. Tuck et al., "Reduction in Plasma Catecholamines and Blood Pressure During Weight Loss in Obese Subjects," *Acta Endocrinologica (Copenhagen)* 102 (1983): 252–257; and "The Effect of Weight Reduction on Blood Pressure Plasma Renin Activity and Plasma Aldosterone Levels in Obese Patients," *New England Journal of Medicine* 304 (1981): 930–933.

15. Tuck et al., "Reduction in Plasma Catecholamines and Blood Pressure."

16. Francisco Grande, "Assessment of Body Fat in Man," in George A. Bray, ed., *Obesity in Perspective* (Washington, D.C.: U.S. Government Printing Office, 1975), pp. 189–204.

17. Josef Brozek, Carleton Chapman, and Ancel Keys, "Drastic Food Restriction," *Journal of the American Medical Association* 137 (1948): 1569–1574.

18. Robert H. Rose, "Weight Reduction and Its Remarkable Effect on High Blood Pressure," *New York Medical Journal* 115 (1922): 752–759.

19. Hovel, "Experimental Evidence"; Reisin et al., "Effect of Weight Loss Without Salt Restriction"; Björn Fagerberg et al., "Blood Pressure Control During Weight Reduction in Obese Hypertensive Men: Separate Effects of Sodium and Energy Restriction," *British Medical Journal* 288 (1984): 11–14; Maxwell et al., "Blood Pressure Changes"; Tuck et al., "Reduction in Plasma Catecholamines"; Tuck et al., "Effect of Weight Reduction"; Grande, "Assessment of Body Fat in Man," pp. 189–204; Brozek, Chapman, and Keyes, "Drastic Food Restriction"; Rose, "Weight Reduction"; Frantz W. Ashley and William B. Kannel, "Relation of Weight Change to Changes in Atherogenic Traits: The Framingham Study," *Journal of Chronic Disease* 27 (1974): 103–114; Herman A. Tyroler, Siegfried Heyden, and Curtis G. Hames, "Weight and Hypertension: Evans County Studies of Blacks and Whites," in Paul Oglesby, ed., *Epidemiology and Control of Hypertension* (Miami: Symposia Specialists, 1975), pp. 177–204; L.E. Ramsay et al., "Weight Reduction in Blood Pressure Clinic," *British Medical Journal* 2 (1978): 244–245; K.H. Stokholm, P.E. Nielsen, and F. Quaade, "Correlation between Initial Blood Pressure and Blood Pressure Decrease After Weight Loss," *International Journal of Obesity* 6 (1982): 307–312; Jeremiah Stamler et al., "Prevention and Control of Hypertension by Nutritional-Hygienic Means," *Journal of the American Medical Association* 243 (1980): 1819–1823; and H.E. Eliahou et al., "Body Weight Reduction Necessary to Attain Normotension in the Overweight Hypertensive Patient," *International Journal of Obesity* (Supplement 1) 1981: 157–163.

20. R. Brian Haynes et al., "Failure of Weight Reduction to Reduce Mildly Elevated Blood Pressure: A Randomized Trial," *Journal of Hypertension* 2 (1984): 535–539.

21. Reisin et al., "Effect of Weight Loss Without Salt Restriction."

22. Aldersterg, Coler, and Laval, "Effect of Weight Reduction on Course of Arterial Hypertension."

23. Tyroler, Heyden, and Hames, "Weight and Hypertension"; Ramsay et al., "Weight Reduction in Blood Pressure Clinic"; and Stokholm, Nielsen, and Quaade, "Correlation Between Initial Blood Pressure and Blood Pressure Decrease After Weight Loss."

24. Jeremiah Stamler et al., "Prevention and Control of Hypertension by Nutritional-Hygienic Means," *Journal of the American Medical Association* 243 (1980): 1819–1823.

25. Eliahou et al., "Body Weight Reduction."

26. V. Jorgens et al., "Long-term Effects of Weight Changes on Cardiovascular Risk Factors Over 4.7 Years in 247 Obese Patients" (Abstract), Presented at the 4th International Congress of Obesity, New York, 1983:68a.

27. Reisin et al., "Cardiovascular Changes."

28. Subcommittee on Nonpharmacological Therapy of the 1984 Joint National Committee on Detection, Evaluation and Treatment of High Blood Pressure, "Nonpharmacological Approaches," p. 447.

29. Graham A. MacGregor et al., "Double-Blind Randomized Crossover Trial of Moderate Sodium Restriction in Essential Hypertension," *Lancet* 1 (1982): 351–355.

30. G.C.M. Watt et al., "Dietary Sodium Restriction for Mild Hypertension in General Practice," *British Medical Journal* 286 (1983): 432–436.

31. A. Mark Richards et al., "Blood-Pressure Response to Moderate Sodium Restriction and to Potassium Supplementation in Mild Essential Hypertension," *Lancet* 1 (1984): 757–761.

32. David L. Longworth et al., "Divergent Blood Pressure Responses During Short-Term Sodium Restriction in Hypertension," *Clinical Pharmacology and Therapeutics* 27 (1980): 544–546.

33. P.S. Parfrey et al., "Relation Between Arterial Pressure, Dietary Sodium Intake and Renin System in Essential Hypertension," *British Medical Journal* 283 (1981): 94–97.

34. Alan J. Silman et al., "Evaluation of the Effectiveness of a Low Sodium Diet in the Treatment of Mild to Moderate Hypertension," *Lancet* 1 (1983): 1179–1182.

35. Trevor C. Beard et al., "Randomized Controlled Trial of a No-Added-Sodium Diet for Mild Hypertension," *Lancet* 2 (1982): 455–458.

36. Terukazu Kawasaki et al., "The Effect of High-Sodium and Low-Sodium Intake on Blood Pressure and Other Related Variables in Human Subjects with Idiopathic Hypertension," *American Journal of Medicine* 64 (1978): 193–198.

37. Herbert G. Langford et al., "Dietary Therapy Slows the Return of Hypertension After Stopping Prolonged Medication," *Journal of the American Medical Association* 253 (1985): 657–664.

38. Subcommittee on Nonpharmacological Therapy of the 1984 Joint National Committee on Detection, Evaluation and Treatment of High Blood Pressure, "Nonpharmacological Approaches," p. 450.

39. Charles H. Hennekens, "Alcohol," in Norman M. Kaplan and Jeremiah Stamler, eds., *Prevention of Coronary Heart Disease*, (Philadelphia: W.B. Saunders, 1983), pp. 130–138; Stephen W. MacMahon et al., "Obesity, Alcohol Consumption and Blood Pressure in Australian Men and Women: The National Heart Foundation of Australia Risk Factor Prevalence Study," *Journal of Hypertension* 2 (1984): 85–91; and Gary D. Friedman, Arthur L. Klatsky, and A.B. Siegelaub, "Alcohol, Tobacco and Hypertension," *Hypertension* (Supplement III) 4 (1982): III-43–III-150.

40. J.B. Saunders, D.G. Bevers, and A. Paton, "Alcohol-Induced Hypertension," *Lancet* 2 (1981): 653–656.

41. M.G. Marmot, "Alcohol and Coronary Heart Disease," *International Journal of Epidemiology* 13 (1984): 160–167; and Tavia Gordon and William B. Kannel, "Drinking and Mortality: The Framingham Study," *American Journal of Epidemiology* 120 (1984): 97–107.

42. Subcommittee on Nonpharmacological Therapy of the 1984 Joint National Committee on Detection, Evaluation and Treatment of High Blood Pressure, "Nonpharmacological Approaches," p. 456.

43. Ibid.

44. Ibid.

45. Ibid.

46. Ibid.

47. Susan B. Steckel and Mary A. Swain, "Contracting with Patients to Improve Compliance," *Hospitals* 51 (December 1977): 81–83.

48. Rena R. Wing et al., "Dietary Approaches to the Reduction of Blood Pressure: Independence of Weight and Sodium/Potassium Interventions," *Preventive Medicine* 13 (1984): 233–244.

49. Norman M. Kaplan et al., "Two Techniques to Improve Adherence to Dietary Sodium Restriction in the Treatment of Hypertension," *Archives of Internal Medicine* 142 (1982): 1638–1641; and Charles A. Nugent et al., "Salt Restriction in Hypertensive Patients: Comparison of Advice, Education and Group Management," *Archives of Internal Medicine* 144 (1984): 1415–1417.

50. Melbourne F. Hovel et al., "Experimental Analysis of Adherence Counseling: Implications for Hypertension Management," 14 (1985): 648–654.

51. Susan E. Evers et al., "Lack of Impact of Salt Restriction Advice on Hypertensive Patients," *Preventive Medicine* 16 (1987): 213–220.

52. Jeanne L. Tillotson, Mary C. Winston, and Yolanda Hall, "Critical Behaviors in the Dietary Management of Hypertension," *Journal of the American Dietetic Association* 84 (1984): 290–293; and U.S. Department of Health and Human Services, "Report of the Working Group Critical Patient Behaviors in the Dietary Management of High Blood Pressure," NIH Publication No. 81-2269 (1981).

53. Karen Glanz, "Compliance with Dietary Regimens: Its Magnitude, Measurement and Determinants," *Preventive Medicine* 9 (1980): 787–804.

54. Jorma Takala, Arto Leminen, and Tauno Telaranta, "Strategies for Improving Compliance in Hypertensive Patients," *Scandinavian Journal of Primary Health Care* 3 (1985): 233–238.

55. Judy Z. Miller, Myron H. Weinberger, and Stuart J. Cohen, "Advances in Non-Pharmacologic Treatment of Hypertension: A New Approach to the Problem of Effective Dietary Sodium Restriction, 1. Sodium in the Diet: Patient Compliance," *Indiana Medicine* (October 1985): 893–895.

56. Jan A.C. Kerr, "Multidimensional Health Locus of Control Adherence, and Lowered Diastolic Blood Pressure," *Heart and Lung* 15 (1986): 87–93.

57. David G. Schlundt, Elizabeth C. McDonel, and Herbert G. Langford, "Compliance in Dietary Management of Hypertension," *Comprehensive Therapy* 11 (1985): 59–66; and Stuart J. Cohen, "Improving Patients' Compliance with Antihypertensive Regimens," *Comprehensive Therapy* 11 (1985): 18–21.

58. Schlundt, McDonel, and Langford, "Compliance in Dietary Management."

59. Michael G. Perri et al., "Maintenance Strategies for the Treatment of Obesity: An Evaluation of Relapse Prevention Training and Post-Treatment Contact by Mail and Telephone," *Journal of Consulting and Clinical Psychology* 52 (1984): 404–413.

60. David L. Watson and Roland G. Tharp, *Self-Directed Behavior: Self-Modification for Personal Adjustment* (Monterey, Calif.: Brooks/Cole Publishing, 1972), 85–89.

61. Ibid., 96–97.

62. Ibid., 97–98.

63. Ibid., 99.

64. Ibid., 148.

65. Ibid., 108.

66. Ibid., 117.

Chapter 13

Nutrition Counseling for Cancer Risk Prevention

Objectives for Chapter 13

1. Identify common inappropriate eating behaviors associated with following a fat-controlled eating pattern.
2. Identify how to assess problems associated with inappropriate eating patterns in following a fat-controlled regimen.
3. List strategies to overcome inappropriate eating behaviors associated with eating patterns controlled for fat.

Cancer is the second most common cause of death in Western societies. Because cancer is largely a disease of old age, as the population ages the number of cancer death increases. Most research in this area has been directed toward treatment and cure of cancers as they arise, a singularly unsuccessful policy. The prognosis of individuals with cancer of the lung, breast, large bowel, stomach, prostate, and pancreas is very discouraging. Successful approaches to diseases such as smallpox, rabies, plague, cholera, whooping cough, and diphtheria have focused on prevention rather than treatment.[1]

Approximately 40 percent of human cancers may have dietary causes,[2] but little is known about dietary factors responsible for cancer and dietary changes necessary for cancer prevention.

THEORIES AND FACTS ABOUT NUTRITION AND CANCER

Many population studies have shown that cancers are strongly related to diet. Colon cancer has been linked to high levels of both fat and meat.[3] Breast cancer studies have implicated animal fat as a potential causative agent.[4] Cancer of the endometrium and prostate have been associated with fat.[5] Cancer of the esophagus has been related to undernutrition and excessive intakes of alcohol.[6] Stomach cancer has been associated with poor nutrition, cereals, and salt.[7]

RESEARCH ON ADHERENCE TO EATING PATTERNS IN CANCER RISK PREVENTION

No systematic studies of the role of nutrition education in reducing cancer risk have been completed, although the National Cancer Institute has sponsored field trials for high-risk persons as well as the public. Written materials aimed at promoting cancer risk reduction through nutrition are available for both health professionals and consumers.[8]

Planning nutrition education programs for reducing cancer risk involves many issues. Considerable controversy still exists about the extent to which dietary changes alone can reduce cancer morbidity. There is also much room for confusion about the specificity of cancers that are affected by certain nutrients in the diet. References to cancer in public health education may unnecessarily raise both the fears and expectations of clients. Health professionals planning nutrition education on cancer risk need to weigh the implications of the strategies and messages they plan to use.[9]

Persons diagnosed with cancer may experience anorexia (see Chapter 14) as a consequence of the disease and its treatment.[10] In addition, nausea, swallowing difficulties, reduced senses of taste and smell, anxiety, depression, and pain may result in inadequate nutrition, which weakens the client and reduces resistance to the disease progression. Nutritional modalities for persons with cancer include compulsory feeding, tube feeding, and parenteral nutrition;[11] however, client education is most relevant to oral feeding.

Glanz stressed the importance of support from the family and health care providers.[12] Recommendations to encourage clients to eat and to adapt to special dietary needs have been compiled in a National Cancer Institute publication entitled *Eating Hints: Recipes and Tips for Better Nutrition during Cancer Treatment.*[13] Carson reported on a team approach to nutrition for persons with cancer in which nutritionists help clients solve a variety of diet-related problems and provided information or referral to other team members as necessary. Nutritionists also provided credible information and answered questions about unorthodox dietary practices. Carson's article gave case examples to illustrate these activities.[14] Campbell et al. taught systematic relaxation techniques to 22 persons with cancer in their homes in an effort to promote weight gain in underweight persons. Only 55 percent of these persons practiced the relaxation techniques regularly, but nutritional status and cancer performance status improved among the compliers.[15] This preliminary study suggested that for motivated persons, relaxation techniques may both help with diet and be useful for other purposes, such as pain control and anxiety reduction.

Nutrition education for persons with cancer must be part of the comprehensive treatment program and account for individual needs and preferences. It will probably gain more attention as survival rates for various cancers increase in the years ahead.[16]

This chapter is devoted to a diet recommended during a feasibility study for the National Cancer Institute Clinical Trial—The Women's Health Trial.* The diet is low in fat with a ratio of polyunsaturated fat to saturated fat of one. The text that follows provides an example of how to apply counseling skills to a specific low-fat diet for cancer prevention.

---

*The efforts of the following persons who developed the intervention component of the Women's Health Trial are acknowledged: Laura Coleman, M.S., R.D.; Joanne Csaplar, M.S., R.D.; Johanna Dwyer, D.Sc., R.D.; Carole Palmer, M.Ed., R.D.; and Molly Holland, M.P.H., R.D. Many of the concepts discussed in this chapter were originally printed in materials designed by this group at Frances Stern Medical Center and New England Medical Center Hospitals with funding from the Nutrition Coordinating Unit, Tufts University School of Medicine or the National Institutes of Health.

INAPPROPRIATE EATING BEHAVIORS

For the client who has difficulty with simple math, adding up total grams of fat consumed in a day can be very difficult. For some, just the time the computation takes may be a problem.

The low-fat diet may be very different from the client's traditional high-fat diet. For example, a client might state, "I miss fried meats, fried potatoes, gravy, and vegetables smothered with butter. I don't know how to avoid those favorite dishes."

ASSESSMENT OF EATING BEHAVIORS

Assessing high fat intake might require using several three-day diet records and possibly a quantified food frequency. Initially, the Client Eating Questionnaire for clients following cholesterol- and fat-controlled eating patterns might be of value (Chapter 9).

TREATMENT STRATEGIES

Treatment strategies can be divided into three categories: those dealing with lack of knowledge, forgetfulness, and lack of commitment.

Strategies To Deal with Lack of Knowledge

Three-day diet diaries can be used to identify problem areas. Once the counselor and client have mutually identified a problem area, the counselor can determine exactly where knowledge may be lacking. The following are examples of problem areas:

1. using mathematical skills
2. knowing what to look for on a label
3. knowing how to cut back on fat in favorite ethnic recipes
4. knowing how to cook ethnic high-fat dishes in a low-fat manner.

For the person who has problems using math skills, the counselor can identify exactly where problems are occurring—for example, whether the math calculations for certain meals like breakfast are easier while calculations for other meals may be more difficult because of the variations in foods. The counselor should praise the use of math skills at one meal and build in those for a more difficult meal. For example, Mrs. Jones has no difficulty adding up grams of fat for breakfast. Dinner is a major problem because she eats a wide variety of food, for many of which she is unfamiliar with the total grams of fat.

> CLIENT: "I especially have trouble calculating grams of fat in meat at dinner."
> COUNSELOR: "You have done an excellent job with breakfast. I'm glad you brought up this problem with dinner so that we can try to solve it."
> CLIENT: "I'm no good at math. I can't handle this problem."
> COUNSELOR: "You have proven that you can use math skills in more routine situations at breakfast. Let's use some of those same skills for the dinner meal. You have said meat is a major problem; let's try to calculate it."

A second problem involves lack of knowledge of what to look for on a label. Sometimes examples are unclear or covered too quickly in a nutrition counseling session for the client to gain adequate understanding of how to apply the knowledge to all situations. In subsequent sessions, it is up to the counselor to assess a problem in this area and allow for enough rehearsal to transfer general information adequately to specific individual situations.

> CLIENT: "I just don't know what to look for on food labels. It's so frustrating."
> COUNSELOR: "Can you give me an example of a label that has been difficult to figure out?"
> CLIENT: "Yes, this ingredient list says that there is no fat in this macaroni dish. But I have added margarine to the dry ingredients, so I know fat is included."
> COUNSELOR: "The ingredient list will not include those items added to a product, only items in the box as you buy it. It is very important to count the fat added because it will contribute to your total fat for the day."

Martha has a problem combining the low-fat diet with her past high-fat ethnic eating pattern.

> CLIENT: "I have a difficult time avoiding fried foods. They have become such an important part of my usual eating habits."
> COUNSELOR: "Martha, what food in particular are you concerned about?"
> CLIENT: "I mostly miss fried potatoes."
> COUNSELOR: "Let's try using PAM spray and frying your potatoes with very little fat. Would you be willing to try that?"
> CLIENT: "I hadn't thought of that. It's a great idea."

Knowledge is seldom enough to increase motivation or adherence, but misinformation can definitely undermine success. If a client is motivated but doesn't understand a correct procedure, simply providing the appropriate information can make a great difference. It is important to provide information on *what* to do, *how* to do it and a *rationale* for why it should be done. The tips below are ways to be sure clients understand information adequately:

1. Knowing the rationale for the new eating pattern helps the client remember what information has been provided.
2. Asking the client to repeat information can help in knowledge retention.
3. Adding new information on the low-fat eating pattern to what the client already knows helps retention.
4. Using language the client can understand is important.
5. Reemphasizing the benefits of the new low-fat eating pattern can help clear up the client's misunderstandings about the regimen and increase client involvement in active change.
6. Providing information slowly over time helps eliminate overloading the client with too much information at one time.

7. Practicing use of information in an actual or simulated situation is helpful in maximizing retention of information.
8. Providing identical written information that supports verbally presented material can help retention.

Strategies To Deal with Forgetfulness

Cues to help remind a client to plan to eat a low-fat diet can be very important. Some occasions that call for cueing a client are: vacations, parties, holiday meals, and birthdays.

> CLIENT: "I forgot to ask the waitress to give me salad dressing on the side, and I know I ate too much on the salad."
> COUNSELOR: "What might you have done to avoid this situation?"
> CLIENT: "Sometimes I just need help remembering."
> COUNSELOR: "Who might help remind you?"
> CLIENT: "My husband might remind me."
> COUNSELOR: "That's a great idea. Sometimes reminders from a spouse can turn into nagging. Has that ever happened to you?"
> CLIENT: "Yes, it has. How can I avoid that?"
> COUNSELOR: "One way is to provide your husband with a few specific things of which to help remind you. The salad dressing on the side might be one of three or four specific reminders. This will eliminate constant general nagging."

Parties, holiday meals, and birthdays may be made easier by preplanning. For example, by calling the hostess ahead of time, clients can check out all items on the menu to determine fat content. By preplanning, the client can choose those items lowest in fat and lessen the temptation just to have fun and forget about the diet during the special event.

Aids for remembering can also point to our achievements, which are also frequently forgotten. One woman keeps a list of all of those tasks she must do in a day. (See Adherence Tool 13-6.) A check when each task is completed helps clients feel they have accomplished something.

A sign on the refrigerator with fat scores (tally of total fat eaten in a day) for each day of the week serves as a reminder to strive for a fat score goal.

Strategies To Deal with Lack of Commitment

Three factors contribute to lack of commitment to following a low fat diet: a history of defeats, a negative attitude, and self-doubts.

A client with a history of poor adherence to other diets may have problems following the low-fat eating pattern. Many clients begin a new eating pattern expecting to fail. This type of person needs a great deal of support and encouragement. Counselors should try to encourage the attitude that success is possible even though it may not have been previously. They can emphasize a break from the old habit of going on and off a "diet," stressing instead the idea of a life-style change. The client should know that lapses will occur. Building new skills from past problems is important.

Some clients may have watched family members die of cancer and be very afraid of its consequences. They may feel that nothing can really help them, but following an eating pattern that may reduce risk is at least one way of easing a troubled mind. Counselors can discuss the goal of the new eating pattern with this client and emphasize that the eating plan is a healthy one.

Self-doubts can begin to creep into thoughts.

> CLIENT: "Life isn't spontaneous anymore. I always have to think about what I'm eating. I'm not sure this new eating plan is worth the trouble."
> COUNSELOR: "Look at the successes you have already had. Have you ever done anything that you were proud of or successful at in the past? How did you feel at that time? Did it become easier as time went on? Let's try to build on those past efforts and be successful with this diet also."

Counselors should assist the client in tearing down blocks to adherence, for example, by helping clients develop short-term goals that they can easily achieve. This technique allows for positive self-rewards. By shaping behavior in this way, the counselor helps the client develop a more positive outlook. Counselors can also guide clients in practicing positive self-talk to help identify negative monologues and change them to positive. Positive self-talk can lead to positive changes in eating patterns. (See Appendixes F and G.)

Some clients may benefit from assertiveness training. Feeling confident enough to ask the ingredients of a dish ordered in a restaurant can be a step toward successfully following the low-fat eating pattern.

What a client believes is true can help or hinder success. Below are some examples:

> CLIENT: "I've been reading that diets too low in fat can be bad for you."
> COUNSELOR: "What is your source of information?" [Explain misconceptions]

Some clients have unrealistic beliefs about the low-fat eating style:

> CLIENT: "I already eat a low-fat diet. This will be easy."
> COUNSELOR: "Your diet diaries show that your current eating pattern is low in visible fat but high in hidden fat. Let me show you what I mean."
> CLIENT: "Wow, my diet is high in fat. I'd better start cutting back."

Clients may begin by being unnecessarily fearful.

> CLIENT: "Life will never be the same. I can never again eat just what I want."
> COUNSELOR: "If you feel like forgetting the new eating plan, give yourself a controlled 'day off.' By that I mean increase your fat intake but in a controlled fashion. For example, set aside one meal a week as a high-fat meal."

Many clients find that the higher-fat foods are not so terrific and that, indeed, they have lost their taste for them.

Some behavioral strategies that help increase commitment are (1) successive approximations, or shaping of behaviors, (2) self-monitoring, (3) contracts, (4) self-reward, and (5) group support networks.

Shaping behavior requires a gradual, stepwise process toward change that helps build success in stages, which promotes further success.

> CLIENT: "I know skim milk is lowest in fat, but I grew up on a farm where skim milk was given to livestock. I will never be able to give up whole milk."
>
> COUNSELOR: "Would you be willing to try a gradual movement to skim milk?"
>
> CLIENT: "I guess I can try."
>
> COUNSELOR: "First try using 2 percent milk. You can begin by mixing 2 percent and whole milk and then moving solely to 2 percent. You could then mix 2 percent and 1 percent milk and eventually move to only 1 percent. The same combination of 1 percent and skim would then end in eventual use of only skim milk."

Self-monitoring, another important strategy, encourages self-reliance, provides immediate feedback, shows behavior patterns that undermine or build success, and provides a means of planning for future problems so that they can be minimized. Examples of self-monitoring tools include Adherence Tool 13-1, which allows for adding grams of fat in a day, and Adherence Tool 13-2, which allows weekly budgeting, or eating a little more fat one day and a little less the following day. Adherence Tool 13-3 provides a list of low-fat eating behaviors along with a check-off system to determine success. Adherence Tool 13-4 is a form for recording accomplishments in switching to low-fat foods over one week. Adherence Tool 13-5 is a meal planning chart.

> CLIENT: "Most of my problem eating times seem to be when I am alone and my husband is out of town."
>
> COUNSELOR: "Are there others with whom you can eat when your husband is away to help eliminate boredom?"
>
> CLIENT: "Yes, I have a close friend who might go to the movies with me."

Contracts may work well when nothing seems to help the client achieve the adherence goal of a set number of grams of fat a day. In a contract, the client and counselor write down the goal in a very specific manner, along with some reward.

1. Be sure the contract includes automatic self-rewards such as reading a book, sewing, or anything already available so that extensive shopping or time is not required to obtain the reward.
2. Be sure the client is involved in planning and has responsibility for the outcome.
3. Be sure the client signs the contract to indicate formal commitment.
4. Be sure that rewards are self-administered when goals are achieved.

The counselor provides the support and encouragement while the client plans and carries out the terms of the contract. The client must be involved in making major decisions and striving to fulfill the contract. Adherence Tool 13-5 allows the client to take an active role in meal planning. The contract might specify this as a task instead of eating.

Although nutrition counselors can provide a great deal of reinforcement, if they are not always available, teaching the client to provide self-administered rewards can be helpful. An example is a verbal pat on the back: "You followed your exact grams of fat today without going over your prescription. That's great!" For some clients, verbal rewards may be less important than tangible rewards such as spending the weekend alone with a friend, buying clothes, having hair styled, going to a movie, or reading a book.

Positive thinking as a part of rehearsing what will happen can be beneficial. For example, if following the new eating pattern during a party is the goal, a client can imagine standing before the buffet table making only low-fat choices. This behavior can then be followed by a reinforcing outcome, like feeling healthy or taking a pleasant two-mile walk.

Support from groups can help to increase commitment to following a new low-fat eating pattern. Support can come from others who are following the diet, fellow workers, friends, or family. The group, which can have three or four members or be a buddy system, can offer empathy for similar problems, provide helpful ideas for solving problems, give positive reinforcement when a goal is met, serve as role models, and assist in helping to minimize stress.

When goals are not met, reestablishing goals that are easily attainable is important. While a long-term goal may be to lower total fat to 20 percent of total calories, that goal does not tell the client how to develop realistic steps toward that goal.

> CLIENT: "I love meat. Since it is my major problem, I should probably set my goal at cutting back drastically on it. I really worry about being able to follow this diet."
>
> COUNSELOR: "Just because you see meat as a major barrier to following your new eating plan doesn't mean that you have to tackle it first. What other foods do you eat that are high in fat?"
>
> CLIENT: "I still use whole milk, but I don't use a lot of it and it won't be that difficult to switch to skim."
>
> COUNSELOR: "Let's start with that area first. It sounds as though you are confident that changes in that area won't be too burdensome."

Waning commitment to an eating pattern can begin with lack of support from a spouse, family members, a housemate, or friends. An otherwise supportive spouse may become unsupportive when faced with a rival, the low-fat diet. A spouse may become jealous, threatened, or hurt by the demands of a new eating style.

> CLIENT: "My husband is not supportive. This is an example of how he feels about my new eating style: 'This diet is all yours. I'm not joining you in a feast of rabbit food!' "
>
> COUNSELOR: "Have you ever asked how he feels about the low-fat eating pattern?"
>
> CLIENT: "No, but I think he is hurt that I no longer pay attention to him but devote all my energy to the new eating pattern."
>
> COUNSELOR: "How have you coped with problems like this in the past?"

CLIENT: "We have always talked through our problems."

COUNSELOR: "What might you say now? Perhaps being honest about your feelings would help. For example, 'It makes me feel angry and hurt when you make fun of my eating habits. You don't have to eat my 'rabbit food,' but your support of my new habits would be appreciated.' "

Sometimes children in a family can be a negative influence by making it difficult to change eating patterns. Children can also have many different feelings: jealousy, neglect, and deprivation of their favorite foods.

CLIENT: "My children are so negative sometimes. 'Why do we have to eat this awful low-fat stuff? We are playing basketball and need some good food.' "

COUNSELOR: "What do you think your children would accept as a compromise?"

CLIENT: "They might appreciate a homemade snack that is lower in fat."

COUNSELOR: "That's a great idea. You might also tell them to eat their favorite high-fat meals or snacks at school."

Some children may not take efforts to follow a low-fat diet seriously: "This is just another crazy diet." The family should know that the new low-fat eating pattern may be effective in preventing a disease and that is is very important to be supportive. Clients should involve children in meal planning, calculating a fat score, and helping to avoid temptations.

There are many ways to help increase the support of family members:

1. It is important to discuss openly feelings about the new low-fat eating pattern. If the client tells the family the importance of avoiding high-fat snacks, they will be more likely to comply.
2. It is best to be patient. A family needs time to go through changes.
3. The client must try to provide reinforcement when support is offered, no matter how minor the support.

Holidays, stressful periods and eating out are all potential challenges to adherence. Never going off the new low-fat eating pattern is a very unrealistic expectation and should be avoided as a written goal. There are several suggestions for participants who have trouble during these times:

1. Do not be afraid to ask for help from friends or relatives prior to a special holiday. If the request is made early, the hostess will appreciate having low-fat dishes for the client's benefits.
2. View following the diet as a series of corrections, not as an undeviating straight line.
3. Expect and predict setbacks in a holiday season.
4. Practice saying "no."

Stressful periods can cause changes in strict observance of a dietary pattern. At these times, it is important to identify the cause of the change and the emotion associated with it.

CLIENT: "When I am depressed, tired, or in general under a lot of pressure at work, I turn to my favorite high-fat foods for comfort."

COUNSELOR: "When eating is a way of consoling yourself, you might make a list of those things which provide comfort or positive reinforcement. These should be things that do not involve eating. Can you think of some things now?"

CLIENT: "I like to jog. Sometimes just going to talk with a friend boosts my spirits."

When clients need comfort, other activities that give reinforcement might be taking a bubble bath, listening to music, or calling a friend.

Tension or anxiety may also cause a lapse in adherence. Exercise, like walking or swimming, may relieve stress. Just making a list of things to do along with delegating and prioritizing this list can help manage stress.

When boredom causes the problem, keeping busy may be the answer. Clients can write a list of tasks to be completed or volunteer for an organization, take a class, learn a craft, or participate in any number of other activities.

Eating out is frequently a problem when others make the majority of the decisions. For example, a German meal served family style may lead to eating more than intended. A special occasion on which food is ordered for the client may result in eating inappropriately large amounts of fat. Many occasions call for spontaneity—beer and pizza after a bowling game or an office party.

Many options are available to help with social occasions:

1. The client can call the restaurant ahead of time to determine what is on the menu and eliminate surprises.
2. The client can bring in menus from favorite restaurants for review and role play with the counselor in selecting from a menu in a safe environment.
3. By saving all of the fat for the day and using it only at the special restaurant meal, clients can eat without worrying whether they are adhering to the low-fat eating plan.
4. Positive monologues can help clients work through an adherence-challenging situation.
5. Sometimes making a compromise can help the client through a difficult situation. For example, "I will order the cheese cake, but only eat one-third of it."
6. Eating slowly allows for eating less and prevents others from offering second servings.

Lapses in following the new low-fat eating pattern should not lead to feelings of guilt or anger. Deviation from the new eating pattern is a way to make corrections; past actions are something to forget. Clients can start anew with more appropriate eating behaviors viewing the setback as temporary or short-lived ("a bad day") rather than a forecasting of "never" getting better.

When commitment to the study begins to wane, a specific plan of action to help cope with adherence-challenging situations helps clients achieve goals in spite of the barriers. The following are two examples of plans to help eliminate barriers to adherence:

CLIENT: "I find that I go overboard when I attend parties with my husband."

COUNSELOR: "What are some preliminary planning steps that might help you?"

CLIENT: "I suppose I could do what I've done on other days and save my fat for the cocktail party. This means all of my other meals are virtually fat free."

COUNSELOR: "Are there ways to minimize your feelings of hunger during the party?"

CLIENT: "I could snack on low-fat snacks at home. This might prevent eating on a whim during the party."

COUNSELOR: "Great! One suggestion I might give is to avoid alcohol at the party. It can tend to make you careless and less aware of what you are eating."

A second example of overcoming barriers to success in the new eating pattern follows:

CLIENT: "I frequently eat more when I'm under stress."

COUNSELOR: "Can you describe in detail when stresses occur and what causes them?"

CLIENT: "Usually a hectic day when someone is on vacation is stressful."

COUNSELOR: "What can you do in advance to avoid these situations?"

CLIENT: "I could plan ahead by bringing a sack lunch on days when I know the potential for stress is greatest."

COUNSELOR: "Great idea!"

To be effective, a strategy should include the following:

1. A description of Strategy A to be taken plus an alternative Strategy B if A does not work.
2. Rehearsals of specific strategies through role playing or review mentally.
3. Application of these strategies to specific predictable stressful situations.

Stressful life events, including death or illness in the family, divorce, marriage, or retirement, can cause major changes in commitment. During these times, it is best to maintain changes and avoid making others. Even if a lapse in following an eating pattern occurs at this time, it should be viewed as temporary (one week) with the plan of renewing efforts the next week and maintaining good adherence.

Some clients may feel discouraged at times. The counselor can remind them of how much progress they have already made, focus on these positive changes, such as coming to appointments, and let clients know others experience this same discouragement.

At times clients whose commitment wavers can be encouraged by being asked to use their talents to show they are accomplished in other areas besides eating. For example, a client can bring in a favorite recipe to share with others or an artistic client might help design a handout with patient information.

Counseling on a low-fat eating pattern involves knowledge of the fat content of food and an ability to use that knowledge in designing individualized eating patterns. Knowledge can provide assistance in making social eating more pleasant. Reminders to avoid high-fat foods can be beneficial in maintaining good dietary adherence. When commitment wanes, the counselor's ability to deal with goal setting, positive self-talk, assertiveness training, shaping, self-monitoring, contracts, self-rewards, and group support becomes extremely important.

Adherence Tool 13-1 Monitoring Device

	Fat Grams for One Day
Meal or Snack	Grams of Fat
Breakfast	
	Total _____
Snack	
	Total _____
Lunch	
	Total _____
Snack	
	Total _____
Dinner	
	Total _____
Snack	
	Total _____
	TOTAL _____

Adherence Tool 13-2 Monitoring Device

	Budgeting for Fat in a Two-Day Period
Day	Grams of Fat
1 _____	_____
_____	_____
_____	_____
_____	_____
_____	Total _____
2 _____	_____
_____	_____
_____	_____
_____	_____
_____	Total _____

Adherence Tool 13-3 Monitoring Device

Low-Fat Action List for a Day

Make a list of specific types of eating behaviors involving low-fat eating that you wish to accomplish:

	Check off when accomplished
1.	( )
2.	( )
3.	( )
4.	( )
5.	( )

Examples: 1. Switch from high-fat weiners to lower-fat turkey franks.
2. Use skim milk instead of 1 percent milk.
3. Have fruit compote for dessert instead of a high-fat fruit cobbler.

Source: Courtesy of Laura Coleman, Joanne Csaplar, Johanna Dwyer, Carole Palmer, and Molly Holland.

Adherence Tool 13-4 Monitoring and Cueing Device

Low-Fat Eating Accomplishments

Sunday	Monday	Tuesday	Wednesday	Thursday	Friday	Saturday

Source: Courtesy of Laura Coleman, Joanne Csaplar, Johanna Dwyer, Carole Palmer, and Molly Holland.

Adherence Tool 13-5 Informational Device

Client Planning Chart

Meal planning can help you keep your total fat intake low. Before your next visit, plan three days of meals in which you avoid foods high in fat.

Meal	Day 1	Day 2	Day 3
Breakfast			
Snack			
Lunch			
Snack			
Dinner			
Snack			

Adherence Tool 13-6 Informational and Cueing Device

Stress Management Chart

When you feel overwhelmed, make a "to do" list of everything you need to get done.

Date   Item To Do

When you have finished the list, ask yourself the following questions:
1. Can I delete anything from this list that might be classified as unnecessary?
2. What can I delegate to a relative or friend?
3. What can I pay someone else to do?
4. What is the most important task? Now begin by doing it first.

Source: Courtesy of Laura Coleman, Joanne Csaplar, Johanna Dwyer, Carole Palmer, and Molly Holland.

Review of Chapter 13

(Answers in Appendix I)

1. List two problems associated with inappropriate eating behaviors when following a fat-controlled eating pattern.

    a. _____

    b. _____

2. List two dietary components to assess in modifying a diet for possible cancer risk prevention.

    a. _____

    b. _____

3. List three strategies that might help the client follow a fat-controlled eating pattern.

    a. _____

    b. _____

    c. _____

4. The following describes a problem situation with a client who has been instructed on a fat-controlled eating pattern to reduce risk of breast cancer.

    Mrs. B is trying to follow a low-fat diet. During an assessment of her current eating habits, it was apparent that most difficulties occur with the evening meal, which is traditionally high fat (potatoes with gravy, high-fat meat, buttered vegetable, and high-fat dessert). Mrs. B's family loves these high-fat meals. (a) What additional information might you ask for regarding current eating habits? (b) What strategies would you use to help alleviate the problem? (c) Why did you choose these strategies?

    a. _____

    b. _____

    c. _____

NOTES

1. Michael J. Hill, "Diet and Human Cancer: A New Era for Research," in Jozef V. Joossens, Michael J. Hill, and Jef Geboers, eds., *Diet and Human Carcinogenesis* (New York: Elsevier Science Publishers, 1986), p. 3.

2. Richard Doll and Richard Peto, "Avoidable Risks of Cancer in the United States Today," *Journal of National Cancer Institute* 66 (1981): 1226–1238; and Ernst L. Wynder and Gio B. Gori, "Contribution of the Environment to Cancer Incidence: An Epidemiologic Exercise," *Journal of National Cancer Institute* 58 (1977): 825–831.

3. O. Gregor, R. Toman, and F. Průsová, "Gastrointestinal Cancer and Nutrition," *Gut* 10 (1969): 1031–1034; B. S. Drascar and Doreen Irving, "Environmental Factors and Cancer of the Colon and Breast," *British Journal of Cancer* 27 (1973): 167–172; and Bruce Armstrong and Richard Doll, "Environmental Factors and Cancer Incidence and Mortality in Different Countries, with Special Reference to Dietary Practices," *International Journal of Cancer* 15 (1975): 617–631.

4. Kenneth K. Carroll, "Influence of Diet on Mammary Cancer," *Nutrition and Cancer* 2 (1981): 232–236; Armstrong and Doll, "Environmental Factors and Cancer Incidence and Mortality"; and Drascar and Irving, "Environmental Factors and Cancer of the Colon and Breast."

5. Bruce K. Armstrong, "The Role of Diet in Human Carcinogenesis with Special Reference to Environmental Cancer," in Howard Hiatt, J. D. Watson, and Jay A. Winsten, eds., *Origins of Human Cancer* (Cold Spring Harbor, N.Y.: Cold Spring Harbor Lab Press, 1977), pp. 557–566; and Armstrong and Doll, "Environmental Factors and Cancer Incidence and Mortality."

6. N. E. Day, "Some Aspects of the Epidemiology of Esophageal Cancer," *Cancer Research* 35 (1975): 3304–3307.

7. Pelayo Correa and William Haeszel, *Epidemiology of Cancer of the Digestive Tract* (Boston: Nijhoff, 1982), pp. 59–84; and Jozef V. Joossens and Jef Geboers, "Nutrition and Gastric Cancer," *Nutrition and Cancer* 2 (1981): 250–261.

8. J. M. Rivers and K. K. Collins, "Planning Meals that Lower Cancer Risk: A Reference Guide" (Washington, D.C.: American Institute for Cancer Research, 1984); C. Di Sogra and L. Groll, *Nutrition and Cancer Prevention: A Guide to Food Choices* (Palo Alto: Northern California Cancer Program, 1981); and U.S. Department of Health and Human Services, National Cancer Institute, *Diet, Nutrition, and Cancer Prevention: The Good News,* NIH Publication 87-2878 (Washington, D.C.: U.S. Government Printing Office, 1986).

9. Karen Glanz, "Nutrition Education for Risk Factor Reduction and Patient Education: A Review," *Preventive Medicine,* 14 (1985): 721–752.

10. "Dietary Modifications in Disease—Cancer" (Columbus, Ohio: Ross Laboratories, 1979).

11. Ibid.

12. Glanz, "Nutrition Education."

13. U.S. Department of Health and Human Services, *Eating Hints: Recipes and Tips for Better Nutrition During Cancer Treatment,* National Institutes of Health (NIH) Publication 80-2079 (Washington, D.C.: 1980).

14. Jo Ann S. Carson, "Nutrition in a Team Approach to the Rehabilitation of the Patient with Cancer," *Journal of the American Dietetic Association* 72 (1978): 407–409.

15. Dawn F. Campbell et al., "Relaxation: Its Effect on the Nutritional Status and Performance Status of Clients with Cancer," *Journal of the American Dietetic Association* 84 (1984): 201–204.

16. Glanz, "Nutrition Education."

Chapter 14

Nutrition Counseling in Treatment of Anorexia Nervosa and Bulimia

Objectives for Chapter 14

1. Identify inappropriate eating behaviors associated with anorexia and bulimia.
2. Identify how to assess problems associated with the client diagnosed as having anorexia or bulimia.
3. Identify strategies to treat inappropriate eating behaviors associated with anorexia and bulimia.

This chapter provides suggestions on solving problems encountered in two eating disorders: anorexia nervosa and bulimia. The American Dietetic Association's position on treatment of anorexia nervosa and bulimia includes the following goals:

1. assisting clients in understanding how the psychological and medical aspects of their disease relate to their food and weight behaviors and how they should be seen as a part of the team treatment goals.
2. establishing an alliance with clients concerning their food fears and eating behaviors, followed by gradual implementation of change.
3. involving family members to enhance their understanding of the eating disorder and to increase their support for treatment.[1]

Over the past decade, the understanding of eating disorders has grown. In the past they were diagnosed by excluding medical disorders instead of by using positive, empirical criteria. Diagnosis by this newer approach means finding the positive features of the disorder on psychiatric history and mental status examination.[2] This methodology has gradually displaced the approach of testing for all conceivable medical disorders that might be responsible for weight loss.

Recently more attention has been given to subclassifying anorexia nervosa into persons who are food restrictors and bulimic anorectics, who induce vomiting after unavoidable binges. Bulimics may be subclassified into those with a past history of anorexia nervosa and those without past diagnosis of anorexia nervosa.[3]

THEORIES AND FACTS ABOUT ANOREXIA NERVOSA

In recent years a variety of diagnostic criteria have been applied to anorexia nervosa. Various investigators have proposed a multitude of distinguishing factors,[4] yet several discriminating features continue to be unanimously emphasized:

1. self-inflicted weight loss accompanied by an effort to avoid mature body shape, which cannot be associated with other identifiable psychiatric causes, cachexia-inducing diseases, or externally imposed demands for reduced food intake
2. a morbid and persistent dread of fat
3. the manipulation of body weight through dietary restraint, self-induced vomiting, abuse of purgatives, or excessive exercise
4. poor body image shown in the misrepresentation of actual body dimensions or extreme loathing of body functions
5. amenorrhea and the development of other behavioral-physiological abnormalities associated with starvation.[5]

The physiological abnormalities of anorexia nervosa include amenorrhea, constipation, bloating, abdominal pain, cold intolerance, lethargy, excess energy, hypotension, hypothermia, dry skin, bradycardia, lanugo (down and wooly hair), edema, and petechiae. Mitchell provides an overview of medical complications by organ systems.[6] A brief review based on his chapter follows.

In general, hypoglycemia is common. Renal complications include dehydration and elevated blood urea nitrogen levels. Cardiopulmonary complications include bradycardia resulting from the adaptive metabolic effects of starvation and arrhythmias. Metabolic alkalosis has been frequently described in the anorexic person with hypochloremia and hypokalemia. In a medical workup a primary consideration must be neurological problems such as space-occupying hypothalamic tumors with secondary symptoms of anorexia nervosa. Studies have invariably associated anorexia nervosa with reduced levels of luteinizing hormone (LH) and follicle-stimulating hormone (FSH), with resulting amenorrhea. A major unresolved question is whether the hypothalamic dysfunction seen in clients with anorexia nervosa is a cause or a consequence of the disorder.

Behavioral abnormalities of anorexia nervosa include distorted attitudes about food, weight, and the body. Maladaptive thinking in anorexia nervosa extends beyond food and weight to other areas of experience.[7] Andersen reports several factors that maintain an anorexic pattern:

1. fear of fatness
2. perfectionism
3. enormity of hunger once it is recognized
4. altered perception of body size
5. altered gastric physiology
6. starvation becoming a way out for relief of anxiety from sources other than fear of fatness
7. difficulty letting go of anorexia nervosa symptoms because it means letting go of the one part of life that is under control while feeling inadequate about the rest of one's abilities, and trying something that one is not already good at and may not do perfectly

8. a primary goal in life of weight control and limited indulgence in food
9. fears that are all related to food and weight (an area that can be controlled).[8]

THEORIES AND FACTS ABOUT BULIMIA

The essential feature of bulimia is that clients suffer from actual, rather than feared, episodes of binge eating. The binges are terminated only by physical distress or social interruption and are followed by remorse and attempts to rid oneself of the food. The true bulimic is distinguished from the more universal occasional indulgence that most people experience at holidays by the underlying morbid fear of fatness. It is this fear that prompts the purge. There is no exact number of episodes required to make the diagnosis, but one or two attempts to purge obviously do not qualify a person as bulimic.

In contrast to anorexia nervosa, almost no systematic work has been published on the signs and symptoms reported by clients with bulimia. These clients frequently complain of constipation, bloating, abdominal pain, weakness, and lethargy. Although prolonged amenorrhea is uncommon, many bulimics report irregular menses.[9]

Routine laboratory screening of bulimics reveals normal renal function or, at most, an elevated blood-urea-nitrogen level, including dehydration.[10] Elevated serum amylase levels are common in clients with bulimia.[11] Swelling of the salivary glands has been documented in bulimic clients.[12] Gastric dilatation in bulimia has been reported.[13]

With fluid loss due to vomiting, laxative abuse and diuretic abuse disturbances in electrolytes are common. The commonly encountered changes include metabolic alkalosis, hypochloremia, and hypokalemia.[14] Neurological and endocrine abnormalities are just beginning to be linked to bulimia.[15]

Behavioral features of bulimia follow:

1. Large amounts of foods are usually ingested with great quantities of sweets or fats predominating.
2. Foods are eaten rapidly.
3. Foods are eaten without appreciation of taste, texture, or quality.
4. Foods are eaten in secret.
5. Several factors trigger onset:
   a. hunger
   b. social disappointment
   c. unstructured activities
   d. anxiety
   e. boredom
   f. anger
   g. depression.[16]

There are many shared and contrasting characteristics in persons with anorexia nervosa and those with bulimia. The central two characteristics of both illnesses are a morbid fear of fatness and the pursuit of slimness as a method of solving crises in development or dealing with painful or unacceptable emotions. The illnesses also share a common predisposing sociocultural influence toward overvaluing slimness.

While anorexia nervosa and bulimia may not become a problem until the later teenage years or beyond, the social pressure toward slimness begins earlier in life. This same preoccupation with thinness is usually emphasized within the family. Admonition to diet and avoid overweight is common in the family setting even though the client may have a genetic predisposition to above-average weight. The abundance of food in our society offers a quick "fix" for emotional distress, but the calories are seen as negative and the individual experiences great conflict.

The inability to perceive inner feelings states (hunger, anxiety, sadness, or anger) and the greater ability to deny the urge to eat characterize the food-restricting anorexic client. In contrast, greater awareness of inner states, lessened ability to control urges and impulses or both characterize the bulimic personality.[17]

The client with anorexia nervosa rarely vomits or abuses diuretics or laxatives, unlike the bulimic, who is prone to vomiting and laxative abuse. More severe weight loss is seen in the anorexic patient than in bulimics. Persons with anorexia nervosa tend to be slightly younger; bulimics, slightly older. The anorexic client is more introverted; the bulimic, more extroverted.[18]

In anorexia nervosa, hunger is denied; in bulimia it is experienced. In anorexia the eating behavior is considered normal and a source of esteem, but the eating behaviors of a bulimic are considered foreign and are a source of distress. Sexual inactivity is common in anorexia, while bulimia is associated with more sexual activity. In anorexia an obsessive personality predominates; in bulimia a more hysterical obsessive personality is seen.

The anorexic client usually dies of starvation or suicide when the disease is chronic. Death in the bulimic is usually from hypokalemia or suicide.

The common feature of an anorexic is amenorrhea. Bulimics more frequently experience irregular menses.

The prognosis for a client with anorexia nervosa is more favorable than that of the bulimic. There tend to be fewer behavioral abnormalities associated with anorexia nervosa whereas bulimics have many more problems in this area—stealing, drug and alcohol abuse, and self-mutilation.[19]

ADHERENCE TO TREATMENT PROGRAMS FOR ANOREXIA AND BULIMIA

Anderson summarizes treatment outcomes for anorexia clients who are a part of a program involving nutritional rehabilitation, intensive psychotherapy, maintenance, and discharge and follow-up. Table 14-1 reviews outcomes for clients in this study.[20] The best outcome occurred with clients who were younger, less chronically ill, had fewer hospitalizations, and had reached a less severely lowered weight on admission. This group contained a higher percentage of food-restricting clients than did the worst-outcome group, which included a substantially greater number of individuals with bulimic complications.

Treatment outcomes for bulimics are encouraging. Data below show evidence of success in a treatment program conducted at the University of Cincinnati Medical College in an Eating Disorders Clinic involving group psychotherapy, family therapy, individual therapy, and body image therapy.[21] In general, results (based on episodes of binging and purging) are positive with subjects showing no tendency toward regression and evidence of marked continuing improvement.

Table 14-1 Best, Worst, and Average Outcome after Inpatient Treatment for Anorexia Nervosa

	Best	Average	Worst
Number of clients	11	90	14
Age at admission (yrs)	18.1	22	25.4
Sex	11F	85F; 5M	13F; 1M
Years of illness	2.3	4.65	4.7
Number of previous hospitalizations	0.8	1.5	3
Percent of ideal body weight (IBW) on admission	77%	72.6%	63.6%
Percent of food restricting patients	73%	59%	36%
Months of follow-up	41	33	43
Percent of IBW at follow-up	106%	88.8%	68.3%

Source: Handbook of Eating Disorders: Physiology, Psychology, and Treatment of Obesity, Anorexia, and Bulimia by K. D. Brownell and J. P. Foreyt (Eds.), p. 345, Basic Books, Inc., © 1986.

INAPPROPRIATE EATING BEHAVIORS

General information on eating behaviors is presented above. A few more specific behaviors are described below:

One woman with anorexia nervosa ate the same food every day for six weeks, 300 calories per day. A typical day would be as follows:

Breakfast	*Lunch*	*Dinner*
8 oz. Hot Tea	1 cup Lettuce	2 oz. Broiled Meat ("Squeezed
Artificial Sweetener	¼ cup Green Beans (cooked)	until it is like paper to get rid of the grease") 2 Tbsp. of Lettuce

This person describes not being able to eat in front of people and never with her family. She ate only food from home. If she had to eat in a restaurant, she allowed herself only lettuce salads. If she did not carry food from home with her and lettuce salads weren't available, she ate nothing.

One woman admitted to eating only two foods—pressure-cooked chicken breast and boiled okra.

Anorexics' exercise regimens are exhausting, including taking ten-mile walks each day, going up and down stairways ten times a day, and doing push-ups for one to two hours at a time.

The description of food intake for a bulimic might be as follows:

- two large pizzas
- one cake
- one dozen cookies
- one dozen doughnuts
- one box of cereal and one gallon of milk.

This binge would be followed by vomiting and large doses of a stimulus-type laxative. One client followed this type of ritual every night for close to a year.

ASSESSMENT OF EATING BEHAVIORS

Assessment of eating disorders is a crucial part of disease treatment. Several faulty thinking patterns characterize eating disorders. Dichotomous reasoning, which involves thinking in extreme, absolute, or all-or-nothing terms, is a typical pattern. The client divides food into "good" and "bad" categories. The following are dichotomous examples of persons with eating disorders:

PATIENT 1: "I gained one pound of weight. I can see my stomach bulge. I look horrible."

PATIENT 2: "I ate the skin on that chicken leg. I'm so miserable. I've lost total control over my diet."

PATIENT 3: "My husband is just right." (Actually he is 120 percent over ideal body weight.) "I'm such a fat slob." (She is 10 percent below ideal body weight.)

The anorexic person has idealized often unattainable notions of happiness, contentment, and success.[22]

The anorexic person feels that strangers or casual friends will notice if she gains a pound or eats a high-calorie, "forbidden" food. The client is frequently oversensitive to disapproval from others. Superstitious thinking is often a pattern in persons with eating disorders. For example, after eating a small amount of a forbidden food, a client may take laxatives despite the knowledge that they do not result in malabsorption. Extreme anxiety may result from only a slight deviation from an exercise ritual.

Magnification is characterized by overestimation of the significance of undesirable events. Clients with eating disorders reliably overinterpret small increases in weight, and in self-evaluations they magnify poor performances and minimize accomplishments.

Selective abstraction is also common in eating disorders. An example is the belief that thinness equals self-worth and fatness equals incompetence.

Overgeneralizations involve applying one rule inappropriately to dissimilar situations. Weight loss, the person with an eating disorder thinks, is the secret to competence because a person the client knows is thin and very competent. Another example is the person who remembers being unhappy at normal weight and, therefore, assumes that weight gain will produce unhappiness.

Bruch described underlying assumptions that characterize the thinking of clients with eating disorders, for example, "body shape equals self-worth" or "family members are infallible." These assumptions are common in the thoughts of persons with bulimia and anorexia nervosa.[23]

Researchers distinguished two components of self-concept, a deficit in which is common in eating disorders. The first, self-esteem, is one's sense of own self-worth, and the second, self-awareness, is the ability to identify and respond accurately to inner experiences. Bruch describes the deficits in self-awareness in clinical examples as clients' sense of "not knowing how they feel."[24]

Clients with eating disorders have many misconceptions, faulty reasoning patterns, and erroneous beliefs about their bodies. Counselors must identify and label them without undermining their confidence in thinking for themselves.

The Diagnostic Survey for Eating Disorders (DSED) provides a detailed assessment of background information about symptomatic eating behavior.[25]

TREATMENT STRATEGIES

Treatment Strategies To Deal with Lack of Knowledge

Many anorexics and bulimics do not see themselves as having a disease. One of the first steps in treating eating disorders is to define the problem.

Andersen identified four stages of treatment: nutritional rehabilitation; intensive, individualized psychotherapy; a maintenance or practice period; and a follow-up program. The stages overlap, but they can be thought of as building on one another.[26]

The first stage of this treatment program relies heavily on providing the client with information about the program. Information is also gathered about the client's caloric intake, meal frequency, and meal content. Eating balanced meals in a reasonable amount of time is emphasized. This is *not* a time for discussion of calories or weight; giving that type of information early in the course of treatment can be disastrous. In addition, clients at this time can learn and practice assertiveness training and relaxation. At this time clients take medications only if they are needed for anxiety or depression. Tube feedings, hyperalimentation, phenothiazines, and strict behavior modification are avoided.

Strategies To Deal with Forgetfulness

If medications are recommended, forgetting may become a problem. Adherence Tool 14-1 is an example of form on which clients can record the medication intake.

Strategies To Deal with Lack of Commitment

Much of the treatment of the client with anorexia nervosa involves intensive psychotherapy revolving around individual, group, and family involvement. The therapy is intensive, individualized, and coordinated to include support from a psychiatrist or psychologist, with emphasis on precipitating factors, developmental issues (responsibility and sexuality), features of temperament (perfectionism, self-esteem, sensitivity, obsessionality, need to control), and insight and ability to cope with these features. Specific client-identified issues might be discussed at this time. Other treatments might involve gradual weight increases to goal range, control of vomiting, reduction of excessive, non-goal-directed physical activity, relaxation techniques, and continued assertiveness training.[27]

The last phase of treatment involves returning control to the client, with self-management of food content, quantity, pattern of eating, and time to eat as a goal. Clients should maintain their weight within the normal range, with exercise of the appropriate quantity and balance.

During the final phase preparation for discharge, such as trips to purchase clothing for their new, more appropriate weight and practice in eating situations where most difficulties will arise, is important. Counselors can try to prevent problems before they arise by visiting restaurants with clients and helping them select food, by discussing problems with eating during a social gathering, and by planning scenarios that help clients work through a problem. For example, the counselor and client can plan how to select from an hors d'oeuvre tray instead of bringing food from home to a party. For the bulimic client scenarios might involve planning for three meals a day. Clients can include a friend to make meal times more fun.

Good recordkeeping is essential for outpatient therapy. The record might include time of eating, location, food eaten, events (including binges) and feelings (Adherence Tool 14-2). Andersen has recommended 50-minute outpatient visits once a week.[28] Clients weigh only in the office to avoid too much dependency on weight change. The dietary program is tailored to individual clients. These clients need assurance that they will not become overweight. For younger clients, the family has a large role in food preparation and supervision of eating. By age 16 and older, clients may begin to assume full responsibility for food preparation, but they should not be allowed to have sole control over the kitchen area or to prepare separate meals for themselves. Sessions with individuals might begin with a brief review of the week in general and then a detailed look at food records. The emphasis should be on learning patterns that include emotional states and difficulties in eating.

Cognitive therapy and behavioral methods have been recognized as important for both anorexia nervosa and nonemaciated clients with bulimia.[29] Garner and Bemis have delineated five main features of cognitive therapy:

1. Emphasis is on conscious experience, not unconscious motivation.
2. Targets are meaning and cognitions that account for maladaptive feelings or emotions.
3. Stress is on the use of questioning during an interview.
4. Focus is on the active and directive involvement of the medical team.
5. Importance is attached to behavioral and scientific psychology.[30]

Little can be done about anorexia nervosa until the client has begun to express a desire to change. During the initial phase of cognitive therapy, trust and openness must gradually evolve. Rather than focusing solely on weight, the client is led to understand the emotional distress that has led to weight loss. If the client denies distress, a new approach that focuses on describing the effects of starvation and conveying information about anorexia or bulimia should take priority. The basic goal of the counselor should be to help the client redefine the short-term goals of therapy as eliminating starvation symptoms, not simple weight gain. The counselor should encourage the client to examine long-term consequences of behavior daily.

Garner and Bemis emphasize some practical suggestions for dealing with eating disorders.[31] Most clients do not attribute starvation symptoms to a common cause, and a description of the starvation state helps to integrate experiences. Keys describes the effects of starvation in the following categories: (1) attitudes and behavior toward food, (2) cognitive changes, (3) emotional and social changes, and (4) physical changes.[32]

Many behaviors associated with starvation may go unrecognized by the client with anorexia nervosa. Behaviors toward food include preoccupations with food; unusual eating habits, including binging; increased consumption of coffee, tea, and spices; and collection of recipes, cookbooks and menus. Cognitive changes related to starvation include an inability to concentrate, poor judgment, and apathy. Emotional and social changes are depression, anxiety, irritability, anger, social withdrawal, and personality changes on psychological tests. Some changes are physical, including sleep disturbances, weakness, gastrointestinal disturbances, hyperacuity to noise and light, edema, hypothermia, paresthesia, decreased metabolic rate, and lack of sexual interest.

Garner, Garfinkel, and Bemis recommend that a physician monitor the client's weight if it drops or approaches 75 percent of premorbid weight.[33] Targeting a goal weight should be approached carefully. Garner et al. have recommended a goal weight range of three to five pounds above the client's menstrual weight threshold and as close as can be tolerated to about 10 percent below her highest weight prior to the onset of the disorder.[34] This range is merely a guideline and may require staging to achieve over time.

Monitoring weight should be an ongoing process, and disregarding weight loss is not advisable. The approach to monitoring should be one of concern for the client's physical and psychological well-being.[35] Information on weight statistics should be individualized for clients. Some clients may state: "I would prefer not to know my weight. It upsets me." These persons are told their weight only if there is a constant upward or downward trend over several weeks. Others may say, "I really like to know my weight status."

Meal planning is particularly an informative experience and partially a means of fostering commitment. It helps clients eat "mechanically" according to predetermined, individualized plans.[36] Choices at mealtimes are minimized to assist the client in avoiding the urge to "choose" foods very low in total calories. Structured eating and monitoring of food intake through detailed records may be gradually replaced by more natural eating behavior.

An important step in treating eating disorders is the reintroduction of foods consumed before the onset of the eating disorder into the client's meal plan.[37] Bulimic persons should be presented with evidence that dieting or rigid avoidance of desired foods can lead to cognitive and physiological conditions that increase the probability of binge eating.[38] The idea of reintroducing foods that the client once avoided should be complemented with cognitive methods.

Several basic cognitive techniques described by Garner and Bemis have worked well in treating anorexia nervosa and bulimia.[39] The rationale for the first, articulation of beliefs, is that merely discussing beliefs leads to changes in behavior. For example, one client stated, "Just by talking about my negative attitudes toward obesity, I began to change my ways of thinking. These attitudes toward obesity were very inconsistent with my attitudes toward other minority groups."

Operationalizing beliefs may lead to more realistic thinking. For example, one patient stated, "I automatically define achieving, being popular, and being competent in terms of weight. Maybe that isn't a valid way of looking at the situation."

Decentering or evaluating a belief from a different perspective may foster more realistic attitudes. One woman stated that she considered herself very overweight, but a woman of similar height and weight she described as "too thin." The recognition of this unrealistic way of thinking about weight may lead to its gradual erosion. The goal is to help clients appreciate that their own standards are far more stringent and unforgiving than those they apply to others.

Ellis has described a technique called decatastrophizing, in which the counselor challenges anxiety that results from the arbitrary definition of negative consequences as intolerable, despite evidence to the contrary. One client described her feelings about exercise: "I am petrified to do one fewer than 50 push-ups each day because I'm afraid I will begin gaining weight." To help decatastrophize this situation, the counselor might ask, "What would be the worst thing that could happen if you missed one push-up?" This question helps the client think more clearly about unrealistic consequences. A counselor may also need to challenge the words "should," "must," or "ought."[40] Many of the anorexic client's thoughts about food, weight and performance include these words.[41]

The process of working through cognitions might also be closely tied to behavior change. In the areas of food and weight, behavior change might include going through scenarios of selecting high-calorie foods from a favorite restaurant menu. The thoughts associated with these discussions might also be included.

Asking the client to test out a situation may be important. For example, a client may assume that reduced exercise will have a major impact on weight. To evaluate this idea objectively, the client might reduce exercise and see what her weight is at the next visit. A second client may think that others will see her as gluttonous if she eats a dessert. She might conduct an informal poll to determine people's attitudes about desserts. The counselor might help prepare the client for ways to interpret negative results in a nondestructive manner.

When their reasoning ability is impaired by intense anxiety, clients may be taught techniques of distraction.[42] For example, the client who is overwhelmed by the urge to vomit after eating may interrupt the process by prearranging "coping phrases" such as "I need to have the food stay down to help me gradually return to a positive attitude when I feel full." Going for a walk or talking to someone on the telephone immediately after eating may provide a potent enough distraction to eliminate the urge to vomit.

A major goal of cognitive therapy is to reattribute the eating disorders to failure rather than success and focus on self-concept deficits that have led to the client's identification with the illness. This cognitive process may be summarized in the following steps for each client:

1. Self-monitor thoughts.
2. Recognize connection between dysfunctional thoughts and maladaptive behaviors and emotions.
3. Examine validity of beliefs related to weight, exercise, and food.
4. Substitute realistic interpretations based on the evidence.
5. Modify underlying assumptions that determine dysfunctional beliefs.[43]

For the bulimic, the cognitive strategies just proposed can be of value. Garner and Bemis have also advocated a number of cognitive-behavioral approaches to help break the cycle of binging and purging:

1. gradual exposure and attitude changes to "forbidden" foods
2. challenging dysfunctional attitudes related to body shape
3. information and education
4. self-control
5. self-monitoring
6. stimulus-control
7. developing or strengthening social skills.[44]

In summary, many of the techniques used to treat anorexia and bulimia are identical. The eventual goal is to improve eating behaviors through cognitive therapy and eventual self-management.

Adherence Tool 14-1 Monitoring Device

Record of Medication Taking		
Type of Medication	Time Recommended for Taking	Place an (X) in the Space If Medication Was Taken.

Adherence Tool 14-2 Monitoring Device

		Food Record		
Time	Food Eaten	Location	Events (include binging, vomiting, etc.)	Feelings

Review of Chapter 14
(Answers in Appendix I)

1. Identify inappropriate eating behaviors frequently associated with anorexia.

   a. _____

   b. _____

   c. _____

   d. _____

   e. _____

   f. _____

2. Identify inappropriate eating behaviors frequently associated with bulimia.

   a. _____

   b. _____

   c. _____

3. Identify the dietary component that must be assessed for persons diagnosed with anorexia and bulimia.

   a. _____

4. List strategies that might help clients follow an eating pattern appropriate to treating anorexia and bulimia.

   a. _____

   b. _____

   c. _____

   d. _____

   e. _____

   f. _____

   g. _____

   h. _____

5. The following describes a client who has been diagnosed with anorexia. Identify strategies that might help facilitate weight gain in this client.

   > Mrs. R is 34 years old. She weighs 90 pounds and is five feet six inches tall. She eats mostly lettuce and chicken, which she grinds up and washes to remove "all of the fat." Her family is very unhappy because she refuses to eat out with them. She states that she has a fear of restaurants because nothing on the menu is "right" for her. (a) What additional information might you elicit from the client? (b) What strategies would you use to help alleviate the problem? (Provide a dialogue between the client and the counselor to describe what might happen during an interview.) (c) Why did you choose these strategies?

   a. _____

   b. _____

   c. _____

NOTES

1. American Dietetic Association, "Position of the American Dietetic Association: Nutrition Intervention in the Treatment of Anorexia Nervosa and Bulimia Nervosa," *Journal of the American Dietetic Association* 88 (1988): 68.

2. J.P. Feighner et al., "Diagnostic Criteria for Use in Psychiatric Research," *Archives of General Psychiatry* 26 (1972): 57–63; and American Psychiatric Association, *Diagnostic and Statistical Manual of Mental Disorders,* 3rd ed. (Washington, D.C.: American Psychiatric Association, 1980), pp. 67–71.

3. Gerald Russell, "Bulimia Nervosa: An Ominous Variant of Anorexia Nervosa" *Psychological Medicine* 9 (1979): 429–448; and Christopher Fairburn, "Area Review: Bulimia Nervosa," *Annals of Behavioral Medicine* 9 (1987): 2–7.

4. Peter J. Dally and Joan Gomez *Anorexia Nervosa* (London: William Heinemann Medical Books, Ltd., 1979), pp. 11–24; H. G. Morgan and G. F. M. Russell, "Value of Family Background and Clinical Features as Predictors of Long-term Outcome in Anorexia Nervosa: Four-year Follow-up Study of 41 Patients," *Psychological Medicine* 5 (1975): 355–371; John P. Feighner et al., "Diagnosis Criteria for Use in Psychiatric Research," *Archives of General Psychiatry* 26

(1972): 57–63; Nancy Rollins and Eugene Piazza, "Diagnosis of Anorexia Nervosa: A Critical Appraisal," *Journal of the American Academy of Child Psychiatry,* 17 (1978): 126–137; D. L. Norris, "Clinical Diagnosis Criteria for Primary Anorexia Nervosa," *South African Medical Journal* 56 (1979): 987–992; and American Psychiatric Association, *Diagnosis and Statistical Manual,* pp. 67–69.

5. Michael Stroker, "Anorexia Nervosa: History and Psychological Concepts," in Kelly D. Brownell and John P. Foreyt, eds., *Handbook of Eating Disorders* (New York: Basic Books, 1986), p. 237.

6. James E. Mitchell, "Anorexia Nervosa: Medical and Physiological Aspects," in Brownell and Foreyt, eds. *Handbook of Eating Disorders,* pp. 248–259.

7. David M. Garner, "Cognitive Therapy for Anorexia Nervosa," in Brownell and Foreyt, eds. *Handbook of Eating Disorders,* p. 301.

8. Arnold E. Andersen, *Practical Comprehensive Treatment of Anorexia Nervosa and Bulimia* (Baltimore, Md.: Johns Hopkins University Press, 1985), p. 75.

9. James E. Mitchell, "Bulimia: Medical and Psychological Aspects," in Brownell and Foreyt, eds., *Handbook of Eating Disorders,* pp. 379–380.

10. James E. Mitchell et al., "Electrolyte and Other Physiologic Abnormalities in Patients with Bulimia," *Psychological Medicine* 13 (1983): 273–278.

11. Harry E. Gwirtsman et al., "Neuroendocrine Abnormalities in Bulimia," *American Journal of Psychiatry* 140 (1983): 559–563.

12. J. Dawson and C. Jones, "Vomiting-Induced Hypokalemic Alkalosis and Parotid Swelling," *Practitioner* 218 (1977): 267–268; and Phillip A. Levin et al., "Benign Parotid Enlargement in Bulimia," *Annals of Internal Medicine* 93 (1980): 827–829.

13. James E. Mitchell, Richard L. Pyle, and Richard A. Miner, "Gastric Dilatation as a Complication of Bulimia," *Psychosomatics* 23 (1982): 96–97.

14. Mitchell et al., "Electrolyte and Other Physiologic Abnormalities," pp. 273–278.

15. Mitchell, "Bulimia: Medical and Physiological Aspects," pp. 383–384.

16. Andersen, *Practical Comprehensive Treatment,* p. 106.

17. Ibid., p. 110.

18. Ibid.

19. Ibid.

20. Arnold E. Andersen, "Inpatient and Outpatient Treatment of Anorexia Nervosa," in Brownell and Foreyt, eds. *Handbook of Eating Disorders,* p. 345.

21. Susan C. Wooley and Ann Kearney-Cooke, "Intensive Treatment of Bulimia and Body-Image Disturbance," in Brownell and Foreyt, eds., *Handbook of Eating Disorders,* pp. 496–500.

22. David M. Garner et al., "A Multidimensional Psychotherapy for Anorexia Nervosa," *International Journal of Eating Disorders* 1 (1982): 3–46.

23. Hilde Bruch, *Eating Disorders: Obesity, Anorexia Nervosa, and the Person Within* (New York: Basic Books, 1973), pp. 87–105.

24. David M. Garner and Kelly M. Bemis, "A Cognitive-Behavioral Approach to Anorexia Nervosa," *Cognitive Therapy and Research* 6 (1982): 123–150; Arnold E. Andersen, "Cognitive Therapy for Anorexia Nervosa," in David M. Garner and Paul E. Garfinkel, eds., *Handbook of Psychotherapy for Anorexia Nervosa and Bulimia* (New York: Guilford Press, 1985), pp. 107–146; and H. Bruch, *Eating Disorders,* p. 338.

25. Kelly D. Brownell and John P. Foreyt, *Handbook of Eating Disorders: Physiology, Psychology, and Treatment of Obesity, Anorexia, and Bulimia* (New York: Basic Books, Inc., 1986), pp. 408–428.

26. Arnold E. Andersen, *Practical Comprehensive Treatment,* pp. 54–82.

27. Ibid., pp. 89–90.

28. Ibid., p. 92.

29. Garner and Bemis, "A Cognitive-Behavioral Approach"; Andersen, "Cognitive Therapy for Anorexia Nervosa," in Garner and Garfinkel, eds., *Handbook of Psychotherapy for Anorexia Nervosa and Bulimia,* pp. 107–146; and David M. Garner, Paul E. Garfinkel, and Kelly M. Bemis, "A Multidimensional Psychotherapy for Anorexia Nervosa," *International Journal of Eating Disorders* 1 (1982): 3–46.

30. Garner and Bemis, "Cognitive Therapy for Anorexia Nervosa."

31. Ibid., p. 306.

32. Ancel B. Keys, "Psychological Problems in Starvation," in *The Biology of Human Starvation,* vol. 2 (Minneapolis: University of Minnesota Press, 1950), pp. 767–782.

33. Garner, Garfinkel, and Bemis, "A Multidimensional Psychotherapy for Anorexia Nervosa."

34. David M. Garner et al., "Psychoeducational Principles in the Treatment of Bulimia and Anorexia Nervosa," in Garner and Garfinkel, eds., *Handbook of Psychotherapy for Anorexia Nervosa and Bulimia,* pp. 513–572.

35. Garner and Bemis, "A Cognitive-Behavioral Approach"; and Garner, "Cognitive Therapy for Anorexia Nervosa," p. 306.

36. Garner, "Cognitive Therapy for Anorexia Nervosa," p. 308.

37. Arthur H. Crisp, *Anorexia Nervosa: Let Me Be* (London: Academic Press, 1980), pp. 95–146; and Russell, "Bulimia Nervosa: An Ominous Variant of Anorexia Nervosa."

38. Garner et al., "Psychoeducational Principles in the Treatment of Bulimia and Anorexia Nervosa," pp. 513–572.

39. Garner and Bemis, "Cognitive Therapy for Anorexia Nervosa."

40. Garner and Bemis, "A Cognitive-Behavioral Approach."

41. Garner and Bemis, "Cognitive Therapy for Anorexia Nervosa."

42. Ibid.

43. Ibid., p. 318.

44. Ibid., pp. 319–320.

Chapter 15

Nutrition Counseling in Management of Pregnancy

Objectives for Chapter 15

1. Identify inappropriate eating behaviors in pregnancy.
2. Identify how to assess problems associated with inappropriate eating patterns in pregnancy.
3. Identify strategies to overcome inappropriate eating patterns in pregnancy.

This chapter suggests ways to solve problems of inappropriate eating patterns during pregnancy. The American Dietetic Association's *Handbook of Clinical Dietetics* lists the following as the purpose of nutritional management during pregnancy:

1. assure that energy sources are adjusted to 15 percent above average nonpregnant needs
2. adjust total daily protein intake to 1.3 grams per kilogram of body weight for an adolescent aged 15 to 18, and 1.7 grams per kilogram for younger girls (Two-thirds of total protein intake should be of high biological quality, such as that found in eggs, milk, meat, or soy protein, and adequate total energy intake is essential for optimal protein utilization.)
3. supplement diet with 30 to 60 milligrams of elemental iron daily throughout pregnancy
4. supplement diet with 400 to 800 micrograms per day of folic acid
5. allow prepregnancy intake of sodium and fluids.[1]

THEORIES AND FACTS ABOUT DIET IN PREGNANCY

Poor nutritional practices before pregnancy, during pregnancy, or both are probably the commonest cause of fetal growth retardation in the world.[2] In the developed world, where no serious evidence of malnutrition exists, maternal nutrition affects fetal growth. For example, gestational age held constant, maternal pregravid weight and weight gain during pregnancy are very important determinants of fetal weight.[3] Severe malnutrition, as observed in the Dutch famine,[4] produces its most marked effects when present in the last half to third of pregnancy, when fetal growth is most rapid.[5]

The nutritional requirements of both mother and infant during pregnancy are shown in Table 15-1. This table indicates a set of nonpregnant requirements based on age and size (height and weight) to which is added an extra sum for pregnancy needs. Table 15-2 summarizes the nutrient demands of pregnancy, the increases in nutrients recommended by the National Research Council, the reasons for the increases, and food sources supplying these needs.[6] Extra calories, protein, calcium, zinc, iron, and folacin are required during pregnancy. A healthy young woman who meets the guidelines in Table 15-2 and eats amounts dictated by her appetite will gain more than 20 pounds and be well nourished during pregnancy and lactation.[7] Translated into foods, the guidelines emphasize animal proteins, including milk and milk products, and fresh fruits and vegetables. Since many eating patterns do not include enough iron and folate, supplementation of these nutrients is recommended during pregnancy.[8]

RESEARCH ON ADHERENCE TO APPROPRIATE EATING PATTERNS IN PREGNANCY

Dietary regimens in pregnancy usually require little change if prepregnancy diets are adequate. Dwyer and Jacobson list factors that may predispose the pregnant woman to need nutrition counseling.[9] Table 15-3 outlines screening criteria for nutrition counseling and types of problems to assess before counseling.

Inappropriate Eating Behaviors

Adherence to the eating pattern described above can be adversely affected by gastrointestinal symptoms and sociocultural influences. (See "Strategies for Dealing with Lack of Knowledge" for suggestions on preventing and solving nutritional problems arising from gastrointestinal symptoms.)

Many pregnant women experience nausea and vomiting during the first trimester of pregnancy.[10] These symptoms can cause major problems with dietary adequacy. In the second and third trimesters, the growth of the uterus alters the position of the stomach. A reflux of the stomach contents into the esophagus because of uterine pressure and decreased gastric motility causes heartburn, which may lead the mother to reduce the intake of certain important nutrients. Eating inappropriately may lead to constipation, as may iron supplementation. If the mother consumes foods high in fiber and minimizes liquid intake, constipation will be an even greater problem.

Culture may greatly influence inappropriate eating behaviors. Many Puerto Rican families, for example, classify foods, diseases, and medicines according to a therapeutic system called the hot-cold theory of disease. Illnesses are classified as hot or cold, and the body needs foods in the opposite classification before it can achieve natural balance. A pregnant woman would be careful to eliminate from her diet hot foods or medications to prevent the baby from being born with a rash. Because iron tablets and vitamins are considered "hot," they are to be avoided unless taken with herb tea or fruit juice, which "neutralize" them. During the first and second trimester, milk of magnesia or antacids are also thought to prevent the baby from being born with a rash.[11] Not all Puerto Rican families adhere to this system, but counselors must recognize these practices in their design of food patterns.

Some Chinese families view foods as yin (cold) and yang (hot), a system analogous to the Puerto Rican family's hot-cold system. A balance between the two is favorable to health: too much yang food leads to a yang illness, which a yin food can counteract. Chicken is a yang food; melon is a yin food. Pregnancy, a yin condition, is believed to

Table 15-1 Recommended Dietary Allowances

		Nonpregnant				Pregnant
	Years	11–14	15–18	19–22	23–50	
Weight	Pounds	101	120	120	120	
Height	Inches	62	64	64	64	
Energy	Calories	2200	2100	2100	2000	+300
Protein	(g)	46	46	44	44	+30
Fat-soluble vitamins						
Vitamin A	(RE)[a]	800	800	800	800	+200
Vitamin D	(mcg)[b]	10	10	7.5	5	+5
Vitamin E	(mg)	8	8	8	8	+2
Water-soluble vitamins						
Ascorbic Acid	(mg)	50	60	60	60	+20
Folacin	(mcg)	400	400	400	400	+400
Niacin	(mg)	15	14	14	13	+2
Riboflavin	(mg)	1.3	1.3	1.3	1.2	+0.3
Thiamin	(mg)	1.1	1.1	1.1	1.0	+0.4
Vitamin B_6	(mg)	1.8	2.0	2.0	2.0	+0.6
Vitamin B_{12}	(mcg)	3.0	3.0	3.0	3.0	+1.0
Minerals						
Calcium	(mg)	1200	1200	800	800	+400
Phosphorus	(mg)	1200	1200	800	800	+400
Iodine	(mcg)	150	150	150	150	+25
Iron	(mg)	18	18	18	18	+18[c]
Magnesium	(mg)	300	300	300	300	+150
Zinc	(mg)	15	15	15	15	+5

[a]Retinol Equivalent (RE) = 5 International Units (IU).
[b]1 mcg = 40 IU.
[c]The use of a 30–60 mg oral iron supplement is recommended.
Source: Adapted from *Recommended Dietary Allowances*, 9th ed., by Food and Nutrition Board, National Research Council, with permission of National Academy of Sciences, © 1980.

weaken the body. Yang foods such as rice, wine, chicken, lychee, and ginger counteract the yin condition following delivery.[12]

Southern blacks who eat large quantities of grits, hot breads, corn bread, and collards and kale cooked with salt pork frequently have inadequate amounts of protein, vitamins, and minerals in their diets.[13]

Although vegetarian diets can be nutritionally adequate during pregnancy, some habits associated with them may be inappropriate. The pregnant vegan who consumes unfortified soybean milk in lieu of dairy products may need supplements of vitamin B_{12}, vitamin D, riboflavin, calcium, and iron.[14]

Some pregnant women experience pica, a craving for an unusual substance. Common substances eaten are clay or laundry soap. This practice is frequently seen in the black woman with cultural roots in the poor South.[15]

Lower economic status is associated with many inappropriate eating behaviors in the pregnant woman as well as problems of accessibility of prenatal care and proper nutrients for adequate health.[16] For poor persons to whom health care is unavailable, unaccepted, or inaccessible, home remedies and self-medications may be an integral part of health care and may influence nutritional status.[17]

Table 15-2 Nutrient Needs of Pregnancy

| Nutrient | Amount (NRC) | | Reasons for Increased Nutrient Need in Pregnancy | Food Sources |
	Nonpregnant Adult Need	Pregnancy Need		
Protein	44 gm	74-100 gm	Rapid fetal tissue growth Amniotic fluid Placenta growth and development Maternal tissue growth: uterus, breasts Increased maternal circulating blood volume: a. Hemoglobin increase b. Plasma protein increase Maternal storage reserves for labor, delivery, and lactation	Milk Cheese Egg Meat Grains Legumes Nuts
Calories	2100	2400	Increased BMR, energy needs Protein sparing	Carbohydrates Fats Proteins
Minerals				
Calcium	800 mg	1200 mg	Fetal skeleton formation Fetal tooth bud formation Increased maternal calcium metabolism	Milk Cheese Whole grains Leafy vegetables Egg yolk
Phosphorus	800 mg	1200 mg	Fetal skeleton formation Fetal tooth bud formation Increased maternal phosphorus metabolism	Milk Cheese Lean meats
Iron	18 mg	18+ mg (+30-60 mg supplement)	Increased maternal circulating blood volume, increased hemoglobin Fetal liver iron storage High iron cost of pregnancy	Liver Meats Egg Whole or enriched grain Leafy vegetables Nuts Legumes Dried fruits
Iodine	150 μg	175 μg	Increased BMR—increased thyroxine production	Iodized salt

Table 15-2 continued

Nutrient	Amount (NRC)		Reasons for Increased Nutrient Need in Pregnancy	Food Sources
	Nonpregnant Adult Need	Pregnancy Need		
Magnesium	300 mg	450 mg	Coenzyme in energy and protein metabolism Enzyme activator Tissue growth, cell metabolism Muscle action	Nuts Soybeans Cocoa Seafood Whole grains Dried beans and peas
Vitamins				
A	800 µg RE (4000 IU)	1000 µg RE (5000 IU)	Essential for cell development, hence tissue growth Tooth bud formation (development of enamel-forming cells in gum tissue) Bone growth	Butter Cream Fortified margarine Green and yellow vegetables
D	5-10 µg cholecalciferol (200-400 IU)	10-15 µg cholecalciferol (400-600 IU)	Absorption of calcium and phosphorus, mineralization of bone tissue, tooth buds	Fortified milk Fortified margarine
E	8 mg αTE	10 mg αTE	Tissue growth, cell wall integrity Red blood cell integrity	Vegetable oils Leafy vegetables Cereals Meat Egg Milk
C	60 mg	80 mg	Tissue formation and integrity Cement substance in connective and vascular tissues Increases iron absorption	Citrus fruits Berries Melons Tomatoes Chili peppers Green leafy vegetables Broccoli Potatoes
Folic acid	400 µg	800 µg (+200-400 µg supplement)	Increased metabolic demand in pregnancy Prevention of megaloblastic anemia in high-risk patients Increased heme production for hemoglobin Production of cell nucleus material	Liver Green leafy vegetables

continues

Table 15-2 continued

| Nutrient | Amount (NRC) | | Reasons for Increased Nutrient Need in Pregnancy | Food Sources |
	Nonpregnant Adult Need	Pregnancy Need		
Niacin	13 mg	15 mg	Coenzyme in energy metabolism	Meat
				Peanuts
			Coenzyme in protein metabolism	Beans and peas
				Enriched grains
Riboflavin	1.2 mg	1.5 mg	Coenzyme in energy metabolism and protein metabolism	Milk
				Liver
				Enriched grains
Thiamine	1.1 mg	1.5 mg	Coenzyme for energy metabolism	Pork, beef
				Liver
				Whole or enriched grains
				Legumes
B$_6$ (pyridoxine)	2.0 mg	2.6 mg	Coenzyme in protein metabolism	Wheat, corn
				Liver
			Increased fetal growth requirement	Meat
B$_{12}$	3.0 μg	4.0 μg	Coenzyme in protein metabolism, especially vital cell proteins such as nucleic acid	Milk
				Egg
				Meat
				Liver
			Formation of red blood cells	Cheese

Source: Adapted from *Handbook of Maternal and Infant Nutrition* by S. Williams, SRW Productions, Inc., © 1976.

ASSESSMENT OF EATING BEHAVIORS

Physiological, psychological, and sociocultural influences on nutrition should all be assessed in the pregnant woman. Some problems in these areas are described above. Table 15-4 provides a summary of dietary preferences for various ethnic groups and lists possible problems to help direct the nutrition counselor in probing during an interview.[18] For example, the American Indian may be prone to a variety of physiological problems during pregnancy, such as obesity, diabetes, alcoholism, iron-deficiency anemias, and dental problems. Sociocultural influence is associated with an excessive intake of sweets. Psychological influences are individual and should be assessed as such. For example, whether or not the pregnant woman is happy about the thought of rearing a child may affect eating habits. Adherence Tool 15-1 provides a list of areas to cover in assessing factors related to current eating patterns and their nutritional adequacy.[19] Adherence Tool 15-2 focuses on specific nutrition-related behaviors.

Table 15-3 Screening Criteria for Women at High Nutritional Risk

I. Likely to Need Therapeutic Diets
Maternal Weight
  Obesity
  Low prepregnancy weight
  Insufficient weight gain during
    pregnancy

Poor Obstetrical History
  History of low-birth-weight
    infants
  Other poor outcomes:
    Past difficulty with conception,
      especially if associated with
      weight deviation
    Repeated spontaneous abor-
      tion
    Stillbirth
    Neonatal death
    Abruptio placenta
    Spontaneous premature labor
  Toxemia, preeclampsia, or eclamp-
    sia
  Previous cesarian section or
    therapeutic abortion

Addictions
  Heroin
  Alcohol
  Pica

*Preexisting Medical Complications
Or Those Developing during
Gestation*
  Diabetes mellitus: overt or gesta-
    tional diabetes
  Anemia (especially iron defi-
    ciency and folate deficiency)
  Preexisting heart disease
  Infectious disease, especially:
    chronic asymptomatic condi-
      tions such as pulmonary
      and renal tuberculosis
    asymptomatic bacteriuria
  Liver disease:
    viral hepatitis
    history of other liver disease
    drug addiction
  Gastrointestinal disease:
    cholelithiasis, cholecystitis
    pancreatitis and pancreatic in-
      sufficiency

  hiatus hernia
  peptic ulcer
  gastric atrophy
  regional iletis
  ulcerative colitis
  protein-losing enteropathy
  disaccharide intolerance
  major gastric or bowel resec-
    tion
  intestinal parasitism with mal-
    absorption
Preexisting hypertension or renal
  disease (including collagen
  vascular disorders)
Other:
  poorly controlled hyperthy-
    roidism
  hyperlipemias
  certain inborn errors of metab-
    olism (phenylketonuria,
    cystinuria, Wilson's
    disease)

II. Likely To Need Lengthy Nutrition
    Counseling

*Age, Parity, and Short Interconceptional
Period*
  Adolescents, particularly if preg-
    nant and under 17
  Short interconceptional periods
    or high multiparity

Low Income or Limited Food Budget
  Low income
  Other situations in which food
    budget is limited, such as
    large families or nonsupport,
    compulsive gambling, drink-
    ing or drug addiction by
    spouse

Ethnic or Language Problems

Unusual Eating Habits
  Vegetarians
  Health food enthusiasts
  Certain religious groups with
    special food proscriptions

continues

Table 15-3 continued

Inadequate Knowledge of Nutrition or
Food Resource Management
   Limited knowledge or ability to
     make required dietary
     changes with ordinary coun-
     seling (e.g., low I.Q., illi-
     teracy, etc.)
   Special family food management
     problems (e.g., handicapped,
     one-parent household)
   Inaccessiblity or lack of knowl-
     edge of food distribution
     programs among eligibles
   Lack of budgeting or cooking
     skills

Lack of infant feeding skill

Poor Somatic Growth Among Offspring

III. Likely To Need Some Nutritional
    Advice of a Special Nature
    Smokers Who are Giving Up the Habit
    Twin Pregnancy
    Out-of-Wedlock Pregnancy
    Emotional Stress or Disturbance
    Dwellers in Area Where Food Distri-
    bution Programs Are Lacking or
    Badly Operated

Source: "Maternal Nutrition: Its Implication for Health Officers, Part II" by J. T. Dwyer and H. N. Jacobson in *Public Health Currents,* Vol. 14, pp. 1-5, © 1974.

After obtaining the client's diet history, by food record and by interview, the nutrition counselor can analyze the findings in terms of the increased nutritional demands of pregnancy. Two methods of analysis are nutrient calculation and nutrient check by food groups. In nutrient calculation, the counselor obtains specific nutrient intake data by calculating the protein, calories, and key vitamins and minerals in foods consumed from food value tables in standard references.[20] Totals for each nutrient may be compared with the National Research Council's RDA for pregnancy[21] or with the values in Table 15-2.

In most cases, however, the counselor can check the adequacy of the mother's food pattern with her using basic groupings of foods according to major nutrient contributions. Counselor and client determine the amounts of food from each group that meet the increased needs for key nutrients during pregnancy. Adherence Tool 15-4 is a guide for this procedure.

First, the counselor should familiarize the mother with the food groups and the basis of the groupings—the major nutrients each contains—and then ask her to name some foods in each group. This process provides a basis for reviewing the basic nutrients needed during pregnancy and the reasons for each. The counselor should emphasize protein, calories, and key vitamins and minerals, with basic core foods emerging to fill these needs. Third, the nutritionist should review the food record and the findings of the nutrition interview with the mother by taking one food group at a time and asking the mother to list all the food items in her own current eating pattern that belong in that food group, with the amount of each food that she usually eats. Continuing in this way with each of the food groups fills in the "My Intake" column in Adherence Tool 15-4.

Finally, taking one group at a time, the nutrition counselor might ask the mother to compare her food intake with the recommended increased amount listed on the sheet for each food group to meet the needs of her pregnancy. As a result of this comparison, the mother might be asked to state her dietary needs in each food group. Then, on the basis of this analysis, the nutrition counselor develops with her a food plan to meet personal nutritional needs for pregnancy as discovered in the nutrition interview.

TREATMENT STRATEGIES

Many of the strategies below fall into the category of lack of knowledge. Because culture greatly influences eating habits, commitment to a new eating pattern may be low for some ethnic groups. Clients may need strategies to jog memory in taking iron and folate supplements.

Strategies To Deal with Lack of Knowledge

On the basis of individual findings, the nutrition counselor should plan with the client a personal food guide. A diet consisting of a variety of foods can supply needed nutrients and make eating a pleasure. A core plan, such as that in Adherence Tool 15-4, may be used initially. Additional foods may be added or changed according to individual needs, cultural patterns, or personal life styles. Adherence Tool 15-5, a follow-up checklist of basic foods to include in a daily food plan, may be used for continual reinforcement.

The food plan must be realistic to be useful. Many women have broad food habits with few, if any, limitations. For these women basic guidance and encouragement suffice. Some women with problems and risks for a successful pregnancy, however, need extremely careful and supportive counseling that may well determine the outcome of their pregnancies.

Some form of follow-up support and evaluation should be built into the continuing plan of care. Ongoing nutrition awareness and concern should be an integral part of every clinic visit, and the nutrition counselor should show positive interest in continuance of the food plan, continue to look for problems that need adjustment, and use occasional food records for continuing evaluation of nutritional needs. Often the mother is greatly encouraged to see visible means that show her food habit changes are indeed increasing her nutrient intake and hence meeting her nutritional requirements.

Knowledge of how to modify intake to deal with gastrointestinal problems can help ensure adequate nutrition during pregnancy. For nausea and vomiting, simple treatment generally improves food toleration. Pregnant women commonly tolerate small frequent, fairly dry meals, and consisting chiefly of easily digested energy foods such as carbohydrates. Liquids are best taken prior to a meal instead of with food. If the condition persists and develops into hyperemesis (severe, prolonged, persistent vomiting), the physician will probably hospitalize the client and feed her intravenously to prevent complications and dehydration. Such an increase in the symptoms is usually rare. Most conditions pass early in pregnancy and respond to the simple dietary remedies given here.

Increased fluid intake, naturally laxative foods such as whole grains with added bran, dried fruits (especially prunes and figs), and other fruits and juices generally induce regularity and relieve constipation. Pregnant women should take laxatives only in special situations under medical supervision.

Complaints of heartburn or full feeling are generally remedied by dividing the day's food intake into a number of small meals during the day, rather than two or three large meals. Attention to relaxation, adequate chewing, eating slowly, and avoiding tensions during meals may also help.

Vegetarian food patterns may cause problems with nutritional adequacy. The counselor must first explore the level or type of vegetarian pattern the woman is following. Many vegetarian food plans exclude only meat; some even allow fish. Women

Table 15-4 Dietary Habits and Acceptable Foods

Ethnic Group	Milk Group	Meat Group	Fruits and Vegetables
American Indian (many tribal variations: many "Americanized")	Fresh milk Evaporated milk for cooking Ice cream Cream pies	Pork, beef, lamb, rabbit Fowl, fish, eggs Legumes Sunflower seeds Nuts: walnut, acorn, pine, peanut butter	Green peas, beans Beets, turnips Leafy green and other vegetables Grapes, bananas, peaches, other fresh fruits
Middle Eastern (Armenian, Greek, Syrian, Turkish)	Yogurt Little butter	Lamb Nuts Dried peas, beans, lentils	Peppers Tomatoes Cabbage Grape leaves Cucumbers Squash Dried apricots, raisins
Black	Milk Ice cream Puddings Cheese: longhorn, American	Pork: all cuts plus organs, chitterlings Beef, lamb Chicken, giblets Eggs Nuts Legumes Fish, game	Leafy vegetables Green and yellow vegetables Potatoes: white, sweet Stewed fruit Bananas and other fruit
Chinese (Cantonese most prevalent)	Cheese Milk: water buffalo; tofu	Pork sausage‡ Eggs and pigeon eggs Fish Lamb, beef, goat Fowl Nuts Legumes	Many vegetables Radish leaves Bean, bamboo sprouts
Filipino (Spanish-Chinese influence)	Flavored milk Milk in coffee Cheese: gouda, Cheddar	Pork, beef, goat, rabbit Chicken Fish Eggs Nuts Legumes	Many vegetables and fruits

*Olive oil is all fat, with no other nutrient value.

†Light molasses (first extraction): 1 tbsp = 50 calories, 33 mg of calcium, 0.9 mg of iron, 0.01 mg each of vitamins B_1 and B_2; dark molasses (third extraction): 1 tbsp =45 calories, 137 mg of calcium, 3.2 mg iron, 0.02 mg of vitamin B_1, 0.04 mg of vitamin B_2, 0.4 mg of niacin.

‡Lower in fat content than regular sausage.

Table 15-4 continued

Breads and Cereals	*Possible Dietary Problems*

Refined bread
Whole wheat
Cornmeal
Rice
Dry cereals
	In California major problems: obesity, diabetes, alcoholism,
	    nutritional deficiencies expressed in dental problems and
	    iron-deficiency anemia
	Inadequate amounts of all nutrients
	Excessive use of sugar

Cracked wheat and dark
   bread
	Fry many meats and vegetables
	Lack of fresh fruits
	Insufficient foods from milk group (use olive oil* in place of
	   butter)
	Like sweetening, lamb fat, and olive oil

Cornmeal and hominy grits Rice Biscuits, pancakes, white breads Puddings: bread, rice Molasses†	Extensive use of frying, "smothering," or simmering Fats: salt pork, bacon drippings, lard, and gravies Like sweets Insufficient citrus and enriched breads Vegetables often boiled for long periods Limited amounts from milk group

Rice/rice flour products
Cereals, noodles
Wheat, corn, millet seed
	Tendency of northern China (Mandarin), coastal China
	   (Shanghai), and inland China (Szechwan) emigrants to use
	   more grease in cooking
	Limited use of milk and milk products
	Often low in protein, calories, or both
	May wash rice before cooking

Rice, cooked cereals Noodles: rice, wheat	Limited use of milk and milk products Tend to prewash rice May have only small portions of protein foods

continues

Table 15-4 continued

Ethnic Group	Milk Group	Meat Group	Fruits and Vegetables
Italian	Cheese Some ice cream	Meat Eggs Dried beans	Leafy vegetables Potatoes Eggplant Spinach Fruits
Japanese (Isei, more Japanese influence; Nisei, more westernized)	Increasing amounts being used by younger generations Tofu	Pork, beef, chicken Fish Eggs Legumes: soya, red, lima beans Nuts	Many vegetables and fruits Seaweed
Mexican-Spanish	Milk Cheese Flan Ice Cream	Beef, pork, lamb, chicken, tripe, hot sausage, beef intestines Fish Eggs Nuts Dried beans: pinto, chick peas	Spinach, wild greens, tomatoes, chilies, corn, cactus leaves, cabbage, avocado Pumpkin, zapote, peaches, guava, papaya, citrus
Polish	Milk Sour cream Cheese Butter	Pork (preferred) Chicken	Vegetables Cabbage Roots Fruits
Puerto Rican	Limited use of milk products	Pork Poultry Eggs (Fridays) Dried codfish Beans	Avocado, okra Eggplant Sweet yams
Scandinavian: Danish, Finnish, Norwegian, Swedish	Cream Butter	Wild game Reindeer Fish Eggs	Fruit, berries Dried fruit Vegetables: cole slaw, roots, avocado

Source: Reproduced by permission from *Maternity and Gynecologic Care,* 3rd ed., by M. D. Jensen and I. M. Bobak (Eds.), pp. 367–368, The C. V. Mosby Company, St. Louis, © 1985.

Table 15-4 continued

Breads and Cereals	Possible Dietary Problems
Macaroni White breads, some whole Farina Cereals	Prefer expensive imported cheeses; reluctant to substitute less-expensive domestic varieties Tendency to overcook vegetables Limited use of whole grains Enjoy sweets Extensive use of olive oil Insufficient servings from milk group
Rice, rice cakes Wheat noodles Refined bread, noodles	Excessive salt: pickles, salty crisp seaweed Insufficient servings from milk group May use refined or prewashed rice
Rice, oats, cornmeal Sweet bread Tortilla Biscuits Fideo	Limited meats primarily because of economics Limited use of milk and milk products Some tendency toward increasing the use of flour tortillas over the more nutritious corn tortillas Large amounts of lard (*manteca*) Abundant use of sugar Tendency to boil vegetables for long periods
Dark rye	Like sweets Tendency to overcook vegetables Limited fruits (especially citrus), raw vegetables, and meats
Rice Cornmeal	Use small amounts of pork and poultry Use fat, lard, salt pork, and olive oil extensively Lack of butter and other milk products

Whole wheat, rye, barley,
  sweets
  (molasses for flavoring)
	Insufficient fresh fruits and vegetables
	Like sweets, pickled salted meats, and fish

Table 15-5 Vegetarian Food Guide

General guidelines
1. Follow nutrition guide for regular food plan during pregnancy as outlined in Adherence Tools 15-5 and 15-6.
2. Eat a wide variety of foods, including milk and milk products and eggs.
3. If no milk is allowed, use a supplement of 4 µg of vitamin B_{12} daily. If goat and soymilk are used, partial supplementation may be needed.
4. If no milk is taken, also use supplements of 1200 mg of calcium and 10 µg of vitamin D daily. Partial supplementation will be necessary if less than four servings of milk and milk products are consumed.
5. Select a variety of plant foods (especially grains, legumes, nuts, and seeds) to obtain "complete" proteins by complementary combinations, as indicated in the list below.
6. Use iodized salt.

Complementary plant protein combinations

Food	Amino acids deficient	Complementary protein food combinations
Grains	Isoleucine Lysine	Rice + legumes
		Corn + legumes
		Wheat + legumes
		Wheat + peanut + milk
		Wheat + sesame + soybean
		Rice + Brewer's yeast
Legumes	Tryptophan Methionine	Legumes + rice
		Beans + wheat
		Beans + corn
		Soybeans + rice + wheat
		Soybeans + corn + milk
		Soybeans + wheat + sesame
		Soybeans + peanuts + sesame
		Soybeans + peanuts + wheat + rice
		Soybeans + sesame + wheat
Nuts and seeds	Isoleucine Lysine	Peanuts + sesame + soybeans
		Sesame + beans
		Sesame + soybeans + wheat
		Peanuts + sunflower seeds
Vegetables	Isoleucine Methionine	Lima beans ⎫
		Green beans ⎪
		Brussels sprouts ⎬ + Sesame seeds or
		Cauliflower ⎪ Brazil nuts or
		Broccoli ⎭ mushrooms
		Greens + millet or rice

Source: *Diet for a Small Planet* by F. M. Lappé, Ballantine Books, Inc., © 1971.

following these patterns may obtain ample protein from dairy foods and eggs. However, a woman following a strict vegetarian pattern needs to plan extremely carefully to obtain sufficient complete protein from mixtures of plant food sources. A vegetarian food guide is given in Table 15-5.

Dealing with pica can be very difficult, depending on how habitual the problem is. One method of solving this problem is gradually to substitute for the eating behavior an activity selected by the client that is motivating, enjoyable, easily attained, and within economic limits.

"Inappropriate Eating Behaviors" above contains a description of ethnic preferences, along with examples of ways in which culture can influence eating behaviors adversely. Table 15-6 provides some sample menus that allow for ethnic food preferences and provide adequate nutrition.[22] The counselor may discuss the basic four food groups with the family and explain simply the rationale for providing proteins, carbohydrates, fats, and vitamins and minerals. Culture may dictate that certain elements of the basic four food groups be eliminated, and the counselor should suggest appropriate substitutions.

A food record (Adherence Tool 15-3) can be valuable in tailoring the eating habits of the pregnant woman. With this tool, the woman writes down everything she eats in a three-day period, including one weekend day. The counselor analyzes the diet with both the woman and the family members. Throughout the counseling session the counselor should praise positive aspects of the diet while indicating relationships between diet and needs during pregnancy. The nutrition counselor should focus on planning meals that fall within the economic needs of the family. Food assistance programs available through government such as Women, Infants, and Children (WIC); church; or lodge groups might be suggested. Consultation with a social worker will provide guidance.

Strategies To Deal with Forgetfulness

Remembering to take the two major prescriptions during pregnancy, iron and folate, may be a problem for some women. Pill boxes set at the dinner table can act as cueing devices. A note on the bathroom mirror with the pill bottle below may also serve as a memory jogger and help keep adherence to supplementation at 100 percent.

Strategies To Deal with Lack of Commitment

Involving the family in positively reinforcing good eating habits and consistent medication taking can be helpful. Showing the pregnant woman how to reward herself positively for eating appropriately can also be a major step in achieving optimum adherence. Tailoring diet to each individual's culture may also foster commitment. Table 15-6 provides menus for various ethnic groups that can serve as a first step toward appropriate eating behaviors.

Commitment to the diet may change as the pregnant woman demonstrates various "cognitive styles" throughout gestation.[23] In the first three months of pregnancy, dietary counseling might focus on the mother rather than the fetus because in many cases the baby is not a reality to her. In the second three months, as the pregnant woman focuses on the baby, the nutrition counselor may educate the pregnant woman and family on both nutrient needs and the growth and development of the fetus. In the third trimester, as the family becomes concerned with the labor and delivery experience, counseling can be directed at labor and delivery, the neonatal period, and nutrients needed in this stage of pregnancy.

Lack of commitment may also be related to stress during pregnancy. Reading and others describe the effects of anxiety common in most pregnancies on the course of pregnancy (see Figure 15-1).[24] Anxiety here refers to state anxiety as distinct from enduring personality predispositions or traits. The model acknowledges that the impact of "stressors," in whatever form, is moderated by a number of factors, including:

Table 15-6 Sample Menus

	Regular	Mexican	Black
Breakfast			
2 energy foods	1 cup cream of wheat	2 corn tortillas	1 cup grits
	1 tbsp. sugar	2 tbsp. jelly	1 tbsp. sugar
1 calcium protein food	1 cup milk	½ cup evaporated milk in coffee	1 cup milk
1 vitamin C food	1 cup orange juice	1 cup orange juice	1 cup orange juice
Lunch			
1 energy food	1 slice bread	1 tortilla	½ in square corn bread
2 protein foods	2 1-oz slices cheese	1 cup beans	1 cup pork and beans
1 calcium protein food	1 cup milk	½ cup evaporated milk and choco-late	1 cup milk
1 vitamin A food	½ cup spinach	½ cup spinach 1 green pepper	½ cup collard greens
1 vitamin/mineral food	1 banana	1 banana	1 banana
Dinner			
1 energy food	1 small baked potato	½ cup Spanish rice	2 halves candied yams
3 protein foods	3 oz beef roast	1 cup beans 1 cup caldo	3½ oz fried pork chops
1 calcium/protein food	1 cup milk	½ cup evaporated milk and coffee	1 cup milk
2 vitamin/mineral foods	1 stalk broccoli 1 cup fruited Jell-O	1 cup fruited Jell-O	1 cup peas 1 cup fruited Jell-O
Snacks			
1 calcium/protein food	1 cup custard	1 cup flan	1 cup custard
1 vitamin/mineral food	1 pear	1 pear	1 pear
1 energy food	2 oatmeal-raisin cookies	2 oatmeal-raisin cookies	2 oatmeal-raisin cookies

The above menus show the cultural variations possible when planning a nutritionally adequate prenatal diet. All meet the Recommended Dietary Allowances for calories, provide a minimum of 90 grams of protein, and exceed the Recommended Dietary Allowances for vitamins A and C and calcium. Only the Black and Mexican dietary pattern meets the Recommended Dietary Allowances for iron, providing 21.9 mg and 23.1 mg. The Regular, American-Indian, and the Oriental pattern provide 15.3 mg, 15.8, and 15.3 respectively. The Lacto-Ovo plan provides only 12.0 mg.

Source: Reprinted from "Prenatal Diet Counseling" by A. T. Cross and H. E. Walsh in *Journal of Reproductive Medicine,* Vol. 7, p. 265, with permission of Journal of Reproductive Medicine, Inc., © 1971.

Table 15-6 continued

Oriental	American Indian	Lacto-Ovo
1 cup rice	1 cup corn mush	1 cup brown rice
1 tsp. sugar (in tea) 1 cup milk	1 tbsp. sugar 1 cup milk	1 tbsp. honey 1 cup milk
1 cup orange juice	1 cup orange juice	1 cup orange juice
½ cup rice	1 slice Indian fried bread	1 slice whole wheat bread
3½ oz tofu 1 egg 1 cup milk	1 cup pinto beans 1 cup milk	1 cup lentils 1 cup milk
3/5 bok choy	½ cup spinach	½ cup spinach
1 banana	1 apple	1 banana
½ cup rice	½ cup fried potatoes	1 small baked potato
Okazu (stewing beef 3 oz and ½ cup broccoli and 2 oz tofu) 1 cup milk 1 cup fruited Jell-O	3½ oz fish 1 cup milk 1 stalk broccoli 1 cup fruited Jell-O	3½ oz cheese (Cheddar) 1 cup milk 1 stalk broccoli ½ cup fruited Jell-O
1 cup custard	1 cup custard	1 cup custard
1 pear	1 pear	1 pear
1 oatmeal-raisin cookie	2 oatmeal-raisin cookies	2 oatmeal-raisin cookies

1. trait anxiety, or the predisposition to react emotionally in stressful circumstances and to perceive events as threatening
2. negative or ambivalent attitudes to the pregnancy that may amplify the impact of stressful life events
3. the woman's appraisal of the impact of a "stressor," which reflects the outcome of both the stress and her ability to use coping mechanism to offset the difficulties encountered
4. the level of support available to the pregnant woman, which has a protective effect
5. the coping resources available and effectiveness of such coping strategies, which have an effect on the reduction of the stress.

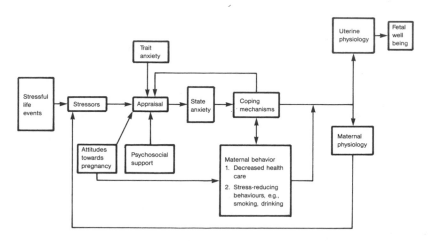

Figure 15-1 The Influence of Maternal Anxiety on the Course and Outcome of the Pregnancy. *Source:* Reprinted from *Psychological Aspects of Pregnancy* by A. Reading, p. 18, with permission of Longman Group Ltd., © 1983.

Figure 15-1 points to the way anxiety may affect fetal well-being indirectly through its effect on behavior. Stress may stimulate certain countertherapeutic behaviors, such as smoking, alcohol abuse, improper eating, and lack of exercise. Anxiety may reduce the likelihood of compliance with health advice, in terms of decreased attendance for antenatal care or birth preparation classes, through preoccupation with the source of the stress. To combat this problem, the client can make a list of activities contributing to the stress and formulate a plan to overcome the stress by prioritizing them (see Adherence Tool 15-7). The woman thus is given a coping mechanism. Involving the client's family in making the stressors less of a burden can be beneficial. In reviewing the list of tasks to be accomplished, the pregnant woman might delegate many responsibilities. Dealing with stresses during pregnancy allows the woman to focus on a major priority, proper nutrition.

Counseling skills for management of nutrition problems in pregnancy require a knowledge of special ethnic nutrient alteration during pregnancy and an understanding of how to realistically apply ethnic choices to recommended dietary allowances. Strategies to ensure medication taking in pregnancy require use of cueing devices. To maintain commitment, several areas are addressed: self-rewards, tailoring, dealing with special "cognitive styles" related to pregnancy, and coping with stress.

Adherence Tool 15-1 Monitoring Device

Questionnaire for Eating Patterns and
Nutritional Assessment in Pregnancy

Age _____

Occupation _____

Medical History: Diabetes _____

                      Heart Disease _____

                      Renal Disease _____

                      Thyroid Disease _____

                      Hypertension_____

Habits: Sleeping patterns: _____

          Eating patterns: _____

          Pica: _____

          Urinary and bowel habits: _____

          Drugs: _____

          Alcohol: _____

          Cigarettes: _____

          Methods of exercise: _____

REVIEW OF SYSTEMS

  1. General appearance: Is she alert and responsive? _____

                        Does she look tired and apathetic? _____

  2. Weight: What was weight during previous pregnancies? _____

          What was the pattern of weight gain? _____

          What was the reaction to weight gain with regard to body image? _____

          Was the woman ever on any weight-reducing program? _____

          Method? _____

          Is weight appropriate for height and body build? _____

  3. Skin, hair, nails: What is texture of skin and hair? _____

                    Does skin appear rough and bruise easily? _____

                    Are nails brittle and spoon shaped? _____

                    (These are signs of vitamin A, C, and riboflavin deficiencies.)

  4. Eyes: Are the eyes bright and shiny? _____

          Are these symptoms related to night blindness? _____

          Are the palpebral conjunctivas pale? _____

          (These may indicate vitamin A and iron deficiency.)

Adherence Tool 15-1 continued

5. Mouth: Do the mucous membranes look pink and healthy? _____
   Is there swelling, recession, or bleeding of the gums? _____
   Are there any fissures in the lips? _____
   (These may be signs of riboflavin, vitamin A, and vitamin C deficiencies.)
   Are there any signs of dental caries and missing teeth? _____
6. Gastrointestinal System: Is nausea and vomiting a problem? _____
   When does this symptom occur in relation to foods, meals and time of day? _____

   What are food preferences? _____

   Is there any constipation or diarrhea? _____
   Is there an increase or decrease in appetite?

7. Musculoskeletal System: Are muscles well developed with good tone?

   Are there any malformations of the skeleton, such as bow legs and chest deformities?

   Are there muscles cramps? _____
   (These may be signs of chronic protein and mineral deficiencies.)
8. Neurologic System: Is the woman irritable and restless? _____
   Are there any signs of paresthesia, weakness of muscles, and depression? _____
   (These may be symptoms of calcium, thiamine, and iron deficiencies.)
9. Cardiovascular System: Does the woman have any problems with dyspnea or orthopnea? _____
   Are there signs of tachycardia, abnormal rhythm, and elevated blood pressure? _____
   (These may be signs of severe nutritional deficiencies.)
10. Reproductive System: Is there a history of increased bleeding with menstruation?

   Previous maternity history: gravida, para, number of live births, abortions, weights of other babies; methods of feeding children, methods of contraception used. _____

   (This information will give the practitioner baseline information about maternal nutrient reserves.)

Source: Maternal and Child Nutrition: Assessment and Counseling by J. Slattery, G. Pearson, and C. Torre, pp. 32-34, Appleton & Lange, © 1979.

Adherence Tool 15-2 Monitoring Device

Name _____ Date _____
Age _____ Height _____ Prepregnant weight _____
Gravida _____ Education _____ Present weight _____
Nutrition Interview
ACTIVITY-ASSOCIATED GENERAL DAY'S FOOD INTAKE PATTERN
Living situation
  Housing _____
  Members of household _____
  Culture _____
  Occupation: Husband _____
          Self _____
Recreation, physical activity _____

Present food habits	Place	Time	Checklist
Morning			Protein foods
			Milk Fish
			Cheese Poultry
			Meat Eggs
			Breads, cereals, legumes
Noon			Breads (whole-grain, enriched)
			Cereals
			Pastas
			Dried beans, peas, lentils
Evening			Vegetables
			Dark yellow Potato
			Deep green Others
			Fruits Fats and oils
Snacks			Citrus Butter
			Others Margarine
			Others
			Desserts, sweets
			Soft drinks, candy
Comments			Alcohol
			Vitamin, mineral supplements
			Medications, drugs

Source: Handbook of Maternal and Infant Nutrition by S. Williams, SRW Productions, Inc., ©
1976.

Adherence Tool 15-3 Monitoring Device

Food Record				Name _____ Date _____		
TOTAL FOOD INTAKE						COMMENTS
Meal and snacks		Description of food items				Any related factors?— associated activity, place, persons, money, feelings, hunger, nausea, heartburn, constipation, etc.
Time	Place	Food	Amount	Type or preparation	With whom eaten?	

Source: Handbook of Maternal and Infant Nutrition by S. Williams, SRW Productions, Inc., © 1976.

Adherence Tool 15-4 Informational Device

Food Groups	Major Nutrient Contributions	Recommended Daily Intake (Number of Servings)	My Intake	Analysis of Food Needs
Nutritional Analysis Sheet				
Protein-rich foods				
Milk-cheese	Protein (complete, high biological value); Ca, P, Mg; vitamin D; riboflavin	1 qt milk 2 oz cheese or ½ cup cottage cheese		
Egg-meat	Protein (complete, high biological value); B complex vitamins; folic acid (liver); vitamin A (liver); iron (liver especially)	2 eggs* 2 servings meat (3-4 oz each) Liver once a week at least*		
Vitamin- and mineral-rich foods				
Grains, whole or enriched, breads or cereals, legumes	Protein (incomplete, supplementary); B complex vitamins; iron, Ca, P, Mg; energy (protein sparing)	4 or more servings		
Green and yellow vegetables	Vitamin A; folic acid	1-2 servings		
Citrus fruits and other vitamin C-rich fruits and vegetables	Vitamin C	2 servings		
Potatoes and other vegetables and fruits	Energy (protein sparing); added vitamins and minerals	1 serving or as needed for calories		
Fats—margarine, butter, and oils	Vitamin A (butter, fortified margarine); vitamin E (vegetable oils); energy (protein sparing)	1-2 tbsp as needed for calories		
Iodized salt	Iodine	Use with food to taste		

*For persons with a history of heart disease use of eggs and liver in the amounts and frequency listed would be contraindicated.

Source: *Handbook of Maternal and Infant Nutrition* by S. Williams, SRW Productions, Inc., © 1976.

Adherence Tool 15-5 Informational Device

Daily Food Plan for Pregnancy		
Foods	Daily Amount	Suggested Uses
Protein-rich foods		
Primary protein		
Dairy products	1 qt milk	Beverage, in cooking, or milk-based
Milk, cheese	2+ oz brick cheese	desserts such as ice milk, custards,
	or ½ cup+	puddings, cream soups; cheese in
	cottage cheese	cooked dishes, salads, or snacks
		throughout the day
Eggs	2	Breakfast use, chopped or sliced
		hard eggs, in salads, custards,
		whole boiled eggs, deviled eggs,
		plain or in sandwiches
Meat	2 servings (total of	Main dish, sandwich, salad, snack
	6 to 8 oz) liver	
	frequently, 1-2	
	times per week	
Supplementary		
protein		
Grains	4 to 5 slices or	Bread, plain or toast, sandwiches,
Enriched or	servings whole	with meals, snacks, cereal
whole grains,	grain or enriched	(breakfast or snack), cooked grain
breads, cereals,		as meal accompaniment (corn,
crackers		rice, pasta, grits, hominy, hot
		breads: corn bread, biscuits, etc.)
Legumes, seeds,	Occasional servings	Cooked and served alone or in
nuts	as meat or grain	combination with grains, cheese,
Dried beans and	substitute or in	or meat; soups, salads; nuts as
peas	combination with	snacks or in salads; peanut butter
Lentils	meat or grains	sandwich
Mineral-rich foods		
Calcium-rich		
Dairy products	1 qt milk (as above)	As above
Grains, whole or	4-5 slices or	As above
enriched	servings (as	
	above)	Cooked or raw in salads
Green leafy	1 serving	
vegetables		
Iron-rich		
Organ meats,	1-2 servings per	
especially liver	week	
Grains, enriched	4-5 slices or	Breakfast cereals, main dish, or
	servings	combination with meats, cheese,
		egg, cooked grain foods, enriched
		breads
Egg yolk	2	As above
Green, leafy	1-2 servings	Cooked or stewed, raw in salads,
vegetables or		snacks
dried fruits		

Adherence Tool 15-5 continued

Foods	Daily Amount	Suggested Uses
	Daily Food Plan for Pregnancy	
Iodine-rich		
Iodized salt	Daily in cooking and on foods	On salads, in cooked food dishes, according to taste
Seafood	1-2 servings per week	Main dish, salad, sandwiches
Vitamin-rich foods		
Vitamin A		
Animal sources		
Butter fat (whole milk, cream, butter)	2 tbsp butter (or fortified margarine)	In cooking or on foods
Liver	1-2 servings per week	Main dish
Egg yolk	2 (as above)	As above
Plant sources		
Dark green or deep yellow vegetables or fruits	1-2 servings	Cooked dishes, salads, snacks
Fortified margarine	2 tbsp	In cooking and on foods
Vitamin C		
Fruits		
Citrus	1 or 2 servings	Snacks, salads, juices
Other fruits— papayas, strawberries, melons	Occasional serving to substitute for one citrus portion	Salads, snacks
Vegetables		
Broccoli, potatoes, tomato, cabbage, green or chili peppers	1 serving as a substitute for 1 citrus occasionally	Cooked, snacks, salads, juices
Folic acid		
Liver, dark green vegetables, dried beans, lentils, nuts (peanuts, walnuts, filberts)	1 serving	Cooked as main dish or soups, snacks, in salads

Source: Handbook of Maternal and Infant Nutrition by S. Williams, SRW Productions, Inc., ©
1976.

Adherence Tool 15-6 Informational Device

Checklist of Foods Recommended during Pregnancy

Foods	Daily Amount
Milk	1 qt
Eggs	1-2
Meat	2 servings (liver often)
Cheese	1-2 servings, additional snacks
Grains (whole, enriched)	4-5 slices or servings
Legumes, nuts	1-2 servings a week
Green and yellow fruits, vegetables	1-2 servings
Citrus fruit	2
Additional vitamin C foods	Frequently, as desired
Other vegetables and fruits	1-2 servings
Butter, fortified margarine	2 tbsp (or as needed)
Other foods: grains, fruits, vegetables other proteins	As needed for energy and added vitamins and minerals

Source: Handbook of Maternal and Infant Nutrition by S. Williams, SRW Production, Inc., © 1976.

Adherence Tool 15-7 Informational and Cueing Device

Stress Management Chart

When you feel overwhelmed, make a "to do" list of everything you need to get done.

Date	Item to Do

Source: Courtesy of Laura Coleman, Joanne Csaplar, Johanna Dwyer, Carole Palmer, and Molly Holland.

When you have finished the list, ask yourself the following questions:

1. Can I delete anything from this list that might be unnecessary?
2. What can I delegate to a relative or friend?
3. What can I pay someone else to do?
4. What is the most important task? Now begin by doing it first.

Review of Chapter 15
(Answers in Appendix I)

1. Identify inappropriate eating behaviors frequently seen in pregnancy.

   a. _____

   b. _____

   c. _____

   d. _____

2. Identify the dietary components that must be assessed during pregnancy.

   a. _____

   b. _____

   c. _____

   d. _____

   e. _____

   f. _____

3. List strategies that might help the client follow an eating pattern appropriate in pregnancy.

   a. _____

   b. _____

   c. _____

   d. _____

   e. _____

4. The following describes a problem situation with a client who has been instructed on a appropriate diet for pregnancy. Identify a strategy that might help solve this client's problem and explain your reason.

   > Mrs. C is a 32-year-old female who is in her second trimester of pregnancy. She is an immigrant from northern China. Her family is supportive in some areas but unwilling to change their food preferences to accommodate her new eating pattern. They frequently make unsupportive remarks about her efforts to change her eating habits. Mrs. C already has five children and frequently feels overwhelmed. (a) What additional information might you elicit from the client? (b) What strategies would you use to help alleviate the problem? (c) Why did you choose these strategies?

a. _____

b. _____

c. _____

NOTES

1. American Dietetic Association, *Handbook of Clinical Dietetics* (New Haven, Conn.: Yale University Press, 1981), pp. A51–A52.

2. JoAnne Brasel, "Normal Nutritional Requirements and Unusual Nutritional Practices," in Myron Winick, ed., *Feeding the Mother and Infant* (New York: John Wiley & Sons, 1985), p. 1; and Frank Falkner, "Maternal Nutrition and Fetal Growth," *American Journal of Clinical Nutrition* 34 (1981): 769–774.

3. Pedro Rosso, "Placental Growth, Development, and Function in Relation to Maternal Nutrition," *Federal Proceedings* 39 (1980): 250–254; and Mervyn Susser, "Prenatal Nutrition, Birthweight, and Psychological Development: An Overview of Experiments, Quasi-Experiments and Natural Experiments in the Past Decade," *American Journal of Clinical Nutrition* 34 (1981): 784–803.

4. Pedro Rosso, "Nutrition and Maternal-Fetal Exchange," *American Journal of Clinical Nutrition* 34 (1981): 744–755.

5. Brasel, "Normal Nutritional Requirements," p. 2.

6. Bonnie S. Worthington-Roberts, Joyce Vwermeersch, and Sue Rodwell Williams, *Nutrition in Pregnancy and Lactation* (St. Louis, Mo.: C. V. Mosby Co., 1981), pp. 86–88.

7. Brasel, "Normal Nutritional Requirements," p. 3.

8. Ibid.

9. Johanna T. Dwyer and H. N. Jacobson, "Maternal Nutrition—Its Implication for Health Officers, Part Two," *Public Health Currents* 14 (1974): 1–5.

10. Frank E. Hytten and Isabella Leitch, *The Physiology of Human Pregnancy,* 2d ed. (Philadelphia: Davis, 1971), p. 60.

11. Helen S. Mitchell et al., *Nutrition in Health and Disease,* 16th ed. (Philadelphia: J. B. Lippincott, 1976), p. 204.

12. Jill S. Slattery, Gayle Angus Pearson, and Carolyn Talley Torre, *Maternal and Child Nutrition, Assessment and Counseling* (New York: Appleton, Century, Crofts, 1979), p. 22.

13. Mitchell et al., *Nutrition in Health and Disease,* p. 203.

14. Slattery, Pearson, and Torre, *Maternal and Child Nutrition,* p. 119.

15. Eleanor R. Williams, "Nutrition: Vegetarian Diets in Pregnancy," *Birth and the Family Journal* 3 (1976): 83–86.

16. Slattery, Pearson, and Torre, *Maternal and Child Nutrition,* p. 129.

17. Ibid., p. 25.

18. Ibid., pp. 26–29.

19. Ibid., pp. 32–34.

20. Jean A. T. Pennington and Helen Nichols Church, *Food Values of Portions Commonly Used,* 14 ed. (New York: Harper & Row Publishers, 1985); Consumer and Food Economics Research Division Agricultural Research Service, "Nutritive Value of Foods," Home and Garden Bulletin No. 72 (Washington D.C.: United States Department of Agriculture, 1970); and Bernice K. Watt and Annabel L. Merrill, "Composition of Foods: Raw, Processed, Prepared," Agricultural Handbook No. 8 (Washington, D.C.: U.S. Department of Agriculture, 1976).

21. Food and Nutrition Board, National Research Council, National Academy of Sciences, *Recommended Dietary Allowances,* 9th ed. (Washington, D.C.: U.S. Government Printing Office, 1980).

22. Slattery, Pearson, and Torre, *Maternal and Child Nutrition,* pp. 30–31.

23. Reva Rubin, "Cognitive Style of Pregnancy," *American Journal of Nursing* 70 (1970): 502–508.

24. Anthony Reading, *Psychological Aspects of Pregnancy* (Essex, England: Longman Group Ltd., 1983), pp. 10–24; James W. Selby et al., *Psychology and Human Reproduction* (New York: The Free Press, 1980), pp. 3–38; and Myra Leifer, *Psychological Effects of Motherhood* (New York: Praeger Pubs., 1980), pp. 43–56, 181–186.

Part IV

Ending Counseling Sessions

This section describes techniques for assessing each counseling session and gives suggestions for client follow-up.

Chapter 16

Evaluation and Follow-Up

Objectives for Chapter 16

1. Identify elements necessary for evaluating both client and counselor.
2. Identify strategies to ensure dietary adherence after ceasing reinforcement.
3. Generate the reinstitution of an intervention or treatment plan.

EVALUATION OF COUNSELOR PROGRESS

Evaluation of the counselor's individual progress forms an important part of the client's success. A counselor becomes ineffective in facilitating client success for a variety of reasons. The questions below are a way to begin defining potential problems. It helps review the success of the interview from the practitioners' viewpoint. The questions also might be made more specific for each client.

1. Did the counseling session address the client's major problem?
2. Was assessment prior to designing a modified eating pattern adequate to prepare a dietary regimen compatible with the client's life style?
3. Did the client's goal appear to have been achieved?
4. Were the strategies for altering eating behaviors carried out efficiently?
5. Did I use appropriate verbal and nonverbal interviewing skills?
6. Where might changes have been made?

_____

_____

7. Did I use appropriate counseling skills? _____
8. Where might changes have been made? _____

_____

_____

9. What general changes would I make in the next counseling interview with a similar client?

_____

_____

_____

Each list should be made more specific as the situations require and can be adapted depending on answers given during the interview.

EVALUATION OF CLIENT PROGRESS

Evaluating the client's progress is crucial to maintenance of a modified eating pattern. Booster sessions to assist in solving problems may be a direct result of careful evaluation.

Following each session, the counselor can appraise the client's success. Below is a list of questions the client might ask to determine whether behavior has changed successfully:

1. Are my dietary patterns different but still compatible with my life style?
2. Have my misconceptions about foods and what they contain been replaced with factual information?
3. Are social occasions less of a problem now than when I first began my diet?
4. Is my family providing needed positive reinforcement?

These very general questions provide insight into potential problems with dietary adherence. Evaluation of client progress is an ongoing process that should be a part of all client counseling sessions. The client should feel a sense of control in changing inappropriate eating behaviors; self-management of problem eating behaviors is crucial to eventual maintenance of dietary goals.

STRATEGIES TO MAINTAIN DIETARY ADHERENCE

Follow-up interviewing sessions are extremely important to counseling on nutrition-related issues. The number of return visits depends on the success of efforts in following a diet. There is always a point at which the nutrition practitioner and client must end a set of counseling sessions. This is the point at which the counselor must be sure that the client can follow the diet without continued help. At that time, the goal of the counseling session is tested: Can the client function adequately in the real world?

Counselors must be sure that their clients are given ample opportunity during the sessions to practice eating behaviors and must be reinforced for them in the natural environment. This can be done by asking them for records of foods consumed, times eating takes place, persons present during the meal or snack, and the type of situation (where and what type of function). These records should be discussed thoroughly with the clients, and problem areas and their solutions noted.

To help with reinforcement in the natural setting, clients are asked to list times and places where their eating behaviors can be supported. The counselors then help them plan for natural situations that reinforce the new eating pattern. If new behaviors are really adjustive, clients should find natural support and natural reinforcements.

In early stages of termination, counselors should help clients identify chains of events that bolster behavior. A woman who had succeeded in losing ten pounds found that her colleagues at work responded very warmly to her. She was asked out more often and spent more time in discussions with colleagues. She eliminated her clothes-buying reinforcement and instead posted a sign on her refrigerator door: "Dieting keeps the telephone ringing!"

After an eating behavior has been solidified in relation to one antecedent condition, clients can make that behavior even more frequent by gradually increasing the range of situations in which reinforcement occurs. They should test for generalization by looking at how reinforcement can be a part of many situations. By keeping a list of all situations in which either appropriate or inappropriate eating behaviors occur, nutritionists can work on problem situations before counseling is terminated.

A most important issue to address before termination is building in resistance to extinction. The best way to ensure that an appropriate eating behavior continues is to work out an intermittent reinforcement schedule. A treatment plan should never be stopped abruptly.

Once an acceptable upper level of behavior has been established, the ratio of its reinforcement can be reduced. Instead of clients' always buying presents for themselves, such as clothing, after eating an appropriate meal, sporadic buying can be used as a reinforcement, i.e., 75 percent of the time, then 50 percent, then 25 percent, and so on.

During this gradual reduction in positive reinforcement, both counselors and clients must continue to count the frequency of the appropriate behaviors. There is some danger that these will decline. Alternating between periods of 50 percent and 100 percent reinforcement can keep their frequency at an acceptably high level if the natural supporters are slow to evolve.

Counselors should ensure that adequate practice of the reinforcement has occurred during intervention or treatment. In general, acceptable behaviors are made more probable by providing a certain number of trials on a reinforcement schedule. Practice is important.

This need for practice implies, correctly, that nutrition counselors will not want to terminate the program as soon as the goal is reached. Instead, it would be wise to continue the plan for a week or two, or perhaps more, depending on the frequency of the opportunities to practice. The number of practices depends on many factors in the intervention plan. For example, a more complicated dietary regimen may require division of practice into small segments, each focusing on one exchange category.

However, a trial at reducing reinforcement is a good test of the degree to which an eating behavior can be maintained after termination. If the frequency of the targeted behavior drops alarmingly as soon as a reduction in reinforcement begins, it means more practice is necessary. In that case, the 100 percent reinforcement schedule should be resumed, along with more practice. For this reason, the frequency of an eating behavior should be recorded after termination of reinforcement until the rate has stabilized.

REINSTITUTION OF INTERVENTION OR TREATMENT

Nutrition counselors may find that an intervention plan must be restarted if gradually decreasing reinforcement seems to be causing an appropriate eating behavior to decrease. At that point, practitioners must be closely attuned to client needs.

Because clients must deal with many life stresses, their attention to an intervention strategy of gradually decreasing reinforcement may be diverted, resulting in total lack of support. By working with clients' significant others, practitioners can suggest persons who are aware of the importance of reinforcing good eating behaviors in the absence of nutrition counseling sessions.

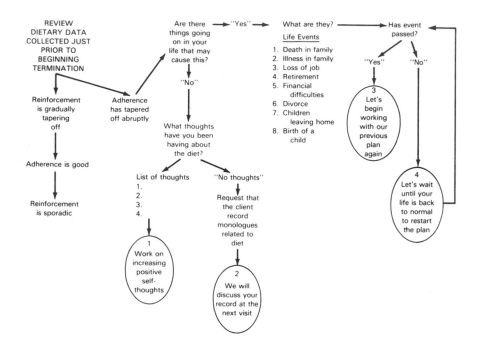

Figure 16-1 Algorithm for Nutrition Counseling Termination

THE TERMINATION PROCESS

The algorithm in Figure 16-1 indicates a step procedure to use in terminating nutrition counseling. TERMINATION should always be approached gradually. The algorithm indicates four possible situations:

1. Some clients begin having negative thoughts. The algorithm suggests listing those thoughts and working on them.
2. Clients occasionally may refuse to discuss them, in which case they should be asked to record both negative and positive monologues for discussion later.
3. Other clients may admit to having a drastic change in their life styles. Those changes may be temporary. In that case, the intervention plan is reinstituted and reinforcements decreased gradually.
4. Clients in some cases may be in the midst of a change in life style. If so, counselors should wait until they seem ready to restart the intervention plan, meanwhile keeping in close contact so that the diet is not totally forgotten.

Termination is different for each client. Counselors should be prepared to restart a strategy to help ensure adherence to the diet over long periods. They might call or write to the client periodically to check on progress. Such attention to the client's needs after the counseling has ended will show a sense of caring and may help maintain the individual's motivation.

A gradual fading process of termination rather than an abrupt "goodbye" is essential. If clients are to be successful on their own, they must prove that success is possible. Nutrition counselors can help clients find this success on their own. A gradual termination can prevent regression to problem eating behaviors.

Review of Chapter 16
(Answers in Appendix I)

1. Identify questions you might ask to evaluate counselor progress.

    a. _____

    b. _____

    c. _____

    d. _____

    e. _____

    f. _____

    g. _____

    h. _____

    i. _____

2. Identify questions you might ask to evaluate client progress.

    a. _____

    b. _____

    c. _____

    d. _____

3. Identify five ways in which you as a counselor might facilitate the continuation of appropriate dietary behaviors in clients who no longer will be coming in for interviews and must live with the regimen in the real world.

    a. _____

    b. _____

    c. _____

    d. _____

    e. _____

4. Mr. Y. has been slipping in his adherence to low-sodium regimen he was following so well when counseling sessions were frequent. What questions might you use to determine exactly what has happened to the reinforcement schedule?

    _____

    _____

    _____

5. What intervention plan can you recommend to help clients maintain dietary adherence? _____

    _____

    _____

    _____

SUGGESTED READINGS

Aronson, Virginia and Fitzgerald, Barbara D. *Guidebook for Nutrition Counselors.* North Quincy, Mass.: The Christopher Publishing House, 1980.

Cormier, L. Sherilyn; Cormier, William H.; and Weisser, Roland J., Jr. *Interviewing and Helping Skills for Health Professionals.* Monterey, Calif.: Wadsworth Health Sciences Division, 1984.

Curry-Bartley, Katherine. *Dietetic Practitioner Skills: Nutrition Education, Counseling and Management.* New York: Macmillan, 1987.

DiMatteo, M. Robin, and DiNicola, D. Dante. *Achieving Patient Compliance: The Psychology of the Medical Practitioner's Role.* New York: Pergamon Press, 1982.

Holroyd, Kenneth A., and Creer, Thomas L., eds. *Self-Management of Chronic Disease, Handbook of Clinical Interventions and Research.* New York: Academic Press, 1986.

Okun, Barbara F. *Effective Helping, Interviewing and Counseling Techniques,* 2nd ed. Monterey, Calif.: Brooks/Cole Publishing Co., 1982.

Seligman, Linda. *Diagnosis and Treatment Planning in Counseling.* New York: Human Sciences Press, Inc., 1986.

Thomas, Edwin J. *Designing Interventions for the Helping Professions.* London: Sage Publication, 1984.

Checklist of Counselor Self-Image

Check the items that are most descriptive of you.

1. *Competence Assessment*

_____ 1. Constructive negative feedback about myself doesn't make me feel incompetent or uncertain of myself.

_____ 2. I tend to put myself down frequently.

_____ 3. I feel fairly confident about myself as a helper.

_____ 4. I often am preoccupied with thinking that I'm not going to be a competent nutrition counselor.

_____ 5. When I am involved in a conflict, I don't go out of my way to ignore or avoid it.

_____ 6. When I get positive feedback about myself, I often don't believe it's true.

_____ 7. I set realistic goals for myself as a helper that are within reach.

_____ 8. I believe that a confronting, hostile client could make me feel uneasy or incompetent.

_____ 9. I often find myself apologizing for myself or my behavior.

_____ 10. I'm fairly confident I can or will be a successful counselor.

_____ 11. I find myself worrying a lot about "not making it" as a counselor.

_____ 12. I'm likely to be a little scared by clients who would idealize me.

_____ 13. A lot of times I will set standards or goals for myself that are too tough to attain.

_____ 14. I tend to avoid negative feedback when I can.

_____ 15. Doing well or being successful does not make me feel uneasy.

2. *Power Assessment*

_____ 1. If I'm really honest, I think my counseling methods are a little superior to other people's.

Note: From *Interviewing Strategies for Helpers,* 2nd ed., by W. H. Cormier and L. S. Cormier. Copyright © 1985, 1979 by Wadsworth Inc. Reprinted by permission of Brooks/Cole Publishing Company, Pacific Grove, California 93950.

_____ 2. A lot of times I try to get people to do what I want. I might get pretty defensive or upset if the client disagreed with what I wanted to do or did not follow my direction in the interview.

_____ 3. I believe there is (or will be) a balance in the interviews between my participation and the client's.

_____ 4. I could feel angry when working with a resistant or stubborn client.

_____ 5. I can see that I might be tempted to get some of my own ideology across to the client.

_____ 6. As a counselor, "preaching" is not likely to be a problem for me.

_____ 7. Sometimes I feel impatient with clients who have a different way of looking at the world than I do.

_____ 8. I know there are times when I would be reluctant to refer my clients to someone else, especially if the other counselor's style differed from mine.

_____ 9. Sometimes I feel rejecting or intolerant of clients whose values and life styles are very different from mine.

_____ 10. It is hard for me to avoid getting in a power struggle with some clients.

3. *Intimacy Assessment*

_____ 1. There are times when I act more gruff than I really feel.

_____ 2. It's hard for me to express positive feelings to a client.

_____ 3. There are some clients I would really like to be my friends more than my clients.

_____ 4. It would upset me if a client didn't like me.

_____ 5. If I sense a client has some negative feelings toward me, I try to talk about it rather than avoid it.

_____ 6. Many times I go out of my way to avoid offending clients.

_____ 7. I feel more comfortable maintaining a professional distance between myself and the client.

_____ 8. Being close to people is something that does not make me feel uncomfortable.

_____ 9. I am more comfortable when I am a little aloof.

_____ 10. I am very sensitive to how clients feel about me, especially if it is negative.

_____ 11. I can accept positive feedback from clients fairly easily.

_____ 12. It is difficult for me to confront a client.

Learning Activity Reaction:
Applications to Your Counseling

1. For each of the three assessment areas above, look over your responses and determine the areas that seem to be OK and the areas that may be a problem for you or something to watch out for. You may find more problems in one area than another.

2. Do your "trouble spots" seem to occur with mostly everyone, or just with certain types of people? In all situations or some situations?

3. Compare yourself now to where you might have been four years ago or where you may be four years from now.

4. Identify any areas you feel you could use some help with, from a colleague, a supervisor, or a counselor.

Checklist of Nutrition Counselor's Nonverbal Behavior

Instructions: Determine whether the counselor did or did not demonstrate the desired nonverbal behaviors listed in the right column. Check "yes" or "no" in the left column to indicate your judgment.

Demonstrated Behaviors		*Desired Behaviors*
Yes	*No*	
___	___	*Eye contact*—Maintained persistent eye contact without gazing
1. Eyes		or staring.
___	___	*Facial expression*—Punctuated interaction with occasional head
2. Head nods		nods.
___	___	*Mouth*—Punctuated interaction with occasional smiles.
3. Smiles		
___	___	*Body orientation and posture*—Faced the other
4. Facing client		person, slight lean forward (from waist up), body appeared relaxed.
___	___	
5. Leaning forward		
___	___	
6. Relaxed body		

Note: From *Interviewing Strategies for Helpers,* 2nd ed., by W. H. Cormier and L. S. Cormier. Copyright © 1985, 1979 by Wadsworth Inc. Reprinted by permission of Brooks/Cole Publishing Company, Pacific Grove, California 93950.

____   ____   *Paralinguistics*—completed sentences without "who" or hesita-
7. Completed   tions in delivery, asked one question at a time, did not ramble.
sentences

____   ____
8. Smooth
delivery
—no speech
errors

____   ____   *Distance*—Seats of counselor and client were between 3 feet, or 1
9. Distance   meter, and 5 feet or 1½ meters apart.

Measures of Nutritional Status

ANTHROPOMETRY

Elbow breadth, three skinfold thicknesses—triceps, biceps, and subscapular—and midarm circumference are described below. The purpose of the elbow breadth measurement is to classify the subject's frame size according to the appropriate column of the standard weight tables. The skinfold and arm circumference measures are used to determine body fatness and arm muscle area. The repeated measurements will be used to assess change in body fat and muscle mass.

Preparation

The skinfold calipers must measure accurately at different thicknesses of skinfolds. Use the calibration block to check the caliper calibration before measuring each client. A constant error of 1 mm is acceptable and should be added to or subtracted from the actual reading. A greater error requires repair or replacement of the calipers.

Measurement

Elbow Breadth

The client extends the right arm forward, perpendicular to the body, with the arm bent so the angle at the elbow measures 90 degrees and with the fingers pointing up and the dorsal part of the wrist toward the measurer. Apply the sliding caliper across the greatest breadth of the elbow joint (at the medial and lateral condyles of the humerus) along the axis of the upper arm. Approximate the arms of the caliper with firm pressure and read the breadth in millimeters.

Have the client repeat the arm maneuver and remeasure. Repeat the reading aloud and record. If the two measurements are within 1 mm, use the second measurement as the elbow breadth for the weight table. If the second measure differs by more than one mm from the first, repeat until two consecutive measures are within one mm. Use the last of the measures as the elbow breadth. Table C-1 gives framesize from height and elbow breadth.

Table C-1 Frame Size from Height and Elbow Breadth[1]

Men
Elbow Breadth

Height* (centimeters)	Small frame (millimeters)	Medium frame (millimeters)	Large frame (millimeters)
150–154	< 62	62–71	> 71
155–158	< 64	64–72	> 72
159–168	< 67	67–74	> 74
169–178	< 69	69–76	> 76
179–188	< 71	71–78	> 78
189–190	< 74	74–81	> 81
191–194	< 76	76–82	> 82
195–199	< 78	78–83	> 83
200–204	< 79	79–85	> 85
205–209	< 80	80–88	> 89

Women
Elbow Breadth

Height* (centimeters)	Small frame (millimeters)	Medium frame (millimeters)	Large frame (millimeters)
145–148	< 56	56–64	> 64
149–158	< 58	58–65	> 65
159–168	< 59	59–66	> 66
169–178	< 61	61–68	> 68
179–180	< 62	62–69	> 69
181–184	< 63	63–70	> 70
185–189	< 64	64–71	> 71
190–194	< 65	65–72	> 72
195–199	< 66	66–73	> 73

*Without shoes.
[1]The medium frame elbow breadths for men, <155 cm or ≥191 cm, and women, ≥181 cm, were determined by extrapolation on a semilog graph.
Source: Table 3, Statistical Bulletin, Metropolitan Life Foundation, January–June, 1983.

Upper Arm Circumference

The client flexes the right arm to 90 degrees at the elbow. Use the steel tape to measure the distance from the acromion to the end of the humerus. Mark the lateral part of the arm at the midpoint with a pen or skin marker. With the arm hanging freely, place the lower edge of the tape at skin mark and measure the circumference. The tape should fit snugly to the arm without compressing tissue. State the reading in millimeters and record. Repeat the maneuver. Successive measures should be within 5 mm. Record the last measure as the midarm circumference.

Skinfolds

Pick up a fold of skin and subcutaneous tissue between the thumb and index finger of the left hand and lift it firmly away from the underlying muscle. Hold the fold between the fingers throughout the time the measurement is being taken. Apply the calipers to the fold 1 cm below the fingertip so that pressure on the fold at the point measured is exerted by the caliper faces only, and not by the fingers. The calipers are applied to the skinfold by removing the thumb of the right hand from the trigger lever of the caliper.

The value registered on the calipers sometimes decreases as one watches the pointer of the dial. This decrease can usually be stopped by taking a firmer pinch with the left hand; if it continues, the reading must be taken immediately after application of the spring pressure.

All measurements are read to the nearest 1 mm. Obtain two measurements at each site. If the two measures are within 5 percent, record the last measure as the skinfold thickness. If the difference between the measures exceeds 5 percent, repeat the maneuver until two successive measures are within 5 percent.

Most skinfolds are measured in the vertical plane except when the Lines of Linn (natural skinfold lines) result in torsion of the skinfold, in which case the skinfold is taken along these lines.

Triceps skinfold. The client should be standing with right arm relaxed and suspended along midaxillary line. The point of measurement is at the skin mark made for arm circumference measurement. Pinch the skin and subcutaneous tissue (do not include muscle) between the thumb and index finger of your left hand. The pinch should be 1 cm above the skin mark and parallel to the long axis of the arm. The jaws of the calipers are placed perpendicular to the fold at the marked level.

Biceps skinfold. The client should be standing with right arm relaxed and suspended along midaxillary line. Pick up the skinfold on the front of the right arm directly above the center of the cubital fossa at the same level as that at which the triceps skinfold is measured.

Subscapular skinfold. The client should be standing and relaxed. Grasp the skin and subcutaneous tissue just below the inferior angle of the right scapula between your left thumb and index finger. Lines of Linn will determine the angle of the skinfold.

Calculation of Percent Body Fat

Percent body fat is determined from (1) a regression equation for the prediction of body density from the triceps, biceps, and subscapular skinfolds and (2) an equation using the known relationship between body density and the proportion of fat in the body.[1]

1. Body density (Y) is calculated as follows:

   $Y = C - M$ (log of the sum of the skinfolds)
   The coefficients C and M are obtained from Table C-2 for the appropriate age and sex group.

2. Percent body fat is calculated as follows:

   $$\% \text{ Fat} = (\frac{4.95}{Y} - 4.5)(100)$$

Table C-2 Linear Regression Coefficients for the Estimation of Body Density × 10³ (kg/m³) from the Logarithm of the Skinfold Thickness (Biceps + Triceps + Subscapular)

	Males		Females	
Age (years)	C	M	C	M
Age categories				
17–19	1.1643	0.0727	1.1509	0.0715
20–29	1.1593	0.0694	1.1605	0.0777
30–39	1.1213	0.0487	1.1385	0.0654
40–49	1.1530	0.0730	1.1303	0.0635
50+	1.1569	0.0780	1.1372	0.0710
Overall				
17–72	1.1689	0.0793	1.1543	0.0756

Source: Reprinted from "Body Fat Assessment from Total Body Density and Its Estimation from Skinfold Thickness: Measurements on 481 Men and Women Aged from 16 to 72 Years" by J. Durnin and J. Wormersley in *British Journal of Nutrition,* Vol. 32, p. 77, with permission of Cambridge University Press, © 1974.

3. Example: A 45-year-old female has a sum of the three skinfolds of 50 millimeters.

$$Y = 1.1303 - 0.0635 \, (\log 50)$$
$$= 1.0224$$

$$\% \, \text{Fat} = (\frac{4.95}{1.0224} - 4.5) \, (100)$$

$$= 34.1$$

Arm Muscle Area

The arm muscle area (AMA) is determined by two measurements: (1) triceps skinfold in millimeters (TSF) and (2) midarm circumference in millimeters (MAC).[2] The following formula is used to calculate arm muscle area:

$$AMA = \frac{(MAC - II \times TSF)^2}{4 \, II}.$$

A corrected AMA_c ("available" arm muscle area) is then calculated separately for men and women as follows:

$$\text{Men } AMA_c = AMA - 19$$
$$\text{Women } AMA_c = AMA - 15.5.$$

Evaluation

Continued changes to lowered arm muscle area may indicate early signs of malnutrition. Large decreases in weight to less than 75 percent of standard body weight (as indicated in height and weight Table C-3) should prompt the nutritionist to also look at change in arm muscle area. In the weight-loss client a decrease in body fat as opposed to muscle area would be preferable.

Table C-3 Height and Weight Tables[+]

Men Weight in Kilograms				Women Weight in Kilograms			
Height[1] (cm)	Small Frame[2]	Medium Frame[2]	Large Frame[2]	Height[1] (cm)	Small Frame[2]	Medium Frame[2]	Large Frame[2]
153	59.0	61.2	64.7	145	48.5	52.4	56.8
154	59.3	61.5	65.2	146	48.8	52.8	57.2
155	59.7	61.9	65.6	147	49.0	53.1	57.7
156	60.0	62.2	66.0	148	49.3	53.6	58.1
157	60.4	62.6	66.5	149	49.6	54.1	58.6
158	60.7	62.9	66.9	150	50.0	54.5	59.0
159	61.1	63.3	67.4	151	50.4	55.0	59.6
160	61.4	63.7	67.8	152	50.9	55.4	60.2
161	61.8	64.1	68.4	153	51.3	55.9	60.7
162	62.2	64.6	68.9	154	51.7	56.4	61.2
163	62.5	65.0	69.4	155	52.3	57.0	61.9
164	62.9	65.5	70.0	156	52.8	57.5	62.5
165	63.2	66.0	70.6	157	53.3	58.1	63.1
166	63.7	66.6	71.2	158	53.8	58.6	63.7
167	64.1	67.1	71.8	159	54.4	59.1	64.3
168	64.6	67.6	72.4	160	54.9	59.6	64.9
169	65.0	68.1	73.0	161	55.5	60.2	65.5
170	65.5	68.7	73.7	162	56.0	60.7	66.1
171	65.9	69.2	74.3	163	56.6	61.3	66.8
172	66.3	69.7	74.9	164	57.1	61.9	67.5
173	66.8	70.3	75.5	165	57.6	62.4	68.1
174	67.3	70.8	76.2	166	58.2	62.9	68.7
175	67.7	71.3	76.8	167	58.7	63.4	69.3
176	68.1	71.9	77.4	168	59.2	63.9	69.9
177	68.6	72.4	78.1	169	59.7	64.5	70.5
178	69.1	73.0	78.7	170	60.3	65.0	71.2

continues

Table C-3 continued

	Men Weight in Kilograms				Women Weight in Kilograms		
Height[1] (cm)	Small Frame[2]	Medium Frame[2]	Large Frame[2]	Height[1] (cm)	Small Frame[2]	Medium Frame[2]	Large Frame[2]
179	69.6	73.6	79.3	171	60.8	65.5	71.7
180	70.2	74.3	80.0	172	61.3	66.0	72.2
181	70.8	74.9	80.7	173	61.9	66.6	72.6
182	71.4	75.5	81.4	174	62.5	67.2	73.3
183	72.0	76.2	82.1	175	63.0	67.7	73.8
184	72.7	76.9	82.9	176	63.5	68.3	74.4
185	73.3	77.6	83.7	177	64.0	68.9	74.9
186	73.9	78.2	84.5	178	64.6	69.3	75.5
187	74.5	78.8	85.3	179	65.1	69.8	76.0
188	75.3	79.6	86.2	180	65.6	70.3	76.5
189	76.0	80.4	87.1	181	66.1	70.8	77.0
190	76.7	81.2	88.0	182	66.6	71.3	77.5
191	77.3	81.8	88.9	183	67.1	71.8	78.0
192	78.1	82.6	89.9	184	67.6	72.3	78.5
193	78.9	83.5	91.0	185	68.1	72.8	79.0
194	79.7	84.3	92.0	186	68.6	73.3	79.5
195	80.5	85.1	93.0	187	69.1	73.9	80.0
196	81.1	85.7	94.0	188	69.6	74.4	80.5
197	81.9	86.6	95.2	189	70.1	75.0	81.0
198	82.8	87.5	96.4	190	70.6	75.5	81.5
199	83.7	88.4	97.6				
200	84.6	89.3	98.8				

+Weights for heights in men below 155 cm and over 190 cm and in women over 180 cm estimated by extrapolation.

1. Height without shoes.

2. Frame size from Table C-1.

Source: Height and Weight Tables, Statistical Bulletin, Metropolitan Life Foundation, January–June, 1983.

NOTES

1. J.V.G.A. Durnin and J. Wormersley, "Body Fat Assessment from Total Body Density and Its Estimation from Skinfold Thickness: Measurements on 481 Men and Women," *British Journal of Nutrition* 32 (1974): 77–97.

2. Steven B. Heymsfield et al., "Anthropometric Measurements of Muscle Mass: Revised Equations for Calculating Bone-Free Arm Muscle Area," *American Journal of Clinical Nutrition* 36 (1982): 680–690.

Appendix D

Behavioral Chart

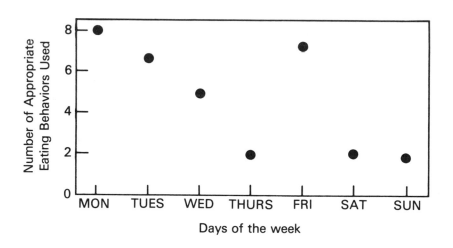

Behavioral Log

Date	Time	Setting	Event	Actual Reaction	Desired Reaction

Appendix F

Logs of Thoughts Related to Food

Baseline Log

Time	Thoughts
7:30	"I'd really like a doughnut but I'm not going to blow my day."
8:15	"It's not fair, I'm really trying and I haven't lost anything."
9:10	"Wish I had a doughnut or something. I'm hungry."
10:00	"It's not fair, it's snack time and all I get is water."
11:30	"Nothing tastes as good when I know there's no dessert."
12:10	"Look at them. They stuff themselves with sweets and stay skinny."
1:15	"Maybe I could have just a couple of cookies after school. I've earned them."
2:30	"Look at them running off to their afternoon snacks. It's not fair."
3:15	"I don't care if I'm fat. I'll never lose anyway. It's not worth it."
4:30	"I might as well eat and enjoy it. I'll never lose anyway. It's not worth it."
5:45	"You pig. Now you feel stuffed and you've ruined your day."
7:30	"What a failure I am. I don't deserve to be thin."
9:00	"I'll never learn, will I? It's no use."
10:30	"I feel hopeless. I've tried everything and I always blow it."

Note: Reprinted from *Permanent Weight Control, A Total Solution to the Dieter's Dilemma* by Michael J. Mahoney and Kathryn Mahoney by permission of W.W. Norton & Company, Inc. Copyright © 1976 by W.W. Norton & Company, Inc.

Replacement Log

Problem Category	Negative Monologues	Appropriate Monologues
Pounds Lost	"I'm not losing fast enough." "I've starved myself and haven't lost a thing." "I've been more consistent than Mary and she is losing faster than I am. It's not fair."	"Pounds don't count. If I continue my eating habits, the pounds will be lost." "Have patience—those pounds took a long time to get there. As long as they stay off permanently, I'll settle for any progress." "It takes a while to break down fat and absorb the extra water produced. I'm not going to worry about it."
Capabilities	"I just don't have the will-power." "I'm just naturally fat." "Why should this work— nothing else has." "I'll probably just regain it." "What the heck—I'd rather be fat than miserable. Besides, I'm not that heavy."	"There's no such thing as lack of willpower—just poor planning." "If I make a few improvements here and there and take things one day at a time, I can be very successful." "It's going to be nice to be permanently rid of all this extra baggage. I'm starting to feel better already."
Excuses	"If it weren't for my job and the kids, I could lose weight." "It's just impossible to eat right with a schedule like mine." "I'm just so nervous all the time—I have to eat to satisfy my psychological needs." "Maybe next time. . . ."	"My schedule isn't any worse than anyone else's. What I need to do is be a bit more creative in how to improve my eating." "Eating doesn't satisfy psychological problems—it creates them." "Job, kids, or whatever, I'm the one in control."

Replacement Log continued

Goals	"Well, there goes my diet. That coffee cake probably cost me two pounds, and after I promised myself—no more sweets." "I always blow it on the weekends." "Fine—I start the day off with a doughnut. I may as well enjoy myself today."	"What is this—the Olympics? I don't need perfect habits, just improved ones." "Why should one sweet or an extra portion blow it for me? I'll cut back elsewhere." "Those high standards are unrealistic." "Fantastic—I had a small piece of cake and it didn't blow the day."
Food Thoughts	"I can't stop thinking about sweets." "I had images of cakes and pies all afternoon—it must mean that I need sugar." "When we order food at a restaurant, I continue thinking about what I have ordered until it arrives."	"Whenever I find myself thinking about food, I quickly change the topic to some other pleasant experience." "If I see a magazine ad or commercial for food and I start thinking about it, I distract my attention by doing something else (phoning a friend, getting the mail, etc.)."

Daily Record of Cognitive Restructuring

Date: _____		Record of: _____	
Description of Situation	Coping Thoughts Used	Positive Self-Statements Used	Date and Time

Source: Adapted from *Interviewing Strategies for Helpers* by William H. Cormier and L. Sherilyn Cormier with permission of Brooks/Cole Publishing Company, © 1979, p. 370.

Food Composition Table[1] (Fat and Cholesterol Content of Certain Foods)

Product[2]	Unit of Measure[3]	Choles-terol (mg)	Total Fats (g)	Total SFA[4] (g)	Total PFA[5] (g)
Egg, 11g[6]	50.00	274.00	5.58	1.68	.73
LRC Meat Composite[7]	28.35	29.77	3.98	2.25	.28
Beef					
Lean (10%)	28.35	25.80	2.18	.95	.13
Med. Fat (15%)	28.35	25.80	4.22	1.83	.20
Pork					
Lean (10%)[8]	28.35	27.22	3.02	1.04	.37
Med. Fat (15%)[9]	28.35	25.52	3.94	1.36	.48
Organ Meats and Cold Cuts					
Beef Bologna (1 slice = 23g)	23.00	12.88	6.52	2.68	.24
Frankfurter (1 link = 43g)	43.00	20.64	12.65	5.14	.50
Liver					
Pork and Beef	28.35	124.07	2.69	.99	.56
Chicken	28.35	178.89	1.55	.52	.26
Poultry, Chicken					
With skin (light)	28.35	22.68	2.72	.77	.61
(dark)	28.35	25.52	3.87	1.11	.93
Without skin (light)	28.35	21.83	1.10	.33	.26
(dark)	28.35	25.23	2.40	.72	.63

[1]All figures from 1987 Nutrition Coordinating Center (NCC), University of Minnesota, Food Table, version 14.0.
[2]Unless otherwise specified, all meats are cooked.
[3]1 ounce = 28.35 grams.
[4]Saturated fatty acids.
[5]Polyunsaturated fatty acids.
[6]Grams.
[7]Percent of total consumption from meat.
[8]Actual percentage of fat is a range, 7.5–12.4 percent.
[9]Actual percentage of fat is a range, 12.5–17.4 percent.

Product[2]	Unit of Measure[3]	Choles-terol (mg)	Total Fats (g)	Total SFA[4] (g)	Total PFA[5] (g)
Fish[10]					
Flat (uncooked) (0–2.9%)	28.35	17.01	.26	.05	.10
(3.0–6.9%)	28.35	22.68	1.28	.29	.42
(11.0–14.9%)	28.35	22.68	3.69	.91	.94
Shellfish					
Shrimp	28.35	42.69	.68	.10	.22
Scallops (1 piece = 20.00g)	20.00	10.60	.28	.07	.07
Clams (1 piece = 16.67g)	16.67	10.50	.42	.08	.09
Oysters (1 piece = 16.67g)	16.67	7.50	.38	.09	.17
Lobster (1 medium = 104.00g)	104.00	156.00	3.54	.42	1.30
Crab	28.35	28.35	.45	.06	.18
Milk					
Whole	8 fl. oz.	34.16	8.15	5.08	.29
2%	8 fl. oz.	19.52	4.68	2.93	.17
1%	8 fl. oz.	9.76	2.59	1.61	.10
Skim	8 fl. oz.	4.88	.44	.29	.02
Chocolate (Skim)	8 fl. oz.	17.50	5.00	3.10	.18
Chocolate (Whole)	8 fl. oz.	30.00	8.48	5.25	.30
Meat Fat[11]					
Gravy, Meat (¼ cup = 58.20g)	58.20	1.76	1.60	.80	.08
Gravy, Poultry/Giblets (¼ cup = 49.00g)	49.00	72.00	1.84	.56	.40
Bacon Fat (1 t[12] = 4.27g)	4.27	2.95	3.11	1.25	.23
Bacon (1 slice = 6.33g)	6.33	5.38	3.12	1.10	.37

Lean Fish (Approximately 2% fat)	Fish (Approximately 6% fat Range = 4.0–8.9%)	Fish (Approximately 12% fat; More than 9% fat)
Bass	Carp	Eel
Bullhead	Trout	Herring, fresh
Catfish	Swordfish	Atlantic, Pacific
Cod		Mackerel
Flounder		Salmon, fresh
Haddock		Sardine, fresh
Halibut		Trout, Lake
Herring, Lake		Trout, Rainbow
Perch		
Pickerel (Walleye)		
Pike (Northern)		
Red Snapper		
Sole		
Trout, brook		
Tuna, fresh		
Turbot		

[10]Fish Guide (List of the most common flat fish)
[11]Gravy without milk added; figures for beef and poultry fat used.
[12]Teaspoon.
Source: Taken from 1978 Nutrition Coding Center Food Table, Version 07.

Product[2]	Unit of Measure[3]	Choles- terol (mg)	Total Fats (g)	Total SFA[4] (g)	Total PFA[5] (g)
Lard (1 t = 4.27g)	4.27	4.06	4.27	1.67	.48
Beef Fat (1 t = 4.27g)	4.27	4.65	4.27	2.13	.17
Baked Products					
Doughnut, Cake	42.00	32.76	7.57	3.40	.71
Cake, Mix					
(1 serving = 4.50g)	4.50	2.67	.41	.15	.07
Pie Crust, Double, Conv.					
(1 slice = 6.42g)	6.42	1.20	2.19	.88	.25
Sweet Roll					
(1 medium = 50.00g)	50.00	25.68	7.94	2.10	1.32
Coffee Cake, Yeast, w/o nuts w/o topping					
(1 piece = 41.22g)	41.22	17.12	3.84	1.15	.61
Quick Bread					
(1 piece = 70.20g)	70.20	36.39	7.18	3.19	.69
Biscuit					
(1 medium = 38.00g)	38.00	2.85	6.62	1.93	1.06
Pancake					
(1 medium = 27.00g)	27.00	18.13	2.42	.80	.35
Muffin, Bran					
(1 medium = 40.00g)	40.00	14.29	2.48	1.03	.33
Cookie, Medium Fat, Commercial					
(1 piece = 13.50g)		8.44	2.17	.72	.30
Cookie, Medium Fat, Homemade					
(1 piece = 11.14)		3.24	1.82	.71	.22
Generic Baked Product (1 serving, average of above items)		14.79	4.06	1.46	.54
Cream					
Heavy (37% fat)					
(1 T[13] = 14.88g)	14.88	20.39	5.51	3.43	.16
Light, Sour (20% fat)					
(1 T = 15.00g)	15.00	9.90	2.90	1.80	.11
Half and Half (10–12% fat)					
(1 T = 15.13g)	15.13	5.60	1.74	1.08	.07
Imitation Sour Cream					
(1 T = 14.38g)	14.38	0	2.81	2.56	.01
Imitation Creamer					
Liquid, Saturated Vegetable Fat					
(1 T = 15.00g)	15.00	0	1.50	1.40	0
Liquid, P/S = 2.0–3.5					
(Poly Perx) (1 T = 15.00g)	15.00	0	1.50	.22	.56

[13]Tablespoon.

Product[2]	Unit of Measure[3]	Choles-terol (mg)	Total Fats (g)	Total SFA[4] (g)	Total PFA[5] (g)
Liquid, P/S = 1.0–2.0					
(1 T = 15.00g)	15.00	0	1.50	.27	.46
Ice Cream (10% fat)					
(½ cup = 66.50g)	66.50	29.93	7.16	4.46	.27
Ice Milk (or soft serve 5% fat)					
(½ cup = 65.50 g)	65.50	9.17	2.82	1.76	.11
Yogurt (1–2% fat) (unflavored					
or plain) (1 cup = 227.00g)	227.00	9.08	2.45	1.59	.07
Cheese					
Cottage (1% fat)					
(½ cup = 113.00g)	105.00	4.52	1.15	.72	.03
Cottage (2% fat)					
(½ cup = 113.00g)	113.00	9.04	2.18	1.38	.07
Cottage, Creamed (4% fat)					
(½ cup = 105.00g)	113.00	15.75	4.74	2.99	.15
Cream Cheese (35% fat)					
(1 T = 14.00g)	14.00	15.40	4.88	3.08	.18
Neufchatel Cream Cheese					
(20% fat) (1 T = 14.00g)	14.00	10.64	3.28	2.07	.09
Mozarella (part skim)	28.35	15.31	4.85	3.08	.14
Cheese (20% fat)					
(Natural Cheese)	28.35	22.96	9.00	5.57	.33
Cheese (15% fat)					
(Light and Lively and					
Light Line)	28.35	2.27	4.39	2.77	.14
Cheese (5–10% fat)					
(Borden Lite-Line)	28.35	9.07	2.27	1.41	.07
American Cheese	28.35	26.65	8.86	5.58	.28
Cheddar Cheese	28.35	29.77	9.40	5.98	.27
Cheese Foods and Spreads					
(Velveeta and Cheese Whiz)	28.35	17.01	6.49	4.08	.19
Butter (1 t = 4.73g)	4.73	10.36	3.84	2.39	.14
Vegetable Products					
Mayonnaise, Commercial					
(HSOY/SAFF) (1 T = 13.80g)	13.80	8.14	10.96	1.19	7.59
Miracle Whip (1 T = 14.70g)	14.70	3.82	4.90	.72	2.65
Mixed Oil (90% soy, 10%					
cottonseed) (1 t = 4.54g)	4.54	0	4.54	.71	2.60
Corn Oil (1 t = 4.54g)	4.54	0	4.54	.58	2.66
Safflower Oil (1 t = 4.54g)	4.54	0	4.54	.41	3.38
Soybean Oil, Partially					
Hydrogenated (1 t = 4.54g)	4.54	0	4.54	.68	1.71
Sunflower Seed Oil (1 t = 4.54g)	4.54	0	4.54	.47	2.98
Puritan Oil (95% Sunflower,					
5% Soy) (1 t = 4.27g)	4.27	0	4.27	1.06	1.22

Product[2]	Unit of Measure[3]	Choles- terol (mg)	Total Fats (g)	Total SFA[4] (g)	Total PFA[5] (g)
Peanut Butter (1 t = 5.38g)	5.38	0	2.75	.46	.83
Peanuts (unsalted) (1 cup = 145.00g)	145.00	0	71.33	9.93	22.62
Chocolate					
Sweet or semisweet					
(1 oz. = 28.35g)	28.35	.28	9.95	5.94	.30
Bitter baking (1 oz. = 28.35g)	28.35	0	15.03	8.97	.45

MARGARINES

Brand Name Margarine	Major Ingredient Oil	Polyunsaturated Fat/ Saturated Fat (P/S)
Blue Bonnet, Whipped, Regular Tub	Soybean/Cottonseed	0.8/0.99
Blue Bonnet, Regular, Stick	Soybean/Cottonseed	1.4/1.59
Blue Bonnet, Regular, Tub	Soybean/Cottonseed	1.4/1.59
Blue Ribbon, Regular, Stick	Soybean/Cottonseed	1.4/1.59
Chiffon, Regular, Stick	Soybean/Cottonseed	1.6/1.79
Chiffon, Regular, Tub	Soybean/Cottonseed	1.6/1.79
Country Morning Blend 60%	Corn	1.2/1.39
40%	Butter	0.06
Fleischmann's, Regular, Stick	Corn	2.0/2.19
Fleischmann's, Regular, Tub	Corn	2.2/2.39
Fleischmann's, Light, Spread 60%	Corn	1.2/1.39
Fleischmann's, Diet 40%	Corn	2.0/2.19
Imperial, Stick	Soybean/Cottonseed	1.4/1.59
Imperial, Tub	Soybean/Cottonseed	1.4/1.59
Imperial, Light, Spread 45%, Tub	Soybean/Cottonseed	1.6/1.79
Meadow Gold, Regular, Stick	Soybean	1.6/1.79
Mrs. Filbert's, Soft Golden, Regular, Tub	Soybean	1.6/1.79
Parkay, Regular, Stick	Soybean	1.6/1.79
Parkay, Regular, Tub	Soybean	1.6/1.79
Promise, Spread 72%, Stick	Sunflower	2.2/2.39
Promise, Spread 72%, Tub	Sunflower	2.8/2.99
Promise, Extra Lite, Spread 53%, Stick	Sunflower	2.2/2.39
Promise, Extra Lite, Spread 53%, Tub	Sunflower	2.8/2.99
Shedd's (Soy), Spread 52%, Stick	Soybean	0.8/0.99
Shedd's (Corn), Spread 52%, Tub	Corn	2.2/2.39
Shedd's Country Crock, Spread 64%, Stick	Soybean/Cottonseed	1.4/1.59
Shedd's Country Crock, Spread 52%, Tub	Soybean	2.2/2.39
Shurfresh (Shurfine), Regular, Stick	Soybean	1.6/1.79
Weight Watcher's Diet, 40%, Tub	Soybean	2.8/2.99

Product	Unit of Measure	Choles- terol (mg)	Total Fats (g)	Total SFA (g)	Total PFA (g)
Margarine, Stick or Tub, 80% fat, corn oil: P/S = 2.0–2.19; saturated fat (g/100g) = 13.00–13.99 (1 t = 4.70g) (Fleischmann's Regular, Stick)	4.70	0	3.78	.63	1.27
Margarine, Stick or Tub, 80% fat, corn oil: P/S = 2.2–2.39; saturated fat (g/100g) = 17.00–17.99 (1 t = 4.70g) (Fleischmann's, Regular, Tub)	4.70	0	3.78	.66	1.47
Margarine, Stick or Tub, 80% fat, partially hydrogenated soybean oil: P/S = 1.6/1.79; saturated fat (g/100g) = 12.00–12.99 (1 t = 4.70g) (Chiffon, Regular, Stick, Chiffon, Regular, Tub)	4.70	0	3.77	.57	.95
Margarine, Stick or Tub, 80% fat, partially hydrogenated soybean oil: P/S = 1.60–1.79; saturated fat (g/100g) = 15.00–15.99 (1 t = 4.70g) (Shurfresh [Shurfine] Regular, Stick; Parkay, Regular, Stick; Parkay, Regular, Tub; Mrs. Filbert's, Soft Golden, Regular, Tub; Meadow Gold, Regular Stick)	4.70	0	3.78	.74	1.24
Margarine, Stick or Tub, 80% fat, corn oil: P/S = 1.2–1.39; saturated fat (g/100g) = 17.00–17.99 (1 t = 4.70g) (Country Morning Blend, 60% corn oil)	4.70	0	3.79	.81	1.10
Margarine, Stick or Tub, 80% fat, partially hydrogenated soybean oil and cottonseed oil: P/S = 1.4–1.59; saturated fat (g/100g) = 15.00–15.99, (1 t = 4.70g) (Blue Bonnet, Regular, Stick; Blue Bonnet, Regular, Tub; Blue Ribbon, Regular, Stick)	4.70	0	3.77	.73	1.08

Product	Unit of Measure	Choles- terol (mg)	Total Fats (g)	Total SFA (g)	Total PFA (g)
Margarine, Stick or Tub, 80% fat, partially hydrogenated soybean oil and cottonseed oil: P/S = 1.4–1.59; saturated fat (g/100g) =14.00–14.99 (1 t = 4.70g) (Imperial, Stick; Imperial, Tub)	4.70	0	3.77	.69	1.10
Margarine, Whipped, 80% fat, partially hydrogenated soybean oil and cottonseed oil: P/S = .8–.99; saturated fat (g/100g) =15.00–15.99 (1 t = 3.16) (Blue Bonnet, Whipped, Regular, Tub)	3.16	0	2.54	.48	.46
Margarine, Spread, 72% fat, sunflower oil: P/S = 2.2–2.39; saturated fat (g/100g) = 12.00–12.99 (1 t = 4.80g) (Promise, Spread 72%, Stick)	4.80	0	3.46	.59	1.37
Margarine, Spread, 72% fat, sunflower oil: P/S = 2.8–2.99; saturated fat (g/100g) = 11.00–11.99 (1 t = 4.80g) (Promise, Spread 72%, Tub)	4.80	0	3.46	.55	1.59
Margarine, Spread, 60% fat, partially hydrogenated soybean oil and cottonseed oil: P/S = 1.4–1.59; saturated fat (g/100g) = 11.00–11.99 (1 t = 4.80) (Shedd's Country Crock, Spread 64%, Stick)	4.80	0	2.92	.57	.84
Margarine, Spread, Low Sodium, 60% fat, corn oil: P/S = 1.2–1.39; saturated fat (g/100g) = 9.00–9.99 (1 t = 4.80g) (Fleischmann's, Light, Spread 60%)	4.80	0	2.92	.48	.65
Margarine, Spread, 52% fat, corn oil: P/S = 2.2–2.39; saturated fat (g/100g) = 9.00–9.99 (1 t = 4.80g) (Shedd's [corn], Spread, 52% fat, Tub)	4.80	0	2.50	.44	.97

Product	Unit of Measure	Choles-terol (mg)	Total Fats (g)	Total SFA (g)	Total PFA (g)
Margarine, Spread, 52% fat, partially hydrogenated soybean oil: P/S = .8–.99; saturated fat (g/100g) = 7.00–7.99 (1 t = 4.80g) (Shedd's [soy], spread 52%, stick)	4.80	0	2.50	.37	.34
Margarine, Spread, 52% fat, sunflower oil: P/S = 2.2–2.39; saturated fat (g/100g) = 8.0–8.99 (1 t = 4.80g) (Promise, Extra Lite, Spread 53%, Stick)	4.80	0	2.54	.43	1.01
Margarine, Diet, 40% fat, partially hydrogenated soybean oil: P/S = 2.8–2.99; saturated fat (g/100g) = 6.0–6.99 (1 t = 4.80g) (Weight Watcher's Diet, 40%, Tub)	4.80	0	1.86	.28	.81
Margarine, Diet, 40% fat, corn oil: P/S = 2.0–2.19; saturated fat (g/100g) = 6.00–6.99 (1 t = 4.80g) (Fleischmann's, Diet, 40%)	4.80	0	1.86	.43	1.01
Margarine, Spread, 52% fat, sunflower oil: P/S = 2.8–2.99; saturated fat (g/100g) = 8.00–8.99 (1 t = 4.80g) (Promise, Extra Lite, Spread 53%, Stick)	4.80	0	2.54	.40	1.17
Margarine, Spread, 52% fat, partially hydrogenated soybean oil: P/S = 2.2–2.39; saturated fat (g/100g) = 8.0–8.99 (1 t = 4.80g) (Shedd's Country Crock, Spread 52%, Tub)	4.80	0	2.50	.43	1.02

OILS

Brand Name Oil	Type of Oil	Polyunsaturated Fat/ Saturated fat (P/S)
Crisco Oil	Partially Hydrogenated Soybean	2.0/3.5
Fleischmann's Corn Oil	Corn	3.0/4.5
Kraft Corn Oil	Corn	3.0/4.5
Kraft Pure Safflower Oil	Safflower	7.0/10.0
Kraft Pure Vegetable Oil	Soybean/Cottonseed	2.5/3.5
Mazola Corn Oil	Corn	3.0/4.5
Mrs. Tucker's Corn Oil	Corn	3.0/4.5
Mrs. Tucker's Soy Salad Oil	Partially Hydro-genated Soybean	2.0/3.5
Orville Redenbacher's Popcorn Oil	Partially Hydro-genated Soybean with Beta-Carotene	2.0/3.5
Planter's Peanut Oil	Peanut	2.0
Puritan	Canbra (Rapeseed)	5.3
Saffola Safflower Oil	Safflower	7.5/10.0
Shurfine Oil	Partially Hydrogen-ated Soybean	2.0/3.5
Sunlite Oil (Wesson)	Sunflower	4.5/6.0
Wesson Corn Oil	Corn	4.0
Wesson Oil	Soybean/Cottonseed	2.5/3.5

Product	Unit of Measure	Choles-terol (mg)	Total Fats (g)	Total SFA (g)	Total PFA (g)
Oil, Corn (1 t = 4.54g) (Fleischmann's Corn Oil, Kraft Corn Oil, Mazola Corn Oil, Mrs. Tucker's Corn Oil, Wesson Corn Oil)	4.54	0	4.54	.58	2.66
Oil, Safflower (1 t = 4.54g) (Saffola Safflower Oil, Kraft Pure Safflower Oil)	4.54	0	4.54	.41	3.38
Oil, Sunflower (1 t = 4.54g) (Sunlite Oil, Wesson)	4.54	0	4.54	.47	2.98
Oil, Popcorn, Partially Hydrogenated Soybean Oil with Beta-Carotene (1 t = 4.54g) (Orville Reddenbacher's Popcorn Oil)	4.54	0	4.54	.68	1.71
Oil Blend, 90% Soybean, 10% Cottonseed (1 t = 4.54g) (Kraft Pure Vegetable Oil, Wesson Oil)	4.54	0	4.54	.71	2.60

Product	Unit of Measure	Choles- terol (mg)	Total Fats (g)	Total SFA (g)	Total PFA (g)
Oil, Soybean, Partially Hydrogenated, specially processed (1 t = 4.54g) (Mrs. Tucker's Corn Oil, Crisco Oil, Shurfine Oil)	4.54	0	4.54	.68	1.71
Oil, Peanut (1 t = 4.50g) (Planter's Peanut Oil)	4.50	0	4.50	.76	1.44
Oil, Canbra (Rapeseed) (1 t = 4.54g) (Puritan Oil)	4.54	0	4.54	.31	1.51

SHORTENING

Brand Name Shortening	Type of Fat	Polyunsaturated Fat/ Saturated Fat (P/S)
Crisco	Soybean/Palm	1.2/1.39
Crisco, Butter Flavor	Soybean/Palm	1.0/1.19
Fluffo	Soybean/Cottonseed	1.0/1.19
Fluffo, Butter-like Color	Soybean/Palm	1.0/1.19
Fryman	Soybean/Cottonseed	1.0/1.19

Product	Unit of Measure	Choles- terol (mg)	Total Fats (g)	Total SFA (g)	Total PFA (g)
Shortening, Household, partially hydrogenated soybean oil and cottonseed oil, P/S = 1.0–1.19 (1 t = 4.27g) (Fluffo, Frymax)	4.27	0	4.27	1.07	1.11
Shortening, Household, butter- like color, partially hydrogenated soybean oil and palm oil, P/S = 1.0–1.19 (1 t = 4.27 g) (Fluffo, Butter-Like Color and Crisco, Butter Flavor)	4.27	0	4.27	1.06	1.22
Shortening, Household, partially hydrogenated soybean oil and palm oil, P/S = 1.2–1.39 (1 t = 4.27g) (Crisco)	4.27	0	4.27	1.02	1.26

Appendix I

Answers to Chapter Reviews

Each answer should be discussed in depth. The responses provided here are intended only as general suggestions to help initiate discussion.

Answers to Review of Chapter 8

1. a. "I'm off that rotten diet now" syndrome.
   b. "I'm such a rotten person, what's the use" syndrome.
2. a. Identify the general problem.
   b. Collect data.
   c. Identify inappropriate eating pattern and possible ways toward improvement.
3. a. Substituting non-food-related activities.
   b. Interposing time.
   c. Eliminating cues.
   d. Involving spouse, family, and friends.
   e. Thinking positively.
   f. Engaging in physical activity.
4. For the client who has a very negative self-concept, I would use the positive thinking strategy. By substituting positive thoughts for negative, self-concepts may become more positive.

Answers to Review of Chapter 9

1. a. "Any vegetable oil is OK on a fat-modified diet."
   b. "One single food will lower my cholesterol so I really don't need to worry about eating other foods."
   c. "My family makes me eat high-fat crackers."
   d. "I can't get by on only six ounces of meat. It's not healthy."
   e. "That low-fat cheese is terrible!"
   f. "I practically drink vegetable oil because I know it will lower my cholesterol level."
2. a. Cholesterol.
   b. Saturated fat.
   c. Polyunsaturated fat.
   d. Monosaturated fat.
3. a. Tailor the diet to take past eating habits into consideration.
   b. Stage the diet instruction.
   c. Clear up misconceptions about fat and cholesterol.

4.

	Choles-terol	Total Fat	Saturated Fat	Polyun-saturated Fat	Monoun-saturated Fat
0 egg/week	0	0	0	0	0
7 oz. meat/day (med. fat beef)	181	29.54	12.81	1.40	15.33
0 dairy	0	0	0	0	0
3 tsps. Fleischmann's Regular, Tub, margarine/day	0	11.34	1.98	4.44	4.95
3 tsps. Mazola oil/day	0	13.62	1.74	7.98	3.90
	181	54.50	16.53	13.82	24.18
		P/S = .83			
(% of 2,400 calories)		(20%)	(6%)	(5%)	(9%)

Strategies: Jim might tell his friends how important it is to his health to eat foods low in cholesterol and fat. He also might ask his family to help by positively reinforcing his efforts on social occasions. Supplements would provide needed calcium.

Answers to Review of Chapter 10

1. a. Social pressures.
   b. Giving up old eating habits.
   c. Avoiding unpalatable commercial substitutes.
2. a. Complex carbohydrates.
   b. Simple carbohydrates.
3. a. Tailoring the eating pattern.
   b. Staging the diet instruction.
   c. Changing behaviors for social occasions.
   d. Involving the family.
4. a. Ask questions to elicit thought patterns surrounding the problem.
   b. Encourage food substitutes and positive thinking.
   c. The goal in using these strategies is to (1) provide added dietary information and (2) help in beginning a program of positive thinking when unplanned and unrecommended eating is avoided.

Answers to Review of Chapter 11

1. a. Too many changes at one time.
   b. Social pressures.
   c. Giving up old eating habits.
   d. Unpalatable commercial substitutes.
2. a. Protein.
   b. Phosphorus.
   c. Potassium.

   d. Sodium.
   e. Fluid.
3. a. Tailoring.
   b. Staging.
   c. Behavior change for social occasions.
   d. Family involvement.
4. a. There are many correct answers to this question. One basic strategy is to
      initiate added spouse involvement in the interview. If the wife is given a sense
      of belonging to the dietary change process, she may become a more positive
      influence on her husband. The dietary changes can be approached in small
      steps with subgoals so that the new eating pattern seems less overwhelming.
   b. The goal in using these strategies is to: (1) focus on increasing spouse support
      and (2) assist in making dietary changes more manageable by setting
      subgoals.

Answers to Review of Chapter 12

1. a. Loss of familiar flavors.
   b. Limited food choices.
   c. Changing old habits.
   d. Unpalatable commercial substitutes.
2. a. Collect data on the sodium content of the baseline diet.
   b. Identify the general problem.
   c. Identify inappropriate eating patterns and possible solutions.
3. a. Tailoring.
   b. Staging.
   c. Flavoring substitutes.
   d. Altering eating style through family involvement.
4. a. One of many areas to assess is family involvement. If the family members'
      attitudes toward the sodium restriction are negative, an increase in their
      involvement is a possible first step. By reviewing baseline information it may
      be possible to substitute foods low in sodium for cheese and cold cuts. The
      client and counselor can build a self-reward system when low-sodium foods
      are eaten and high-sodium foods avoided.
   b. The goal in using these strategies is to: (1) provide necessary dietary informa-
      tion and (2) design a system of self-rewards to help in maintaining good
      adherence.

Answers to Review of Chapter 13

1. a. Lack of math skills.
   b. Familiar high-fat eating pattern.
2. a. Fat.
   b. Calories (for persons at ideal body weight, nonfat sources of calories will need
      to be substituted in the new eating pattern).
3. a. Providing information gradually.
   b. Posting fat scores for the day on the refrigerator.
   c. Recording positive monologues.

4. a. Ask questions to elicit current successes with changing this high-fat meal. Inquire about family response to these efforts at change.
   b. Organize a session in which the family is told how important they are to Mrs. B's success and provide tips on how to be supportive. Ask Mrs. B to keep a list for the week of her low-fat accomplishments in changing foods eaten in this meal.
   c. The goals in using these strategies were to: (1) focus on increasing family support and (2) focus on the positive by listing accomplishments in modifying the meal to be lower in total fat.

Answers to Review of Chapter 14

1. a. Limits the types of foods eaten.
   b. Takes extreme care in removing all fat from meat and totally eliminating it as an addition to other foods.
   c. Does not eat in front of other people and never with her family.
   d. Eats only lettuce in restaurants.
   e. If lettuce is not available, nothing is eaten.
   f. Exercises to exhaustion.
2. a. Eats a large quantity of a single food, such as two large pizzas, one cake, or one dozen doughnuts.
   b. Binges and vomits.
   c. Takes large doses of stimulus-type laxatives.
3. a. Calories. (Certainly other nutrients are limited, but as foods are added overall nutrient intake will increase. Eventually an assessment of all nutrients will be important to an assessment of health status.)
4. a. Provide the client with information on how meals might be more balanced following an assessment of caloric intake, meal frequency, and content.
   b. If pills are taken, provide a medication record.
   c. Increase weight gradually to goal range.
   d. Reduce excessive, non-goal-directed physical activity.
   e. Instruct the client in relaxation techniques.
   f. Introduce assertiveness skills.
   g. Teach self-management techniques.
   h. Use cognitive therapy techniques.
   i. Use behavior change therapy.
5. a. Ask the client to provide information on family members' response to the client's not eating with them and her fear of eating out with them.
   b. Ask the client to keep a record of time of eating, location, food eaten, events (which include binges), and feelings. Based upon these data, begin to discuss thoughts surrounding eating. Begin with articulation of beliefs about eating and move to operationalizing beliefs, finally evaluating these beliefs.

   COUNSELOR: "What are some of your thoughts about overweight people?"
   CLIENT: "I see them as ugly, unmotivated, and unhappy, and I don't want to be one of them."
   COUNSELOR: "How do you feel about minorities?"
   CLIENT: "Oh, you mean persons of another race. Oh that's different."

COUNSELOR: "Why?"

CLIENT: "Well, maybe you're right. I guess I have an attitude toward obesity that is different from my attitude toward the human race in general. I guess I automatically define thinness as equivalent to intelligent, beautiful, and prosperous."

COUNSELOR: "How would your describe Mrs. C, who was in the waiting room with you?"

CLIENT: "She looks too thin."

COUNSELOR: "She is the same height, weight, and build as you are."

Move on to the area of behavior change. Discuss how to select high-calorie food from a favorite restaurant menu. Allow the client time to make her own choices.

    c. The rationale in using these strategies is first to identify the problems in terms of eating behaviors and thought patterns and then to change beliefs through analogies, rehearsal and self-management.

Answers to Review of Chapter 15

1. a. Decreased caloric and nutrient intake due to nausea and vomiting.
   b. Inappropriate eating behaviors as a result of cultural misinformation.
   c. Inappropriate eating behaviors associated with vegetarianism.
   d. Pica.
2. a. Calories.
   b. Protein.
   c. Calcium.
   d. Zinc.
   e. Iron.
   f. Folacin.
3. a. Information on dietary intake appropriate during pregnancy as it relates specifically to the client's individual and cultural food preferences.
   b. Pill box.
   c. Positive reinforcement by others and self-reinforcement.
   d. Tailoring.
   e. Stress management.
4. a. Toward what specific food behaviors are the family member responses most negative? When are they supportive? By what types of tasks is Mrs. C feeling overwhelmed?
   b. Build on the positive by talking with the family and praising them for positively reinforcing Mrs. C. Request that they use the same reinforcement at times when they are currently negative. List tasks during the day that overwhelm Mrs. C. Try to decide which tasks others might do and which tasks someone could be paid to do. Last, prioritize tasks. Work on the most important task first. Always make time for good dietary practices.
   c. These strategies were designed to focus on the following:
      •Emphasize the positive.
      •Increase positive reinforcement from family members.
      •Help Mrs. C manage stress in her life and allow time for making good eating habits a priority in her day.

Answers to Review of Chapter 16

1. a. Did the counseling session address the client's major problem?
   b. Was assessment prior to designing a modified eating pattern adequate to prepare a dietary regimen compatible with the client's life style?
   c. Did the client's goal appear to have been achieved?
   d. Were the strategies for altering eating behaviors carried out efficiently?
   e. Did I use appropriate verbal and nonverbal interviewing skills?
   f. Where might changes have been made?
   g. Did I use appropriate counseling skills?
   h. Where might changes have been made?
   i. What general changes would I make in the next counseling interview with a similar client?
2. a. Have my dietary patterns changed but remained compatible with my life style?
   b. Have my misconceptions about foods and what they contain been replaced with factual information?
   c. Are social occasions less of a problem now than when I first began my diet?
   d. Is my family providing needed positive reinforcement?
3. a. Reinforce and practice in the new environment.
   b. Promote generalization to many situations.
   c. Build in resistance to extinction.
   d. Practice new behaviors sufficiently.
   e. Promote social support.
4. a. Are there things going on in your life that may cause this?
   b. If "yes," what are they?
   c. Has the intervening event passed?
5. Check with the client to determine the most useful strategy used in the past to maintain adherence. Reinstitute that plan and monitor behavior.

Index

A

ABC model, 58
Active responses
  attributing, 40
  confronting, 40-43
  definition, 38-39
  immediacy, 45-46
  interpreting, 43
  probing, 39-40
  self-disclosure, 44-45
Adherence
  cancer and, 406-407
  computer uses, 143-149
  coronary heart disease and, 239, 242,
    248-249
  cueing and, 79
  diabetes and, 179-180, 315-317
  dietary stage factors, 115-116
  eating disorders and, 425
  educational focus factors, 68
  factors influencing, 64-65, 114-115
  hypertension and, 388-389
  maintenance strategies, 470-471
  monitoring methods, 82-83
  obesity and, 206-209
  predictors, 65-66
  pregnancy and, 438
  promotion strategies, 66-68
  renal disease and, 353
  stress and, 179-180, 187-189
  See also Monitoring

Adherence tools, 201-202
  cancer, 417-420
  coronary heart disease, 251-281
  diabetes, 329-341
  eating disorders, 432-433
  hypertension, 399-400
  obesity treatment, 217-227
  pregnancy, 455-462
  renal disease, 361-378
Alcohol use
  diabetes and, 296
  hypertension and, 386
Alternate responses, 80
Amino-acid supplementation, 350, 351
Anorexia nervosa
  adherence and, 425
  assessment, 427-428
  characteristics, 423-425
  eating behavior problems, 426
  goals of treatment, 422
  monitoring devices, 107, 432, 433
  treatment strategies, 428-432
Aspartame, 295
Assessment
  biochemical, 82
  cancer, 408
  computer use, 143, 144
  coronary heart disease, 242
  data collection instruments, 94-98
  data needs, 92-93

data types, 56-57
definition, 91
diabetes, 318-319
eating disorders, 427-428
hypertension, 390
importance, 91-92
instrument selection factors, 98-101
learning performance, 155
medical term involvement, 101-102
monitoring and, 103-104
needs specification, 57-58
obesity, 209-212
object setting, 102-103
pregnancy, 442, 444, 455-459
reliability, 99
renal disease, 354-355
system model, 10
use factors, 92
validity, 99-100
See also Adherence tools; Evaluation;
   Monitoring
Attention gaining, 152-153
Attributing, 40
Autogenic training, 183

B

Bar graphs, 144, 147
Behavioral change
   adherence promotion, 66-67
   cancer and, 411-413
   hypertension and, 389
   motivation strategies, 72-76
   obesity and, 206-209, 212-216
   renal disease and, 353
   stimulus control and, 79-80
   weight loss and, 206-209
Behavioral data, 57, 63, 486, 487. *See also*
   Data collection
Behavioral objectives, 102-103, 113
Behavioral therapy, 7-8
Biochemical assessment. *See* Physiological
   measures
Biofeedback, 180-181, 183-184
Biologic data, 56. *See also* Data collection;
   Physiological measures
Blood glucose
   alcohol and, 296
   calories and, 294
   carbohydrates and, 288-293
   exercise and, 296

fats and, 293-294, 321-325
graphing, 319, 330
monitoring, 108, 297-298, 316, 323
protein and, 294
salt and, 294
sweeteners and, 294-295
treatment strategies, 319-320
Brand name nutrient values, 131-132
Bulimia
   adherence and, 425
   assessment, 427-428
   characteristics, 424-425
   eating behavior problems, 426-427
   goals of treatment, 422
   monitoring devices, 107, 432, 433
   treatment strategies, 428-432
Burke-type dietary history, 98

C

Caffeine, 185-186
Calcium
   hypertension and, 387
   renal disease and, 352
Cancer
   adherence and, 406-407
   assessment, 408
   cueing devices, 418, 420
   eating behavior problems, 408
   informational devices, 419, 420
   monitoring devices, 417-418
   nutrition and, 406
   treatment strategies, 408-417
Carbohydrates, 288-293
Center for Science in the Public Interest, 125
Cholesterol, 236-240, 492-501
Clarification, 36
Closed-ended questions, 40
Cognitive-behavioral therapy, 186-187, 189
Cognitive restructuring
   cancer and, 411, 418, 488-491
   coronary heart disease and, 248
   daily record, 491
   description, 73-74
   obesity and, 214
   renal disease, 360-361, 378
Commercial products
   label reading, 319, 341
   low-fat, 240, 246
   low-protein, 357, 373
   low-sodium, 389, 390

nutrient value software, 131-132
Commitment strategies
    cancer, 410-416
    coronary heart disease, 248-249
    diabetes, 326-328
    eating disorders, 428
    hypertension, 397-399
    obesity, 214-216
    pregnancy, 451, 453-454
    renal disease, 358-361
Compliance. See Adherence
Computers
    adherence-related uses, 143-149
    data base factors, 130-133
    dietary analysis systems, 96
    graphics, 130, 144-149
    software types, 124
    spreadsheet applications, 124, 134-143
    stand-alone software, 124-133, 135
    uses, 123-124, 143
Confrontation, 40-42, 328, 360
Congruence, 22
"Continuing Survey for Individual Intakes"
    (CSFII), 132, 133
Contracting
    cancer and, 412-413
    coronary heart disease and, 248
    description, 76
    diabetes and, 326, 328
    hypertension and, 397-398
    obesity and, 215
    renal disease and, 360, 377
Conversational style, 34-35
Coping styles, 182, 189
Coping thoughts, 73
Coronary heart disease
    adherence and, 239, 242, 248-249, 263-265
    assessment, 242
    eating behavior problems, 240-242, 246
    eating questionnaire, 251-262
    informational devices, 267-281
    meal planning, 267-280
    misinformation device, 260
    monitoring devices, 251-266
    nutrition and, 235-239
    prevention recommendations, 231, 235
    P/S ratios, 281
    treatment strategies, 239, 245-250
Counseling skills
    assessment, 56-58
    evaluation, 81-83
    initial information provision, 55-56
    overview, 12
    treatment planning, 58-68
    treatment strategies, 68-81
Counselor-client relationship, 18-21
Counselor performance evaluations, 83,
    202-203, 477-478
Covert modeling, 70, 80
Covert reinforcement, 80-81
Covert sensitization, 81
Cueing
    behavior change and, 72, 80
    cancer and, 410, 418, 420
    coronary heart disease and, 247-248
    diabetes and, 325
    interview and, 33
    obesity and, 212-214
    pregnancy and, 462
    renal disease, 358, 374-377

D

Daily records, 82, 242, 366, 400, 491
Data bases, 130-133
Data collection
    coronary heart disease, 242, 253-264
    eating behaviors, 63, 486, 487
    hypertension, 390-393
    obesity, 209, 217-224
    prospective methods, 94-95
    renal disease, 354-355, 361-366
    retrospective methods, 95-98
    types of data, 56-57, 63
Decatastrophizing, 430-431
Decentering, 430
Decision making, 77
Depression monitoring, 109
Diabetes mellitus
    adherence and, 179-180, 315-317
    alcohol and, 296
    assessment, 318-319
    blood glucose monitoring, 108, 297-298,
        316-323
    diet pattern spreadsheets, 138
    diet therapy, 299-300, 313-315
    eating behavior problems, 317-318
    exchange lists, 301-312
    exercise and, 296
    informational devices, 332-341
    instructional plan, 156-164, 319
    insulin management, 298-300, 313-315,

323-325, 332
monitoring devices, 108-109, 114, 318-319, 329-332
non-insulin-dependent, 287
nutrition and, 287-296
physiology, 178-179
stress and, 177-181, 326-328
treatment, 180-181, 287, 296-300, 313-315
treatment strategies, 319-328
Diaries, 94, 242, 392, 408
Dietary concern identification, 61-62
Dietary histories, 98, 318
Dietary intake
   assessment factors, 99, 111
   cancer and, 408
   computer-based assessments, 143, 144
   coronary heart disease and, 242, 253-264, 266, 267
   data collection factors, 56-57, 99
   diabetes and, 318, 329
   hypertension and, 390-392, 400
   renal disease and, 355, 366
Diet pattern spreadsheets, 137-139
Diet records. *See* Food records
Digestible carbohydrates, 288-291, 294-295
Disaccharides, 289
Discrimination, 154
Distraction, 431
Duplicate portion analysis, 95

E

Eating behaviors
   cancer, 408
   coronary heart disease and, 240-242
   data collection, 63, 486, 487
   diabetes and, 317-319
   eating disorders and, 426-427
   hypertension and, 389-392
   obesity and, 208-212
   pregnancy and, 438-439, 442, 444
   renal disease and, 353-355
Eating disorders. *See* Anorexia nervosa; Bulimia
Eliciting performance, 155
Emotion-focused stress management, 182, 188
Emotive modeling, 70
Environmental data, 57
Evaluation
   client progress, 470
   counselor progress, 82-83, 469-470
   counselor role, 12

focus of, 81
   methods, 82-83
   process, 15, 81-82
   purposes, 81
Exchanges
   computer-based, 137-139
   diabetes, 299-313, 332, 333-337
   renal disease, 356, 370
Exercise
   diabetes and, 296
   obesity and, 209, 212, 214-215
   stress and, 184-185
Extinction, 75, 471

F

Family support. *See* Social support
Family therapy, 8-9
Fats
   cancer and, 406, 417
   coronary heart disease and, 242, 281
   diabetes and, 293-294, 320-323
   food composition table, 492-501
Fatty acids, 236-240
Feedback, 155
Fiber, 291
Focus identification, 35-36
Food code entry, 127
Food diaries, 94, 242, 392, 408
Food frequency recalls, 96-97, 242, 318
Food name entry, 127
Food plans, 445, 460-461
Food product resource files, 246
Food records
   computer-based, 144
   diabetes and, 318, 329, 330
   eating disorders and, 429, 433
   hypertension and, 396, 400
   pregnancy and, 451, 458
   renal disease and, 366
Forgetfulness strategies
   cancer, 410
   coronary heart disease, 247-248
   diabetes, 325
   eating disorders, 428-432
   hypertension, 396
   obesity, 214
   pregnancy, 451
   renal disease, 358
Fructose, 289, 294-295

G

Gestalt therapy, 8
Glucose level monitoring. *See* Blood glucose
Glycemic index, 292
Glycosylated hemoglobin levels, 297, 319, 331
Goal setting, 13-14, 58-61, 413
Graphing
   computer-based, 130, 144-149
   coronary heart disease monitoring, 262, 263
   diabetes monitoring, 318-319, 330-331
   renal disease monitoring, 355, 367
Group sessions, 182-183, 215-216
Growth facilitation, 20-21

H

Hassle Scale, 169-170, 175, 176
Heart disease. *See* Coronary heart disease
Helping strategies, 63-64
"Home and Garden Bulletin No. 72," 132
Hyperlipidemia monitoring, 109
Hypertension
   adherence and, 388
   assessment, 390-392
   blood pressure level classification, 383
   eating behavior problems, 389-390
   informational devices, 399
   monitoring devices, 110, 400
   nutrition and, 383-388
   treatment strategies, 392-399
   weight control and, 383-385
Hypnosis, 183

I

Idaho Extension Services, 125
Identification of dietary concerns, 61-62
Imagined aversive consequences, 81
Imitation, 8
Immediacy, 45-46
Indigestible carbohydrate, 291
Informational strategies
   cancer, 408-410
   coronary heart disease, 239, 264, 269-283
   diabetes, 315-317, 319-325, 332-341
   eating disorders, 428
   guidelines for, 48-49, 64
   obesity, 212, 217-224
   pregnancy, 445, 450-451, 459-462
Instructional plans, 319
   materials and activities, 156

   objectives, 150-152
   overview, 150
   sample, 157-164
   teaching steps, 152-156
Instructions, 46-47
Insulin, 298-300, 313-315, 323-325, 332
Intake and output records, 95
Interpreting, 43-44
Interview for Recent Life Events, 174
Interviewing, 12
   action responses, 38-46
   client evaluation, 82
   counselor-client relationship, 18-21
   counselor evaluation, 202-203
   data collection methods, 95-98
   listening responses, 36-38
   nonverbal communication, 21-34, 477-478
   response selection, 49-51
   structural elements, 55-56
   teaching responses, 46-49
   verbal communication, 34-36

K

Ketoacid amino-acid supplements, 350
Ketone levels, 297-298
Keyword entry, 127
Kidney disease. *See* Renal disease
Kinesics, 22
Knowledge strategies
   cancer, 408-410
   coronary heart disease, 245-247
   diabetes, 319-325
   eating disorders, 428
   hypertension, 392-393, 396
   obesity, 212-214
   pregnancy, 445, 450-451
   renal disease, 356

L

Lapses, 105, 389, 415. *See also* Commitment
   strategies
Learning guidance, 154
Learning responses, 36-38
Life events stress, 169, 174, 176, 326-327,
   359, 416
Life Experiences Survey (LES), 174
Limit setting, 56
Line graphs, 147
Lipoproteins, 235-239

M

Macros, 143
Magnesium, 388
Meal planning
  cancer and, 412-413, 419
  computer-based, 139-141, 144
  coronary heart disease and, 245, 267-280
  diabetes and, 301-312, 319, 332, 340
  eating disorders and, 430
  renal diseases and, 357, 369
Medical team, 101-102, 113
Medications
  coronary heart disease, 247-248
  diabetes, 287, 296, 298-300, 313-315
  eating disorders, 428, 432
  pregnancy, 451
  renal disease, 355, 358, 366, 367, 374-376
  stress management, 185
Meditation, 183, 184
Memorization, 155
Mixed messages, 33
Modeling, 8, 68-71, 80
Monitoring
  assessment and, 103-104
  blood glucose, 295-296, 314, 321
  cancer, 412, 417-418
  coronary heart disease, 242, 251-266
  definition, 103
  diabetes, 297-298, 316, 318-319, 329-332
  eating disorders, 430, 432, 433
  hypertension, 388, 400
  importance of, 103-104
  instrument selection, 111-113
  instrument types, 107-111
  medical team involvement, 113
  methods, 82
  obesity, 217-225
  objectives factors, 106-107
  participants, 105-106
  pregnancy, 455-458
  renal disease, 355, 361-368
  use factors, 104-105
Monosaccharides, 289-290, 294-295

N

National Library of Agriculture, 127
Negative thinking. *See* Cognitive restructuring;
  Thought stopping
Nonverbal communication
  checklist, 23-32

client behavior, 22
  counselor behavior, 34, 477-478
  counselor response, 22, 33
Nutrient intake analysis, 57, 124-130, 444
Nutritional status measures, 479-485
Nutrition counseling
  client attitudes and, 5-6
  counselor roles, 4, 11, 15
  definition, 3
  dietary adherence factors, 9-10
  history of, 3-5
  importance of, 9
  skills, 12-15
  structure-related elements, 55-56
  systems approach, 10-12
  theories of, 6-9
Nutrition needs specification, 57-58
Nutrition Wizard software, 125

O

Obesity
  adherence and, 206-209
  assessment, 209-212
  cueing devices, 226-227
  diabetes and, 287
  eating behavior problems, 208, 212
  eating questionnaire, 217-224
  goal attainment chart, 225
  hypertension and, 383-385
  informational devices, 226-227
  monitoring devices, 107, 217-225
  nutrition and, 205-206
  treatment strategies, 212-216
Objective setting, 102-103, 113-114, 150-152
Objectives review, 153
Open-ended questions, 39-40, 326
Operant conditioning, 8
Operationalizing beliefs, 430

P

Pantry surveys, 80, 242, 266
Paralinguistics, 22
Paraphrasing, 37, 326
Peer monitoring, 106
Perceived stress, 171, 175, 176
Person-centered therapy, 6-7
Phosphorus, 351, 352
Photographic records, 94-95
Physiological measures

blood glucose, 108, 297-298, 316, 323
diabetes, 108, 297-298, 316, 319, 323
effectiveness of, 82
hypertension, 388
ketone levels, 297-298
obesity, 211-212
renal disease, 355, 368
types, 479-485
Pica, 109, 439, 450
Pie graphs, 147
Polysaccharides, 289, 291
Positive thinking. *See* Cognitive restructuring
Potassium, 352-353, 387
Pregnancy
    adherence and, 438
    assessment, 442, 444, 455-459
    cueing devices, 462
    eating behavior problems, 438-439
    ethnic factors, 438-439, 446-449, 451, 454
    informational devices, 459-462
    monitoring devices, 455-458
    nutritional management goals, 437
    nutritional requirements, 437-438
    stress factors, 451, 453-454, 462
    treatment strategies, 445, 450-451, 453-454
Printouts, 130
Probing, 39-40
Problem definition, 58, 326
Problem-focused stress management, 182, 188
Problem solving, 155
Progressive muscle relaxation (PMR), 183
Prospective records, 94-95
Protein
    diabetes and, 290, 294
    renal disease and, 349-352
Proxemics, 22
P/S ratios, 245, 281

Q

Qualitative evaluations, 202
Quantitative evaluations, 203
Questioning, 39-40, 324, 392

R

Rational emotive therapy (RET), 7
Recall stimulation, 153
Reflection, 37
Refocusing, 33
Reinforcement

covert, 80-81
hypertension, 397-399
overview, 74-75
renal disease, 360
termination and, 470-471
Relaxation treatment, 180-181, 183, 184
Renal disease
    adherence and, 353
    assessment, 354-355
    commitment-related devices, 377-378
    cueing devices, 374-376
    eating behavior problems, 353-354
    eating questionnaire, 361-366
    informational devices, 357, 369-372
    monitoring devices, 109-110, 361-368
    nutrition and, 349-353
    nutrition management goals, 348
    treatment strategies, 356-361
Respiratory One Method, 183
Response consequence alterations, 80-81
Restaurant eating
    cancer and, 415
    coronary heart disease and, 268, 272-274, 278-280
    diabetes and, 320, 325
    renal disease and, 357
Restrained eating, 104
Retention, 156
Retrospective records, 95-98
Rewards. *See* Reinforcement
Role playing, 78
Rules, 154-155

S

Saccharin, 293
Salt. *See* Sodium
Satiation, 75
Screen displays, 129, 130
Screening, 92
Self-defeating thoughts, 73. *See also* Thought stopping
Self-direction, 77-81
Self-disclosure, 44-45
Self-evaluation, 12, 15, 82-83
Self-image, 19, 475-476
Self-management, 78
Self-monitoring, 78-81, 103, 106. *See also* Monitoring
Semiquantitative food frequency questionnaires, 96-97

Sequenced learning, 66-67
Shaping, 76, 411-412
Sharing responses, 44-46
Shopping guides, 240
Silence, 33
Simulation, 71-72, 144
Social Provisions Scale, 175
Social Readjustment Rating Scale (SRRS), 169
Social support
  cancer and, 413
  coronary heart disease and, 239, 249
  diabetes and, 317, 318, 327-328
  maintenance phase and, 115, 116
  renal disease and, 360
  stress and, 172-173, 175-176
Sodium
  diabetes and, 294
  hypertension and, 385-386, 388-391, 393,
    396, 399, 400
  renal disease and, 352, 353
  stress and, 186
Software
  costs, 124-125
  functionality factors, 126-127
  graphics, 147
  types, 124
Sorbitol, 295
Spreadsheets
  characteristics of, 135
  design of, 136-137
  dietary intake assessment, 143
  exchange diet patterning, 137-139
  macro programming, 143
  meal planning, 139-141, 144
  overview, 134-135
  uses, 124
Staging
  coronary heart disease and, 245
  hypertension and, 392-393
  renal disease and, 356-357
"Standard Reference Data Base," 132
Starches, 290-291, 293
Stimulating recall, 153
Stimulus control, 79-80
Stimulus presentation, 154
Strategies. *See* Treatment strategies
Stress
  daily hassles, 169-170, 175, 176
  definition, 166-167, 189
  diabetes and, 177-181
  event characteristics, 171-172

illness and, 176-177
life events, 169, 174, 176, 324-325, 359, 416
measurement, 173-176
perceived, 171, 175, 176
physiology, 167-168, 173-174
renal disease and, 359-360
self-reported, 168-176
social support and, 172-173, 175-176
Stress Inoculation Training (SIT), 186-187
Stress management
  approaches, 182-183
  cancer and, 414-416, 420
  objectives, 181-182
  pregnancy and, 451, 453-454, 462
  techniques, 183-187
Substitutions, 393
Sugars, 287-288
Summarization, 37-38
Sweeteners, 294-295
Symbolic modeling, 70
Systems model, 10-12

T

Tailoring
  coronary heart disease and, 245
  description, 75-76
  diabetes and, 319-320, 325, 332
  hypertension and, 392
  renal disease and, 356
Teaching responses
  information giving, 48-49
  instructions, 46-47
  verbal setting operations, 47-48
Teaching steps, 152-156
Telephone interviews, 94
Termination, 12, 470-473
Thought stopping, 73, 488-490
Total Available Glucose (TAG) system,
  299-300, 313-314, 318-324, 333-339
Transcendental Meditation (TM), 183
Treatment planning
  adherence predictors, 65-66
  adherence-related factors, 64-65
  behavior change steps, 66-67
  educational focus, 68
  goal setting, 58-61
  helping strategies, 63-64
  identification of concerns, 61-63
  strategy selection, 66
Treatment strategies

behavior change, 72-76
coronary heart disease, 239, 245-250
definition, 68
eating disorders, 428-432
helping, 63-64
hypertension, 392-399
implementation factors, 68, 69
learning response, 68, 70-71
obesity, 212-216
pregnancy, 445, 450-451, 453-454
renal disease, 353, 356-361
selection of, 66
self-direction, 77-81
24-hour recalls, 95-96, 143, 318

U

Urea nitrogen appearance, 109-110

U.S. Department of Agriculture (USDA), 124, 125, 131-133

V

Vegetarian diets, 445, 450
Verbal communication, 34-35
Verbal setting operations, 47-48

W

Weighed intakes, 94
Weight loss, 206-208, 287, 383. *See also* Obesity

X

Xylitol, 293

About the Author

LINDA G. SNETSELAAR graduated from Iowa State University with a Bachelor of Science Degree in Food and Nutrition in 1972. She did a dietetic internship at the University of Iowa and became a registered dietitian in 1973. Dr. Snetselaar received a Master of Science Degree from the University of Iowa in Nutrition in 1975, and a Doctor of Philosophy Degree in Instructional Design (Health Sciences Education) in 1983.

She has worked as a clinical dietitian instructing patients on modified diets, and as a research nutritionist counseling cardiovascular patients on diet and medication. As head research nutritionist she directed the Foods and Nutrition Resource Center for Lipid Research Clinic's Coronary Primary Prevention Trial (a clinical trial funded by the National Institutes of Health).

She is now involved in three studies funded by the National Institutes of Health. Each involves dietary modification to prevent disease and its complications: the Diabetes Control and Complications Trial, the Modification of Diet in Renal Disease, and Dietary Intervention Study in Children with elevated low-density lipoprotein levels.

Dr. Snetselaar is an adjunct assistant professor in the Department of Preventive Medicine and an assistant research scientist in the Department of Internal Medicine at the University of Iowa. She team teaches courses in dietetics, chronic disease and nutrition epidemiology, and behavior modification.

She has directed seven workshops funded by the National Institutes of Health on counseling skills applied to nutrition. She has also given numerous talks on the topic. In 1978 Dr. Snetselaar was named Recognized Young Dietitian of the Year in Iowa and received the honor of being named an Outstanding Young Woman in America for 1982.